Fodor's 91
New England

Fodor's Travel Publications, Inc.
New York and London

ISBN 0-679-01936-7

Fodor's New England

Editors: Vernon Nahrgang, Jillian Magalaner
Associate Editors: Staci Capobianco, Chris Heath
Editorial Contributors: Suzanne Brown, Mary H. Frakes, Candice Gianetti, Kimberly Grant, Shawn Hartley Hancock, Marjorie Ingall, Deborah Kovacs, David Laskin, Betty Lowry, Anne Merewood, Janet Nelson, Arthur S. Rosenblatt, William G. Scheller, Linda K. Schmidt
Art Director: Fabrizio La Rocca
Cartographer: David Lindroth
Illustrator: Karl Tanner
Cover Photograph: Peter Guttman

Design: Vignelli Associates

Special Sales

Contents

Foreword

This year's completely rewritten edition of *Fodor's New England* contains two new features intended to make more accessible two of the region's principal attractions: its ski areas and its coastline.

The topical chapter **Skiing New England** surveys 50 ski resorts in five states, describing the trails, the facilities, and the amenities at each area, with details of other activities, day-care provisions, and lodging and nightlife where appropriate.

The second innovation, a **comprehensive coastal tour,** begins in the south at Greenwich ("The Coast: Southwestern Connecticut") and continues north to Acadia National Park in Maine ("The Coast: Acadia"). The 12 segments of the tour, each titled "The Coast," can be located on the Contents page and read in sequence through the state chapters, enabling travelers to join the tour at any stage and proceed as far north along the coast as they please.

While every care has been taken to ensure the accuracy of the information in this guide, the passage of time will always bring change, and consequently the publisher cannot accept responsibility for errors that may occur.

All prices and opening times quoted here are based on information supplied to us at press time. Hours and admission fees may change, however, and the prudent traveler will avoid inconvenience by calling ahead.

Fodor's wants to hear about your travel experiences, both pleasant and unpleasant. When a hotel or restaurant fails to live up to its billing, let us know and we will investigate the complaint and revise our entries where the facts warrant it. Send your letters to the editors of Fodor's Travel Publications, 201 E. 50th Street, New York, NY 10022.

Highlights'91 and Fodor's Choice

Highlights '91

Massachusetts Visitors to Boston in 1991 will find **Faneuil Hall** and the **Old State House** closed for renovation and, at the Charlestown Navy Yard, the USS *Constitution* about to go into Drydock I for restoration in preparation for the celebration of the ship's bicentennial in 1997. The ongoing reconstruction of the **Central Artery** may make travel by auto in the city even more difficult in the coming months, whether or not the city expands its taxi fleet.

Boston's **Marriott Long Wharf** and **Eliot** hotels expect to complete their refurbishing projects by the end of 1991, while the **Copley Plaza** has just been extensively remodeled and the **Ramada Hotel** has added new rooms. On Beacon Hill, the **State House** has a new principal public access in Ashburton Park, behind the building, and a new Great Hall will be a palazzo-style ceremonial area. Harvard's **Busch-Reisinger Museum,** with its collections of Central and Northern European art, expects to reopen in its new building at the end of 1991.

The first season (1989) of high-speed catamaran service to Martha's Vineyard and Nantucket from Boston was also the last, the company having failed; its Boston–Providence ferry is now being operated by a new company formed by employees of the failed company.

On Martha's Vineyard, renovations of the century-old **Harbor View Hotel** in Edgartown and its sister inn, the adjacent **Kelley House,** are scheduled for completion by the 1991 summer season. The Harbor View interior was stripped and everything replaced; the exterior will boast a Victorian gazebo and turrets. Both hotels will remain open year-round.

Following extensive renovations, Nantucket's **Oldest House,** a saltbox of 1686 that was severely damaged by lightning in 1987, reopened for the 1990 season.

Connecticut Major repairs on Connecticut's bridges and highways continue to be made, often creating severe traffic problems; wise motorists will pay close attention to traffic reports on local radio stations throughout the summer. Some of the rush hour traffic on I–95 may have been alleviated with the inauguration in 1990 of **commuter rail service** between New Haven and Old Saybrook, with stops at Branford, Guilford, Madison, Clinton, and Westbrook.

South Norwalk's new 5-acre **Maritime Center** allows visitors to board an oyster sloop, a steam tender, and other vessels in its presentation of the ecology, history, and marine life of Long Island Sound. Further east, Bridgeport's recently renovated **Barnum Museum** highlights the life and interests of the prototypical American showman, Phineas T. Barnum.

In Hartford, a revitalized **Union Station Transportation Center** has consolidated bus and train stations and energized a neighborhood with new dining opportunities and, across Station Place, an array of clubs and bistros. In Salisbury, the newly restored **White Hart Inn** lays claim to a tradition of first-class food and lodging dating to the early 19th century.

Rhode Island Newport's stately **Bellevue Avenue** has a new look: The original brick sidewalks have been re-created, the street repaved and widened slightly, and some trees removed. Drivers may find that approaching Newport from the west during the morning rush hour (and heading west from Newport during the evening rush hour) can be difficult because of ongoing repairs and new construction at the **Jamestown Bridge.**

A new **Providence Bus Terminal** has opened on Cemetery Street, off Exit 25 from I–95; and the creation of an entirely new downtown Providence, in a series of projects that will utilize the air rights above the railroad tracks, is under way at the **Capitol Center.** This construction is expected to take years to complete. Meanwhile, the repair work on I–195 in Providence and on the Fall River Bridge has been finished.

Vermont The bicentennial of **Vermont statehood** will be commemorated in towns and cities throughout the state in 1991, with a statewide folk festival planned for Montpelier in September. On Statehood Day, March 4, Bennington will host a constume ball and other activities. The Vermont Bicentennial Commission (Box 6833, Rutland 05702, tel. 802/775–0800) will have details of the plans in other communities as they are finalized.

One of New England's **longest covered bridges,** a venerable structure that spans the Connecticut River fromWindsor to Cornish, New Hampshire, was reopened to traffic in 1990 after having been closed two years for repairs.

New Hampshire The licensing and startup of the **Seabrook nuclear power plant** may have concluded a long political and ecological controversy that often made headlines across the nation; the surrounding communities of coastal New Hampshire, like so many others in America, are resigned to living with a productive but potentially hazardous neighbor.

Black flies, the scourge of springtime New England, have been greatly reduced in number in the area of **The Balsams Grand Resort Hotel** in Dixville Notch. This is the consequence of The Balsams's five-year pilot program of introducing *bacillus thuringiensis israelensis* (BIT), a naturally occurring organism, into the flies' breeding streams.

In Bretton Woods, the landmark **Mount Washington Hotel** expects to reopen in 1991, following a $20 million renovation of its rooms, suites, and public facilities and the addition of a new recreation center with pool, spa, tennis courts, and 36 holes of golf. And New Hampshire continues to attract shoppers simply by being the state without a retail sales tax.

Maine   Maine's center of culture and the arts continues to be Portland, where the **Old Port Exchange District** has become even more appealing with the opening of the 95-room **Port Regency Hotel** and its health club. Portland's **Western Promenade,** a Victorian residential neighborhood near downtown, has a couple of new and sophisticated bed-and-breakfasts.

In Bethel, the resort complex known as the **Bethel Inn and Country Club** has completed a golf course expansion and opened additional condominium units on the fairway.

The crowding of the Maine coastal resorts during the summer months has led discriminating travelers to discover the pleasures of the off-season (weather on the coast remains fine well into October) and the offshore islands—especially **Vinalhaven** and **Islesboro** in Penobscot Bay—in summer.

Fodor's Choice

No two people will agree on what makes a perfect vacation, but it's fun and helpful to know what others think. We hope you'll have a chance to experience some of Fodor's Choices yourself while visiting New England. For detailed information about each entry, refer to the appropriate chapters in this guidebook.

Sights

Long Island Sound from the tip of Water Street in Stonington Village, CT

The mansions of Bellevue Avenue, Newport, RI

The purple-hued cranberry bogs of Cape Cod just before the harvest in the fall

The candy-colored Victorian cottages of the Oak Bluffs Camp Ground on Martha's Vineyard

The Elizabeth Islands, seen from the Gay Head Cliffs on Martha's Vineyard

Quechee Gorge, Quechee, VT

Early October on the Kancamagus Highway between Lincoln and Conway, NH

The beach at Naskeag Point, ME, on a perfect summer day

Taste Treats

Tiramisu at the Venetian in Torrington, CT

Johnnycakes at The Commons Lunch, Little Compton, RI

Clam chowder at The Flume, Mashpee, MA

Portuguese kale soup at Land Ho, Orleans, MA

San Angel autentica salsa chipotle in Stowe, VT

Sugar on snow at a maple sugar house in Vermont or New Hampshire

Lobster at a lobster pound on the Maine coast

Fresh goat cheese at the farmers market, Blue Hill, ME

Special Moments

Sunset at Napatree Point, Watch Hill, Westerly, RI

Riding horseback through the dunes of Provincetown at sunset

Glimpsing Nantucket town from the approaching ferry

Watching a whale surface from beneath your whale-watch boat off Portsmouth, NH

Picnicking at Smugglers' Notch, VT

Seeing moose feeding at dusk at Sandy Stream Pond, Baxter State Park, ME

Skiing the first run of the day following a snowstorm at Sugarloaf/USA, ME

Attractions for Kids

Mystic Aquarium, Mystic, CT

The Children's Museum and the Computer Museum, Boston, MA

Old Sturbridge Village, Sturbridge, MA

Green Mountain Flyer excursion train, Bellows Falls, VT

Mt. Washington Cog Railway to the top of Mt. Washington (when the weather is good), Bretton Woods, NH

A ferry ride to the Cranberry Isles from Northeast Harbor, Mount Desert Island, ME

Shopping

Main Street, Mystic, CT

The Peacable Kingdom, Providence, RI

Crafts and antiques shops along Route 6A, Cape Cod, MA

Odyssey Bookstore, South Hadley, MA

Vermont Country Store, Weston, VT

League of New Hampshire Craftsmen shops in Exeter, Concord, Hanover, Lincoln, Manchester, Meredith, North Conway, Sandwich, and Wolfeboro, NH

L. L. Bean and the nearby outlet stores, Freeport, ME

Ski Resorts

Killington, VT, for learning to ski

Jay Peak, VT, for the international ambience

Mad River Glen, VT, for challenging terrain

Stowe, VT, for an overall great place to ski

Woodstock Inn and Resort at Suicide Six, VT, for lodging

Waterville Valley, NH, for vacation packages

Saddleback, ME, for scenic wilderness views

Museums

Barnum Museum, Bridgeport, CT

Rhode Island School of Design Museum, Providence, RI

Whaling Museum, Nantucket, MA

Sterling and Francine Clark Art Institute, Williamstown, MA

Shelburne Museum, Shelburne, VT

Hood Museum of Art, Dartmouth College, Hanover, NH

Portland Museum of Art, Portland, ME

Places to Stay

The Homestead Inn, Greenwich, CT (Expensive)

The Inn at Castle Hill, Newport, RI (Moderate–Expensive)

The Charles Hotel, Cambridge, MA (Very Expensive)

Captain's House Inn, Chatham, MA (Expensive)

Chillingsworth, Brewster, MA (Very Expensive)

Clark Currier Inn, Newburyport, MA (Moderate)

Vermont Marble Inn, Fair Haven (Rutland), VT (Very Expensive)

Fitzwilliam Inn, Fitzwilliam, NH (Inexpensive)

Claremont Hotel, Southwest Harbor, ME (Expensive–Very Expensive)

Places to Eat

Truc Orient Express, Hartford, CT (Moderate–Expensive)

Manisses, Block Island, RI (Expensive)

Le Marquis de Lafayette, Boston, MA (Very Expensive)

Giordano's, Martha's Vineyard, MA (Inexpensive)

Chanticleer, Nantucket, MA (Very Expensive)

Yankee Pedlar Inn, Holyoke, MA (Moderate)

The Arlington Inn, Arlington, VT (Expensive)

Henry David's, Keene, NH (Inexpensive–Moderate)

Fisherman's Friend, Stonington, ME (Inexpensive)

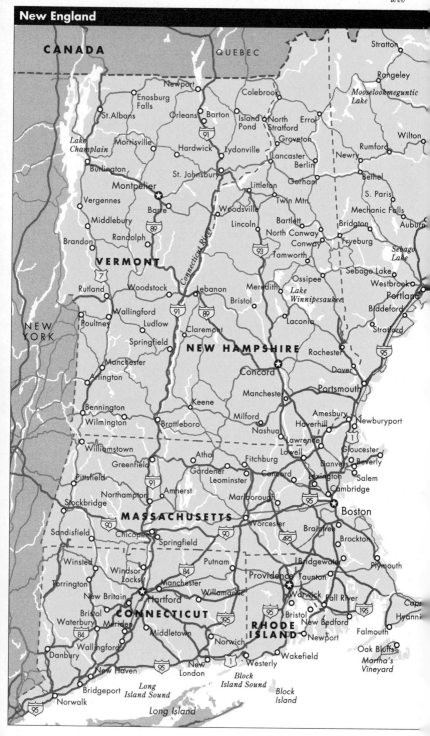

New England

CANADA QUEBEC

Stratton
Rangeley
Mooselookmeguntic Lake
Wilton
Newport
Enosburg Falls
Colebrook
St. Albans
Orleans Barton
Island Pond
North Stratford
Errol
Groveton
Newry
Rumford
Lake Champlain
Morrisville
Hardwick
Lydonville
Lancaster
Berlin
Bethel
S. Paris
Burlington
St. Johnsbury
Gorham
Mechanic Falls
Montpelier
Littleton
Twin Mtn.
Auburn
Vergennes
Barre
Woodsville
Bartlett
Bridgton
Fryeburg
Sebago Lake
Middlebury
Randolph
Lincoln
North Conway
Conway
Sebago Lake
Brandon
Conway
Westbrook
VERMONT
7
Woodstock
Lebanon
Meredith
Lake Winnipesaukee
Portland
Rutland
Bristol
Biddeford
Wallingford
Ludlow
Claremont
Laconia
Stratford
Poultney
Springfield
95
Manchester
Rochester
Arlington
NEW HAMPSHIRE
Dover
Concord
Portsmouth
Bennington
Keene
Manchester
Wilmington
Brattleboro
Milford
Amesbury
Newburyport
Nashua
Haverhill
Williamstown
Lawrence
Lowell
Gloucester
Atho
Fitchburg
Beverly
Greenfield
Gardener
Concord
Danvers
Pittsfield
Leominster
Lexington
Salem
Northampton
Amherst
Cambridge
Stockbridge
Marlborough
90
MASSACHUSETTS
Worcester
Boston
Sandisfield
Chicopee
Braintree
Brockton
Springfield
495
Winsted
Putnam
Bridgewater
Plymouth
Windsor Locks
84
Providence
Taunton
Torrington
Manchester
Warwick
Fall River
New Britain
Willamantic
195
Bristol
Hartford
Bristol
New Bedford
Cape
Waterbury
Merider
CONNECTICUT
RHODE ISLAND
Newport
Hyanni
Danbury
Middletown
395
Falmouth
Wallingford
Norwich
Oak Bluffs
New Haven
95
Wakefield
Martha's Vineyard
Bridgeport
New London
Westerly
Norwalk
Long Island Sound
Block Island Sound
Block Island
Long Island

NEW YORK
89
91
93
89
91

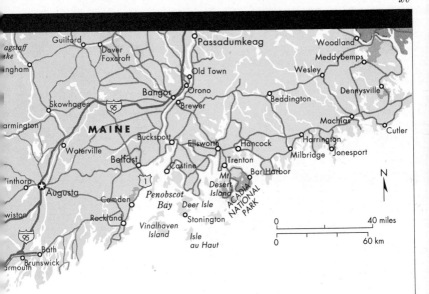

ATLANTIC OCEAN

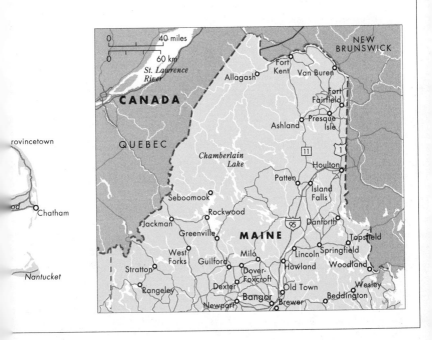

xvi

World Time Zones

Numbers below vertical bands relate each zone to Greenwich Mean Time (0 hrs.).
Local times frequently differ from these general indications,
as indicated by light-face numbers on map.

Algiers, **29**	Berlin, **34**	Delhi, **48**	Istanbul, **40**
Anchorage, **3**	Bogotá, **19**	Denver, **8**	Jerusalem, **42**
Athens, **41**	Budapest, **37**	Djakarta, **53**	Johannesburg, **44**
Auckland, **1**	Buenos Aires, **24**	Dublin, **26**	Lima, **20**
Baghdad, **46**	Caracas, **22**	Edmonton, **7**	Lisbon, **28**
Bangkok, **50**	Chicago, **9**	Hong Kong, **56**	London (Greenwich), **27**
Beijing, **54**	Copenhagen, **33**	Honolulu, **2**	Los Angeles, **6**
	Dallas, **10**		Madrid, **38**
			Manila, **57**

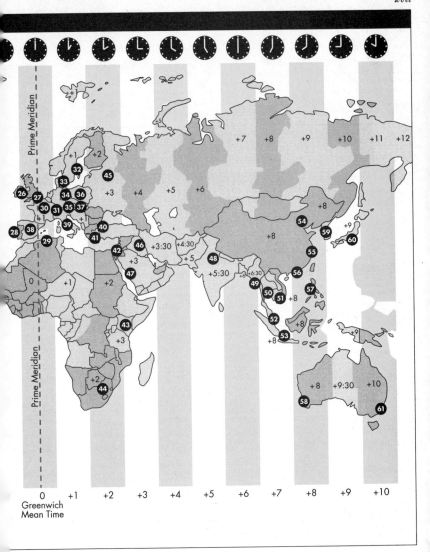

Prime Meridian

Prime Meridian

| 0 | +1 | +2 | +3 | +4 | +5 | +6 | +7 | +8 | +9 | +10 |

Greenwich
Mean Time

Introduction

by William G. Scheller

A contributing editor to National Geographic Traveler, *William Scheller writes frequently on travel; his books* New Hampshire Backroads *and* New Hampshire: Portrait of the Land and Its People *appeared in 1989 and 1988.*

The man was a professor from Vermont who had spent four months of a sabbatical in Palo Alto, California. He had liked it well enough at first, but after a while it began to wear on him, and he was happy to get back to New England.

Asked what it was that bothered him about Palo Alto, the professor gave an answer that might strike anyone but a New Englander as more than a little odd: "Day after day," he said, "it was just so *beautiful.* It never rained. The sky never clouded over. It never got too hot or too cold."

Thus the Vermonter writes off paradise; thus the man from New England voices his suspicion of a place where it is never November.

More than a few observers, both in and outside New England, would be quick to conclude that the professor's remarks are yet another indication of the region's lingering Calvinism, of its mistrust of too much real or metaphoric good weather. Ishmael of *Moby-Dick*, a creation of an adopted New Englander, confessed to experiencing "a damp, drizzly November in my soul." Is that a model phrase for describing the way people feel here?

Not really; psychologizing about the lowering of Calvinist doom clouds over the collective New England brow is a silly academic game. Yet the habit is so pervasive that it is even regularly suggested that the reason the Boston Red Sox fall short of a championship each year is that they are predestined to disappoint us, to chasten the exuberant and mock the vanity of human wishes. But we should leave Cotton Mather out of it; the real problems for the Red Sox are inconsistent pitching and stranding men on base.

In fact, New England has something that none of her partisans would trade for an endless spate of California weather, and that something is October. The knowledge of October —or of bright May at the year's antipodes—sustains a New Englander through the hottest August or the muddiest March. No one who prefers a place where May is perpetual could understand such a thing. We are not, in these six small states, won over to Puritan gloom; we simply have a taste for hills and valleys in our weather as in our landscape. Listen again to Melville, who wrote that "truly to enjoy bodily warmth, some small part of you must be cold, for there is no quality in this world that is not what it is merely by contrast . . . If you flatter yourself that you are all over comfortable, and have been so a long time, then you cannot be said to be comfortable any more." We are comfortable up here, by Melville's lights.

Hills and valleys, sun and shadow: New England lives by variety. To the rest of America, this region is usually summed up in the visual shorthand of a white steeple rising above a village green. But lovely—and actual—as that image might be, it says nothing of the roadless spruce forest of northern Maine; the empty brick mills of Manchester, New Hampshire; the thicket of old and new suburbs surrounding Boston; or the busy streets of downtown Hartford and New Haven. And along with that white Georgian steeple, a score or more of architectural styles compete to define New England's built environment. The clean-line country saltboxes, the boxlike yet peerlessly graceful Federalist mansions of Salem and Portsmouth, and the Greek Revival farmhouses that look like democratic temples in an Arcadian wood all have one abiding virtue: their seemliness in a varied landscape. They fit the hills and valleys of New England like a land-hugging Wright house fits the prairie.

As for the diversity of its people, don't let folklore's sly country Yankees and proper Bostonians even begin to crowd New England's stage. Look at the roster of famous individuals this place has put before the world, and you'll find the names of Paul Revere and John Hancock, James Michael Curley and Marvelous Marvin Hagler, Leonard Bernstein and Martin Luther King (he studied divinity at Boston University), Julia Child and Jay Leno. The local literary reputation is one of which you will have heard; it was earned not only by the Brahmin poets Oliver Wendell Holmes and Robert Lowell, and by Ralph Waldo Emerson and Robert Frost (who made of plain New England speech one of the great poetic languages of the world), but by a French Canadian printer's son from Lowell, Massachusetts, who dreamed by the banks of the Merrimack and at tenement windows long before he went on the road: Jack Kerouac was a great New England voice and the scion of one of its most important ethnic strains.

For all this diversity, and for all our protestations that the dour echoes of Puritanism are but a part of the New England legacy, we have to admit that there is a prevailing *seriousness* here. Or perhaps *earnestness* is the word. It comes across sometimes on Town Meeting Day, when the residents of this or that obscure hamlet vote to advise the president on the proper course of action in Central America or South Africa. It comes across every day in the letters to the editor of the *Boston Globe:* Just when you think the last word has been said on a subject—or that no word need be said—someone from Cohasset or Damariscotta will check in with an epistolary rap on the knuckles. A recent letter to the *Globe* went on for three paragraphs about how we ought to wear our hats when it's cold out; another writer explained that she and her husband didn't feel comfortable about sweetening food with honey because it exploited the bees. The tradition of *right thinking* runs deep in this part of the world, and one never knows when a New Englander is going to spring out from behind a maple tree and tell you how to behave.

Fortunately, this strain of behavior is countered by the legendary Yankee independent-mindedness, which is based on the notion that while you have the right to put your two cents in, I have the right not to listen to a thing you say. Henry David Thoreau, who is something of a patron saint in some New England circles (and elsewhere), exemplified both sides of the regional character. He was never at a loss for astonishment, yet he celebrated the person who hears a "different drummer" and goes his or her own way.

"New England," the writer Bernard DeVoto stated nearly 60 years ago, "is a finished place. It is the first old civilization, the first permanent civilization in America." Do these words still apply? No doubt New England is old, in terms of civilization in North America, and if not permanent it is at least exceedingly durable. As to whether it is "finished"— well, what is ever finished until it has finished living? New England certainly hasn't, no matter how carefully it husbands its past. If there is truth and a positive meaning in DeVoto's words, it is that New England has done a better job than most places of defining the terms of its growth and the tenor of its changes. It figured out, somewhere along the way, what it wants to be. Sometimes it tries in earnest and in large measure succeeds, as in Vermont's heroic effort to maintain a rural character even as it welcomes tourism and light industry. Sometimes, as in Boston's struggle to maintain its civilized image in the face of a growing susceptibility to modern urban ills, the results are less impressive. But even New England's failings are held against a certain standard, a certain sense of the proper order of things.

Perhaps most important, New England has earned the love and loyalty of its people. A Massachusetts senator named Leverett Saltonstall once observed that "the real New England Yankee is a person who takes the midnight train home from New York." Or makes sure he is back from Palo Alto by Christmas.

1 Essential Information

Before You Go

Visitor Information

Connecticut Department of Economic Development, 865 Brook St., Rocky Hill, CT 06037, tel. 203/258–4200 or 800/282–6863.

Maine Publicity Bureau, 97 Winthrop St., Hallowell, ME 04347, tel. 207/289–2423 or 800/533–9595.

Maine Innkeepers Association, 142 Free St., Portland, ME 04101, tel. 207/773–7670.

Massachusetts Office of Travel and Tourism, 100 Cambridge St., Boston, MA 02202, tel. 617/727–3201.

New Hampshire Office of Vacation Travel, Box 856, Concord, NH 03301, tel. 603/271–2666; 603/224–2525 or 800/258–3608 for a recorded message about seasonal events.

Rhode Island Tourism Division, 7 Jackson Walkway, Providence, RI 02903, tel. 401/277–2601 or 800/556–2484 in the northeastern United States.

Vermont Travel Division, 134 State St., Montpelier, VT 05602, tel. 802/828–3236.

Vermont Chamber of Commerce, Department of Travel and Tourism, Box 37, Montpelier, VT 05602, tel. 802/223–3443.

Tour Groups

Those who want to see as much of New England as possible in a realistic amount of time might consider an escorted motorcoach tour. Group tours generally pack a lot of sightseeing into a relatively short time span, traversing the six New England states in a week or so. In this way you'll hit all the traditional attractions and perhaps a few out-of-the-way places you might not find on your own. If freedom and flexibility are more important to you, pick up a map, decide where you want to go, and experience New England on your own. Most major rental-car companies offer weekly rates.

When considering a tour, be sure to find out (1) exactly what expenses are included, in particular, tips, taxes, side trips, meals, and entertainment; (2) the ratings of all hotels on the itinerary and the facilities they offer; (3) the additional cost of single accommodations when you are traveling alone; and (4) the number of travelers in your group. Learn whether the tour operator reserves the right to change hotels, routes, or even prices after you've booked, and determine the operator's policy with regard to cancellations, complaints, and trip-interruption insurance.

The following sampling of operators and packages should give you an idea of what is available. For additional resources, contact your travel agent or the tourist offices listed above. Many tour operators request that bookings be made through a travel agent; there is no additional charge for doing so.

General-Interest Tours

American Express Vacations (Box 5014, Atlanta, GA 30302, tel. 800/241–1700; 800/282–0800 in Georgia) has a 12-day tour to eastern Canada, Maine, Massachusetts, Rhode Island, and Connecticut.

Casser Tours (46 W. 43rd St., New York, NY 10036, tel. 212/840–6500 or 800/251–1411) treks the New England coast for six days of sightseeing; a six-day fall foliage tour is available.

Collette Tours (124 Broad St., Pawtucket, RI 02860, tel. 401/728–1000 or 800/832–4656) has package tours by coach throughout New England.

Domenico Tours (751 Broadway, Bayonne, NJ 07002, tel. 201/823–8687 or 800/554–8687) offers a five-day jaunt that stretches from New York to Acadia National Park in Maine and three-day and four-day tours to Boston, Cape Cod, Martha's Vineyard, Nantucket, and coastal Maine.

Globus-Gateway (69 Austin St., Forest Hills, NY 11375, tel. 212/268–7000 or 800/221–0090) offers seven-day and eight-day autumn excursions as well as one-day excursions up the New England coastline. **Cosmos,** a budget-minded affiliate, offers a nine-day trip.

Gray Line (275 Tremont St., Boston, MA 02116, tel. 617/426–8805) runs one-day excursions along the New England coastline.

Maupintour (Box 807, Lawrence, KA 66044, tel. 913/843–1211 or 800/255–4266) has a 15-day tour that combines the best of New England with French Canada, the Gaspé Peninsula and Laurentian resorts; Maupintour also offers fall foliage tours.

Mayflower Tours (1225 Warren Ave., Downers Grove, IL 60515, tel. 312/960–3430) has an eight-day tour that begins in Boston and meanders through Maine, New Hampshire, Vermont, Rhode Island, and Cape Cod.

New England Vacation Tours (Box 947, West Dover, VT 05356, tel. 802/464–2076 or 800/742–7669) offers a weeklong coach tour of the region.

Paragon Tours (680 Purchase St., New Bedford, MA 02740, tel. 508/996–8276) has tours of Maine, New Hampshire, and Vermont.

Tauck Tours (11 Wilton Rd., Westport, CT 06881, tel. 203/226–6911 or 800/468–2825) offers both summer and fall tours from 7 to 11 days in length, as well as a 10-day cruise/tour aboard the *Newport Clipper.*

Special-Interest Tours

Art and Architecture

Uncommon Boston Ltd. (437 Boylston St., Boston, MA 02116, tel. 617/424–9468) will custom-design tours for travelers with special interests in and around Boston. The company has more than 150 escorts with specialty interests who lead walking or driving tours organized around such themes as literature, art and architecture, antiques—even chocolate. The company schedules special tours for Halloween and St. Patrick's Day, and there are coach tours to Sturbridge Village, Lexington and Concord, and Plimoth Plantation.

Food

Beckham Reception Services (587 Washington St., Canton, MA 02021, tel. 617/821–5990 or 800/343–4323) runs a clambake tour to Bar Harbor, Maine.

Shopping **Golden Age Festival** (5501 New Jersey Ave., Wildwood Crest, NJ 08260, tel. 609/522–6316 or 800/257–8920) offers a four-night coach tour to Maine for senior citizens that includes shopping at outlet stores in Kittery and Freeport.

Package Deals for Independent Travelers

New England Travel (884 Washington St., Norwood, MA 02062, tel. 617/762–1100) arranges air tickets and hotel accommodations for travelers who want to plan their own schedules.

Tips for British Travelers

Visitor Information The **U.S. Travel and Tourism Administration** (22 Sackville St., London W1X 2EA, tel. 071/439–7433) has information and brochures.

Passports and Visas You need a valid 10-year passport to enter the United States (cost £15 for a standard 32-page passport, £30 for a 94-page passport). Application forms are available from most travel agents and major post offices and from the **Passport Office** (Clive House, 70 Petty France, London SW1H 9HD, tel. 071/279–3434 for recorded information, or 071/279–4000). You do not need a visa if you are visiting either on business or pleasure, are staying less than 90 days, have a return ticket, are traveling with a major airline (in effect, any airline that flies from the United Kingdom to the United States), and complete visa waiver form I791, which is supplied either at the airport of departure or on the plane. If you fail to comply with any one of these requirements or are entering the United States by land, you will need a visa. Apply to a travel agent or the **United States Embassy** (Visa and Immigration Department, 5 Upper Grosvenor St., London W1A 2JB, tel. 071/499–3443 for a recorded message, or 071/499–7010). Visa applications to the U.S. Embassy must be made by mail, not in person. Visas can be given only to holders of 10-year passports, although visas in expired passports remain valid.

Airports and Airlines Flying time from all British airports is about 6½ hours on most flights, about 4 hours on the Concorde.

Three airlines fly to Boston from London Heathrow: **British Airways** (tel. 071/897–4000), **Northwest** (tel. 0293/576955), and **TWA** (tel. 071/439–0707). Northwest also has four flights a week to Boston from Prestwick, near Glasgow in Scotland. There are no flights to Boston from London's Gatwick airport.

British travelers combining a New England trip with a visit to New York should consider flying into New York's JFK or Newark airports, which offer more flights from Britain than Boston does. Six airlines fly to New York from London Heathrow: **British Airways, TWA, Air India** (tel. 071/491–7979), **El Al** (tel. 071/437–9255), **Kuwait Airways** (tel. 071/935–8795), and **Pan Am** (tel. 071/935–5400). British Airways has as many as six flights a day, two on the Concorde. Three airlines fly to New York from London Gatwick: **British Airways, Continental** (tel. 0293/567–955), and **Virgin Atlantic** (tel. 0293/567711); British Airways also flies to New York from Manchester, England.

Airfares vary enormously, depending on the type of ticket you buy and the time of year you travel. Full-fare prices start at

£700 round trip for economy (coach class); £1,760 round trip for business class; and £3,270 round trip for first class. Concorde to New York costs £2,125 one way. Round-trip tourist tickets in peak season start at around £360, however, and fares are even lower mid-January to mid-March, ranging from as little as £150 round-trip, though £250 is an average price. Ticket agencies such as Trail Finders, STA, and Travel Cuts also offer good deals.

Customs Entering the United States, a visitor 21 or over can bring in 200 cigarettes or 50 cigars or 3 pounds of tobacco; 1 U.S. quart of alcohol; duty-free gifts to a value of $100. You may not bring in meat or meat products, seeds, plants, or fruit.

Returning to the United Kingdom, a traveler 17 or over can take home (1) 200 cigarettes or 100 cigarillos or 50 cigars or 250 grams of tobacco; (2) one liter of alcoholic drink over 22% volume *or* two liters of alcoholic drink under 22% volume *or* two liters of fortified or sparkling wine; (3) two liters of still table wine; (4) 60 ml of perfume and 250 ml of toilet water; (5) other goods to a value of £32.

Insurance We recommend that you take out insurance to guard against health problems, motoring mishaps, theft, flight cancellation, and loss of luggage. Most major tour operators offer holiday insurance, and details are given in brochures. For free general advice on all aspects of holiday insurance, contact the **Association of British Insurers** (Aldermary House, Queen St., London EC4N 1TT, tel. 071/248–4477). A proven leader in the holiday insurance field is **Europ Assistance** (252 High St., Croydon, Surrey CRO 1NF, tel. 081/680–1234).

Tour Operators The following is a selection of companies that offer tour packages to New England. For details of these and other resources, consult a travel agent.

Bales Worldwide Tours (Bales House, Barrington Rd., Dorking, Surrey RH4 3EJ, tel. 0306/76881), in conjunction with Tauck Tours, offers a 10-day autumn tour of New England that covers Massachusetts, New Hampshire, Vermont, and upper New York State. Tours are timed to coincide with the peak of the New England fall foliage season; prices start at £1,370.

Jetlife Holidays (33 Swanley Centre, Swanley, Kent BR8 7TL, tel. 0322/614801) has an 11-night "Grand New England Coach Tour" that visits Boston, Portland, Mount Canon, Springfield, and Cape Cod; prices range from £989 to £1,089. The "Complete New England Fly/Drive" package gives you 14 nights at prices from £799 to £1,139. Jetlife will also help you plan your own driving holiday in New England.

Kuoni Travel (Kuoni House, Dorking, Surrey RH5 4AZ, tel. 0306/76711) sponsors a 10-night "Grand New England" tour that covers the region's highlights and New York as well; prices start at £959. Kuoni's 7-day "Autumn New England" tour, with prices from £625, not including airfare, is offered in conjunction with Tauck Tours.

Serenissima Travel (21 Dorset Sq., London NW1 6QG, tel. 071/730–9841) offers a lavish "Autumn Colour in New England" tour that emphasizes museum-going as much as foliage-viewing. Accommodations for 12 nights are in first-class ho-

tels, and a guide and lecturer accompanies the tour; prices
start at £1,595.

When to Go

All six New England states are largely year-round destinations. While summer is a favored time all over New England,
fall is balmy and idyllically colorful, and winter's snow makes
for great skiing. The only times vacationers might want to stay
away are during mud season in April and black-fly season in the
last two weeks of May. Note that many country museums and
attractions are open only from Memorial Day to mid-October,
at other times by appointment only.

Summer is a time for festivals throughout New England (*see*
Festivals and Seasonal Events in each of the state chapters below). Outdoor music festivals draw crowds to Tanglewood in
the Massachusetts Berkshire Mountains; to Newport, Rhode
Island; and to Bretton Woods in New Hampshire. (Reservations for these popular events should be made months in
advance.) Memorial Day is the start of the migration to the
beaches and the mountains, and summer begins in earnest on
July 4. Those who are driving to Cape Cod in July or August
should know that Friday and Sunday are the days weekenders
clog the overburdened Route 6; a better time to visit the beach
areas and the islands may be after Labor Day.

Fall is the most colorful season in New England, a time when
many inns and hotels are booked months in advance by foliage-
viewing visitors. The first scarlet and gold colors emerge in
mid-September in northern areas; "peak" color occurs at different times from year to year. Generally, it is best to visit the
northern reaches in early October and then to move southward
as the month progresses.

All leaves are off the trees by Halloween, and hotel rates fall as
the leaves do, dropping significantly until ski season begins.
November and early December are hunting season in much of
New England; those who venture into the woods then should
wear bright red or orange clothing.

Winter is the time for downhill and cross-country skiing. New
England's major ski resorts, having seen dark days in years
when snowfall was meager, now have snowmaking equipment.

In spring, despite mud season, maple sugaring goes on in
Maine, New Hampshire, and Vermont, and the fragrant scent
of lilacs is never far behind.

Climate What follows are average daily maximum and minimum temperatures for some major cities in New England.

Hartford, CT								
Jan.	36F	2C	**May**	70F	21C	**Sept.**	74F	23C
	20	−7		47	8		52	11
Feb.	38F	3C	**June**	81F	27C	**Oct.**	65F	18C
	20	−7		56	13		43	6
Mar.	45F	7C	**July**	85F	29C	**Nov.**	52F	11C
	27	−3		63	17		32	0
Apr.	59F	15C	**Aug.**	83F	28C	**Dec.**	38F	3C
	38	3		61	16		22	−6

Boston, MA	Jan.	36F	2C	May	67F	19C	Sept.	72F	22C
		20	−7		49	9		56	13
	Feb.	38F	3C	June	76F	24C	Oct.	63F	17C
		22	−6		58	14		47	8
	Mar.	43F	6C	July	81F	27C	Nov.	49F	9C
		29	−2		63	17		36	2
	Apr.	54F	12C	Aug.	79F	26C	Dec.	40F	4C
		38	3		63	17		25	−4

Burlington, VT	Jan.	29F	−2C	May	67F	19C	Sept.	74F	23C
		11	−12		45	7		50	10
	Feb.	31F	−1C	June	77F	25C	Oct.	59F	15C
		11	−12		56	13		40	4
	Mar.	40F	4C	July	83F	28C	Nov.	45F	7C
		22	−6		59	15		31	−1
	Apr.	54F	12C	Aug.	79F	26C	Dec.	31F	−1C
		34	1		58	14		16	−9

Portland, ME	Jan.	31F	−1C	May	61F	16C	Sept.	68F	20C
		16	−9		47	8		52	11
	Feb.	32F	0C	June	72F	22C	Oct.	58F	14C
		16	−9		54	15		43	6
	Mar.	40F	4C	July	76F	24C	Nov.	45F	7C
		27	−3		61	16		32	0
	Apr.	50F	10C	Aug.	74F	23C	Dec.	34F	1C
		36	2		59	15		22	−6

WeatherTrak provides information on more than 750 cities around the world, 450 of them in the United States. Dialing 900/370–8725 will connect you to a computer, with which you can communicate by touch tone (at a cost of 75¢ for the first minute and 50¢ a minute thereafter). A recording tells you to dial a three-digit access code for the destination you're interested in; the code is either the area code (in the United States) or the first three letters of the name of the foreign city. For a list of access codes, send a self-addressed stamped envelope to Cities, Box 7000, Dallas, TX 75209, or call 800/247–3282.

What to Pack

Clothing The principal rule on weather in New England is that there are no rules. A cold, foggy morning can and often does become a bright, 60-degree afternoon. A summer breeze can suddenly turn chilly, and rain often appears with little warning. Thus the best advice on how to dress may be to layer your clothing so that you can peel off or add garments as needed for comfort. Showers are frequent, so pack a raincoat or an umbrella. Even in summer you should bring long pants and a sweater or two, for evenings are often chilly and the sea spray can make things cool on a whale-watch or deep-sea fishing trip. Winter requires heavy clothing, gloves, a hat, warm socks, and waterproof shoes or boots. Keep in mind that the temperature in winter may be less meaningful than the wind-chill factor.

Casual sportswear—walking shoes and jeans—will take you almost everywhere in New England, but swim suits and bare feet will not: Shirts and shoes are required attire at even the most casual venues. Boston is the most cosmopolitan New England city, and you may want to dress up a bit there. Jacket and tie are required in some of the better Boston restaurants, at a number of inns in the Berkshires, and in the occasional more formal dining room in the other states.

Miscellaneous Remember to pack sunscreen lotion, a hat, and an extra pair of glasses, contact lenses, or prescription sunglasses. It's also important to pack any prescription medicines you use regularly, as well as any allergy medication you may need. Drugstores, especially in rural areas, are frequently closed on Sunday. Remember also to pack insect repellent—and use it! Recent outbreaks of Lyme disease all over the East Coast make it imperative (even in urban areas) that you protect yourself from ticks from early spring through the summer.

Carry-on Luggage Passengers aboard major U.S. carriers are usually limited to two carry-on bags. Bags stored under the seat must not exceed 9″ × 14″ × 22″. Bags hung in a closet can be no larger than 4″ × 23″ × 45″. The maximum dimensions for bags stored in an overhead bin are 10″ × 14″ × 36″. Any item that exceeds the specified dimensions will generally be rejected as a carryon and handled as checked baggage. Keep in mind that an airline can adapt these rules to circumstances; on a crowded flight, you may be allowed to take only one carry-on bag aboard.

In addition to the two carryons, passengers may bring aboard: a handbag, an overcoat or wrap, an umbrella, a camera, a reasonable amount of reading material, an infant bag, and crutches, braces, a cane, or other prosthetic device upon which the passenger is dependent. Infant/child safety seats can also be brought aboard if parents have purchased a ticket for the child or if there is space in the cabin.

Checked Luggage Luggage allowances vary slightly among airlines. Many carriers allow three checked pieces; some allow only two. It is best to consult with the airline before you go. In all cases, checked luggage cannot weigh more than 70 pounds per piece or be larger than 62 inches (length + width + height).

Cash Machines

Virtually all U.S. banks belong to a network of ATMs (Automatic Teller Machines) that dispense cash 24 hours a day in cities throughout the country. There are some eight major networks in the United States, the largest of which are Cirrus, owned by MasterCard, and Plus, affiliated with Visa. Some banks belong to more than one network. To receive a card for one of these systems, you must apply for it. Cards issued by Visa and MasterCard also may be used in the ATMs, but the fees are usually higher than the fees on bank cards. There is also a daily interest charge on credit card "loans," even if monthly bills are paid on time. Each network has a toll-free number you can call to locate machines in a given city. The Cirrus number is 800/424–7787; the Plus number is 800/843–7587. Check with your bank for information on fees and on the amount of cash you can withdraw on any given day.

Traveling with Film

If your camera is new, shoot and develop a few rolls of film before leaving home. Pack some lens tissue and an extra battery for your built-in light meter. Invest about $10 in a skylight filter: It will protect the lens and reduce haze.

Film doesn't like hot weather, so if you're driving in summer, don't store film in the glove compartment or on the shelf under the rear window. Put it behind the front seat on the floor, on the side opposite the exhaust pipe.

On a plane trip, never pack unprocessed film in checked luggage; if your bags get X-rayed, say goodbye to your pictures. Always carry undeveloped film with you through security and ask to have it inspected by hand. (It helps to keep your film in a plastic bag, ready for quick inspection.) Inspectors at American airports are required by law to honor requests for hand inspection. The newer airport scanning machines used in all U.S. airports are safe for anything from five to 500 scans, depending on the speed of your film. The effects are cumulative; you can put the same roll of film through several scans without worry. After five scans, though, you're asking for trouble.

If your film gets fogged and you want an explanation, send it to the **National Association of Photographic Manufacturers** (550 Mamaroneck Ave., Harrison, NY 10528). It will try to determine what went wrong. The service is free.

Traveling with Children

New England is largely a family-oriented destination; kids are welcome at all restaurants and included in almost every event. Because some country inns, especially those that specialize in a quiet, romantic atmosphere or those that are furnished with antiques, are wary of having children as guests, those who are traveling with children should discuss the issue when making a reservation. Don't expect innkeepers to baby-sit, either, though most hosts can recommend baby-sitters. Major hotel chains gladly accept children, and concierges can often arrange baby-sitting services.

Visitors to New Hampshire will find supervised children's activities at the weeklong Craftsman's Fair at Lake Sunapee, a children's day at the Farm Museum in Milton, a miniature-horse petting farm in Pittsfield, and hands-on children's museums in Portsmouth and Keene. Visitors to Massachusetts will find programs for kids at the Children's Museum and the outstanding Museum of Science in Boston, as well as the Battleship Massachusetts in Fall River and the Whaling Museum in New Bedford. The **Ritz-Carlton Hotel** in Boston (2 Arlington St., tel. 617/536–5700) features a junior presidential suite, an activity-packed guest room for kids where all the fixtures are sized for children age 3–12.

Renting a vacation home can be the least expensive way to house a family on vacation in New England. A guide to cottage rentals in Vermont, *Four Seasons Vacation Rentals*, is available from the **Vermont Travel Division** (134 State St., Montpelier, VT 05602, tel. 802/828–3236).

Home Exchange One surprisingly low-cost way to vacation in New England is through an exchange of homes. **Vacation Exchange Club** (12006 111th Ave., Unit 12, Youngstown, AZ 85363, tel. 602/972–2186) specializes in domestic home exchanges. The club publishes an annual directory in February and a supplement in April. Membership, at $24.70 per year, entitles you to one listing; photos cost another $9; listing a second home costs $6.

Loan-a-Home (2 Park La., Mount Vernon, NY 10552) is popular with the academic community on sabbatical and with businesspeople on temporary assignment. There's no annual membership fee or charge for listing your home, but one directory and a supplement costs $30. Loan-a-Home publishes two directories (in December and June) and two supplements (in March and September). The cost of all four books in one year is $40.

Publications *Just for Kids: The New England Guide and Activity Book for Young Travelers*, by Ed and Roon Frost (Glove Compartment Books, Box 1602, Fort Smith, NH 03801), is available by mail for $7.95 plus $3 shipping and handling.

Family Travel Times is a newsletter published 10 times a year by Travel With Your Children (TWYCH, 80 8th Ave., New York, NY 10011, tel. 212/206–0688). A one-year subscription for $35 includes access to back issues and twice-weekly opportunities to call for specific advice.

Getting There On domestic flights, children under 2 not occupying a seat travel free. Various discounts apply to children age 2–12. If possible, reserve a seat behind the bulkhead of the plane; these offer more legroom and usually enough space to fit a bassinet (supplied by the airlines). At the same time, inquire about special children's meals or snacks, which are also offered by most airlines. (See "TWYCH's Airline Guide," in the February 1990 issue of *Family Travel Times*, for a rundown on children's services offered by 46 airlines.) Ask the airline if you can bring aboard your child's car seat. For the booklet *Child/Infant Safety Seats Acceptable for Use in Aircraft*, write the Community and Consumer Liaison Division (APA–400 Federal Aviation Administration, Washington, DC 20591, tel. 202/267–3479).

Hints for Disabled Travelers

Recent Vermont laws requiring new construction to include facilities for the handicapped mean that all newer hotels and those that have recently been renovated are likely to have handicapped-access and handicapped-equipped rooms. A list of such facilities is available from the **Vermont Travel Division** (134 State St., Montpelier, VT 05602, tel. 802/828–3236). The official Vermont state map indicates which public-recreation areas at state parks are handicapped-accessible.

The state of New Hampshire publishes a directory for the disabled traveler that lists special facilities, events and their level of difficulty, where guides and assistance can be found, and other information. The directory is available from the **New Hampshire Office of Vacation Travel** (Box 856, Concord, NH 03301, tel. 603/271–2666).

The **Information Center for Individuals with Disabilities** (Fort Point Pl., 27–43 Wormwood St., Boston, MA 02210, tel. 617/727–5540) offers useful problem-solving assistance, including lists of travel agents who specialize in tours for the disabled.

Moss Rehabilitation Hospital Travel Information Service (12th St. and Tabor Rd., Philadelphia, PA 19141, tel. 215/329–5715) provides information on tourist sites, transportation, and accommodations in destinations around the world for a small fee.

Travel Industry and Disabled Exchange (TIDE, 5435 Donna Ave., Tarzana, CA 91356, tel. 818/368–5648), for a $15 (per person) annual membership fee, provides a quarterly newsletter and a directory of travel agencies that specialize in service to the disabled.

Mobility International USA (Box 3551, Eugene, OR 97403, tel. 503/343–1284) is an internationally affiliated organization with 500 members. For a $20 annual fee, it coordinates exchange programs for disabled people in the United States and around the world and offers information on accommodations and organized study programs.

Amtrak (tel. 800/872–7245) advises that you request redcap service, special seats, or wheelchair assistance when you make reservations. (Not all stations are equipped to provide these services.) All handicapped passengers are entitled to a 25% discount on regular coach fares. A special children's handicapped fare is also available, offering qualified kids age 2–12 a 50% discount on already discounted children's fares. Check with Amtrak to be sure discounts are available when you plan to travel. For a free copy of Amtrak's *Travel Planner*, which outlines all its services for the elderly and handicapped, contact Amtrak (National Railroad Corp., 400 N. Capitol St. NW, Washington, DC 20001, tel. 800/872–7245).

Greyhound Lines will carry a disabled person and companion for the price of a single fare. Contact any Greyhound ticket office for details.

Publications Twin Peaks Press publishes three useful resources: *Travel for the Disabled* ($9.95), *Directory of Travel Agencies for the Disabled* ($12.95), and *Wheelchair Vagabond* ($9.95). Order through a bookstore or from the publisher, Twin Peaks Press (Box 129, Vancouver, WA 98666, tel. 206/694–2462). When ordering by mail, add $2 postage for one book, $1 for each additional book.

Access to the World: A Travel Guide for the Handicapped, by Louise Weiss, offers tips on travel and accessibility around the world. It is available from Henry Holt & Co. for $12.95 (tel. 800/247–3912; order number 0805001417).

Access America: An Atlas and Guide to the National Parks for Visitors with Disabilities, published by Northern Cartographic (Box 133, Burlington, VT 05402, tel. 802/655–4321), contains detailed information on access for the 37 largest and most heavily visited national parks in the United States. Available directly from the publisher, the award-winning book costs $44.95 plus $5 shipping.

Fly Rights, a free brochure available on request from the U.S. Department of Transportation (tel. 202/366–2220), gives airline access information for the handicapped.

Hints for Older Travelers

Many country inns will accommodate requests for rooms on the ground floor if innkeepers are notified when reservations are made. Older travelers may want to request a room with a shower or ask that they not be put in a room with a Victorian clawfoot tub that requires climbing in and out.

The **American Association of Retired Persons** (AARP, 1909 K St. NW, Washington, DC 20049, tel. 202/662–4850) has two programs for independent travelers: (1) the **Purchase Privilege Program,** which offers discounts on hotels, airfare, car rentals, RV rentals, and sightseeing; and (2) the **AARP Motoring Plan,** which furnishes emergency aid (road service) and trip-routing information for an annual fee of $33.95 per person or couple. (Both programs include the member and member's spouse or the member and another person who shares the household.) The AARP also arranges group tours at reduced rates through two companies: **Olson-Travelworld** (100 N. Sepulveda Blvd., El Segundo, CA 90245, tel. 213/323–7323). As of January 1991, tours will be arranged by **American Express Vacations** (*see* Tour Groups, above). AARP members must be 50 years or older; annual dues are $5 per person or per couple.

Elderhostel (80 Boylston St., Suite 400, Boston, MA 02116, tel. 617/426–7788) is an innovative 17-year-old educational program for people 60 and older. Participants live in dorms on some 1,200 campuses around the world. Mornings are devoted to lectures and seminars, afternoons to sightseeing and field trips. Fees for two- to three-week trips, including room, board, tuition, and round-trip transportation, range from $1,700 to $3,200. The catalog is free for the first year (and if you participate in a program); after that it costs $10.

National Council of Senior Citizens (925 15th St. NW, Washington DC 20005, tel. 202/347–8800) is a nonprofit advocacy group with some 5,000 local clubs across the country. Annual membership ($12 per person or per couple) brings you a monthly newspaper with travel information and an ID card for reduced-rate hotels and car rentals.

Mature Outlook (6001 N. Clark St., Chicago, IL 60660, tel. 800/336–6330), a subsidiary of Sears Roebuck & Co., is a travel club for people over 50, with hotel and motel discounts and a bimonthly newsletter. Annual membership is $9.95; there are 800,000 members currently. Instant membership is available at participating Holiday Inns.

Golden Age Passport is a free lifetime pass to all parks, monuments, and recreation areas run by the federal government. People over age 62 can pick one up at any national park that charges admission. The passport also provides a 50% discount on camping, boat launching, and parking (lodging is not included). A driver's license or other proof of age is required.

Saga International Holidays (120 Boylston St., Boston, MA 02116, tel. 800/343–0273) specializes in group travel for people over 60, offering a variety of tour packages at various prices.

September Days Club (tel. 800/241–5050) is run by the moderately priced Days Inns of America. The $12 annual membership fee for individuals or couples over 50 entitles them to reduced car-rental rates and reductions of 15%–50% at most of the chain's 350 motels.

Amtrak (tel. 800/872–7245) requests advance notice to provide redcap service, special seats, or wheelchair assistance at stations that are equipped to provide these services. Elderly passengers are entitled to a 25% discount on regular coach fares. (Check with Amtrak about possible exceptions to these discounts.) For a free copy of Amtrak's *Travel Planner*, which outlines its services for elderly and handicapped travelers, contact Amtrak (National Railroad Corp., 400 N. Capitol St. NW, Washington, DC 20001).

Greyhound Lines has special fares for senior citizens, subject to date and destination restrictions. Contact any Greyhound ticket office for details.

When using an AARP or other discount identification card, ask for reduced hotel rates when you make your reservation, not when you check out. At restaurants, show your card to the maitre d' before you're seated, since discounts may be limited to certain set menus, days, or hours. When renting a car, remember that economy cars, priced at promotional rates, may cost less than cars available with your discount ID card.

Publications   *The International Health Guide for Senior Citizen Travelers*, by W. Robert Lange, M.D., is available for $4.95 plus $1 shipping, and *The Senior Citizens Guide to Budget Travel in the United States and Canada*, by Paige Palmer, is available for $4.95 plus $1 shipping, both from Pilot Books (103 Cooper St., Babylon, NY 11702, tel. 516/422–2225).

The Discount Guide for Travelers Over 55, by Caroline and Walter Weintz, lists helpful addresses, package tours, and reduced-rate car rentals in the United States and abroad. To order, send $7.95 plus $1.50 shipping to Penguin USA/NAL (120 Woodbine St., Bergenfield, NJ 07621, tel. 800/526–0275; order number ISBN 0–525–483–58–6).

Further Reading

New England has been home to some of America's classic authors, among them Herman Melville, Henry David Thoreau, Edith Wharton, Mark Twain, Robert Frost, and Emily Dickinson. Thoreau wrote about New England in *Cape Cod*, *Maine Woods*, and his masterpiece, *Walden*. Melville's *Moby-Dick*, set on a 19th-century Nantucket whaler, captures the spirit of the whaling era. Nathaniel Hawthorne portrayed early New England life in his novels *The Scarlet Letter* and *The House of the Seven Gables* (the actual house, in Salem, Massachusetts, is open to the public for guided tours). *The Country of the Pointed Firs*, by Sarah Orne Jewett, is a collection of sketches about the Maine coast at the turn of the century.

Inside New England, by Judson Hale, the longtime editor of *Yankee* magazine, examines with humor all aspects of the six states, including small-town life, language, legends, even the weather. David Laskin's *Eastern Islands* tours many of the unbridged islands of the East Coast from Maine to Florida, including Nantucket, Martha's Vineyard, and Block Island.

Maine, A Guide Downeast, edited by Dorris A. Isaacson, and *Maine: An Explorer's Guide*, by Christina Tree and Mimi Steadman, are useful guides to sights, hotels, and restaurants throughout Maine. Among books written about the Maine Islands are Philip Conkling's *Islands in Time*, Bill Caldwell's *Islands of Maine*, and Charlotte Fardelmann's *Islands Down East*. The Kennebunk resident Kenneth Roberts set a series of historical novels, beginning with *Arundel*, in the coastal Kennebunk region during the Revolutionary War. Carolyn Chute's *The Beans of Egypt, Maine* offers a fictional glimpse of the hardships of contemporary rural life in that state.

A Guide to the Salem Witchcraft Hysteria of 1692, by David C. Brown, explores the witchcraft hysteria that swept the North Shore of Massachusetts and the Puritan culture behind it. The naturalist Henry Beston's *The Outermost House* chronicles Cape Cod's seasons during a solitary year the author spent in a cabin at the ocean's edge. Practical information about the Cape and the islands is available in *Short Bike Rides on Cape Cod, Nantucket and the Vineyard*, by Edwin Mullen and Jane Griffith; *Short Nature Walks on Cape Cod and the Vineyard*, by Hugh and Heather Sadlier; *Cape Cod, Its People and Their History*, by Henry C. Kittredge (first published in 1930); and *Nantucket: The Life of an Island*, by Edwin P. Hoyt.

Vermont: An Explorers Guide, by Christina Tree and Peter Jennison, is a comprehensive guide to virtually every back road, event, attraction, town, and recreational opportunity in Vermont. Charles Morrissey's *Vermont: A History* delivers just what the title promises. Peter S. Jennison's *Roadside History of Vermont* travels the most popular highways and gives historical background on points along the way. *Without a Farmhouse Near*, by Deborah Rawson, describes the impact of change on small Vermont communities. *Real Vermonters Don't Milk Goats*, by Frank Bryan and Bill Mares, looks at the lighter side of life in the Green Mountain state.

Visitors to New Hampshire may enjoy *New Hampshire Beautiful*, by Wallace Nutting; *The White Mountains: Their Legends, Landscape, and Poetry*, by Starr King; and *The Great Stone Face and Other Tales of the White Mountains*, by Nathaniel Hawthorne. New Hampshire was also blessed with the poet Robert Frost, whose first books, *A Boy's Way* and *North of Boston*, are set here. It's commonly accepted that the Grover's Corners of Thornton Wilder's *Our Town* is the real-life Peterborough, New Hampshire.

Magnificent photographs fill the pages of *Connecticut*, by William Hubbell, with text by Roger Eddy. Sloan Wilson's novel *The Man in the Gray Flannel Suit* describes Connecticut suburban commuter life in the 1950s. A portrait of Newport, Rhode Island, in its social heyday will be found in Thorton Wilder's novel *Theophilus North*.

Arriving and Departing

By Plane

When booking a flight, air travelers will want to keep in mind the distinction between *nonstop flights* (your destination is the only scheduled stop), *direct flights* (one or more stops are scheduled before you reach your destination), and *connecting flights* (you'll stop and change planes before you reach your destination).

Airports **Logan International Airport,** in Boston, the largest airport in New England, is served by most major carriers. **Bradley International Airport,** in Windsor Locks, Connecticut, north of Hartford, is convenient to southern Massachusetts and all of Connecticut. **Theodore Francis Green State Airport,** just outside Providence, Rhode Island, is another major airport. Additional New England airports served by major carriers include those in Manchester, New Hampshire; Portland and

Bangor, Maine; Burlington, Vermont; and Worcester, Massachusetts.

Smoking The Federal Aviation Administration has banned smoking on all scheduled flights within the 48 contiguous states, within the states of Alaska and Hawaii; to and from the U.S. Virgin Islands and Puerto Rico; and on flights of under six hours to and from Alaska and Hawaii. The rules apply to both domestic and foreign carriers. When necessary, a request for a seat in a nonsmoking section should be made at the time you make your reservation.

Lost Luggage On domestic flights, airlines are responsible for up to $1,250 per passenger in lost or damaged property. If you're carrying valuables, either take them with you on the plane or purchase additional insurance for lost luggage. Some airlines will issue luggage insurance when you check in, but many do not. Insurance for lost, damaged, or stolen luggage is available through travel agents or directly through insurance companies. Luggage-loss coverage is usually part of a comprehensive travel-insurance package that includes insurance against personal accident, trip cancellation, and sometimes default and bankruptcy. Two companies that issue luggage insurance are **Tele-Trip** (Box 31685, 3201 Farnam St., Omaha, NE 68131, tel. 800/228-9792), a subsidiary of Mutual of Omaha, and the **Travelers Insurance Co.** (Ticket and Travel Dept., 1 Tower Sq., Hartford, CT 06183, tel. 203/277-0111 or 800/243-3174). Tele-Trip operates sales booths at airports and issues insurance through travel agents. Tele-Trip will insure checked luggage with a valuation of $500-$3,000 for up to 180 days. Rates for $500 valuation are $8.25 for 1-3 days, $100 for 180 days. The Travelers Insurance Co. will insure checked or hand luggage with a valuation of $500-$2,000 per person for up to 180 days. Rates for $500 valuation are $10 for 1-5 days, $85 for 180 days. Other companies with comprehensive policies include **Access America,** a subsidiary of Blue Cross-Blue Shield (Box 807, New York, NY 10163, tel. 212/490-5345 or 800/284-8300) and **Near Services** (450 Prairie Ave., Calumet City, IL 60409, tel. 708/868-6700 or 800/654-6700).

By Car

Because the six New England states form a relatively compact region with an effective network of interstate highways and other good roads linking the many cities, towns, and recreational and shopping areas that attract visitors, a car is the most effective and convenient means of travel throughout the region. Yet driving is not without its frustrations; traffic can be heavy on coastal routes and beach-access highways on weekends and in midsummer, and Newport in summer and Boston all year long are inhospitable to automobiles. Each of the states makes available, free on request, an official state map that has directories, mileage, and other useful information in addition to routings. The speed limit in New England is 55 miles per hour.

Car Rentals Avis (tel. 800/331-1212), **Budget** (tel. 800/527-0700), **Dollar** (tel. 800/421-6868), **Hertz** (tel. 800/654-3131), **National** (tel. 800/328-4567), and **Thrifty** (tel. 800/367-2277) maintain airport and city locations throughout New England.

By Train

Amtrak (tel. 800/872–7245) offers frequent daily service along its Northeast Corridor route from Washington and New York to Boston, making two stops in Connecticut (New Haven and New London) and two in Rhode Island (Westerly and Providence). Amtrak's *Montrealer* crosses Massachusetts and makes stops in New Hampshire and Vermont on its overnight run between New York and Montreal.

For rail travel within the region, the **Massachusetts Bay Transportation Authority** (tel. 617/227–3200) connects Boston with outlying areas on the north and south shores. Maine's only passenger rail service is offered by Canada's **VIA Rail** (tel. 800/361 –3677), which crosses the state on its service between Montreal and Halifax, stopping at Jackman, Greenville, Brownville Junction, Mattawamkeag, Danforth, and Vanceboro.

By Bus

Greyhound Lines (tel. 800/237–8211) provides bus service to Boston and other major cities and towns in New England. **Vermont Transit** (tel. 207/772–6587) has service between Maine and Vermont. **Peter Pan Bus Lines** (tel. 413/781–3320) serves western Massachusetts and southern Connecticut.

Staying In New England

Shopping

Antiques, crafts, maple syrup and sugar, fresh produce, and the greatly varied offerings of the factory outlets are the principal merchandise that lures shoppers to New England's outlet stores, flea markets, shopping malls, bazaars, yard sales, country stores, and farmers' markets. You'll find few trendy boutiques outside Boston, Newport, and some resort areas on the Cape, but their overstocks are sold in the many designer outlets that are commonplace in all six states. The area around New Bedford in southeastern Massachusetts is a factory outlet paradise; in Maine the outlet area runs along the coast, in Freeport, Kennebunkport, Wells, Searsport, and Bridgton; in New Hampshire the largest outlet concentration is in North Conway.

Boston, Cape Cod, and the Berkshires harbor active artists' communities and many antiques shops, but the days of bargain prices have passed. Local newspapers and the bulletin boards of country stores carry notices of flea markets, shows, and sales that can be lots of fun—and a source of bargains as well.

Opportunities abound for obtaining fresh farm produce from the source; some farms allow you to pick your own strawberries, raspberries, and blueberries, and there are maple syrup producers who demonstrate for visitors the processes involved. The **Massachusetts Association of Roadside Stands** (721 Parker St., East Longmeadow, MA 01028, tel. 413/525–4147) prepares a list of pick-your-own fruit farms in that state. The **Massachusetts Maple Producers Association** (Box 377, Ashfield, MA 01330) has a list of maple sugar houses. The **New Hampshire Department of Agriculture** (Box 2042, Concord, NH 03301) pub-

lishes lists of maple syrup producers and farmers' markets in
New Hampshire.

Sports and Outdoor Activities

Biking   Cape Cod has miles of bike trails, some paralleling the National
Seashore, most on level terrain. Other favorite areas for bicyc-
ling are the Massachusetts Berkshires and the New Hampshire
lakes region. Biking in Maine is especially scenic in and around
Kennebunkport, Camden, and Deer Isle; the carriage paths in
Acadia National Park make ideal bike routes.

Boating and   At most lakeside and coastal resort areas, sailboats and power-
Sailing   boats can be rented at a local marina. Newport, Rhode Island,
is a famous sailing area, and Penobscot Bay in Maine has fine
cruising grounds. The lakes in New Hampshire and Vermont
are splendid for all kinds of boating. The Connecticut River in
the Pioneer Valley and the Housatonic River in the Berkshires
are popular for canoeing.

Camping   Many state parks throughout New England have private campgrounds. A list of private campgrounds in Massachusetts can
be obtained from the **Massachusetts Association of Campgrounds** (100 Cambridge St., 13th fl., Boston, MA 02202). A list
of the national, state, and private campgrounds of New Hampshire is available from the **New Hampshire Campground
Association** (Box 141, Twin Mountain, NH 13595, tel. 603/846–
5511). For a list of private campgrounds in Maine, contact the
Maine Campground Owners Association (655 Main St., Lewiston, ME 04240, tel. 207/782–5874).

Hiking   For information on hiking the Appalachian Trail, which runs
through New England, contact the **Appalachian Mountain Club**
(Box 298, Pinkham Notch, NH 03581, tel. 603/466–2725) or the
White Mountain National Forest (U.S. Forest Service, Box 638,
Laconia, NH 03246, tel. 603/524–6450). **Road's End Farm Hiking Center** (Jackson Hill Rd., Chesterfield, NH 03443, tel. 603/
363–4703) is open from May to December, and the **Audubon Society of New Hampshire** (Box 528B, Concord, NH 03302, tel.
603/224–9909) maintains marked trails for hikers. Nearly all
state parks in Massachusetts provide hiking trails; for a brochure detailing them, write the **Department of Environmental
Management** (Division of Forests and Parks, 100 Cambridge
St., Boston, MA 02202, tel. 617/727–3159).

Hunting and   Maine's north woods are loaded with trout and salmon as well
Fishing   as moose, bear, deer, and game birds. For information, contact
the **Maine Department of Inland Fisheries and Wildlife** (284
State St., Augusta, ME 04333, tel. 207/289–2043). The **Massachusetts Division of Fisheries and Wildlife** (100 Cambridge St.,
Boston, MA 02202) prepares "A Guide to Freshwater Fishing"
and a leaflet on fish and wildlife laws.

Skiing   When there's snow enough on the ground, New Englanders can
be seen skiing on golf courses, in parks, across farmland, and
along quiet roads and streets. For the downhill skier, more
than 50 ski resorts, large and small, can be found in the hills and
mountains of five New England states (*see* Chapter 2, Skiing
New England, for activities and facilities at these resorts).

Beaches

Many state and town beaches in New England have lifeguards on duty, and many beaches have picnic facilities. The waters are at their warmest in August, though even at the height of summer the waters along much of the Maine coast are still cold. The most popular beach areas are on Cape Cod, Martha's Vineyard, Nantucket, and the shore areas north and south of Boston; in the Kennebunk area of Maine; and on Long Island Sound in Connecticut and Rhode Island.

Dining

Seafood is king throughout New England. Clams, quahogs, lobster, and scrod are prepared here in an infinite number of ways, some fancy and expensive, others simple and moderately priced. One of the best ways to enjoy seafood is "in the rough," off paper plates on a picnic table at a real New England clamboil or clambake—or at one of the many shacklike eating places along the coast, where you can smell the salt air!

At inland resorts and inns, traditional fare—rack of lamb, game birds, familiar specialties from other cultures—dominates the menu. Among the quintessentially New England dishes are Indian pudding, clam chowder, fried clams, and cranberry anything. You can also find multicultural variations on old themes, such as Portuguese *chouricco* (a spicy red sausage that transforms a clamboil into something heavenly) and the minced-meat pie made with pork in the tradition of the French Canadians who populate the northern regions.

Dining dress is generally casual, except at some of the distinguished restaurants of Boston; Newport, Rhode Island; Kennebunkport, Maine; and at occasional inns in the Berkshires and elsewhere.

Lodging

Hotel and motel chains provide standard rooms and desired amenities in major cities and at or near traditional vacation destinations. Elsewhere the majority of facilities for travelers are small inns where each room is different and the amenities vary in number and quality. Price isn't always a reliable indicator here; fortunately, when you call to make reservations, most hosts will be happy to give all manner of details about their properties, down to the color scheme of the handmade quilts—so ask all your questions before you book. Don't expect telephone, TV, or honor bar in your room; you might even have to share a bathroom. Most inns offer breakfast—hence the name bed-and-breakfast—yet this formula varies, too; at one B&B you may be served muffins and coffee, at another a multicourse feast with fresh flowers on the table. Many inns prohibit smoking, which is a fire hazard in older buildings, and some are wary of children. Almost all say no to pets.

At many larger resorts and inns with restaurants, the Modified American Plan (MAP), in which rates include breakfast and dinner, is an option or even standard policy during peak summer season. Other resorts may give guests a dinner credit.

Inexpensive accommodations are hard to find in downtown Boston and in the desirable resort areas, especially during high season, but accommodation packages for weekend getaways, local sports, or cultural events are frequently available, and it can pay to ask about them.

Credit Cards

The following credit card abbreviations have been used: AE, American Express; CB, Carte Blanche; D, Discover; DC, Diners Club; MC, MasterCard; V, Visa. It's always a good idea to call ahead and confirm an establishment's credit card policy.

Great Itineraries

The following recommended itineraries, arranged by theme, are offered as a guide in planning individual travel.

Scenic Coastal Tour

From southwestern Connecticut through Rhode Island and Massachusetts to Maine, New England's coastline is a picturesque succession of rocky headlands, sand-rimmed coves, and small towns built on shipbuilding, fishing, and other seaside trades. For more detailed information, follow in individual state chapters the tours noted as "The Coast."

Length of Trip   Six to 10 days

The Main Route   One to two nights: Travel through such classic Connecticut towns as Old Lyme and Mystic, passing through Rhode Island's South County to end up in Newport, with its magnificent turn-of-the-century mansions open for tours.

One to three nights: Stop off in the classic whaling port of New Bedford, Massachusetts, then head for one of the charming summer resort towns of Cape Cod.

One night: Drive north to Boston, one of the country's oldest thriving port cities.

One night: Head north through historic North Shore fishing towns such as Marblehead, Gloucester, and Rockport; visit sea captains' mansions in Newburyport.

Two to three nights: Swing through the Kennebunks and Portland to the small towns and islands around Penobscot Bay.

Factory Outlet Shopping

While this tour generally follows the same coastline as the preceding tour, its focus is less on picturesque surroundings and more on the challenge of finding bargains at New England's wealth of factory outlet stores.

Length of Trip   Four days

The Main Route   One night: Norwalk, Connecticut, has several outlet stores; Mystic, Connecticut, has just opened a factory outlet mall off Route 95, behind the Olde Mistick Village mall.

One night: Bypass Newport, taking I-95 through Providence instead of the slower coastal road, to visit the Fall River and New Bedford area, where there are several outlet malls.

Two nights: Pick up I–495 to bypass Boston and head north for the Maine towns of Freeport, Wells, and Searsport, where outlet shopping abounds.

Historical Preservations

Although they appear to be simply villages that time forgot, these meticulously preserved hamlets are the product of years of research and painstaking restoration, providing a living lesson in American history that's surprisingly free of commercial gloss. Tour escorts are likely to be immensely learned, and costumed interpreters on site give the eerie impression of having just stepped out of a time machine.

Length of Trip Four to six days

The Main Route Two nights: From a base in Boston, venture south to Plimoth Plantation for a glimpse of the lives of the first Puritan settlers. Then refresh your sense of Colonial history by following the Freedom Trail, a route of fine historic sites in the middle of busy modern Boston.

One night: Head west on the Massachusetts Turnpike to Old Sturbridge Village, which brings to life a prosperous farm town of the 1830s.

One night: I–395 will take you to Mystic, Connecticut, and Mystic Seaport, a large, lively restoration that focuses on the whaling and shipbuilding industries of the mid- and late 19th century. Some may wish to end this tour here.

One night: A long half-day's drive to Hartford and then up I–91 into western Massachusetts will take you to Old Deerfield, a tranquil pre-Revolutionary settlement preserved as a National Historic District.

One night: Take either the Massachusetts Turnpike or the more scenic Mohawk Trail west, then take Route 7 to Hancock, Massachusetts, where the Hancock Shaker Village offers an historic glimpse of a way of life that has always stood apart from America's mainstream.

College Towns

As one of the first settled areas in the United States, New England was the site of some of the nation's first colleges and universities. As those fine institutions were joined by others over the years, they enshrined in the American imagination an image of imposing ivy-clad buildings on green, shady campuses. College towns have an added attraction in that they usually offer excellent bookstores and museums, great inexpensive restaurants, and plenty of friendly, casual street life.

Length of Trip Five to 10 days

The Main Route One to three nights: In Boston, perhaps the premier college town in the United States, visit the Cambridge campuses of Harvard University and the Massachusetts Institute of Technology and the busy urban campus of Boston University, centered on Kenmore Square. Head to the suburbs to visit Tufts University (Medford), Brandeis University (Waltham), Boston College (Newton), or Wellesley College (Wellesley).

One to two nights: Drive west to the five-college region of the Pioneer Valley, where you can visit Amherst College, Hampshire College, and the University of Massachusetts in Amherst; Mount Holyoke College in the quaint village of South Hadley; and Smith College in the bustling county seat of Northampton.

One to two nights: Head west to Williamstown, home of Williams College, in the Berkshires. Then swing north into Vermont to Bennington, where you'll find Bennington College.

One to two nights: Travel east to Keene State College, in Keene, a well-kept college town with one of the widest main streets in the world. Head southeast through Worcester, Massachusetts, where Holy Cross is only the best known of several colleges in town, and on to Providence, Rhode Island, where Brown University and the Rhode Island School of Design share a fine hillside site.

One night: An eastward drive along I–95 will take you to New Haven, Connecticut, the home of Yale University, with its gothic-style quadrangles of gray stone.

Kancamagus Trail

This circuit takes in some of the most spectacular parts of the White and Green Mountains, along with the upper Connecticut River Valley. In this area the antiques hunting is exemplary and the traffic often almost nonexistent. The scenery evokes the spirit of Currier & Ives—or at least the opening sequence of the *Newhart* TV series.

Length of Trip   Three to six days

The Main Route   One to three days: From the New Hampshire coast, head inland to Wolfeboro, perhaps detouring to explore around Lake Winnepesaukee. Take Route 16 north to Conway, then follow Route 112 east along the scenic Kancamagus Pass through the White Mountains to the Vermont border.

One to two days: Head south along the Connecticut River, past scenic Hanover, New Hampshire, home of Dartmouth College. At White River Junction, cross into Vermont. You may want to follow Route 4 through the lovely town of Woodstock to Killington, then along Route 100 and I–89 to complete the loop back to White River Junction. Otherwise, simply proceed south along I–91, with stops at such pleasant Vermont towns as Putney and Brattleboro.

One to two days: Take Route 119 east to Rhododendron State Park in Fitzwilliam, New Hampshire. Nearby is Mount Monadnock, the most-climbed mountain in the United States; in Jaffrey take the trail to the top. Dawdle along back roads to visit the preserved villages of Harrisville, Dublin, and Hancock, then continue along Route 101 to return to the coast.

Cape Cod and the Islands

Cape Cod, Martha's Vineyard, and Nantucket are favorite resort areas in and out of season. Because the Cape is only some 70 miles from end to end, day trips from a single base are easily managed. A visit to Martha's Vineyard or Nantucket takes about 2 hours each way from Hyannis (and it's only 45 minutes to the Vineyard from Woods Hole), so you may want to plan to stay overnight on an island, though a day trip is certainly feasible.

Length of Trip Three to five days

The Main Route One day: Drive east on Route 6A to experience old Cape Cod, sampling some of the Cape's best antiques and crafts shops and looking into the historic sites and museums that interest you. Here, too, are charming restaurants and intimate B&Bs. A stop at Scargo Hill Tower allows a view of the lake, the bay, and the village below.

One day: Take Route 6 east to Provincetown. Do a whale-watch in the morning, spend the afternoon browsing the shops and galleries of the main street, and at sunset go for a Jeep or horseback ride through the dunes of the Province Lands. Try one of Provincetown's fine restaurants—or drive to Chatham for dinner and theater.

One day: Take Route 6 to the Salt Pond Visitor Center in Eastham and choose your activity: swimming or surf-fishing at Coast Guard or Nauset Light Beach, wandering the bike path, taking a self-guided nature walk, or joining in one of the National Seashore programs. On the way there, you might look into some of the galleries or crafts shops of Wellfleet.

Four to five days: From Hyannis, take a ferry to either Martha's Vineyard or Nantucket. If you choose the Vineyard, visit the Camp Meeting Grounds and the old carousel in Oak Bluffs, then head for the sunset at Gay Head Cliffs before returning on the evening ferry; if you stay over, explore a nature preserve or the historic streets of Edgartown the next day. In Nantucket, you might explore the Whaling Museum, the mansions, and the shops; if you stay over, bike or take a bus to 'Sconset for a stroll around this village of rose-covered cottages and perhaps a swim at a fairly uncrowded beach.

2 Skiing New England

*by Janet Nelson,
with reviews of
lodging and
nightlife by the
authors of the
state chapters*

*A skier for more
than 20 years,
Janet Nelson
writes on skiing
and other sports
for the* New York
Times *and
numerous
magazines.*

For close to 100 years the softly rounded peaks of New England have attracted people who want to ski. When blanketed with snow, these mountains generate a quiet beauty that lingers in the mind long after one has left them.

In the beginning you had to climb a mountain in order to realize the experience of skiing down it. Then came the lifts; the first rope tow in the United States was installed at Suicide Six in Woodstock, Vermont. T-bars and chairlifts soon followed, and gondolas and tram cars enclosed and protected skiers from the elements on long rides to mountaintops. Today's high-speed chairlifts move skiers up the mountain in half the time of the older lifts.

Ski lifts made the sport widely accessible, and the development of technology for manufacturing and treating snow when nature fell short has made skiing less dependent on weather conditions. The costs of these facilities—and those of safety features and insurance—are borne by the skier in the price of the lift ticket.

Lift Tickets Lift tickets come in many configurations. During the winter of 1990, the price of a one-day lift ticket, purchased separately, was between $15 and $36 midweek, between $26 and $37 on a weekend or a holiday, depending on the resort and the season. Lift tickets are also commonly available as part of two-day, three-day, five-day, or seven-day packages or with discounts for groups, seniors, juniors, or even men or women on particular days of the week. The price range of five-day lift ticket packages during the winter of 1990 was $75–$150.

Several associations of ski areas offer omnibus lift tickets that allow skiers on an extended visit to experience the terrain, facilities, and amenities of several ski areas at a saving over the cost of daily lift tickets. Ski the Vermont Classics and New Hampshire's One Pass and the Valley Pass are the most notable examples of this type.

In recent years some resorts—Ascutney in Vermont and Bretton Woods in New Hampshire among them—have been stopping the sale of lift tickets when lift lines become too long. This does not happen often, but on holidays and busy weekends in February and March it may be prudent to learn what policy is in effect and to reserve your lift ticket by phone when possible.

Accommodations Lodging may be the most important consideration for skiers who plan more than a day trip. While some of the ski areas described in this chapter are small and draw only day trippers, often from nearby towns, most ski areas offer a variety of accommodations—lodges, condominiums, hotels, motels, inns, bed-and-breakfasts—close to or at a short distance from the action. Where appropriate, the resort reviews that follow include a selection of lodging options. Another useful source of information and help are the reservations services that many ski areas operate.

Weekend accommodations can be arranged easily by telephone; for a longer vacation, one should request and study the resort area's accommodations brochure. For stays of three days or more, a package rate may offer the best deal. Packages vary in composition, price, and availability throughout the season; their components may include a room, meals, lift tickets, ski lessons, rental equipment, transfers to the mountain, parties, races, and use of a sports center. Tips and taxes may also be included. Most packages require a deposit upon making the reservation, and a penalty for cancellation usually applies. Package prices are highest during the holidays in December and throughout February, lowest in November and April. Some areas offer mid-season packages in January and March.

Equipment Rental Rental equipment is available at all ski areas, at ski shops around ski resorts, and even in cities distant from ski areas. Shop personnel will advise customers on the appropriate equipment for an individual's size and ability and on how to operate the equipment. It's a good idea to rent ski equipment until you're certain you will stick with the sport and you're competent enough on skis to manage the easy slopes on most mountains.

First-time skiers may find that the best way to start is a one-day outing as close to home as possible. On arrival at the ski area, go to the base lodge and ask at an information desk (general information, ski school, or lift ticket sales) about the arrangements for beginners that most ski areas have. They generally include basic equipment (rental skis with bindings, ski boots, ski poles), a lesson lasting one hour or more, and a lift ticket that may be valid only on the beginners' slopes.

Ski areas have devised standards for rating and marking trails and slopes that offer fairly accurate guides. Trails are rated: Easier (green circle), More Difficult (blue square), and Most Difficult (black diamond). Keep in mind that trail difficulty is measured relative to other trails *at the same ski area*, not those of an area down the road, in another state, or in another part of the country; a black-diamond trail at one area may rate only a blue square at a neighboring area. Yet the trail-marking system throughout New England is remarkably consistent and reliable.

Lessons Within the United States, the Professional Ski Instructors of America (PSIA) have devised a teaching system that is used with relatively little variation at most ski schools. This allows skiers to take lessons at ski schools in different ski areas and still make progress. Class lessons usually last 1½–2 hours and are limited in size to 10 participants.

The skill-transfer feature also applies to children taking lessons. Most ski schools have adopted the PSIA teaching system for children, and many also use Skiwee, which awards progress cards and applies other standardized teaching approaches. Classes for children are normally formed according to age and ability. Many ski schools offer half-day or full-day sessions in which the children ski together with an instructor, eat together, and take their breaks together.

Child Care Nurseries can be found at virtually all ski areas, and some accept kids as young as 6 weeks and as old as 6 years. Parents must usually supply formula and diapers for infants; some youngsters may want to bring their own toys. Reservations are advisable to be certain that a nursery has space for a child. While skiing may be offered for children at age 3, this activity is geared more to play than to serious learning.

A few words about safety: The cartoon image of a person with a leg in a cast lounging before a fireplace at a ski resort seems to stick in people's minds and is a picture many nonskiers associ-

Vermont

Ascutney Mountain Resort, **12**
Bolton Valley Resort, **4**
Bromley Mountain, **13**
Burke Mountain, **5**
Haystack Mountain, **17**
Jay Peak, **1**
Killington, **9**
Mad River Glen, **7**
Magic Mountain, **14**
Mount Snow, **16**
Okemo Mountain, **11**
Pico Ski Resort, **8**
Smugglers' Notch, **3**
Stowe, **2**
Stratton, **15**
Sugarbush, **6**
Suicide Six, **10**

New Hampshire

Attitash, **24**
Balsams Wilderness, **18**
Black Mountain, **22**
Bretton Woods, **19**
Cannon Mountain, **21**
Gunstock, **28**
King Ridge, **29**
Loon Mountain, **23**
Mount Cranmore, **25**
Mount Sunapee, **30**
Pats Peak, **31**
Tenney Mountain, **27**
Waterville Valley, **26**
Wildcat Mountain, **20**

Maine

Big Squaw Mountain, **32**
Mount Abram, **36**
Saddleback Ski and Summer Lake Preserve, **34**
Shawnee Peak at Pleasant Mountain, **37**
Sugarloaf/USA, **33**
Sunday River, **35**

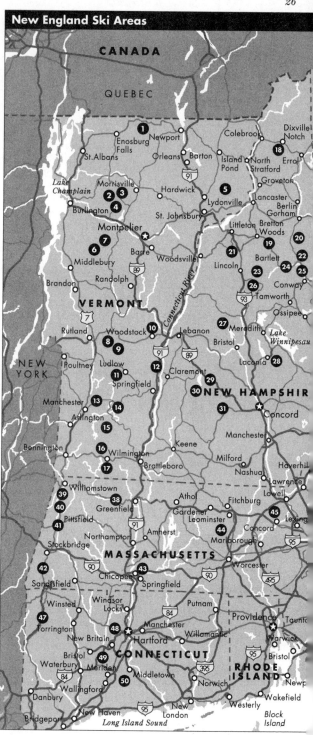

New England Ski Areas

Massachusetts
Berkshire East, **38**
Blue Hills, **46**
Bousquet Ski Area, **41**
Brodie, **39**
Butternut Basin, **42**
Jiminy Peak, **40**
Mt. Tom, **43**
Nashoba Valley, **45**
Wachusett
Mountain, **44**

Connecticut
Mohawk Mountain, **47**
Mount Southington, **49**
Powder Ridge, **50**
Ski Sundown, **48**

ate with the sport. That image is a carryover from the days of stiff skis, soft boots, and nonreleasing bindings, aggravated by icy slopes and a thin snow-cover. Equipment and facilities have improved even in the last 10 years; according to statistics, skiing today is no more hazardous than most other participant sports. Yet accidents occur and people are hurt. All ski areas in the United States have trained Ski Patrolers ready to come to the aid of injured skiers.

For those who are reluctant to ski, and for skiers who want to take a day off during a ski vacation, most larger resorts offer a range of other activities: cross-country skiing on scenic trails, indoor tennis, racquetball, swimming, and the facilities of exercise centers. In addition, villages in the vicinity of many New England ski areas have shops and sites that make a winter's day seem much too short.

Lodging   The following rate categories apply to the hotels and inns described in this chapter.

Category	Cost*
Very Expensive	over $150
Expensive	$100–$150
Moderate	$60–$100
Inexpensive	under $60

All prices are for a standard double room during peak season, with no meals unless noted, and excluding any service charge and local taxes.

Vermont Skiing

The Green Mountains run through the middle of Vermont like a bumpy spine, visible from almost every point in the state, and generous accumulations of snow make the mountains an ideal site for skiing. Today Vermont has 23 Alpine ski resorts with more than 900 trails and over 4,000 acres of skiable terrain. They offer 175 lifts with the capacity to carry nearly 200,000 skiers per hour. In addition, the area offers a wide variety of accommodations and dining options, from inexpensive dormitories to luxurious inns, at the base of most ski mountains or within an easy drive.

Several Vermont ski areas participate in the Ski Vermont's Classics interchangeable lift ticket program. For a nominal fee above the regular price of a lift ticket, you can purchase a ticket that permits skiing at Bolton Valley, Jay Peak, Smugglers' Notch, Stowe, and Sugarbush. The Vermont Ski Areas Association (tel. 802/233–2439) and the participating resorts can provide details of the program.

Ascutney Mountain Resort
Box 129, Brownsville 05037
Tel. 802/484–7711; for snow conditions, 802/484–7711

Ascutney is a new-old ski resort. Its first trails date to 1938, but its present-day configuration was launched in 1983, when new management poured big money into the area. Today it's a modern resort with two base lodges and a village featuring a four-story hotel, condominiums, restaurants, shops, a sports and fitness center, and meeting and conference space. Service, free shuttle buses, and the lack of crowds are big attractions. Another big plus is the fact that the resort limits lift ticket sales, which means lift-line crowds are limited, even on peak days. The area caters to new skiers and families and offers packages ranging from two-day weekends to five days and nights of intensive race-training. The Vermont Handicapped Ski Foundation offers lessons and ski equipment for disabled people.

Downhill Skiing Ascutney's skiing has two distinct parts: the upper mountain's mostly steep, expert pitches, and the lower mountain's gentle, easy runs. A fair number of slopes are designated intermediate, but sections of these could be deceivingly easy or difficult. The 31 trails wind and dip to points for scenic views. Four chairlifts, two of them triples, take skiers up the 1,500 vertical feet. At the base is a pleasant beginner's section.

Cross-Country Skiing For cross-country skiers, Ascutney has 34 kilometers (21 miles) of trails, most of them groomed.

Other Activities The Racquet, Sports and Fitness Center has an indoor pool, Nautilus and free-weight equipment, aerobics space, two racquetball courts, whirlpool, saunas, and massage rooms. An outdoor pool and seven tennis courts are available in summer.

Child Care Children under 6 ski free or can participate in the Teddy Bears day-care program for ages 3 for half or full days, which includes short ski lessons. The Polar Bear program is directed at youngsters in the same age group who have more skiing experience. For those 6–12, Skiwee lessons emphasize the basics and are available for either half or full days.

Lodging **Inn at Weathersfield.** Less than a 30-minute drive from Killington, Magic Mountain, Bromley Mountain, and Ascutney, this 1795 Colonial inn situated on 21 acres combines Colonial and Victorian influences to achieve its comfortable atmosphere. Exposed beams, wide-plank floors, oriental and braided rugs, antiques, and live piano music during dinner set the mood of this retreat. Breakfast, high tea, and dinner are served in the converted carriage-house dining room. *Box 165, Rte. 106, Weathersfield 05151, tel. 802/263–9217, fax 802/263–9219. 12 rooms with bath, 2 suites. Facilities: restaurant, recreation room, sauna, exercise equipment, pool table, videos, swimming/skating pond, horsedrawn sleighs and carriages. AE, D, MC, V. Rates are MAP. Very Expensive.*

Ascutney Mountain Resort. This large, Colonial-style complex, located next to a ski lift, has accommodations that range from simple, modern hotel rooms to three-bedroom suites with kitchen, fireplace, and outdoor deck. *Rte. 44, Box 129, Brownsville 05037, tel. 802/484–7711 or 800/243–0011. 250 rooms with bath. Facilities: 2 restaurants, bar, fitness center, indoor pool, outdoor pool, 7 tennis courts, 2 racquetball courts. AE, DC, MC, V. Expensive.*

Nightlife In addition to the **Winners' Circle Lounge** (tel. 802/484–7711) at the resort, there are night spots in Hanover, New Hampshire. In Ascutney, 5 miles from the resort, **Moguls** (tel. 802/672–9965) has rock bands and dancing. The lounge of the **Coolidge**

Hotel (tel. 802/295–3118) in White River Junction has small bands on weekends.

Bolton Valley Resort
Box 300, Bolton 05477
Tel. 802/434–2131 or 800/451–3220

Although some skiers come for the day, most of the people at Bolton Valley stay at one of the hotels or condominium complexes at the base of the mountain, all within easy walking of the ski lifts. Because of this proximity and the relatively gentle skiing, Bolton attracts more family groups and beginners than singles. The mood is easygoing, the dress and atmosphere casual; there is a ski shop, a country store, and meeting and convention space. Package vacation plans, a specialty at Bolton Valley, range from the All-Frills Vacation for two to five days (with hotel accommodations, breakfast and dinner, ski lifts, daily ski lessons, use of the sports center, night skiing, and cross-country skiing) to a Super Saver low-season package that provides accommodations and lift tickets. A Ski Vermont's Classics lift ticket is available here.

Downhill Skiing Most of the 40 interconnecting trails on Bolton's two mountains, each with a vertical drop of 1,625 feet, are intermediate and novice in difficulty. The new Timberline Peak trail network, with a vertical of 1,000 feet, offers more challenging terrain and wider slopes. Serving these trails are one quadruple chair, four doubles, and one surface lift—enough to prevent long lift lines on all but the most crowded days. Trails are lit for night skiing 6–11 P.M.

Cross-Country Skiing Bolton Valley has 100 kilometers (62 miles) of cross-country trails.

Other Activities The sports center has an indoor pool, Jacuzzi, sauna, one indoor tennis court, and an exercise room. Practically every weekend the resort features on-slope events, parties, festivals, or races. In summer there are eight outdoor tennis courts and a nature center offering guided tours of the region.

Child Care The HoneyBear day-care facility offers supervised play and games, indoors and outdoors, for children 4–6 and nursery care for infants from 3 months to 2 years. For children who want to learn to ski, Bolton Cubs program is for ages 5–7, the Bolton Bears for ages 6–12.

Lodging **Bolton Valley Resort.** Like the ski area, this self-contained resort 20 miles west of Montpelier is geared to families. Hotel units have either a fireplace or a kitchenette, and there are condominium units with as many as four bedrooms. *Bolton Valley 05477, tel. 802/434–2131. 145 rooms with bath. Facilities: 2 restaurants, deli, pub, fitness center, 9 tennis courts, indoor and outdoor pools, sauna, whirlpool. AE, CB, D, DC, MC, V. Expensive.*
Black Bear Inn. The innkeeper made the quilts for the beds in the guest rooms, many of which have balconies and—you guessed it—bears. The in-room movie (a different one each night) is a nice touch at this modern, two-level ski lodge. *Mountain Rd., Bolton Valley 05477, tel. 802/434–2126 or 802/434–2920. 24 rooms with bath. Facilities: restaurant, access to sports club, cable TV, outdoor pool. MC, V. Inexpensive–Moderate.*

Nightlife The Bolton Valley Resort's **James Moore Tavern** (tel. 802/434–2131) has live entertainment, and the **Sports Bar** (tel. 802/434–2131) features sports on TV.

Bromley Mountain
Box 1130, Manchester Center 05255
Tel. 802/824–5522

Venerable Bromley, whose first trails were cut in 1937, is where thousands of skiers learned to ski and learned to love the sport. Bromley today attracts families who enjoy its low-key atmosphere as well as experienced skiers who seek their skiing roots. The area has a comfortable red-clapboard base lodge with a large ski shop and a small condominium complex adjacent to the slopes.

Downhill Skiing While most ski areas are laid out to face the north or west, away from the sun's melting rays, Bromley faces south and east, making it one of the warmer spots to ski in New England. The bulk of its 35 trails are beginner and intermediate, with a few shorter runs in the Most Difficult category. The vertical drop is 1,300 feet. Six double chairlifts, one quad lift, a J-bar, and a surface lift for beginners provide transportation. On weekends and holidays a low-price, two-day lift pass offers a day each at Bromley and at nearby Magic Mountain.

Other Activities Snowboarding and telemark skiing lessons are offered by the ski school. On weekends the area holds a variety of ski races. In summer an Alpine slide with mountain rides is a major attraction for adults and children, and the condominium village has a heated outdoor pool and tennis courts.

Child Care As one of the first ski areas with a nursery, Bromley has maintained its reputation as a good place to bring children. Besides a nursery with half-day and all-day sessions, there is ski instruction in the Mighty Moose Club for children ages 3–5. For children 6–14, the All-Day Discover School includes lunch.

Lodging The town of Manchester, a center of activity for the resorts of Bromley Mountain, Magic Mountain, and Stratton, offers a large variety of accommodations; additional selections will be found under Manchester Lodging and Newfane Lodging in the Southern Vermont section of the Vermont chapter.

Johnny Seasaw's. In the central living room of this Adirondack-style shingled cottage are a circular fireplace, a game room with pool table, and a raised alcove dubbed the "seducerie." Rooms vary from dormitory style to individual cottages with working fireplaces. *Rte. 11/30, Peru 05152, tel. 802/824–5533. 25 rooms with bath. Facilities: restaurant, tennis court, outdoor pool. AE, MC, V. Closed Apr.–mid-May, late Oct. Moderate.*

Kandahar. This 1950 ski lodge has an ambience similar to that of a large chain hotel. Rooms 25–26 have a great view of the 2-acre trout pond in back. *Rte. 11/30, Box 1841, Manchester Center 05255, tel. 802/824–5531. 27 rooms with bath. Facilities: restaurant, lounge, sauna, outdoor pool, cable TV, paddleboat, canoe for trout pond. AE, CB, D, DC, MC, V. Moderate.*

Nightlife Après-ski action is largely located in Manchester. The biggest dance club there is **Alfie's** (tel. 802/362–2637), which has four dance floors and features rock and oldies. The **Marsh Tavern**

(tel. 802/362–4700) at the Equinox Hotel has more subdued pop and cabaret music. (*See* also Nightlife in Stratton, below.)

Burke Mountain
Box 247, East Burke 05832
Tel. 802/626–3305 or 800/541–5480

Burke has a reputation for being a racer's mountain, for the Burke Mountain Academy, adjacent to the ski area, has developed many top racers. In reality, Burke has plenty of terrain for tenderfeet and intermediate skiers. Burke also has slope-side lodging and vacation packages, many of which are significantly less expensive than those at other Vermont areas.

Downhill Skiing With a 2,000-foot vertical drop, Burke is something of a sleeper among the larger eastern ski areas. Although there is limited snowmaking on the mountain, its northern location and exposure assure plenty of natural snow. It has one quad, one double chairlift, and three surface lifts.

Cross-Country Skiing About a mile from the base lodge is a cross-country center with more than 50 kilometers (31 miles) of groomed trails, some leading to high points with scenic views of the countryside.

Child Care A nursery takes children age 4–6 for brief outings on skis to get the feel of sliding. Skiwee lessons through the ski school are for children 5–12. Teenagers are eligible for the Holiday Race Program, which has lots of gate running.

Lodging **Old Cutter Inn.** Only ½ mile from the Burke Mountain base lodge, this small converted farmhouse has a two-bedroom apartment in a separate building. The restaurant features Continental cuisine. *RR 1, Box 62, East Burke 05832, tel. 802/626–5152. 10 rooms, 5 with bath. Facilities: restaurant, lounge, outdoor pool. MC, V. Closed Apr., Nov. Inexpensive.*

Nightlife **Burke Mountain ski resort** (tel. 802/626–3305) hosts dances on Saturday night during the season. In nearby Lindenville, **Gumby's** (tel. 802/626–9898) and **The Packing House** (tel. 802/626–8777) have live music Friday and Saturday during the season.

Haystack Mountain
RR 1, Box 173, Wilmington 05363
Tel. 802/464–5321

Haystack, much smaller than Mt. Snow 4 miles away, offers a more personal, service-oriented atmosphere. The area's original main lodge was an inconvenient distance from the bottom of the mountain, but that problem has been overcome with the addition of a modern, comfortable base lodge close to the lifts. A condominium village at the base of the mountain and three condo complexes around the golf course provide on-site accommodations; a free shuttle connects skiers to all services.

Downhill Skiing Most of the 43 trails on the mountain are pleasantly wide with bumps and rolls and straight fall lines—good-cruising, intermediate runs. A new section was recently opened with three double black-diamond trails—very steep but short. A beginner section, safely tucked below the main-mountain trails, provides a haven for lessons and slow skiing. The area has three triple and two double chairlifts and one T-bar serving its 1,400 vertical feet.

Other Activities Adjacent to Haystack Mountain, the Haystack Golf Club has an 18-hole course designed by Desmond Muirhead.

Child Care A Junior Development Program for children 7–18 allows weekend skiers to learn racing. All-day classes for children 3–12 include lunch. A nursery for ages 3 and 4 has daylong sessions with lunch but no skiing.

Lodging and Nightlife *See* Lodging and Nightlife for Mount Snow, below.

Jay Peak
Rte. 242, Jay 05859
Tel. 802/988–2611 or 800/451–4449

Jay Peak boasts the most natural snow of any ski area in the East. Sticking up out of the flat farmland, Jay catches an abundance of precipitation from the Maritime provinces of Canada. Its proximity to Quebec gives an international flavor to the area—French-speaking and English-speaking skiers mix on the slopes, in the base lodges, at the Hotel Jay, and at the adjacent Jay Peak condominiums. Although Jay is a popular weekend outing for Montrealers, its distance from metropolitan centers along the Eastern seaboard has led to the availability of bargain midweek packages designed to induce skiers to drive the extra hour beyond other northern-Vermont areas. In January, for instance, guests of the Hotel Jay or the condominiums ski free Monday through Friday. A Ski Vermont's Classics lift ticket is available here.

Downhill Skiing Jay Peak is in fact two mountains, the highest reaching nearly 4,000 feet with a vertical drop of 2,150 feet, served by a 60-passenger tram. The area also has a quad, a triple, and a double chairlift and two T-bars. The smaller mountain has more straight-fall-line, expert terrain, while the tram-side peak has many curving and meandering trails perfectly suited for intermediate and beginning skiers. Every morning the ski school offers a free tour, from the tram down one trail, to anyone who shows up at 9 AM.

Cross-Country Skiing A touring center at the base of the mountain has 40 kilometers (25 miles) of cross-country trails.

Child Care An indoor nursery for youngsters 2–7 is open from 9 to 4 at the mountain Child Care Center. Guests of Hotel Jay or the Jay Peak condominiums get this nursery care free, as well as evening care and supervised dining at the hotel. For children 5–12, an all-day Skiwee program includes lunch.

Lodging **Hotel Jay.** Ski-lodge simplicity sets the tone here, with wood paneling in the rooms, built-in headboards, and vinyl wallpaper in the bathroom. Since it's right at the lifts, few come here unless they plan to spend most of their time on the slopes. Rooms on the southwest side have a view of Jay Peak, those on the north overlook the valley, and upper floors have balconies. Summer rates are very low. *Rte. 242, Jay 05859, tel. 802/988–2611 or 800/451–4449. 48 rooms with bath. Facilities: restaurant, bar, 4 tennis courts, outdoor pool, game room, satellite TV, sauna, whirlpool. AE, CB, D, DC, MC, V. Rates are MAP and include lift tickets. Very Expensive.*
Snowline. One side of the hallway in this small lodge used to be a building exterior before it was enclosed, and the decor includes hooked-rug wall hangings. Most important, this retreat

is convenient to the lifts. The small restaurant offers steaks and burgers. *Rte. 242, Jay 05859, tel. 802/988–2822. 10 rooms with bath. Facilities: restaurant, lounge, TV in public area. AE, D, MC, V. Inexpensive–Moderate.*

Nightlife The **International** restaurant at the Hotel Jay (tel. 802/988–2611) has a rock band and dancing on Saturday night during ski season, and there's often a pianist in the hotel's **Sports Lounge.**

Killington
400 Killington Rd., Killington 05751
Tel. 802/422–3333 or 802/773–0755; for snow conditions, 802/422–3261

"Megamountain," "the General Motors of skiing," and just plain "big" are appropriate descriptions of Killington. This is the largest ski resort in the East, the one with the most slopes and the greatest number of skiers. Killington manages its crowds well, if somewhat impersonally, but despite its extensive facilities and terrain, lift lines on weekends—especially holiday weekends–can be long. Killington is a great place to learn to ski, and it has the longest ski season in the East and the best package plans anywhere. With a single telephone call, skiers can select price, date, and type of ski week they want; choose accommodations; book air or railroad transportation; and arrange for rental equipment and ski lessons. More than 100 lodging establishments serve the Killington region, though only a few of them are within walking distance of the lifts. On the Bear Mountain side, there are slope-side condominiums in the Sunrise Mountain Village. Some lodges have free shuttles to the area, and there is a scheduled mountain bus-service. Five base lodges serve the mountains, and there's a restaurant/cafeteria on Killington Peak.

Downhill Skiing It would probably take a good skier a week to test all 107 trails on the six mountains of the Killington complex, even though everything interconnects. About half the 721 acres of skiing can be covered with machine-made snow, and that's still more snowmaking than any other area in the world can manage—an indication of how much terrain there is here. Transporting skiers to the peaks of this complex are a 3.5-mile gondola plus five quad, four triple, and six double chairlifts and two surface lifts. That's a total of 18 ski lifts, a few of which reach the area's highest elevation, at 4,241 feet off Killington Peak, and a vertical drop of 3,175 feet to the base of the gondola. The range of skiing includes everything from Outer Limits, one of the steepest and most challenging trails anywhere, to the Snowshed beginners' area.

Other Activities Killington proper is for skiing, but elsewhere in the region—up and down the access road—there are health clubs, indoor tennis and racquetball courts, ski touring centers, ice skating, and sleigh rides. In summer, Killington has an 18-hole golf course adjacent to a condominium complex; outdoor tennis courts and a tennis school; a concert series; and ballet, theater, and chamber music performances.

Child Care Nursery care is available for children from infants to 8 years old. For youngsters 3–8, the Introduction to Skiing program provides an hour of instruction in the morning or afternoon. The Superstars Program for children 6–12 has all-day care with lunch.

Lodging **Summit Lodge.** Just 3 miles from Mt. Killington on an access road, this rambling, rustic two-story country lodge caters to a varied crowd of ski enthusiasts. Country decor and antiques blend with modern conveniences to create a relaxed atmosphere. Two restaurants allow formal and informal dining. *Killington Rd., Killington 05751, tel. 802/422–3535 or 800/635 –6343, fax 802/422–3536. 45 rooms with bath, 2 suites. Facilities: 2 restaurants, indoor racquetball courts, saunas, Jacuzzi, massage, recreation rooms, fireplace lounge, live entertainment, ice-skating pond. AE, CB, DC, MC, V. Very Expensive.*

The Inn at Long Trail. Only ¼ mile from the Pico ski slopes, this 1938 inn has a Gaelic flavor (Guinness beer is on tap). The decor, with boulders that span inside and outside, makes nature a part of the interior. *Rte. 4, Box 267, Killington 05751, tel. 802/ 775–7181 or 800/325–2540. 26 rooms, 14 with bath; 6 suites. Facilities: restaurant, bar. MC, V. Closed June, mid-Oct.– Thanksgiving. Expensive–Very Expensive.*

Killington Village Inn. This inn, situated in the large, Villages of Killington condominium development, has access to all the facilities of a major resort, including a summer theater and golf course. A fieldstone fireplace dominates the lobby of the chalet-style ski lodge. There's a complimentary shuttle to the base lodge, but the lodge is within walking distance. *Killington Rd., Killington 05751, tel. 802/422–3451 or 800/451–4105. 29 rooms with bath. Facilities: restaurant, pub, tennis court, Jacuzzi, cable TV and movies in rooms. AE, CB, D, DC, MC, V. Rates include full breakfast. Expensive.*

Cortina Inn. The large luxury lodge features small-scale exhibits by local artists and diverse activities. About two-thirds of the rooms have private balconies. *Rte. 4, Killington 05751, tel. 802/773–3331 or 800/451–6108. 98 rooms with bath. Facilities: restaurant, lounge, shuttle service to slopes, 8 tennis courts, indoor pool, fitness center with whirlpools, saunas. AE, D, DC, MC, V. Moderate–Expensive.*

Mountain Inn. This may be a ski lodge, but it has the feeling of a small luxury resort. Popular for conferences, it's within walking distance of Killington's lifts. *RR 1, Box 2850, Killington 05751, tel. 802/422–3595 or 800/842–8909. 50 rooms with bath. Facilities: restaurant, lounge, outdoor pool, whirlpool, sauna, steam room, game room. AE, DC, MC, V. Closed mid-Apr.– late June, mid-Oct–Thanksgiving. Moderate–Expensive.*

Additional accommodations sections will be found under Rutland Lodging in the Central Vermont section of the Vermont chapter.

Nightlife Among the many night spots on the Killington access road are the **Pickle Barrel** (tel. 802/422–3035), which specializes in big rock bands; the **Wobbly Barn** (tel. 802/422–3392), with dancing to blues and rock during the season; and the **Nightspot** (tel. 802/ 422–9885), a singles-oriented dance club. Near Pico, the lounge at the **Inn at Long Trail** (tel. 802/775–7181) features Irish music on weekends.

Mad River Glen
Rte. 17, Waitsfield 05673
Tel. 802/496–3551; for snow conditions, 802/496–2001 or 800/ 696–2001

Mad River Glen was developed in the late 1940s and has changed relatively little since then; the single chairlift may be the only lift of its vintage still carrying skiers. There is a rugged and unkempt aura about this place that for 40 years has attracted core groups of skiers from among wealthy families in the East as well as rugged individualists looking for a less-polished atmosphere.

Downhill Skiing Mad River is steep. More than the usual 25% of the runs are justly classified as expert, and they are often narrow and receive only a bit of grooming during the winter season. Snowmaking is in short supply (12 acres on the entire mountain of 33 trails), but grooming vehicles are used fairly regularly on intermediate and beginner terrain. Besides that old single chairlift, which serves the area's 2,000 vertical feet, Mad River has three double chairlifts.

Child Care The Cricket Club nursery takes children infant and older, while the ski school has Skiwee classes for children 4–12. Junior Racing is available weekends and during holiday periods.

Lodging and Nightlife *See* Lodging and Nightlife in Sugarbush, below.

Magic Mountain
RFD 1, Box 32, Londonderry 05148
Tel. 802/824–5566

About 25 years ago Magic Mountain was conceived and built as a challenge for serious skiers. Serious skiers, it was thought, didn't care for such trimmings as snowmaking and modern lifts, so Magic stood still. In 1985 the area's new owners acquired the adjacent Timber Ridge ski area and connected the two. Today the combined areas, while not fancy, are favorites of local skiers, offering short lift-lines, good snowmaking and grooming, and a down-home atmosphere. Overnighters choose from two condominium complexes at slope-side, two lodges a short walk from the lifts, and lodging at nearby Bromley or Stratton.

Downhill Skiing Magicside, the original Magic ski area, has black-diamond runs off the 1,600-foot vertical. Toward the bottom and angling to the Timberside (the newly acquired and connected Timber Ridge area), the trails are gentle-beginner and cruising-intermediate. Between the two sides are one triple and four double chairlifts and two T-bars. On weekends, a low-price lift ticket allows one day each at Magic and Bromley (about 9 miles away); lift prices are even lower midweek.

Cross-Country Skiing Timberside's cross-country center has 32 kilometers (20 miles) of trails.

Child Care A nursery for children 3–6, located in the base lodge, has indoor activities and outdoor sledding and play. Through the ski school, lessons are available for children 3 and older; 6 and older take classes with other children. A junior race program is also offered.

Lodging The town of Manchester, a center of activity for the resorts of Magic Mountain, Stratton, and Bromley Mountain, offers a large variety of accommodations; additional sections will be found under Manchester Lodging and Newfane Lodging in the Southern Vermont section of the Vermont chapter.

Inn on Magic. Just 125 yards from the lifts of Magic Mountain, this Swiss-style, stucco-and-wood-beam retreat boasts 25 rooms with private bath, color TV, and in some rooms a fireplace. Ski storage lockers provide extra space. At breakfast and dinner choose from American and Continental cuisines. *R.R. 1, Box 30, Magic Mountain Rd., Londonderry 05148, tel. 802/824–6100 or 800/624–4246, 25 rooms with bath. Facilities: restaurant, lounge, game room, widescreen TV, videos, sauna, ski storage. AE, D, MC, V. Closed Apr.–May, Nov. Rates are MAP. Expensive.*

Nightlife *See* Nightlife in Bromley, above, and Stratton, below.

Mount Snow

400 Mountain Rd., Mount Snow 05356
Tel. 802/464–3333 or 802/464–8501; for snow conditions, 802/464–2151.

Established in the 1950s, Mount Snow was promoted as a place where ordinary people could come and feel that they had become skiers. Although the area's ownership and management has changed—in 1977 it was purchased by SKI, Ltd., the owners of Killington—Mount Snow still retains that aura. Both the bustling Main Base Lodge and the Sundance Base Lodge have food service and other amenities. The Carinthia Base Lodge (site of the old Carinthia ski area, absorbed by Mount Snow in 1986) is usually the least crowded and most easily accessible from the parking lot. On weekends the area tends to be crowded, although lines are not as long as you might expect. Mount Snow attracts a good mix of families and single skiers, and it often holds theme weeks for special groups such as college students, families, couples, and racers. A hotel and several condominiums are within walking distance of the lifts.

Downhill Skiing Mount Snow is a remarkably well-formed mountain. From its 1,700-foot vertical summit, most of the trails down the face are intermediate, wide, and sunny. Toward the bottom and in the Carinthia section, are the beginner slopes; most of the expert terrain is on the North Face. In all, there are 77 trails, of which about two-thirds are intermediate. They are served by one quad, six triple, and eight double chairlifts and two surface lifts. The ski school's EXCL instruction program is designed to help intermediate skiers. On the Lower Exhibition trail, skiers can be videotaped and critiqued free of charge; they can then take a one-hour class with one or two other skiers who need the same type of instruction.

Cross-Country Skiing Four cross-country trail areas within 4 miles of the resort provide more than 100 kilometers (62 miles) of varied terrain.

Other Activities Ice skating and sleigh rides head the list of nonskiing winter activities at Mount Snow. In summer, Mount Snow has an 18-hole golf course and a golf school that runs from May to September. The area also conducts a mountain-biking instruction program and rents bikes for use on its trails.

Child Care The Pumkin Patch nursery takes children age 6 weeks to 8 years and provides indoor and outdoor supervised play. The ski school offers Skiwee programs, with full-day or half-day sessions for ages 3–12.

Lodging **Inn at Sawmill Farm.** This small, aristocratic inn is a touch on the formal side: The decor has the country look one finds in the glossy magazines, and men must wear jackets in the public areas after 6 PM. The 10 outside rooms are the largest and have working fireplaces. The dining room has a sophisticated menu and wine list. *Rte. 100, West Dover 05356, tel. 802/464-8131. 21 rooms with bath. Facilities: outdoor pool, tennis court. No credit cards. Closed mid-Apr.–mid-May. Very Expensive.*

The White House at Wilmington. The grand staircase in this Federal-style mansion leads to spacious rooms that are individually decorated and have antique bathrooms, brass wall sconces, mah-jongg sets, and in some cases the home's original wallpaper. The newer section has more contemporary plumbing; some rooms have fireplaces and lofts. The inn is set back from busy Route 9, so road noise is no problem. A description of the public rooms—heavy velvet drapes, tufted leather wingchairs—suggests formality, yet the atmosphere here is casual and comfortable. Although it's just a short drive to the downhill skiing of Mt. Snow and Haystack, the White House is primarily a cross-country ski touring center, with a rental shop and extensive trails. Instruction is also available. *Rte. 9, Wilmington 05363, tel. 802/464-2135. 12 rooms with bath. Facilities: restaurant, lounge, Jacuzzi, sauna, indoor and outdoor pools. AE, CB, DC, MC, V. Rates are MAP. Very Expensive.*

The Hermitage. Everywhere you look there is evidence of the owner Jim McGovern's passion for decoys, wine, and Michel Delacroix prints. The duck pond and the roaming game-birds make staying at this 19th-century estate like visiting the country during the hunt season. Rooms are in two buildings—the Wine House is the newest, built 12 years ago; the Brookbound Inn, which has the most modest rooms, is ¼ mile down the road. *Coldbrook Rd., Box 457, Wilmington 05363, tel. 802/464-3511. 15 rooms with bath in the main inn, 14 rooms with bath at Brookbound. Facilities: restaurant, lounge, sauna, tennis court. AE, DC, MC, V. Rates are MAP. Expensive–Very Expensive.*

Nutmeg Inn. This cozy inn has all the Colonial touches appropriate 'to a 210-year-old farmhouse: an old butter churn, antique dressers, rag rugs, mason jars with dried flowers, and hand-hewn beams in the low-ceiling living room. Added touches are fresh quilts on the brass beds and thick carpeting. Rooms in the barn are smaller but get less road noise, and the king suite has a private balcony with a terrific view of Haystack Mountain. *Rte. 9 West, Wilmington 05363, tel. 802/464-3351. 13 rooms. MC, V. Rates include full breakfast. Moderate–Expensive.*

Nightlife The **Spiral Lounge** at Snow Lake Lodge (tel. 802/464-3333) and the **Snow Barn** (tel. 802/464-3333), both near the base of Mount Snow, have live entertainment nightly during the season; a little further down Route 100, **Deacon's Den Tavern** (tel. 802/464-9361) and the **Sitzmark** (tel. 802/464-3384) have live bands on weekends. In nearby Wilmington, **Poncho's Wreck** (tel. 802/464-9320) is lively during the season. For a quieter après-ski experience, there's **Le Petit Chef** (tel. 802/464-8437), which usually has a folk singer or instrumentalist on Monday and Thursday, or the **Dover Forge** (tel. 802/464-9361).

Okemo Mountain
RFD 1, Ludlow 05149
Tel. 802/228–4041 or 802/228–5571; for snow conditions, 802/228–5222

Layer upon layer, Okemo has evolved and emerged in recent years as an almost ideal ski area for families with children. The main attraction is a long, broad, gentle slope with two beginner lifts just above the base lodge. All the facilities at the bottom of the mountain are close together, so family members can re-group easily during the ski day. Condominium housing is located at the base and along some of the lower trails. The net effect is efficient, not fancy.

Downhill Skiing Above the broad beginner's slope at the base, the upper part of Okemo has a varied network of trails: long, winding, easy trails for beginners, straight fall-line runs for experts, and curving cruising slopes for intermediates. The 70 trails are served by three quad, three triple, and two double chairlifts and two sur-face lifts. From the summit to the base lodge, the vertical drop is 2,150 feet. The ski school offers a complimentary Ski Tip sta-tion where skiers can get an evaluation and a free run with an instructor.

Child Care The area's nursery, for children 1–8 years of age, has a broad range of indoor activities plus supervised outings. Children 3 and up can get brief introduction-to-skiing lessons. All-day or half-day Skiwee lessons are available.

Lodging **Okemo Mountain Lodge.** The three-story, brown-clapboard building has balconies and fireplaces in all guest rooms, and the one-bedroom condominiums clustered around the base of the ski lifts are close to restaurants, shops, and the resort's clock tower. *Rte. 100, RFD 1, Ludlow 05149, tel. 802/228–5571 or 802/228–4041. 76 rooms with bath. Facilities: restaurant, lounge, cable TV, shuttle bus to Ludlow. AE, MC, V. Expensive–Very Expensive.*

Nightlife **Priority's** (tel. 802/228–5571), at Okemo Mountain Lodge, has entertainers; **Dadd's** (tel. 802/228–9820) has electronic games and bands for a little harder rocking.

Pico Ski Resort
2 Sherburne Pass, Rutland 05701
Tel. 802/775–4346; for snow conditions, 802/775–4345 or 800/225–7426

Although it's only 10 miles down the road from Killington, Pico has long been an underground favorite among people looking for uncrowded, low-key skiing. In recent years that friendly patina seemed to be threatened when modern lifts were in-stalled and a village square constructed at the base, but the new condo-hotel, restaurants, and shops have not altered the essential nature of Pico.

Downhill Skiing From the area's 2,000-foot summit, most of the trails are ad-vanced to expert, with one intermediate bail-out trail for the timid. The rest of the mountain's terrain is intermediate or eas-ier. The lifts for these slopes and trails are two quad, two triple, and three double chairlifts, plus two surface lifts. The ski school's one-on-one package combines the lift ticket and a one-hour private lesson.

Other Activities A sports center at the base of the mountain has fitness facilities, a 75-foot pool, Jacuzzi, saunas, and a massage room.

Child Care The nursery takes children from 6 months to 6 years old and provides indoor activities, outdoor play, and optional ski instruction. The ski school has an Explorers instruction program for children 3–6 and Mountaineers classes for ages 6–12; either can be taken for full- or half-day periods.

Lodging **Pico Village.** This resort at the base of Pico Mountain, a stone's throw from the ski lift, offers condominiums with hotel services. Condos have full kitchen, modern bath, fireplace, daily maid service, and use of the sports center. Two restaurants serve American and Italian cuisine, and there's a convenience store on the premises. Live entertainment is scheduled daily in the late afternoon in the base lodge. *Sherburne Pass 05701, tel. 802/747–3000 or 800/848–7325, fax 802/773–2502. 150 units. Facilities: 2 restaurants, indoor pool, sports center, Jacuzzi, sauna, TV lounge. MC, V. Moderate–Expensive.*

Additional accommodations selections will be found under Rutland Lodging in the Central Vermont section of the Vermont chapter.

Nightlife *See* Nightlife in Killington, above.

Smugglers' Notch
Smugglers' Notch 05464
Tel. 802/644–8851 or 800/451–8752

This resort complex has condominiums, restaurants, a grocery store, bars, meeting and convention facilities, and even a post office at the base of the lifts. Most skiers stay at the resort, and a large majority take advantage of the reasonably priced package plans that cover everything but meals. A Ski Vermont's Classics lift ticket is available here.

Downhill Skiing Smugglers' is made up of three mountains. The highest, Madonna, with a vertical drop of 2,160 feet, is in the center and connected with a trail network to Sterling (1,500-foot vertical). The third mountain, Morse, is more remote, but you can visit all three without removing your skis. The tops of each of the mountains have expert terrain—a couple of double black-diamonds make Madonna memorable—while intermediate trails fill the lower sections. Morse specializes in beginner trails. The 53 trails are served by four double chairlifts and one surface lift, which is something of a shortcoming. The area has improved its grooming and snowmaking capabilities in recent years.

Cross-Country Skiing Thirty-seven kilometers (23 miles) of cross-country trails have been laid out here.

Other Activities Management committed itself to developing an activities center long before the concept was adopted by other ski resorts. The area has ice skating, sleigh rides, and horseback riding. For indoor sports, there are hot tubs, tennis courts, and a pool. In summer, Smugglers' offers mountain biking, a water playground, minature golf, shuffleboard, outdoor tennis courts, and an outdoor pool.

Child Care The Alice's Wonderland nursery is a spacious facility that takes children from newborns to 6 years. The Discovery Ski Camp gives children 3–6 lessons, movies, games, and story-time entertainment. The Adventure Ski Camp for ages 7–12 has all-day skiing and other activities.

Lodging **The Village at Smugglers' Notch.** The large year-round resort complex offers condos with contemporary furnishings that may include tiled fireplaces, cane Marcel Breuer chairs, and blond Scandinavian-design furniture. Most guests stay several nights as part of a ski- or tennis-package plan. *Rte. 108, Jeffersonville 05464, tel. 802/644–8851 or 800/451–8752. 279 rooms with bath. Facilities: 2 restaurants, lounge, 2 indoor and 8 outdoor tennis courts, hot tub, indoor pool, exercise equipment, tanning machines, saunas, outdoor ice rink, child-care center, game room, water slide. AE, MC, V. Expensive–Very Expensive.*

Three Mountain Lodge. Originally a hostel for University of Vermont students, the tiny lodge 1 mile from the ski area has an excellent small restaurant. The timbered rooms of the log cabin are rustic, the porch swing offers great relaxing, and the huge fieldstone fireplace downstairs warms the public area. *Rte. 108, Jeffersonville 05464, tel. 802/644–5736. 3 rooms, 1 with bath. Facilities: restaurant. AE, DC, MC, V. Rates include full breakfast. Inexpensive–Moderate.*

Nightlife Most après-ski action centers on **The Meeting House,** which has live bands for dancing on weekends, and the **Club Lounge** (tel. 802/644–8851, ext. 247) with a wall-size video screen. **Smugglers' Lounge** (tel. 802/644–8851, ext. 143) in the Village Restaurant has a big-screen TV and entertainment four nights a week. **The Brewski** (tel. 802/644–5432), on Route 108 just outside the village, has weekend entertainment.

Stowe

Box 1310, Stowe 05672
Tel. 802/253–7311 or 800/247–8693; for snow conditions, 800/637–8693

To be precise, the name of the village is Stowe, the name of the mountain is Mt. Mansfield, but to generations of skiers the area, the complex, and the region are just plain Stowe. This classic resort, steeped in tradition, dates to the 1930s when the sport of skiing was a pup, and the area's mystique still attracts more serious skiers than social skiers. In recent years, on-mountain lodging; free shuttle buses that gather skiers from lodges, inn, and motels along the Mountain Road; improved snowmaking; and new lifts have added convenience to the Stowe experience. Yet the traditions remain: the Winter Carnival in January, the Sugar Slalom in April, ski weeks all winter. So committed is the ski school to improvements that even noninstruction package plans include one free ski lesson. Four base lodges provide plenty of essentials plus two on-mountain restaurants. A Ski Vermont's Classics lift ticket is available here.

Downhill Skiing Mt. Mansfield, with a vertical drop of 2,360 feet, is one of the giants among Eastern ski mountains. Its symmetrical shape allows skiers of all abilities long, satisfying runs from the summit. The famous Front Four runs (National, Liftline, Starr, and Goat) are the intimidating centerpieces for tough, expert runs, yet there is plenty of mellow intermediate skiing and one long beginner trail from the top that ends at the Toll House, where there is easier terrain. Mansfield's satellite sector is a network of intermediate and one expert trail off a basin served by a gondola. Spruce Peak, separate from the main mountain, is a teaching hill and a pleasant experience for inter-mediates and beginners. In addition to the four-passenger gondola, Stowe has one triple and six double chairlifts, plus one surface lift serving its 45 trails.

Cross-Country Skiing The area has 30 kilometers (18 miles) of groomed cross-country trails and 20 kilometers (12 miles) of back-country trails.

Other Activities In addition to sleighing and tobogganing facilities, Stowe boasts a public ice-skating rink with rental skates.

Child Care The Kanga Pocket infant care center takes children age 1 month to 3 years; Pooh's Corner day-care center takes ages 3–12. The ski school has two instruction programs: Winnie the Pooh for ages 3–7, Stowemeisters for 7–12. Children with ski-ing experience are eligible for all-day skiing with an instructor in the Mountain Adventure program.

Lodging The Trapp Family Lodge and additional nearby accommoda-tions are described under Stowe Lodging in the Northern Vermont section of the Vermont chapter.

Mt. Mansfield Resort. This is the lodging closest to the lifts, owned and operated by the same company that built the ski op-eration. The resort includes hotel rooms, town houses, and 35 individual lodges. In the hotel, which was converted from a mo-tel in the 1960s, rooms feature balconies, folk-art prints, a refrigerator, and chain-hotel-style furnishings. *Mountain Rd., Stowe 05672, tel. 802/253–7311 or 800/253–4754. 77 rooms with bath. Facilities: restaurant, tennis court, golf course, out-door swimming pool, cable TV, exercise equipment, whirlpool, sauna, trout pond. AE, CB, DC, MC, V. Rates are MAP. Very Expensive.*

Topnotch at Stowe. The 25-year-old resort is one of the state's most posh. Floor-to-ceiling windows, a freestanding circular stone fireplace, and cathedral ceilings make the lobby an im-posing setting, appropriate for the afternoon tea served from a rolling cart. Redecorated in 1989, the rooms have thick rust-color carpeting, a small shelf of books, and perhaps a barnboard wall or an Italian print. The restaurant is renowned, and there's a newly installed health spa. *Mountain Rd., Stowe 05672, tel. 802/253–8585 or 800/451–8686. 92 rooms with bath, 8 suites. Facilities: restaurant, lounge, 4 indoor tennis courts, 8 outdoor tennis courts, 18-hole golf course, indoor and outdoor pools, cable TV, 24-hour room service, riding stables. AE, DC, MC, V. Very Expensive.*

The Gables. The converted farmhouse is a rabbit warren of charming, antique-filled rooms. Those in the carriage house, renovated in 1989, have cathedral ceilings and a porch with white Adirondack chairs for contemplating the view of Mt. Mansfield. The tiny plant-filled sunroom is fine for lazy morn-ings, and the innkeepers are known for generous breakfasts. *Mountain Rd., Stowe 05672, tel. 802/253–7730 or 800/422–5371. 17 rooms with bath. Facilities: cable TV in public area, hot tub, outdoor pool, handicapped-equipped room. AE, MC, V. Rates include full breakfast. Closed late Apr.–May. Expensive–Very Expensive.*

Green Mountain Inn. A two-story Colonial-style inn built in 1833, the Green Mountain attracts skiers of all ages. Its com-munal living room and library provide a comfortable atmosphere for relaxation before dinner in one of the two house restaurants. MAP rates are optional; both formal dining and bistro fare are available. *Box 60, Main St., Stowe 05672, tel. 802/253-7301 or 800/445-6629. 52 rooms with bath, 2 suites. Facilities: 2 restaurants, conference rooms, living room, library, health club. AE, MC, V. Expensive.*

Nightlife The **Matterhorn Night Club** (tel. 802/253-8198) has 1940s and 1950s music for dancing, and the **Rusty Nail Saloon** (tel. 802/253-9444) has rock. Other options include the lounges at **Topnotch at Stowe** (tel. 802/253-8585) and the less-expensive **Stoweflake Inn** (tel. 802/253-7355).

Stratton
Stratton Mountain 05155
Tel. 802/297-2200 or 800/843-6867; for snow conditions, 802/297-2211

Since its creation in 1959, Stratton has undergone several physical transformations and upgrades, yet the area's sophisticated character has been retained. It has been the special province of well-to-do families and, more recently, young professionals from the New York–Boston corridor. In recent years an entire village, with a covered parking structure for 950 cars, has arisen at the base of the mountain. Adjacent to the base lodge are a condo-hotel, restaurants, and about 25 shops lining a minimall. Beyond that complex are many condominiums and town houses minutes away from the slopes. Across the main road and accessible by shuttle are three more good-size hotel-inns. Package plans are available, and conventions and meetings can be accommodated.

Downhill Skiing Stratton's skiing comprises three sectors. The first is the lower mountain directly in front of the base lodge-village-condo complex; a number of lifts reach midmountain from this entry point, and practically all skiing is beginner or low-intermediate. Above that, the upper mountain, with a vertical drop of 2,000 feet, is graced with a high-speed, 12-passenger gondola, *Starship XII*, that was installed during the 1988–89 season. Down the face are the expert trails, while on either side are intermediate cruising runs with a smattering of wide beginner slopes. The third sector, the Sun Bowl, is off to one side with a couple of lifts, a base lodge, and mostly intermediate terrain. In all, Stratton has 92 slopes and trails served by the gondola and four quad, one triple, and six double chairlifts.

Cross-Country Skiing The area has 32 kilometers (20 miles) of cross-country skiing.

Other Activities The area's sports center has two indoor tennis courts, three racquetball courts, a 25-meter indoor swimming pool, a Jacuzzi, steam room, a fitness facility with Nautilus equipment, and a restaurant. The summertime facilities include 15 additional outdoor tennis courts, 27 holes of golf, horseback riding, and mountain biking. Instruction programs in tennis and golf are offered.

Child Care The day-care center takes children ages 6 weeks to 5 years for indoor activities and outdoor excursions in mild weather. The ski school has a Little Cub program for ages 3–6 and Big Cub for 6–12; both are day-long programs with lunch. A junior racing program and special instruction groups are aimed at more-experienced junior skiers.

Lodging   The town of Manchester, a center of activity for the resorts of Stratton, Bromley Mountain, and Magic Mountain, offers a large variety of accommodations; additional selections will be found under Manchester Lodging and Newfane Lodging in the Southern Vermont section of the Vermont chapter.

Stratton Mountain Inn and Resort. The complex includes a 125-room inn—the largest on the mountain—and a 91-room lodge built in 1985, which has studio units. Ski packages that include lift tickets bring down room rates. *Stratton Mountain Rd., Stratton Mountain 05155, tel. 802/297–2200 or 800/843–6867. 216 rooms with bath. Facilities: 4 restaurants, golf course, indoor pool, exercise machines, 2 racquetball courts, 19 tennis courts, saunas, whirlpool, cable TV. AE, D, MC, V. Expensive–Very Expensive.*

Windham Hill Inn. In the converted dairy barn, two rooms share an enormous deck that overlooks the West River Valley. Rooms in the main building (some have a balcony) are more formal. Personal touches abound; the innkeeper's fascination with antique shoes is evident everywhere, and the antiques-filled rooms might be decorated with a child's white dress or a chenille bedspread. Guests can choose to be seated at a communal table for dinner. *West Townshend 05359, tel. 802/874–4080. 15 rooms with bath. Facilities: restaurant, lounge, phones, fireplaces in common areas, skating pond. Closed Apr.–mid-May, Nov. 1–Thanksgiving. AE, MC, V. Expensive.*

Nightlife   Among the lounges at Stratton Mountain are **A. J. Pimento's** (tel. 802/297–9899), with a dance floor and 1950s and 1960s music; and **Cafe Applause** at the Stratton Mountain Inn (tel. 802/297–2500), with a live band, cabaret, or comedy. Within walking distance of the slopes, **Mulligan's** (tel. 802/297–9293) has three bars on three floors, American cuisine, and dancing to DJs and live bands. **Haig's** (tel. 802/297–1300) in Bondville, 5 miles from Stratton, has live entertainment and dancing in winter. (*See* also Nightlife in Bromley, above.)

Sugarbush
RR Box 350, Warren 05674
Tel. 802/583–2381 or 802/583–3333; for snow conditions, 802/583–7669

In the early 1960s Sugarbush had the reputation of being an outpost of an affluent and sophisticated crowd from New York. While that reputation has faded, Sugarbush has maintained a with-it aura for the smart set—not that anyone would feel uncomfortable here. The base of the mountain has a village of condominiums, restaurants, shops, bars, and a sports center, and just down the road is the Sugarbush Inn, recently acquired by the ski area. A Ski Vermont's Classics lift ticket is available here.

Downhill Skiing   Sugarbush is two distinct mountain complexes. The South Basin area is what old-timers recall as Sugarbush Mountain, with a vertical of 2,400 feet; it is known for formidable steeps toward the top and in front of the main base lodge. In recent years, intermediate trails that twist and turn off most of the lifts have been widened and regraded to make them more inviting. This sector has three triple and four double chairlifts and two surface lifts. The *Mount Ellen* peak offers what the South Basin has in short supply: beginner runs. Mount Ellen also has steep fall-line pitches and intermediate cruisers off its 2,600 vertical feet. This mountain has five double chairlifts and two surface lifts. There are plans to connect the two mountains with a series of lifts and trails, but for the present a shuttle bus takes skiers back and forth.

Cross-Country Skiing More than 35 kilometers (22 miles) of marked cross-country trails are adjacent to the Sugarbush Inn.

Other Activities Two sports centers within walking distance of the ski lifts have Nautilus and Universal equipment; tennis, squash, and racquetball courts; Jacuzzi, sauna, and steam rooms; an indoor pool; and outdoor skating. In summer there are 35 outdoor tennis courts, 10 outdoor pools, and an 18-hole golf course on the Sugarbush property.

Child Care The Sugarbush Day School accepts children ages 6 weeks to 6 years; older children have indoor play and outdoor excursions. The Minibear Program introduces kids ages 4–5 to skiing as an adjunct to the nursery. For children 6–10, the Sugarbear instruction program operates half days or full days.

Lodging **Sugarbush Inn.** This white-clapboard country inn is a resort in itself, with activities to interest all family members. The plant-filled public areas are spacious, and bedrooms have Colonial-style maple furnishings. The large enclosed porch is used as a dining area. Standard rooms have small, square bathtubs. *Warren 05674, tel. 802/583–2301. 45 rooms with bath. Facilities: 2 restaurants, lounge, 11 tennis courts, 18-hole golf course, weight room, game room, outdoor ice rink, indoor pool, whirlpool. AE, D, DC, MC, V. Moderate–Very Expensive.*

PowderHound Resort. Most of the rooms in this century-old farmhouse converted into an inn are part of two-room suites that have living area, bath, and kitchenette. *Rte. 100, Box 369, Warren 05674, tel. 802/496–5100 or 800/548–4022. 44 rooms with bath. Facilities: restaurant, lounge, tennis court, volleyball, croquet, cable TV. AE, MC, V. Moderate–Expensive.*

Christmas Tree Inn. A modern country-style inn 3 miles from Sugarbush and 12 miles from Mad River, the Christmas Tree attracts couples and families. In addition to the 12 country-yet-contemporary rooms in the main house, on the grounds are 29 condos, each with one or three bedrooms. Antiques and Laura Ashley accents set the tone throughout. Breakfast and an informal afternoon tea are served in the dining room. Hand-made jigsaw puzzles are set out around the large fireplace in the main room to challenge guests. *Sugarbush Access Rd., Warren 05674, tel. 802/583–2211 or 800/535–5622. 12 rooms with bath, 29 condos. Facilities: outdoor pool and tennis courts in summer. AE, MC, V. Rates include breakfast. Moderate.*

Golden Lion. At the base of the road to the Sugarbush ski area, this small, riverside, family motel is guarded by a golden chainsaw-carved lion. The fireside lobby, where Continental breakfast is served, is cozy; rooms are standard motel decor. *Rte. 100 at Access Rd., Box 336, Warren 05674, tel. 802/496–3084. 12 rooms with bath; 1 efficiency; 1 apartment. Facilities: cable TV, riverside beach. AE, D, MC, V. Rates include Continental breakfast. Inexpensive–Moderate.*

Nightlife In Sugarbush Village, **Chez Henri** (tel. 802/583–2600) boasts of being the only disco in the Mad River Valley. The **Blue Tooth** (tel. 802/583–2656) has a variety of live entertainment and dancing during ski season and is popular with the singles crowd; it's on the access road to Sugarbush.

Suicide Six
Woodstock 05091
Tel. 802/457–1666; for snow conditions, 802/457–1622

Suicide Six is a tail wagging a dog, the canine being the Wood-stock Inn, owner of the ski resort. The Inn, located 3 miles from the ski area in Woodstock village, offers package plans that are remarkably inexpensive, considering the quality of the accommodations. In addition to skiers interested in exploring Woodstock, the area attracts students and Olympic trainees from nearby Dartmouth College.

Downhill Skiing Despite Suicide Six's short vertical of only 650 feet, the area offers challenging skiing. There are several steep runs down "the face" and intermediate trails that wind around the hill. Beginner terrain is mostly toward the bottom. The 18 trails are serviced by two double chairlifts and one surface lift.

Cross-Country Skiing The ski touring center has 75 kilometers (47 miles) of trails.

Other Activities A sports center near the Woodstock Inn has an indoor lap pool; indoor tennis, squash, and racquetball courts; whirlpool, steam, sauna, and massage rooms; and Nautilus workout equipment. Outdoor tennis courts, lighted paddle courts, croquet space, and an 18-hole golf course are available in the summer.

Child Care Although the ski area has no nursery, babysitting can be arranged. Lessons for children are given by the ski-school staff.

Lodging **Woodstock Inn and Resort.** The present facility is the latest in a series of Woodstock Inns that have presided over the village green since 1793. The hotel's floor-to-ceiling fieldstone fireplace with its massive wood-beam mantel has a distinctive New England character, and it comes as no surprise to learn that the resort is owned by the Rockefeller family, which has been instrumental in preserving the town's charm. In the guest rooms the modern ash furnishings are enlivened by patchwork quilts on the beds and original art that depicts bucolic Vermont scenes. *Rte. 4, Woodstock 05091, tel. 802/457–1100 or 800/448–7900. 106 rooms with bath. Facilities: restaurant, lounge, conference rooms, indoor and outdoor pools, 2 indoor and 10 outdoor tennis courts, sports center with fitness equipment, 2 squash courts, 2 racquetball courts, whirlpool, saunas; 18-hole Robert Trent Jones golf course, gift shop, cable TV. AE, MC, V. Expensive–Very Expensive.*

Additional accommodations selections will be found under Quechee Lodging and Woodstock Lodging in the Central Vermont section of the Vermont chapter.

Nightlife **Bentley's** (tel. 802/457–3232) in Woodstock has a DJ and dancing on weekends.

New Hampshire Skiing

Magnificent Mt. Washington, which looms like a beacon over the White Mountains, may have been the original attraction in the northern region of New Hampshire. Scandinavian settlers who came to the high, handsome, rugged peaks in the late 1800s brought their skis with them. Skiing got its modern start in the Granite State in the 1920s, with the cutting of trails on Cannon Mountain.

Today there are 28 ski areas in New Hampshire, ranging from the old, established slopes (Cannon, Cranmore, Wildcat) to the most contemporary (Attitash, Loon, Waterville Valley). Whatever the age of the area, traditional activities—carnivals, races, ski instruction, family services—are important aspects of the skiing experience. On the slopes, skiers encounter some of the toughest runs in the country alongside some of the gentlest, and the middle range is a wide one.

New Hampshire ski areas offer two special lift-ticket promotions. The five-day One Pass lift ticket allows skiing at any of 10 areas: Attitash, Balsams Wilderness, Black Mountain, Bretton Woods, Cannon Mountain, Loon Mountain, Mount Cranmore, Tenney Mountain, Waterville Valley, and Wildcat. Skiers visiting the Mt. Washington Valley region may want to take advantage of the three-day Valley Pass, which can be used at Attitash, Black Mountain, Mount Cranmore, and Wildcat.

Attitash
Rte. 302, Bartlett 03812
Tel. 603/374-2369

In the 1980s a new, young management at Attitash directed the resort's appeal to active young people and families. Keeping a high and busy profile, the area hosts many activities, race camps, and demo equipment days. Lodging at the base of the mountain is available in condominiums and motel-style units. The Valley Pass and One Pass lift tickets are available here, and a frequent-skier program allows participants to collect credits toward free lift tickets.

Downhill Skiing   Enhanced with massive snowmaking, the trails and lifts have expanded significantly in recent years. There are expert pitches at the top of the mountain (try Idiot's Option, for example), but the bulk of the skiing is geared to advanced-intermediates and below, with wide fall-line runs from midmountain. Beginners have a share of good terrain on the low-er mountain. Serving the 22 miles of trails and the 1,750 vertical drop are two triple and four double chairlifts.

Other Activities   Attitash has two Alpine slides and five water slides in summertime, and concerts, stock theater, and a horse show are held on premises.

Child Care   The nursery takes children ages 1–6, and those 5 and under can ski free. The Attitots program, with fun and games, is for children 3–5 who want to take lessons. The Attiteam program, for ages 6–12, offers daylong supervision and group lessons.

Lodging   **Attitash Mountain Village & Conference Center.** Opened in 1989, this condo-motel complex has a glass-enclosed pool and units that will accommodate 2–14 people. Some quarters with fireplaces and kitchenettes are especially good for families. The style is Alpine-contemporary; the staff, young and enthusiastic. *Rte. 302, Bartlett 03812, tel. 603/374-6501 or 800/862-1600. 250 rooms with bath. Facilities: restaurant, pub, game room, indoor pool, sauna, whirlpool. AE, MC, V. Expensive.*
Best Western Storybook Resort Inn. This family-owned, family-run motor inn is especially well suited to families. The larger rooms are those on the hillside. Copperfield's Restaurant has

gingerbread, sticky buns, farmer's omelets, and a special children's menu. *Box 129, Glen Junction 03838, tel. 603/383–6800 or 800/528–1234. 78 rooms with bath. Facilities: restaurant, outdoor pool, sauna, cable TV. No pets. AE, DC, MC, V. Inexpensive–Moderate.*

Nightlife   *See* Nightlife in Mt. Cranmore and Wildcat, below.

Balsams Wilderness
Dixville Notch 03576
Tel. 603/255–3400 or 800/255–0600; for snow conditions, 603/255–3951

Maintaining the tradition of a grand resort hotel is the primary goal at Balsams Wilderness; skiing is secondary. Restoration and renovation of the large, sprawling structure that dates to the late 19th century has been going on since the early 1970s. Guests will find many nice touches: valet parking, gourmet meals, dancing and entertainment nightly, and stretch clinics. The One Pass lift ticket is available here.

Downhill Skiing   Sanguinary, Umbagog, Magalloway—the slope names sound tough, but at most they are only moderately difficult, leaning toward intermediate. There are trails from the top of the 1,000-foot vertical drop for every skill level. One double chairlift and two T-bars carry skiers up the mountain.

Cross-Country Skiing   Balsams Wilderness has 50 kilometers (31 miles) of cross-country skiing, with natural-history markers annotating some trails.

Other Activities   In winter, the area offers skating, sleigh rides, snowshoeing, and snowmobiling. In summer, the resort has 27 holes of golf; six tennis courts; two trap fields; a heated outdoor pool; boating, swimming, and fly fishing on Lake Gloriette; and trails for hiking and climbing.

Child Care   The nursery takes children out of diapers to age 6. Wind Whistle lessons are designed to introduce skiing to children 3–5 years old. For those 5 and up, group lessons are available.

Lodging   **Balsams Grand Resort Hotel.** The famous full-service retreat with 15,000 acres of outdoor facilities and wilderness leaves nothing undone—and there's no reason to leave the grounds! The hotel is genuinely Victorian, retaining a touch of 1873 class. Dinner in the dining room requires jacket and tie, but other meals are informal. *Dixville Notch 03576, tel. 603/255–3400 or 800/255–0600. 232 rooms with bath. Facilities: restaurant, billiard room, children's program, day nursery, dancing, movie theater, heated outdoor pool, skating, skiing, sleigh rides, snowmobiling. AE, D, MC, V. Rates include all meals and activities. Very Expensive.*

Additional accommodations selections will be found under Lodging in the White Mountains section of the New Hampshire chapter.

Black Mountain
Rte. 16B, Jackson 03846
Tel. 603/383–4490

The setting is 1950s, the atmosphere is friendly, and the customers have fun here. There's a country feeling at the big base building that resembles an old farmhouse and at the skiing facilities that generally have no lines. The Black has the essentials for families and singles who want a low-key skiing holiday. The Valley Pass and One Pass lift tickets are available.

Downhill Skiing The bulk of the terrain is easy to middling, with intermediate trails that wander over the 1,100-vertical-foot mountain, but every now and then a zinger is steep, narrow, and treacherous. The lifts are a triple and a double chairlift and two surface tows.

Child Care The nursery takes children up to 6 months old. The ski school has an all-day Youth Proficiency Program on weekends and holidays for children 5–12.

Lodging **Whitney's Inn.** Three generations, counting the preschool set, are involved in running this country inn at the base of the mountain. You'll find antiques in the living room, period pieces in the one-of-a-kind bedrooms (some with sitting area), and suites that can take the bang of ski-week families. The windows of the dining room look out onto the slopes. *Box W, Jackson 03846, tel. 603/383–6886 or 800/252–5622. 35 rooms, 30 with bath. Facilities: restaurant, game room, pond. No pets. AE, DC, MC, V. Rates are MAP. Expensive.*

Nordic Village. The light wood and white walls of these deluxe condos are as Scandinavian as the snowy views. The Club House has a pool and spa, and there is a nightly bonfire at Nordic Falls. Fireplaces, full kitchens, and Jacuzzis can be found in the larger units; some economy cottages have wood stoves and kitchenettes. *Rte. 26, Jackson 03846, tel. 603/383–9101 or 800/ 472–5207. 90 apartments. Facilities: heated indoor pool, heated outdoor pool, therapy spa, steam room, skating area, sleigh rides, whirlpool. MC, V. Moderate–Expensive.*

Additional accommodations selections will be found under Lodging in the White Mountains section of the New Hampshire chapter.

Nightlife The **Shovel Handle Pub** in Whitney's Inn (tel. 603/383–6886) is the après-ski bar nearest the slopes.

Bretton Woods
Rte. 302, Bretton Woods 03575
Tel. 603/278–5000

Bretton Woods offers comfort and convenience in the three-level open-space base lodge, the drop-off area, the easy parking, and the uncrowded setting that make skiing a pleasant experience for families. A few town houses are on the mountain, and reasonably priced packages are available through the resort. The spectacular views of Mt. Washington alone are worth the visit. The One Pass lift ticket is available here.

Downhill Skiing The skiing is mostly gentle, with a few intermediate pitches near the top of the 1,500-foot vertical. Black diamonds are short and sparse. The 26 trails are served by one quad, one triple, and two double chairlifts and one T-bar. The area has night skiing Friday and Saturday, and a limited lift-ticket policy helps keep lines to a 10-minute maximum wait.

Cross-Country Skiing A short distance from the base of the mountain, the ski area has a large cross-country center with 100 kilometers (62 miles) of trails, 85 of them groomed and 65 track-set.

Other Activities A recreation center has racquetball, saunas and whirlpools, indoor swimming, an exercise room, and a game room. In summer, 27 holes of golf, 12 tennis courts, an outdoor pool, fly fishing, and hiking are available at the Mount Washington Hotel.

Child Care The nursery takes children ages 2 months to 4 years. The ski school has all-day programs for children of varied ages and abilities: The Pippins are beginner skiers, the Bilbos are skiers who can turn and ride lifts, the Frodos are ready for mountain skiing, the Aragorns are experienced mountain skiers, and the Wizzards are advanced skiers. The racing program is for children 8–18.

Lodging **Bretton Arms.** Built in 1896, this restored historic inn predates even the grande dame Hotel Mt. Washington across the way, so you *know* that the trendsetters of the last century stayed here. Reservations, required in the dining room, should be made on arrival. Guests are invited to use the facilities of the Hotel Mt. Washington when open, but that hotel is undergoing a major renovation in 1990. *Rte. 302, Bretton Woods 03575, tel. 603/ 278–3000 or 800/258–0330. 30 rooms with bath. Facilities: restaurant, color TV. AE, D, DC, MC, V. Rates include full breakfast. Expensive.*

Lodge at Bretton Woods. Rooms have contemporary furnishings, a balcony, and views of the Presidential Range. Darby's Restaurant serves Continental cuisine around a circular fireplace, and the bar is a hangout for après skiers. The lodge, across the road from the Mt. Washington Hotel, shares its facilities in summer. *Rte. 302, Bretton Woods 03575, tel. 603/278– 1000 or 800/258–0330. 50 rooms with bath. Facilities: restaurant, indoor pool, spa pool, sauna, whirlpool. No pets. AE, D, MC, V. Moderate.*

Additional accommodations selections will be found under Lodging in the White Mountains section of the New Hampshire chapter.

Cannon Mountain
Franconia Notch State Park, Franconia 03580
Tel. 603/823–5563; for snow conditions, 603/823–7771 or 800/ 552–1234

Nowhere is the granite of the Granite State more pronounced than at Cannon Mountain, where you'll find the essentials for feeling the thrill of downhill. One of the first ski areas in the United States, the massif has retained the basic qualities that make the sport unique—the camaraderie of young people who are there for challenge and family fun. The New England Ski Museum is located adjacent to the base of the tramway. The One Pass lift ticket is available here.

Downhill Skiing The Peabody slopes, cut in the 1960s, were regarded as too easy for Cannon's diehards when at most ski areas the slopes would have been considered tough enough. The tone of this mountain's skiing is reflected in the narrow, steep pitches off the peak of the 2,150 feet of vertical rise. Some trails marked intermediate may seem more difficult because of the sidehill slant of the slopes (rather than the steepness). Under a new fall of snow, Cannon has challenge not often found at modern ski areas. There is an 80-passenger tramway to the top, one triple and two double chairlifts, and three surface lifts.

Cross-Country Skiing The area has 8 kilometers (5 miles) of cross-country trails and ski jumping.

Child Care The nursery takes children 13 months and older. All-day and half-day Junior Workshops are available for children of all ages, and seasonlong instruction can be arranged.

Lodging **Horse and Hound Inn.** Off the beaten path and yet convenient to the Cannon Mountain tram 2¾ miles away, this traditional inn is set on 8 acres surrounded by the White Mountain National Forest. Antiques and assorted collectibles offer guests a cheery atmosphere, and on the grounds are 10 kilometers (6 miles) of cross-country ski trails. *R.R. Box 33, Wells Rd., Franconia 03580, tel. 603/823–5501. 10 rooms, 8 with bath. Facilities: restaurant, bar, lounge, pool table, videos. AE, CB, DC, MC, V. Closed Apr. Rates include breakfast. Moderate.*

Indian Head Resort. Views of Indian Head Rock, the Great Stone Face, and the Franconia Mountains are available across the 180 acres of this resort/motel. Take Exit 33 from I–93, then Route 3 north. *Rte. 3, North Lincoln 03251, tel. 603/745–8000 or 800/343–8000. 98 rooms with bath. Facilities: restaurant, game room, outdoor pool, indoor pool, sauna, cable TV, whirlpool, 2 tennis courts. AE, CB, DC, MC, V. Moderate.*

Additional accommodations selections will be found under Lodging in the White Mountains section of the New Hampshire chapter.

Nightlife Live nightly entertainment in the **Thunderbird Lounge** at the Indian Head Resort (tel. 603/745–8000) attracts a young crowd. **Hillwinds** (tel. 603/823–5533) and the **Village House Restaurant** (tel. 603/823–5912), both on Main Street in Franconia, also offer live entertainment weekends.

Gunstock
Box 336, Laconia 03247
Tel. 603/293–4341; for snow conditions, 603/293–4345

High above Lake Winnipesaukee, the pleasant, all-purpose ski area of Gunstock attracts some skiers for overnight stays and others—many from Boston and its suburbs—for the day's skiing. Gunstock allows skiers to return lift tickets for a cash refund for any reason—weather, snow conditions, health, equipment problems. That policy plus a staff of customer-service people give a bit of class to an old-timey ski area.

Downhill Skiing Some clever trail cutting, summer grooming, and surface sculpting have made this otherwise pedestrian mountain an interesting place for intermediates. That's how most of the 19 trails and five open slopes are rated, with designated sections for slow skiers and learners. The 1,700 feet of vertical has one quad, two triple, and two double chairlifts and two surface tows.

Cross-Country Skiing There are 14 kilometers (9 miles) of cross-country trails.

Child Care The nursery takes children from infants up. The ski school teaches the Skiwee system to children 3–12.

Lodging **B. Mae's Resort Inn.** This new resort complex and conference center has weekend entertainment in The Greenhouse at B. Mae Denny's Eating & Drinking Establishment, also on the property. All rooms are large; some two-room luxury suites have kitchens. *Rte. 11, Gilford 03246, tel. 603/293–7526 or 800/ 458–3877. 83 rooms with bath. Facilities: restaurant, game room, indoor pool, cable TV, whirlpool. No pets. AE, D, MC, V. Moderate–Expensive.*

Gunstock Inn and Health Club. This country-style resort and motor inn about a minute's drive from the Gunstock recreation area has rooms of various size, all furnished with American antiques, all with views of the mountains and Lake Winnipesaukee. *580 Cherry Valley Rd. (Rte. 11A), Gilford 03246, tel. 603/293–2021. 27 rooms with bath. Facilities: restaurant, health club, indoor pool, spa, cable TV. No pets. AE, D, MC, V. Moderate–Expensive.*

King Ridge

RR 1, Box 3130, New London 03257
Tel. 603/526–6966; for snow conditions, 800/343–1312

They call it a summit village, which accurately—if a bit dramatically—describes the base facilities at King Ridge. The lodge and all attendant services are located at the *top* of the ski area, with the trails spinning off to points below. Skiers and family groups who come here quickly make the adjustment and appreciate the efficient and agreeable skiing.

Downhill Skiing Upside down it may be, but King Ridge's 850 vertical feet has the right kind of challenge for novices and low-level intermediates. Most of the terrain is for beginners, but several long intermediate runs are rewarding, and three advanced trails are fun if not exciting. Two triple and one double chairlift and four surface lifts transport skiers. Weekday and nonpeak weekend lift ticket prices are low.

Child Care The nursery takes children 4 months to 6 years old and offers Playtime on Skis lessons to ages 4–6. On nonvacation weekdays, nursery care is free. All-day Skiwee lessons are available through the ski school for children 5–12.

Lodging **Follansbee Inn.** Built in 1840, this quintessential country inn on the shore of Lake Kezar is a perfect fit in the 19th-century village of North Sutton, about 4 miles south of New London. Common rooms and bedrooms alike are full of collectibles and antiques. You can ice-fish on the lake as well as ski across it. *Rte. 114, North Sutton 03260, tel. 603/927–4221. 23 rooms, 11 with bath. Facilities: dining room (guests only), cross-country trails, skating, tobogganing. No pets. No smoking. MC, V. Rates include full breakfast. Moderate.*

Pleasant Lake Inn. *Pleasant* well describes this quiet family-run inn near the lake. The herbs, preserves, and other yummy things on the table were grown on the property; all the baked goods come from the inn kitchen. The original farmhouse dates from 1790, and that early country look has been maintained with stenciled walls, painted floors, fireplace, and woodstove. There are even sheep in the barn. *Pleasant St., Box 1070, New London 03257, tel. 603/526–6271. 13 rooms, 11 with bath. Facilities: dining room (guests only). No pets. No smoking in bedrooms. MC, V. Rates include full breakfast. Moderate.*

Loon Mountain

Kancamagus Hwy., Lincoln 03251
Tel. 603/745–8111; for snow conditions, 603/745–8100

Between the Kancamagus Highway and the Pemigewasset River is the modern Loon Mountain resort. Begun in the 1960s, Loon saw serious development in the 1980s, adding more mountain facilities, base lodges, and a large hotel near the main lifts at the bottom of the mountain. The result attracts a broad cross-section of skiers. In the base lodge, on the mountain, and around the area are a large number of food-service and lounge facilities. The Mountain Club hotel, an elegant addition, has guest rooms within walking distance of the lifts, and there are on-slope and nearby condominium complexes. The One Pass lift ticket is available here.

Downhill Skiing Wide, straight, and consistent intermediate trails prevail at Loon, which makes it ideal for plain fun or for advancing one's skills. Beginner trails and slopes are set off, so faster skiers won't interfere. Most advanced runs are grouped on tne North Peak section farther from the main mountain. The vertical is 2,100 feet; a four-passenger gondola, two triple and four double chairlifts, and one surface lift serve the 22 trails and slopes.

Cross-Country Skiing The touring center has 35 kilometers (22 miles) of cross-country trails.

Other Activities The Mountain Club has a fitness center with a whirlpool, lap pool, saunas, steam rooms, an exercise room, and racquetball and squash courts. Massages and aerobics classes are available. An outdoor pool, two tennis courts, horseback riding, archery, skeet shooting, mountain biking, and gondola rides to the summit are available in summer.

Child Care The Honeybear nursery takes children as young as 6 weeks. Nonintensive ski instruction is offered to youngsters of nursery ages. The ski school has a Mountain Trekkers program for children 6–12. Children 5 and under ski free every day, while those 6–12 ski free midweek during nonholiday periods when parents participate in a five-day ski week.

Lodging **The Mountain Club on Loon.** A new resort hotel right at the slopes has a full range of activities including nightly live entertainment in the lounge. Suites sleep as many as six; some are studio style with fold-in-the-wall beds; 70 have kitchens. Take Exit 2 from I–93 (Kancamagus Highway). *Rte. 112, Lincoln 03584, tel. 603/745–8111 or 800/433–3413. 140 rooms with bath. Facilities: restaurant, fitness center, garage, indoor pool, racquetball court, squash court, sauna, cable TV. AE, CB, DC, MC, V. Moderate–Very Expensive.*

Mill House Inn. A bed-and-breakfast hotel on the western edge of the Kancamagus Highway offers country-inn style along with free transportation to Loon and Waterville Valley during ski season. Nonskiers will have plenty to do, too: shopping, a four-screen cinema, and the North Country Center for the Performing Arts nearby. *Box 696, Lincoln 03251, tel. 603/745–6261 or 800/654–6183. 96 rooms with bath. Facilities: restaurant, nightclub, exercise room, outdoor pool, indoor pool, sauna, tennis court, whirlpools. AE, D, DC, MC, V. Rates include Continental breakfast. Expensive.*

Additional accommodations selections will be found under Lodging in the White Mountains section of the New Hampshire chapter.

Nightlife Après-ski activity will be found at the **Granite Bar** at the Mountain Club (tel. 603/745–8111), and there's dancing at the **Loon**

Saloon, also at the Mountain Club. **Dickens** (tel. 603/745–2278) has live musical entertainment most weekends.

Mount Cranmore
Box 1640, North Conway 03860
Tel. 603/356–5543; for snow conditions, 800/323–0488

The ski area at Mount Cranmore, on the outskirts of North Conway, came into existence in 1938 when local residents saw an opportunity to make the most of their mountain. One early innovation, the Skimobile lift (a haul-rope track that conveys small cars to the top), still operates. In recent years new owners have put more money into condominium complexes and updated base facilities than into mountain improvements, hoping to broaden the area's attraction for families as well as diehard regulars. The Valley Pass and One Pass lift tickets are available here.

Downhill Skiing The mountain and trail system at Cranmore needs little attention to remain first class. Most of the runs are naturally formed intermediate-levels that weave in and out of glades. Beginners have several slopes and routes from the 1,160-foot summit, while experts must be content with a few short but steep pitches. The Skimobile and one triple and four double chairlifts carry skiers to the top. There is night skiing Wednesday through Saturday.

Cross-Country Skiing Sixty kilometers (37 miles) of groomed cross-country trails weave through North Conway and the countryside.

Other Activities A fitness center contains four indoor tennis courts, exercise equipment, an indoor pool, aerobics workout space, and a climbing wall. There is outdoor skating and, in summer, four outdoor tennis courts.

Child Care The nursery takes children from 6 months up. For children 4–12, the Skiwee program offers all-day skiing and instruction. The Rattlesnake Youth Development Program offers season-long ski instruction for children in the same age range.

Lodging **Fox Ridge Resort Inn.** One mile from North Conway Village on a 300-acre resort estate, Fox Ridge offers family rooms with loft sleeping areas, and suites that have a kitchen and a living room with a convertible couch. *Box 990, White Mountain Hwy., North Conway 03860, tel. 603/356–3151 or 800/343–1804. 136 rooms with bath. Facilities: restaurant, lounge, exercise room, game room, indoor pool, saunas, cable TV, whirlpool. No pets. AE, MC, V. Moderate–Expensive.*
Eastern Slope Inn Resort and Conference Center. Although this has been an operating inn for more than a century, recent restoration and refurbishing have updated its image and its facilities. The resort has the ambience of a historic site along with such modern amenities as an enclosed pool. Jackson Square, the inn restaurant, serves French, Cajun, and Creole food in a glassed-in courtyard. *Main St., North Conway 03860, tel. 603/356–6321 or 800/258–4708. 125 rooms with bath. Facilities: restaurant, pub, game room, indoor pool, sauna, whirlpool. AE, MC, V. Moderate.*

Additional accommodations selections will be found under Lodging in the White Mountains section of the New Hampshire chapter.

Nightlife For rock and roll go to **Barnaby's** (tel. 603/356–5781), the **Cranmore Pub** (tel. 603/356–2472), or the **White Horse Pub** (tel. 603/356–2831), all in North Conway. The **Fox Ridge Resort** (tel. 603/356–3151) offers soft music on weekends, as does the **Darby Field Inn** (tel. 603/447–2181). The **Red Jacket Mountain View Inn** (tel. 603/356–5411), with a piano bar, attracts a more up-scale crowd. See also Nightlife for Wildcat Mountain.

Mount Sunapee
Mt. Sunapee State Park, Rte. 103 Mt. Sunapee, 03772
Tel. 603/763–2356; for snow conditions, 603/763–5256 or 800/322–3300

Without glitz or glamour, Sunapee remains popular among lo-cal residents and skiers from Boston and the coast for its low-key atmosphere and easy skiing. Two base lodges supply the essentials.

Downhill Skiing This mountain of 1,500 vertical feet has 18 miles of gentle-to-moderate terrain with a couple of pitches that could be called steep. A nice beginner's section is located beyond the base facil-ities, well away and well protected from other trails. Three triple and three double chairlifts and one surface lift transport skiers.

Child Care The Duckling Nursery takes children from 12 months to 6 years of age. Little Indians ski instruction gives ages 3 and 4 a taste of skiing, while Skiwee lessons are available for ages 5–12.

Lodging **Bradford Inn.** This delightfully old-fashioned country inn in the village of Bradford has two common rooms and a popular res-taurant, J. Albert's, that features New England cooking. Rooms have details circa 1898, and there are family suites. Sen-ior citizen discounts and facilities for the handicapped are available. *Main St., Bradford 03221, tel. 603/938–5309. 20 rooms with bath. Facilities: restaurant. MC, V. Rates include full breakfast. Moderate.*
Inn at Sunapee. This onetime farmhouse is now a cozy, rustic inn with books to read by the fire. *Box 336, Burke Haven Hill, Sunapee 03782, tel. 603/763–4444. 16 rooms with bath. Facili-ties: restaurant, outdoor pool, tennis court. MC, V. Rates include full breakfast. Moderate.*

Additional accommodations selections will be found under Lodging in the Dartmouth–Lake Sunapee section of the New Hampshire chapter.

Pats Peak
Rte. 114, Henniker 03242
Tel. 603/428–3245

This small area near the Boston and coastal metropolitan re-gions is ideally suited to families. Base facilities are simple, and friendly personal attention is the rule.

Downhill Skiing Despite its size of only 700 vertical feet, with 14 trails and slopes, Pats Peak has something for everyone: New skiers are well served with a wide slope, chairlift, and several short trails; intermediates have wider trails from the top; and advanced ski-ers have a small selection that includes a couple of real thrillers. One triple and two double chairlifts, two T-bars, and two sur-face lifts serve the runs.

Child Care The nursery takes children ages 6 months to 5 years. For children 6 and up, there are group lessons. All-day lessons for children 4–13 are scheduled throughout the season.

Lodging **Colby Hill Inn.** The fireplace still has a bake oven and the Indian shutters are tightly closed on frosty evenings, just as they were in homestead days. Expansion has meant the conversion of the old carriage house to bedrooms (a tad smaller than those in the main house), but the one-of-a-kind approach to decorating is maintained throughout. *Box 778, Henniker 03242, tel. 603/478–3135. 15 rooms with bath. Facilities: restaurant, outdoor pool. AE, MC, V. Rates include full breakfast. Moderate.*
Meeting House Country Inn. The 200-year-old farmhouse, located conveniently at the base of Pats Peak, serves a country breakfast in bed to guests. A solar-sided pub and restaurant occupy the old barn. *Rte. 114 (Flanders Rd.), Henniker 03242, tel. 603/428–3228. 6 rooms with bath. Facilities: restaurant, pub, hot tub, sauna. AE, MC, V. Rates include full breakfast. Moderate.*

Tenney Mountain
RFD 4, Box 1300, Plymouth 03264
Tel. 603/536–1717

Tenney has always attracted families because the skiing is good and the prices are right, and new ownership has added amenities that promise to expand the skier base. New trailside condominium housing eliminates the need for a long drive to one's accommodation. The area regularly hosts races and special events for particular groups (firefighters, students, snowboarders, weather reporters). Tenney has a frequent-skier program and low midweek prices for lift tickets. The One Pass lift ticket is available here.

Downhill Skiing Tenney specializes in the pitch that keeps intermediate skiers happy. There is advanced terrain as well, and a small number of slopes for beginners. With a vertical drop of 1,400 feet, the area has one triple and one double chairlift and two surface lifts.

Child Care The nursery takes children from infants to 6 years. The Mountain Munchers program offers introductory skiing lessons for ages 4–7; 5 and under ski free. Children 7–12 are eligible for Mountain Patrollers, with all-day or half-day sessions. Group and private lessons are available.

Waterville Valley
Waterville Valley 03215
Tel. 603/236–8311; for snow conditions, 603/236–4144

Everything in the valley belongs to or is licensed by the mountain company, and the overall effect is that of an enclave. There are inns, lodges, and condominiums; restaurants, taverns, and cafés; shops, boutiques, and a grocery store; conference facilities, a post office, and a sports center. Everything has been built with taste and regard for the New England sensibility, and the resort attracts hordes from Boston and environs. An array of three-day to five-day vacation packages is available. The One Pass lift ticket is available here.

Downhill Skiing Mount Tecumseh, a short shuttle ride from the Town Square and accommodations, has been laid out with great care and attention to detail. A good selection of the 48 trails offer most advanced skiers an adequate challenge, and there are slopes and trails for beginners. Yet the bulk of the skiing is intermediate: straight down the fall line, wide, and agreeably long. The variety is great enough that no one will be bored on a weekend visit. The lifts serving the 2,000 feet of vertical rise are one quad, three triple, and four double chairlifts, plus four surface lifts. A second mountain, Snow's, about 2 miles away, is open on weekends and takes some of the overflow; it has five fairly easy trails and one double chairlift off a 580-foot vertical.

Cross-Country Skiing   A cross-country center, located in the Town Square, has 100 kilometers (62 miles) of trails, 70 of them groomed.

Other Activities   An ice skating arena is adjacent to the Town Square, and sleigh rides depart from here as well. The Sports/Fitness Center has two tennis courts, racquetball, and squash courts; a 25-meter indoor pool; jogging track; exercise equipment; whirlpools, saunas, and steam rooms; massage service and a game room. In summer, there is an outdoor pool, 18 tennis courts, nine holes of golf, biking, horseback riding, and water sports on Corcoran's Pond. In July and August the Bridge Music Festival takes place at the resort.

Child Care   The nursery takes children 6 weeks and older. Children ages 6–12 who want to ski have a choice of class lessons or half-day or full-day Skiwee lessons. Petite Skiwee is designed for children 3–5, Skiwee is for ages 6–8, and Grand Skiwee is for ages 9–12. The Kinderpark, a children's slope, has a slow-running lift and special props to hold children's attention. Children under 5 ski free anytime; midweek, those under 12 ski free and receive free nursery care.

Lodging   **Black Bear Lodge.** The condo-motel has one-bedroom and two-bedroom apartments with hotel service, heated indoor and outdoor pools, a sauna, a steam room, and bus service to the slopes. *Snow's Brook Rd., Box 357, Waterville Valley 03215, tel. 603/236-4501 or 800/468-2553. 107 suites. Facilities: indoor and outdoor pools, access to sports center, cable TV, saunas, steam room. No pets. AE, D, DC, MC, V. Rates include morning coffee. Expensive–Very Expensive.*
Snowy Owl Inn. The central fieldstone fireplace, one of seven, is three stories tall, and the surrounding atrium is supported by single-log posts. Yet the inn is cozy and intimate, the fourth-floor bunk-bed loft rooms ideal for families, the first-floor rooms suitable for those who want a quiet getaway. You'll see lots of prints and watercolors of snowy owls. Four restaurants are within walking distance. *Box 407, Snow's Brook Rd., Waterville Valley 03215, tel. 603/236-8383 or 800/468-2553. 80 rooms with bath. Facilities: indoor pool, saunas, sports center access, cable TV, whirlpool. No pets. AE, D, DC, MC, V. Rates include breakfast. Moderate–Expensive.*
Valley Inn and Tavern. Soft, muted colors and antiques welcome guests at this country inn. In the fireplace lobby, chocolate chip cookies and jigsaw puzzles await guests in the afternoon. MAP, EP, and B&B rates are available. *Box 1, Waterville Valley 03215, tel. 603/236-8336 or 800/343-9069, fax 603/236-4294. 45 rooms with bath. Facilities: restaurant, lounge with weekend entertainment, indoor/outdoor pool, Jacuzzi, sauna, exercise room, tanning bed. AE, CB, D, DC, MC, V. Moderate.*

Nightlife   The valley teems with lounges, taverns, and cafés. **The Yacht Club,** overlooking Corcoran's Pond, has a piano bar. **O'Keefe's** (tel. 603/236-8331) offers a pianist during the week, live bands on weekends. Away from the valley, the **Granite Rock Cafe** (tel. 603/726–3782), off I–93 in Compton, has entertainment nightly.

Wildcat Mountain
Pinkham Notch, Rte. 16, Jackson 03846
Tel. 603/466–3326; for snow conditions, 800/552–8952

As tough as Cannon, as easy as Bretton Woods—Wildcat works hard at living down its name and reputation for difficulty. The area is a favorite of local residents, and attractive pricing (junior lift tickets extend to 15-year-olds instead of the usual 12-year age limit) has made it ideal for families. Races and special events for ski clubs and groups also set Wildcat apart. The area has weekend, three-day, and five-day packages at reasonable rates. The Valley Pass and One Pass lift tickets are available here.

Downhill Skiing Wildcat's expert trails deserve their designations and then some. Intermediates have a fair share, too, although their trails tend to be wider and less winding. Beginners will find gentle terrain and a broad teaching slope. The 30 trails with a 2,100-foot vertical drop are served by a two-passenger gondola and one double and four triple chairlifts. On a clear day, from the 4,000-foot summit, views of Mt. Washington in the near distance are spectacular.

Child Care The Kitten Club nursery takes children 6 months and up. All-day Skiwee instruction is offered to children 5–12. A separate slope is used for teaching children to ski.

Lodging **Eagle Mountain House.** When this country estate of 1879 was restored and modernized in 1986, it became a showplace. The public rooms are rustic-palatial, in keeping with the period of tycoon roughing-it; the bedrooms are large and furnished with period pieces. *Carter Notch Rd., Jackson 03846, tel. 603/383–9111 or 800/527–5022. 94 rooms with bath. Facilities: restaurant, health club, outdoor pool, saunas, whirlpool. No pets. AE, MC, V. Moderate–Expensive.*
Wildcat Inn & Tavern. Located in the center of Jackson Village, the restaurant in this small 19th-century inn is a lodestone for skiers in nearby condos and B&Bs. The fragrance of home-baking rises to the guest rooms, which are full of interesting furniture and knickknacks. *Rte. 16A, Jackson 03846, tel. 603/383–4245. 15 rooms, 8 with bath. Facilities: restaurant. AE, MC, V. Rates include breakfast. Inexpensive–Moderate.*

Nightlife The **Wildcat Inn & Tavern** (tel. 603/383–4245) can become very lively in the evening. The **Tavern at Eagle Mountain House** (tel. 603/383–9111) has weekend entertainment. In Glen, the **Bernhof Inn** (tel. 603/383–4414) is the setting for an evening of fondue and soft music by the fireside, and the **Red Parka Club** (tel. 603/383–4344) is nearby. *See* Nightlife in Mt. Cranmore, above, for additional suggestions.

Maine Skiing

Weather patterns that create snow cover for Maine ski areas may come from the Atlantic or from Canada, and Maine may have snow when other New England states do not—and vice versa. In recent years ski-area operators in Maine have discovered snowmaking with a vengeance, and they now have the capacity to cover thousand-foot-plus mountains with the deep white. In turn, more skiers have discovered Maine skiing, yet in most cases this has still not resulted in crowds, hassles, or lines.

Further good news for Maine ski areas is the building of more and better housing; best news of all is that skiers find lower prices here for practically every component of a ski vacation or a day's outing: lift tickets, accommodations, lessons, equipment, and meals. Nightlife activities at most resorts center on the ski areas and lodgings.

Big Squaw Mountain
Box D, Greenville 04441
Tel. 207/695-2272

Remote but pretty, Big Squaw is an attractive place for family ski vacations and one that offers appealing package rates. A hotel at the base of the mountain, integrated into the main base lodge, has a restaurant, bar, and other services and offers ski packages.

Downhill Skiing Trails are laid out according to difficulty, with the easy slopes toward the bottom, intermediate trails weaving from midpoint, and steeper runs high up off the 1,750-vertical-foot peak. The 17 trails are served by one triple and one double chairlift and two surface lifts.

Cross-Country Skiing The 45 kilometers (28 miles) of cross-country trails begins at a center about a mile from the base of the mountain.

Other Activities The base hotel has a pool and sauna. Moosehead Lake and other ponds and streams provide fishing, sailing, canoeing, swimming, and lake-boat cruising in summer. At the mountain there are two tennis courts, hiking, and lawn games. A recreation program for children functions midweek in summer.

Child Care The nursery takes children from infants to age 6 and provides skiing lessons for those who want them. The ski school has daily lessons and racing classes for children of all ages and abilities.

Lodging **Big Squaw Mountain Resort.** From the door of the resort you can ski to the slopes and to cross-country trails. The motel-style units and dorm rooms have picture windows opening onto the woods or the slopes, and Katahdin and Moosehead Lake (6 miles away) can be seen from the lawn. The restaurant has Cajun and Oriental specialties, pork chops, and steaks. The Saturday night buffet is popular, and weekends often bring entertainment. American Plan and ski packages are available. *Rte. 15, Greenville 04441, tel. 207/695-2272 or 800/842-6743 in Maine. 61 rooms with bath. Facilities: restaurant, cafeteria, ski shop, ski school, nursery, playground, volleyball, 2 all-weather tennis courts. AE, MC, V. Moderate.*

Mount Abram
Rte. 26, Box 189, Locke Mills 04255
Tel. 207/875-2601

This complete resort has a friendly, rustic Maine feeling. Package rates for slope-side condominiums are reasonable, and there's just the right amount of low-key après-ski activity.

Downhill Skiing The mountain reaches just over 1,000 vertical feet, the majority of its terrain intermediate, with a few fall-line steep runs and a separate small hill for beginner and novice skiers. The area has two double chairlifts and three T-bars. In addition to regular instruction classes, the Plus Program, a series of six weekend classes, is designed to upgrade adult skills.

Cross-Country Skiing Twenty-four kilometers (15 miles) of cross-country trails depart from the base area.

Child Care A nursery takes children from 6 months to 6 years. The ski school offers class lessons on weekends and during vacation weeks to children 3–6 who are enrolled in the nursery. For juniors 6–16 there are individual classes plus a series of eight two-hour lessons on weekends.

Saddleback Ski and Summer Lake Preserve
Box 490, Rangeley 04970
Tel. 207/864–5671; for snow conditions, 207/864–3380

A down-home, laid-back atmosphere prevails for families that come to Saddleback, where the quiet and the absence of crowds, even on busy weekends, draw return visitors. The base area has the feeling of a small community for the guests at trailside homes and condominiums. Midweek lift tickets and packages come at attractively low rates.

Downhill Skiing The expert terrain is short and concentrated at the top of the mountain, and an upper lift makes the trails easily accessible for skiers who want to stick with them. The middle of the mountain is mainly intermediate, with a few meandering easy trails, while the beginner or novice slopes are located toward the bottom. Two double chairlifts and three T-bars (usually without lines) carry skiers to the 40 trails on the 1,830 feet of vertical.

Cross-Country Skiing Fifty kilometers (31 miles) of cross-country trails spread out from the base area and circle Saddleback Lake and several ponds and rivers.

Other Activities In summer these waterways provide swimming, boating, and fishing within an easy walk of accommodations. Hiking and biking the mountain in search of spectacular views are significant summertime activities, along with paddle tennis.

Child Care The nursery takes children ages 6 weeks to 8 years. For those who are new to skiing, Snoopy classes offer a half day or full day of lessons for children 4–7. The goal at Saddleback is to get children into the Junior Masters Program, in which Levels One and Two are for 5-year-olds and up with beginning and intermediate skiing skills and the Ski Meisters is for 9-year-olds and up who can ski in control. A Junior Racing Program serves three age groups: 9–11, 12–14, and 15 and up.

Lodging **Country Club Inn.** Cathedral ceilings, 2 fieldstone fireplaces, sitting areas, game tables, and views of the mountains and lake from the 2,000-foot elevation accentuate a stay at this contemporary inn. Dining in the restaurant provides another opportunity to enjoy the spectacular view. MAP rates are available. *Box 680, Country Club Dr., Rangeley 04970, tel. 207/864–3831. 10 rooms with bath during peak season, 20 during off-peak season. Facilities: restaurant, bar/lounge, pool table. AE, MC, V. Closed Apr., Nov. Expensive.*
Rangeley Inn and Motor Lodge. From Main Street you see only the massive, three-story, blue inn building (circa 1907), but be-

hind it the newer motel wing commands Haley Pond, a lawn, and a garden. The traditional lobby and a smaller parlor have 12-foot ceilings, a jumble of rocking chairs and easy chairs, and polished wood. Sizable guest rooms boast iron and brass bedsteads, subdued wallpaper, and a clawfoot tub in the bath. Motel units contain Queen Anne reproduction furniture, velvet chairs, and a whirlpool bath. French cuisine is the rule in the spacious dining room with the Williamsburg brass chandeliers. Modified American Plan is available. *Main St., Rangeley 04970, tel. 207/864-3341 or 800/624-6380. 36 rooms with bath, 15 motel units with bath. Facilities: dining room, bar, conference and meeting room. AE, MC, V. Inexpensive–Moderate.*

Town & Lake Motel. This complex of efficiencies, motel units, and cottages alongside the highway and on Rangeley Lake is just down the road from the shops and restaurants of downtown Rangeley. Two-bedroom cottages with well-equipped kitchens are farther from the highway, and some face Saddleback. Pets are welcome. *Rte. 16, Rangeley 04970, tel. 207/864-3755. 16 motel units with bath, 9 cottages. Facilities: swimming, canoes, boat rental. AE, MC, V. Inexpensive.*

Shawnee Peak at Pleasant Mountain
Box 734, Rte. 302, Bridgton 04009
Tel. 207/647-8444

Situated on the New Hampshire border, Pleasant Mountain draws many skiers from the North Conway region 18 miles away and from Portland, 40 miles distant. It's a relative sleeper owned by the Shawnee Group, a resort enterprise whose aim is to attract families for vacations. With condominiums on the mountain and an upgraded base lodge, the area promises to expand without compromising its hospitable atmosphere.

Downhill Skiing Recent lighting installations have opened more trails for night skiing off the 1,300-foot vertical. Most trails are pleasant cruisers for intermediates, with some beginner slopes and a few pitches suitable for advanced skiers. One triple and three double chairlifts and a T-bar service the 31 ski runs.

Child Care The area's nursery takes children from 6 months to 7 years. Skiwee instruction for children 4–12 lasts six hours a day and includes lunch. Mighty Mite classes are for children 6–12 who know how to ski. The Youth Ski League has instruction for aspiring racers.

Lodging **Westways.** A stay at Westways on Kezar Lake can be like a visit with posh relatives. Built in the 1920s, the gray-shingle main lodge has a palatial living room with a massive fireplace, wood floors, and overstuffed easy chairs. Among the guest rooms, the masculine Horses Room sports hunting prints, maple furniture, and the best lake view; the Maple Room in the southwest corner has Italian Renaissance prints, floral bedspreads, and a water view from every window; the east-wing rooms are smaller, spartan, and less expensive. The dining room, open to nonguests by reservation, is a glassed-in porch facing the lake. Six cottages for rent by the week through the inn are tucked away on the densely wooded grounds and are suitable for families. *Center Lovell 04016, tel. 207/928-2663. 7 rooms, 3 with bath; 6 cottages with 3–7 bedrooms. Facilities: clay tennis court, swimming and boating, bowling, Ping Pong, billiards. AE, MC, V. Closed Apr., Nov., Dec. 25. Expensive–Very Expensive.*

Sugarloaf/USA
Carrabassett Valley 04947
Tel. 207/237–2000

The 1980s saw Sugarloaf emerge as a major ski resort with two sizeable hotels, a complex of condominiums, a cluster of restaurants, conference and meeting facilities, a shopping mall, and —most important but last to come—an extensive snowmaking system. Despite its charm, vigor, and amenities, the area had suffered several bad years when natural snow was lean; now skiers are rediscovering this sophisticated resort. Lots of special packages, activities, and programs are offered.

Downhill Skiing The vertical of Sugarloaf, 2,640 feet, makes it slightly shorter than Killington (Vermont) but taller than any other New England ski peak. The advanced terrain begins with the steep snowfields on top, wide open and treeless. Coming down the face of the mountain, there are black-diamond runs everywhere, often blending into easier terrain. A substantial number of intermediate trails can be found down the front face, and a couple more come off the summit. Easier runs are predominantly toward the bottom, with a few long, winding runs that twist and turn from higher elevations. The 45 miles of trails are served by one four-passenger gondola; two quad, one triple, and eight double chairlifts; and two T-bars.

Cross-Country Skiing The Touring Center has 80 kilometers (50 miles) of cross-country trails that loop and wind through the valley.

Other Activities The Sugartree Health Club features an indoor pool, six indoor and outdoor hot pools, two racquetball courts, weightlifting equipment, aerobics machines, saunas, steam rooms, a massage room, and a beauty salon. For summer, there is an 18-hole golf course and six tennis courts.

Child Care A nursery takes children from 6 weeks to 3 years. Once they reach 3, children are provided with free ski equipment if they are interested in trying the sport. A night nursery is open on Wednesday and Saturday, 6–10 PM. Mountain Magic provides instruction for ages 4–6 on a half-day or full-day basis; and Mountain Adventure, with half-day and full-day instruction, is offered to two age groups: 7–12 and 13–16.

Lodging **Sugarloaf Inn Resort.** This lodge provides ski-on access to Sugarloaf/USA, a complete health club, and rooms that range from king size on the fourth floor to dorm style (bunk beds) on the ground floor. A greenhouse section of the Seasons restaurant affords views of the slopes: At breakfast the sunlight pours in, and at dinner you can watch the snow-grooming machines prepare your favorite run. *RR 1, Box 5000, Kingfield 04947, tel. 207/237–2000 or 800/843–5623. 36 rooms with bath, 6 dorm rooms. Facilities: restaurant, lounge, health club, sauna, Jacuzzi, aerobics classes, video arcade, conference facilities. AE, MC, V. Expensive–Very Expensive.*
Sugarloaf Mountain Hotel. This six-story brick structure at the base of the lifts on Sugarloaf combines a New England ambience with full hotel service in the European manner. Oak and redwood paneling in the main rooms is enhanced by contemporary furnishings. Valet parking, ski tuning, lockers, and mountain guides are available through the concierge. *Box 518, Carrabassett Valley 04947, tel. 207/527–9879 or 207/237–2874. 90 rooms with bath, 26 suites. Facilities: 2 restaurants, pub,*

spa, 2 hot tubs, sauna, tanning booth, message, concierge. AE, MC, V. Expensive–Very Expensive.

Lumberjack Lodge. Located on the access road, ½ mile from Sugarloaf, this informal lodge is the closest accommodation to the mountain. The Tyrolean-style building contains eight efficiency units, each with living and dining area, kitchenette, full bath, bedroom, and no phone or TV. Units sleep up to 8 people. A free shuttle to the lifts operates during the peak season. Restaurants nearby serve those who may not want to prepare their own meals. *Rte. 27, Carrabassett 04947, tel. 207/237–2141. 8 units. Facilities: recreation room with fireplace and cable TV, video games, Ping Pong, bumper pool, sauna. AE, MC, V. Closed May–Sept. Inexpensive.*

Sunday River
Box 450, Bethel 04217
Tel. 207/824–3000; for snow conditions, 207/824–6400

From a sleepy little ski area with minimal facilities, Sunday River came on in the 1980s like state-of-the-art. Spread throughout the valley are three base areas, trail-side condominiums, town houses, a ski dorm, and condotels that provide the essentials. Lots of imaginatively packaged ski weeks are promoted to appeal to skiers with specialized interests: college students, Canadians, and handicapped skiers, among others. Beginners are offered a program that guarantees they will learn to ski in one day or their money will be refunded.

Downhill Skiing Billed as the steepest, longest, widest lift-served trail in the East, White Heat is the latest in a line of trails opened at Sunday River in recent years. At present the area has 60 trails, the majority in the intermediate range. Expert and advanced runs are grouped from the peaks, and most beginner slopes are located near the base of the area. Some trails representing all difficulty levels spread down from five peaks (the tallest with a vertical drop of 1,650 feet) that are served by four quad, four triple, and two double chairlifts and one T-bar.

Other Activities Throughout the housing complexes are three indoor pools, three outdoor heated pools, saunas, and Jacuzzis for winter and summer. For summer, there are two tennis courts, a volleyball court, and mountain biking. In the fall an arts and crafts festival is held.

Child Care The nursery takes children ages 6 weeks to 2 years; the Day Care Center takes them from 2 to 6 years. The Skiwee program accommodates children 4–6, and Sunday Rapids is available for ages 7–12. Both programs are all-day sessions that include lift tickets, lessons, lunch, and rental equipment.

Lodging **Bethel Inn and Country Club.** Bethel's grandest accommodation is a full-service resort with a health club, conference facilities, and lodgings ranging from old-fashioned inn rooms to slick new condos on the fairway. Guest rooms in the main inn, sparsely furnished with Colonial reproductions and George Washington bedspreads, are the most desirable; choice rooms have fireplaces and face the mountains over the golf course. Four cottages on the town common have plain rooms, and the condos echo the inn's Colonial decor. The formal dining room, done in lemon yellow with pewter accents, serves elaborate dinners. *Village Common, Box 49, Bethel 04217, tel. 207/824–2175 or 800/654–0125, fax 207/824–2233. 57 rooms with bath, 80* *two-bedroom condo units. Facilities: restaurant, tavern with weekend entertainment, all-weather tennis court, golf course, health club, conference center. AE, CB, D, DC, MC, V. Rates are MAP or EP. Expensive–Very Expensive.*

Sunday River Inn. Conveniently located at the base of the Sunday River ski area, this modern chalet offers private rooms for families and dorm rooms (bring your sleeping bag) for groups and students. Hearty meals are served buffet-style, and the comfy living room is dominated by a stone hearth. *Sunday River Rd., RFD 2, Box 1688, Bethel 04217, tel. 207/824–2410. 8 rooms, 4 dorms, 1 apartment. Facilities: cross-country skiing, Finnish sauna. AE, MC, V. Rates are MAP. Closed Apr.– Thanksgiving. Inexpensive.*

Massachusetts Skiing

Because the Massachusetts Berkshires are in fact foothills of the Green Mountains of Vermont, many of the ski areas have significant vertical drops of just over 1,000 feet, usually on gentle-beginner to intermediate terrain. This can be the ideal environment for an introduction to skiing and for family outings on winter weekends. City and suburban ski shops run busloads of skiers to the areas on Saturday and Sunday, adding to the crowds and the lift lines. Although most skiers go to the Berkshires for day skiing, there are numerous places to stay overnight, and two ski areas can be visited comfortably in one weekend. Good restaurants are found in large number here.

In the Boston and Springfield areas the hills may be smaller, but the numbers of skiers tend to rival those in the Berkshires. These ski areas offer the same mix of people—beginners, families, and bus groups—and provide excellent opportunities for learning the sport.

Berkshire East
Box 0, South River Rd., Charlemont 01339
Tel. 413/339–6617

Berkshire East has been around for some years, yet it seems to attract little more than a college crowd from the region and loyal families and youngsters interested in the area's racing program. Improvements may change that; a 326-unit condominium development under construction at the base of the area should draw a wider spectrum of skiers to an area where accommodations have been scarce.

Downhill Skiing The 1,200-foot vertical was once considered more difficult than that of neighboring ski areas. Recent blasting, widening, and sculpting tamed many of the steeper trails, but you can still find steep pitches toward the top. Wide, cruisable intermediate slopes are plentiful, and beginner terrain is abundant. Four dou-ble chairlifts and two surface lifts serve the 25 trails. There's night skiing Thursday through Saturday.

Child Care The nursery takes children from infants to 8 years; children under 6 ski free. For older children the ski school offers instructional classes. For aspiring racers, 5–18, the race-training program is Saturday and Sunday.

Lodging **The Inn at Charlemont.** This rambling old inn just two minutes' drive from Berkshire East was reopened recently by new owners who are now in the throes of renovation. Guest rooms have uneven wood floors and rather basic furnishings; those that have been restored are more comfortable, with quilts and country-style decorations. Bunk beds are available for skiers, and individual packages, including lift-ticket discounts, can be arranged. *Rte. 2, Charlemont 01339, tel. 413/339–5796. 14 rooms share 7 baths. Facilities: restaurant, bar, TV lounge. AE, CB, D, DC, MC, V. Closed Dec. 25. Inexpensive.*

Nightlife The Inn at Charlemont is the main resource for skiers at Berkshire East, an area that hardly throbs with activity. On Friday and Saturday evenings blues and reggae bands perform; on Sunday there's a "warm-up" hour, with blues, piano, and saxophone entertainment beginning as skiers leave the slopes, at around 4 PM.

Blue Hills

Canton 02186
Tel. 671/828–7490; for ski school, 617/828–5090; for snow conditions, 617/828–5070

Situated just 30 minutes south of downtown Boston, Blue Hills is a day and night outpost for suburban skiers. On most midweek afternoons the slopes are filled with groups of children from schools and recreation programs taking part in beginner to junior classes. Evenings attract a cross-section of skiers; weekends see mostly families.

Downhill Skiing The vertical is only 365 feet, which doesn't allow much variety. Most of the slopes are easy; a double chairlift and three surface lifts carry skiers.

Bousquet Ski Area

Tamarack Rd., Pittsfield 01201
Tel. 413/442–8316; for snow conditions, 413/442–2436

In 1935, when skiing was a novelty sport, the installation of a state-of-the-art rope tow at Bousquet made it a true destination resort. Ski trains from New York City brought skiers by the hundreds throughout the winter. In 1936 a group of engineers from General Electric devised a way to light the slopes for night skiing, which further propelled Bousquet into the heady modern era of skiing. Sad to say, the area's time in the limelight ended in the 1960s when bigger and more glamorous ski areas came on the scene. Yet Bousquet remains a fixture in Pittsfield with its inexpensive midweek lift-ticket policy, night skiing Monday through Saturday, and bargain packages that include lodging, lift tickets, and lunch at the base lodge.

Downhill Skiing The area brochure counts 21 trails, but that includes every change in steepness, cutoff, and merging slope. In fact, there is a good selection of beginner and intermediate runs, with a few steeper pitches, off a 750-foot vertical drop. The area has two double chairlifts and two surface lifts.

Other Activities A center at the base offers four handball courts, six indoor tennis courts, saunas, and a whirlpool.

Child Care While there are no nursery or special children's programs, ski instruction classes are offered twice daily on weekends and holidays, at noon on weekdays.

Lodging **Wheatleigh.** This is an undeniably grand, even baronial accommodation; the sheer style of the great hall with its gallery is amazing. But what are those modern chrome chairs doing here?

Why is the hall carpeting a utilitarian gray, the wallpaper a blue bamboo print? Guest rooms vary in size from vast to medium and are generally elegant if sparsely furnished; several have fireplaces. *W. Hawthorne Rd., Lenox 01240, tel. 413/637–0610. 17 rooms with bath. Facilities: dining room, lounge, outdoor pool, tennis court, steam room, exercise room. AE, CB, DC, MC, V. Very Expensive.*

Cliffwood Inn. This classic Colonial-style building sits unobtrusively on a residential street in Lenox. Six of the seven guest rooms have fireplaces (one in a bathroom!), and there are four more fireplaces in the lounge, hall, and breakfast room downstairs. Much of the furniture comes from Europe—the innkeepers have lived in Paris, Brussels, and in Italy—and most rooms have canopy beds. *25 Cliffwood St., Lenox 01240, tel. 413/637–3330. 7 rooms with bath. Facilities: dining room, lounge, music room, outdoor pool. No credit cards. Rates include Continental breakfast on winter weekends. Expensive–Very Expensive.*

Dalton House. This bed-and-breakfast enterprise has expanded over the years, the owners adding a sunny breakfast room, with pine chairs and tables, to the front of the 170-year-old house and converting the carriage house into deluxe rooms. Guests share a split-level sitting room, with cathedral ceiling, exposed beams, and a wood-burning stove. Bedrooms in the main house are cheerful, of average size, with floral print drapes and wallpaper and rocking chairs. The spacious carriage-house rooms are more impressive: They have exposed beams, period furnishings, quilts, and views of the pool and garden. Ski packages, which include dinner, are offered in season. *955 Main St., Dalton 01226, tel. 413/684–3854. 9 rooms with bath, 2 suites. Facilities: outdoor pool, lounge, 2 hall phones. AE, MC, V. Rates include breakfast. Moderate.*

Nightlife In addition to the many restaurants in the Lenox and Pittsfield area, **Brannigan's** (1015 South St., Lenox, tel. 413/443–6228) is a well-known nightclub, with a disco and DJ downstairs and live bands upstairs. **Bucksteep Manor** (Washington Mountain Rd., Washington, tel. 413/623–5535) offers après-ski entertainment, with folk singers between 3 and 5 PM. On weekends Bucksteep often showcases local bands.

Brodie

U.S. 7, New Ashford 01237
Tel. 413/443–4752 or 413/443–6597; for snow conditions, 413/443–4751

Color it green and you might be skiing at Brodie, where the snow can be green, the beer is often green, and the decor is always green. Yet there's more here than an Irish ambience to attract young crowds to the weekend and night skiing. The base lodge has a restaurant and bar with live entertainment, lodging is within walking distance of the lifts, and trailers can be accommodated on the grounds.

Downhill Skiing Almost all trails are beginner and intermediate despite the black diamonds, which designate steeper (not expert) runs. They are served by four double chairlifts and two surface lifts off 1,250 feet of vertical.

Cross-Country Skiing The area's cross-country skiing covers 25 kilometers (16 miles) of trails.

Other Activities A sports center has five indoor courts for tennis and five for racquetball, an exercise room, and a cocktail lounge.

Child Care The nursery takes infants to age 8 by the hour, half day, or full day. Afternoon ski instruction programs teach youngsters from beginning to racing techniques.

Lodging **Best Western Springs Motor Inn.** This pleasant motel overlooks Brodie Mountain across Route 7. Rooms have modern furnishings and white cinderblock walls; those on the second tier are larger, with better views and more luxurious appointments. Some rooms have refrigerators. *Rte. 7, New Ashford 01237, tel. 413/458–5945. 38 rooms with bath, 2 suites. Facilities: restaurant, lounge, breakfast bar, outdoor pool, game room. AE, CB, D, DC, MC, V. Expensive.*

Field Farm Guest House. Built in 1948 on 254 acres of private grounds, the house was designed primarily to exhibit its owner's art collection (which went to the Williams College Museum of Art on his death). Guest rooms are large, some of them huge, with big windows and expansive views over the grounds and pond. Three rooms have private decks, two have working fireplaces decorated with tiles depicting animals, birds, and butterflies. The place resembles a modern museum: Most of the furniture was handmade by the owner-collector, and there are sculptures in the garden. Cross-country ski trails begin at the door. *554 Sloan Rd. (off Rte. 43), Williamstown 01267, tel. 413/458–3135. 5 rooms with bath. Facilities: dining room, lounge, outdoor pool, tennis court. No credit cards. Expensive.*

Nightlife Brodie is not a focal point for nightlife; skiers seeking après-ski entertainment usually head north to Williamstown, where there are collegiate bars and a number of restaurants.

Butternut Basin
Great Barrington 01230
Tel. 413/528–2000; for ski school, 413/528–4433

The friendly Butternut Basin has good base facilities, pleasant skiing, and tasty food in the base lodge, attracting skiers by the score and often producing long lift lines on weekends. Yet skiers from New York's Long Island and Westchester County and Fairfield County in Connecticut continue to flock to the area.

Downhill Skiing Only a steep chute or two interrupts the mellow intermediate terrain. There are slopes for beginners and something for everyone off the area's 1,000-foot vertical. One triple and five double chairlifts plus one surface lift keep skier traffic spread out.

Cross-Country Skiing There are 7 kilometers (4 miles) of groomed cross-country trails.

Child Care The nursery takes children ages 2½–6 for indoor and outdoor activities on weekends and holidays. The ski school's highly successful Skiwee program is for children 4–12. During midweek, youngsters can get group lessons any day.

Lodging **Weathervane Inn.** The open fireplace and beehive oven in the lounge of this friendly, family-run inn date to the 1760s, when the original building was constructed. The more formal parlor has striking reproduction wallpaper, and guest rooms are pleasantly decorated with stencils, country curtains, wreaths, Norman Rockwell prints, and rocking chairs. The inn has had a varied past; at one period it served as dog kennels, and one of the guest bathrooms has inherited an original dog-sized bathtub! *Rte. 23, South Egremont 01258, tel. 413/528-9580. 10 rooms with bath. Facilities: 2 dining rooms, lounge, TV lounge, outdoor pool. AE, MC, V. Closed Dec. 20-26. Rates include full breakfast. Expensive-Very Expensive.*

Turning Point Inn. Located ½ mile east of Butternut Basin, this 200-year-old inn used to be the Pixie Tavern, a stagecoach stop. The whole of the upstairs—now guest rooms—was then a ballroom. Guests share a large living room, with two fireplaces and a piano, as well as a kitchen area, with a woodstove. Bedrooms, with uneven, wide-board floors, are of varying sizes, and several have sloping roofs; they are furnished with antiques. Breakfasts are a specialty—the hosts are natural-foods advocates and serve up multigrain hot cereals, fritata omelets with fresh garden vegetables, buckwheat pancakes, eggs, and home-baked muffins or cakes. The barn was recently converted into a two-bedroom cottage, which has modern furnishings, a full kitchen, and screened porch. *Rte. 23 and Lake Buel Rd., RD2, Box 140, Great Barrington 01230, tel. 413/528-4777. 7 rooms, 1 with bath, 1 cottage. Facilities: kitchen, lounge, hall phone, cross-country ski trail. No smoking, no pets. No credit cards. Rates include full breakfast. Expensive.*

Mountain View Motel. This is the closest motel to Butternut, situated a mile west of the ski area on Route 23. Rooms have in-room coffee and Rockwell prints. *304 State Rd. (Rte. 23E), Great Barrington 01230, tel. 413/528-0250. 16 rooms with bath, 1 suite, 1 efficiency. AE, MC, V. Moderate.*

Nightlife Sampling the cuisine at a nearby inn is probably the principal evening entertainment at Butternut. Those who are determined to seek out more active nightlife should head for the **Lion's Den,** beneath the Red Lion Inn (tel. 413/298-5545) in Stockbridge, which has live entertainment and is located 20 minutes from the ski area by car.

Jiminy Peak
Corey Rd., Hancock 01237
Tel. 413/738-5500 or 413/445-5500

Just three hours from midtown New York City or Boston, Jiminy Peak has all the amenities of a major mountain resort. A country inn and condominiums are within walking distance of the ski lifts, more condominium complexes are nearby, and two restaurants and bars are at the slopes. These services attract families and nearby residents for day and night skiing. Rentals from one night to one week to three months are available, and there is meeting and convention space.

Downhill Skiing With a vertical of 1,140 feet, Jiminy can claim big-time status. The steeper black-diamond sections are toward the top of the mountain, and there is enough good intermediate terrain to satisfy most skiers. Beginners, too, are well served. The area has one triple and three double chairlifts and one surface lift for its 24 trails. Night skiing is an option every night of the week.

Other Activities Jiminy has seven outdoor tennis courts in summer, an outdoor pool, an Alpine slide, an 18-hole putting course, and a pond stocked for fishing. Tennis instruction is available for one or a series of lessons.

Child Care The nursery takes children from age 2. Children 5-12 can take daily Skiwee lessons, and for ages 6-15 the Patriot program offers a series of eight weekends of instruction with the same teacher.

Lodging **The Country Inn at Jiminy Peak.** The massive stone fireplaces in the lobby and lounge areas give this year-round hotel a ski-lodge atmosphere. All rooms are modern, condo-style suites, their neat kitchenettes—separated from the living area by a bar and high stools—supplied with crockery, cooker, dishwasher, and refrigerator. Rooms at the rear of the building overlook the slopes. *Corey Rd., Hancock 01237, tel. 413/445–5500, fax 413/738–5729. 105 suites. Facilities: restaurant, lounge, 4 outdoor pools, 2 saunas, Jacuzzi, exercise room, massage, 7 tennis courts, minigolf, meeting rooms. AE, CB, D, DC, MC, V. Very Expensive.*

Hancock Inn. The inn dates to the late 1700s and provides cozy "olde worlde" accommodation a mile from Jiminy Peak. Dinner at the inn's restaurant is well recommended. *Rte. 43, Hancock 01237, tel. 413/738–5873. 6 rooms with bath. Facilities: 2 dining rooms, bar, lounge. AE, MC, V. Rates include breakfast. Expensive.*

Nightlife The Country Inn at Jiminy Peak has a dining room overlooking the slopes and an adjoining bar lounge, both open throughout the evening. (*See* also Nightlife in Brodie, above.)

Mt. Tom
Rte. 5, Holyoke 01041
Tel. 413/536–0516; for ski school, 413/536–1575

Just minutes from Springfield and several colleges, Mt. Tom attracts skiers for day and night skiing, offering six-week series of ski-lesson packages for children and adults. In addition, the area holds races and special events for local groups. At midweek, high school youngsters ski in the afternoon and retired people use season passes when the weather is at its best. There is a restaurant and banquet facilities.

Downhill Skiing Slopes and trails at Mt. Tom tend to be extra wide, if not long, off the vertical of 680 feet. The trails are mostly for intermediates and beginners, with a few steeper pitches. Serving the 17 trails are three double chairlifts, two T-bars, and two surface lifts.

Other Activities Mt. Tom has a wave pool and Alpine slide in summer.

Child Care In addition to daily group lessons on weekends, day camps provide an entire day of instruction for children 6–14. During vacation periods in December and February, five-day lesson programs are offered. Mt. Tom has midweek instruction programs for schoolchildren.

Lodging **Susse Chalet.** This chain motel 2 miles from Mt. Tom provides comfortable modern furnishings. The 35-year-old facility has no restaurant, but there is one within walking distance. *Rte. 5, Holyoke 01040, tel. 413/536–1980. 52 rooms with bath. AE, MC, V. Moderate.*

Riviera Motel. The budget-style accommodations at this basic motel are a little more than a mile north of the ski area on Route 5. *59 Northampton St. (Rte. 5), Smiths Ferry, Holyoke 01040, tel. 413/536–3377. 17 rooms with bath. AE, MC, V. Inexpensive–Moderate.*

Nightlife Local residents, asked for nightlife recommendations, may suggest a visit to the Ingleside shopping mall. Those who seek something on the order of a nightclub will have to travel south to Springfield.

Nashoba Valley
Power Rd., Westford 01886
Tel. 508/692–3033

Close to Boston, Nashoba attracts suburban families for day and night skiing. Package instruction programs are offered to adults in the morning and evening, to children in the afternoon.

Downhill Skiing The area has two wide-open intermediate slopes with a smattering of trees, plus a couple of narrow trails that wind around the 250-foot hill. One double and two triple chairlifts and six surface lifts provide transport.

Child Care For children ages 4 and 5, a series of four consecutive one-hour morning classes is offered Monday through Friday. For students in grades 1 to 12, six consecutive one-hour lessons are offered midweek in the morning and afternoon. For children in grades 7 to 12, the six-lesson series is also offered in the evening.

Lodging **The Westford Regency.** Just five minutes' drive from Nashoba Valley's slopes, this luxurious hotel offers ideal facilities for the skier—a sauna, Jacuzzi, steam room, and indoor pool—and the choice of formal or informal dining. Guest rooms have either modern furnishings or reproduction antiques. *219 Littleton Rd., Rte. 110, Westford 02886, tel. 508/692–8200 or 800/543–7801. 193 rooms with bath, 5 suites. Facilities: 2 dining rooms, bar, pool, Jacuzzi, steam room, exercise room, 4 racquetball courts, massage, tanning, meeting rooms. AE, CB, DC, MC, V. Moderate–Expensive.*

Nightlife The skier's best bet for nightlife here is to travel 20 miles to Boston.

Wachusett Mountain
499 Mountain Rd., Princeton 01541
Tel. 617/464–5101; for snow conditions, 800/696–7669

Wachusett, one hour from Boston, offers a good-size mountain and a large base lodge with facilities usually found only at bigger resorts. It attracts family skiers for day skiing and provides numerous ski-instruction programs for school groups midweek and on weekends.

Downhill Skiing Wachusett has two peaks, the higher with a vertical drop of 1,000 feet. The more difficult terrain is located toward the top of the higher peak; most of the rest is intermediate. Beginner slopes are separated from the main traffic. The area has two triple and one double chairlift and one surface lift.

Cross-Country Skiing Twenty-five kilometers (16 miles) of cross-country trails circle the mountain.

Child Care At the Polar Club Den in the base building, children meet for classes, take hot-chocolate breaks, and have lunch. The Polar Cub ski instruction program for children 3–12 incorporates full-day Skiwee lessons on weekends, and Lollipop has half-day lessons on weekday mornings.

Lodging **Harrington Farm.** One can ski cross-country to Wachusett from this B&B, and it's only three minutes by car. The farmhouse, built in 1763, has Colonial-style furnishings, antiques, and hand-stenciling on the walls. *178 Westminster Rd., Princeton 01541, tel. 508/464–5600. 8 rooms, 2 with bath. Facilities: dining room, 2 lounges, spring-fed outdoor swimming pond. MC, V. Moderate.*

Town Crier Motel. This is the nearest motel to the ski resort 3 miles away. Rooms have Colonial decor; some rooms have waterbeds. Restaurants will be found in the immediate area. Ski packages and discounts are available. *Jct. Rtes. 2, 2A, 140, Westminster 01473, tel. 508/874–5951. 31 rooms with bath. MC, V. Inexpensive–Moderate.*

Nightlife The lodge at Wachusett Mountain, open late, offers a restaurant and a lounge (with live entertainment on special occasions). The area's next best bet is **Abigail's Restaurant** in the Days Inn (Betty Spring Rd., Gardner, tel. 508/630–2500), where live bands perform Friday and Saturday night.

Connecticut Skiing

Who would imagine there could be ski areas in Connecticut? The soft, rolling hills along the northern tier may not be high, but with the help of snowmaking systems, several ski areas flourish in this region. One reason for the success of Connecticut skiing is a large local population of families; most ski areas have active instruction and racing programs for youngsters and a warm atmosphere that caters to children of all ages.

Mohawk Mountain
Box 27, Cornwall, 06753
Tel. 203/672–6100; for snow conditions, 203/672–6464

Located in the foothills of the Berkshires, Mohawk Mountain was opened in 1948 by Walt Schoenknecht, who later founded and developed Mount Snow in Vermont. Mohawk was a testing ground for early innovations in the ski-area business: Snowmaking was first tried here, and wide-open fall-line slopes were conceived on this mountain. In 1989 Mohawk was the victim of a five-force, triple-funnel tornado that ripped apart the entire base of the mountain—trees, buildings, lifts, equipment—yet the area rebuilt quickly, with a little help from other ski areas and equipment manufacturers. Midweek this is a busy place, with junior racing programs and special discount days; the weekend attracts families from nearby metropolitan areas.

Downhill Skiing Mohawk always had wide slopes, but since the tornado of 1989, the lower sections have been one continuous broad field of snow. There is a lot of easy beginner terrain and plenty of intermediate trails, with a few steeper sections toward the top of the 660-foot vertical. The 25 trails are served by one triple and four double chairlifts and one surface lift.

Child Care For ages 5–12, Mohawk has an active Skiwee program, weekends and holidays, 10 AM–3 PM. A half-day session for younger children starts at 1 PM. A racing camp for boys and girls is held in December.

Lodging **Hitching Post Country Motel.** This old-fashioned but well-maintained motel is the closest to the ski trails and is easy to find on the main approach to the area. The Bonanza bus stops nearby at the "general store." *Rte. 7, Cornwall 06754, tel. 203/672–6219. 9 rooms with bath, 1 suite, 1 efficiency. MC, V. Moderate.*

Nightlife Restaurants in nearby Kent often feature live entertainment, particularly on weekends. Head north on Route 7 to reach the **Interlaken Inn** (tel. 203/435–9878) on Route 112 in Winsted, which has live entertainment nightly.

Mount Southington
Box 347, Southington 06489
Tel. 203/628–0954; for snow conditions, 800/982–6828

A feeling of fun pervades Mount Southington, where the formula is parties, races, and enjoying the sport. The area is an easy drive for skiers from Waterbury, Danbury, Hartford, and New Haven, and its programs include night skiing and racing camps for adults and juniors.

Downhill Skiing The 12 trails off the 425 feet of vertical are basic beginner and low intermediate, with a touch of steeper stuff here and there. One triple and two double chairlifts and two surface lifts carry skiers.

Child Care Skiwee classes for ages 4–12 take place on Saturday and Sunday. Group lessons are available during the week, and school and recreation groups take lessons and race almost every afternoon.

Lodging **Comfort Inn.** Some rooms have whirlpool baths; all rooms justify the name of the lodging. *120 Laning St. (I–84, Exit 32), Southington 06489, tel. 203/228–5150. 122 rooms with bath. Facilities: outdoor pool. MC, V. Rates include Continental breakfast. Moderate–Expensive.*
Howard Johnson Lodge. The familiar Howard Johnson food-and-lodging formula meets expectations here. Rooms have a certain ski-lodge ambience. *I–84 and Rte. 10 (I–84, Exit 32), Southington 06489, tel. 203/628–0921 or 800/543–2000. 72 rooms with bath. Facilities: restaurant, coffee shop, outdoor pool. AE, CB, DC, MC, V. Moderate–Expensive.*
Susse Chalet Motor Lodge. Rooms are sparsely but adequately furnished, and this budget motel is always busy. *462 Queen St. (I–84, Exit 32), Southington 06489, tel. 203/621–0181. 148 rooms with bath. Facilities: outdoor pool. AE, CB, DC, MC, V. Inexpensive–Moderate.*

Powder Ridge
Powder Hill Rd., Middlefield 06455
Tel. 203/349–3454

Right here in the heart of Connecticut is a day hill substantial enough for real skiing. Powder Ridge gathers suburbanites from metropolitan New York, Danbury, Hartford, and New Haven; families and kids come all week long and on weekends. The restaurant at the base offers a good view of the activities on the hill.

Downhill Skiing It's a ridge indeed, 500 feet high, with ski trails that drop straight down. Most trails are slightly more difficult toward the top and ease up at the bottom of the hill. Serving these slopes are one quad and three double chairlifts and one surface tow. There is night skiing every night, until 1 AM Friday and Saturday, and timed tickets allow skiers to buy four-hour or eight-hour segments of skiing for any time of the day or night.

Other Activities In summer, Powder Ridge has an outdoor pool, two tennis courts, playing fields, and catering services for special events.

Child Care The Kinder School program takes children 4–8 for half-day sessions Saturday and Sunday. Classes range from play to instruction, and reservations are required.

Ski Sundown
Box 208, New Hartford 06057
Tel. 203/279–9851

Close to the Massachusetts border in the Litchfield Hills, Ski Sundown has some neat touches—a sundeck on the mountain, racing classes for adults and children, and a Mountaineers social club for skiers 55 and older. These attractions plus state-of-the-art facilities and equipment draw skiers from all over Connecticut and New York.

Downhill Skiing The mountain looks impressive for Connecticut, with trails for all abilities spread out and winding to the bottom. Beginner and intermediate levels share the bulk of the terrain, but one good-size advanced run drops straight down from the 625-foot vertical. Three triple chairlifts and one surface lift take skiers to the top with reasonable waits at the bottom. A wide variety of lesson programs are offered to all ages and levels of ability in four-week and seven-week packages.

Child Care Ski Puffins is a series of five lessons for preschoolers on weekdays. Beyond that, Mogul Mites are ages 5–8; Ski Scooters, 7–13, should be experienced skiers; and Mogul Masters, 9–13, can be any ability level. All these programs are offered on consecutive weekends in four-lesson series. The Afterschool Club is for ages 8–18, and vacation camps are offered in December and February during school breaks for ages 9–16.

Lodging **Avon Old Farms Motel.** A luxurious country-style hotel with a restaurant of established reputation, the Avon Old Farms attracts visitors to nearby Hartford. *Rtes. 44 and 10, Avon 06001, tel. 203/677–1651 or 800/228–1651. 161 rooms with bath, 3 suites. Facilities: restaurant, coffee shop, lounge, outdoor pool, health club, sauna. AE, CB, D, DC, MC, V. Very Expensive.*
Hillside Motel. This motel, operating at the thrifty end of the spectrum, offers simple, neat rooms. *671 Albany Tpke. (Rte. 44), Canton 06019, tel. 203/693–4951. 14 rooms with bath, 2 efficiencies. AE, MC, V. Inexpensive.*

3 Connecticut

by Arthur S.
Rosenblatt, with
an introduction by
William G.
Scheller

The author of 16
books for children,
Arthur S.
Rosenblatt is also
a frequent
contributor to
Food & Wine and
Poets & Writers.

When Mark Twain decided to make his time-traveling Yankee a Connecticut man, he wasn't just nodding to his adopted state. The Connecticut Yankee was a mechanic whose genius at tinkering earned him the title Sir Boss at King Arthur's court. Any of Twain's 19th-century readers would have understood the type, for Connecticut, perhaps more than any other New England state, fostered the concept of American know-how and set in motion the wheels of precision technology. Waterbury and Hartford were the Silicon Valley or Route 128 of their day.

Although Connecticut's economy today is based largely on service industries, the state offers many examples of the world that was assembled meticulously by those tinkering Yankees of the 19th century. In Bristol the American Clock and Watch Museum celebrates the accomplishments of two great technicians of time, Seth Thomas and Eli Terry, for whom nearby Thomasville and Terryville are named. Terryville is the home of the Lock Museum of America, which honors another great industry built from small parts carefully put together.

Small parts can be put together with greater efficiency and precision when they are made to be interchangeable—a fact we take for granted today, but one that was the pioneering achievement of a Connecticut Yankee named Eli Whitney at the beginning of the last century. Whitney's development of interchangeable parts made possible America's manufacturing revolution and fostered the phenomenal success of another Connecticut entrepreneur, the revolver inventor Samuel Colt.

Connecticut's early industrialization and small size has made it one of the most densely populated states. Although most of its cities lie along a corridor that reaches from Hartford south through the Long Island Sound communities of New Haven, Bridgeport, and Stamford, urban and rural Connecticut are not as distinct from each other as a glance at the map might suggest; much of the state is within such easy reach of the cities that suburbanization has blurred the distinctions between town and country. Agriculture survives—this is the only New England state with an appreciable tobacco crop, of all things— yet Connecticut's character is more suburban than that of any other section of the six-state area, with the exception of the Providence–Boston corridor.

Because so much of that suburban territory (primarily Fairfield County) lies within a commuter's reach of New York City, it has become common for residents of the region's more distant corners to suggest that Connecticut really shouldn't be considered part of New England at all—as though the state could be blackballed from the club for the offense of consorting too freely with Gotham. It's possible, of course, that the talk of exclusion is simply sour grapes on the part of Boston, which resents New Englanders' bowing in any direction other than its own. Rumor has it that there were people in Fairfield County who rooted for the Mets against the Red Sox in the 1986 World Series, a truly unforgiveable sin.

Despite its overall dissimilarity to northern New England, Connecticut boasts some of the most beautiful villages and rural areas in the region. In the west, along the valley of the Housatonic and in the southern Berkshire Hills near the borders of Massachusetts and New York, the character of the

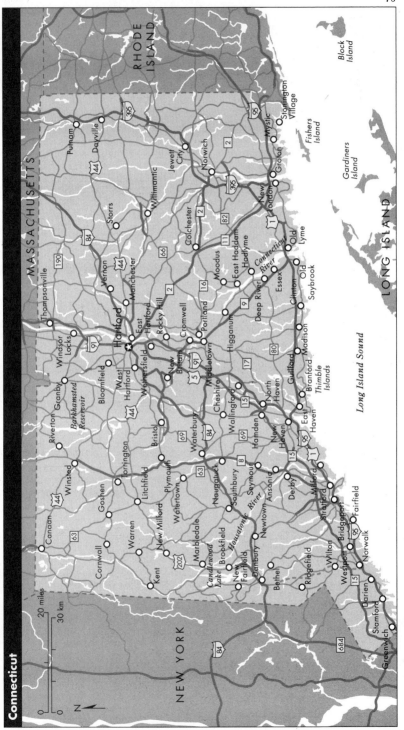

Connecticut

RHODE ISLAND

MASSACHUSETTS

NEW YORK

LONG ISLAND

Block Island

Fishers Island

Gardiners Island

Long Island Sound

Putnam
Dayville
Thompsonville
Storrs
Willimantic
Jewett City
Norwich
Mystic
Stonington Village
Groton
New London
Old Lyme
Old Saybrook
Clinton
Madison
Guilford
Branford
Thimble Islands
East Haven
New Haven
North Haven
Hamden
Wallingford
Cheshire
Meriden
Middletown
New Britain
Rocky Hill
Cromwell
Portland
Higganum
Moodus
East Haddam
Hadlyme
Essex
Deep River
Connecticut River
Colchester
Vernon
Manchester
East Hartford
Hartford
Wethersfield
West Hartford
Bloomfield
Windsor Locks
Riverton
Granby
Barkhamsted Reservoir
Winsted
Canaan
Cornwall
Goshen
Warren
Litchfield
Torrington
Bristol
Plymouth
Watertown
New Milford
Kent
Marbledale
Candlewood Lake
Brookfield
New Fairfield
Danbury
Bethel
Ridgefield
Newtown
Southbury
Naugatuck
Seymour
Ansonia
Derby
Housatonic River
Milford
Stratford
Bridgeport
Fairfield
Westport
Wilton
Norwalk
Darien
Stamford
Greenwich

20 miles
30 km

N

countryside is more self-consciously "exurban," more meticulously cultivated as the apotheosis of New England charm. Villages such as Ridgefield and Litchfield epitomize the country-inn mystique and are groomed so carefully that the visitor immediately suspects that the tainted Manhattan dollars have been working as hard here as any Old Money.

Northeastern Connecticut presents a different prospect. The villages are pretty, but they don't look as though they're posing for magazines, and there aren't so many of them. The rolling countryside is so oddly underpopulated, given its proximity to Hartford, Providence, Worcester, and Boston, that airline pilots flying Northeast Corridor routes are known to comment that this is one of the few dark spots that they look down upon.

The Connecticut countryside is only one reason to dismiss those who say this state isn't New England. There's the old tradition of precision manufacturing in cities where water power once reigned supreme, the proud seafaring heritage represented by Mystic and its preserved whaling vessels, and even the requisite Ivy League college, Yale, in New Haven. And if there is further need for proof that the Connecticut Yankees are just that, consider the nickname Nutmeg State. The legend says that it dates from the days when local traders passed off wooden nutmegs as the real thing. If that's not sharp Yankee practice, what is?

Essential Information

Visitor Information

Department of Economic Development (865 Brook St., Rocky Hill, tel. 203/258–4200 or 800/282–6863).

Tour Groups

General-Interest Tours **Classics Limited** (855 Ridge Rd., Wethersfield 06109, tel. 203/563–0848) offers individual and group tours by private car, limousine, van, and coach.

Discover Connecticut (40 Berwyn Rd., West Hartford 06107, tel. 203/521–3955 or 203/243–0177) has half-day and daylong theme tours to historic homes, sports events, and cultural events.

Heritage Trails (Box 138, Farmington 06034, tel. 203/677–8867) runs daily tours of historic places and candlelight dinner tours. Guide services are available.

Unique Auto Tours (Box 879, Canton 06019, tel. 203/693–0007) lets you follow your own itinerary in a chauffeur-driven antique Rolls Royce or Bentley. Four-day and seven-day packages are available, July to October.

Special-Interest Tours **Down River Canoes** (Box 283, Haddam 06438, tel. 203/346–3308 or 203/345–8355) offers trips of one to three days with barbecues and pig roasts. Instruction, guides, and equipment are available from March through November.

North American Canoe Tours (65 Black Point Rd., Niantic 06357, tel. 203/739–0791) runs guided canoe trips on the Connecticut River, including weekend retreats with camping, paddling, and hiking.

When to Go

In summer the communities on Long Island Sound draw most visitors, as do some waterfront resorts along the Connecticut River. Those seeking a cooler summer climate may prefer the northwest corner, those Litchfield County hills where the performing arts flourish between Memorial Day and Labor Day. For a few brief weeks in mid-autumn, when the foliage is at its peak, Connecticut vies with its northern neighbors in the brilliant colors of the foliage. Those who enjoy winter sports will find Connecticut's small country inns and lodges particularly welcoming. Many rent ski equipment and can outfit you for a day on the slopes. Cross-country skiing has become popular, too, in recent years. Early spring thaws bring mud season, any time from mid-March on, and then outdoor Connecticut is least appealing.

Festivals and Seasonal Events

Jan.–Mar.: Warm Up to Winter schedules weekend events throughout the Farmington River valley. *Tel. 203/674–1035.*
Mid-May: A Taste of Hartford highlights the specialties of more than 40 local restaurants, with outdoor music, dance, comedy, and magic. *Tel. 203/728–6789.*

Late May: Lobster Weekend at Mystic Seaport includes entertainment. *Tel. 203/672–0711.*

Early June: Farmington Antiques Weekend shows the wares of 600 dealers. *Tel. 508/839–9735.*

Early June: Yale–Harvard Regatta, along the Thames River in New London, is said to be the oldest intercollegiate athletic event in the country. *Tel. 203/432–1413.*

Mid-June: Festival of the Arts, in Stamford, salutes the performing and visual arts. *Tel. 203/732–6008.*

Late June–early July: Barnum Festival culminates in an enormous parade through Bridgeport. *Tel. 203/367–8495.*

Late June, July: Jazz Festival, the second-largest free jazz festival in the United States, takes place on New Haven's historic green. *Tel. 203/669–1662.*

Early July: Sail Festival, at New London's City Pier, features sail races, outdoor concerts, fireworks, food, and the Ugliest Dog Contest. *Tel. 203/443–8331.*

July: Litchfield's Open House Tour allows visitors inside historic homes in the area. *Tel. 203/567–9423.*

Late July: Antique and Classic Boat Rendezvous shows vintage powerboats and sailboats at Mystic Seaport. *Tel. 203/572–0711.*

Early Aug.: The Great Connecticut Traditional Jazz Festival offers traditional, Dixieland, and ragtime jazz aboard an old-fashioned steam train. *Tel. 203/453–6543.*

Early Aug.: Mystic Outdoor Arts Festival hosts the sidewalk art of 300 artists. *Tel. 203/536–9644.*

Late Aug.–early Sept.: Woodstock Fair is an agricultural fair with horse and ox pulls, livestock shows, Colonial crafts, puppet shows, food, and a petting zoo. *Tel. 203/928–3246.*

Mid-Sept.: Fall Antiques Show in New Haven is New England's oldest antiques show and one of its largest. *Tel. 203/387–7006.*

Early Oct.: Mum Festival in Bristol includes arts and crafts, drama, a beauty pageant, and a parade. *Tel. 203/589–4111.*

Dec.: Christmas at Mystic Seaport features costumed guides who escort visitors to the activities. *Tel. 203/572–0711.*

Early Dec.: Christmas Torchlight Parade and Muster of Ancient Fife and Drum Corps ends with a carol sing at the Church Green in Old Saybrook. *Tel. 203/399–9460 or 203/399–6571.*

Dec. 31: First Night in Stamford celebrates the last night of the year with live entertainment. *Tel. 203/327–0555.*

What to Pack

Outside the business community, Connecticut places little emphasis on dress-up attire, even in the major cities. Dining at top restaurants will sometimes require that men wear jackets, but insistence on a necktie is rare. Rainwear and an umbrella are frequently useful, and comfortable footwear is important for any outdoor activity, here as elsewhere. The baseball cap and the sunshade are commonly seen during the warmer months, notably at beaches and sporting events.

Arriving and Departing

By Plane **Bradley International Airport** (tel. 203/627–3000), 12 miles north of Hartford and New England's second-largest airport, has scheduled daily flights by most of the major U.S. airlines.

Igor Sikorsky Memorial Airport (tel. 203/576–7498), 4 miles south of Stratford, is served by **Business Express** (tel. 800/345–3400) and **Piedmont** (tel. 800/368–5425).

Tweed/New Haven Airport (tel. 203/787–8283), 5 miles southeast of the city, is served by **USAir** (tel. 800/428–4322) and **Continental** (tel. 800/525–0280).

By Car I–95 reaches all the major cities of coastal Connecticut, linking them with New York in the west and Rhode Island and Massachusetts in the east. I–91, I–84, and I–395 bring traffic from central Massachusetts to the Hartford area and eastern Connecticut.

By Train **Amtrak** (tel. 800/872–7245) service between New York and Boston makes stops from Greenwich to New Haven, then heads north to Hartford and east to New London.

Metro North (tel. 800/522–5624) stops along the coast from Greenwich to New Haven and farther north at New Canaan, Danbury, and Waterbury.

By Bus **Greyhound Lines** (tel. 203/722–2470) and **Bonanza Bus Lines** (tel. 800/556–3815) join Hartford, Middletown, New London, Stamford, Bridgeport, New Haven, and smaller towns with major cities of the eastern United States.

Getting Around Connecticut

By Car The older state highways—the Merritt Parkway and the northern sections of Route 7—are scenic drives, but traffic can become heavy on the narrow roads. The interstate highways offer the fastest means of reaching most destinations in Connecticut. The official state map, available free from the Connecticut Department of Economic Development, is useful for routings.

Shopping

The state's golden age of manufacturing has long since faded, and consumer goods are no longer produced in quantity; factory stores have been supplanted by factory outlets for goods made elsewhere by prominent manufacturers. Connecticut is a prime source of antiques, for its buyers scour the world and bring home treasures to sell in shops throughout the state. The state retail sales tax is 8%.

Sports and Outdoor Activities

Fishing The **Department of Environmental Protection** (165 Capitol Ave., Hartford 06106, tel. 203/566–2287) provides information on licenses and fishing seasons. There's hardly a spot along the coast where the saltwater anglers cannot drop a line, and no license is required for ocean fishing. The Long Island Sound has good saltwater fishing year-round, from striped bass and winter flounder in the bleak months to the heyday of bluefish, from midsummer to early autumn.

Fishing boats are available at rates from $20 per person for a half day to $32 per person for a full day (generally $100 a day for tuna fishing). Bait is usually supplied, but tackle must be rented. These craft, licensed by the U.S. Coast Guard, may carry from six to 150 passengers.

Charter boats are also available in the Sound, ranging in size from 24 feet to 47 feet, most carrying up to six passengers. Tackle is normally supplied, but bait or chum may cost extra. To rent a boat, you'll spend from $275 to $375 for half a day, $450 and up for a full day.

Skiing *The skiing facilities of Connecticut are reviewed in Chapter 2, Skiing New England.*

Beaches

Traditional beach bathing can be a challenge, for there are only a few state-operated public beaches, and access to strips of sandy shore is usually restricted to residents with windshield permits for limited parking areas. If you manage to get to a beach by foot or by pedal, and you don't make a fuss, chances are no one else will. Despite the constant efforts of environmentalists, the southern Connecticut coastline of the Long Island Sound is not always an attractive milieu for splashing about.

Dining

At one time you could expect to find the same handful of items on just about every restaurant menu in the state—New England clam chowder, broiled haddock, seafood platter, Boston Cream Pie, and so on. Today, with new and different restaurants opening every month, the emphasis is on fresh food prepared to order, often by chefs working under the New American or Eclectic banners. A large variety of ethnic cuisines is available, too, and you may find exceptionally good Vietnamese, Tex-Mex, or Nouvelle French cooking, often in the most unexpected places. At the same time, many older establishments have innovated, with more and more of them baking their own breads and pastry.

Highly recommended restaurants in each price category are indicated by a star ★ .

Category	Cost*
Very Expensive	over $25
Expensive	$20–$25
Moderate	$12–$20
Inexpensive	under $12

average cost of a three-course dinner, per person, excluding drinks, service, and 8% sales tax

Lodging

Connecticut offers a large selection of hotels, motels, inns, and bed-and-breakfasts, many located in the vicinity of major highways. The traveler who seeks exceptional accommodations or personal attention may have to make several stops; many of the neon-lit motels along the old highways, for example, have only adequate facilities. Seasonal and weekend rates can be found in all regions, with higher tariffs in the warmer months and bargain rates in winter. The 8% state lodging tax is added to all bills.

Highly recommended lodgings in each price category are indicated by a ★.

Category	Cost*
Very Expensive	over $100
Expensive	$75–$100
Moderate	$50–$75
Inexpensive	under $50

All prices are for a standard double room during peak season, with no meals unless noted, and excluding service charge and 8% state lodging tax.

The Coast: Southwestern Connecticut

The Connecticut coast west of New Haven continues the metropolitan sprawl that fans out from New York City, though most residents of Fairfield County claim that the atmosphere is distinctive here. Beyond the area's occasional opportunities for bathing, numerous nature centers and wilderness preserves offer hiking, bird-watching, and exhibits. The region's Colonial heritage is reflected in several well-preserved 18th-century homes.

Bridgeport, the state's largest city, is still struggling to pull itself up from the urban decline seen most vividly in its downtown area, but other cities have improved their appearance considerably in recent years. Stamford is now a corporate center whose contemporary high rises reflect mirrored facades onto a bustling downtown. Norwalk has turned a derelict area into a lively development of boutiques and restaurants concentrated on the new Maritime Center. Similar projects are taking place all along the shore.

Important Addresses and Numbers

Visitor Information
Bridgeport Convention and Visitors Commission (303 State St., Bridgeport 06604, tel. 203/576–8494).

Greater Stamford Convention and Visitors Bureau (2 Landmark Sq., Stamford 06901, tel. 203/359–3305).

Hill and Harbor Convention and Visitors District (605 Broad St., Suite 208, Stratford 06497, tel. 203/381–9433).

New Haven Convention and Visitors Bureau (900 Chapel St., Suite 344, New Haven 06510, tel. 203/787–8822 or 203/787–8367).

Yankee Heritage District (297 West Ave., The Gate-Lodge, Matthews Park, Norwalk 06850, tel. 203/854–7825).

Emergencies **Yale–New Haven Hospital** (20 York St., tel. 203/785–2222).

Late-night Pharmacy **CVS Pharmacy** (1168 Whalley Ave., New Haven, tel. 203/389–4714).

Getting Around Southwestern Connecticut

By Car The Merritt Parkway and I–95 are the principal highways on the coast, and both are subject to traffic jams, especially during rush hours and construction; it's wise to have a map that shows alternate routes. Travel time from Greenwich to New Haven, when there is no major delay, is approximately one hour.

By Bus **Connecticut Transit** (tel. 203/327–7433) provides bus service in the Stamford, Hartford, and New Haven areas.

Guided Tours

Hello New Haven (Box 5085, Hamden 06585, tel. 203/787–9660) provides one- or two-hour guided car or bus tours of Yale University, museums, architecture, and historical attractions.

Tours of the Shubert (Shubert Performing Arts Center, 247 College St., New Haven 06510, tel. 203/624–1825) offers 40-minute tours, including an audiovisual presentation, of this landmark theater in New Haven which has operated since 1914. Tours are Saturday at 11 AM.

Exploring Southwestern Connecticut

Numbers in the margin correspond with the numbered points of interest on the Southwestern Connecticut map.

I–95 and the Merritt Parkway are the principal highways of this tour of coastal Connecticut that begins at Greenwich, 5 miles inside the state line, and proceeds east to New Haven.

❶ In north **Greenwich** the 485-acre **Audubon Center** offers 8 miles of secluded hiking trails, exhibits about the environment, a gift shop, and a bookshop. *613 Riversville Rd. (Rte. 15, Exit 28), tel. 203/869–5272. Admission: $2 adults, $1 children and senior citizens. Open Tues.–Sun. 9–2.*

The **Bruce Museum** looks a little like a smaller version of the Bates house in *Psycho*, with a concrete-block addition. It has wildlife dioramas, a worthwhile small collection of American Impressionist paintings, and many exhibits on the area. *1 Museum Dr. (I–95, Exit 3), tel. 203/869–0386. Admission: $2 adults, $1.50 senior citizens, $1 children. Open Tues.–Sat. 10–5.*

Follow the signs to Route 1, also known as Putnam Avenue and Boston Post Road, then turn and head east on Route 1. A little more than a mile ahead, on your left, you'll see a small, barn-red cottage with strangely scalloped shingles and a small stone appendage on its eastern side. This is **Putnam Cottage**, built about 1690, and known as Knapp's Tavern during the Revolutionary War. Inside is an enormous stone fireplace and Colonial furniture; outside, the original herb garden still blooms. *243 E. Putnam Ave., tel. 203/869–9697. Admission: $2 adults. Open Mon., Wed., Fri. 10–noon, 2–4.*

The **Bush–Holley House,** built in 1685, is now the headquarters of the Greenwich Historical Society. In the late 1800s the Holley family turned the two-story white-clapboard structure into an inn, where Childe Hassam, John Twachtman, Willa Cather, and Lincoln Steffens later congregated. Currently on display are paintings by Hassam, Twachtman, and Elmer Liv-

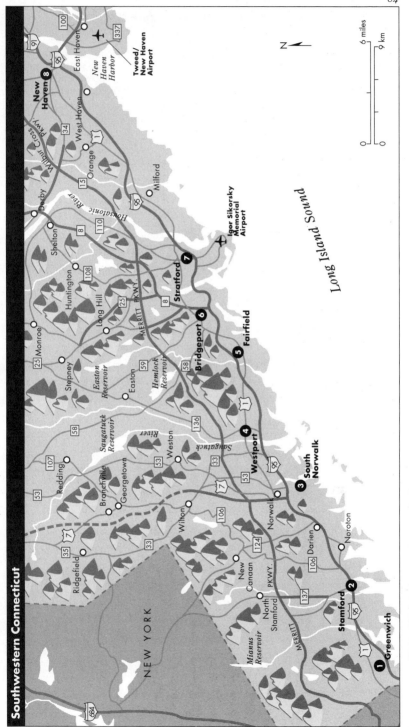

Southwestern Connecticut

Long Island Sound

NEW YORK

Tweed/
New Haven
Airport

New Haven Harbor

East Haven

New Haven 8

West Haven

Orange

Milford

Derby

Shelton

Huntington

Long Hill

Monroe

Stepney

Easton

Houstatonic River

Stratford 7

Bridgeport 6

Fairfield 5

Igor Sikorsky
Memorial Airport

Hemlock Reservoir

Easton Reservoir

Saugatuck Reservoir

Redding

Branchville

Georgetown

Weston

Saugatuck River

Westport 4

South Norwalk 3

Ridgefield

Wilton

Norwalk

Darien

Noroton

New Canaan

North Stamford

Mianus Reservoir

Stamford 2

Greenwich 1

MERRITT PKWY.

6 miles

9 km

N

ingston MacRae, sculpture by John Rogers, and pottery by Leon Volkmar. *39 Strickland Rd., Cos Cob (I–95, Exit 4), tel. 203/869–6899. Admission: $2 adults, $1 senior citizens and students, 50¢ children under 12. Open Tues.–Fri. noon–4. Closed major holidays.*

2 **Stamford's** shoreline may be given over primarily to industry and commerce, but to the north is the 118-acre **Stamford Museum and Nature Center,** a 19th-century working farm and country store. It has permanent exhibits of farm tools, local Native American life, and early American artifacts, and an observatory and planetarium with shows on Sunday at 3. *39 Scofieldtown Rd. (Merritt Pkwy., Exit 35), tel. 203/322–1646. Admission: $3 adults, $2 senior citizens and children 5–16. Open Mon.–Sat. 9–5, Sun., holidays 1–5. Closed Thanksgiving, Dec. 25, Jan. 1.*

Return to the Merritt Parkway and travel north to Exit 36. Follow Route 106 south to the first traffic light and turn right onto Camp Avenue. At the next light, take a left onto Hope Street. At the fourth traffic light you'll discover **United House Wrecking,** where acres of architectural artifacts, decorative accessories, antiques, collectibles, nautical items, lawn and garden furnishings, and other less valuable but certainly unusual items await you. *535 Hope St., tel. 203/348–5371. Admission free. Open Mon.–Sat. 9:30–5:30, Thurs. 9:30–8.*

On your way back into town, take a look at the **First Presbyterian Church** of 1958. The fish-shaped structure was designed by Wallace Harrison, and its famous stained-glass windows catch the light from many angles. Inside you may feel as though you're in the belly of a whale. The 56-bell carillon was added a decade later. *1101 Bedford St., tel. 203/324–9522. Open weekdays 9–5, weekends 9–1.*

The Fairfield County branch of New York's venerable **Whitney Museum of American Art** is located on the street level of the Champion International Corporation building, in the heart of downtown. Works range from George Bellows's *Dempsey and Firpo* (1924) to Roy Lichtenstein's *Little Big Painting* (1965), and there are recent acquisitions as well. Sculpture, folk art, and furniture are also displayed here. *Atlantic St. and Tresser Blvd., tel. 203/358–7630. Admission free. Open Tues.–Sat. 11–5.*

3 The new **Maritime Center** is the cornerstone of the **South Norwalk** (SoNo) redevelopment. Built around a restored 19th-century redbrick factory on the west bank of the Norwalk River, the 5-acre waterfront center brings to life the ecology and history of Long Island Sound through state-of-the-art technology. A huge aquarium competes for attention with actual marine vessels such as the 30-foot steam tender *Glory Days* and the 56-foot oyster sloop *Hope*, both of which may be boarded in the comfort of an indoor display hall. A 340-seat Image Maximum (IMAX) theater is exactly that—an immense curving screen rising six stories and extending 80 feet, beyond the edges of peripheral vision. Special activities include scuba diving and the tracking and tagging of lobsters. *10 N. Water St. (I–95, Exit 14N or 15S), tel. 203/852–0700 or 800/243–2280. Admission: $5.50, aquarium and marine hall or IMAX theater; $9.50 adults combined; $7.50 combined, senior citizens* *and children 4–12. Open Sun.–Wed. 11–6, Thurs.–Sat. 11–10. Closed Dec. 25.*

Steps away from the Maritime Center, the thriving **SoNo commercial district** teems with art galleries, restaurants, and trendy boutiques.

A monument to a different time is found in the **Lockwood–Matthews Mansion Museum,** to the north on West Avenue. The vast display of Victorian decorative art is almost overwhelming to the 20th-century eye—it's hard not to be impressed by the octagonal rotunda and 50 rooms of gilt, fresco, marble, ornate woodwork, and etched glass. *295 West Ave. (I–95, Exit 14S or 15N), tel. 203/838–1434. Admission: $3 adults, $2 senior citizens. Open Tues.–Fri. 11–3, Sun. 1–4. Closed mid-Dec.–Feb.*

At the intersection of Smith and East Wall streets you'll find a cluster of reconstructed 18th- and 19th-century buildings that comprise **Mill Hill Historic Park** (tel. 203/846–0525). A one-room schoolhouse, jail, and the Fitch House law office are among them.

4 In the northern section of **Westport** you'll find the **Nature Center for Environmental Activities,** a 62-acre wildlife sanctuary containing several carefully designed trails through woods, fields, and streams. A Sensitivity Trail for the visually handicapped gets you as close as possible to flora and fauna in their natural habitat. *10 Woodside Ave. (Merritt Pkwy., Exit 41), tel. 203/227–7253. Admission: $1 adults, 50¢ children. Open Mon.–Sat. 9–5, Sun. 1–4.*

During the summer months, visitors to Westport congregate at **Sherwood Island State Park.** In addition to its long sweep of sandy beach, it boasts two picnic groves on the water and several food concessions. Sunbathing, swimming, and fishing are the chief attractions at the only truly public beach between Greenwich and New Haven. *I–95, Exit 18, tel. 203/226–6983. Open Memorial Day–Sept.*

The headquarters of the **Connecticut Audubon Society** maintain
5 a 160-acre wildlife sanctuary in **Fairfield** that includes 6 miles of rugged hiking trails and special walks for the visually handicapped, disabled, and elderly. There's also a well-stocked gift shop and reference library. *2325 Burr St. (I–95, Exit 21), tel. 203/259–6305. Admission: building free; sanctuary, $1 adults, 50¢ children. Building open Tues.–Sat. 9–4:30; sanctuary open daily dawn to dusk.*

The society operates a smaller sanctuary and **Birdcraft Museum** that features a children's activity corner, along with 6 acres of trails and a pond that attracts seasonal waterfowl. *314 Unquowa (I–95, Exit 21), tel. 203/259–0416. Admission: $1 adults, 50¢ children. Open weekends noon–5.*

Time Out | **Rawley's,** the ramshackle red-shingle structure at 1886 Post Road in Fairfield, has a few parking slots outside, a small counter inside, and a firm local reputation for serving the best hot dog in the world. Hot dogs, fixins, and cold soft drinks are the entire bill of fare.

6 **Bridgeport** is making strides in urban renewal, drawing on every possible resource. One of its chief assets is the **Barnum Museum,** associated with a past resident and mayor, the entrepreneur Phineas T. Barnum, who was one of the great show-men of his day. Barnum's will provided for the establishment of an Institute of Science and Industry in the city he loved, and the early original building has been incorporated into the present museum, which was renovated and reopened in 1989. The fun here is in the permanent exhibits associated with Barnum's show-business career, which feature such characters as General Tom Thumb and Jenny Lind, the Swedish Nightingale. You can tour a scaled-down model of Barnum's famous creation, the three-ring circus. The great canvas tent may be gone now, but the spirit of the Big Top lives on at the Barnum Museum. *820 Main St. (I–95, Exit 27), tel. 203/331–1104. Admission: $4 adults, $3 senior citizens, $2 children 4–18. Open Tues.–Sat. 10–4:30, Sun. noon–4:30. Closed major holidays.*

The city's **Museum of Art, Science and Industry** tries to cover all bases with an eclectic collection of art from Renaissance to contemporary, a planetarium, several hands-on science exhibits, and a children's museum. It also offers demonstrations, lectures, and workshops. *4450 Park Ave. (Merritt Pkwy., Exit 47), tel. 203/372–3521. Admission: $4 adults, $2 senior citizens and children 4–18. Open Tues.–Fri. 11–5, Sun. noon–5.*

Beardsley Zoological Gardens is Connecticut's largest zoo. The 30-acre site houses more than 200 animals, ranging from North American mammals such as the mountain lion, elk, and bison to the exotic Siberian tiger. A smaller children's zoo (in a farmlike setting) offers pony rides. *Noble Ave., Beardsley Park (I–95, Exit 27A), tel. 203/576–8082. Admission: $1 adults, 50¢ children 5–12, senior citizens free. Open daily 9–4. Closed Thanksgiving, Dec. 25, Jan. 1.*

At the foot of Bostwick Avenue, at **Captain's Cove Seaport,** a replica of the British warship HMS *Rose* is berthed. Before boarding the Revolutionary War ship, check out the craft shops and restaurants in the area. *1 Bostwick Ave. (I–95, Exit 26), tel. 203/335–1433. Admission: $3 adults, $2 children. Open May–Oct.*

7 In northern **Stratford, Boothe Memorial Park** contains a number of unusual buildings, including a blacksmith shop, carriage and tool barns, and a museum that includes a history of the trolley among its displays. There's also a children's playground. *Main St. (Merrit Pkwy., Exit 53), tel. 203/378–9895. Admission free. Park open 9–5; museum open Tues.–Fri. 11–1, weekends 1–4. Closed Nov.–May.*

8 While **New Haven** enjoys a reputation as a manufacturing center dating back to Eli Whitney's 19th-century development of the principle of interchangeable parts, its greater fame rests on an earlier "Eli." In 1718, a donation by wealthy resident Elihu Yale enabled the Collegiate School, founded in 1701, to settle in New Haven, where it changed its name to **Yale University** to honor its benefactor. The university provides knowledgeable guides for one-hour walking tours that include Connecticut Hall in the Old Campus, which housed the young Nathan Hale, William Howard Taft, and Noah Webster during their student days. *344 College St., Phelps Gateway (I–95, Exit 47), tel. 203/432–2300. Tours free. Tours leave weekdays at 10:30 and 2, weekends at 1:30.*

Sterling Memorial Library and the **Beinecke Rare Book Library** house major collections, a Gutenberg Bible, illuminated manuscripts, and original Audubon bird prints. *121 Wall St., tel. 203/432-2977.. Beinecke open weekdays 8:30-5, Sat. 10-5. Closed Sat. June-Aug., major holidays. Sterling open Mon.-Sat. 8:30-5. Closed Sat. in Aug., major holidays.*

The **Yale Art Gallery,** the country's oldest college art museum, contains Renaissance paintings, American, African, Near and Far Eastern Art, and European art of the 20th century. Don't miss the remarkable reconstruction of a Mithraic shrine. *1111 Chapel St., tel. 203/432-0600. Admission free. Open Tues.-Sat. 10-5, Sun. 2-5. Closed major holidays.*

The **Peabody Museum of Natural History** is the largest of its kind in New England. Along with exhibits of dinosaur fossils and meteorites, emphasis is placed on Connecticut's environment, including early Indian life and birds. *170 Whitney Ave., tel. 203/432-5050 or 203/432-5799 (recorded announcement). Admission: $2 adults, $1.50 senior citizens, $1 children 5-15; Tues. free. Open Mon.-Sat. 9-4:45, Sun. 1-4:45.*

More than 850 instruments, some dating to the 16th century, make up the university's **Collection of Musical Instruments.** An annual concert series is given using some of these instruments. *15 Hillhouse Ave., tel. 203/432-0822. Admission free. Open Tues.-Thurs. 1-4. Closed Aug., university recesses.*

The **Yale Center for British Art** has a sizeable collection of British paintings, drawings, prints, sculpture, and rare books from the Elizabethan period to the present. Anglophiles will enjoy the well-stocked gift shop. *1080 Chapel St., tel. 203/432-2800. Admission free. Open Tues.-Sat. 10-5, Sun. 2-5. Closed major holidays.*

Time Out At the bright, contemporary **Atticus Bookstore-Cafe** (1082 Chapel St.), next to the Yale Center for British Art, one can sit at the counter or at a tiny table, sip tea or freshly brewed coffee, munch on a croissant or muffin, and read. It's the kind of place where spontaneous conversations become prolonged discussions.

The most notable example of the campus's collegiate-Gothic architecture is the **Harkness Tower,** with its famous motto, sometimes described as the world's greatest anticlimax: "For God, for country, and for Yale."

Across from the old campus, the **New Haven Green** offers impressive architecture as well as a superb example of urban planning. As early as 1638, village elders set aside the 16-acre plot as a town common. Three churches, added from 1812 to 1814—the Gothic-style Trinity Episcopal Church, the Georgian-style Center Congregational Church, and the predominantly Federalist United Church—contribute to its present appeal.

At opposite ends of New Haven, two popular outdoor attractions are **East Rock Park** (East Rock Rd., tel. 203/787-8021) and **West Rock Nature Center** (Wintergreen Ave., tel. 203/787-8016). East Rock is a large municipal park, complete with picnic and recreation facilities, playgrounds, a bird sanctuary, and nature trails. West Rock is more a zoo with live animals in outdoor settings and reptiles and smaller creatures indoors. There are also picnic and hiking facilities. Follow the Regicides Trail to the infamous Judges' Cave—two of the men who signed the warrant for the execution of England's Charles I fled to the cave after the Restoration.

Black Rock Fort and **Ft. Nathan Hale** are reconstructions of forts from the Revolutionary and Civil wars, and they present a spectacular view of New Haven Harbor. *Woodward Ave., tel. 203/787–8790. Open Memorial Day–Labor Day, daily; weekends in the fall.*

To get to the city's southeastern tip, take Exit 50 off I–95 and follow Lighthouse Road. The **Pardee–Morris House,** built in 1750, was burned by the Redcoats in 1779, then rebuilt in 1780 on the original foundation. Furnishings from its earliest days to those used during the early part of the 19th century give a picture of life in those times. *325 Lighthouse Rd., tel. 203/562–4183. Admission: $2 adults, $1 senior citizens and children 6–18. Open June–Aug. 11:30–4. Closed Mon., holidays.*

Lighthouse Point (tel. 203/787–8005), at the end of the road, is an 82-acre park with a public beach, nature trails, a picnic grove, and an antique carousel set in a turn-of-the-century beach pavilion. *Open Memorial Day–Labor Day.*

Southwestern Connecticut for Free

United House Wrecking, Stamford

Whitney Museum of American Art, Stamford

Boothe Memorial Park and Museum, Stratford

Yale University, New Haven

What to See and Do with Children

Virtually all the nature centers feature special attractions for children, including hands-on exhibits.

Maritime Center, South Norwalk

Barnum Museum, Bridgeport

Peabody Museum of Natural History, New Haven

Shopping

Bridgeport "Off-price shopping" is the local term for the bargains available at a number of mostly clothing discount stores. The **Hi–Ho Center** (303 State St., tel. 203/366–3271) is the city's largest shopping mall.

New Haven Opposite the green, the **Chapel Square Mall** (900 Chapel St., tel. 203/777–6661) has 63 shops and a parking garage.

The **Yale Co-op** (77 Broadway, tel. 203/772–2200), larger than many campus bookstores, carries Yale-emblem goods from T-shirts to tennis togs, bar glasses to wall pennants, and a vast stock of books and records.

Norwalk **Antique Trail** (brochures and map at 140 Main St., tel. 203/846–1242) organizes the city's antiques shops. Discount outlets range from **Decker's** (666 West Ave., tel. 203/866–5593), with clothing for the family, to **Villeroy & Boch** (75 Main St., tel. 203/847–8540), which has china, crystal, porcelain, and gifts at reduced prices.

Stew Leonard's Dairy (100 Westport Ave., Rte. 1, tel. 203/847–7213) boldly proclaims itself "The Disneyland of Supermarkets." You never know what's going to be on sale in the main store, but just as much fun is the children's animal farm where the kids get to touch the sources of some of the amazing bargains.

Stamford The **Stamford Town Center** (100 Greyrock Pl., tel. 203/356–9700), a multistory mall, is the hub of retail activity, with 130 shops and a parking garage.

Westport Shops on Main Street lean toward the cute and the expensive. Antiques seekers will discover "finds" rather than genuine bargains in the shops near the meeting of Riverside Avenue and Post Road West.

Sports and Outdoor Activities

Fishing **Open boats** are provided by **Yacht Haven** (Washington Blvd., Stamford, tel. 203/359–4500), **Stratford Marina** (Broad St., Stratford, tel. 203/377–4477), and **Caswell Cove Marina** (231 Pope Island Rd., Milford, tel. 203/878–1780).

Fishing boats can be chartered from **Yacht Haven East** (Stamford, tel. 203/348–3386), **Norwalk Cove Marina** (Norwalk, tel. 203/853–2522 or 203/259–7719), and **Bridge Square** (Westport, tel. 203/255–5653).

Water Sports **Longshore Sailing School** (Cove Island Park, Stamford, tel. 203/348–6100) rents small boats; **Rick's Surf City** (570 Boston Post Rd., Milford, tel. 203/877–4257), rents sailboards and surfboards; and **Sail New Haven** (2 Lighthouse Rd., New Haven, tel. 203/469–6754) rents sailboards and sailboats, and offers lessons.

Spectator Sports

Hockey The **New Haven Night Hawks** of the American Hockey League skate at the New Haven Coliseum (tel. 203/787–0101).

Jai-Alai **Bridgeport Jai-Alai** (255 Kossuth St., tel. 203/576–1976 or 800/243–9490) and **Milford Jai-Alai** (311 Old Gate La., tel. 203/877–4242) host the fast-moving sport.

Dining and Lodging

Bridgeport Dining **Ocean Sea Grill.** You'll have to make your way through derelict surroundings to reach this Art Deco fortress, a survivor of urban blight. Inside all is pleasant, uncluttered, and reassuringly contemporary-cum-deco. For more than 50 years the restaurant has served fresh seafood with an Italian influence—and chocolate mousse cake to follow. *1328 Main St., tel. 203/336–2132. Reservations advised. Dress: casual. AE, CB, DC, MC, V. Closed Sun., Thanksgiving, Dec. 25. Moderate–Expensive.*
Tumbleweed's. Tex-Mex has come to Bridgeport's north end, at the Brookside Center shopping mall. Beneath a sign proclaiming "Home Sweet Home" and amid a clutter of cactus, Southwestern and international concoctions are served, among them sirloin teriyaki and Mississippi mud pie. *4485 Main St., tel. 203/374–0234. Reservations advised. Dress: casual. AE, CB, DC, MC, V. Closed major holidays. Inexpensive.*

Bridgeport Lodging

Bridgeport Hilton. Smack in the middle of downtown, this member of the Hilton chain offers comfortable lodging with particular appeal to the business trade. Rooms have modern furniture in soft color combinations of rose and off-white. The best accommodations are the named suites on the top floor; the lower floors, although well-insulated from noise, may be penetrated by city sounds from below. The bar and lounge off the lobby draw a convivial crowd. *1070 Main St., 06604, tel. 203/334–1234 or 800/445–8667. 224 rooms with bath, 10 suites. Facilities: restaurant, lounge, health club, indoor pool, sauna. AE, CB, DC, MC, V. Expensive.*

Fairfield Lodging

Fairfield Motor Inn. The light-brick hotel with the white pillars offers attractively furnished modern bedrooms and large, full baths. The lobby, the small breakfast room, and the lounge (with a working fireplace) all have a light decor that suggests a Scandinavian influence. *417 Post Rd., 06430, tel. 203/255–0491. 80 rooms with bath. Facilities: restaurant, outdoor pool, airport limo service. AE, CB, DC, MC, V. Rates include breakfast. Moderate–Expensive.*

Greenwich Dining

★ **Bertrand.** The spectacular brick-vault interior of this main-street restaurant provides a classic setting of small, candlelit tables for a menu of classic and nouvelle French cuisine. The confit of duck with sorrel sauce, and salmon in a pastry crust, seem more at home in this onetime bank than stacks of money bags. Financial matters pale beside the nougat ice cream—until the check comes. *253 Greenwich Ave., tel. 203/869–4459 or 203/869–4618. Reservations advised. Jacket and tie required. AE, CB, DC, MC, V. No lunch Sat., Sun. Closed Jan. 1, Dec. 25. Very Expensive.*

★ **Homestead Inn.** This restaurant provides the perfect setting for Jacques Thiebeult's imaginative variations on classic French cuisine. In any of the cozy nooks that comprise the dining area, all-agleam with sparkling silver and crystal, you might opt for the perennial favorite Billi Bi, mussel soup, or the veal sweetbreads with chanterelles. For dessert, try the triple chocolate cake. *420 Field Point Rd., tel. 203/869–7500. Reservations advised. Jacket required. AE, MC, V. Very Expensive.*

★ **Restaurant Jean Louis.** The roses in silver bud-vases, the Villeroy & Boch china, and the crisp, white cloths with lace underskirts are complemented by careful service of extraordinary food. A few of Jean Louis's specialties are the quail-and-vegetable ragout with foie gras sauce; scallopine of salmon on a bed of leeks with fresh herb sauce; and for dessert lemon-and-pear gratin. *61 Lewis St., tel. 203/622–8450. Reservations advised. Jacket and tie required. AE, CB, DC, MC, V. No lunch Sat. Closed Sun., Thanksgiving, Dec. 25. Very Expensive.*

Manero's. The sign outside exhorts you to "bring the kids," and most patrons do: The place echoes with renditions of "Happy Birthday" at every meal. However, the beef aged on the premises is deservedly famous, so ignore the hokey surroundings and treat yourself to chateaubriand. An adjacent retail meat-market offers the same beef for domestic consumption. *559 Steamboat Rd. (I–95, Exit 3), tel. 230/869–0049. No reservations. Dress: casual. AE, CB, DC, MC, V. Moderate.*

Greenwich Lodging

★ **Homestead Inn.** Those interested in the art of hospitality should visit this inn for a graduate course. In the last decade, since its total renovation, the Homestead has achieved well-deserved renown for the superiority of its restaurant and accommodations. Each individually designed bedroom is decorated with attractive period furniture and reproductions arranged to provide respite for the weary and allure for the romantic. Clock radios and electric blankets, one firm pillow and one soft for each guest, and good reading lights are standard equipment, along with plush robes and a bouquet of bathroom goodies. *420 Field Point Rd., 06830, tel. 203/869–7500. 23 rooms with bath. Facilities: dining room. AE, DC, MC, V. Rates include Continental breakfast. Expensive.*

★ **Hyatt Regency Greenwich.** Once upon a time the Condé Nast publishing empire was ruled from the four-story turreted tower and spire of this modern edifice. Inside, a vast but comfortable atrium boasts its own flourishing lawn and abundant flora. Spacious rooms offer all the amenities, including telephones that are modem-compatible for laptop-computer users. *1800 E. Putnam (I–95, Exit 5), 06870, tel. 203/737–1234 or 800/233–1234. 353 rooms with bath. Facilities: 2 restaurants, jazz bar, atrium lounge, valet parking, indoor pool, health club, sauna, steam room, open-air sun court. AE, CB, D, DC, MC, V. Expensive.*

Stanton House Inn. This large, Federal-period mansion within walking distance of downtown underwent considerable redesign by the noted architect Stanford White in 1900. It has been carefully refurbished and redecorated in traditional style, with a mixture of antiques and tasteful reproductions. *76 Maple Ave., 06830, tel. 203/869–2110. 27 rooms with bath. AE, MC, V. Rates include Continental breakfast. Moderate–Expensive.*

New Haven Dining
★ **Robert Henry's.** From the quiet comfort of the main dining room, with its huge stone fireplace, you can gaze out the windows at the bustle of Chapel Street. The slightly smaller but equally embracing Club Room features fine china and crystal on crisp tablecloths. Traditional and contemporary French cuisine and seasonal treats make up the menu, which includes medallions of venison, warm truffled pheasant sausage, and the restaurant's signature duck-leg confit. You may have trouble resisting the *chocolate plaisir*, a cake with bittersweet chocolate and vanilla mousse served with a chocolate sauce. *1032 Chapel St., tel. 203/789–1010. Reservations required. Jacket required. AE, CB, DC, MC, V. No lunch. Closed Sun., July 4, Labor Day, Dec. 25. Expensive.*

★ **Azteca's.** This restaurant draws a crowd of aficionados who appreciate its elegant presentation of Mexican and Southwestern dishes in a modern, appropriately subdued setting. The artwork on the walls changes monthly; the innovative menu changes somewhat less frequently. Among the favorites are black buck-antelope tenderloin; broiled Norwegian salmon with Texas ruby-red grapefruit sauce; and chicken mole with a rich and spicy sauce. *14 Mechanic St., tel. 203/624–2454. Reservations advised. Dress: casual but neat. MC, V. No lunch. Closed Sun., major holidays. Moderate–Expensive.*

Bruxelles. In the heart of New Haven's theater district, this elegant, modern brasserie has a cosmopolitan menu that ranges from selections prepared on an open rotisserie to *pasta raccio* —tricolor tortellini with slivers of duck, fresh tomatoes, watercress, mushrooms, and a light Parmesan cream. The second-floor dining room is at once formal and madcap, with starched cloth napkins standing at attention in stemmed glasses on top of tablecloths covered with butcher's paper for doodling with the crayons provided. *220 College St., tel. 203/777–7752. No* *reservations. Dress: casual but neat. AE, MC, V. Closed Dec. 25. Moderate–Expensive.*

Carbone's. Under the pressed-tin ceiling of this restaurant, diners at green-cloth-covered tables dig into traditional Italian favorites such as the *zuppa di pesce* (shellfish and saltwater fish in tomato or cream sauce, served over linguine) and veal *paggliacei* (veal parmigiana with escarole and eggplant). Somewhat incongruous but luxurious is the California mud pie, a chocolate mousse pie with Oreo cookies and fudge topping. *100 Wooster St., tel. 203/773–1866. Reservations advised. Dress: casual. AE, MC, V. No lunch on weekends. Closed Mon., Thanksgiving, Dec. 25. Moderate–Expensive.*

Christopher Martins. This neighborhood bistro offers a long, informal bar with a few tables and a more formal dining room with cloth-covered tables and soft, indirect lighting. The Continental menu changes often, but there's sure to be a featured veal dish such as the veal Christopher, with port wine, pignoli nuts, and mushrooms. Chances are there will also be a devastating white-chocolate mousse. *860 State St., tel. 203/772–3613. Reservations advised. Dress: casual. AE, CB, DC, MC, V. No lunch weekends. Closed Thanksgiving, Dec. 25. Moderate–Expensive.*

★ **Elm City Diner.** High on the lists of those who revere the brushed-chrome-and-neon, art-deco look of a bygone era, this place is still a diner when it comes to food. It pays its dues to the trendy with a blue-plate-special selection that ranges from Cajun fish-and-chips, to pizza with broccoli, but you're sure to find the basics, too. A grand piano in the center of it all comes into play on weekend nights. *1228 Chapel St., tel. 203/776–5050. Reservations advised. Dress: casual. AE, CB, DC, MC, V. Closed Thanksgiving, Dec. 25. Inexpensive.*

Frank Pepe's. One of the major combatants in the pizza wars of Wooster Street, this contender has served pies since 1925. The big ovens on the back wall bake pizzas that are served by smart-mouthed waitresses who could teach bad manners to the legendary waiters at Lindy's in New York. On weekend evenings the wait for a table can be more than an hour, but the pizza, the sole item on the menu, is worth it. *157 Wooster St., tel. 203/865–5762. No reservations. Dress: casual. No credit cards. No lunch Mon., Wed., Thurs. Closed Tues. Inexpensive.*

Sally's. The loyal clientele of this small pizza restaurant continues to line up outdoors in all weather, having seen no change in quality since the owner and founder of the family-operated eatery died a few years ago. *237 Wooster St., tel. 203/624–5271. No reservations. Dress: casual. No credit cards. Closed Thanksgiving, Dec. 25. Inexpensive.*

New Haven Lodging

The Inn at Chapel West. Technically a bed-and-breakfast, this inn in a restored Victorian mansion provides comfortable lodging in a big-city environment. Ten guest rooms, some with fireplaces, are furnished with a mix of antiques and modern conveniences, and breakfast is served in the dining room downstairs. *1201 Chapel St., 06511, tel. 203/777–1201. 10 rooms with bath. Facilities: concierge services, conference facilities, afternoon refreshments. AE, CB, DC, MC, V. Rates include Continental breakfast. Very Expensive.*

Colony Inn. Set in the center of the Chapel Street hotel district, the inn offers sidewalk dining in its glass-enclosed Greenhouse Restaurant. The eclectic lobby, with an ornate chandelier, appears to be a mix of grand Baroque and Victorian. Guest rooms were refurbished in 1987, and the Colonial-reproduction furnishings and modern baths are still attractive. Some rooms on the higher floors have excellent views of the Yale campus. *1157 Chapel St., 06511, tel. 203/776–1234 or 800/458–8810, fax 203/772–3929. 80 rooms with bath, 6 suites. Facilities: restaurant, lounge, airport limo. AE, DC, MC, V. Expensive.*

Holiday Inn Downtown. A renovation completed in 1988 left a comfortable modern decor with soft, restful colors. The best rooms in this hotel on the edge of the Yale campus are on the eighth floor, high above the traffic outside. *31 Whalley Ave., 06511, tel. 203/777–6221 or 800/465–4329, fax 203/772–1089. 154 rooms with bath, 6 suites. Facilities: restaurant, lounge, health club, outdoor pool, free parking. AE, CB, DC, MC, V. Moderate–Expensive.*

Park Plaza Hotel. This contemporary downtown hotel, slightly overlit, is a hub of activity near the theater district, with access to an adjacent shopping mall and parking garage. But the graffiti-scarred elevator doors suggest that the hotel, built in 1966 and since refurbished, has seen better days. Rooms are attractively furnished and modern-looking. *155 Temple St., 06510, tel. 203/772–1700 or 800/243–4221, fax 203/624–2683. 295 rooms with bath, 5 suites. Facilities: outdoor pool. AE, DC, MC, V. Moderate–Expensive.*

Norwalk Dining
★

Silvermine Tavern. The dining area is enormous, but a low ceiling, Colonial decor, and many windows make this landmark restaurant an intimate setting for hearty meals. Glowing candles and gleaming silver add to the romantic atmosphere. Traditional New England favorites, such as crisp roast duckling with apple-cider sauce, are the order of the day. Chocolate silk pie is the outstanding dessert. *194 Perry Ave. (Merritt Pkwy., Exit 39), tel. 203/847–4558. Reservations advised. Dress: casual. Closed Tues. (Sept.–May). Moderate–Expensive.*

Norwalk Lodging
★

Silvermine Tavern. Best known for its extraordinary restaurant, the lodgings, parts of which date back to 1642, are equally attractive. Each room has a different configuration and is furnished with a variety of antiques and period pieces, as well as some modern touches. Idiosyncracies abound: Room T–8 is entered through its bathroom but is particularly cozy. Some rooms have tubs but no showers because of the slanted ceilings. All of the accommodations share the ambience of the remarkable main-floor lobby and lounges. *194 Perry Ave. (Merritt Pkwy., Exit 39), 06850, tel. 203/847–4558. 10 rooms with bath. Facilities: restaurant. AE, DC, MC, V. Rates include Continental breakfast. Expensive.*

Courtyard by Marriott. A new addition to the fast-growing corporate strip north of the Merritt Parkway, this Marriott features all the state-of-the art comforts of a modern hotel—from security cards instead of room keys, to coffeemakers in each room, and comfortable, modern furniture. Within the courtyard, a gazebo is surrounded by a perfectly groomed lawn, and a pool so serene it almost defies trespass. *474 Main Ave. (Rte. 7N), 06851, tel. 203/849–9111 or 800/321–2211, fax 203/849–8144. 133 rooms with bath, 12 suites. Facilities: restaurant, lounge, health club, whirlpool, indoor pool. AE, CB, DC, MC, V. Moderate–Expensive.*

Day's Inn. Built in 1988, this hotel retains its freshly minted atmosphere by attention to maintenance. The small lobby is efficient, if not cheery, and rooms contain modern furnishings in soft colors. A top-floor room will protect you from traffic noise, but none of the views is particularly interesting. *426 Main Ave. (Rte. 7N). tel. 203/849–9828 or 800/325–2525. 119 rooms with bath. Facilities: restaurant, lounge, health club. AE, CB, DC, MC, V. Moderate–Expensive.*

South Norwalk Dining

Coyote Cafe & Saloon. Tex-Mex favorites are served here, in a setting of bare floors, exposed brick, and bright oilcloth-covered tables. In addition to taquitos, burritos, and fajitas there are specialties such as chicken and shrimp *Tchopatoulis* (sautéed with pimentos, mild green chilies, artichoke hearts, mushrooms), and andouille sausage with linguine. If these dishes don't raise your temperature, a display of more than 100 bottled hot-sauces that lines the walls might do the trick. *50 Water St., tel. 203/854–9630. Reservations advised. Dress: casual. AE, DC, MC, V. No lunch Sat. No dinner Mon. Closed major holidays. Moderate.*

★ **SoNo's Little Kitchen.** A simple storefront turned into kitchen and dining room, this restaurant seduces you with aromas the minute you cross the threshold. You also get to watch the owner and chef Jeanette Hart prepare her specialty: Jamaican cuisine at its finest. Nibble on some Jamaican CoCo bread while you contemplate the curried goat or the jerk chicken or pork—meat that's been marinated with pimento, cloves, nutmeg, cinnamon, and peppers and is then barbecued. Hart smokes her own bluefish and serves it with sweet pepper or tomato-basil sauce. For dessert, the coconut pastry *gazada* deserves a try. *49 S. Main St., tel. 203/855–8515. Reservations advised. Dress: casual. No credit cards. No dinner Mon.–Wed. Closed Sun., Jan. 1, Thanksgiving, Dec. 25. Inexpensive.*

Stamford Dining

Pellicci's. Fifties glitz, complete with fake stained-glass ceiling, provides the setting for traditional Italian and Continental favorites at this large, longtime favorite in a neighborhood that is undergoing rapid change. Corporate execs mingle with the local folk over specialties such as veal marsala, shrimp marinara, and baked ziti. *96 Stillwater Ave., tel. 203/323–2542. Reservations advised. Dress: casual. AE, CB, DC, MC, V. Closed Mon., Easter, Dec. 25. Moderate.*

Stamford Lodging

Sheraton Stamford Hotel and Towers. The drive leading to the ultramodern entrance of this downtown luxury hotel should prepare you for the dramatic atrium lobby inside, with its brass-and-glass-enclosed gazebo. High-tech haywire to some, the lobby is actually the well-organized axis from which the hotel's services flow. Attractive, contemporary furnishings in the rooms are complemented by amenities such as massaging showerheads in the spacious bathrooms. The Towers section contains accommodations for the carriage trade and has its own lounge and concierge service. Topping everything off is an awe-inspiring skylit swimming pool. *1 First Stamford Pl. (I–95, Exit 7N or 6S), tel. 203/967–2222 or 800/325–3535. 471 rooms with bath, 34 suites. Facilities: 2 restaurants, lounge, health club, sauna, indoor pool. AE, CB, DC, MC, V. Expensive.*

Stamford Marriott. One of the first of the downtown hotels built to accommodate Stamford's growth as a corporate hub, the Marriott stands out for its convenience to transportation and its up-to-date facilities. Modern and comfortable, if unmemorable, furnishings are found throughout. The large, busy lobby is a favorite meeting place for the city's movers and shakers, who frequently head for one of several meeting rooms or to Le Carrousel, which is at press time the only revolving rooftop restaurant in the state. *2 Stamford Forum (I–95, Exit 8), 06901, tel. 203/357–9555 or 800/228–9290. 500 rooms with bath, 7 suites. Facilities: 2 restaurants, 2 lounges, health club, sauna, rooftop jogging track, indoor and outdoor pools, 2 racquetball courts, game room, valet, laundry service, free parking, airport limousine. AE, CB, DC, MC, V. Expensive.*

Tara Stamford. Formerly the Westin, this cavernous, modern, five-story hotel reopened as the Tara in January 1989. Geared to serve the corporate community, the dark-brick, glass-covered atrium, with its lack of floral relief, sacrifices intimacy to high-tech efficiency. Rooms, however, are spacious and tastefully decorated. *2701 Summer St., 06905, tel. 203/359–1300 or 800/321–2042. 457 rooms with bath, 35 suites. Facilities: restaurant, lounge, 2 lighted tennis courts, health club, saunas, indoor pool, 23,000-square-foot meeting space, complimentary ballroom parking. AE, CB, D, DC, MC, V. Expensive.*

Westport Dining **Le Chambord.** Tiny oil lamps set on each pale-almond-colored tablecloth cast a romantic glow on gleaming silver and crystal, and quiet, attentive service accompanies trusted classic French favorites such as *canard à l'orange* (duckling with orange sauce), and baby rack of lamb with tiny vegetables. The arrival of the Grand Marnier soufflé inevitably draws sighs of pleasure. *1572 Post Rd. E, tel. 203/255–2654. Reservations advised. Dress: casual. AE, CB, DC, MC, V. No lunch Sat. Closed Sun., all major holidays. Very Expensive.*

Nistico's Red Barn. Under the aged beams and wagon-wheel chandeliers, tables here are decorated with crisp white cloths, pink napkins, and candle lamps. An enormous stone fireplace divides the main dining areas and provides warmth in blustery weather. Particularly cozy is the "Louis Room," to the right of the entrance, with its low ceiling and fireplace. Specialties include enormous Maine lobsters and a 32-ounce porterhouse steak. For the less ambitious, there's the 24-ounce New York strip sirloin or the 12-ounce filet mignon. *292 Wilton Rd. (Merritt Pkwy., Exit 41), tel. 203/222–9549. Reservations advised. Dress: casual. AE, DC, MC, V. Closed Thanksgiving, Dec. 25. Expensive.*

Tanglewoods. The country-modern decor in this restaurant includes ceiling fans, Tiffany-style lamps, and bentwood and rattan chairs placed around tile-topped tables. An international menu ranges from *poisson à la champagne* (fresh cod fillet baked in a champagne white sauce), to Black Angus T-bone steak. There's also a bread pudding in bourbon sauce, made on the premises. *833 Post Rd. E, tel. 203/226–2880. Reservations advised. Dress: casual. AE, CB, DC, MC, V. Sun. brunch. Closed Thanksgiving, Dec. 25. Inexpensive–Moderate.*

★ **International Deli & Restaurant.** Despite the modern, Scandinavian-influenced decor, the zesty scent of corned beef and kosher pickles tells you you're in a bona fide deli. Whether you stop at the voluminous counter to buy some takeout, or settle down at a table, you'll find all the traditional deli favorites—potato pancakes, cheese blintzes, borscht, and brisket, to mention a few. The creamy New York–style cheesecake is irresistible. *1385 Post Rd. E, tel. 203/255–7900. Reservations advised for 4 or more. Dress: casual. AE, MC, V. Closed Jan. 1, Dec. 25. Inexpensive.*

Mario's. Directly opposite the southbound side of the Westport train station, this restaurant serves Italian-American food to devotees who have come here for nearly a quarter of a century. Stop off for a drink at the long bar, swap a few stories, then stick around for the seafood platter served with linguine or the veal parmigiana with spaghetti. *36 Station Pl., tel. 203/227–9217. Reservations advised. Dress: casual. AE, CB, DC, MC, V. Closed Easter, Thanksgiving, Dec. 25. Inexpensive.*

Westport Lodging
★

The Inn at Longshore. There are very few grand hotels in the Nutmeg State, but Longshore makes a strong claim for that distinction. Although small, this late-19th-century mansion is located on one of the most beautiful sites on the Connecticut shore. As you drive up the entranceway's long alley of stately oaks, you know you're in for a treat. And the inn itself, after being taken over by private management five years ago, has been renovated and refurbished with tasteful, traditional reproductions. All rooms have a view of the water or the park. Even Room 217, rented only when there isn't a bit of space left, looks beyond an exhaust vent to the water. *260 South Compo Rd., 06880, tel. 203/226–3316. 14 rooms with bath, 3 suites. Facilities: restaurant, guest privileges at tennis courts, handball courts, 18-hole golf course, Olympic-size adult and children's outdoor pools, sailing, windsurfing. AE, DC, MC, V. Very Expensive.*

The Westport Inn. Vigorous new management has taken this veteran inn of two decades in hand and shaken it up, all to the good. Bedrooms have been refurbished with attractive contemporary furniture; a new restaurant is scheduled to open in 1990; and even the apples on the front counter are polished. Rooms surrounding the large indoor pool are set back nicely and are slightly larger than those in the nonpoolside section. *1595 Post Rd. (Rte. 1), 06880, tel. 203/259–5236 or 800/223–0888. 112 rooms with bath, 2 suites. Facilities: restaurant, poolside cafe and bar, health club, sauna, indoor pool, airport-limo stop, room service. AE, DC, MC, V. Expensive.*

Connecticut River Valley

The Connecticut River rises in the hills of northern New England, winds its way across western Massachusetts and south through the center of Connecticut, and flows into Long Island Sound between Old Saybrook and Old Lyme. The river valley, an extent of less than 100 miles in Connecticut, offers wilderness and primitive campground experiences as well as Colonial history and sophisticated nightlife. Less well-visited than the coastal areas, the valley escapes the fierce crowds that the Long Island shore may experience in summer.

Important Addresses and Numbers

Visitor Information

Connecticut Valley Tourism Commission (393 Main St., Middletown 06457, tel. 203/347–6924).

Greater Hartford Convention and Visitors Bureau (1 Civic Center Plaza, Hartford 06103, tel. 203/728–6789).

Olde Towne Tourism District (800 Main St., Rocky Hill 06067, tel. 203/257–9299).

Emergencies Hartford Hospital (80 Seymour St., tel. 203/524–2525).

Late-night **Community Pharmacy** (197 Main St., Deep River, tel. 203/525–
Pharmacies 5379 or 203/526–9100).

CVS (1099 New Britain Ave., West Hartford, tel. 203/236–6181).

Arriving and Departing

By Plane Airport Taxi (tel. 203/627–3210) has scheduled limousine service between Bradley International Airport and downtown Hartford (and points farther south).

By Train and Bus Hartford's **Union Station** (1 Union Pl., tel. 203/247–5329), a modern, renovated facility, is the terminal for train service by **Amtrak** (tel. 800/872–7245) and bus service by **Greyhound Lines** (tel. 203/547–1500), **Bonanza Bus Lines** (tel. 800/556–3815), and **Peter Pan Bus Lines** (tel. 203/724–5200).

Getting Around the Connecticut River Valley

By Car The major roads through the valley are Route 9, from I–95 in the south to I–91 mid-state, and I–91 north from that junction.

By Bus **Connecticut Transit** (tel. 203/525–9181) provides local bus service in and around Hartford; the fare is 75¢.

Guided Tours

Chester Airport (Winthrop Rd., Chester, tel. 203/526–4321) hosts 15-minute scenic orientation flights over the lower Connecticut River valley, weather permitting.

Greater Hartford Architecture Conservancy (278 Farmington Ave., tel. 203/525–0279) sponsors *Hartford on Tour*, one-hour and two-hour walking tours of Hartford's historic neighborhoods, Sunday only, June through August.

Exploring the Connecticut River Valley

Numbers in the margin correspond with the numbered points of interest on the Connecticut River Valley map.

❶ Our tour of the valley begins in the south, on the west bank of the Connecticut River, 3 miles north of I–95, at **Essex.** On the way into Essex on Route 9, signs direct you to **Pratt House,** a center-chimney Colonial dwelling of 1732–34 that contains an extensive collection of 17th-, 18th-, and 19th-century furnishings, notably Connecticut redware and Chinese courting mirrors. *19 West Ave., tel. 203/767–2220. Admission: $1.50 adults, $1 senior citizens. Open June–Labor Day, weekends 1–4.*

The **Valley Railroad,** near Exit 3 from Route 9 in Essex, carries passengers on a one-hour rail journey along the Connecticut River and lower valley to Deep River. At Deep River, passengers have the opportunity to return to Essex by riverboat, a trip of about 70 minutes. *Tel. 203/767–0103. Train fare: $7.95 adults, $3.95 children 2–11. Combined train and boat fare: $12.95 adults, $5.95 children 2–11. 10% discount for senior citizens. Operates May–Oct.*

At the end of Main Street you'll find the **Connecticut River Museum.** In addition to artifacts and displays telling the story of

99

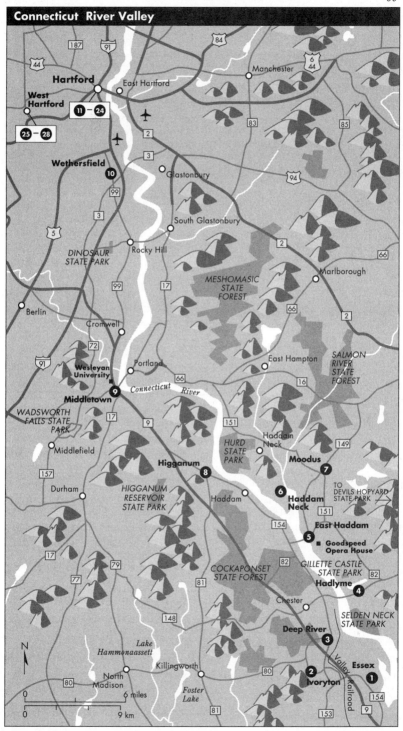

Connecticut River Valley

the area from pre-Colonial days, there's a full-size reproduction of the world's first submarine, the *American Turtle.* The adjacent waterfront park has superb river views. *Box 261, Steamboat Dock, Essex, tel. 203/767–8269. Admission: $2.50 adults. Open Tues.–Sun. 10–5 (reduced hours during winter). Closed major holidays.*

② On the other side of the highway at Exit 3 is **Ivoryton,** best known for its summer theater, the **Ivoryton Playhouse.** The **Museum of Fife and Drum** is here also, with a lively collection of Americana on parade since the Revolutionary War. You'll see martial sheet music, instruments, and uniforms, as well as a special exhibit on the Civil War. Live musical performances are given during the summer. *62 N. Main St., tel. 203/767–2220. Admission: $1 adults, 50¢ senior citizens. Open May, June, Oct., weekends 1–5; July–Sept., Fri.–Sun. 1–5.*

③ Farther north on Route 9 is **Deep River.** The **Stone House,** built in the 19th century, has a Charter Oak piano, Native American artifacts, and locally made cut-glass. *S. Main St. (Rte. 154), tel. 203/526–2609. Admission free (donation requested). Open July–Aug., Sun., Tues., Thurs. 2–4.*

④ At Exit 6 on Route 9, in **Hadlyme,** numerous signs will lead you to the region's leading oddity, **Gillette Castle State Park.** The unusual 24-room, oak-and-granite hilltop castle was built by the actor William Gillette between 1914 and 1919, and you can see the remains of the 3-mile private railroad that toured the property until the owner's death in 1937. Now a state park, the grounds offer excellent hiking, picnicking, and viewing of the river and surrounding foliage. *67 River Rd. (off Rte. 82), Hadlyme, tel. 203/526–2236. Admission: $2 adults, $1 senior citizens and children. Open Memorial Day–Columbus Day, daily 11–5; Columbus Day–last weekend before Christmas, weekends 10–4.*

⑤ Follow the road along the river a few miles north to **East Haddam,** home of the **Goodspeed Opera House.** Built in 1876 for mercantile interests, the upper floors have served as a venue for theatrical performances for more than 100 years. The views of Goodspeed from the bridge over the river are a photographer's delight. *Rte. 82, East Haddam, tel. 203/873–8668. Tour admission: $1 adults, 50¢ children under 12. Tours given July–Oct., Mon. 1–3. Performances Apr.–Dec.*

On East Haddam's Main Street you'll find the **schoolhouse** where Nathan Hale taught from 1773 to 1774. On display are some of his possessions and other items of local history. *Rte. 149 (rear of St. Stephen's Church), East Haddam, tel. 203/873–9547. Admission: 25¢. Open Memorial Day–Labor Day, weekends and holidays 2–4.*

⑥ A few miles north, just off Route 151, in **Haddam Neck,** is the **Connecticut Yankee Energy Information Center.** On the grounds of the nuclear power plant, the center demonstrates the basics of energy production through hands-on exhibits, multimedia shows, computer games, and films. *Injun Hollow Rd. (Rte. 9, Exit 7), East Hampton, tel. 203/267–9279. Admission free. Open July–Aug., weekdays 9–4, Sat. 10–6, Sun. 12–5; Sept.–June, weekends 9–4. Closed major holidays.*

Take Route 151 east to Route 149, and a few miles south on **⑦** Route 149, in **Moodus,** is **Down on the Farm.** This onetime poultry farm now houses studios for artists whose crafts are for sale in the adjacent galleries. *Banner Rd., tel. 203/873-9905. Admission free. Open Apr.–June, Thurs.–Sun. 11–5; July–Jan., Tues.–Sun. 11–5.*

8 Return westward to Route 9, and at Exit 9 take Route 81 east to its intersection with I–95, in **Higganum.** Follow Braut Hill Road to its end, bear right, and follow signs to **Sundial Herb Farm.** The 1970 restoration of this Colonial farmstead led to the development of its three unusual gardens—a knot garden of interlocking hedges, a typical 18th-century geometric garden with central sundial, and a topiary garden. In the barn shop you'll find herbs in every form. *59 Hidden Lake Rd., tel. 203/ 345–4290. Admission free. Open Apr. 15–Oct., weekends 10–5; Nov.–Dec. 24, daily 10–5.*

9 Our next stop on Route 9 heading north is **Middletown,** the home of **Wesleyan University** (tel. 203/347–9711), founded in 1831. Wesleyan's **Center for the Arts** (between Washington Terrace and Wyllys Avenue) hosts concerts, theater performances, cinema, and art exhibits throughout the year.

The Federal-style **General Mansfield House,** built in 1810, houses 18th- and 19th-century furniture, Civil War memorabilia and firearms, and local artifacts. *151 Main St., tel. 203/346– 0746. Admission: $1. Open Sun. 2–4:30, Mon. 10–noon, 1–4. Closed major holiday weekends.*

On the main western road leading out of town, Route 66, the **Submarine Library Museum** maintains an extensive collection of submarine memorabilia and artifacts from both world wars. *440 Washington St., tel. 203/346–0388. Admission free. Open Apr.–Nov., weekends 10–5.*

Five miles south of Middletown on Route 157 you can smell the air grow sweeter at **Lyman Orchards,** where you can pick your own fruits and vegetables from June to October—berries, peaches, pears, apples, even golden white-tasseled sweet corn. The Apple Barrel Farm store sells what others have picked, plus bakery goods and cheese. *Jct. Rtes. 147 and 157, Middlefield, tel. 203/349–1566. Open Nov.–July, daily 9–6, Aug.– Oct., daily 9–7.*

10 Follow Route 9 north to I–91, then continue north 4 miles on I–91 to Route 99, which will take you north to **Wethersfield,** where the **Joseph Webb House** (1752), **Silas Deane House** (1766), and **Isaac Stevens House** (1788) form a joint museum. Well-preserved examples of Colonial architecture, they also reflect their individual owners' lifestyles—those of a merchant, a diplomat, and a tradesman respectively. The Webb House was the site of the strategy conference between Washington and Rochambeau that led to the British defeat at Yorktown. *203–211– 215 Main St. (I–91, Exit 26), tel. 203/529–0612. Admission: $2 adults per house, $5 all three houses, 75¢ children per house. Open Oct. 16–May 14, Tues.–Sat. 10–4; May 15–Oct. 15, Sun. 1–4.*

The **Buttolph-Williams House,** built in 1692, has a remarkable hand-hewn overhang and small casement windows suggesting medieval architecture. The well-preserved kitchen is one of the best of its period in New England. *249 Broad St. (I–95, Exit 26), tel. 203/529–0460 or 203/247–8996. Admission: $2 adults,*

$1 senior citizens, 50¢ children 5–18. Open May 15–Oct. 15, Tues.–Sun. 12–4.

⓫ I–91 is just one of the main roads that lead to **Hartford.**

Exploring Hartford

Numbers in the margin correspond with the numbered points of interest on the Downtown Hartford and Greater Hartford maps.

⓬ Our tour of the city begins at the **Old State House,** a distinctive building designed by Charles Bulfinch, architect of the U.S. Capitol, and occupied by the state legislature from 1796 to 1878. The restored Senate chamber contains a Gilbert Stuart portrait of George Washington. *800 Main St., tel. 203/522–6766. Admission free. Open Mon.–Sat. 10–5, Sun. noon–5.*

⓭ Farther north on Main Street is **The Richardson** (formerly the Cheney Building), built in 1877 by the architect H. H. Richardson. Once the headquarters and family residence of a prominent silk manufacturer, it now houses specialty shops and luxury apartments.

⓮ Steps away from **Constitution Plaza,** an urban park in the heart of downtown, is the green, curved-glass, boat-shaped tower of the **Phoenix Mutual Life Insurance Company,** the world's first two-sided building, and a Hartford landmark since 1964. Exhibits on insurance history are displayed in the lobby. *Constitution Plaza, tel. 203/275–5000. Open weekdays 8–4.*

On the second floor banking room of the **Connecticut Bank and Trust Co.** (1 Constitution Plaza, tel. 203/244–5000) is a huge Alexander Calder mobile.

At the south end of the plaza, a brick path leads you to the **Travelers Companies Tower** (1 Tower Sq., tel. 203/277–2431), headquarters of the prominent insurance company that underwrote construction of the plaza, and the city's tallest observation point. If you make it up the 72-step climb, the view from the top takes in the entire city and surrounding suburbs and stretches to the fields of shade-grown tobacco in outlying areas.

⓯ A return to Main Street brings you to the civic strip that starts with the **Wadsworth Atheneum,** the first public art museum in the country. Today, its more than 40,000 works span 5,000 years of art. Its "Lions Gallery of the Senses" offers exhibits designed for the visually impaired. *600 Main St., tel. 203/247–9111 or 203/278–2670. Admission: $3 adults, $1.50 senior citizens, admission free Sat. 11–1 and Thurs. Open Tues.–Sun. 11–5. Closed major holidays.*

⓰ Before you get to the Municipal Building next door, pause at the **Burr Mall,** a small park that contains Calder's famous *Stegosaurus* sculpture.

⓱ The daily business of running the city goes on at the **Municipal Building,** the seat of local government since 1914. Inside, walk up the grand staircase to the higher level, and you'll find yourself standing on the frosted-glass ceiling of the floor below.

⓲ Continue down the block to the defunct **Hartford Times building,** a 160-year-old structure that witnessed many historical events, described on the plaques outside.

Amos Bull House, **20**
Burr Mall, **16**
Bushnell Park, **22**
Butler-McCook
Homestead, **19**
Center Church and
Ancient Burying
Ground, **21**
Constitution Plaza, **14**
Hartford Times
building, **18**
Municipal Building, **17**
Old State House, **12**
Raymond E. Baldwin
Museum of
Connecticut
History, **24**
The Richardson, **13**
State Capitol, **23**
Wadsworth
Atheneum, **15**

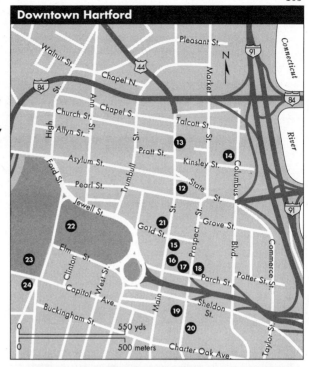

Museum of American
Political Life, **28**
Noah Webster House
and Museum, **27**
Nook Farm, **25**
Science Museum of
Connecticut, **26**

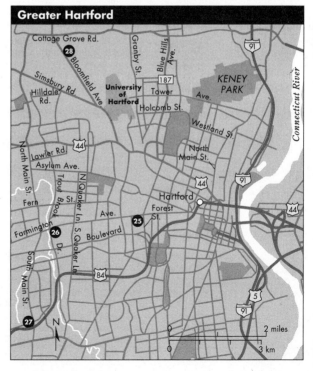

⑲ A few more blocks south you'll find the **Butler-McCook Homestead,** built in 1782. This house was occupied continuously by the same family until 1971. The furnishings show the evolution of tastes over time, with the Victorian era predominating. *396 Main St., tel. 203/247–8996 or 203/522–1806. Admission: $2 adults, $1 senior citizens, 50¢ children. Open May 15–Oct. 16, Tues., Thurs., Sun. noon–4. Closed major holidays.*

From the garden of the Butler-McCook Homestead you can see
⑳ the **Amos Bull House,** built in 1788 by a local character who set up a school here with the third of his five wives. Today it's the home of the **Connecticut Historical Commission,** and it's not open to the public.

㉑ At the intersection of Main and Gold streets is the **Center Church and Ancient Burying Ground.** The present structure of the 350-year-old parish was built in 1807 and is patterned after the Church of St. Martin-in-the-Fields on London's Trafalgar Square. The Center Church's stained-glass windows were created by Louis Tiffany. In the burial ground lie the remains of several of Hartford's first settlers and prominent families. *Main and Gold Sts., tel. 203/249–5631. Open daily noon–3.*

㉒ **Bushnell Park,** which fans out from the State Capitol building, was the first public space in the country to use natural landscaping rather than a traditional village green. The park was created by the firm of Frederick Law Olmsted, the Hartford landscape architect who designed New York City's Central Park. On the Bushnell's 40 acres you'll find 150 varieties of trees as well as manmade landmarks. The **Soldiers and Sailors Memorial Arch** is a huge, brownstone, Gothic-and-Romanesque-Revival monument to the local citizens who served in the Civil War; and the 30-foot **Corning Fountain** celebrates the bravery and heritage of Native Americans.

Another attraction that never fails to please during its working hours is the **Bushnell Park Carousel,** a gem of a merry-go-round with 48 hand-carved horses prancing beneath twinkling lights. First erected in 1914, the carousel is accompanied by a wheezing 1925 Wurlitzer band organ. The 25¢ ride seems never to last long enough. *Jewell St., tel. 203/728–3089. Open mid-May–Aug., Tues.–Sun. 11–5; mid-Apr.–mid-May, Sept., weekends 11–5.*

The crowning gem rising above the park and seen from all over
㉓ the city is the **State Capitol,** a wonder of gingerbread Victorian architecture, built in 1879. The gold-domed structure houses the governor's office and legislative chambers, and, with the new, architecturally commanding Legislative Office Building opened in 1988, forms the true seat of government for the state. Within these two buildings are historic murals, statuary, flags, and furnishings. *210 Capitol Ave., tel. 203/240–0222. Open weekdays 9–3.*

㉔ Across from the Capitol building is the **Raymond E. Baldwin Museum of Connecticut History,** with exhibits of Connecticut memorabilia including the original Colonial charter. It also contains the vast Colt collection of firearms. *231 Capitol Ave., tel. 203/566–3056. Admission free. Open weekdays 9–4:45, Sat. 9–12:45. Closed Sun., state holidays.*

Head west on Farmington Avenue to reach the spot where Samuel Langhorne Clemens, better known as Mark Twain, **㉕** built his own Victorian mansion at **Nook Farm** in 1874. The neighboring cottage, built in 1871, was the home of Harriet Beecher Stowe, the author of *Uncle Tom's Cabin*. During his residency here, Twain published seven major novels, including *Tom Sawyer, Huckleberry Finn,* and *The Prince and the Pauper*. Personal memorabilia and original furnishings of both writers are on display. A visitor center and a gift shop serve both houses. *Farmington Ave. at Forest St., tel. 203/525–9317. Admission for tour of both houses: $6.50 adults, $2.75 children 6–16. Open June–Columbus Day, Mon.–Sat. 9:30–4, Sun. noon–4. Closed Mon., Columbus Day–May.*

㉖ Continuing west on Farmington Avenue will take you into **West Hartford** and the **Science Museum of Connecticut,** which includes an aquarium with a hands-on tank, a mini-zoo, and a planetarium. You're greeted at the museum's entrance by a life-size, walk-through replica of a 60-foot sperm whale. There are daily animal- and planetarium shows plus changing exhibits whose subjects range from the human heart to computers. *950 Trout Brook Dr., tel. 203/236–2961. Admission: $3.50 adults, $2 senior citizens and children under 13. Open Mon.–Sat. 10–5, Sun. 1–5. Closed Jan. 1, Labor Day, Thanksgiving, Dec. 25.*

㉗ Head west on I–84 to reach the **Noah Webster House and Museum,** birthplace of the famed author of the *Blue-Backed Speller* and the *American Dictionary*. The 18th-century farmhouse contains Webster memorabilia and period furnishings along with changing exhibits. *227 S. Main St., tel. 203/521–5362. Admission: $2 adults, $1.50 senior citizens, $1 children 6–150. Open mid-June–Sept., Mon., Tues., Thurs., Fri. 10–4, weekends 1–4; Oct.–mid-June, Mon., Tues., Thurs.–Sun. 1–4.*

At the **University of Hartford** you'll find the newly opened **㉘** **Museum of American Political Life** (200 Bloomfield Ave., Rte. 189, tel. 203/523–1182). A broad range of displays includes artifacts of U.S. presidents and their campaigns as well as memorabilia of various political movements, including the women's rights movement and the temperance-Prohibition crusade.

Connecticut River Valley for Free

The Stone House, Deep River

Sundial Herb Farm, Higganum

The **Historical Museum of Medicine and Dentistry** has instruments and medicine used by early practitioners of these professions. There's a probing history of anesthesia, and a medical library. *230 Scarborough St., Hartford, tel. 203/236–5613. Open weekdays 10–4.*

Inside the working Tudor-style **Pump House Gallery** you'll find works of Connecticut artists and artisans. *Bushnell Park, Hartford tel. 203/772–6440 or 203/722–6536. Open Tues.–Fri. 11–2, Sun. noon–3.*

What to See and Do with Children

Valley Railroad, Essex

Dinosaur State Park (*see* State Parks, below)

Bushnell Park Carousel, Hartford

Science Museum of Connecticut, West Hartford

Off the Beaten Track

The **New England Air Museum** at Bradley International Airport has more than 75 aircraft on display—bombers, fighters, helicopters, gliders, and today's commercial planes. A jet fighter cockpit simulator will give you the shakes, as will some of the aviation films. *Rte. 75 (at Bradley Airport), Windsor Locks, tel. 203/623–3305. Admission: $5 adults, $4 senior citizens, $2 children 6–11. Open daily 10–5. Closed Thanksgiving, Dec. 25.*

Brown's Harvest offers free hayrides out to the pumpkin fields. *Rte. 75, Windsor, tel. 203/683–0266. Weekends during harvest only.*

A bit west of West Hartford in the town of Farmington is the **Hill–Stead Museum,** a private home converted to a museum by its unusual owner, Theodate Pope, the woman who designed it in 1899 with the prestigious architectural firm of McKim, Mead, and White. The Colonial-Revival farmhouse contains a superb collection of Impressionist art. This may be the only drawing room in America with Monet haystacks at either end and Manet's *The Guitar Player* in the middle. *35 Mountain Rd., (I–84, Exit 39), tel. 203/677–4787. Admission: $5 adults, $4 senior citizens, $2 children 6–12. Open Wed.–Fri. 2–5, weekends 1–5.*

Shopping

Deep River The town seems like an enormous antiques fair, with a concentration of dealers on Main Street and at the intersection of Routes 80 and 145.

Hartford Three large shopping centers can be found downtown. The **Civic Center** (1 Civic Center Plaza, tel. 203/275–6100) has more than 60 shops as well as a 16,500-seat arena, **The Richardson Mall** (942 Main St., tel. 203/525–9711) has more than 40 shops selling everything from hats to video games, and the art deco **Pavilion** (State House Sq., tel. 203/241–0100) has 25 shops.

About 7 miles from the downtown area is **Westfarms Mall** (I–84, Exit 40, tel. 203/561–3024), with 140 shops amid lots of marble and greenery.

Old Saybrook **The Antiques Village** (985 Middlesex Tpke., tel. 203/388–0689) has more than 80 dealers.

Sports and Outdoor Activities

Camping **Wolf's Den Family Campsites** (Town St., Rte. 82, East Haddam, tel. 203/824–7051 or 800/422–2267), **Markham Meadows Campground** (7 Markham Rd., East Hampton, tel. 203/267–9738), and **Nelson's Family Compound** (71C Mott Hill Rd., East Hampton, tel. 203/267–4561 or 203/237–6157) have camping.

Spectator Sports

Hockey   The **Hartford Whalers** (tel. 203/728–6637 or 203/728–3366) of the National Hockey League play their home games at the Civic Center in Hartford.

Jai-Alai   Berenson's **Hartford Jai Alai** (89 Weston St., tel. 203/525–8611), the first jai-alai fronton in the Northeast, draws many top players and features pari-mutuel wagering.

State Parks

East Haddam   **Devil's Hopyard.** The 60-foot cascades flowing down Chapman Falls are the highlight of this 860-acre park. It's said that the potholes at the base of the falls were made by the Devil hopping from one stone to the next to stay dry. There are 20 campsites available. *3 mi north of the junction of Rtes. 82 and 156, tel. 203/873–8566. Open mid-Apr.–Sept.*

East Hampton   **Hurd** (Rte. 151). High on the east bank of the river, Hurd offers excellent views in spring and summer.

Haddam   **Cockaponset** (Rte. 148, tel. 203/345–8521). Connecticut's second-largest state forest was named for an Indian chief buried nearby. Its 15,652 acres allow a full range of outdoor activities.

Haddam Meadows (Rte. 154). The predominantly flat ground of this 175-acre meadowland is great for field sports.

Hadlyme   **Gillette Castle** (*see* Exploring above).

Middlefield   **Wadsworth Falls** (Rte. 157, Middlefield, tel. 203/344–2950). A beautiful waterfall dominates this 285-acre park. Colorful laurel displays are a highlight of the spring season.

Rocky Neck   **Dinosaur State Park.** Dinosaurs may have roamed hereabouts. Jurassic-period tracks (185 million years old) are preserved under a giant geodesic dome here, and you can even make plaster casts. There are also 40 acres of nature trails. *West St. (I–91, Exit 23), tel. 203/529–8423. Open daily 9–4:30.*

Dining and Lodging

Centerbrook   **Fine Bouche.** A Victorian mansion on Main Street is home to
Dining   some of the finest contemporary French cooking in the state.
★   Its handsome dining room has candlelit, white-napped tables with settings of Villeroy & Boch pink-iris china. Entrées on a recent menu were *faisan fécampoise* (sautéed pheasant breast with apples and Benedictine) and *grillade de thon à la Provençal* (grilled fresh tuna with caper sauce and tomato puree). The *marjolaine* is four layers of almond-and-hazelnut meringue cake with crème fraîche, pralines, and a semisweet chocolate coating—and the pâtisserie up front sells the restaurant's pastries to take away. Fine Bouche has periodic wine tastings with special menus. *78 Main St., tel. 203/767–1277. Reservations advised. Dress: casual. AC, MC, V. No lunch. Closed Mon., Thanksgiving, Dec. 25. Very Expensive.*

Chester Dining   **The Chart House.** This century-old, former brush factory offers possibly the most exciting entrance to dining in the state. Leaving the parking lot, you walk across a trellis-sided footbridge that spans the waters of the Pattaconk River as they tumble over a waterfall. In keeping with the building's 19th-century origins, antique machinery components are suspended discreetly from the ceiling. A traditional New England menu offers fresh seafood as well as prime beef. The restaurant is so famous for its blue-cheese salad dressing that it provides printed copies of the recipe to customers. *W. Main St. at Rte. 9, tel. 203/526–9898. Reservations advised. AE, CB, D, DC, MC, V. No lunch. Closed Thanksgiving, Dec. 25. Inexpensive–Expensive.*

Pattaconk Inn. Remember what a small, downtown, storefront restaurant was like about three decades ago? The Pattaconk Inn is one such establishment, serving the basics in unpretentious surroundings. The locals routinely catch the game on the TV, while enjoying a frothy mug and the fish of the day. *33 Main St., tel. 203/526–9285. Reservations advised for 6 or more. Dress: casual. No credit cards. Closed Dec. 25. Inexpensive.*

Chester Lodging   **The Inn at Chester.** About as far west on Main Street as you can go without reaching the next town, this once-historic inn has been so modernized that only the faintest traces of its origins are visible, mostly in the oddly shaped bedrooms in the older section. Behind its Colonial, mustard-colored clapboards lies a contemporary, full-service conference center. Complimentary copies of the *Wall Street Journal* and The *New York Times* are provided. Rooms are generally spacious and equipped with TV sets hidden in antique-reproduction cupboards. *318 Main St. (Rte. 148), tel. 203/526–4961. 48 rooms with bath, 1 suite. Facilities: restaurant, lounge, tennis court, health club, sauna, free bicycles. AE, DC, MC, V. Expensive.*

Cromwell Lodging   **Treadway Hartford Hotel.** This modern, sprawling, full-service hotel has come a long way from its origin as the Lord Cromwell Motor Inn. Guest rooms are reproduction Colonial with modern conveniences. Some overlook the busy interior pool and restaurant under the glass dome. Finding your way around the contorted ground level can be confusing. *100 Berlin Rd. (I–91, Exit 21), 06416, tel. 203/635–2000 or 800/631–2392. 212 rooms with bath, 2 suites. Facilities: indoor heated pool, health club, saunas, adjacent garage parking, in-room coffeemakers. AE, CB, DC, MC, V. Rates include breakfast. Expensive.*

Holiday Inn of Cromwell. Blonde wood is the keynote of the light, airy decor throughout this hotel, lobby, and the rooms all have simple, contemporary furnishings in soft colors. During the early evening, mellow music is played on the baby-grand piano in the lounge. *4 Sebethe Dr. (I–91, Exit 21), 06416, tel. 203/635–1001 or 800/465–4329. 145 rooms with bath, 2 suites. Facilities: restaurant, lounge, indoor heated pool, health club, saunas, handicapped access, waterbeds in some rooms. AE, CB, D, DC, MC, V. Moderate–Expensive.*

Knight's Inn. Directly across the street from and operated by the Treadway, it offers budget rooms at budget prices, and use of the larger establishment's facilities. *111 Berlin Rd. (I–91, Exit 21), 06416, tel. 203/635–2000 or 800/631–2392. 77 rooms with bath. AE, CB, DC, MC, V. Inexpensive.*

Deep River Lodging ★   **Riverwind.** Miss Hickory, the feline ruler of this charming B&B, may be found napping in front of any one of the impressive fireplaces of the restored Victorian town house. Each guest room has been decorated with thematic integrity, from the canopied bird's-eye-maple four-poster in the Willow Room to the red, white, and blue furnishings of the Smithfield Room. The Champagne and Roses Room has an impressive mahogany pencil-post bed topped by a fishnet-lace canopy. An enormous homemade breakfast is served beside a cozy hearth on the main floor. *209 Main St., 06417, 203/526–2014. 8 rooms with bath. Facilities: dining room, game room, reading room, parlor. AE (5% surcharge), MC, V (3% surcharge). Rates include full breakfast. Expensive.*

Essex Dining **The Griswold Inn.** This 200-year-old landmark claims to be "America's oldest and most famous inn." Charm abounds, from the worn floorboards to the exposed ceiling beams, in every tchachka-filled nook and cranny. The no-frills, traditional American menu features hearty portions of prime beef and fresh seafood. *36 Main St., tel. 203/767–1776. Reservations advised. Dress: casual. AE, MC, V. Closed Dec. 25. Moderate.*

Essex Lodging **Griswold Inn.** A lodging place since 1776, the "Gris" gets a little carried away with marine memorabilia in trying to sustain a nautical character. Bedrooms furnished with antique and re-production pieces maintain a precarious balance between original beamed ceilings and push-button telephones. There are no TVs or radios in the rooms, but one can tune in to a cen-tral music system. Located in the middle of downtown Essex, the inn is within easy walking distance of local attractions. *36 Main St., 06426, tel. 203/767–1776. 20 rooms with bath. Facili-ties: dining rooms, taproom, library. AE, MC, V. Expensive.*

East Haddam **Austin's Stonecroft Inn.** Period furnishings in this Federal-
Lodging style B&B recall a gracious era that is echoed in the warm present-day welcome you receive here. And you're only steps away from the Goodspeed Opera House. *17 Main St. (at Goodspeed Landing), 06423, tel. 203/873–1754. 5 rooms with bath. No credit cards. Rates include full breakfast. Moderate–Expensive.*

Hartford Dining **L'Americain.** Hartford's ultimate word in elegant dining can be
★ found within a renovated factory block on the edge of down-town. In the tastefully appointed dining rooms, exotic and luxurious coexist happily in entrées such as lime-and-sauternes shrimp (with leeks and white grapes served over black pepper pasta), and tequila buffalo (marinated sirloin of buffalo with blue-cornmeal polenta and cactus-pear game sauce). A compa-rable menu for dieters lists nutritional contents. *2 Hartford Sq. W, tel. 203/522–6500. Reservations advised. Dress: casual. AE, CB, DC, MC, V. No lunch. Closed Sun., Thanksgiving, Dec. 25. Very Expensive.*

Carbone's. There's a timeless comfort in the warm, brown-and-beige decor of this bastion of Italian–American cuisine. Sub-dued lighting and candlelit tables add to the romantic aura. A family member is always on duty and can recommend a daily offering, be it *vitello cuscinetto* (veal slices with prosciutto, ar-tichoke, and cheese, sautéed with lemon and sherry), or *pesce spada Genovese* (baked swordfish with pesto in a sherry sauce). The killer dessert is *bocce balls* (chocolate-dipped vanilla ice cream flamed with Grand Marnier sauce). *588 Franklin Ave., tel. 203/296–9646. Reservations advised. Dress: casual. AE, MC, V. No lunch Sat. Closed major holidays. Very Expensive.*

Chuck's Steak House. Beyond the long, book-lined, paneled en-trance is a steakhouse in the time-honored tradition. Steak, prime rib, or the fresh fish of the day is rushed to your table, allowing plenty of time for you to make a hockey game, concert, or other event nearby. The menu is painted on wine-jugs. *1 Civic Center Plaza, tel. 203/241–9100. No Reservations. Dress: casual. AE, CB, D, DC, MC, V. Closed Thanksgiving, Dec. 25. Expensive.*

★ **Frank's Restaurant.** A favorite among the prominent of Hartford for nearly half a century, this restaurant has a new setting beside the entrance to City Place, opposite the Civic Center. The traditional Italian-Continental menu includes San Francisco *cioppino* (fresh fish and shellfish baked with an oreganato or tomato sauce and served over linguine). Leave room for the zabaglione. The ceilings are high, the lighting soft and soothing; even when the restaurant is crowded, an air of calm prevails. *185 Asylum St., tel. 203/527–9291. Reservations advised. Dress: casual but neat. AE, DC, MC, V. Closed Dec. 25. Expensive.*

Max on Main. Don't dismiss as "trendy" this sophisticated dining room; there's good dining here. Calamari and carpaccio are served with spicy touches, and the Stone Pies are a superb variation on pedestrian pizza. The late-night crowd swears by the Stone Pie with smoked chicken, pancetta, sweet peppers, scallions, and Monterey Jack cheese; or the version with shrimp, sun-dried tomatoes, pesto, calamata olives, and two cheeses. *205 Main St., tel. 203/522–2530. Reservations advised. Dress: neat but casual. AE, DC, MC, V. No lunch Sat. Closed Sun., Jan. 1, Thanksgiving, Dec. 25. Moderate–Expensive.*

★ **Truc Orient Express.** Head south on broad Wethersfield Avenue to this outpost of Vietnamese cuisine served in bright and comfortable premises. The signature *Banh Xeo* (Happy Pancake), a stuffed rice-batter crepe, might be followed by *Bo Luc Lac* (Shaking Beef), cubes of marinated filet mignon sautéed with garlic; or *Ga Xoi Mo* (Five-Spice Chicken), marinated Cornish hen with tamarind sauce. The *Bo 4 Mon* (Beef in Four Dishes), for two persons, will delight gourmet beef-eaters. *735 Wethersfield Ave., tel. 203/296–2818. Reservations advised for 4 or more. Dress: casual. AE, CB, DC, MC, V. No lunch Sun., Mon. Closed major holidays. Moderate–Expensive.*

Margaritaville. Standard Mexican fare is offered here, along with trendy, Southwest-influenced novelties such as chicken and beef fajitas. The traditional decor includes tin lanterns and awning-stripe seat coverings. Lunch is served downstairs in the Cantina, where, after 3 PM, you'll find only appetizers and snacks—along with enormous margaritas. *1 Civic Center Plaza, tel. 203/724–3331. Dress: casual. AE, CB, D, DC, MC, V. Cantina closed Sun. Moderate.*

Kashmir. The furnishings in this small, intimate dining room complement the traditional menu. The classic Moghul cuisine ranges from Bombay to Bengal, from mildly spicy to eyeball-popping hot. The menu explains the gradations, from the Tandoori Chicken on the mild side to the Chicken Vindaloo at the other end of the thermometer. In between are such offerings as lamb *saag* (braised in a spinach sauce), and shrimp *dopiaza* (cooked with onions in a tumeric–cumin sauce). *481 Wethersfield Ave., tel. 203/278–9685. Reservations advised. Dress: casual. AE, MC, V. No lunch Sun. Closed major holidays. Inexpensive–Moderate.*

Municipal Restaurant. At one time, every major city in the country had a downtown cafeteria like this, but few remain today. Since 1924 the Municipal has been serving cafeteria food that's ordered at the counter and consumed in bare-bones surroundings. If sawdust on the floor weren't outlawed, you'd find it here. Under the pressed-tin ceiling the menu boards list the daily fare: Turkey plate with mashed potatoes and gravy, meat loaf with green beans, and smoky pea soup are typical staples. *485 Main St., tel. 203/278–4210. No reservations. Dress: casual. AE, MC, V. No dinner Mon.–Tues. Closed Sun. Inexpensive.*

Hartford Lodging **Sheraton-Hartford.** Built in 1975, the 15-story Sheraton is the city's largest hotel. Connected to the Civic Center by an enclosed bridge, it's within easy walking distance of the downtown area. The preferred rooms are on floors one through nine, which were refurbished with period reproductions in 1985. This is not a "grand hotel," but it does have touches of elegance, including the street-level lobby abloom with fresh flowers. *315 Trumbull St. at the Civic Center Plaza, 06103, tel. 203/728–5151 or 800/325–3535. 400 rooms with bath, 6 suites. Facilities: restaurant, lounge, health club, sauna, indoor pool, motor entrance and direct-access parking garage. AE, CB, D, DC, MC, V. Very Expensive.*

Holiday Inn Downtown. There's no easy way to get to this hotel, wedged as it is between one-way streets, the highway, and ongoing construction. And when you arrive there's no free parking, even temporarily, so you must pay for the antiquated garage, with its grim entrance to the hotel. Inside, the modern rooms have big windows with sweeping views of the distant hills beyond the urban landscape. *50 Morgan St., 06120, tel. 203/549–2400, 203/549–7844. 347 rooms with bath, 4 suites. Facilities: restaurant, lounge, coffee shop, health club, sauna, outdoor pool. AE, CB, DC, MC, V. Expensive.*

Ramada Inn. Situated beside Bushnell Park, this two decade-old hotel has an unobstructed view of the Capitol. Those rooms facing the rear, however, overlook the train station, a parking lot, and the busy highway. The hotel's location, around the corner from Union Station, is convenient; and the food should be good when the New England Culinary Institute moves in (spring 1990) to run the restaurant. *440 Asylum St., 06103, tel. 203/246–6591 or 800/228–2828. 96 rooms with bath, 4 suites. Facilities: room service, direct access to parking. AE, CB, DC, MC, V. Moderate.*

Ivoryton Dining **Copper Beech Inn.** Fresh flowers, gleaming silver and crystal, ★ and soft candlelight set the scene in each of the comfortable dining rooms at this gracious, inviting country inn. Equally impressive is the distinctive country-French menu, which has already garnered numerous awards. The availability of fresh ingredients dictates daily changes in the country pâté, the fish of the day, and the seasonal game. Year-round treats include the *filet mignon aux echalotes* (grilled twin tenderloins with a sauce of shallot, white wine, and veal stock, garnished with a shallot confit), and the chocolate crepes filled with chocolate mousse. *46 Main St., tel. 203/767–0330. Reservations required on weekends, advised weekdays. Dress: casual. AE, CB, DC, MC, V. No lunch. Closed Mon., Jan. 1, Dec. 25. Expensive–Very Expensive.*

Daniel's Table. Traditional Colonial decor accompanies an international menu that features local fish and game in season. Entrées on a recent menu included warm duck salad with raspberry-walnut vinaigrette; and game hen filled with wild mushrooms and Madeira cream. *Ivoryton Inn, Main St., tel.*

203/767–8914. Reservations advised. Dress: casual. AE, MC, V. No lunch. Closed Mon. Expensive.

Ivoryton Lodging
★ **Copper Beech Inn.** A magnificent copper beech tree shades the imposing Victorian main building, once the residence of the ivory importer A. W. Comstock and now housing several dining rooms and four guest rooms, each with an old-fashioned tub in the bathroom. The present innkeepers have refurnished the rooms here and in the renovated carriage house with period pieces. Rooms in the carriage house have private decks and large Jacuzzis. Seven acres of wooded grounds and groomed terrace gardens creates an atmosphere of privileged seclusion. *46 Main St., 06442, tel. 203/767–0330. 13 rooms with bath. Facilities: dining rooms, greenhouse lounge. AE, CB, DC, MC, V. Rates include Continental breakfast. Closed Jan. 1, Dec. 25. Expensive.*

The Arts

Listings may be found in the *Hartford Courant, Middletown Press, Hartford Monthly, Connecticut Magazine,* and *New England Monthly.* The Civic Center publishes *Center View,* a monthly guide to all that's happening in that location, appearing as a supplement to the *Hartford Courant.*

Dance The **Hartford Ballet** (166 Capitol Ave., Hartford, tel. 203/527–0713) performs classical and contemporary productions, including a holiday *Nutcracker,* seasonally at The Bushnell.

Music **Hartford Symphony,** musical luminaries, symphony orchestras, and soloists perform at The Bushnell (tel. 203/246–6807).

Cathedral Theatre (45 Church St., Hartford, tel. 203/232–0085) is the site of Chamber Music Plus concerts.

Hartford Camerata Conservatory (834 Asylum Ave., Hartford, tel. 203/246–2588) presents numerous recitals.

Bronson & Hutensky Theater (233 Pearl St., Hartford, tel. 203/232–1006) is home to the Real Art Ways Music Series which presents up-to-the-minute new works.

Theater **Goodspeed Opera House** (Rte. 82, East Haddam, tel. 203/873–8668) presents an annual season of revivals of neglected great musicals and some on their way to Broadway. Past successes have included *Man of La Mancha* and *Annie.* The season starts in early spring and runs through early December. The tiny stage and theater in this gem of Victorian architecture offer the highest quality musical theater.

Goodspeed at Chester operates a second company at the **Norma Terris Theatre** (North Main St., Rte. 82, Chester, tel. 203/873–8668) where it presents new works in development.

The Tony-award-winning **Hartford Stage Company** (50 Church St., Hartford, tel. 203/527–2151) has turned out its share of Broadway hits, including *Other People's Money* and *A Shayna Maidel,* as well as innovative productions of Shakespeare, the classics, and exciting new plays.

Theatreworks (233 Pearl St., Hartford, tel. 203/527–7838), the Hartford equivalent of off-Broadway, presents a series of creative theater works including experimental new dramas.

The **National Theatre of the Deaf** (5 W. Main St., Chester, tel. 203/526–4971) originates here the spectacular productions it takes on tour throughout the state and country.

Nightlife

Comedy Clubs **Brown Thomson's Last Laugh Club** (942 Main St., Hartford, tel. 203/525–1600) showcases comics from Boston and New York on weekend evenings.

Dance Clubs **Citi Lites** (70 Union Pl., Hartford, tel. 203/525–1014) features a large dance floor and tunes ranging from Top 40 to Motown.

The Club Car (50 Union Pl., Hartford, tel. 203/529–5444) has a high-tech dance floor upstairs and a glitzy restaurant and jazz club downstairs. The music ranges from live jazz to country and western.

The Hartford Trading Company (315 Trumbull St., Hartford, tel. 203/728–5151) has 12 video screens surrounding a large central screen.

Jazz Clubs **The 880 Club** (880 Maple Ave., Hartford, tel. 203/525–2428), the oldest jazz club in Hartford, presents live acts in an intimate atmosphere.

Shenanigan's (1 Gold St., Hartford, tel. 203/522–4117) offers live piano music, usually jazz, seven nights a week and during Sunday brunch.

Nightclubs **The Russian Lady Cafe** (191 Ann St., Hartford, tel. 203/525–3003) swings into the wee hours with rock, R&B, and pop music.

Rock Clubs **The Arch Street Tavern** (86 Arch St., Hartford, tel. 203/246–7610) presents local rock bands in one room that can hold 120 people.

Litchfield Hills

The modest rise of the Litchfield Hills in the northwest corner of the state is a relatively tranquil area where resorts and camps abound and traffic is a problem only on holiday weekends and during the summer season, when parents arrive to visit campers. The absence of major industry and big cities leaves the region relatively free of the urban problems one encounters elsewhere in the state.

Important Addresses and Numbers

Visitor Information **Litchfield Hills Travel Council** (Box 1776, Marbledale 06777, tel. 203/868–2214).

Emergencies **Sharon Hospital** (Sharon, tel. 203/364–4111).

Charlotte Hungerford Hospital (Torrington, tel. 203/496–6666).

Winsted Memorial Hospital (Winsted, tel. 203/379–3351).

Late-night Pharmacies **Sharon Pharmacy** (Sharon, tel. 203/364–5272).

North End Drug Store (470 Main St., Torrington, tel. 203/489–3743 or 203/482–9090).

Getting Around the Litchfield Hills

By Car The principal north–south highways in the area are Route 8 in the east and Route 7 in the west; the best east–west highways are Route 44 in the north and Route 4. Torrington has the largest number of auto rental companies.

Exploring the Litchfield Hills

Numbers in the margin correspond with the numbered points of interest on the Litchfield Hills map.

❶ . The oversize hamlet of **Riverton** springs to life during the annual Riverton Fair and on summer weekends, when travelers stop at the Hitchcock Chair Factory Store or look in on the show of 19th-century furniture at the **Hitchcock Museum,** located in the Old Union Church. Lambert Hitchcock made his first chair here in 1826—and the town was once called Hitchcockville. *Rte. 20, tel. 203/379–1003. Admission free. Open Apr.–May, Sat. 1–4; June–Oct., Wed.–Sat. 11–4, Sun. 1–4.*

One of the prettier drives in the area is along the Farmington River, as it winds through the **People's State Forest.** Follow signs to Pleasant Valley and Route 318. When you reach the metal bridge spanning the river, turn right on Route 318 and follow the winding road to Route 44. Turn right and head west on Route 44.

❷ The **Solomon Rockwell house,** in **Winsted,** has survived the Great Winsted Flood of 1957 and many other disasters. Built in 1813, the Greek-Revival building was once the home of a prosperous iron manufacturer and today displays furnishings and memorabilia dating from the Revolutionary and Civil wars. *225 Prospect St. (Rte. 263 west off Rte. 44), tel. 203/379–8433. Admission: $1 adults. Open mid-June–mid-Sept., Thurs.–Sun. 1:30–4.*

Follow Route 263 for 4 miles, to the **Winchester Center Green.** This peaceful spot surrounded by traditional, white Colonial architecture is steps away from the unusual **Kerosene Lamp Museum,** where you'll find a remarkable private collection of more than 500 hanging and standing kerosene-powered lamps dating from 1856 to 1880. *100 Waterbury Tpke. (Rte. 263), tel. 203/379–2612. Admission free. Open daily 9:30–4.*

❸ Retrace your path to Route 44, turn left (west) through downtown, and continue to **Norfolk.** At the southern tip of the village green is an elaborate drinking fountain designed by Stanford White. More of the town's past may be discovered at the **Norfolk Historical Society Museum,** which is housed in the former Norfolk Academy, built about 1840. *The Green, tel. 203/542–5761. Admission free. Open mid-June–mid-Sept., weekends 10–5.*

❹ Continue west on Route 44 to **Canaan.** The town's railroad depot played an important role during the booming days of iron mining. **Union Station** (Rtes. 44 and 7, tel. 203/824–0339), built in 1872 and presently the starting point for the scenic **Housatonic Railroad,** is the oldest train station in continuous use in the country. The "Housy" offers scenic rides over short distances between Memorial Day and early fall.

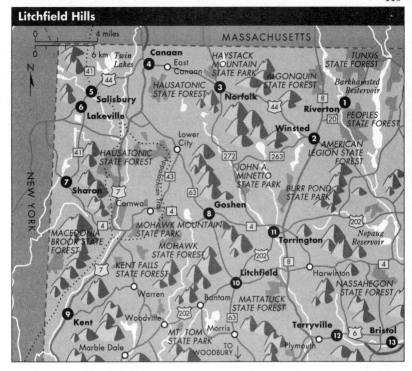

Litchfield Hills

MASSACHUSETTS

⑤ The next 10 miles, from Canaan to **Salisbury** on Route 44, take you by well-preserved country inns and gracious estates set back from the road. Don't miss the controversial architecture of the new **Salisbury Town Hall.**

⑥ In **Lakeville,** at the intersection with Route 41 south, you'll find the **Holley Williams House.** Built in 1808 by a local iron baron, this Classical-Revival house contains original furnishings, including several important Colonial primitive paintings. *Rtes. 44 and 41, Lakeville, tel. 203/435–2878. Admission free. Open July–mid-Oct., Thurs., Sat. 2–4.*

⑦ Route 41 south leads to **Sharon.** In the center of town, amid the sloping lawns and tree-shaded houses, is the ornate stone **Hotchkiss Clock Tower,** at the junction with Route 4. Continue east on this road to the **Northeast Audubon Center.** This 684-acre sanctuary operated by the National Audubon Society has several well-marked trails, as well as a main building housing natural history displays, a gift shop, and a bookstore. There is also a Children's Discovery Room. *Rte. 4, tel. 203/364–0520. Admission: $2 adults, $1 children. Open Mon.–Sat. 9–5, Sun. 1–5; trails open dawn to dusk. Closed major holidays.*

⑧ Continuing east on Route 4 toward **Goshen,** you pass broad fields, cleared farmland, and a small, one-room building with a flagpole and nearby **monument.** This memorial to the Civil War General Meade, who hailed from these parts, is surrounded by stone walls and rolling meadows and is a quiet reminder of a time when battles were fought on fields just like these.

9 Back on Route 7, continue south to **Kent.** Just before you get to the busy Main Street, you'll see a sign pointing to the right for the **Sloane–Stanley Museum,** which was built by the author and artist Eric Sloane, whose work celebrates Early American woodworking and craftsmanship. Tools and implements, many from the 17th century, are on display. The ruins of the **Kent Iron Furnace,** in operation from 1826 to 1892, are also on the grounds. *Rte. 7, tel. 203/927–3849. Admission: $3 adults, $1.50 senior citizens and children. Open mid-May–Oct., Wed.–Sun. 10–4:30.*

At the southern end of Main Street, at the monument in the middle of the road, turn right and head west toward the Kent Preparatory School. Immediately after crossing the bridge over the Housatonic River, turn left on Schagticoke Road. This partially dirt road follows the river and passes the small enclave of the **Schagticoke Indian Reservation** and tiny burial ground. Although there are no provisions for visitors and not much to be seen beyond the road, the river view is commanding, particularly late in the summer when the fireweed is abloom, and later during foliage season.

At the end of the road, make a left turn and you'll cross two bridges, one modern and one covered. According to local wags, the latter, **Bull's Bridge,** is celebrated as the site of a mishap suffered by George Washington. The story claims that his horse stumbled here on a rotted plank, and the general was forced to spend the night nearby.

Return north on Route 7 to the intersection with Route 341. Turn right and head east through the villages of Warren and Woodville to Route 202 in Bantam. Turn left and continue **10** northeast to **Litchfield,** the county seat. Many of the old homes set well behind the broad avenue on North and South Main Street (Route 63) bear plaques giving their dates of construction and historic credentials. There are many period houses to see (among them Sheldon's Tavern, Pierce Academy, and the birthplace of Harriet Beecher Stowe); the **Litchfield Historical Society Museum** provides information on all of them. Here you'll find changing exhibits of 18th-century portraits and items of local history. The reference library can satisfy your curiosity about anything that has happened hereabouts in the last four centuries. *East and South Sts., tel. 203/567–4501. Admission: $1 adults. Open Tues.–Sat. 11–5, subject to seasonal changes.*

The **Tapping Reeve House and Law School,** America's first law school, was founded in 1773. Graduates include Aaron Burr and John C. Calhoun, and 130 former students have served as members of Congress. *South St., tel. 203/567–8919. Admission: $1 adults. Open mid-Apr.–mid-Nov., Thurs.–Mon. noon–4.*

The **Haight Vineyard and Winery** flourishes in Litchfield despite the town's often severe climate. Partake of vineyard walks, winery tours, and tastings. *Chestnut Hill Rd. (off Rte. 118, 1 mi east of town center), tel. 203/567–4045. Admission free. Open Mon.–Sat. 10:30–5, Sun. noon–5.*

The 4,000-acre **White Memorial Foundation** is the state's largest nature center and wildlife sanctuary, with 35 miles of hiking and horseback riding trails as well as seasonal activities ranging from cross-country skiing to fishing. There are also permanent bird-watching platforms, two family campgrounds, and the main conservation center, which offers nature exhibits, a library, gift shop, and special "touch-me" exhibits for children. *Rte. 202, tel. 203/567-0857 (foundation) or 203/567-0015 (conservation center). Admission to foundation grounds free; conservation center, $1 adults, 50¢ children under 12. Foundation grounds open daily; conservation center open spring–fall, Tues.–Sat. 8:30–4:30, Sun. 11–5; winter, Tues.–Sat. 9–5, Sun. 11–5.*

⑪ Probably the most notable event that has taken place in **Torrington** was the birth of the abolitionist John Brown in 1800. The natal site has long since disappeared, but the town's history has been well-preserved in the **Hotchkiss-Fyler House,** a Victorian mansion built in 1900, containing original family furnishings. The adjacent museum displays local artifacts. *192 Main St. (Rte. 8, Exit 43), tel. 203/482-8260.*

The area's great seasonal treat is the opening of **The Christmas Village,** in early December. Here, in Santa's Room, kids can sit on St. Nick's lap, make their requests, and then tour his workshop to see the elves hard at work. *Church St., tel. 203/ 489-2274. Admission free. Open early Dec.–Dec. 24, daily 1:30–4:30, 6–8:30. Children must be accompanied by an adult.*

Litchfield Hills for Free

Hitchcock Museum, Riverton

Kerosene Museum, Winchester

Holley Williams House, Lakeville

Haight Vineyard, Litchfield

What to See and Do with Children

The **Housatonic Railroad,** Canaan

White Memorial Conservation Center, Litchfield

Northeast Audubon Center, Sharon

Off the Beaten Track

The **Lourdes of Litchfield Shrine** (Rte. 118, Litchfield, tel. 203/ 567-8434) was built and is operated by the Montfort Missionaries. The 35-acre complex contains a replica of the famous grotto at Lourdes, France, as well as a remarkably commanding Stations of the Cross path. During Pilgrimage Season, May through mid-October, outdoor services are held on Sundays at 3 PM. Picnickers are welcome.

Lock Museum of America. Located on Route 6, in the center of
⑫ **Terryville,** about 13 miles southest of Litchfield, the museum stands on the site of the old Eagle Lock Company factory. Housing the largest collection of locks, keys, and ornate hardware in America, the museum includes among its possessions an 1846 combination padlock said to be worth $20,000 and an Egyptian-style tumbler lock that dates to the time of the Crusades. Group tours can be accommodated by calling ahead. *Rte. 6, Terryville, tel. 203/589-6359. Admission: $2. Open May–Oct., daily 1:30–4:30.*

American Clock and Watch Museum. Housed in the historic
❸ Miles Lewis house (1801) in **Bristol,** this collection of more than
3,000 New England–made clocks and watches is the most extensive of its kind in America. Guided tours and slide
orientations brief visitors on the measurement of time through
the ages and on the history of Bristol as the clock capital of
19th-century America. The striking of the hour by 300 clocks is
usually a big hit with kids. The museum is south of Route 6,
about 18 miles west of Hartford. *100 Maple St., Bristol, tel.
203/583–6070. Admission: $3 adults, $2.50 senior citizens,
$1.50 children 8–15, $8 families. Open Mar.–Nov., daily 11–5.
Closed Thanksgiving.*

Shopping

The best shopping in the area is for antiques and locally made
crafts. There are no large shopping malls in this part of the
state.

Antiques **Gilyard's Antiques** (Rte. 202, tel. 203/567–4204), a restored
Bantam house built in 1756 features 18th- and 19th-century country furniture and decorative items.

Gooseboro Brook Antiques (Old Turnpike Rd., tel. 203/567–
5245) sells antique furniture, baskets, quilts, stoneware, and
collectibles galore.

Richard Phelps Antiques and Design (Rte. 202, tel. 203/567–
4388) has a large selection of country furniture and furnishings.

Goshen **Goshen Antiques Center** (North St., tel. 203/491–2320), a historic 1830's house dating to the 1830s, now contains the varied
wares of 28 antiques dealers.

Tradewinds (Rte. 63, tel. 203/491–2141), in a house built in
1749, sells Oriental antiques and contemporary art works.

Kent **Molly Bloom Vintage Clothing** (tel. 203/927–3621) fills a
Beatrix Potter-style house with the threads of yesteryear as
well as accessories.

Woodbury **British Country Antiques** (50 Main St. N., tel. 203/263–5100)
specializes in polished pine and country furniture from England and France.

Country Loft Antiques (88 Main St. N., tel. 203/266–4500) has
English and French furniture, plus a collection of rare Oriental
rugs.

Monique Shay (92 Main St. S., tel. 203/263–3186) specializes in
Canadian country antiques.

Simpatico (345 Main St., tel. 203/266–0067) sells Spanish imports.

Crafts **Cornwall Bridge Pottery Store** (off Rte. 7, Cornwall Bridge, tel.
Cornwall 203/672–6545) sells its own pottery as well as glass by Simon
Pearce, fabric by Pierre Deux, and paintings by local artists.

Ian Ingersoll Cabinetmakers (Main St., West Cornwall, tel. 203/
672–6344), specializes in reproduction Shaker-style rockers
and chairs.

East Canaan The **Connecticut Woodcarvers Gallery** (Rte. 44, tel. 203/824–
0883) sells the work of professional woodcarvers—colonial ea-
gles, pineapples, birds, even clocks and mirrors.

Kent **Kent Carved Signs** (Kent Station Sq., tel. 203/927–3013) makes the handcarved signs you see throughout New England.

Housatonic Trading Co./Country Things (27 Kent Rd., tel. 203/927–4411), right on the river, has a selection of the folk art of more than 200 local craftspeople.

Food Stores **Pacific Isles Oriental Mart** (Rte. 202, Harris Plains, Litchfield, tel. 203/567–9857) can provide the ingredients for a superb Oriental meal.

Sports and Outdoor Activities

Camping **White Pines Campground** (232 Old North Rd., Winsted; tel. 203/379–0124), **Loan Oak Campsites** (Rte. 44, East Canaan, tel. 824–7051 or 800/422–2267), **Valley in the Pines** (Box 5, Goshen, tel. 203/491–2032), and **Hemlock Hill Camp Resort** (Box 368, Litchfield, tel. 203/567–0920), offer camping.

Canoeing **Clarke Outdoors** (Rte. 7, Box 302, West Cornwall 06796, tel. 203/672–6365) offers canoe and kayak rentals as well as 10-mile trips from Falls Village to Housatonic Meadow State Park. Flatwater and Class I and II whitewater equipment and instruction are available for beginners and experts.

Main Stream Canoe Corp. (Rte. 44, Box 448, New Hartford 06057, tel. 203/379–6657) does flatwater and whitewater day trips on the Farmington River, and moonlight trips on summer evenings. Equipment rentals are available.

Riverrunning Expeditions (Main St., Falls Village 06031, tel. 203/824–5579) services the Housatonic River crowd with rentals, instruction, guides, and trips that begin in Falls Village and end at Cornwall Bridge. Main St., Falls Village, 06031, tel. 203/824–5579 or 203/824–5286.

Tubing All it takes is an old automobile (or preferably larger vehicle) tire inner tube, and a body of water. But if you want a little adventure as well, try Tubing Through Satan's Kingdom, a 2-3 hour trip down the Farmington River starting in New Hartford, just east of Winsted, and ending in Canton. Tube rental, Coast Guard approved flotation device, and pickup at end of trip are part of the package provided by **North American Canoe Tours** (65 Black Point Rd., Niantic 06357, tel. 203/693–6465).

Fishing Trout season runs from mid-April through February, and a license is required.

Good places to pick up tackle and tips on what's biting are **Trips Sporting Goods and Variety Store** (7 Willow St., Torrington, tel. 203/489–2256), **Bantam Sportsman** (Lake Rd., Litchfield, tel. 203/567–8517), and **Housatonic Meadows Fly Shop** (Rte. 7 at Cornwall Bridge, Cornwall, tel. 203/672–6064).

Horseback Riding **Rustling Wind Stables** (Mountain Rd., Falls Village, tel. 203/824–7634) gives lessons and takes riders along the beautiful trails of Canaan Mountain.

Spectator Sports

Auto Racing **Lime Rock Park** (Rte. 112, Lakeville, tel. 203/435–2571 or 203/435–0896) has recently gained fame as Paul Newman's favorite course.

State Parks

Kent **Kent Falls** (Rte. 7) displays the state's most scenic cascade.

Macedonia Brook (Rte. 341) has two peaks with excellent views of the Catskills and Taconic mountains.

Litchfield **Mt. Tom** (Rte. 202) contains a large lake for swimmers and boaters on its 232 acres. There's also a stone tower at the summit of the 1,325-foot hill; the trail to reach it is a mile long.

Norfolk **Dennis Hill** (Rte. 272) is topped by a stone pavilion that was once the summer home of its previous owner. The view from the 1,626-foot summit is panoramic.

Haystack Mountain (Rte. 272) has a 1,716-foot hill, and on a clear day you can see the Long Island Sound from the stone tower.

Campbell Falls (Rte. 272), a natural cascade, is surrounded by picnic grounds and hiking trails.

Sharon **Housatonic Meadows** (Rte. 7) borders the Housatonic River and is a popular stopping-off point for hikers along the Appalachian Trail, which crosses nearby.

Torrington **Burr Pond** (Rte. 8) is the site of Mr. Borden's first condensed-milk factory in America. A well-marked trail circles the pond in the center of the 438-acre preserve. Admission charge.

John A. Minetto Park (Rte. 272), formerly known as Hall Meadow, is popular with cross-country skiiers in winter and picnickers at all times of the year.

Dining and Lodging

Canaan Dining **Cannery Cafe.** The Cajun influence of the owner and chef is re-
★ flected in the grilled shrimp served over angel-hair pasta with lemon-butter sauce; and the mixed grill, a combination of beef tenderloin, duck, Cajun sausage, and pork loin. Be sure to try the Chocolate Decadence, a small, rich, torte-like truffle with ganache icing, served with light raspberry cream. *85 Main St. (Rtes. 44 and 7), tel. 203/824–7333. Reservations advised. Dress: casual but neat. MC, V. No lunch Sun., closed Mon. and Dec. 25. Moderate.*

Cornwall Lodging **Cornwall Inn and Restaurant.** On busy Route 7, amid the Litchfield Hills, sits this barn-red cluster of buildings, the oldest of which dates to 1810. Renovations are always in progress, and some rooms reflect a wise decorator's touch in the selection of country-style furnishings. The least appealing accommodations are in the so-called motel, on the far side of the parking lot. Individual suites are also available as well as two-bedroom apartments with complete kitchen. *Rte. 7, Cornwall Bridge, 06754, tel. 203/672–6884. 17 rooms with bath. Facilities: restaurant, outdoor pool. MC, V. Moderate.*

Kent Dining **Fife 'n Drum.** Renowned deservedly for gracious dining, this restaurant's exposed brick and dark, wood-paneled walls are warmed by candlelit tables where tableside preparation is a specialty. Live piano music supplies a gentle counterpoint to a superb *filet au poivre* or Dover sole *almondine.* Subdued gasps frequently greet the Grand Marnier soufflé. *Rte. 7, Main St.,* *tel. 203/927–3509. Reservations advised. Dress: casual. AE, CB, DC, MC, V. Closed Tues. Expensive.*

Milk Pail Restaurant. This restaurant-cum-art-gallery features a different exhibit every month, usually by local artists, and prides itself on unembellished American cooking. Freshness is the byword (the kitchen boasts neither a can opener nor a freezer). Maybe it's the fresh ingredients that give zest to the broiled bluefish with apple-onion topping. During the day, request a table in the sun room overlooking a rolling meadow and the playing fields of the Kent School. *Rte. 7, tel. 203/927–3136. Reservations advised. Dress: casual but neat. AE, DC, MC, V. No dinner Sun. Closed Mon. Moderate–Expensive.*

Kent Station Restaurant. What may once have been a large waiting room now comprises this bistro specializing in fresh American food with an international flourish. The bare wooden floor and the schoolhouse lights suspended from the high ceiling provide a simple setting for favorites like shrimp Leo— broiled shrimp with prosciutto, tomato, Madeira, and garlic butter. Soak up the tasty sauce with home-baked bread. *Rte. 7, Main St., tel. 203/927–4751. Reservations advised. Dress: casual. AE, MC, V. Closed Wed., Thurs. Inexpensive–Moderate.*

Lakeville Dining **The Woodland.** Behind the plain roadhouse exterior lurks an up-to-date setting for exemplary New American cuisine. Though billed as a "country restaurant," chefs Jon Everin and Robert Peters bring an urbane touch to favorites such as grilled Nova Scotia salmon with Key-lime mustard hollandaise, and sautéed chicken with leeks and wild mushrooms. For peaceful dining, steer clear of the rowdy bar during major sporting events. *Rte. 41, tel. 203/435–0578. Reservations advised for 5 or more. Dress: casual. MC, V. No lunch Sun. Closed Mon. Expensive.*

Lakeville Lodging **Interlaken Inn and Resort.** Interlaken's 26 acres offer all the facilities for a self-contained holiday, including water sports at the unpronounceable Lake Wononscopumic, directly across the highway from the resort. In addition to standard, comfortably furnished rooms in the main building, a handful of separate structures, mostly clever conversions of 19th-century mansions, contains rooms with more charm. The attractive Vineyard restaurant is known for its rack of lamb and puff-pastry desserts, and the popular lounge features live entertainment and dancing nightly. *Rte. 112, 06039, tel. 203/435–9878 or 800/222–2909. 73 rooms with bath, 8 suites. Facilities: restaurant, lounge, outdoor heated pool, 2 all-weather lighted tennis courts, pitch-and-putt golf and adjacent 9-hole golf course, recreation center/health club, saunas; rowboats, canoes, and paddleboats provided at lake. AE, MC, V. Expensive.*

Wake Robin Inn. A country inn since 1913, the original, Georgian-Colonial edifice built in 1896 has been extensively renovated. At the end of a winding driveway, 15 acres harbor an abundance of wildflowers, including the inn's signature *trillium*, the dark crimson "Wake Robin." Rooms in the main house are the most desirable, each tastefully decorated with period furnishings such as sleigh beds, spool beds, wash stands, and odd-looking though comfortable chairs. The annex, undergoing renovation in 1990, and the motel offer more basic rooms. The Savarin dining room features live easy-listening and piano music during dinner hours. *Rte. 41, 06039, tel. 203/435–2515. 41 rooms with bath, 2 suites. Facilities: restaurant,* *breakfast room, sauna, outdoor pool. AE, MC, V. Moderate–Expensive.*

Iron Masters Motor Inne. Despite the management's well-meaning attempts to create a contemporary refuge, the long strip of park-in-front units betrays its 1950s sensibilities. Some of the hand-hewn beams in the gift shop that shares the lobby date back to the original structure, circa 1675, but all else is basic roadside-motel, though clean and well-maintained. *Main St., Rte. 44, 06039, tel. 203/435–9844. 26 rooms with bath. Facilities: outdoor heated pool. AE, DC, MC, V. Inexpensive–Moderate.*

Litchfield Dining **Toll Gate Hill Inn and Restaurant.** The 18th-century dining rooms are a perfect setting for the modern New England cuisine. While the menu changes daily to reflect the availability of fresh produce, two favorite entrées are the Toll Gate shellfish pie (shrimp, lobster, and scallops in a light sauce, baked in puff pastry) and grilled pork loin with white beans, escarole, and tomatoes. *Rte. 202, tel. 203/567–4545. Reservations advised. Dress: casual. AE, DC, MC, V. Closed Tues. Nov.–Mar. Expensive.*

Litchfield Lodging **Toll Gate Hill Inn and Restaurant.** Located on the old stagecoach route to Albany, midway between Torrington and Litchfield, the original structure of 1745 is sheltered from the busy highway by thick evergreens. Rooms in the main building and the old schoolhouse a few steps away are decorated with proper respect for Colonial fashion, for the inn is listed in the National Register of Historic Places; many rooms have canopy beds and working fireplaces. A new structure with 10 rooms is scheduled for completion in 1990. *Rte. 202, 06759, tel. 203/567–4545. 10 rooms with bath. Facilities: dining room. AE, DC, MC, V. Rates include Continental breakfast. Expensive.*

Litchfield Inn. Set back from the road, this modern inn attempts to capture the Colonial elegance of the stately homes that line Main Street. Telling details betray the architectural newness, but inside there's a stronger sense of a bygone era. A gleaming 9-foot chandelier hangs in the well of a delicately curved staircase that leads to the guest rooms. Rooms are furnished with Hitchcock and Colonial reproductions, fine fabrics, and wallcoverings. Among the reception rooms on the main floor, a formal sitting room and tack room has saddlery, harness, and a huge fireplace that's always ablaze in chilly weather. Wood beams and wainscoting are features of the main dining room, the Terrace Room has greenery, and there's an English-style pub. *Rte. 202, 06759, tel. 203/567–4503. 31 rooms with bath. Facilities: 3 restaurants, lounge (with weekend entertainment), piano bar, meeting rooms. AE, CB, D, DC, MC, V. Moderate–Expensive.*

Salisbury Lodging **White Hart Inn.** Following a total renovation of its interior, this
★ celebrated country inn, built in 1815, reopened in February 1990. Both the main building and the adjacent Gideon Smith House are furnished throughout with Chippendale reproductions and country pine pieces. Waverly prints on wall coverings and fabrics complement soft rose or muted blue carpeting; period brass lamps and fixtures contribute to the Colonial ambience. In the pleasantly dim Tap Room, original artifacts and clever carpentry combine to bridge past and present. *Junction Rtes. 44 and 41N; Box 385, 06068, tel. 203/435–0030, fax 203/ 435–0040. 23 rooms with bath, 3 suites. Facilities: restau-*

rant, lounge, tap room, banquet facilities. AE, CB, D, DC, MC, V. Expensive–Very Expensive.

Under Mountain Inn. The nearest neighbors of this white-clapboard farmhouse north of Main Street are the horses grazing in the field across the road. Indoors there are antiques, knickknacks, and homey objets d'art in every corner of the house, and the hospitality has a pronounced British flavor: an English newspaper, a properly brewed cup of tea, an authentic steak-and-kidney pie. *482 Under Mountain Rd. (Rte. 41), 06068, tel. 203/435–0242. 7 rooms, 6 with bath. Facilities: walking trail. No pets. AE, D, MC, V. May be closed mid-Mar.–mid-Apr. Expensive.*

Ragamont Inn. The tall white pillars of the 160-year-old downtown edifice signal a cozy country inn and fine restaurant. Five rooms are furnished in the Colonial style with assorted antiques; three contemporary rooms in the annex have king-size beds, color TV, and air-conditioning; a small suite has a charming sitting room with a fireplace. *Main St., 06068, tel. 203/435–2372. 9 rooms with bath. Facilities: restaurant. No credit cards. Closed Nov.–Apr. Moderate.*

Yesterday's Yankee Bed & Breakfast. Three upstairs guest rooms share one bath in this Cape Colonial home built in 1744. Hearty breakfasts (with home-baked muffins, rolls, or bread) are served at a large trestle table before the fireplace. *Main St. (Rte. 44), Box 442, 06068, tel. 203/435–9539. 3 rooms. Facilities: box lunches prepared. No pets. MC, V. Moderate.*

Torrington Dining
★

Venetian. The frescoes on the walls cry Venice; the cuisine is described as Roma-Napoli (and prepared with a knowing touch). Freshly made pasta gives authenticity to the linguine *alla putanesca* and the gnocchi. For dessert, *tiramisu* ("pick me up") is a bracing blend of mascarpone, eggs, rum, marsala, espresso, chocolate, and biscuits. *52 E. Main St., tel. 203/489–8592. Reservations advised. Dress: casual but neat. AE, MC, V. No lunch weekends. Closed Tues. Moderate–Expensive.*

West Cornwall Dining
★

Freshfields. This dining oasis is set beside a covered bridge, in a picture-perfect hamlet between the Housatonic and a mill stream. "Cozy-contemporary" best describes the spacious dining areas that spill onto the deck above the stream. The kitchen provides a selection of subtly flavored delights, including chunky tomato-basil bisque; grilled swordfish with lime butter and black-bean sauce; and lemon mousse served with fresh berries. *Rte. 128 (off Rte. 7, directly across bridge), tel. 203/672–6601. Reservations advised. Dress: casual. AE, MC, V. Closed Tues., one week in Mar., Dec. 25. Expensive.*

Winsted Dining
★

Jessie's Restaurant. Home-style Italian cooking rises high above the ordinary in this converted turn-of-the-century clapboard house with enough separate rooms to offer choice seating for nonsmokers. Try the pasta primavera (the pasta of your choice served with fresh vegetables gently sautéed with garlic) or Joanie's veal (lightly sautéed in marsala, with mushrooms, prosciutto, and shrimp). So many customers have asked for the recipe for spicy clam soup with homemade sausage and tomato that copies are now available upon request. There's a lounge upstairs and a garden for dining al fresco. *142 Main St., tel. 203/379–0109. Reservations advised. Dress: casual. AE, MC, V. Closed Tues. Inexpensive–Moderate.*

The Arts

Film   The newest way to watch movies in public is seated around small tables having a light meal, snack, or drinks. The **Gilson Cafe and Cinema** (354 Main St., Rte. 44, Winsted, tel. 203/379–5108) a refurbished Art Deco movie house, keeps the service going unobtrusively during the movie, every evening from Tuesday through Sunday. Because alcohol is served, you must be 21 or older to attend.

Music   **Music Mountain** (Falls Village, tel. 203/496–1222) presents chamber music concerts on weekends with distinguished guest artists such as the Manhattan String Quartet, from mid-June to mid-September.

The former Battell–Stoeckel estate in Norfolk is the site of the **Yale School of Music and Art** summer session and the **Norfolk Chamber Music Festival** (tel. 203/432–1966 or 203/542–5537). Friday and Saturday evenings, and some Sunday afternoons, such groups as the Tokyo String Quartet, the New York Woodwind Quintet, and the New York Brass Quintet make music in an extraordinary concert "shed."

Theater   **The Warner Theatre** (69 Main St., Torrington, tel. 203/489–7180 or 203/489–1219), a former Art Deco movie palace, presents live entertainment, including Broadway musicals, the repertory season of the local Nutmeg Ballet, and concerts by touring pop and classical musicians.

The Sharon Playhouse (Rte. 343, Sharon, tel. 203/364–5909), one of the country's oldest summer theaters, has played host to many stars doing the straw-hat circuit. It offers a warm-weather season of Broadway hits and occasional pre-Broadway tryouts.

Nightlife

For most visitors to the northwest corner of the state, after-dark entertainment means listening to the bug-zapper on the front porch, but Torrington's **Water Street Station** (131 Water St., tel. 203/496–9872) offers live entertainment Thursday through Saturday. Local and national acts are featured, especially rock, R & B, and jazz groups.

The Coast: Southeastern Connecticut

The urban buildup that characterizes the Connecticut coast west of New Haven appears to dissipate as you drive east from the New Haven hub on I-95; there are long stretches here where you won't see even a single manmade interruption. Activities along the eastern shore center on Long Island Sound, which opens to the Atlantic Ocean in the northeast, and where saltwater anglers go after the big ones.

Important Addresses and Numbers

Visitor Information   **Shoreline Visitors Bureau** (115 State Sq., Guilford 06437, tel. 203/397–5250).

Southeastern Connecticut Tourism District (27 Masonic St., Box 89, New London 06320, tel. 203/444–2206 or 800/222–6783).

Emergencies **Lawrence & Memorial Hospital** (365 Montauk Ave., New London, tel. 203/442–0711).

Getting Around Southeastern Connecticut

By Car I–95 is the principal route through the coastal area, from New Haven to the Rhode Island border.

By Train **Connecticut Department of Transportation** (tel. 800/243–2855) has commuter rail service (Monday to Friday, westbound in the morning, eastbound in the evening) between New Haven, Branford, Guilford, Madison, Clinton, Westbrook, and Old Saybrook.

By Bus **Southeastern Area Rapid Transit** (tel. 203/886–2631) has local bus service in the eastern half of the area, between East Lyme and Stonington.

Exploring Southeastern Connecticut

Numbers in the margin correspond with the numbered points of interest on the Southeastern Connecticut map.

❶ A tour of coastal Connecticut resumes just south of I–95, 3 miles east of New Haven, in the town of **East Haven.** The principal attraction here is the **Shore Line Trolley Museum,** which houses more than 100 classic trolleys, among them the oldest rapid transit car and the world's first electric freight locomotive. Admission includes unlimited rides aboard a vintage trolley on a 3-mile track. *17 River St. (Exits 51N, 52S from I–95), tel. 203/467–6927. Admission: $3.50 adults, $2.50 senior citizens, $1.50 children 2–11. Open June–Aug., daily 11–5; May, Sept., Oct., Dec., weekends 11–5; Apr., Nov., Sun. 11–5. Closed Dec. 25.*

❷ **Branford** is 4 miles east of East Haven on Route 1, which becomes Main Street in Branford. Here, the restored two-story clapboard **Harrison House,** built in 1774, has a fine collection of late 18th- and early 19th-century furnishings and a Colonial herb garden. *124 Main St., tel. 203/488–4828. Admission free. Open June–Sept., Wed.–Sat. 2–5.*

Continue down the road and you'll come upon **Bittersweet Farm,** where the **Branford Craft Village** is located. These 85 acres have been a working farm for over 150 years, though the sale of a wide variety of crafts made on the premises predominates today. There's a small play area on the grounds, and a café serves refreshments. *779 E. Main St., tel. 203/488–4689. Admission free. Open Tues.–Sat. 11–5, Sun. noon–5.*

❸ Leave I–95 at Exit 56 and follow Leetes Island Road south to the village of Stony Creek, the departure point for cruises to the **Thimble Islands.** This group of 365 tiny islands was named for their abundance of thimbleberries, which are similar to gooseberries. Legend has it that Captain Kidd buried pirate gold on one island. Two sightseeing vessels vie for your patronage, the *Volsunga III* (tel. 203/481–2234 or 203/488–9978) and the *Sea Mist* (tel. 203/481–4841). Both offer daily trips from early May through Columbus Day, departing from the Town Dock at the end of Thimble Island Road.

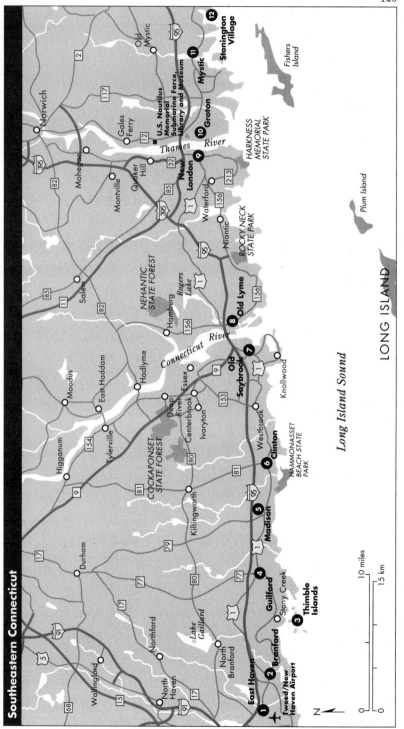

Southeastern Connecticut

LONG ISLAND

Long Island Sound

Fishers Island

Plum Island

Stonington Village 12

Mystic 11

Groton 10

U.S. Nautilus Memorial Force, Submarine Library and Museum

Old Mystic

Norwich

Gales Ferry

Thames River

New London 9

HARKNESS MEMORIAL STATE PARK

Waterford

Quaker Hill

Mohegan

Montville

Niantic

ROCKY NECK STATE PARK

Salem

NEHANTIC STATE FOREST

Rogers Lake

Hamburg

Old Lyme 8

Old Saybrook 7

Connecticut River

Moodus

East Haddam

Hadlyme

Essex

Deep River

Centerbrook

Ivoryton

Knollwood

Higganum

Tylerville

COCKAPONSET STATE FOREST

Killingworth

Westbrook

Clinton 6

HAMMONASSET BEACH STATE PARK

Durham

Madison 5

Guilford 4

Lake Gaillard

Stony Creek

Thimble Islands 3

Wallingford

Northford

North Branford

North Haven

Branford 2

East Haven 1

Tweed/New Haven Airport

N

0   10 miles
0   15 km

➍ **Guilford** is the next stop off I–95, at Exit 58. Among the well-preserved houses surrounding the village green is New England's oldest stone house, built by Reverend Henry Whitfield, an English vicar who settled here in 1639. The **Whitfield House Museum** was originally a village stronghold and meeting hall as well as the minister's home. The late-medieval-style building houses a collection of 17th-century furnishings. *Old Whitfield St., tel. 203/453–2457 or 203/566–3005. Admission: $3 adults, $1.50 senior citizens and children. Open Apr.–Nov., Wed.–Sun. 10–5, Dec.–May, Wed.–Sun. 10–4. Closed Thanksgiving, Dec. 15–Jan. 15.*

In the same neighborhood, on Boston Street, is the **Hyland House,** a Colonial saltbox built in 1666, with five fireplaces and hand-hewn floorboards, still held together by the original handwrought nails and bolts. A 1720 addition contains a sophisticated Bolection molding around the fireplace. *84 Boston St., tel. 203/453–9477. Admission: $1.50. Open June–Sept., 10–4:30. Closed Mon.*

Farther down the street is another Colonial saltbox, the **Thomas Griswold House,** built in 1774, displaying clothing, furniture, farm tools, books, and photographs of early residents. There's also a restored blacksmith shop and Colonial garden. *171 Boston St., tel. 203/453–3176 or 203/453–5452. Admission: $1 adults, 50¢ children 12–18. Open mid-June–mid-Sept., Tues.–Sun. 11–4.*

➎ Continuing eastward to **Madison,** summertime traffic thickens as the crowds head for the sand and surf of **Hammonasset Beach State Park** (I–95, Exit 62, tel. 203/245–2785), the largest of the state's shoreline parks. The 2-mile beach along the eastern edge of town has facilities for swimming, camping, and picnicking. A large concession stand offers the usual beachfront food and beverages.

Back in town is the **Allis-Bushnell House and Museum,** built about 1785. Along with period rooms containing antique furnishings and costumes, you'll find an early doctor's office with period medical equipment. *853 Boston Post Rd. (I–95, Exit 61), tel. 203/245–4567 or 203/245–7891. Admission free. Open June–Labor Day, Wed.–Sun. 1–4.*

➏ The Marquis de Lafayette stayed at the **Stanton House** in **Clinton,** in 1824, in a bed still displayed in its original surroundings. Built about 1790, the Stanton House was once a general store and now exhibits items it might have sold back then as well as a large collection of antique American and Staffordshire dinnerware. *63 E. Main St., Clinton, (I–95, Exit 63), tel. 203/669–2132. Admission free. Open June–Sept., Tues.–Sun. 2–5, and by appt.*

➐ Located on the western side of the mouth of the Connecticut River, **Old Saybrook** was once a lively shipbuilding and fishing town. Today the bustle comes mostly from its many summer vacationers.

The Georgian-style **General William Hart House,** once the residence of a prosperous merchant and politician, was built about 1767. One of its eight corner fireplaces is decorated with Sadler and Green transfer-print tiles that illustrate Aesop's fables. *350 Main St. (I–95, Exit 67 or Rte. 9, Exit 2), tel. 203/388–*

*2622. Admission free (donation suggested). Open late May–
Sept., Fri.–Sun. 12:30–4.*

8 On the other side of the river mouth is **Old Lyme,** renowned
among art lovers throughout the world. Central to its reputation is the **Florence Griswold Museum,** the former home of a
great patron of the arts. Built in 1817, the mansion housed an
art colony that included Willard Metcalfe, Clark Voorhees, and
Childe Hassam. Many of their works are still on display here,
along with early furnishings and decorative items. *96 Lyme St.
(I–95, Exit 70, 1 block west), tel. 203/434–5542. Admission:
$2 adults. Open June–Oct., Tues.–Sat. 10–5, Sun. 1–5; Nov.–
May, Wed.–Sun. 1–5. Closed Jan. 1, Easter, Dec. 25.*

A few steps away is the **Lyme Academy of Fine Arts,** housed in a
Federal-style former private home built in 1817. Today it's a
popular gallery featuring works by contemporary artists. *84
Lyme St., tel. 203/434–5232. Admission free. Open weekdays
9–4:30, weekends by appt.*

9 **New London** is widely known as the home of the **U.S. Coast
Guard Academy.** The 100-acre cluster of traditional redbrick
buildings includes a museum and visitors' pavilion with a gift
shop. When the three-masted training bark the USCGC *Eagle*
is in port, you may board from Friday to Sunday, noon to 5 PM.
*I–95, Exit 83 (1 mi north), tel. 203/444–8270. Admission free.
Academy open daily. Museum open weekdays, also weekends
May–Oct. Visitors' pavilion open May–Oct., daily 9–5.*

Across from the academy entrance, step back in time at the **Lyman Allyn Art Museum,** with its small, selective collection of
art and antiques—including an impressive array of dolls, dollhouses, and toys—dating from the 18th and 19th centuries. *625
Williams St., tel. 203/443–2545. Admission free. Open Tues.–
Sat. 11–5, Sun. 1–5. Closed major holidays.*

Just off Williams Street is the **Thames Science Center,** a
regional science museum with a permanent "Time and the River" exhibit and changing presentations focusing on the river
basin, such as "Birds of the Basin." *Gallows La. (I–95, Exit
83), tel. 203/442–0391. Admission: $1 adults, 50¢ children.
Open Mon.–Sat. 9–5, Sun. 1–5. Closed major holidays.*

The **Joshua Hempstead House,** built in 1678, is the oldest house
in New London; today it showcases early American furnishings. Nearly a century later, Nathaniel Hempstead built the
nearby cut-stone house and its outdoor stone beehive bake
oven, where occasional demonstrations of open-hearth cooking
are given. *11 Hempstead St. (I–95, Exit 84S, 83N), tel. 203/
443–7949 or 203/247–8996. Admission: $2 adults, $1 senior citizens, 50¢ children 5–18. Open mid-May–mid-Oct., Tues.–
Sun. 1–5.*

Nathan Hale Schoolhouse, where the state's Revolutionary
War hero taught prior to his military service, is located at the
foot of Captain's Walk, the pedestrians-only main street in the
heart of town. *No phone. Admission free. Open mid-June–
Aug., weekdays, 10–3.*

Other highlights of **Captain's Walk** are a beautifully restored
19th-century train station designed by H. H. Richardson, and
the **Shaw Mansion,** a stone residence with unique, paneled-
cement fireplace walls. Built in 1756, it was visited during the
Revolutionary War by Washington and Lafayette, to the de-

light of the Shaw family, whose furnishings and portraits abound. *11 Blinman St., tel. 203/443–1209. Admission: $1 adults, 50¢ children 6–12. Open Tues.–Sat. 1–4. Closed major holidays.*

The **Monte Cristo Cottage,** in the downtown area, was the boyhood home of the playwright Eugene O'Neill and was named for his actor-father's greatest role, as the literary count. The setting figures in two of O'Neill's landmark plays, *Ah, Wilderness!* and *Long Day's Journey into Night. 325 Pequot Ave., tel. 203/443–0051. Admission: $3 adults, $1 students and children. Open Apr.–mid-Dec., weekdays 1–4.*

During the summer, sightseers turn into beachgoers at **Ocean Beach Park,** a 3-mile strip of shoreline that offers a choice of ocean or saltwater pool. Children have their own pool and playground, complete with triple waterslide. There's also miniature golf, a picnic area, mechanical rides, a games arcade, food concessions, and a sit-down dining area. *Foot of Ocean Beach, tel. 203/447–3031, or 800/962–0284 in CT. Admission: $1 adults, 50¢ children 5–16. Open Memorial Day weekend–Labor Day, daily 9 AM–10 PM.*

🔟 After crossing the river to **Groton,** you're in submarine country. There's no escaping the impact of the **U.S. submarine base** on the area. Just outside the entrance to the base is the **U.S. Nautilus Memorial/Submarine Force Library and Museum.** The world's first nuclear-powered submarine, the *Nautilus,* launched from Groton in 1954, is now permanently berthed here and welcomes you aboard. The adjacent library-museum contains submarine memorabilia, artifacts, and displays, including working periscopes and controls. *Rte. 12 (I–95, Exit 86), tel. 203/449–3174. Admission free. Open Apr. 15–Oct. 14, Wed.–Mon. 9–5; Oct. 15–Apr. 14, Wed.–Mon. 9–3:30. Closed 3rd week of Mar., 1st week of June, 3rd week of Sept., 2nd week of Dec., Jan. 1, Thanksgiving, Dec. 25.*

The best way to see the subs is by boat. The *River Queen II* conducts sightseeing and sunset cruises past the *Nautilus; the sub base; the Eagle* across the river when it's in home port; the Coast Guard Academy; a panoply of local craft; and whatever other ships are at berth. Evenings get a little jazzier with dinner and Dixieland as part of the scene. *193 Thames St. (departs from Harbour Inn), tel. 203/445–9516. Harbor tour fare: $6 adults, $3.50 children. Tours: Memorial Day weekend–mid-June, mid-Sept.–Columbus Day, weekends 11:15–3; mid-June–Labor Day, daily 10–3.*

Project Oceanology offers another way to explore the wonders of the briny deep aboard the **Enviro-Lab,** a 50-foot oceanographic research vessel. It's a great way to discover more about marine life, navigation, seawater, and the sea bottom during a 2½-hour cruise that takes you past lighthouses, islands, and submarines. *University of CT, Avery Point Campus, tel. 203/445–9007. Admission: $11 adults, $9 children. Cruises late June–Labor Day, Sun.–Fri. 10 and 1, Sat. 9, noon, and 3; Sept.–early Oct., weekends 10 and 1.*

⓫ A few miles down I–95 or Route 1 take you from state-of-the-art marine biology, to **Mystic's** earlier perspective on the seven seas. Some people think the name of the town is **The Mystic Seaport,** and it very well might be, given the lure of the museum that goes by that name. It is the nation's largest maritime museum, and its 17 riverfront acres feature authentic 19th-century sailing vessels you can board; a maritime village with historic homes; working craftspeople who give demonstrations; steamboat cruises; and small boat rentals. There are seasonal special events, shops, restaurants, and art exhibits. *50 Greenmanville Ave. (I–95, Exit 90, Rte. 27), tel. 203/572–0711. Admission: $12 adults, $6 children 5–18. Open May–Oct., 9–5, Nov.–Apr., 9–4. Closed Dec. 25.*

At the same I–95 exit, you're steps away from **Olde Mistick Village,** a recreation of what an American village might have looked like at about 1720. It truly is picturesque, but it's also quite commercial, with as much emphasis on the stores selling crafts, clothing, souvenirs, and food, as on the country church and old barn. *Coogan Blvd. (I–95, Exit 90), tel. 203/536–4941. Admission free. Open Mon.–Sat. 10–5:30, Sun. noon–5:30.*

Within strolling distance is the **Mystic Marinelife Aquarium** with more than 6,000 specimens and 49 live exhibits of sea life. Seal Island, a 2.5-acre outdoor exhibit, features seals and sea lions from around the world. Dolphins and sea lions perform every hour on the half hour at the marine theater. *55 Coogan Blvd. (I–95, Exit 90), tel. 203/536–3323. Admission: $7 adults, $6 senior citizens, $4 children 5–17. Open July–Labor Day, 9–5:30; Labor Day–June, 9–4:40. Closed Jan. 1, Thanksgiving, Dec. 25.*

Also in the cluster of attractions in this area is **Whitehall,** a country mansion, dating to the 1770s, that has been restored with authentic furnishings. The kitchen contains a rare brick "trimer arch" supporting the hearthstone of the fireplace in the room directly above. *Rte. 27 (I–95, Exit 90), tel. 203/536–2428. Admission: $2 adults, 50¢ children 6–12. Open May–Oct., Tues.–Sun. 2–4.*

Take Route 27 south along the Mystic River and you'll come to Main Street. Cross over to West Main Street and you're in an area of remarkably well-preserved, beautiful 19th-century houses.

⑫ Back on I–95 and heading east again, **Stonington Village** is a few miles south of the highway. Explore the historic buildings that surround the green and continue down Water Street to the **Old Lighthouse Museum** at the very tip. The granite building with its octagonal-towered lighthouse was the first government-operated facility of its kind in the state. Built in 1823, it was moved to higher ground in 1840. Today you'll find a wealth of displays related to shipping, whaling, and early village life. Climb to the top of the tower for a spectacular view of the sound. *7 Water St. (I–95, Exit 91), tel. 203/535–1440. Admission: $2 adults, $1 children 6–12. Open May–Oct., Tues.–Sun., 11:30–4:30.*

Within the same borough are the **Stonington Vineyards,** a small coastal winery that has grown premium vinifera and French hybrid grape varieties since 1979. Look over the winery, stroll through the vineyard and taste samples of the wines on sale. *Taugwonk Rd. (I–95, Exit 91), tel. 203/535–1222. Admission free. Open Tues.–Sun. 11–5.*

Just before you reach the Rhode Island border on I–95, you come to the town of **North Stonington** and the **Crosswoods Vineyards,** a modern winery with 35 acres of vineyards on a plateau overlooking the waters of Long Island Sound. *75 Chester Maine Rd. (I–95, Exit 92), tel. 203/535–2205. Admission free. Open daily noon–4:30.*

Southeastern Connecticut for Free

Military Historians Headquarters Museum has a large collection of American military uniforms, including unit insignias and completely restored and operable vehicles that range from a World War II Weasel to a Jeep used in Vietnam. *N. Main St., Westbrook (I–95, Exit 65), tel. 203/399–9460. Admission free. Open Tues.–Fri. 8:30–4.*

Milestone Energy Center at the Milestone Nuclear Power Station shows exhibits on nuclear and other energy sources and features computer energy games and multimedia programs. *278 Main St., Niantic (I–95, Exit 74), tel. 203/444–4234. Admission free. Open summer, Mon.–Tues. 9–4, Wed.–Fri. 9–7, weekends noon–5; other seasons, weekdays 9–4.*

Ebenezer Avery House, a center-chimney Colonial home built by one of the great local Revolutionary War heroes, has a restored kitchen and a weaving room that are particularly well furnished. *Ft. Griswold, Groton (I–95, Exit 85), tel. 203/446–9257. Admission free. Open Memorial Day–Labor Day, weekends 1–5.*

What to See and Do with Children

Shore Line Trolley Museum, East Haven

Thames Science Center, New London

The Mystic Seaport, Mystic

Mystic Marinelife Aquarium, Mystic

Memory Lane Doll and Toy Museum schedules free entertainment for kids on weekends from May to mid-October. *Olde Mistick Village, Rte. 27, Mystic, tel. 203/536–1641 or 203/536–4941. Admission free. Open Mon.–Sat. 10–5:30, Sun. noon–5:30.*

Shopping

The New Haven and New London areas have typical concentrations of shopping centers. Downtown Mystic boasts a more interesting collection of shops, many of them offering traditional resort items, and Olde Mistick Village, with street performers and a group of factory outlet stores nearby.

Mystic
Art

Trade Winds Gallery (20 W. Main St., tel. 203/536–0119) shows rare prints and antique maps.

Records

Mystic Disc (10 Steamboat Wharf, tel. 203/536–1312) has the look of a hole-in-the-wall operation and stocks out-of-print albums; musicians stop by here between gigs.

Olde Mistick
Village
Gifts

Franklin's General Store (tel. 203/536–1038) carries New England products, including Vermont maple syrup and Vermont cheddar, and an assortment of pottery.

Toys

The Toy Soldier (tel. 203/536–1554) shows and sells both miniature soldiers and dolls.

Mystic Factory Outlets Across the road from Olde Mistick Village are the **Mystic Factory Outlets** (Coogan Blvd., tel. 203/443–4788), nearly two dozen stores offering discounts on famous-name clothing and other merchandise.

Sports and Outdoor Activities

Biking **Haley Farm** (Brook St., off Rte. 215, Groton) offers an 8-mile bike trail that winds through shoreline farm property.

Camping **Riverdale Farm Campsites** (22 River Rd., Killingworth, tel. 203/669–5388 or 203/663–2712), **River Road Campground** (13 River Rd., Clinton, tel. 203/669–2238), and **Seaport Campground** (Rte. 184, Old Mystic, tel. 203/536–4044) have camping facilities.

Fishing Party fishing boats (or head boats or open boats) take passengers for half-day, full-day, and some overnight trips at fees from $20 to $35 per person; tuna-fishing trips may cost as much as $100 a day. Open-boat providers include **Niantic Beach Marina** (Niantic, tel. 203/443–3662 or 203/739–9296), **Mijoy Dock** (Waterford, tel. 203/443–0663), and **Hel-Cat Dock** (Groton, tel. 203/535–2066 or 203/535–3200).

Private charter boats, whose rentals range from $275 to $375 for a half day, to $450 and up for a full day, are available from **Boats, Inc. Dock** (Waterford, tel. 203/442–9959), **Niantic Fisheries** (Waterford, tel. 203/739–7419), **City Pier** (New London, tel. 203/767–0495 or 203/443–8331), and **Brewer Yacht Yard** (Mystic, tel. 203/536–3259).

Fitness **New London Sports Complex** (145 State Pier Rd., tel. 203/442–0588), a vast, state-of-the-art facility, has a complete Nautilus center, free weights, an aerobics exercise studio, a cardiovascular fitness center, a basketball gym, a volleyball court, racquetball courts, an indoor track, wallyball, and a tanning salon.

Water Sports Surfboards and sailboards can be rented from **Action Sports** (324 W. Main St., Branford, tel. 203/481–5511), **Sunset Bay Surf Shop** (192 Boston Post Rd., Westbrook, tel. 203/669–7873), **Freedom Sailboards** (375 Middlesex Tpke., Old Saybrook, tel. 203/388–0322), **Sailways** (2 Pearl St., Mystic, tel. 203/572–0727), and **Ocean Flyer Wind Surfing** (Rte. 1, Pawcatuck, tel. 203/599–5694).

Boats can be rented or chartered from **Sea Sprite Charters** (113 Harbor Pkwy., Clinton, tel. 203/669–9613), **Colvin Yachts** (Hammock Dock Rd., Westbrook–Old Saybrook, tel. 203/399–9300), **Cardinal Cove Marina** (Rte. 1, Mystic, tel. 203/535–0060), **Shaffer's Boat Livery** (Mason's Island Rd., Mystic, tel. 203/536–8713), and **Dodson Boat Yard** (184 Water St., Stonington, tel. 203/535–1507).

State Parks

Selden Neck (Lyme, no phone). This 528-acre island park, located in the Connecticut River, is accessible only by water; primitive campsites are available May–September.

Harkness Memorial State Park (Rte. 213, Waterford, tel. 203/443–5725). This former summer estate of the Harkness family contains formal gardens, picnic areas, a beach for strolling and fishing (not swimming), in addition to the Italian villa-style mansion, Eolia. Come for the summer music festival in July and August.

Ft. Griswold State Park (Monument St. and Park Ave., Groton, I–95, Exit 85, tel. 203/445–1729). Battle emplacements and historic displays mark the site of the massacre of American defenders by Benedict Arnold's British troops in 1781. From the top of the memorial tower you get a sweeping view of the shoreline.

Beaches

Rocky Neck State Park (Rte. 156, Niantic, I–95, Exit 72, tel. 203/739–5471). This mile-long crescent beach is one of the finest saltwater bathing sites in the state. Facilities include family campgrounds, picnicking sites and shelter, food concessions, fishing, and public bath houses.

Ocean Beach Park (Ocean Ave., New London, I–95, Exit 82A N/83S), tel. 203/447–3031 or 800/962–0284, in CT). Swim in the waters of Long Island Sound or in the Olympic-size outdoor pool with a triple waterslide. The kids have their own pool and playground, and everyone can enjoy the amusement park, miniature golf, arcade, boardwalk, picnic area, food concessions, and restaurant with an ocean view.

Dining and Lodging

Groton Lodging   **Thames Harbour Inn.** Located right on the bank of the Thames River, the inn offers boat dockage and fishing for guests. And it's within minutes of all the attractions in the Groton–New London area. Spacious rooms with modern furnishings all have refrigerators. *193 Thames St., 06340, tel. 203/445–8111 or 800/243–7779. 22 rooms with bath, 4 suites. AE, CB, DC, MC, V. Moderate–Expensive.*

Mystic Dining   **FloodTide.** This gracious establishment, part of The Inn at Mystic, offers several dining options. One dining room overlooking the harbor serves guest breakfasts and afternoon tea. The lounge, where complimentary hors d'oeuvres are served at cocktail hour, opens onto a breezy deck and outdoor pool. The formal main dining rooms emphasize tableside preparation of such specialties as Caesar salad, chateaubriand, or bananas Foster (bananas flamed with liqueurs and served over vanilla ice cream). *Junction Rtes. 1 and 27, tel. 203/536–8140. Reservations advised. Dress: casual but neat. AE, D, DC, MC, V. Closed Dec. 25.*

Mystic Lodging   **The Taber Inn.** This small compound is made up of the motor inn, Guest House, Town House, Country House, and Farmhouse. The most basic, least expensive rooms are in the motor inn; the fanciest and most expensive are the two-bedroom duplex apartments in the Town House. All rooms are furnished with Colonial reproductions. *29 Williams Ave. (Rte. 1), 06355, tel. 203/536–4904. 40 rooms. Facilities: cable TV, telephones, Jacuzzis in some rooms, tennis privileges at nearby Williams Beach. MC, V. Moderate–Very Expensive.*
The Inn at Mystic. To reach the winding driveway of the inn, follow signs to the "Mystic Motor Inn." The parking lot gives a breathtaking view of the harbor, and from the lot you can walk to the motor inn, the east wing, and the FloodTide restaurant.

Up the hill you'll find the Corinthian-columned main inn and the gate house. Guest rooms are furnished in traditional Colonial style, some with four-posters or canopy beds. The best views are in the old mansion called the main inn. Rooms in the gate house are secluded and have a Jacuzzi and wet bar. *Junction Rtes. 1 and 27, 06355, tel. 203/536–9604 or 800/237–2415. 68 rooms with bath. Facilities: restaurant, private dock with canoes and sailboats, outdoor pool and hot spa, landscaped walking trail. AE, CB, D, DC, MC, V. Expensive–Very Expensive.*

New London
Lodging
Radisson Hotel. The downtown location makes it convenient to Captain's Walk, I–95, and the Amtrak station. Rooms have nondescript modern furnishings but are quiet and spacious. *35 Gov. Winthrop Blvd. (I–95, Exit 83/86S), 06320, tel. 203/443–7000 or 800/333–3333. 114 rooms with bath, 6 suites. Facilities: restaurant, lounge, exercise room, Jacuzzi, indoor pool. AE, CB, DC, MC, V. Expensive–Very Expensive.*

Holiday Inn. You can't miss the bright neon sign on I–95. This link in the Holiday Inn chain is typical, with well-furnished rooms that offer no surprises. *I–95 and Frontage Rd. (I–95, Exit 82A N/83S), 06320, tel. 203/442–0631. 135 rooms. Facilities: restaurant, lounge, health club, outdoor pool. AE, CB, DC, MC, V. Expensive.*

North Stonington
Dining
★
Randall's Ordinary. Authentic Colonial dishes are prepared at the open hearth of this house, built in about 1685. "Ordinary" refers to the original town ordinance that made it possible for this site to provide food and lodging; the victuals served today in its small, intimate, low-ceiling dining rooms are anything but ordinary. Though the menu changes seasonally, you'll probably find Nantucket scallops, lightly breaded and sautéed in butter, with scallions, garlic, and paprika, prepared on a hanging skillet. Try the spider bread, a crisp cornbread named for the footed cast-iron pan in which it's cooked. For dessert, the Thomas Jefferson bread pudding is laced with brandy. *Rte. 2, tel. 203/599–4540. Reservations required for dinner, advised for lunch. Dress: casual but neat. AE, MC, V. Very Expensive.*

North Stonington
Lodging
Randall's Ordinary. This inn is famed for its open-hearth cooking. The original structure, the John Randall House, provides lodging on the second floor. The Jacob Terpenning Barn (built in 1819, moved from upstate New York in 1989, and renovated) now offers accommodation, in wonderfully irregular rooms. Most have fireplaces, and all are furnished in an authentic, early Colonial manner, with canopy beds, four-posters, trundle beds, and simple chairs and tables. The lack of carpets and scarcity of pictures on the walls make the guest rooms somewhat cheerless, despite the occasional antique knickknacks. *Rte. 2, Box 243, 06359, tel. 203/599–4540. 12 rooms with bath. Facilities: whirlpool bath, shower. AE, MC, V. Rates include Continental breakfast. Expensive.*

★
Antiques and Accommodations. The English influence is evident in the Georgian formality of this Victorian country home, built about 1861. Exquisite furniture and accessories, all for sale, are found throughout the common rooms and guest rooms of the main building. Simpler furnishings are found in the separate, multibedroom barn-efficiency across the yard. Breakfast, served by candlelight at the formal dining table, includes seasonal fruits, local eggs, and home-baked goods. Aromatic candles and fresh flowers create a warm and inviting atmos-

phere. *32 Main St., 06359, tel. 203/535–1736. 4 rooms, 3 with bath. Facilities: cable TV on main floor and in barn house. No smoking. No credit cards. Rates include full breakfast. Moderate–Expensive.*

Stonington Dining

Sailor Ed's. This family-style restaurant is decorated with knotty-pine panels and nautical motifs and features abundant servings of fresh seafood, excellent prime rib, and steaks. Many diners opt for the New England Shore Dinner—clam chowder, boiled fresh lobster, potato, corn on the cob, and Indian pudding. Try a crisp mountain of "Howard's Outrageous Onion Rings." *Rte. 1, Old Stonington Rd. (1 mi east of Mystic), tel. 203/572–9524. Reservations advised. Dress: casual but neat. AE, MC, V. No lunch Sun. Closed Thanksgiving, Dec. 25. Inexpensive.*

Stonington Lodging

Sea Breeze Motel. Behind its vibrant, mustard-and-white exterior are basic, modern rooms, each with two double beds, simple contemporary furnishings, and a stall shower in the bathroom. *Rte. 1, 06378, tel. 203/535–2843. 26 rooms with bath. Facilities: cable TV. AE, MC, V. Inexpensive.*

Stonington Village Dining

Harbor View. Chef Bill Geary continues a 17-year tradition of fine French cuisine in romantic dining rooms with crisp blue linens and candlelit tables. The large, old-fashioned taproom in front offers a contrast, with its bare wooden floor and kegs hung from the ceiling. Specialties include *homard Melanie* (pan-roasted lobster with bourbon and chervil-butter) and *ris de veau Guesclin* (braised veal sweetbreads with wild mushrooms in a puff-pastry shell). *60 Water St. (Cannon Sq.), tel. 203/535–2720. Reservations advised. Dress: casual but neat. AE, CB, DC, MC, V. Closed Dec. 25. Moderate–Expensive.*

Skipper's Dock. This seafood restaurant is located on the dock behind the parking lot of the Harbor View and is run by the same management. Surrounded by its nautical artifacts, you might well choose the kettle of fisherman's stew Portuguese (clams, mussels, shrimp, native fish, and chourico sausage in broth with tomato and peppers). On the weekend, prime rib is served in two generous sizes. *66 Water St. (on the pier), tel. 203/535–2000. No reservations. Dress: casual. AE, CB, DC, MC, V. Closed Mon. and Tues. during fall and winter, Dec. 25. Moderate–Expensive.*

Stonington Village Lodging

Lasbury's Guest House. On a quiet side street, overlooking a salt marsh to the rear, sits a frame house with a small, red, Colonial building a few steps behind it. A nautical theme, along with framed posters for the annual Stonington Fair, provides the decoration in these neat, trim surroundings. A Continental breakfast is delivered to each room in a tiny basket. *24 Orchard St., 06378, tel. 203/535–2681. 3 rooms, 2 with bath. No credit cards. Moderate.*

Waterford Lodging

Blue Anchor Motel. Near the banks of the Niantic River, the Blue Anchor offers cottages and efficiencies for those planning to spend a few days in the area. Swimming, boating, and golf are nearby. *563 Boston Post Rd. (I–95, Exit 75), 06385, tel. 203/422–2072. 15 units. MC, V. Inexpensive–Moderate.*

The Arts

Southeastern Connecticut Guide, available at hotels and restaurants throughout the area, has news and listings of arts events.

Dance Connecticut College's **Palmer Auditorium** (Mohegan Ave., New London, tel. 203/447–7610) presents dance and theater programs.

Music **Eastern Connecticut Symphony Orchestra** (tel. 203/443–2876) performs at the **Garde Arts Center** (325 Captain's Walk, New London, tel. 203/444–6766).
Shoreline Alliance for the Arts (tel. 203/453–3890) sponsors concert offerings throughout the western part of the region.
East Haven Cultural Arts Council produces a concert series at the East Haven Community Center (91 Taylor Ave., tel. 203/468–2963).
Branford Folk Music Society (Box 441, Branford, tel. 203/488–7715) presents music on the green at Trinity Church.
The **Madison Green and Beach Department** (tel. 203/245–5623) sponsors Sunday concerts on the Madison green.

Theater **Puppet House Theatre** (128 Thimble Island Rd., Stony Creek, tel. 203/773–8080) has a lively season of comedy, drama, and musical productions by three companies.

Nightlife

Blues Clubs **Bank St. Cafe** (639 Bank St., New London, tel. 203/444–7932) bills itself as the top live blues club on the East Coast, with music Thursday through Saturday and a Sunday jam session at 5.

Rock Clubs **El 'n' Gee Club** (86 Goden St., New London, tel. 203/443–9227) has different programs nightly—heavy metal, reggae, local bands, and national acts.

4 Rhode Island

by Deborah
Kovacs and
Marjorie Ingall,
with an
introduction by
William G.
Scheller

Deborah Kovacs
is the author of
12 children's
books; Marjorie
Ingall, who wrote
the Providence
tour for this
chapter, has
contributed to
travel guides on
Greece and
Cyprus.

Rhode Island, which shares with New Jersey the distinction of being one of the two most densely populated states in the Union, has at least one other characteristic in common with the Garden State: Its image suffers from the fact that all too often it is a place people pass through on their way to somewhere else. The culprit in both cases is Interstate 95, but for Rhode Island the problem is compounded by its size. With dimensions of 48 by 37 miles, the state can come and go without the notice of someone who is paying close attention to the car radio. The one fact that nearly everyone in America seems to know about Rhode Island is that it's the smallest of the 50 states.

The way to experience Rhode Island as something other than a "pass-through" is to stay off the interstate. Traveling the city streets and blacktop roads of this tiny corner of New England reveals a place where changes in landscape and character come abruptly.

Take the 5 miles or so of Route 1 just above Wickford. On the face of it, this is as crass and tacky an example of modern strip-mall Americana as any stretch of asphalt in the country. But if you turn off the highway onto a discreetly marked drive in North Kingstown, you'll pass through a grove of trees and enter the 17th-century world of Smith's Castle, a beautifully preserved saltbox plantation house on the quiet shore of an arm of Narragansett Bay. Little appears to have changed here since Richard Smith built his "castle" after buying the surrounding property from Rhode Island's founder, Roger Williams, in 1651. Head back onto the highway, and you'll find a little place run by two emigrés from Texas who serve some of the best barbecue in New England. Follow Route 1 a bit farther south to Route 1A, and the scene will change once again: The bayside town of Wickford is the kind of almost-too-perfect, salty New England period piece that is usually conjured up only in books and movies—and rumor says that this was John Updike's model for the New England of his novel *The Witches of Eastwick*. (Questioned about this, Updike told the writer that he would leave the putative similarities between Wickford and Eastwick "to conjecture.")

So there it is: a run of tawdry highway development, a restored relic of a house that was once the seat of a 17,000-acre plantation, great barbecued ribs, and a picture-perfect seacoast town that may or may not have suggested the locale for a novel of contemporary witchcraft. Pick the Rhode Island you want; all are cheek by jowl and none is visible from I–95. Nor is the 2,600-acre Great Swamp south of Kingston, the thinly populated rural fastness of northwestern Rhode Island, the Victorian shore resort of Watch Hill, or the exquisite desolation of Block Island, way out in Long Island Sound.

If you are traveling Route 1 to Wickford, you are likely to be driving between the two poles of Rhode Island, Providence and Newport. Providence, the capital, is the hub of New England's second-largest urban conglomerate (after Boston); in its density, heavy ethnic concentrations, and old industrial infrastructure, it suggests yet another comparison with New Jersey. But Providence has one resource that is typically New England: the handsomely restored cluster of 18th- and early 19th-century homes in the district surrounding Benefit Street, near the Brown University campus. Here is a reminder of the wealth brought to Rhode Island by the triangular trade of slaves, rum,

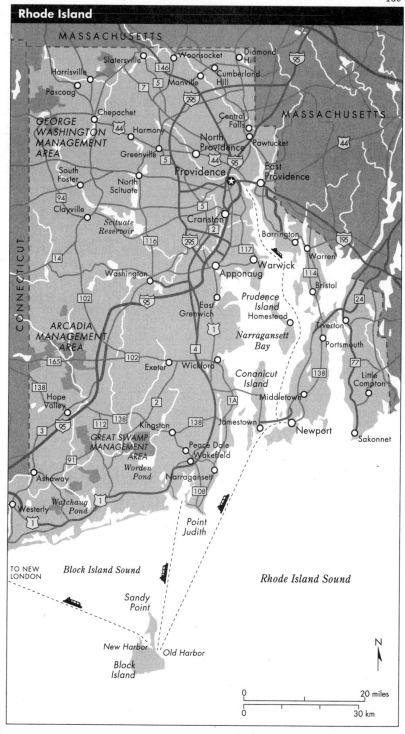

Rhode Island

MASSACHUSETTS

MASSACHUSETTS

CONNECTICUT

Slatersville

Harrisville

Pascoag

Woonsocket

Diamond Hill

Cumberland Hill

Manville

Chepachet

Harmony

GEORGE WASHINGTON MANAGEMENT AREA

Central Falls

North Providence

Pawtucket

Greenville

Providence

East Providence

South Foster

North Scituate

Clayville

Scituate Reservoir

Cranston

Barrington

Warren

Washington

Apponaug

Warwick

Bristol

ARCADIA MANAGEMENT AREA

East Greenwich

Prudence Island

Homestead

Narragansett Bay

Tiverton

Portsmouth

Exeter

Wickford

Conanicut Island

Little Compton

Hope Valley

Middletown

Kingston

GREAT SWAMP MANAGEMENT AREA

Peace Dale

Wakefield

Jamestown

Newport

Sakonnet

Ashaway

Worden Pond

Narragansett

Westerly

Watchaug Pond

Point Judith

TO NEW LONDON

Block Island Sound

Rhode Island Sound

Sandy Point

New Harbor

Old Harbor

Block Island

N

0		20 miles
0		30 km

and molasses in Colonial times—and a reminder that neighborhoods long thought past their prime can be brought back to fashion, given a timely influx of ambitious "rehabbers." Throughout the 1980s, much of Providence beyond Benefit Street was discovered by erstwhile Bostonians looking for drastically cheaper real estate even though it meant enduring commuting times of an hour or more.

Newport evokes memories of another kind of wealth, riches not made in Rhode Island but imported by the titans of the Gilded Age and translated into the fabulous "cottages" overlooking the Atlantic. The masters and mistresses of estates such as Marble House and the Breakers lived in luxury unimaginable even to royalty or New York developers today; ironically, the local citizens one society matron once referred to as "footstools" now earn a good deal of their tourism income from visitors to the palaces by the sea.

The "footstools" weathered the days of ersatz feudalism and made the best of the world the wealthy left behind. The photographer and humorist Chris Maynard, a native of Woonsocket, points out that "whenever several Rhode Islanders get together, they end up trading arcane facts about the state. Rather than give in to self-consciousness about Rhode Island's size, they become proud experts in its minutiae."

Essential Information

Visitor Information

Rhode Island Department of Economic Development, Tourism Division (7 Jackson Walkway, Providence 02903, tel. 401/277–2601 or 800/556–2484).

Tour Groups

Stumpf Balloons (Box 1143, Providence, tel. 401/253–0111) offers fall foliage tours of Rhode Island by balloon—with champagne.

When to Go

Rhode Island is most beautiful in the fall. Although the colors of the fall foliage may not be as striking as those of Vermont or New Hampshire, the combination of yellow and orange leaves, clear blue skies, and sparkling ocean can be spectacular. Those who do not enjoy crowds will want to avoid Newport at the height of the summer season.

Festivals and Seasonal Events

June: Providence's stately homes are visited on tours (some by candlelight) sponsored by the Providence Preservation Society. *Tel. 401/831–7440.*
July 4: Bristol's **Fourth of July Parade** is the nation's senior Independence Day parade. Floats, marchers, and bands combine to provide quite a show. *Tel. 401/253–8397.*
Mid-July: Newport Music Festival brings together celebrated musicians for a two-week schedule of morning, afternoon, and evening concerts in Newport mansions. *Tel. 401/846–1133.*
Mid-July: Volvo Tennis Hall of Fame Championship matches take place on grass courts at Newport Casino. *Tel. 401/849–3990.*
Mid-July: Virginia Slims of Newport is a tournament for professional women players. *Tel. 401/849–3990.*
Late July: Newport Folk Festival, at Ft. Adams State Park in Newport, is the nation's premier folk festival. *Box 605, Newport 02840, Tel. 401/847–3709.*
Late July: Black Ships Festival, the last weekend of the month in Newport, commemorates the treaty negotiated with Japan by Commodore Matthew Perry in 1865. The citywide events include fireworks. *Tel. 401/272–7790.*
Mid-Aug: The **JVC Jazz Festival** brings renowned performers to Ft. Adams State Park in Newport. *Tel. 401/847–3700.*
Early Sept.: Annual Pasta Challenge sees a one-day pasta cookoff among 25 Providence restaurants. *Tel. 401/351–6440.*
Early Sept.: Providence Waterfront Festival is a weekend of arts, crafts, ethnic foods, musical entertainment, and boat races. *Tel. 401/781–8470.*
Dec.: Christmas celebrations begin in late November and last until early January. In Newport several Bellevue Avenue mansions open for the holidays, and there are crafts fairs, holiday concerts, and candlelight tours of Colonial homes throughout the month. *Tel. 401/849–6454.*
Dec. 31: First Night is Providence's citywide alcohol-free New

Year's celebration. One $5 button is your admission to dozens of music, theater, dance, and choral performances around the city. *Tel. 401/521-1166.*

Arriving and Departing

By Plane   **Theodore Francis Green State Airport** (tel. 401/737-4000), north of Warwick, has scheduled daily flights by seven major U.S. airlines and additional service by regional carriers.

By Car   Interstate 95 cuts diagonally across the state, the fastest route to Providence from Boston, coastal Connecticut, and New York City. I-195 links Providence with New Bedford and Cape Cod. Route 1 follows much of the Rhode Island coast east from Connecticut before turning north to Providence.

By Train   **Amtrak** (tel. 800/872-7245) service between New York City and Boston makes stops at Westerly, Kingston, and Providence's **Union Station** (100 Gaspee St.).

       MBTA Commuter rail service (tel. 401/727-7382) connects Boston and Providence during weekday morning and evening rush hours at about half the cost of Amtrak's regular service.

By Bus   **Greyhound Lines** and **Bonanza Bus Lines** link cities of the northeastern United States with the **Providence Bus Terminal** (Cemetery St., off Exit 25 from I-95, tel. 401/751-8800). A shuttle service connects the terminal with Kennedy Plaza in downtown Providence.

Getting Around Rhode Island

By Car   In Rhode Island cars are allowed to turn right on a red light after coming to a full stop and looking for oncoming traffic. The official state map, available free from the Rhode Island Department of Economic Development, is useful for routings and for area directories.

By Bus   **Rhode Island Public Transit Authority** (tel. 401/781-9400) provides comprehensive local transportation.

By Ferry   Ferries leave Providence for Newport and Block Island from the **India Street Pier** (tel. 203/442-7891). Ferries from Point Judith to Block Island depart from **Galilee State Pier** (tel. 401/783-4613). Reservations are required for cars, and service is curtailed in the off-season.

Shopping

Rhode Island is home to many antiques fairs and flea markets, most held on weekends. The *Providence Journal, The Observer, Rhode Island Magazine,* and notices posted on telephone poles give specific times and places.

Sports and Outdoor Activities

Biking   Beautiful biking spots can be found all over Rhode Island. Bellevue Avenue in Newport, along the row of mansions, is the most attractive city route. Other scenic rides are through the vineyard country of Sakonnet and Little Compton, in Jamestown, or in Bristol. Bristol's bike path is unusually wide, closed to traffic, and perfect for a family ride. **The Rhode Island Bicyc-**

le Coalition (Box 4781, Rumford 02916) has information and maps.

Fishing   Block Island Sound is famous for striped bass, bluefish, weak-fish, mackerel, and bluefin tuna. These species all migrate, and they first appear in Rhode Island waters during the spring or early summer. Cod, pollock, and flounder are caught throughout the year. No license is required for surf casting.

Freshwater fishing is popular in protected shoreline areas throughout Rhode Island—but you'll need a license. Call **The Department of Environmental Management, Division of Fish and Wildlife** (tel. 401/789–3094) for license information. Trout season opens the second Saturday in April and lasts through March.

Saltwater sport fishing is also available in Rhode Island. Many charter boats make day trips into Narragansett Bay and beyond. No license is necessary for saltwater fishing in Rhode Island, but you do need one to sell any fish that are caught.

For the brochure *Boating and Fishing in Rhode Island*, which includes regulations, as well as a complete list of anchorages, marinas, yacht clubs, and excursion boats, contact the **Rhode Island Department of Economic Development, Tourism Division** (*see* Visitor Information, above).

Beaches

Rhode Island is filled with beautiful beaches. One of the largest is at **Misquamicut State Park,** near Westerly. One of the quietest is **Goosewing,** at Little Compton. Surfers favor **Second Beach** at Newport.

State Parks

Five state parks permit camping: **Burlingame State Park, Charlestown Breachway, Fishermen's Memorial State Park, George Washington Camping Area,** and the **Ninigret Conservation Area.** For information on state and privately owned camping areas, contact the **Rhode Island Department of Economic Development, Tourism Division** (*see* Visitor Information, above).

Dining

Rhode Island is home to much traditional regional fare. John-nycakes are a sort of corn cake cooked on a griddle, and the native clam, the quahog (pronounced KO-hog) is served in chowder, stuffed clams, fried clams, and even clam pie. Particularly popular are "shore dinners," which include clam chowder, steamers, clam cakes, baked sausage, corn-on-the-cob, lobster, watermelon, and Indian pudding (a steamed pudding made with cornmeal and molasses).

Dinners in Rhode Island tend to be early affairs; don't be surprised to find many restaurants, especially in the smaller towns, closed by eight. The 6% sales tax is added to restaurant bills throughout the state. A service charge is not usually added to restaurant bills unless specified.

Highly recommended restaurants in each price category are indicated by a star ★ .

Category	Cost*
Expensive	over $20
Moderate	$10–$20
Inexpensive	under $10

average cost of a three-course dinner, per person, excluding drinks, service, and 6% sales tax

Lodging

While the big chain hotels are represented in Rhode Island, many visitors prefer to stay in smaller inns and bed-and-breakfasts. Bed and Breakfast of Rhode Island, Inc. (Box 3291, Newport 02840, tel. 401/849–1298) provides information on bed-and-breakfast arrangements in the state. In considering one of these smaller places, be aware that the amenities, while clean, may be old-fashioned. Chairs may wobble, wallpaper may not be brand-new, but as a rule the accommodations will be warm and welcoming. Throughout the state a 5% hotel tax plus the 6% sales will be added to lodging bills. A service charge is not usually added to hotel bills unless specified.

Highly recommended lodgings in each price category are indicated by a star ★ .

Category	Cost*
Expensive	over $100
Moderate	$60–$100
Inexpensive	under $60

All prices are for a standard double room, with no meals unless noted, and excluding 11% in hotel and sales taxes.

Providence

Founded by Roger Williams in October 1635 as a refuge for freethinkers and religious dissenters, Providence remains a community that tolerates difference and fosters cultural inquiry and diversity. Brown University, the Rhode Island School of Design (RISD), and the Trinity Square Repertory Company are major forces in New England's intellectual and cultural life.

After Roger Williams, the most significant name in Providence history may have been Brown. Four Brown brothers had a major part in the city's development in the 18th century: John Brown, who traded in slaves, opened trade with China and aided the American Revolution; his mansion on the East Side is a must-see. Joseph Brown's designs—including his brother's mansion and the First Baptist Meeting House—changed the face of the city. Moses Brown, an abolitionist and a pacifist, funded the Quaker School that bears his name. Nicholas Brown rescued the failing Rhode Island College—known today as Brown University.

While downtown Providence is largely colorless—perhaps the uncovering of the built-over Providence River, now in progress, will enliven the area—many neighborhoods are attractive for strolling: Fox Point's Portuguese community, Federal Hill's Italian section, the historically Yankee and now predominantly Jewish East Side, and the young and hip College Hill. The city's restaurants include several that have won national recognition and quite a few that reflect the variety of cuisines of the city's ethnic populations. Many residents will argue that it is this ethnicity that makes Providence special.

Important Addresses and Numbers

Visitor Information
Greater Providence Convention and Visitors Bureau (30 Exchange Terr., 02903, tel. 401/274–1636).

Getting Around Providence

By Car Overnight parking is not allowed on Providence streets.

By Bus **Rhode Island Public Transit Authority** (tel. 401/781–9400 or 800/662–5088; 401/461–9400 for the hearing-impaired) provides bus service in the Providence area; the fare is 70¢. A free trolley (painted green and orange) circles the downtown area from 11 AM to 2 PM weekdays, making a loop every 15 minutes between Davol Square and the State House. Catch it at Kennedy Plaza.

Bonanza Bus Lines (tel. 401/751–8800) has service between the airport and downtown Providence.

By Taxi Taxis can be ordered from **Airport Taxi** (tel. 401/737–2868), **Checker Cab** (tel. 401/273–2222), **East Side Taxi Service** (tel. 401/521–4200), and **Yellow Cab** (tel. 401/941–1122). Taxi fare is 90¢ at the flag drop and 10¢ each additional ⅑-mile. Taxis from the airport take about 15 minutes; the fare is about $15.

Guided Tours

Providence Preservation Society (21 Meeting St., tel. 401/831–7440) offers 90-minute cassette tours of the East Side, College Hill (including Brown and the Rhode Island School of Design), and the downtown area. The society runs the popular Historic Houses tour in the first week of June, which allows you to explore stunningly furnished private homes. Three additional tours visit historic houses whose architecture ranges from pre-Revolutionary to Federal, from Greek Revival to Victorian.

Exploring Providence

Numbers in the margin correspond with the numbered points of interest on the Central Providence map.

❶ Begin your exploration of Providence at the **admissions office of Brown University** (45 Prospect St., tel. 401/863–2378), where you can orient yourself to the history and layout of the university and even join a tour of the National Historic Landmark campus. A walk on Thayer Street will acquaint you with the campus's principal commercial thoroughfare.

Time Out **Peaberry's**, at 258 Thayer Street, is a comforting little shop that sells tempting varieties of fresh-brewed coffee and rich homemade pastries. Here you can sit and watch intense Brown students fervently debate Derrida.

Leave the campus via Prospect Street, where you'll face the
② John Hay Library. This structure of 1910, named for Abraham
Lincoln's secretary, houses 11,000 items related to the 16th
president. The library also has American drama and poetry collections, 500,000 pieces of American sheet music, the Webster
Knight Stamp Collection, the letters of the early horror and
science fiction writer H. P. Lovecraft, military prints, and a
collection of toy soldiers. *20 Prospect St., tel. 401/863–2146.
Open weekdays 9–5.*

Walk 2 blocks down College Street and turn left onto Benefit
③ Street. The Providence Athenaeum, a Greek Revival structure,
was built in 1856, making it one of the oldest lending libraries in
the country. Here Edgar Allan Poe, visiting Providence to lecture at Brown, met and courted Sarah Helen Whitman, who
was said to be the inspiration for his poem "Annabel Lee."
Whitman lived nearby at 88 Benefit Street. The library has a
collection of Rhode Island art and artifacts; an ivory piece by
Edward Malbone is said to be the most valuable miniature in
the country. *251 Benefit St., tel. 401/421–6970. Open weekdays
8:30–5:30, Sat. 9:30–5:30.*

④ The Rhode Island School of Design Museum of Art, a small museum down the street from the Athenaeum, is one of the most
comprehensive of its size in the country. In addition to about 25
changing exhibitions each year, many involving textiles (a
longstanding Rhode Island industry), the permanent holdings
contain the Abby Aldrich Rockefeller collection of Japanese
prints, Paul Revere silver, 18th-century porcelain, and French
Impressionist paintings. Especially popular with young
museumgoers are the 10-foot statue of Buddha and the mummy
from the Ptolemaic period (c. 300 BC). The RISD Museum is connected to **Pendleton House,** a replica of an early 19th-century
Providence house, with furnishings of the 18th and 19th centuries. *224 Benefit St., tel. 401/331–3511. Admission: $1
adults, 50¢ senior citizens, 25¢ children under 18; free Sat.
Open Tues.–Wed., Fri.–Sat. 10:30–5, Thurs. noon–8, Sun.
2–5.*

**⑤ Follow College Street west to South Water Street and Market
House** (Market Sq., South Main St.), designed by Joseph
Brown. Opening onto the Providence River, this brick structure was central to Colonial Providence's trading economy. Tea
was burned there in March 1775, and the upper floors were
used as a barracks during the Revolutionary War. Afterward
Market House was the seat of city government from 1832 to
1878. A plaque shows the height reached by floodwaters during
the Great Hurricane of 1938.

Head north on South Water Street, turn west onto Westmin-
⑥ ster Mall, and you'll soon reach the Arcade, America's very first
indoor shopping mall. Built in 1828 and now a National Historic
Landmark, the Greek Revival Arcade boasts a facade with six
gigantic Ionic columns, cast-iron railings, and three tiers of
shops: The shops on the lower level have clothing, furnishings,
jewelry, paper goods, and toys. Examine the different
Weybosset Street and Westminster Street facades—one has a
pediment, the other stone panels. The reason for this discrep-
ancy is that the Butler who owned only half the land on which
his arcade was to be built could not agree with the other owners
on an architect, so they hired two—each of whom insisted on

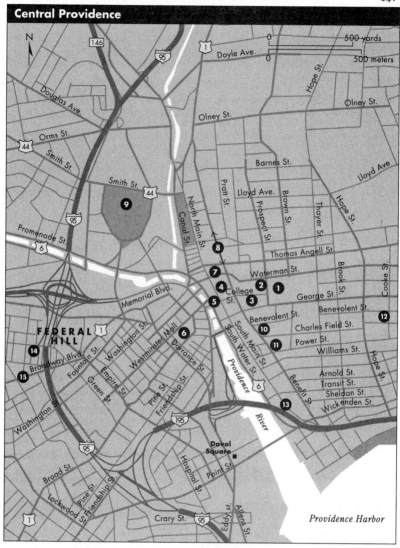

Central Providence

Admissions office,
Brown University, **1**

Arcade, **6**

Benefit Street, **8**

Broadway, **15**

Federal Hill, **14**

First Baptist Church
in America, **7**

Fox Point, **13**

John Brown House, **11**

John Hay Library, **2**

Market House, **5**

Museum of Rhode
Island History, Aldrich
House, **12**

Providence
Athenaeum, **3**

Rhode Island School of
Design Museum of
Art, **4**

State House, **9**

Unitarian church, **10**

carrying out his own conception. *65 Weybosset St., tel. 401/456–5403. Open Mon.–Sat. 11–6; Sun. noon–5; Dec., Thurs. 11–8.*

Time Out The **Providence Cookie Co.** on the ground floor of the Arcade has chocolate chip for traditionalists, white chocolate macadamia nut for the more adventurous.

7 Return to North Main Street and walk north until you cross Waterman Street, and the **First Baptist Church in America** will be on your right. Designed by Joseph Brown and built in 1775 for a congregation established in 1638 by Roger Williams and his fellow dissenters, the church has carved wood, a "meeting-house sage" decor, and features a Waterford crystal chandelier and graceful but austere Ionic columns. It was rebuilt by ships' carpenters in 1775, and so it survived the Gale of 1875 and the 1938 hurricane. *75 North Main St., tel. 401/751–2266. Open weekdays 10–3; Sat. 10–noon; Sun. tour at 12:15.*

8 Turn left onto **Benefit Street,** the "Mile of History." A bumpy cobblestone sidewalk leads past a long row of mostly small, early Federal and 19th-century candy-colored houses, crammed shoulder-to-shoulder, on a steep hill overlooking downtown Providence. The houses form a portrait of a time gone by. Try to stroll along it at dusk, when there is still some daylight but the old-fashioned streetlights have already lit up. **Ambrose Burnside's mansion** (314 Benefit St.), a redbrick Victorian with a turret, was built in 1850. Burnside was the Civil War general who led the Rhode Island army in defense of Washington, and later he became governor. Today he is known best for his facial hair: Sideburns are named after him.

9 Head west on Smith Street to Rhode Island's **State House,** built in 1900, and the first unsupported marble dome in America. The dome is the world's second-largest, after St. Peter's Basilica in Rome, after which Rhode Island's version was modeled. The ornate white Georgian marble exterior is topped by the gilded statue of *Independent Man*, designed by George T. Brewster. The interior features a full-length portrait of George Washington by Rhode Islander Gilbert Stuart, the same artist who created the likeness on the $1 bill. You'll also see the original parchment charter granted by King Charles to the colony of Rhode Island in 1663, and military accoutrements of Nathanael Greene, Washington's second-in-command during the Revolutionary War. *82 Smith St., tel. 401/277–2311 or 277–2357. Open weekdays 8:30–4:30.*

10 Return to Benefit Street and walk quite a few blocks south. On your left you'll see the first **Unitarian church** in Rhode Island. The bell tower houses the largest bell ever cast in Paul Revere's foundry, a 2,500-pounder. From the church you can enjoy a panoramic view of Brown. *1 Benevolent St., tel. 401/421–7970. Service daily 10:30 AM in the Meeting House.*

11 Walk another block down Benefit Street to Power Street and the **John Brown House,** designed by Joseph Brown for his brother in 1786. This three-story Georgian mansion suggests that the slave trade was good to John; John Quincy Adams called it "the most magnificent and elegant mansion that I have ever seen on this continent." Abolitionist brother Moses wasn't impressed; through his organization, the Anti-Slavery Society, Moses brought charges against John for illegally engaging in the buying and selling of human lives. In addition to opening trade with China, John is famous for his role in the burning of the British customs ship *Gaspee*. George Washington slept here—and he probably found it lovely: The house is replete with elaborate woodwork and filled with examples of decorative arts, furniture, silver, pewter, glass, linens, and Chinese porcelain from the late 18th and early 19th centuries. Children may enjoy the antique doll collection. *52 Power St., tel. 401/331-8575. Admission: $3.50 adults, $2.50 senior citizens and students. Open Tues.–Sat. 11–4, Sun. 1–4.*

⑫ Walk east on Charles Field Street to Hope Street. Turn left, and then right onto Benevolent Street. The **Museum of Rhode Island History, Aldrich House,** has no permanent collection but offers two to five exhibits a year on the history, culture, architecture, and crafts of Rhode Island. *110 Benevolent St., tel. 401/331-8575. Admission: $1.50 adults, $1 senior citizens and students. Open weekdays 10–4, Sat. 11–4, Sun. 1–4.*

⑬ Walk south on Hope Street to Wickenden Street. **Fox Point** used to be a Portuguese neighborhood, but gentrification is rapidly changing its character. Yet many of the houses along Wickenden, Transit, Gano, and neighboring streets are painted the pastel colors of Portuguese homes, and people still sit out on their stoops on hot summer evenings. Follow Wickenden across the Point Street Bridge to **Davol Square,** an 1874 rubber factory converted to an enclosed shopping plaza.

Time Out   **Taj Mahal** (230 Wickenden St.) and **Taste of India** (221 Wickenden St.) are dueling Indian restaurants, both cheap, located across the street from one another. The hours and prices are the same (the owners used to be in business together); choose the one that has no wait for a table.

⑭ The Italian community is vital to Providence's culture and sense of self, and **Federal Hill** is its center. Entering the neighborhood via Atwells Avenue might make you think you're walking down a main street in a small Italian town—you're as likely to hear Italian as English. The slats of the curved little park benches are painted red, white, and green, as is the stripe down the middle of the avenue. A huge pignolia (pine nut), an Italian symbol of hospitality, hangs above you on an arch soaring over the street and adorns the decorative fountain. From the pine nut, stroll down Atwells Avenue. The hardware shop may sell bocce sets and the corner store may sell little china statues of saints, but The Avenue, as locals call it, isn't cutesy. The St. Joseph's and Columbus Day seasonal celebrations, with music, street food, and parades, are not to be missed.

Places to visit include the **Grotta Azzura** (210 Atwells Ave., tel. 401/272–9030), a great old-world restaurant, and **Plaza Grille** (64 DePasqualle Ave., tel. 401/274–8684), on a side street behind the pignolia-topped statue. The former is for more formal dining, the latter serves bistro-style burgers and omelets in a cozy, pink, exposed-brick setting. You can create your own Italian feast at home if you stop by **Venda's** (219 Atwells Ave., tel. 401/421–9105) to take out some fresh, homemade ravioli or gnocchi. Gourmets in particular will enjoy the neighborhood grocery store, **Tony's Colonial** (311 Atwells Ave., tel. 401/621–8675), which has dried pasta of every conceivable shape, color, and size, Orzata almond syrup, Abruzzese sausage, and Ghirardelli chocolate for baking or eating. Other interesting stops are two clothing stores, **Julia's Apparel** (200 Atwells Ave., tel. 401/273–8580) and **Zuccolo's Fine Men's Clothing** (200 Atwells Ave., tel. 401/521–0646). Think leather, silk, and lots of detailing.

⑮ **Broadway** is a Victorian boulevard first developed in the 1830s by Irish immigrants. They built the large, rambling ginger-bread houses frosted with external bric-a-brac and details like porticos, turrets, towers, and small stained glass windows. To-ward the turn of the century, the Broadway gradually turned Italian, like neighboring Federal Hill. **"Barnaby's Castle,"** the huge mansion at No. 229—adorned with a four-story, twelve-sided tower—was owned by J. B. Barnaby, "the Rhode Island Clothing Prince." Barnaby's wife was the victim in a famous murder, brought to trial in 1891, when her doctor sent her a New Year's present of whiskey laced with arsenic. Other par-ticularly stunning houses are at No. 514 and No. 380. The houses vary in style from Greek Revival to Italianate to Queen Anne to Gothic Revival; there's even a row of brownstones (rare in Providence).

Time Out **Leon's on the West Side** (500 Broadway) is great for breakfast scones and lunch. The fettucine with prosciutto and asparagus in a ricotta cream sauce was a winner of the Pasta Challenge cookoff at one year's Waterfront Festival.

Providence for Free

Brown University
John Hay Library
Athenaeum
State House
Wickenden Street
Federal Hill, Fox Point, and Davol Square

What to See and Do with Children

Slater Mill Historic Site. A 16,000-pound wheel operates the first water-powered mill in the country, a 19th-century thread-spinning mill that inaugurated America's Industrial Age. The story goes that Samuel Slater, a lowly apprentice to an English watermill owner, memorized the mill's complex plans, came to America, reproduced them, and started his own mill with the financial backing of Moses Brown. There's also a 1758 worker's cottage on the site, where spinning and weaving techniques are illustrated. The mill offers classes in the Colonial crafts of chair-caning and basketry. *727 Roosevelt Ave., Pawtucket, tel. 401/725–8638. Admission: $3 adults, $2 senior citizens and children 6–14. Open June–Labor Day, Tues.–Sat. 10–5, Sun. 1–5; Mar.–May, Labor Day–Dec. 21, weekends 1–5; Jan.–Feb., weekdays for group tours by appointment only.*

The **Roger Williams Park and Zoo** is popular with kids and dogs. With 430 acres, there's plenty of room to run, tumble, and shriek. Have a picnic, take out a paddleboat, feed the ducks in the lakes, take a pony ride. There's even ice-skating in the winter, and tennis in the warmer months. Then you and the kids can mellow out in the restful Oriental Garden, created by the Works Projects Administration in 1930. At the only accred-ited zoo in New England, you can call to the birds flying free in the aviary, watch the penguins, and pet the animals in the petting zoo (but do not feed Norman and Trixie, the polar bears). The museum on the grounds has exhibits on local history, wildlife, and Narragansett Bay. *950 Elmwood Ave., tel. 401/785–9450. Admission: $2 adults, $1 children 5–12. Admission free Jan.–Feb. Zoo open Mon.–Thurs. 10–4 in summer; Fri.–Sun. 10–7; daily 1–4 in winter. Museum open Tues.–Fri. 10–4, weekends noon–5.*

The **Children's Museum of Rhode Island** is a "please touch" museum. Great-Grandmother's Kitchen encourages kids to rifle through cabinets filled with Victorian utensils, letting them see what cooking was like long ago; the Puzzle Room lets kids build and celebrate their creativity. They can also paint on acrylic, and visit a room-size map of Rhode Island. *58 Wolcott St., Pawtucket, tel. 401/726–2590. Admission: $3. Open Tues., Thurs., Sun. 1–5; Fri.–Sat. 10–5. Closed in summer.*

Off the Beaten Track

Kind of seedy, kind of musty, the **Cable Car Cinema** is a relic from another time. Sit on old couches, munch popcorn and Steve's Ice Cream, and watch low-budget, foreign, and cult films you can't see anywhere else in Providence. Before the show, watch the street-theater artists perform. *204 S. Main St., tel. 401/272–3970. Admission: $5.*

Shopping

Malls The absence of a sales tax makes Providence a shopper's mecca near the borders of tax-laden Massachusetts and New York. For grimly serious shopping, the malls just outside the city are the place to go. Two of the more interesting ones are the **Rhode Island Mall** (intersection of Rtes. 2 and 113, tel. 401/739–7500) with 100 stores, and the **Warwick Mall** (intersection of Rtes. 2 and 5, tel. 401/739–7500) with 70 stores. For down-and-dirty bargain hunting, Providence residents head to Fall River, in Massachusetts.

Shopping Complexes The Arcade (*see* Exploring Providence, above).

Davol Square (Point and Eddy Sts., tel. 401/273–9700) is housed in a former rubber factory built about 1874. This appealing brick building now bustles with restaurants, carts of inexpensive little items to buy on whim, and small (generally expensive) boutiques like **Talbots** and **Laura Ashley.** Unlike the Arcade, it's still bopping into the night.

Specialty Stores
Antiques **The Cat's Pajamas** (241 Wickenden St., tel. 401/751–8440) specializes in kitschy clothing, accessories, and furnishings from the 1950s. Younger shoppers scream in delight at the clean lines and funky patterns they've never seen before; older ones moan at the memory of the same items in their childhood homes—long since given away and now collectible.

Roxy Deluxe (224 Thayer St., tel. 401/861–4606) sells glamorous antique clothing, such as beaded sweaters from the 1950s, Edwardian women's underwear and gowns, and men's vests, hats, and overcoats.

Art Galleries **The Alaimo Gallery** (Tilden-Thurber Building, 292 Westminster St., tel. 401/421–5360) specializes in ephemera: antique posters, handcolored engravings, magazine and playbill covers, political cartoons, antique prints, book pages, and box labels. The gallery is run by the former director of the picture collection at RISD.

JRS Fine Art (218 Wickenden St., tel. 401/331–4380) sells contemporary jewelry, paintings, and sculpture.

The Peaceable Kingdom (116 Ives St., tel. 401/351–3472) offers folk art, with strengths in Native American jewelry and crafts, kilims, and brilliantly colored, finely detailed, embroidered Hmong story cloths. (A large community of Hmong has established itself in the state, and Joan Ritchie, the owner of the store, has written about the cloths made by these people from Laos.)

Men's Clothing   **Briggs Ltd.** (61 Weybosset St., tel. 401/331–5000) features men's suits, shirts, and dress wear both off the rack and custom made.

Toys   **The Game Keeper** (36 Arcade Building, 65 Weybosset St., tel. 401/351–0362), on the third floor of The Arcade, sells board games, puzzles, electronic games, and many little spur-of-the-moment gadgets.

Women's Clothing   **Frugal Fannie's Fashion Warehouse** (Garden City, Cranston, Exit 14 off I–95 onto Rte. 2, tel. 401/946–2200) is a trove of inexpensive, quality women's clothes. The store is strong in career-wear, especially suits.

Urban Cargo (224 Thayer St., tel. 401/421–7179) smack in the middle of collegeland, features young, casual, and moderately priced clothing and a selection of costume jewelry.

Sports and Outdoor Activities

Bicycling   For information on trails in the city, call the **Department of Public Parks** (tel. 401/785–9450). For general information on biking in Providence, and a bike map of metropolitan Providence, write to the **Rhode Island Bicycle Coalition** (Box 4781, Rumford 02916). Biking from Providence, you can easily get to the farm country of Seekonk in Massachusetts and to the shores of Narragansett Bay.

Boating   In addition to the Roger Williams Park paddleboats, boating is available on the Seekonk River and in Narragansett Bay. For more information, contact the **Narragansett Boat Club** (River Rd., Providence, tel. 401/272–1838).

Jogging and Fitness   Join members of the Brown track team as they work out on Blackstone Boulevard on Providence's East Side. The 3-mile boulevard is surrounded by trees and features plenty of benches and a dirt track.

Spectator Sports

Baseball   Following a much-publicized cleanup effort in 1987, the **Pawtucket Red Sox,** the Boston Red Sox farm team, provides a gentler ballpark experience. The fans generally behave; the atmosphere is rowdy but communal; and the emphasis remains more on the game than on the beer. You'll see former Bosox stars and stars to be. The Pawsox made the International League playoffs in 1987, and 60% of its players eventually get called up to the majors. *McCoy Stadium, Pawtucket, tel. 401/724–7300. Take I–95S to Exit 2A; follow Newport Ave. for 2 mi,* *then go right onto Columbus at the light. 71 home games from Apr. to Sept.*

Football If you want to sit in the cold, scream till you're hoarse, and watch mediocre but enthusiastic play, there's always the autumn joy of Ivy League football at **Brown Stadium** (Elmgrove and Sessions Sts., Providence, tel. 401/863–1893). The halftime show may be better than the game. You can see the real thing, the Patriots themselves, in training camp at **Bryant College** (Smithfield, tel. 401/232–6070 or 617/543–7911). They're in the Ocean State during July and August.

Greyhound Racing You might want to catch this Rhode Island tradition at Lincoln Greyhound Park *Louisquisset Pike, Lincoln, tel. 401/723–3200.*

Other Sports Events The Providence College Friars play Big East basketball at the Providence Civic Center (1 LaSalle Sq., tel. 401/331–6700). The Boston Celtics and Boston Bruins play exhibition games at the Civic Center, and there are regularly scheduled wrestling and boxing matches there.

Beaches

Public beaches closest to Providence are in Middletown, Newport, and South Kingstown. Moonstone Beach in South Kingstown, the only nude beach in the state, was closed in 1990 in an effort to protect the rare piping plover, a bird that uses the Moonstone area as a breeding ground.

Dining

Providence restaurants are generally less expensive than those of Boston and New York, and the city's many ethnic groups are well represented.

American **Trapper John's.** This restaurant is run by Providence's colorful former mayor and current talk-show personality, Buddy Cianci. Olive drab is the dominant color, the walls are decked with stretchers, the restrooms are labeled latrines. The "mess hall chow" (meat loaf, codfish balls, and the like) is cheap, and there's real food as well: salads, sandwiches, upscale meat and fish dishes. *75 Plain St., tel. 401/273–9111. Reservations advised for 6 or more. Dress: casual. AE, DC, MC, V. Closed Sun. Moderate.*

Troye's Southwestern Grill. There's a definite trendiness here, with bovine-print chairs, exposed pipes, and cacti galore, but the feeling of a neighborhood restaurant remains. Gazpacho, blue-corn nachos, and tortilla pizzas are among the offerings. Savor your vegetarian black-bean chili and think what you'd pay for the same food in Greenwich Village. *404 Wickenden St., tel. 401/861–1430. Reservations advised. Dress: casual. AE, V. No lunch. Closed Mon. Moderate.*

★ **Wes' Rib House.** Sure, there are vegetable kabobs for vegetarians, but this Providence institution is for those who want to tear into sticky, meaty viands. Order wood-fire barbecued ribs by the piece, damn your cholesterol count, and dig in. Late diners will appreciate the fact that Wes' stays open until 2 AM weeknights, 4 AM weekends. *38 Dike St., tel. 401/421–9090. Dress: casual. No credit cards. Moderate.*

Continental **Al Forno.** This restaurant (with its sister restaurant, Lucky's)
★ cemented Providence's reputation as a culinary center in New
England. The fare includes grilled pizzas, pastas, and veal
dishes, all with fresh ingredients, and sinful desserts. *577 S.
Main St., tel. 401/273–9760. No reservations; expect a wait on
weekends. Dress: casual. AE, MC, V. No lunch Tues.–Sat.
Expensive.*

Ethnic **Andreas.** Gyros, souvlaki, Greek salads, and plenty of options
for vegetarians make Andreas a healthy resource. *268 Thayer
St., tel. 401/331–7879. Reservations advised for 10 or more.
Dress: casual. AE, DC, MC, V. Moderate–Expensive.*

In-Prov. This tapas place is great for grazers; portions are
smallish, the menu wildly varied. You'll want to go with people
you like so you can eat off all their plates. Highlights include
grilled seafood chowder with tomato fumé; pizza with chorizo,
grilled peppers and wild mushrooms; and Chinese duck in ginger, soy, and saki sauce with pancakes and red currant sauce.
*Fleet Center, 50 Kennedy Plaza, tel. 401/351–8770. Reserva-
tions advised. Dress: casual but neat. AE, MC, V. No lunch
Sat. Closed Sun. Moderate–Expensive.*

Thailand Restaurant. What's a nice Thai restaurant doing
smack in the middle of a staunchly Italian neighborhood? It's
introducing the Italian community to the wonders of *To Ka Gai*
(chicken soup in a coconut and lime broth with cilantro and ginger); and *Pla Rard Prik* (deep-fried fish in fiery chili sauce).
The decor is minimalist: white tables and a few flowers. *224
Atwells Ave., tel. 401/331–0346. Reservations advised. Dress:
casual but neat. No credit cards. BYOB. No lunch Sun. Moderate.*

Cecilia's West African Restaurant. The neighborhood downtown isn't particularly inviting, but the Liberian food and
reggae on weekends make it worth the trip. Steaming stews
and meat in exotic sauces—cassava and palm butter—are
served in wooden bowls. *488 Friendship St., tel. 401/621–8031.
Reservations advised. Dress: casual. No credit cards. Inexpensive.*

French **Rue de l'Espoir.** This restaurant's creative menu includes
shrimp with oyster, Brie, and brioche pâté; veal medallions
with porcini mushrooms and a madeira glaze; roasted grilled
duck with caramelized onions and lingonberries; and crêpes
and salads. Eye-pleasing art, including a great mural on the
walls around the bar, and homey decor add to the appeal. The
crusty bread from Palmieri's is a local institution. *99 Hope St.,
tel. 401/751–8890. Reservations advised. Dress: casual. AE,
DC, MC, V. Closed Mon. Expensive.*

Italian **Adesso.** Upscale California-influenced Italian, including the
★ requisite enthusiasm for radicchio, reigns here. The pizzas are
big enough to share, but you might not want to. For dessert,
the *tiramisu* (creamy mascarpone cheese, Italian ladyfingers,
Dutch chocolate, espresso, and rum) is to swoon for. *161 Cush-
ing St., tel. 401/521–0770. No reservations. Dress: casual. AE,
CB, MC, V. No lunch Sun. Moderate–Expensive.*

Angelo's Civita Farnese. On Federal Hill, in the heart of Little
Italy, this family-run place has vinyl booths, oil paintings of the
family, fresh and simply prepared pasta. The portions are
large, the place is loud. *141 Atwells Ave., tel. 401/621–8171. No
reservations. Dress: casual. AE, V. Closed Sun. Inexpensive.*

Seafood **Hemenway's.** When you want to marvel at the city's revitalizing
★ downtown, this is one of the bright spots. The seafood is superb, the lighting makes everyone look good, and the atmosphere is loud and cheerful. New England Clambake (a seafood sampler), seasonal stone or softshell crabs, and
Norwegian salmon can be recommended. *1 Old Stone Sq., tel.
401/351–8570. Reservations advised for 8 or more. Dress: casual. AE, DC, MC, V. No lunch. Expensive.*

Ocean Express. The neon lobster and fish out front beckon
youngsters, and even the most finicky kid usually finds something appealing to eat here. The house promises the freshest
seafood, oysters, clams, and lobster, with a raw bar. Oak and
brass furnishings are brightened by green and burgundy decor, and there are plants everywhere. *800 Allens Ave., tel. 401/
461–3434. Reservations advised for 6 or more. Dress: casual.
AE, MC, V. No lunch weekends. Moderate.*

Lodging

Marriott Inn. While it lacks the Biltmore's old-fashioned elegance, some travelers will prefer the Marriott's larger size and
modern conveniences. The two swimming pools are a draw.
*Near Exit 23 on I–95. Charles and Orms Sts., tel. 401/272–
2400 or 800/228–9290. 339 rooms with bath, 6 suites. Facilities:
restaurant, indoor and outdoor pools, health club, saunas,
convention facilities, weekend packages. AE, MC, V. Expensive.*

Omni Biltmore Hotel. The Biltmore, completed in 1922, has a
sleek Art Deco exterior, old-world charm, and an external
glass elevator that offers attractive views of Providence at
night. *11 Dorrance St., Kennedy Plaza, tel. 401/421–0700 or
800/843–6664. 269 rooms with bath, 20 suites. Facilities: restaurant, café, garage parking, convention facilities, health
club, weekend packages. AE, CB, DC, MC, V. Expensive.*

Day's Hotel on the Harbor. Despite its small lobby (modern,
with marble floors and ficus trees), Providence's newest hotel
affords a sense of openness: You can even watch the chef at
work. *220 Gano St., tel. 401/272–5577. 140 rooms with bath. Facilities: restaurant, free garage parking, exercise room,
Jacuzzi, convention facilities, disco, airport shuttle, free shuttle service to areas within 3 mi of downtown Providence. AE,
CB, DC, MC, V. Moderate.*

Holiday Inn. This newly refurbished high-rise motel is close to
Exit 21 on I–95, near the Providence Civic Center. The comfortable piano bar (early American decor, with nautical
overtones) off the lobby, is designed for relaxed conversation.
*21 Atwells Ave., tel. 401/831–3900 or 800/465–4329. 274 rooms
with bath. Facilities: restaurant, lounge, indoor pool, Jacuzzi,
exercise room, free garage parking, meeting rooms, free airport shuttle. AE, CB, DC, MC, V. Moderate.*

The Arts

For comprehensive entertainment listings, see the *Providence
Journal*, the *Newpaper* (available free in restaurants and bookstores; extensive rock/funk/blues coverage), and *Rhode Island
Magazine*. Look for free speakers and performances at Brown
and RISD.

Music **Providence Civic Center** (1 LaSalle Sq., tel. 401/331–6700) with 14,500 seats, hosts touring rock groups, including the very pro-Providence Grateful Dead.

Providence Performing Arts Center (220 Weybosset St., tel. 401/421–2787) is a 3,200-seat hall that is home to touring Broadway shows, concerts, and other large-scale happenings. Opened in 1928, it boasts a lavish interior filled with painted frescoes, Art Deco chandeliers, gilt, bronze moldings, and marble floors.

Rhode Island Philharmonic (tel. 401/831–3123) offers 10 concerts between October and May.

Veterans Memorial Auditorium (Brownell St., tel. 401/277–3150) hosts concerts, children's theater, and ballet—both traveling productions and short-run performances.

Theater **Trinity Square Repertory Company** (201 Washington St., tel. 401/351–4242) has become nationally known for Tony Award-winning plays. In the renovated old Majestic Movie House downtown, the Rep generally offers a varied season: classics, foreign plays, new works. Audiences from all over New England support the repertory actors in what can be unusual and risky works.

Several smaller companies stage contemporary works:

Alias Stage (50 Aleppo St., tel. 401/521–2312), an ambitious offshoot of Trinity, presents original works.

Second Story Theatre Company (75 John St., tel. 401/421–5776).

Wickenden Gate Theatre (134 Mathewson St., tel. 401/421–9680).

Brown University (Leeds Theatre, 77 Waterman St., tel. 401/863–2838) mounts productions that range from contemporary works to classics to avant-garde and student pieces.

Nightlife

Bars and Nightclubs **The Hot Club** (575 S. Water St., tel. 401/861–9007) is just that, a hip place—with plants, a jukebox, and nice lighting—that was an early entry in the movement to revive nightlife on the waterfront.

Oliver's (83 Benevolent St., tel. 401/272–8795) with a pool table, bar, and jukebox upstairs, good pub food, booths, and brass downstairs, is a hangout for Brown University people.

Sports-Scoreboard (1055 Westminster St., tel. 401/831–2211) a downtown bar offering table games, caters to Providence College and Rhode Island College guys.

Dance Clubs **American Cafe** (1 Throop Alley, tel. 401/861–1996) offers mostly classic rock and roll, with live music (sometimes jazz or reggae) during the week and a DJ on the weekend.

Sh-Booms (108 N. Main St., tel. 401/751–1200) has a 1950s theme, good dance music, a pink Cadillac as part of the decor, and some hairy chests and chains.

Folk Clubs **Stone Soup Coffee House** (655 Hope St., tel. 401/781–7504) is nestled in the basement of the Church of the Redeemer. The decor isn't much—long institutional tables and paper coffee cups—but the music and homey atmosphere are tops. Shows Saturday at 8 PM.

Jazz Clubs **The Bluepoint Oyster Bar** (99 N. Main St., tel. 401/272–6145) promises seafood, a dark and cozy setting, and jazz. It's open until 11:30 on weeknights, midnight on weekends.

Caffe Roscoe (762½ Hope St., tel. 401/751–5010) features desserts in a cozy, painting- and sculpture-bedecked atmosphere and jazz on weekends.

Rock Clubs **AS220** (71 Richmond St., tel. 401/831–9327), a gallery and performance space, features paintings, plays, and performance art primarily for the young and the funky. Musical styles run the gamut from techno-pop and hip-hop to traditional Hmong folk music and dance.

The Last Call Saloon (15 Elbow St., tel. 401/421–7170) is a good spot for rock and blues.

The Living Room (212 Promenade St., tel. 401/521–2520) showcases national and local bands, like Roomful of Blues, Scruffy the Cat, Marshall Crenshaw, NRBQ, and Jimmy Cliff.

Rocket (73 Richmond St., tel. 401/273–9619) attracts a downtown, artsy crowd.

The Coast: South County

Coastal Rhode Island from Westerly to Narragansett is known within the state as the South County. You won't find South County on a map—its origins and boundaries have not been clearly defined—but that won't stop you from exploring the rolling farmland and beautiful beaches of a lovely, slow-paced area.

When the principal interstate traffic shifted from the coastal Route 1 to the new I–95, coastal Rhode Island was left behind in time, largely escaping the advance of malls and tract housing developments that has overtaken other, more accessible, areas. More popular with visitors today than in recent years, the region is still undervisited compared to other parts of New England; its vast stretches of sandy beaches, wilderness, and interesting historic sites escape the crush of tourists that can make a vacation a nightmare.

With 19 preserves, state parks, beaches, and forest areas, including Charlestown's Burlingame State Park, Ninigret Park, and the Trustom Pond Wildlife Refuge, South County is a region that respects the concept of wilderness.

Important Addresses and Numbers

Visitor Information **Chamber of Commerce Information office** (The Towers, Ocean Rd., tel. 401/783–7121).

South County Tourism Council (Box 651, Narragansett 02882, tel. 401/789–4422 or 800/548–4662).

State of Rhode Island's **Visitor Information Center** on I–95 at the Connecticut border is open during the summer months.

Emergencies **South County Hospital** (95 Kenyon Ave., Wakefield, tel. 401/
Hospitals 783–3361).

Westerly Hospital (Wells St., Westerly, tel. 401/596–6000).

Late-night **Bonnet Bay Pharmacy** (885 Boston Neck Rd., Narragansett,
Pharmacies tel. 401/782–3500).

Granite Drug (Granite Shopping Center, Westerly, tel. 401/
596–0306).

Getting Around South County

By Car I–95 passes just north of Westerly at the western edge of coastal Rhode Island. Travelers touring the New England coast may
approach from southeastern Connecticut on Route 1, the former interstate. While Routes 1 and 1A may be a little bumpy in
places, they are the principal routes for seeing the coastline of
the state.

Exploring South County

*Numbers in the margin correspond with the numbered points
of interest on the Rhode Island Coast map.*

1 **Watch Hill** is a pretty Victorian-era resort town, with miles of
beautiful beaches, a number of Native American settlements,
and an active fishing port; it's a good place to shop for jewelry,
summer clothing, and antiques.

To reach Watch Hill, drive south on Route 1A to Watch Hill
Road. At the end of Watch Hill Road, turn onto Everett Ave-
nue, which becomes Westerly Road. Take Westerly to Plimpton
Street, Plimpton to Bay Street, and you will encounter Watch
Hill at its most scenic in the westward views of Watch Hill
Cove.

On Bay Street you'll be greeted by a **statue of Ninigret,** a chief
of the Rhode Island branch of the Niantics, first appearing in
Colonial history in 1637. The model for this 19th-century statue
was part of Buffalo Bill Cody's Wild West Review, on tour at
the time in Paris.

Nearby, the **Flying Horse Carousel,** the oldest merry-go-round
in America, was built by the Charles W. F. Dare Co. of New
York in about 1867. The horses, suspended from a center
frame, swinging out when in motion, are each handcarved from
a single piece of wood, and embellished with real tails and
manes, leather saddles, and agate eyes. *Bay St., Ride: 25¢.
Open June 15–Labor Day, weekdays 1–9; weekends and holidays 11–9. Children only.*

The view of the sunset alone is worth the hike up the hill to
Ocean House (2 Bluff Ave., tel. 401/348–8161), one of several
Victorian-era hotels in this part of Watch Hill. Built in about
1868 by George Nash, this is one of the grand hotels that helped
bring Watch Hill fame as a resort in the 19th century. If you're
here during the hotel's short season, from late June to Labor
Day, you might have a bite to eat or a drink on the magnificent
200-foot porch that faces the Atlantic.

A walk to the end of Bay Street and a left into Fort Road will
take you in the direction of the path (at the end of Fort Road) to
Napatree Point, one of the best long beach walks in the entire
state. A sandy spit lying between Watch Hill's Little Narragansett Bay and the ocean, Napatree Point is a protected

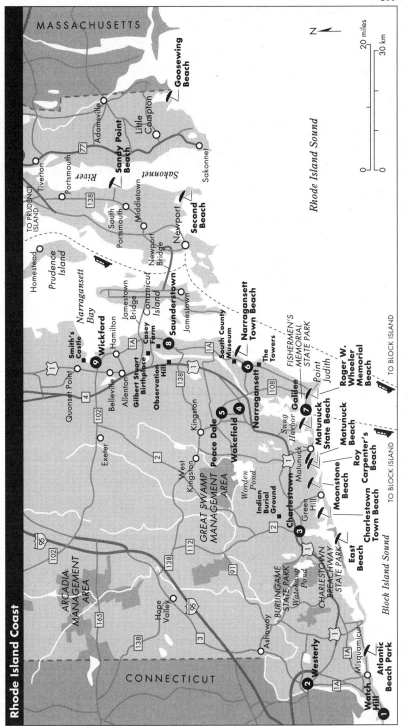

Rhode Island Coast

MASSACHUSETTS

Goosewing Beach

Adamsville

Little Compton

Sandy Point Beach

Tiverton

77

Portsmouth

TO PRUDENCE ISLAND

138

South Portsmouth

Middletown

Sakonnet

Sakonnet River

Second Beach

Newport

Rhode Island Sound

Homestead

Prudence Island

Narragansett Bay

Newport Bridge

Jamestown

Conanicut Island

Jamestown Bridge

Casey Farm

8 Saunderstown

1A

Narragansett Town Beach

9 Wickford

Smith's Castle

Hamilton

South County Museum

1

Quonset Point

4

Belleville

Allenton

Gilbert Stuart Birthplace

1A

Observation Hill

6 Narragansett

The Towers

FISHERMEN'S MEMORIAL STATE PARK

102

Exeter

2

West Kingston

Kingston

138

5

4 Narragansett

108

Galilee

7

Point Judith

Roger W. Wheeler Memorial Beach

TO BLOCK ISLAND

Wakefield

Snug Harbor

Matunuck State Beach

Matunuck Beach

ARCADIA MANAGEMENT AREA

GREAT SWAMP MANAGEMENT AREA

Peace Dale

Worden Pond

112

Matunuck

1

Roy Carpenter's Beach

Moonstone Beach

Indian Burial Ground

Charlestown

Green Hill

Charlestown Town Beach

TO BLOCK ISLAND

95

102

165

Hope Valley

138

91

BURLINGAME STATE PARK

Watchaug Pond

East Beach

CHARLESTOWN BREACHWAY STATE PARK

Ashaway

3

95

138

Westerly

1A

Misquamicut

Atlantic Beach Park

1

2

Watch Hill

1

CONNECTICUT

Block Island Sound

N

20 miles
30 km

0

TO BLOCK ISLAND

conservation area with many species of wildlife. Be careful not to disturb the area above the sand.

A stroll back up Fort Road to Larking Road and then southwest down Light House Road leads to the **U.S. Coast Guard Light Station.** Though you can't venture inside the station, on a clear day this is the place to go for the best view of the exclusive Fisher's Island. *Lighthouse Rd., Watch Hill, tel. 401/348–8923. Open daily 8–4.*

2 Drive north on Watch Hill Road to Route 1A, and head east to Winnipaug Road and **Westerly.** Drive south on Winnipaug Road to **Atlantic Beach Park** at Misquamicut, a mile-long beach featuring an amusement park, a giant waterslide, a carousel, a miniature golf course, a roller rink, and fast-food stands. *Atlantic Ave., Westerly, tel. 401/322–0504. Open daily 9–8. Closed Sept.–May.*

3 Drive north along Winnipaug Road to Route 1A. Follow Route 1A (here it's called Shore Road) west to the intersections of Routes 1 and 2 to reach **Charlestown,** a resort town filled with summer cottages.

Drive east on Routes 1 and 2 to the entrance of **Ninigret National Wildlife Refuge** (tel. 401/364–3106), a wildlife sanctuary maintained by the U.S. Fish and Wildlife Service. This 172-acre park includes picnic grounds, ball fields, a 10-speed bike path, and the Frosty Drew Nature Center.

A few minutes northwest, on Kings Factory Road, you'll find **Burlingame State Park** (tel. 401/322–7337 or 322–7994), a 2,100-acre park offering freshwater swimming, camping, and picnic areas, as well as boating and fishing on Watchaug Pond.

Return to the intersection of Kings Factory Road and Route 1e/1A. Drive east on Route 1A to Fort Neck Road, and drive south, back into Charlestown proper. **Fort Ninigret** is the remains of an earthwork fort built by Dutch traders during the early 1600s.

Return to Route 1. Make a U-turn after the Cross Mills exit, and drive north to Lewis Trail on Route 2/112. Charlestown retains much of the history of the Narragansett Indians, natives to the area. The **Indian Church** (tel. 401/364–6411) is the last of three Christian Indian Churches built in Rhode Island.

Drive south on Route 2/112, to Narrow Lane. About 1 mile southeast you'll find the **Indian Burial Ground,** the resting place of *sachems* (chiefs), and families of the Narragansett tribe.

A 15-minute drive east on Route 1 brings you to **South Kingstown,** a large area made up of many small villages, including Green Hill, Matunuck, Snug Harbor, Wakefield, Peacedale, Rocky Brook, and West Kingston. The University of Rhode Island is here, as is rowdy Matunuck Beach (*see* Beaches, below). South Kingstown is a good place to spend a warm summer day —or a crisp fall afternoon.

4 Five miles to the northeast is the village of **Wakefield,** where the old **Washington County Jail,** built in 1792, now houses the Pettaquamscutt Historical Society. Here you can see jail cells and rooms from the Colonial period, a Colonial garden, and changing exhibits that depict South County life during the last

300 years. *1348 Kingstown Rd., tel. 401/783–1328. Open May–Oct., Tues., Thurs., Sat. 1–4.*

Drive north on Kingstown Road to Curtis Corner Road. Turn left here and then left again on Asa Pond Road. In the village of **Peace Dale,** the Winding Creek Trail (tel. 401/789–9331, ext. 245), a barrier-free nature trail, is specially equipped for the handicapped and elderly. The trail features ponds, swamps, a fishing pier, and many types of flora and fauna.

Head north on Route 108 to Route 138. Turn left onto Route 1. As you leave South Kingstown, you may want to pause to climb the 100-foot, open-air wooden **Observation Tower,** at the top of McSparren Hill. Your reward: a beautiful panoramic view of the Rhode Island coastline.

Travel east on Route 1 to Route 1A (called Kingstown Road here), and continue on to **Sprague Park** at the intersection of Kingstown Road and Strathmore Street in **Narrangansett,** the dining and lodging hub of the South County. Convenient to both Newport and the Block Island Ferry, it makes a logical home base for a tour of Rhode Island.

The section of Narragansett known as **Narragansett Pier** was a posh resort at the end of the 19th century, when it was linked by rail with New York and Boston and the wealthy streamed in from those cities and beyond. The town was also a major stop on the steamboat line that ran between New York and Newport. Wealthy Newporters might have taken the steamboat to Narragansett for luncheon at the Narragansett Casino, a portion of which still stands, now known in Narragansett as The Towers.

At Sprague Park you can see the **Narragansett Indian Monument.** Donated to the town by the sculptor Peter Toth, the 23-foot monument weighs 10,000 pounds and is made from a single piece of wood, the trunk of a giant Douglas fir. To create the sculpture, Toth worked with hammer and chisel 12 hours a day for two months, then applied 100 coats of preservative.

Head east on Route 1A (called Narragansett Avenue here), to Beach Street. Turn right on Beach Street to Central Street, and head east to Ocean Road. Turn right on Ocean Road. For a sense of what Narragansett looked like at the height of the Victorian era, visit **The Towers** (tel. 401/783–7121). This turret structure is the last remaining section of the Narragansett Pier Casino after a fire in September 1900. The massive building arching over the roadway, designed by McKim, Mead, and White in 1885, functioned as a hub of social activity in the late 1800s. The Towers now houses the Narragansett Chamber of Commerce.

Drive south to the end of Ocean Road to find beautiful beaches and the **Point Judith Lighthouse.** A beautiful ocean vista awaits travelers who make it to land's end at this point. *1460 Ocean Rd., tel. 401/789–0444. Open daily 8 AM–9:30 PM.*

Travel north on Ocean Road to Route 108 (called Point Judith Road here), and turn left onto the Galilee Escape Road. Another left onto Great Island Road brings you into the bustling fishing village of **Galilee.** One of the busiest ports on the East Coast, the village has several excellent seafood restaurants. The Southland Ferry (tel. 401/783–2954) leaves from Galilee on a 1¾-hour tour of Point Judith, Galilee, and Jerusalem; or the Super Squirrel II (tel. 401/783–8513) can take you on a whale-watching expedition. This is also a good place to catch the Block Island ferry, run by the Interstate Navigation Company (Galilee State Pier, Point Judith, tel. 401/783–4613).

Travel east on the Galilee Escape Road to Route 108, also called Point Judith Road. Take Route 108 north to Route 1A, and head northeast. On your way out of Narragansett, just after the Narragansett Pavilion on the left side of the road, you'll see the entrance to the **South County Museum.** On the grounds of Canonchet Farm, the museum features reconstructions of many typical New England buildings. Exhibits include a general store, a cobbler's shop, a tack shop, a children's nursery, and a print shop. The museum hosts many special events throughout its season. *Canonchet Farm, tel. 401/783–5400. Admission: $2.50 adults, $1.50 children 6–16. Open June–Aug., Wed.–Sun. 10–4; May, Sept., Oct., weekends 10–4.*

Following Route 1A north will take you to **North Kingstown,** "plantation country," the site of many farms dating to the Colonial era, some of which can be visited. Like South Kingstown, North Kingstown is made up of many villages, including Saunderstown, Hamilton, Allenton, Belleville, Quonset Point, Davisville, and the charming Wickford, a favorite spot of shoppers.

❽ In **Saunderstown** the **Silas Casey Farm,** a working farm of the 18th century, has original furniture, family memorabilia, and many barns; it was the site of Revolutionary War activity. *Tel. 401/294–9182. Open June–Oct., Tues.–Thurs. 1–5, Sun. 1–5.*

Head north on Route 1A to Snuff Mill Road, turn left, and continue 2 miles to the **Gilbert Stuart Birthplace.** Built in 1751, the home of America's foremost portraitist of George Washington has been completely restored. The adjacent 18th-century snuff mill was the first in America. *Tel. 401/294–3001. Admission: $1.50 adults, 50¢ children. Open Mar.–Nov., Sat.–Thurs. 11–5.*

❾ Continue north on Route 1A to the Colonial village of **Wickford,** a part of the town of North Kingstown, which has attractive 18th- and 19th-century homes and interesting shops. Turn right onto Main Street and left onto Church Lane to reach the **Old Narragansett Church,** one of the oldest Episcopal churches in America. *Tel. 401/294–4357. Open July–Aug., Fri. 11–5, Sat. 10–5, Sun. 11–5.*

Drive north through the village of Wickford to the intersection of Routes 1A and 1; take Route 1 north and turn right onto Richard Smith Drive. **Smith's Castle,** built in 1678 by Richard Smith Jr., was the site of many orations by Roger Williams, Rhode Island's most famous historical figure. *41 Richard Smith Dr., tel. 401/294–3521. Admission: $2 adults, 50¢ children. Open Apr.–Oct., Thurs.–Sat. 10–4, Sun. 1–5.*

South County for Free

U.S. Coast Guard Light Station, Watch Hill

Fort Ninigret, Charlestown

Indian Church, Charlestown

Kimball Wildlife Refuge, a parklike Audubon refuge, is on the south side of Watchaug Pond, west of Charlestown. *Prosser*

Trail, Charlestown, tel. 401/231-6444. Open daily dawn-dusk.

Point Judith Lighthouse, Narragansett

Old Narragansett Church, Wickford

What to See and Do with Children

Flying Horse Carousel, Watch Hill

Atlantic Beach Park, Misquamicut

Burlingame State Park, Charlestown

Adventureland in Narragansett has bumper boats, miniature golf, and other attractions. *Rte. 108, Narragansett, tel. 401/789-0030. Admission and hours to be announced.*

South County Museum, Narragansett

Casey Farm, North Kingstown

Off the Beaten Track

Wilcox Park, laid out by Frederick Law Olmsted and Calvert Vaux in 1898, is an 18-acre park in the heart of Westerly with a garden for the visually impaired and handicapped. Signs in Braille identify the plantings of carnations, mint, chives, thyme, bay leaves, and coconut, apple, lemon, and rose-scented geraniums—to touch, smell, and taste. *71½ High St., Westerly, tel. 401/348-8362. Tours by appointment only.*

Shopping

Antiques are a specialty of the region, with more than 30 stores within an hour's drive. Among other specialties are traditional clothing and crafts.

Specialty Stores
Antiques

Artists Guild and Gallery (Post Rd., Rte. 1, Charlestown, tel. 401/322-0506). The shop exhibits 19th- and 20th-century art, and the staff will help with conservation, frame repair, and gilding.

Book and Tackle Shop (7 Bay St., Watch Hill, tel. 401/596-0700). The dealer buys, sells, and appraises old and rare books, prints, autographs, and photographs.

Dove and Distaff Antiques (365 Main St., Wakefield, tel. 401/783-5714). This is a good spot for early American furniture and accessories; restoration and refinishing and an upholstery and drapery workshop are available.

Finitney & Company (Bay St., Watch Hill, tel. 401/596-6210). This shop has antiques, fine art, and linens.

Fox Run Country Antiques (Opposite Charlestown Village, tel. 401/364-3160). This shop near the junction of routes 1 and 2 has country primitives, furniture, jewelry, assorted glassware and china, and a large collection of Oriental jars, dishes and *netsuke*, the small, carved Japanese decorative figures.

Lillian's Antiques (7442 Post Rd., Rte. 1, North Kingstown, tel. 401/885-2512). This shop sells antique jewelry, china, glass, paintings, furniture, and wicker.

Lion's Mane Antiques (Junction Rtes. 1 and 2, Charlestown, tel. 401/364–9104). Antique furniture, watercolors, and engravings are featured; the shop also prepares a monthly catalogue.

Mentor Antiques (7512 Post Rd., Rte. 1, North Kingstown, tel. 401/294–9412). The store receives monthly shipments of English furniture—mahogany, pine, and oak—and has an extensive inventory of armoires.

Peter Pots Authentic Americana (101 Glen Rock Rd., West Kingstown, tel. 401/783–2350). This shop features stoneware, period furniture, and collectibles.

Salt Box Antiques (Post Rd., Rte. 1, Charlestown, tel. 401/322–0598). Country and folk art can be found here.

Sign of the Unicorn Bookshop (1187 Kingstown Rd., Peacedale, tel. 401/295–7867). Rare and out-of-print books from collections and estate libraries are on hand. The staff makes appraisals.

Wickford Antiques Center 1 (16 Main St., tel. 401/295–2966) features wooden kitchen utensils and crocks, country furniture, china, glass, linens, and vintage clothing.

Wickford Antiques Center II (93 Brown St., tel. 401/295–2966) sells large pieces of antique furniture from many periods.

Children's Clothing **Gabrielle's Originals** (1 Fort Rd., Watch Hill, tel. 401/348–8986). "Children are our specialty" is the motto here.

Teddy Bearskins (17 Brown St., tel. 401/295–0282). This shop sells "unique clothing for children."

Crafts **Askham and Telham Inc.** (12 Main St., Wickford, tel. 401/295–0891) has elegant gifts and household accessories.

Puffins of Watch Hill (84 Bay St., tel. 401/596–1140) offers Halcyon Days enamels, Perthshire paperweights, Arthurcourt Designs, Seagull pewter, garden statuary and fountains, and handcrafted jewelry and gifts.

Sportswear **Wilson's of Wickford** (35 Brown St., Wickford; and Rte. 1A, North Kingstown, tel. 401/294–9514). Here you'll find traditional clothing for men and women.

Women's Clothing **Christina's Ltd.** (Bay St., Watch Hill, tel. 401/348–9041). Unique clothing and imported collectibles are the stock here.

Green Ink (17 Brown St., Wickford, tel. 401/294–6266). Here you'll find women's clothing, shoes, and accessories.

John Everets (Larkin Sq., Watch Hill, tel. 401/596–2229). This store features evening wear, daytime dresses, jewelry, wedding apparel, sportswear, and accessories.

Sports and Outdoor Activities

Canoeing Many small rivers and ponds in the South County are perfect spots for canoeing. **Quaker Lane Bait Shop** (4019 Quaker La., North Kingstown, tel. 401/294–9642) has information and rentals.

Fishing Bait and tackle shops in the area include **Ocean House Marina** (12 Town Dock Rd., Charlestown, tel. 401/364–6040), **Quaker**

Lane Bait Shop and **Wickford Bait and Tackle** (1 Phillips St., Wickford, tel. 401/295–8845).

Charters (Snug Harbor, Gooseneck Rd., South Kingstown, tel. 401/783–7766) can tell you about captains who skipper charters.

Hiking   One of the best trail guides for the region is the *AMC Massachusetts and Rhode Island Trail Guide.* Look for this book at local outdoors shops or from the Appalachian Mountain Club (5 Joy St., Boston, MA 02114, tel. 617/523–0636). The **Rhode Island Audubon Society** (40 Bowen St., Providence, tel. 401/521–1670) offers interesting hikes and field expeditions. The **Sierra Club** (3 Joy St., Boston, MA 02114, tel. 617/227–5339) and the **Appalachian Mountain Club** both have active groups in Rhode Island. For hiking, think of South Kingstown's Great Swamp.

Water Sports   **Ocean House Marina, Inc.** (12 Town Dock Rd., Charlestown, tel. 401/364–6060) rents 14-foot motorboats and daysailers. **Narragansett Surf & Sports** (Pier Village, Narragansett, tel. 401/789–2323) rents sailboards, surfboards, and diving equipment. **Windsurfing of Watch Hill** (3 Bay St., tel. 401/596–0079) rents sailboards and gives lessons.

National Parks

Ninigret Park National Wildlife Refuge is a 400-acre park that borders Ninigret Pond, a saltwater home to many species of waterfowl. *Charlestown, tel. 401/364–9124. Open daily, dawn–dusk.*

Beaches

The south coast of Rhode Island boasts mile after mile of beautiful ocean beaches, most of which are open to the public. The beaches are sandy, for the most part, and their water is clear and clean—in some places, the water takes on the turquoise color of Caribbean beaches.

Westerly   **Atlantic State Beach at Misquamicut.** A haven for young people, the crowds throng to this lively, friendly beach in the summertime.

Charlestown   **Charlestown Town Beach** (Charlestown Beach Rd). Don't slide down the sand dunes, covered with tall, rustling sea grass—they are fragile! The waves here can be high, the water turquoise and warm.

East Beach (East Beach Rd.). Two miles of dunes, backed by the crystal-clear waters of Ninigret Pond, make this beach a treasure, especially for the adventurous beachgoer who is willing to hike a distance from the car.

South Kingstown   **East Matunuck State Beach** (Succotash Rd.). This beach, also called Daniel O'Brien State Beach, is popular with the college crowd for its white sand, picnic areas, and bathhouse.

Matunuck Beach (Matunuck Beach Rd.). Unpredictable, high waves make this beach a good spot for surfing and raft-riding.

Moonstone Beach (Moonstone Beach Rd.). This beach is part wildlife refuge, part "clothes optional" bathing area. It is a beautiful beach, although public access is being increasingly restricted in deference to the wildlife refuge.

Roy Carpenter's Beach (Matunuck Beach Rd.). Quiet and out of the way, this beach seems private and secluded, yet there's food and drink within walking distance.

Narragansett **Narragansett Town Beach** (Rte. 1A). This in-town beach has a boardwalk, good surf, and is within walking distance of many Narragansett hotels and guest houses. Its pavilion has changing rooms, showers, and concessions.

Roger W. Wheeler State Beach (Cove Wood Dr.). Picnic areas, a playground, mild surf, and swimming lessons make this beach a good place for families with young children. It's near the fishing port of Galilee.

Scarborough State Beach (Ocean Dr.). With high surf, a bathhouse, and concessions, this beach becomes crowded with teenagers on weekends. *Rhode Island Monthly* says: "Big hair, hard muscles, and more mousse and mascara than Factor 15. Definitely not for the timid or self-conscious."

Dining and Lodging

Casual wear is the rule in the restaurants and dining rooms of South County.

Narragansett **Basil's Restaurant.** The chef prepares classical and provincial
Dining French cooking: mussels *brunoise;* duck à l'orange; vol-au-vent. The desserts, too, are homemade. *22 Kingstown Rd., tel. 401/789–3743. Reservations advised. AE, MC, V. No lunch. Closed Mon., Tues. Expensive.*
Coast Guard House. Frequently cited by those who know it as a favorite locale for a romantic dinner, the restaurant occupies a 1888 building by McKim, Mead, and White that overlooks Narragansett Bay. Dinner entrées feature seafood, pasta, poultry, veal, steak, and lamb. Friday and Saturday nights see entertainment in the Oak Room and a DJ in the upstairs lounge. *40 Ocean Rd., tel. 401/789–0700. AE, CB, DC, MC, V. Closed Dec. 25. Expensive.*
Spain Restaurant. Rhode Island's only true Spanish restaurant features appetizers such as shrimp in garlic sauce, clams marinara, clams Casino, stuffed mushrooms, and Spanish sausages; the main courses are variations on lobster, steak, paella and mariscada, fresh fish, chops, and poultry. *Village Inn, 1 Beach St., tel. 401/783–9770. Reservations advised on Sat. AE, DC, V. Expensive.*
Aunt Carrie's. Here's the place for traditional Rhode Island shore dinners, clam cakes and chowder, seafood, and meat dinners—and there's a children's menu. At the height of the season you may find a line; one alternative is to order from the take-out window and picnic on the grass nearby. Try the enormous but light clam cakes; for the more adventurous, there's the squid burger, served on homemade bread. Indian pudding à la mode is a favorite dessert. *Rte. 108 and Ocean Rd., Point Judith, tel. 401/783–7930. Closed Labor Day–Memorial Day. Moderate.*
★ **Champlin's Seafood.** Whether you like your fried clams as bellies or strips, you have the choice here. For just a bit more money, there are the sweet fried oysters. Other possibilities are a fried seafood platter, lobster, and the snail salad. *Galilee Rd., South Kingstown, tel. 401/783–3152. No reservations. MC, V. Closed weekdays Apr.–May, Nov.–Dec.; closed Jan.–Mar. Moderate.*

George's of Galilee. The lines around the building on summer Saturday nights baffle local residents, who speculate that it might be because of the location at the end of a spit of land in a busy fishing harbor. They insist that it's certainly not the atmosphere (frantic and noisy) or the food (much better, they say, elsewhere in Galilee). Yet it's hard to argue with success, and George's has been a "must" for tourists since 1948. The restaurant offers several chowders and hosts barbecues on the beach on summer weekends. *Galilee Rd., South Kingstown, tel. 401/783–2306. No reservations. MC, V. Closed Nov.–Feb., Fri.–Sun. Moderate.*

Narragansett Lodging ★ **Stone Lea.** The spacious house, more than 100 years old and filled with antiques collected by the owners, is a bed-and-breakfast that has the feel of an inn. Guest rooms have panoramic ocean views, the most striking in rooms 1 and 7; number 5 has a sitting room attached. *40 Newton Ave., 02882, tel. 401/783 –9546. 7 rooms with bath. Facilities: lounge with pool table, player piano. No credit cards. Closed Thanksgiving, Dec. 25, Jan. 1. Expensive.*

South Kingstown Dining **Larchwood Inn.** The owners call this "a country inn with a Scottish flavor." More than 150 years old, the original building is set in a grove of larch trees. Ask for a table near the fireplace in winter, and try for a patio spot under the larch trees in summer. On the menu are halibut stuffed with scallops; and seafood, chicken, beef, and veal preparations. *521 Main St., Wakefield, tel. 401/783–5454. Reservations advised. AE, CB, DC, MC, V. No lunch Sun. Closed Dec. 25. Expensive.*

★ **South Shore Grill.** The restaurant has a wood-fired grill and waterfront views: One wall, overlooking the Wakefield Marina, is all window. Starters are grilled duck; and a South Shore bisque made with fresh rock crab and garnished with beef chips. The entrées include inventive pasta dishes such as penne with pesto, lemon, Parmesan cheese, and roast eggplant. *210 Salt Pond Rd., Wakefield, tel. 401/782–4780. Reservations advised. AE, MC, V. Closed Feb. Expensive.*

South Kingstown Lodging **Admiral Dewey Inn.** Listed on the National Historic Register, the building was constructed as a seaside hotel in 1898 and more recently stood unused until new owners, who live on the premises, began its restoration. The 10 rooms are furnished with Victorian antiques. The inn is in a summer community just across the road from Matunuck Beach. *668 Matunuck Beach Rd., 02881, tel. 401/783–2090. 10 rooms with bath. MC, V. Rates include Continental breakfast. Moderate.*

Watch Hill Dining **Olympia Tea Room.** Step back in time to a small restaurant first opened in 1916, where the soda fountain has a long marble counter and there are varnished wood booths. If you feel up to it, order a marshmallow sundae—or an orangeade. For dinner there's ginger chicken; and mussels steamed in white wine. On the dessert menu, the "world famous Avondale swan" is a fantasy of ice cream, whipped cream, chocolate sauce, and puff pastry. *30 Bay St., tel. 401/348–8211. BYOB. AE, MC, V. Expensive.*

Watch Hill Lodging **Ocean House.** The grand old lady may appear a bit down at the heels, yet hers is one of the best seaside porches in New England. The casual, relaxing, quiet place has a reassuring if faded elegance. Lunch on the deck can be a treat. *Bluff Ave.,*

02891, tel. 401/348–8161. 59 rooms with bath. Facilities: game room. MC, V. Closed Sept.–June. Rates are MAP. Expensive.

Westerly Dining
★ **Shelter Harbor Inn.** Originally a farm established in the early 1800s, the property is now a comfortable, unpretentious country inn with a sun porch and an outdoor terrace for unwinding. An appetizer of smoked bluefish is served with a thick, creamy apple and horseradish sauce. Among the entrées, hazelnut chicken in orange thyme cream sauce is a specialty; broiled lamb chops are accompanied by a mint pesto sauce. The wine list is extensive, and a bowl of warm, buttery Indian pudding makes a solid finish to any dinner. Those who stay the night can look forward to ginger-blueberry pancakes in the morning. *Rte. 1, tel. 401/322–8883. Reservations advised. AE, MC, V. Expensive.*

Westerly Lodging
★ **Shelter Harbor Inn.** Set in a fairly quiet rural area not far from the beach, this place is perfect for a romantic weekend getaway, ruled by simple luxury, comfort, and privacy. The original house, built in the 1800s, has been extensively renovated, as have several outbuildings. Several rooms have both a working fireplace and a deck, and there's another deck, with a barbecue and a hot tub, on the roof. While the owner does not now live at the inn, you may find him mowing the front lawn. *Rte. 1, 02892, tel. 401/322–8883. 24 rooms with bath. Facilities: restaurant, lighted paddle tennis court, croquet court, hot tub, barbecue, van service to beach. AE, DC, MC, V. Expensive.*

The Arts

Theater **Center for the Arts** (116 High St., Westerly, tel. 401/348–5000), housed in a historic building, offers concerts, exhibits, and theater productions.

Colonial Theatre (3 Granite St., Westerly, tel. 401/596–0801), the town's only professional theater, presents musicals, comedies, and dramas throughout the year.

South County Players Children's Theater (High St., Wakefield, tel. 401/783–7202) gives performances by children for children in Father Greenan Hall of St. Francis Church.

Theatre-by-the-Sea (Cards's Pond Rd., off Rte. 1, Matunuck, tel. 401/782–8587), built in 1933 and listed on the National Register of Historic Places, has had a major restoration. The barn-style summer theater presents musicals and children's plays.

Nightlife **Windjammer** (Atlantic Ave., Westerly, tel. 401/322–0271) offers dancing to rock bands in a room that holds 1,800. Performers of national renown who have played here recently include Huey Lewis and the News, Cyndi Lauper, and Joan Jett.

The Coast: Newport

Perched gloriously on the southern tip of Aquidneck Island and bounded on three sides by water, Newport is one of the great sailing cities of the world and the host to world-class jazz, blues, and classical music festivals.

Newport's first age of prosperity was in the late 1700s, when it was a major port city almost on a par with Boston and New

York; many homes and shops built in that era still stand in the Colonial section of the city.

In the 19th century Newport became a summer playground for the wealthiest families in America. Having taken the "grand tour" of Europe and seen its magnificent castles, the well-to-do displayed their newfound sophistication by building European-style mansions that were monuments to themselves, their wealth, and the Gilded Age in America. Each new home constructed on Bellevue Avenue was grander than the one built just before it, until the acme of extravagance was reached with Cornelius Vanderbilt II's home, the Breakers, whose luxurious appointments rival those of world-class museums.

Newport on a summer afternoon can be exasperating, its streets jammed with visitors and the traffic slowed by the procession of air-conditioned sightseeing buses. Yet the quality of Newport's arts festivals persuades many people to brave the crowds. In fall, winter, and spring, visitors enjoy the sights of Newport without the crowds. The weather is pleasant well into November, and the city goes all out to attract visitors in December with the many "Christmas in Newport" activities.

Important Addresses and Numbers

Visitor Information **Newport County Convention and Visitors Bureau** (23 America's Cup Ave., tel. 401/849–8048 or 800/326–6030) has reservations phones to motels, an orientation film, and cassette tours.

Emergencies
Hospital **Newport Hospital** (Friendship St., Newport, tel. 401/846–6400).

Late-night Pharmacy **Douglas Drug** (7 E. Main Rd., tel. 401/849–4600).

Arriving and Departing by Plane

Newport State Airport (tel. 401/846–2200), 3 miles northeast of the city, has connecting flights by charter companies to Theodore Francis Green State Airport in Warwick.

Cozy Cab (tel. 401/846–2500) runs a frequent shuttle service ($11) between the airport and the visitors bureau downtown, and some Newport hotels provide free airport shuttle service to guests.

Getting Around Newport

Newport is a walker's city; whether or not you arrive with a car, in most cases you will want to tour on foot.

By Car A car can be a liability in summer, when traffic thickens on the city's narrow one-way streets. When you need a car, the rental agencies are **Avis** (tel. 401/846–1843), **Hertz** (tel. 401/846–6540), and **Pontiac** (tel. 401/847–5600).

By Bus **Rhode Island Public Transit Authority** (tel. 401/847–0209) provides Newport area bus service.

Guided Tours

General-Interest Tours **Viking Bus Tours of Newport** (Brick Marketplace, tel. 401/847–6921) runs Newport tours on air-conditioned buses.

Old Colony & Newport Railway follows an 8-mile route along Narragansett Bay from Newport to Portsmouth. The round-trip takes a little over two hours. *1 America's Cup Ave., tel. 401/624–6951. Departs Newport Sun. 1:30 (May–Dec.), daily 1:30 and Wed. 6:30 PM (July–Aug.).*

The Spirit of Newport (tel. 401/849–3575) gives one-hour minicruises of Newport harbor and Narragansett Bay, departing from the Treadway Inn on America's Cup Avenue every 90 minutes.

Walking Tours The **Newport Freedom Trail** (tel. 401/351–8700) makes a loop through the downtown area, beginning at the Historical Society on Touro Street and finishing at the Automobile Museum.

Newport Historical Society (82 Touro Street, tel. 401/846–0813) sponsors walking tours on Friday and Saturday in summer.

Exploring Newport

Numbers in the margin correspond with the numbered points of interest on the Newport map.

Our exploration of Newport begins with Colonial Newport, the northwestern section of the city, clustered around the harbor; the second half of the tour turns to Newport of the Gilded Age, the southern part of town, where many of the city's stunning mansions stand. The quality of the attractions here is due in large part to the careful efforts of Newport residents and such organizations as the Newport Preservation Society and the Newport Historical Society, which have restored many important buildings to their original condition and opened them to the public.

A walk around **Colonial Newport,** which should give you a good idea of what the town was like at the time of the Revolutionary War, begins at **Hunter House** on Washington Street. Notice the carved pineapple over the doorway of this beautiful Colonial home of 1748; throughout Colonial America the pineapple was a symbol of hospitality from the days when a seaman's wife placed a fresh pineapple at the front door to announce that her husband had returned from the sea. Notice the elliptical arch (a typical Newport architectural detail) in the central hall. In the northeast parlor, notice the cherubs carved over the cupboard. Much of the house is furnished with pieces made by Newport craftsmen Townsend and Goddard. *54 Washington St., tel. 401/847–1000. Admission: $4.50 adults, $2.50 children. Open May–Oct., daily 10–5.*

Walk north on Washington Street to Walnut Street and east on Walnut to Farewell Street to the 18th-century **Common Burial Ground.** The tombstones offer interesting examples of Colonial stonecarving, much of it the work of the stonecutter John Stevens.

Walk south on Farewell Street to Thames Street (pronounced *Thaymz*), the main street of Colonial Newport. Continue south on Thames Street to Washington Square. The **Brick Market,** built in 1760, was designed by Peter Harrison, who was also responsible for the Touro Synagogue and the Redwood Library. From 1793 to 1799 it was used as a theater, and if you look closely at the east wall, you'll find a trace of one of the theatrical scenes—a seascape of ships. In later years the building was

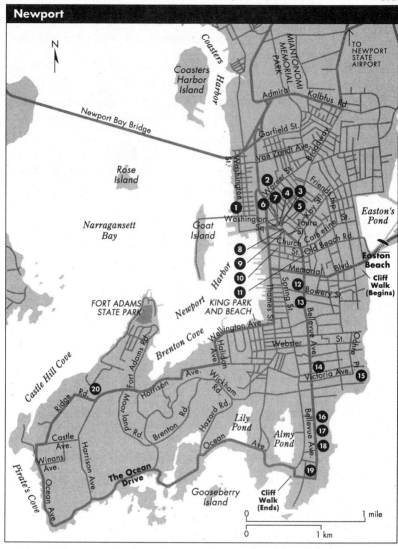

Newport

The Astors'
Beechwood, **17**

Belcourt Castle, **19**

The Breakers, **15**

Brick Market, **3**

Chateau-sur-mer, **14**

Common Burial
Ground, **2**

The Elms, **13**

Friends Meeting
House, **7**

Hammersmith
Farm, **20**

Hunter House, **1**

Kingscote, **12**

Marble House, **18**

Newport Historical
Society, **9**

Old Colony House, **4**

Redwood Library, **11**

Rosecliff, **16**

Touro Synagogue, **8**

Trinity Church, **10**

Wanton-Lyman-
Hazard House, **5**

White Horse Tavern, **6**

used as a town hall. Restored to its original appearance in the 1920s, the building now houses shops. *Tel. 401/846–7482. Open Mon.–Sat. 10–9, Sun. noon–9 in summer; Mon.–Sat. 10–5, Sun. noon–5 in winter.*

④ Facing the Market on Washington Square is the **Old Colony House,** built in 1739. The headquarters of the Colonial and state governments, it was from the balcony of this building that the succession of George III was announced and the Declaration of Independence was read to Newporters. George Washington met General Rochambeau here. *Washington Sq., tel. 401/846–2980. Open by appointment.*

Walk northeast from Washington Square on Broadway to reach
⑤ Newport's oldest house, the **Wanton-Lyman-Hazard House,** which displays a "two-room" plan typical of the time. It also has a Colonial garden, and there are demonstrations of 18th-century cooking. *17 Broadway, tel. 401/846–0813. Admission: $2 adults. Open mid-June–Aug., Tues.–Sat. 10–5.*

Walk west on Broadway and north on Farewell Street to Marl-
⑥ borough Street and the **White Horse Tavern** (tel. 401/849–3600). In operation since 1687, The White Horse claims to be the oldest tavern in America.

⑦ Also on this corner stands the **Friends Meeting House.** Built in 1699, this is the oldest Quaker meeting house in America. *29 Farewell St., tel. 401/846–0813. Open Mon.–Sat. 10–5. Closed Sept.–May.*

Walk south again on Farewell Street to Washington Square, then south across the square to Touro Street. Walk east on Touro Street to the oldest surviving synagogue in the country,
⑧ **Touro Synagogue,** built in 1759 by Peter Harrison. Very simple on the outside, the building's interior is elaborate. Notice the way its design combines the ornate columns and moldings of the Georgian style with Jewish ritualistic requirements. *72 Touro St., tel. 401/847–4791. Open Sun.–Fri. 10–5, and by appointment.*

⑨ At 82 Touro Street you'll find the headquarters of the **Newport Historical Society,** the departure point for walking tours of Newport. The building is also a museum featuring a large collection of Newport memorabilia, furniture, and maritime items. *82 Touro St., tel. 401/846–0813. Open Tues.–Fri. 9:30–4:30.*

Walk south of Washington Square, down Division Street, to the
⑩ corner of Spring and Church streets. Here you'll find **Trinity Church,** a Colonial beauty built in 1724. A special feature of the interior is the three-tiered wineglass pulpit, the only one of its kind in America. *Queen Anne Sq., tel. 401/846–0660. Open daily 10–4.*

For the last stop on our tour of Colonial Newport, walk east along Church Street to the beginning of Bellevue Avenue and
⑪ the **Redwood Library,** built in 1748—the oldest library still in use in the United States. Another magnificent example of the architecture of Peter Harrison, the building, although made of wood, was designed to look like a Roman temple, the exterior being painted to resemble marble. The library houses a wonderful collection of paintings by the important early American artists Gilbert Stuart, Rembrandt Peale, and others. *50 Bellevue Ave., tel. 401/847–0292. Open Mon.–Sat. 9:30–5.*

We turn now to **Gilded Age Newport,** which is largely seen in the splendid mansions of the turn of the century. Contrary to our earlier caution about driving in Newport, you may find a car useful here in covering the considerable distances between the grand homes, for you'll have plenty of walking to do inside the mansions themselves.

It is hard to imagine the sums of money possessed by the wealthy elite who made Newport their summer playground in the late 1800s and early 1900s. The "cottages" they built are almost obscenely grand, laden with ornate rococo detail and designed with a determined one-upmanship.

Six Newport mansions are maintained by the Preservation Society of Newport County (tel. 401/847–1000). A combination ticket—available at any of the society's properties—gives you a discount on individual admission prices. Each mansion provides a guided tour that lasts about one hour.

⓬ We begin at **Kingscote,** just west of Bellevue Avenue, on Bowery Street. Built in 1840 for George Noble Jones, a Savannah, Georgia plantation owner, this mansion serves to remind us that Newport was popular with Southerners before the Civil War. Today it is furnished with antique furniture, glass, and Oriental art. It also has a number of Tiffany windows. *Bowery St., off Bellevue Ave. Admission: $5. Open daily 10–5 in summer. Closed in winter.*

⓭ Head south on Bellevue Avenue and look to your right for **The Elms,** one of Newport's most graceful mansions. The Elms pays homage to the classical design, broad lawn, fountains, and formal gardens of the Chateau d'Asnieres near Paris; it was built for Edward Julius Berwind, a bituminous-coal baron, at the turn of the century. *Bellevue Ave. Admission: $5. Open daily 10–5 in summer, weekends 10–4 in winter.*

⓮ A few blocks south is **Chateau-sur-mer,** the first of Bellevue Avenue's stone mansions. Built in 1852 and enlarged by Richard Morris Hunt for William S. Wetmore, a China trade tycoon, the mansion houses a toy collection. Compared to the more opulent homes built during the 1890s, this one seems rather modest today. A December visit will find the home decorated for a Victorian Christmas. *Bellevue Ave. Admission: $5. Open daily 10–5 in summer, weekends 10–4 in winter.*

⓯ Turn left on Victoria Avenue and continue to Ochre Point Avenue and **The Breakers.** It's easy to understand why it took more than 2,500 workmen two years to create this structure, the most magnificent of the Newport mansions. Built in 1893 for Cornelius Vanderbilt II and his small family, The Breakers has 70 rooms and required 40 servants to keep it running. Just a few of the marvels within the four-story limestone villa are a gold-ceilinged music room, a blue marble fireplace, rose alabaster pillars in the dining room, and a porch whose mosaic ceiling took Italian craftsmen six months, lying on their backs, to install. If it were possible to build The Breakers today, according to recent estimates, it could cost $400 million. *Ochre Point Ave. Admission: $6. Open daily 10–5. Closed in winter.*

⓰ Return to Bellevue Avenue and continue south to **Rosecliff.** Built for Mrs. Hermann Oelrichs, this romantic mansion was completed in 1902. Modeled after the Grand Trianon at Versailles, the 40-room home includes the Court of Love (inspired by a similar room at Versailles) and a heart-shaped staircase designed by Stanford White. It has appeared in several movies, including *The Great Gatsby. Bellevue Ave. Admission: $5. Open daily 10–5. Closed in winter.*

❼ Farther down Bellevue Avenue is **The Astors' Beechwood,** where a succession of actors, dressed in period costume, play the parts of members of the Astor family (including Mrs. Astor, the belle of New York and Newport society), servants, and household guests. The guides involve visitors in much banter, such as noticing a woman's knee-length skirt and asking, "Do your clothes have a shrinkage problem?" If you'd enjoy a touch of time travel, by all means look in. *580 Bellevue Ave., tel. 401/ 846–3772. Admission: $7 adults, $6 senior citizens and children 6–12. Open daily 10–5.*

Continue down Bellevue Avenue, and on your left will be
❽ **Marble House,** with its extravagant gold ballroom, the gift of William Vanderbilt to his wife, Alva, in 1892. Alva divorced William in 1895, and married Oliver Perry Belmont and became the lady of Belcourt Castle (just down the road). When Oliver died in 1908, she returned to Marble House. Mrs. Belmont was involved with the suffragist movement and spent much of her time campaigning for women's rights. In the kitchen you'll see plates marked Votes for Women. The lovely Chinese teahouse behind the estate was built in 1913 by Mrs. Belmont. *Bellevue Ave. Admission: $5. Open daily 10–5 in summer, weekends 10–4 in winter.*

❾ Farther along the avenue is **Belcourt Castle,** designed by Richard Morris Hunt, and based on Louis XIII's hunting lodge. The castle contains an enormous collection of European and Oriental treasures. Sip tea and admire the stained glass and carved wood, and don't miss the Golden Coronation Coach. *Bellevue Ave., tel. 401/846–0669 or 849–1566. Admission: $4.50 adults, $2.50 senior citizens, $10 family (2 adults and 2 children). Open daily 10–5. Closed Feb., Mar.*

❿ Take Ocean Drive all the way along the coast to **Hammersmith Farm,** the childhood summer home of Jacqueline Bouvier Kennedy Onassis, the site of her wedding to John F. Kennedy, and a summer White House during the Kennedy Administration. It is also the only working farm in Newport. Loaded with Bouvier and Kennedy memorabilia, the house is so comfortable that it seems as though its owners have just stepped out of the room. The elaborate gardens were designed by Frederick Law Olmsted, and there are breathtaking views of the ocean. *Ocean Dr., near Ft. Adams, tel. 401/846–7346. Admission: $5 adults, $2 children. Open daily 10–5, summer until 7. Closed mid-Nov.– Mar.*

Exploring East of Newport

Between the city of Newport and the Massachusetts border to the east there are two areas that deserve a visit, either as an excursion from Newport or as the continuation of a coastal tour: Portsmouth and the Sakonnet lands.

It's less than 10 miles from Newport to **Portsmouth,** traveling north on Route 138. Situated on the Sakonnet River on the east side of Aquidneck Island, Portsmouth has seen much development in recent years, a departure from its somewhat rural past.

Turn east from Route 138 onto Sandy Point Avenue to reach **Sandy Point Beach,** where the calm surf of the Sakonnet River creates a choice spot for families and beginning windsurfers.

Leaving the beach area, continue north on Route 138, then head west and look out for the "Green Animals" signs that direct you to a **topiary garden** filled with plants sculpted to look like an elephant, a bear, a giraffe, and other animals, all set on a lovely sloping lawn that descends to Narrangansett Bay. *Cory's La., tel. 401/847–1000. Admission: $4.50 adults, $2.50 children 6–11. Open May–Oct., daily 10–5.*

Route 138 a few miles farther north will take you across the bridge over the Sakonnet River and into the Sakonnet lands. Turn south and take Route 77 to **Tiverton.**

On Lawton Avenue in Tiverton, turn right to reach the remains of **Fort Barton,** named for Colonel William Barton, who captured Newport's British commander during the Revolutionary War. A climb of the observation tower will give you a view of Aquidneck Island.

It's about 12 miles south on Route 77 from Tiverton to the town of **Little Compton.** Turn left on Meetinghouse Lane and take a few minutes to walk on Little Compton commons, a typical New England commons, at the edge of which is a lofty United Congregational Church built in 1832. Examine the gravestones at the nearby church burial ground, laid out in 1675; one honors Benjamin Church, the Indian fighter who took part in the Great Swamp Fight and the execution of King Philip. Across the commons is a Big Toy playground structure that attracts children from miles around.

Museums and Galleries

International Tennis Hall of Fame and the **Tennis Museum.** Housed in a magnificent building by Stanford White, the museum features photographs and other memorabilia of more than a century of tennis history. The first National Tennis Championships were held here in 1881. *Newport Casino, 194 Bellevue Ave., tel. 401/849–3990. Admission: $4 adults, $2 children 6–12, $10 family. Open May–Oct., daily 11–5; Nov.–Apr., daily 11–4.*

Museum of Yachting. Here are galleries of pictures of the incredible yachts of the Vanderbilts, the Astors, and the Belmonts. *Ft. Adams, Ocean Dr., tel. 401/847–1018. Admission: $2 adults, $1 senior citizens, children under 12 free. Open mid–May–Oct., Tues.–Sun. 10–5.*

Newport Art Museum and Art Association. Permanent and changing exhibits of historic contemporary art of Rhode Island and New England are offered. Notice the building's stick-style Victorian architecture, courtesy of designer Richard Morris Hunt. *76 Bellevue Ave., tel. 401/847–0179. Admission: $3 adults, $2 senior citizens and students. Open Tues.–Sat. 10–5, Sun. 1–5.*

Newport for Free

A 3-mile **Cliff Walk,** which begins at Easton's Beach and runs
along Newport's cliffs, offers a water level view of many Newport mansions. This is a challenging walk, not recommended
for the elderly or infirm or for children under six, but it promises breathtaking vistas.

Concerts in Newport parks and **events at Newport Beach Rotunda** on Memorial Boulevard are held throughout the summer.

Kite flying is a popular pastime on Newport's beaches and in its
parks.

Price's Neck along Ocean Drive is a wonderful spot to stop for a
picnic, within sight of the ships at sail in summer and early fall.

What to See and Do with Children

Norman Bird Sanctuary. The 450-acre sanctuary has nature
trails, guided tours, and a small natural history museum. *583
Third Beach Rd., Middletown, tel. 401/846–2577. Admission:
$2 adults. Open daily 9–5.*

The Children's Theatre (Astor's Beechwood, Bellevue Ave., tel.
401/848–0266) puts on several major productions for children
each year.

Shopping

Newport is a shopper's city, though not a city for bargain hunters. Its specialties include antiques, traditional clothing, and
marine supplies. Many of Newport's arts and antiques shops
can be found on Thames Street or near the waterfront, and
others are located on Spring Street, Franklin Street, and at
Bowen's and Bannister's wharves. The Brick Market area—
between Thames Street and America's Cup Avenue—has more
than 50 shops.

Department Stores **Leys** (Long Wharf Mall, opposite Gateway Center, tel. 401/
846–2100), America's oldest department store (established in
1796), offers clothing, linens, home furnishings, and souvenirs.

The Narragansett (11 Memorial Blvd., tel. 401/847–0303) has
leather, cashmere, and silk fashions for men and women.

Specialty Stores **Aardvark Antiques** (475 Thames St., tel. 401/849–7233) has ar-
Antiques chitectural pieces: mantels, doors, and garden ornaments.

Black Sheep Antiques (54 Spring St., tel. 401/846–6810) stocks
an unusual combination of antiques and collectibles. You may
find period glassware, quilts, linens, baskets, furniture, and
lots of nautical antiques.

Full Swing (474 Thames St., tel. 401/849–9494) has collectibles
from the 1920s through the 1950s: odd lamps, ashtrays, books,
dishes, strange furniture, and vintage fabrics.

John Gidley House (22 Franklin St., tel. 401/846–8303) features
Continental furnishings from the 18th and 19th centuries. The
store's own chandeliers and marble are a reminder of what
Newport was like in the Gilded Age.

The Old Fashion Shop (38 Pelham St., tel. 401/849–7330) sells American furniture and accessories, including elegant china, kitchenware, quilts, and glass—and Oriental objects.

Art **The Liberty Tree** (128 Spring St., tel. 401/847–5925) has contemporary folk art, furniture, carvings, and paintings.

Native American Trading Company: Indian Territory (104 Spring St., tel. 401/846–8465) sells paintings and artifacts.

Books **Anchor & Dolphin Books** (30 Franklin St., tel. 401/846–6890) buys, sells, and appraises rare books, libraries, and collections. The store is especially rich in garden history, architecture, and design.

The Armchair Sailor (Lee's Wharf, tel. 401/847–4252) stocks marine and travel books, charts, and maps.

Crafts **Tropea-Puerini** (492 Thames St., tel. 401/846–3344) calls itself the Alternative Bridal Registry and offers interesting pottery, sculpture, jewelry, and other crafts.

Home Furnishings **Rue de France** (78 Thames St., tel. 401/846–3636) specializes in French lace: curtains, pillows, and table linens.

Jewelry **J. H. Breakell & Co.** (69 Mills St., tel. 401/849–3522) shows original designs in gold and silver.

Men's Clothing **JT's Ship Chandlery** (364 Thames St., tel. 401/846–7256) is a major supplier of marine hardware, equipment, and clothing.

Native American Trading Company: Explorer's Club (138 Spring St., tel. 401/846–8465) features quality outdoor sportswear with British and American labels.

Women's Clothing **Native American Trading Company: Ladies' Division** (140 Spring St., tel. 401/846–8465) shows quality shearlings and leathers and other outdoor wear.

Sports and Outdoor Activities

Biking **Ten Speed Spokes** (79 Thames St., tel. 401/847–5609) has bikes; **Newport Rent-a-Ped** (2 Washington St., tel. 401/846–7788) has mopeds.

Boating **Old Port Marine Services** (Sayer's Wharf, tel. 401/847–9109) has boat rentals.

Fishing No license is required for saltwater fishing, although anglers should check with local bait shops for minimum size requirements. Charter fishing boats depart daily from Newport, from the spring through the fall. For bait and tackle, visit **Newport Bait and Tackle** (462 Thames St., tel. 401/423–1170). For charter boats, contact **Black Horse Fishing Charter** (Long Wharf Moorings, tel. 401/846–0540).

Spectator Sports

Newport Jai-alai (150 Admiral Kalbfus Rd., tel. 401/849–5000) has been called "the fastest game on two feet." The season here runs from May to mid-October.

Beaches

Newport **Easton's Beach** (Memorial Blvd.), also known as First Beach, is popular for its carousel for the kids and miniature golf.

Fort Adams State Park (Ocean Dr.), a small beach with a picnic area and lifeguards during the summer, has beautiful views of Newport Harbor.

King Park (Wellington Ave.), with lifeguards patrolling during the summer, is a haven for scuba divers.

Middletown **Sachuest Beach** (Sachuest Point area), or Second Beach, is a beautiful sandy beach adjacent to the Norman Bird Sanctuary. Dunes and a campground make it popular with singles and surfers.

Third Beach (Sachuest Point area), on the Sakonnet River, with a boat ramp, is a favorite of windsurfers.

Dining

Casual wear is the rule in the restaurants of Newport except as noted.

American **The Black Pearl.** At this popular waterfront restaurant with a nautical decor, diners choose between the tavern and the more formal Commodore's Room. The latter offers such appetizers as black and blue tuna with red pepper sauce; and oysters warmed with truffles and cream. Sample entrées on a recent menu were swordfish with dutch pepper butter; salmon with mustard dill hollandaise; and duck breast with green peppercorn sauce. *Bannister's Wharf, tel. 401/846–5264. Reservations advised. Jacket required. AE, DC, MC, V. Expensive.*

Clarke Cooke House. The lamb and the game on the menu are raised here on the farm, and the vegetables are grown locally as well. Chicken breast stuffed with lobster in a lobster sauce; and sole poached in Chardonnay with asparagus are typical offerings at dinner. *Bannister's Wharf, tel. 401/849–2900. Reservations advised; required in summer. Jacket required. AE, MC, V. Expensive.*

Star Clipper Dinner Train. Dine on prime rib or swordfish as you ride clackety-clack from the Newport Depot to the Mount Hope Bridge and back. The four-course meal in transit lasts two hours. *19 America's Cup Ave., tel. 401/849–7550. Reservations required. MC, V. Expensive.*

Brick Alley Pub. An extensive menu includes fresh fish, chowder, steaks, and homemade pasta. *140 Thames St., tel. 401/ 849–6334. Reservations advised. AE, MC, V. Moderate.*

Wave Cafe. One can stop here for a full breakfast and return for a deli lunch or dinner; the principal attractions are a large selection of cheeses and smoked meats, a salad bar, homemade desserts, and fresh-roasted coffee. *580 Thames St., tel. 401/ 846–6060. No reservations. MC, V. BYOB. No dinner Mon. Moderate.*

★ **Commons Lunch.** This is a good place to try johnnycakes, which are grittier than pancakes, and quahog pie. Onion rings are served in generous portions. *Little Compton Commons, tel. 401/635–4388. No reservations. No credit cards. Inexpensive.*

Franklin Spa. Omelets and a thick, hearty beef stew are two attractions of this neighborhood luncheonette. *229 Spring St., tel. 401/847–3540. No reservations. No credit cards. Inexpensive.*

Gary's Handy Lunch. The friendly breakfast and lunch spot is often filled with anglers. *462 Thames St., tel. 401/847–9480. No reservations. No credit cards. No dinner. Inexpensive.*

Continental **White Horse Tavern.** One of the nation's oldest operating tav-
★ erns, the White Horse offers a setting conducive to intimate
dining. Lobster and beef Wellington are standard entrées. *Corner of Marlborough and Farewell Sts., tel. 401/849–3600.
Reservations required. Jacket required. AE, CB, DC, MC, V.
No lunch Tues. Expensive.*

Riviera Family Restaurant. The traditional Portuguese food
served here is a staple of many area residents. Favorite dishes
include kale soup; *clams Bulhao Pato* (clams steamed in garlic,
beer, parsley, olive oil, and *piri-piri,* a Portuguese hot sauce);
and shrimps Mozambique, a spicy shrimp sauté. *1 Bay St.,
Tiverton, tel. 401/624–8268. Reservations advised. MC, V.
Moderate.*

French **Le Bistro.** The friendly, informal, pleasantly crowded restaurant serves such entrées as duck confit; fresh foie gras with
artichokes; and roast rack of lamb. The less expensive luncheon
menu features soups, fancy sandwiches, salads, omelets.
*Bowen's Wharf, tel. 401/849–7778. Reservations advised. AE,
CB, DC, MC, V. Expensive.*

La Petite Auberge. While this romantic French restaurant suggests the 19th century, there are 20th-century surprises on the
menu as well, one of them the Cajun blackened tenderloin. *19
Charles St., tel. 401/849–6669. Reservations advised. AE, MC,
V. Expensive.*

Italian **Puerini's.** This friendly neighborhood restaurant with the long
and intriguing menu presents such selections as green noodles
with chicken in marsala wine sauce; tortellini with seafood; and
cavatelli in four cheeses. *24 Memorial Blvd., tel. 401/847–5506.
No reservations. No smoking. No credit cards. BYOB. No
lunch. Closed Sun. in winter. Moderate.*

Seafood **Anthony's Seafood & Shore Dinner Hall.** The large, light room
with the panoramic views of Newport Harbor is a cafeteria-
style restaurant serving seafood at reasonable prices. Families
find the atmosphere congenial. The adjoining seafood shop has
local specialties. *Lower Thames St., at Waites Wharf, tel. 401/
848–5058. No reservations. MC, V. Closed Oct.–Nov., Mon.–
Wed; Dec.–Mar. Moderate.*

Evelyn's Nanaquaket Drive-In. A favorite of those who enjoy
fried seafood, Evelyn's prepares versions that are low in cholesterol and salt-free. The seafood platter is large enough to be
shared. *2335 Main Rd., Tiverton, tel. 401/624–3100. No reservations. No credit cards. Closed in winter. Moderate.*

★ **The Lobster Pot.** A glass wall provides a view looking onto Narragansett Bay, and the menu offers grilled lobster, crab cakes,
and smelt. *119–121 Hope St., Bristol, tel. 401/253–9100. Reservations advised. AE, MC, V. Closed Mon.; 2 weeks in Feb.;
July 4; Thanksgiving; Dec. 25. Moderate.*

Salas'. Movie posters, red-and-white plastic tablecloths, and
lines of waiting customers create a lively, good-natured waterfront dining spot. Pastas, lobster, clams, and corn-on-the-cob
are the principal fare. *341 Thames St., tel. 401/846–8772. No
reservations. AE, V. Moderate.*

Lodging

The Inntowne. Accommodations are more modest than those of
The Inn at Castle Hill (below), which is under the same management and which sends travelers here when it is fully

booked. Guests use a private beach at Castle Hill, and tea is served in the afternoon. *6 Mary St., 02840, tel. 401/846–9200. 26 rooms, 25 with bath. AE, MC, V. Closed Dec. 24–25. Rates include Continental breakfast. Expensive.*

Brinley Victorian Inn. With two parlors, a library, and a Victorian courtyard, this inn won *Yankee* magazine's Apple Pie contest in 1989. *23 Brinley St., 02840, tel. 401/849–7645. 17 rooms, 13 with bath. Facilities: off-street parking. MC, V. Rates include Continental breakfast. Moderate–Expensive.*

Cliffside Inn. A Victorian home of 1880, Cliffside is near Newport's Cliff Walk. Its atmosphere is homey, the rooms furnished with attractive Victorian antiques. "Miss Beatrice's Room" has two bay windows. *2 Seaview Ave., 02840, tel. 401/847–1811. 11 rooms with bath. Facilities: porch, meeting area. No smoking. AE, MC, V. Moderate–Expensive.*

The Inn at Castle Hill. Built as a summer home in 1874, the inn is popular and requires booking well in advance. In *Theophilus North* Thornton Wilder wrote of the views from the room "in a turret above the house," which can be booked. *Ocean Dr., 02840, tel. 401/849–3800. 10 rooms with bath. Facilities: private beach. AE, MC, V. Closed Dec. 24–25. Rates include Continental breakfast. Moderate–Expensive.*

★ **Ivy Lodge.** The only bed-and-breakfast in the mansion district has the look of a large Victorian home with a wraparound porch. Inside you'll find a 33-foot gothic paneled oak entry with a three-story turned baluster staircase. A fire burns brightly on fall and winter afternoons in the huge brick fireplace built in the shape of a Moorish arch. Rooms are spacious and very private. *12 Clays St., 02840, tel. 401/849–6865. 10 rooms, 8 with bath. MC, V. Rates include Continental breakfast. Moderate–Expensive.*

Victorian Ladies. This bed-and-breakfast is sumptuously decorated with Victorian antiques and is within walking distance of Newport's shops. While the thoroughfare has a fair amount of traffic, the house's insulation muffles the sound significantly. *63 Memorial Blvd., 02840, tel. 401/849–9960. 9 rooms with bath. Facilities: off-street parking. MC, V. Closed Jan. Moderate–Expensive.*

The Marriott. The luxury hotel on the harbor at Long Wharf has an elegant atrium lobby with marble floors and a gazebo. *25 America's Cup Ave., 02840, tel. 401/849–1000 or 800/228–9290. 310 rooms with bath, 7 suites. Facilities: restaurant, cocktail lounge, disco, pool, sauna, 4 racquetball courts, health club, Jacuzzi, conference rooms. AE, DC, MC, V. Moderate.*

Sheraton Islander Inn. This resort hotel, set on its own private island, has an impressive view of the harbor and Colonial Newport. The nautical New England lobby makes it less easily recognizable as a Sheraton. *Goat Island 02840, tel. 401/849–2600 or 800/325–3535. 250 rooms with bath. Facilities: 4 restaurants, indoor pool, outdoor saltwater pool, health center, sauna, beauty salon, 2 racquetball courts, marina, conference rooms. AE, DC, MC, V. Moderate.*

The Arts

Newport County Convention and Visitors Bureau (23 America's Cup Ave., tel. 401/849–8040) has listings of concerts, shows, and special events, as do the Newport and Providence newspapers.

Theater **Blaus Haus Theatre** (Blue Pelican, W. Broadway, tel. 401/847–5675) schedules performances Wednesday through Sunday.
Kinderhook Theater (102 Connell Hwy., tel. 401/847–9910) offers contemporary productions.
Rhode Island Shakespeare Theater (tel. 401/849–7892) performs classic plays at several spaces in Newport.

Nightlife

The Ark (348 Thames St., tel. 401/849–3808) features a piano bar on Friday and Saturday, jazz on Sunday.
Blue Pelican (40 W. Broadway, tel. 401/846–5675) is popular for jazz.
Clark Cooke House (Bannister's Wharf, tel. 401/849–2900) has a piano bar upstairs, disco and swing downstairs.
Viking Hotel (1 Bellevue Ave., tel. 401/847–3300) offers mainstream jazz on Sunday afternoon.

Block Island

Situated 13 miles off the coast, Block Island's 11-square-mile area has been a popular tourist destination since the 19th century. Despite the large number of visitors who come here each year, the island's beauty and privacy have been preserved; its 365 freshwater ponds make it a haven for more than 150 species of migrating birds. Camping and tenting are illegal, as is operating a motorcycle between midnight and 6 AM. Shellfishing without a license is illegal; licenses, when available, may be obtained at the police station. Mopeds can be rented at many locations for riding on the town roads, but they should be used with caution, especially by those unfamiliar with them. Mopeds are prohibited on dirt roads.

Block Island's original inhabitants were the Native Americans who called it Manisses, or Isle of the Little God. In 1524 Verrazano renamed it Claudia, after the mother of the French king. Revisited in 1614 by the Dutch explorer Adrian Block, the island was given the name Adrian's Eyelant, which later became Block Island. In 1661 the island was settled by colonists seeking religious freedom; they established a farming and fishing community that exists today.

Important Addresses and Numbers

Visitor **Block Island Chamber of Commerce** (Drawer D, 02807, tel. 401/
Information 466–2982).

Arriving and Departing by Plane

New England Airlines (tel. 401/596–2460 or 800/243–2460) provides air service from Westerly State Airport to Block Island.

Action Air (tel. 800/243–8623) has flights from Groton, Connecticut to Block Island from June to October.

Several of the island's hotels offer courtesy vans to assist guests with their luggage. Taxis are also available.

Arriving and Departing By Car and Ferry

Interstate Navigation Co. (Galilee State Pier, Point Judith, tel. 401/783–4613) provides ferry service from Galilee (1 hr, 10 min; make reservations for your car well in advance) and passenger boats from Providence via Newport.

Nelseco Navigation (tel. 203/442–7891) runs a ferry from New London, Connecticut (2 hrs) in summer.

Jigger III (tel. 516/668–2214) has ferry service (passengers only) from Montauk, Long Island (2 hrs), June–September.

Getting Around Block Island

By Car   **Block Island Car Rental** (tel. 401/466–2297) and **Block Island Boat Basin** (tel. 401/466–2631) have rentals.

By Bicycle and   **Esta's at Old Harbor** (tel. 401/466–2651), **Old Harbor Bike Shop**
Moped   (tel. 401/466–2029), and **Block Island Boat Basin** (tel. 401/466–2631) have rentals.

By Taxi   The island's dispatch services include **Airport Taxi Dispatch** (tel. 401/466–5668), **Milner Taxi Service** (tel. 401/466–7728), Bob Rice (tel. 401/466–2206), **Monica Hull Shea** (tel. 401/466–5946), **Foy Stiefer** (tel. 401/466–5573), **Mac Todd** (tel. 401/466–2029), and **Wolfie's Taxi** (tel. 401/466–5550).

Exploring Block Island

Numbers in the margin correspond to the numbered points of interest on the Block Island map.

Block Island has two harbors, Old Harbor and New Harbor. The Old Harbor commercial district extends along Water, Dodge, and Main streets. Approaching Block Island by sea, you'll see the Old Harbor and its group of Victorian hotels.

The Old Harbor area is the island's only village—a concentration of shops, boutiques, restaurants, inns, and hotels—accessible on foot from the ferry landing, and near most of the interesting sights of Block Island.

❶ Our tour of the island begins at the **Block Island Historical Society,** where permanent and special exhibits have propagated the island's farming and maritime past since the society opened in 1942. *Old Town Rd., tel. 401/466–2481. Open June–Sept., daily 10–4.*

Head east on Old Town Road, and a short walk north on Corn Neck Road brings you to a string of beautiful beaches known **❷** collectively as **Crescent Beach.** State Beach, patrolled by lifeguards, is good for a swim.

❸ Continue north on Corn Neck Road to find the **Clayhead Nature Trail,** leading first to the east, where you'll hike along oceanside cliffs, then to the north. Don't be afraid to meander down side trails for the best views and wildlife spotting. Guided tours are available in summer.

❹ If you follow the trail to its end, you'll find the stone of **Settler's Rock** on the shores of Chaqum Pond. Erected in 1911, Settler's Rock lists the names of the original settlers and marks the spot where they first landed in 1661.

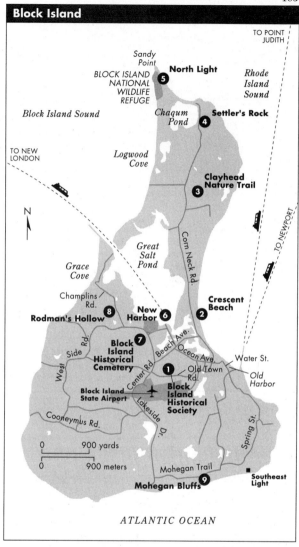

Block Island

TO POINT JUDITH

Sandy Point

BLOCK ISLAND NATIONAL WILDLIFE REFUGE

North Light ⑤

Rhode Island Sound

Block Island Sound

Chaqum Pond

Settler's Rock ④

TO NEW LONDON

Logwood Cove

Clayhead Nature Trail ③

N

Great Salt Pond

Corn Neck Rd.

Grace Cove

Champlins Rd.

Rodman's Hollow ⑧

New Harbor ⑥

Crescent Beach ②

TO NEWPORT

⑦

West Side Rd.

Block Island Historical Cemetery

Beach Ave.

Ocean Ave.

Water St.

Center Rd.

Block Island State Airport

① Old Town Rd.

Block Island Historical Society

Old Harbor

Lakeside Dr.

Cooneymus Rd.

Spring St.

0   900 yards
0   900 meters

Mohegan Trail

Mohegan Bluffs ⑨

■ **Southeast Light**

ATLANTIC OCEAN

⑤ It's a 7-mile hike along the coast to the **North Light at Sandy Point,** the northernmost tip of Block Island; many visitors prefer to rent bikes in town for the trip. Built in 1867 of Connecticut granite hauled to the site by oxen, it's being restored to house a maritime museum. Beware of the many seagulls nesting in the rocks leading up to the lighthouse!

⑥ Follow Corn Neck Road all the way back to town, turn right onto Beach Avenue, and right again onto Ocean Avenue. **New Harbor,** on the inland side of the Great Salt Pond, provides safe anchor for the many small craft that call at Block Island. The harbor also has shops and marina facilities.

⑦ Turn right off Ocean Avenue onto West Side Road and climb to the top of Job's Hill. There the **Block Island Historical Ceme-**

tery houses the remains of island residents since the 1700s. You may have to brush back the tangled growths of vines to study the legends of their lives.

❽ Turn right onto Champlins Road. On your right, **Rodman's Hollow,** one of Block Island's five wildlife refuges, is a natural wonder: a ravine formed by a glacier. With many winding paths, you can follow the deep cleft in the hills all the way down to the sea.

Follow West Side Road east to Center Road, which becomes Lakeside Drive. Turn left along the Mohegan Trail to the **❾** southern tip of the island, the top of **Mohegan Bluffs.** There you'll get dramatic ocean views from a height of 150 feet, and you'll see the Southeast Light, a brick building with gingerbread detail built in 1873.

Shopping

Department Stores **The Shoreline** (Fish Head Bldg., Water St., tel. 401/466–2541) has contemporary clothing by Patagonia, Esprit, Kiko, Cambridge Dry Goods, and B. D. Baggies.

Star Department Store (tel. 401/466–5541), the self-proclaimed "general store of Block Island," stocks saltwater taffy, film, toys, souvenirs, gifts, shoes, hats, and a line of active sportswear. The island's largest selection of T-shirts and sweatshirts can be found here.

Specialty Stores **Emily's** (Ocean Ave., no phone) has vintage clothing, linens,
Antiques antiques, and jewelry.

Art Galleries **Ragged Sailor** (Water St., tel. 401/466–7704) shows paintings, crafts, porcelain, folk art, and photographs.

Square One Gallery (Dodge St., tel. 401/466–5016) exhibits the work of Block Island and other New England artists.

Books **The Book Nook** (Water St., no phone) stocks paperbacks, posters, magazines, and newspapers from major cities in and around New England.

Crafts **The Barn** (Spring St., tel. 401/466–5379), an artist's cooperative, shows and sells handknit baby clothing, stained glass, serigraphs, and other work of island artists and craftspeople.

Scarlett Begonia (Dodge St., tel. 401/466–5024) offers unusual jewelry and crafts.

Miscellaneous **Block Island Boatworks and Block Island Kite Co.** (Corn Neck Rd., tel. 401/466–2033) occupy two buildings, one filled with kites, the other with boating equipment, casual clothing, fine garden furniture, and tools.

Esta's at Old Harbor (Water St., tel. 401/466–2651) has resort wear, sun products, beach supplies, and souvenirs.

Island House, the Irish Shoppe (Water St., tel. 401/466–2309) sells imported Irish merchandise, handknit sweaters, and jewelry.

Toys **The Mouse House** (Beach Ave., no phone) is filled with puzzles and games, dinosaurs, stuffed animals, paper dolls, and lots of books. Many of the toys are imported.

Sports and Outdoor Activities

Boating **Block Island Boat Basin** (tel. 401/466–2631) and **Captain Dick Lemoi** (tel. 401/466–2688) offer charters.

Block Island Club (tel. 401/466–5939) rents sailboats.

Twin Maples (tel. 401/466–5547) has rowboats for rent.

Water Sports Sailboard rentals and lessons are available from **Island Moped** (tel. 401/466–2700).

Sailboards and surfboards can be found at **Claudia's Surf City** (tel. 401/466–2026).

Dining

Casual wear is appropriate in the restaurants of Block Island.

★ **Manisses.** Dine inside by the long, oak bar which once graced a Boston waterfront establishment; under the canopy on the outdoor deck; or in the glassed-in garden terrace. Try the smoked fish or meats from the smokehouse, or enjoy the raw bar or an appetizer of gourmet pizza. Main courses include local seafood; and beef, pork, and veal dishes. Fresh vegetables are grown in the hotel's garden, and delicious homemade desserts are prepared by the pastry chef. The inn was recently featured in *Gourmet* magazine. *Spring St., tel. 401/466–2836. Reservations advised. AE, MC, V. Closed Nov.–mid-Apr. No lunch. Expensive.*

Ballard's Inn. The place to go for lobster, Italian food, or family-style dinners, this noisy, lively spot caters to the boating crowd. Go here if you're looking for a place to polka. *Old Harbor, tel. 401/466–2231. MC, V. Closed Nov.–Apr. Moderate.*

Finn's Seafood Bar. Eat inside, or out on the deck, which offers a panoramic view of the harbor. The smoked bluefish pâté is wonderful. A popular lunch order is the Workman's Special platter—a burger, coleslaw, and french fries. Take-out orders are available. *Water St., tel. 401/466–2473. AE, MC, V. Moderate.*

Harborside Inn. This cheerful restaurant features excellent, fresh native seafood, as well as steaks, and an extensive salad bar. Order the scallops sautéed in butter, or the lobster, swordfish, or steak, and enjoy the view from the pleasant, bustling outdoor terrace. *Ferry Landing, tel. 401/466–5504. Reservations advised. AE, MC, V. Closed Nov.–May. Moderate.*

The Beachhead. This is a favorite local spot, where you can catch up on local gossip or stare out at the sea. Have a burger, or try the spicy chili. *Corn Neck Rd., tel. 401/466–2249. No reservations. No credit cards. No dinner in winter. Closed Dec. 25. Inexpensive.*

Lodging

Atlantic Inn, Perched on a hill, a short walk from the Old Harbor and town, the inn boasts a veranda with sweeping views of the sunset, the harbor, beaches, and bluffs. Built in 1880 and restored in 1986, the Atlantic's rooms are carpeted and simply furnished with antiques. *Box 188, High St., 02807, tel. 401/466–2005. 21 rooms. Facilities: tennis; croquet; conference* *room with telephones, AV equipment, PC interface. Closed Dec.–Mar. Expensive.*

Blue Dory Inn. This restored hotel, with two small additional houses, is decorated with Victorian-era antiques, and each room has either an ocean or harbor view. Continental breakfast, consisting of fresh breads, rolls, pastries, fruits, juices, and coffee or herbal tea, is served each morning in a homey kitchen facing the ocean. *Box 488, Dodge St., 02807, tel. 401/ 466–2254. 13 rooms with bath. MC, V. Expensive.*

★ **Manisses.** Each room is unique in this restored mansion with the Victorian furnishings, where afternoon tea is served in a romantic parlor overlooking the garden. The inn dining room hosts a buffet breakfast, offers gourmet meals, and prepares an elegant picnic basket. *Box 1, 02807; Spring St., tel. 401/466– 2063. 17 rooms with bath. Facilities: restaurant, ceiling fans, Jacuzzi in some rooms. AE, MC, V. Closed Dec.–Mar. Rates include buffet breakfast. Expensive.*

1661 Inn and Guest House. Humphrey the llama greets you at this cozy inn overlooking the Atlantic Ocean and Old Harbor. Guests sup in the dining room or outdoors on a canopied deck with ocean view. The breakfast buffet includes such fare as bluefish, corned beef hash, Boston baked beans, sausage, Belgian waffles, roast potatoes, french toast, scrambled eggs, hot and cold cereal, fruit juice, and fresh muffins. *Spring St., 02807, tel. 401/466–2421 or 466–2063. 26 rooms, 24 with bath. Facilities: some rooms have a deck, some have a Jacuzzi. AE, MC, V. Rates include buffet breakfast. Expensive.*

Rose Farm Inn. Just outside the village of Old Harbor, next to the Atlantic Inn, Rose Farm is convenient to downtown and the beaches. The wallpapered rooms, recently redone, are furnished with antiques, and all have views. Porch and sundeck offer society and relaxation. *Box E, 02807; Roslyn Rd., tel. 401/466–2021. 10 rooms, 9 with bath. AE, MC. Closed Nov.–Apr. Rates include buffet breakfast. Moderate–Expensive.*

National Hotel. This classic Block Island hotel has recently been renovated throughout and the original furniture of the guest rooms restored. The front porch commands a view of the Old Harbor and the Atlantic Ocean and is the setting for breakfast, lunch, and afternoon cocktails. Indoors, the dining room offers seafood and entertainment. The hotel's central location makes it fairly busy, especially during high season; while it may be a great place to stay with the family or a group of friends, it may not have the tranquility that some seek for a romantic getaway weekend. *Box 189, 02807; Water St., tel. 401/466–2901 or 800/225–2449. 43 rooms with bath. Facilities: color TV, telephone. AE, MC, V. Closed Dec.–Feb. Moderate.*

Old Town Inn. A quiet, out-of-the-way inn at the head of Crescent Beach, near the Block Island Airport, the Old Town offers antique furnishings and art. All rooms have distant ocean or harbor views. Breakfast, served in the inn kitchen, features fresh breads, breakfast rolls, pastry, fresh fruit, and juice. *Box 488, 02807; Dodge St., tel. 401/466–5958. 10 rooms with bath. MC, V. Closed Nov.–Apr. Moderate.*

Surf Hotel. Furnished with Victorian antiques, the Surf is famous for its big breakfast, the only meal it serves. The spacious porch with the old-fashioned rockers overlooks Old Harbor.

Dodge St., 02807, tel. 401/466–2633 or 401/466–5990. 40 rooms with bath. MC, V. Closed Nov.–Apr. Inexpensive.

Nightlife

McGovern's Yellow Kittens Tavern (Corn Neck Rd., tel. 401/466–5855), established in 1876, features live music.

5 Massachusetts

*by Anne Merewood
and Candice
Gianetti, with an
introduction by
William G.
Scheller*

*The author of two
travel guides to
Greece, Anne
Merewood writes
frequently on
health and travel
for major
American
magazines.
Candice Gianetti,
who wrote the
Cape Cod,
Martha's
Vineyard, and
Nantucket sections
of this chapter, is
the author of*
Fodor's Cape Cod
1991. *The Boston
section of the
chapter is
abridged from*
Fodor's Boston.

Americans tend to see Massachusetts not just as postcard views of pretty villages and Beacon Hill streetscapes, but as a center of social and political thought. Conservatives call it derisively the People's Republic of Massachusetts; liberals remember it fondly as the only state to vote for George McGovern in the presidential election of 1972. At the same time, the commonwealth is often stereotyped as a bastion of reactionaries, of thin-lipped Yankees who banned books and condemned Sacco and Vanzetti in the 1920s. Yet the image of puritanical rectitude is accompanied by memories of the roguish Boston mayor James Michael Curley, who for most of the first half of this century ran a crony-ridden fiefdom as reform-proof as any Chicago machine.

Unlike the other New England states, Massachusetts is populous enough, rich enough, and influential enough to conceive of itself as playing a substantial role in the scheme of the nation—and to trouble itself over just what that role might be. For generations the Bay State has amounted to something of a national resource, offering brains and conscience in much the same way that the desert yields borax or the Pacific Northwest contributes salmon and logs. (Massachusetts once had marketable supplies of salmon and logs, too, but they ran out years ago.) Great eras of shipping, manufacturing, high technology, investment banking, and insurance have followed one upon the other in the centuries since the first settlers built an economy based on primary resources, and throughout all these epochs ideas have been Massachusetts's greatest stock-in-trade.

The list of Massachusetts men and women who have helped to define American culture—either as builders of a mainstream consensus or as often-cantankerous consciences of the nation—is long indeed. The short list would have to include Cotton Mather, Anne Hutchinson, Benjamin Franklin (even though he moved to Philadelphia early in his career), John Adams, William Ellery Channing, Ralph Waldo Emerson, Henry David Thoreau, Margaret Fuller, Nathaniel Hawthorne, William Lloyd Garrison, Henry Adams, Francis Parkman, Oliver Wendell Holmes, Samuel Eliot Morison, and John F. Kennedy.

How could one small state, even if it is one of the oldest in the Union, have produced so many citizens who made such a difference in our national life? The easiest answer, and perhaps the one most often put forward, is education: Massachusetts has more than a hundred institutions of higher learning, surmounted by the twin pinnacles of Harvard University and the Massachusetts Institute of Technology. Even more important, it has a long tradition of deeply valuing education at all levels, a tradition that dates to the Puritan founders of the Bay Colony.

Yet education alone did not create this galaxy of memorable individuals. Having a hundred colleges and universities is all very well, but the rigor of debate is what has kept Massachusetts intellectually vital, and we honor its heroes not only for what they knew but for the ways in which they often challenged received wisdom. Massachusetts has always been a fertile ground for intellectual controversy, a place where contentious people have had at each other with all the erudition and moral ardor they could muster. In the beginning it was hard-line Calvinists against the theologically unorthodox who in later generations would spark the Unitarian and Transcendentalist movements. In politics the liberal, conservative, and radical el-

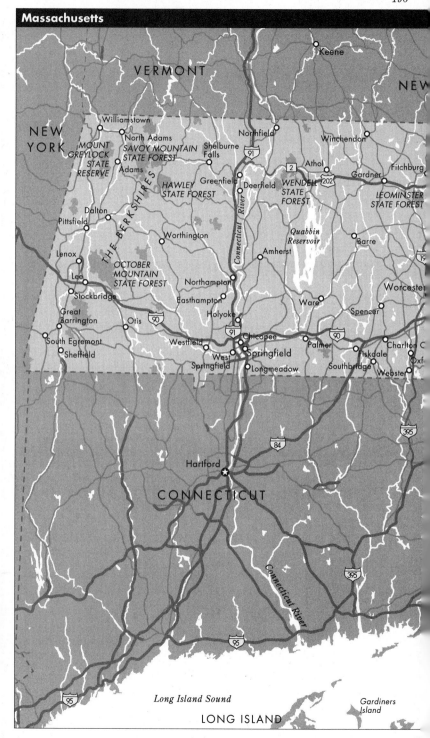

190

Massachusetts

VERMONT

Keene

NEW

NEW
YORK

Williamstown

MOUNT
GREYLOCK
STATE
RESERVE

North Adams

SAVOY MOUNTAIN
STATE FOREST

Shelburne
Falls

Northfield

Winchendon

91

Adams

HAWLEY
STATE
FOREST

Greenfield

Deerfield

2

Athol

202

Gardner

Fitchburg

WENDELL
STATE
FOREST

LEOMINSTER
STATE FOREST

Dalton

Pittsfield

Worthington

Quabbin
Reservoir

Barre

19

Lenox

Amherst

Worcester

Lee

OCTOBER
MOUNTAIN
STATE FOREST

Northampton

Stockbridge

Easthampton

Spencer

Great
Barrington

Otis

Holyoke

90

Ware

South Egremont

Sheffield

Westfield

West
Springfield

91

Chicopee

Springfield

Longmeadow

Palmer

90

Fiskdale

Southbridge

Charlton C

Oxf

Webster

395

84

Hartford

CONNECTICUT

395

95

Connecticut River

Long Island Sound

95

Gardiners
Island

LONG ISLAND

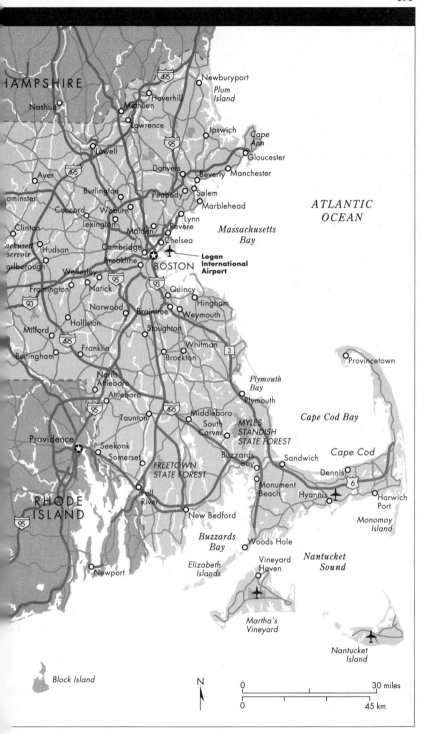

ements fought their way to and through the Revolution; in its aftermath, Federalists and Democrats debated the merits of a weak versus a strong central government, the mercantile versus the agrarian control of economic policy.

The 19th century saw the great debate over slavery, and, while Massachusetts is usually remembered as a hotbed of abolitionism, powerful forces opposed the new movement in a state where fortunes had been built on the slave trade. William Lloyd Garrison, remember, was physically attacked when he spoke in Boston early in his career as an antislavery crusader. In later years the Yankees and the ascendant Irish struggled for power in a clash that was less a contest of ideas than an opposition of temperament and will.

In the end it may not matter what stamp the rest of America puts on the ideas that come out of the state. Massachusetts will live on in the national imagination as a place where people think —and where they make a lot of noise when they do.

Essential Information

Visitor Information

Massachusetts Office of Travel and Tourism (100 Cambridge St., Boston 02202, tel. 617/727–3201).

Tour Groups

Collette Tours (124 Broad St., Pawtucket, RI 02860, tel. 401/728–1000 or 800/832–4656; 800/752–2655 in New England) and **Tauck Tours** (Box 5027, Westport, CT 06881, tel. 203/226–6911 or 800/468–2825) are travel agencies that offer package tours to Massachusetts.

Domenico Tours (751 Broadway, Bayonne, NJ 07002, tel. 800/554–8687) schedules three-day and five-day escorted tours, April through October, to Cape Cod and the islands.

Casser Tours (46 W. 43rd St., New York, NY 10036, tel. 212/840–6500 or 800/251–1411) has three-day tours to the Cape and Newport and four-day tours to the Cape and New Bedford, from Memorial Day to Columbus Day.

Brush Hill Tours (109 Norfolk St., Dorchester, MA 02124, tel. 617/287–1900 or 800/343–1328) runs day trips from Boston to the Cape from Memorial Day through October, with stops in Provincetown, Sandwich, and Hyannis.

Package Deals for Independent Travelers

Amtrak (tel. 800/872–7245) offers three-day "Cape Escape" packages that include hotels and transfers and a four-day Boston and New England package with full-day and half-day tours.

When to Go

The only time visitors avoid Massachusetts is during mud season in April. Northern Massachusetts may see biting black flies in force during the last two weeks of May—not the best time to plan a hiking vacation—and North Shore beaches are affected periodically throughout the summer by biting bugs (when you plan a visit to a supervised area, it's a good idea to call ahead and ask the beach operators for a fly check). But otherwise, the state is a year-round vacation spot. Summer can be hot, fall is balmy and colorful, and winter snows make for family skiing. And while mud season may not be the best time for taking a country walk, it offers a quiet, inexpensive opportunity to explore the state.

Remember that Memorial Day through Labor Day (and in some cases, Columbus Day) is high season on Cape Cod, Martha's Vineyard, and Nantucket; you'll find good beach weather then, but high prices and crowds as well. Spring and fall are best for bird-watching, nature hikes, country drives, and lower prices at inns and restaurants. In winter on the Cape and the islands, many museums, shops, restaurants, and lodging places are closed; the intimate bed-and-breakfasts and inns that remain open—their tariffs as much as 50% below those of high season —can make romantic winter retreats.

Festivals and Seasonal Events

Late Jan.: The **New England Camping and RV Show** takes place at the Bayside Expo Center in Boston. *Tel. 617/242–6092.*

Mid-Feb.: The **New England Boat Show,** the largest in the region, occupies the Bayside Expo Center in Boston. *Tel. 617/242–6092.*

Mar.: Maple-sugaring goes on statewide.

Mar. 17: Boston's **St. Patrick's Day Parade** is one of the largest in the country. *Tel. 617/268–8525.*

Mid-Apr.: Reenactments of Paul Revere's ride and the Battle of Lexington and Concord take place on site the Sunday before Patriot's Day. *Tel. 617/862–1450.*

Mid-Apr.: The **Boston Marathon** is run on Patriot's Day. *Tel. 617/536–4100.*

Late Apr.: Nantucket celebrates spring with a daffodil show, elaborate shop-window displays, and a procession of antique cars. *Tel. 508/228–1700.*

Mid-May: Holyoke's **Shad Fishing Derby** is said to be the largest freshwater fishing derby in North America. *Tel. 413/536–5520.*

Mid-May: The **Brimfield Antiques Fair,** held three times annually, is the largest antiques and collectibles show in New England. *Tel. 508/764–3283.*

Late June: The **ACC Crafts Fair** draws more than 500 exhibitors to the fairgrounds in Springfield. *Tel. 413/787–1040.*

Late June: The **Blessing of the Fleet** in Provincetown on the last Sunday culminates a weekend of festivities—a quahog feed, a public dance, a crafts show. *Tel. 508/487–3424.*

June–Sept.: **Jacob's Pillow Dance Festival** at Becket in the Berkshires hosts performers from various dance traditions. *Tel. 413/243–0745.*

July 4 weekend: The **Mashpee Powwow** brings together Indians from North and South America for three days of dance contests, drumming, a fireball game, and a clambake; Native American food and crafts are sold. *Tel. 508/477–0792.*

Mid-July: **Brimfield Antiques Fair** (*see* Mid-May).

July–Aug.: **Tanglewood Music Festival** at Lenox, the summer home of the Boston Symphony Orchestra, schedules other top performers as well. *Tel. 413/637–1600 or 617/266–1492.*

Late July: The **Eastern National Morgan Horse Show** in Northampton is the largest single-breed horse show in the United States. *Tel. 413/584–7516.*

Late July: **Barnstable County Fair** in Hatchville, Cape Cod's biggest event, is six days of livestock and food judgings, arts and crafts demonstrations, entertainment, rides, and edibles. *Tel. 508/563–3200.*

Early Aug.: **The Hyannis Street Festival** is a three-day weekend of Main Street shopping. *Tel. 508/775–2201.*

Aug.: A **Sandcastle Contest** at Jetties Beach in Nantucket produces amazing sculptures. *Tel. 508/228–1700.*

Mid-Aug.: **Martha's Vineyard Agricultural Fair** promises contests, animal shows, a carnival, and evening entertainment. *Tel. 508/693–0085.*

Mid-Aug.: **Falmouth Road Race,** a world-class event, covers 7.1 miles of coastline. *Tel. 508/540–7000.*

Mid-Aug.: Amherst's **Annual Teddy Bear Rally** attracts teddies and crowds. *Tel. 415/253–9666.*

Early Sept.: **Tivoli Day,** in Oak Bluffs on Martha's Vineyard, involves a minifishing derby for kids, a 50-mile bike race, and a blessing of the fleet. *Tel. 508/693-0085.*

Mid-Sept.: The **Eastern States Exposition** in Springfield is New England's largest agricultural show and fair. *Tel. 413/737-2443.*

Mid-Sept.: The **Bourne Scallopfest** on the weekend following Labor Day attracts thousands to Buzzards Bay for fried scallops and entertainment. *Tel. 508/888-6202.*

Mid-Sept.: Brimfield Antiques Fair (*see* Mid-May).

Mid-Sept.: The **Harwich Cranberry Festival's** 10 days of festivities include a country-and-western jamboree, parade, fireworks, pancake breakfast, and regatta. *Tel. 508/543-0100.*

Mid-Sept.–mid-Oct.: The month-long **Martha's Vineyard Striped Bass and Bluefish Derby** is one of the East Coast's premier fishing contests. *Tel. 508/693-1881.*

Early Dec.: Christmas (or **Shoppers) Stroll,** the first weekend of the month on Nantucket, sees costumed carolers, theatrical performances, art exhibits, and tours of historic homes. *Tel. 508/228-1700.*

Mid-Dec.: Reenactment of the Boston Tea Party takes place on the *Tea Party Ship* in Boston Harbor. *Tel. 617/338-1773.*

Dec. 31: First Night Arts Celebration in Boston. *Tel. 617/542-1399.*

What to Pack

In summer you'll need only light clothing, but bring a sweater for nights along the shore and daytime fishing trips. The constant likelihood of rain in some areas makes it a good idea to travel with a lightweight waterproof coat or umbrella as well. Bug repellent, too, is strongly recommended for summer. Because of the increased incidence of Lyme disease, which is transmitted to human beings by deer ticks, anyone planning to explore the woods, nature areas, or dunes should wear long pants, socks to be drawn up over pants cuffs, and a long-sleeve shirt. Insect repellent applied to clothing before entering infested areas can be effective. Protective sunscreens and sunglasses are also important in the summer months.

Fall evenings are cool, especially along the coast, and Massachusetts winters can be cold. When the sea is frozen and the snow thick, you'll need the warmest winter clothing. Some Berkshire inns require formal dress at dinner; only a few restaurants on Cape Cod, Martha's Vineyard, and Nantucket require jacket and tie, for the area prides itself on its informality.

Arriving and Departing

By Plane Boston's **Logan International Airport,** the largest airport in New England, has scheduled flights by most major U.S. and foreign carriers.

Bradley International Airport, in Windsor Locks, Connecticut, 18 miles south of Springfield on I–91, has scheduled flights by major U.S. airlines.

By Car Boston is the traffic hub of New England, with interstate highways approaching it from every direction and every major city in the northeast. New England's chief coastal highway, I–95, skirts Boston, while I–90 leads west to the Great Lakes and Chicago. Interstate 91 brings visitors to the Pioneer Valley in western Massachusetts from Vermont and Canada in the north and Connecticut and New York to the south.

By Train **Amtrak's Northeast Corridor** service (tel. 800/872–7245) links Boston with principal cities between it and Washington, D.C. The *Lake Shore Limited*, which stops at Springfield and the Berkshires, carries passengers from Chicago to Boston. *The Cape Codder* runs between Hyannis and Washington, DC, weekends only from late June through Labor Day.

By Bus **Greyhound Lines** (tel. 800/531–5332) and **Peter Pan Bus Lines** (tel. 800/237–8747) connect Boston and other major cities in Massachusetts with cities throughout the United States. **Bonanza** (tel. 800/556–3815) serves Boston and the eastern part of the state from Providence with connecting service to New York.

Getting Around Massachusetts

By Plane **Worcester Municipal Airport** is served by Continental Express (tel. 800/525–0280), Eastern Express (tel. 508/228–3672 or 800/327–8376), and USAir (tel. 508/795–7300 or 800/428–4322); **Barnstable Municipal Airport** (in Hyannis on Cape Cod) is served by Delta Connection/Business Express (tel. 800/345–3400), Continental Express, and Nantucket Airlines (tel. 508/228–6234). For **Martha's Vineyard Airport,** there is service on Delta Connection/Business Express, Continental Express, and Express Air (tel. 800/852–2332). **Nantucket Memorial Airport** is served by Delta Connection/Business Express, Continental Express, and Eastern Express. **Provincetown Municipal Airport** is served by Cape Air (tel. 800/352–0714). **New Bedford Airport** is served by Express Air.

By Car The Massachusetts Turnpike (I–90) is the principal east-west route across southern Massachusetts, from Boston through Worcester and Springfield to the Berkshires. To the north, Route 2 joins Boston with Williamstown in the Berkshires. A variety of major highways link Boston with the South Shore, the North Shore, and Cape Cod.

A car is essential for touring Cape Cod, but you won't need one on the islands of Martha's Vineyard or Nantucket unless you plan a long stay, will visit the less accessible areas, or expect to go in the off-season and don't want to take cabs.

By Train The commuter rail service of the **Massachusetts Bay Transportation Authority** (tel. 617/722–3200) connects Boston with the South Shore and the North Shore.

By Boat Ferries join Martha's Vineyard and Nantucket with Cape Cod throughout the year and with New Bedford in season.

Shopping

The Massachusetts sales tax is 5%.

The best areas for antiques hunting are the Berkshires (particularly in the south), Boston's North Shore, and Cape Cod. Stores in the Berkshires are not noted for low prices; each area has an association of antiques dealers who guarantee the authenticity of their merchandise—these addresses are listed under the separate regions. The **Cape Cod Antiques Dealers Association** (Box 1223, Brewster 02631, tel. 508/896–7198) publishes a directory of the Cape's antiques dealers and auctions.

Arts and crafts shops abound; the **Division of Continuing Education** (University of Massachusetts, Amherst 01003) prepares a western Massachusetts crafts guide that lists local studios and galleries.

Farm products are also popular throughout the state. A list of "pick-your-own" fruit farms can be obtained from the **Massachusetts Association of Roadside Stands and Pick Your Own Stands** (721 Parker St., East Longmeadow 01028, tel. 413/525–4147). For a list of maple-sugar houses, write to **Massachusetts Maple Producers Association** (Box 377, Ashfield 01330).

Sports and Outdoor Activities

Biking Cyclists usually head for the gently rolling terrain of the southern Berkshires or the level reaches of Cape Cod and the islands.

Camping A complete list of private campgrounds in the state can be obtained from the **Massachusetts Association of Campgrounds** (c/o Massachusetts Division of Tourism, 100 Cambridge St., Boston 02202). Most state parks have camping facilities, and campgrounds are abundant in the Berkshires. Few camping areas exist in the North Shore region.

Fishing The **State Division of Fisheries and Wildlife** (100 Cambridge St., Boston 02202) prepares a guide to freshwater fishing and a leaflet on fish and wildlife laws.

Hiking Nearly all state parks in Massachusetts provide hiking trails. The Appalachian Mountain Trail, which crosses the Berkshires region, is a favorite of walkers. Seasoned hikers might consider an ascent of Mount Greylock, the state's highest peak, or a trek through one of the North Shore's wildlife reservations.

Skiing *The skiing facilities of Massachusetts are reviewed in Chapter 2, Skiing New England.*

Water Sports Canoeing is popular on the Connecticut River in the Pioneer Valley and on the Housatonic River in the Berkshires. For saltwater canoeing and kayaking, the waters of the Essex River Estuary on the North Shore are generally calm and protected. Marblehead is the pleasure sailing capital of the North Shore. The Cape and the islands offer virtually all water sports, including swimming, surfing, windsurfing, and sailing.

Beaches

Favorite North Shore beaches include Crane's Beach, Ipswich; Plum Island, Newburyport; Singing Beach, Manchester; and Wingaersheek Beach and Good Harbor Beach, Gloucester. Cape Cod National Seashore has the best beaches on the Cape, with high dunes, wide strands of sand, and no development along the shore. Martha's Vineyard and Nantucket islands are ringed with miles of beautiful sandy beaches. The ocean is swimmable June through September, although it is warmest in August.

National and State Parks

National Parks Cape Cod National Seashore, a 40-mile stretch of the Cape between Eastham and Provincetown, is protected from development and offers excellent swimming, bike riding, birdwatching, and nature walks.

State Parks Some of the newest parks in Massachusetts have been created by the Urban Heritage State Park Program, which celebrates the Industrial Revolution of the 19th century in Lowell, Gardner, North Adams, and Holyoke. Entrance is free, and a leaflet describing all Heritage Parks in the state is available from the **Department of Environmental Management** (Division of Forests and Parks, 100 Cambridge St., Boston 02202). The same office prepares *Massachusetts Forests and Parks*, which details the state's outdoor parks and their facilities.

Dining

Apart from the seafood specialties that the state shares with other New England regions, Massachusetts claims fame for inventing the fried clam, a revolutionary event that apparently took place in Essex. Fried clams, therefore, appear on many North Shore menus, especially around the salt marshes of Essex and Ipswich, and on Cape Cod, where clam chowder is another specialty. Eating seafood "in the rough" (from paper plates in shacklike wooden buildings dominated by deepfryers) is a revered local custom.

In recent years Nantucket Island has spawned a number of first-rate gourmet restaurants (with price tags to match), as has Brewster on the Cape. On the North Shore, Rockport is a "dry" town, though you can almost always take your own alcohol into restaurants; most places charge a nominal corking fee. This law leads to early closing hours—many Rockport dining establishments are shut by 9 PM. Martha's Vineyard also has dry towns.

Dining in the state is generally casual, except at certain inns, particularly in the Berkshires, which require formal dress at dinner.

Highly recommended restaurants in each price category are indicated by a star ★.

Category	Cost*
Very Expensive	over $40
Expensive	$25–$40
Moderate	$12–$25
Inexpensive	under $12

average cost of a three-course dinner, per person, excluding drinks, service, and 5% sales tax

Lodging

Some accommodations may not be suitable for young children; check with individual establishments in advance.

Highly recommended lodgings in each price category are indicated by a star ★.

Category	Boston, the Cape, and the islands*	Other Areas*
Very Expensive	over $150	over $100
Expensive	$95–$150	$70–$100
Moderate	$70–$95	$40–$70
Inexpensive	under $70	under $40

All prices are for a standard double room in high season and do not include tax or gratuities. Some inns add a 15% mandatory service charge. The state tax on lodging is 5.6%; individual towns can impose an extra tax of up to 10% more.

Boston

New England's largest and most important city, the cradle of American independence, Boston is 360 years old, far older than the republic it helped to create. Its most famous buildings are not merely civic landmarks but national icons; its great citizens are not the political and financial leaders of today but the Adamses, Reveres, and Hancocks who live at the crossroads of history and myth.

At the same time, Boston is a contemporary center of high finance and higher technology, a place of granite and glass towers rising along what once were rutted village lanes. Its enormous population of students, artists, academics, and young professionals have made the town a haven for foreign movies, late-night bookstores, racquetball, sushi restaurants, New Wave music, and unconventional politics.

Best of all, Boston is meant for walking. Most of its historical and architectural attractions can be found in compact areas, and its varied and distinctive neighborhoods reveal their character and design to visitors who take the time to stroll through them.

Important Addresses and Numbers

Visitor Information **Boston Common Information Kiosk.** A multilingual staff provides maps, brochures, and information about ongoing events. *Tremont St., where the Freedom Trail begins, tel. 617/536–4100. Open daily 9–5.*

National Park Service Visitor Center. The center shows an eight-minute slide show on Boston's historic sites and provides maps and directions. *15 State St., across from the Old State House, tel. 617/242–5642. Open daily 9–5. Closed major holidays.*

Emergencies **Police, fire, ambulance** (tel. 911); **Massachusetts General Hospital** (tel. 617/726–2000); **dental emergency** (tel. 508/651–3521); **poison control** (tel. 617/232–2120); **rape crisis center** (tel. 617/492–7273).

Late-night **Phillips Drug Store** (155 Charles St., tel. 617/523–1028 or 617/
Pharmacy 523–4372).

Opening and Closing Times

Banks are generally open weekdays 9–4. Some branches are
open Sat. 9–noon or 9–1.
Museums are generally open Mon.–Sat. 9 (or 10)–5 (or 6), Sun.
noon–5. Many are closed Mon.
Shops and stores are generally open Mon.–Sat. 9 (or 9:30)–6 (or
7). Many stay open later toward the end of the week. Some, particularly those in malls or tourist areas, are open Sun. noon–5.

Getting Around Boston

From the Airport Only 3 miles—and Boston Harbor—separate Logan Interna-
to Downtown tional Airport from downtown, yet it can seem like 20 miles
Boston when you're caught in one of the many daily traffic jams at the
two tunnels that go under the harbor. Boston traffic is almost
always heavy, and the worst conditions prevail during the
morning (6:30–9) and evening (3:30–6) rush hours.

Cabs can be hired outside each terminal. Fares downtown
should average about $15, including tip.

A 24-hour toll-free ground transport number provides informa-
tion and schedules for Logan Express buses and the **Airport
Water Shuttle** (tel. 800/235–6426), which goes downtown to
Rowes Wharf.

The **MBTA Blue Line** to Airport Station is one of the fastest
ways to reach downtown from the airport. Free shuttle buses
connect the subway station with all airline terminals (tel. 800/
235–6426 or 617/561–1800 for Logan Airport Public Information).

By Subway and The MBTA, or T, operates subways, elevated trains, and trol-
Trolley leys along four connecting lines.

Park Street Station (Common) is the major downtown transfer
point for Red and Green Line trains; the Orange and Blue Lines
cross at State Street. Trains operate from about 5:30 AM to
about 12:30 AM. Current fares on subways and trolleys are 75¢
adults, 35¢ children 5–11, free under 5. An extra fare is required for the distant Green Line stops. Tourist passes are
available for $8 (3 days) and $16 (7 days). The MBTA (tel. 617/
722–3200 or 617/722–5657) has details.

A free map of the entire public transportation system is available at the Park Street Station information stand (street level),
open daily 7:30 AM–11 PM. Bus lines will be marked on this map,
but bus stops and routes are difficult to follow for uninitiated
riders.

By Car Those who cannot avoid bringing a car into Boston should be
able to minimize their frustration by keeping to the main thoroughfares and by parking in lots—no matter how expensive—
rather than on the street.

Major public parking lots are at Government Center; beneath
Boston Common (entrance on Charles Street); at the Prudential Center; at Copley Place; and off Clarendon Street near the
John Hancock Tower. Smaller lots are scattered through the
downtown area. Most are expensive, especially the small out-

door lots; a few city garages are a bargain at about $6–$10 a day.

By Taxi Cabs are not easily hailed on the street, except at the airport; you should use a hotel taxi stand or telephone for a cab. Companies offering 24-hour service include **Checker** (tel. 617/536–7000), **Independent Taxi Operators Association** or ITOA (tel. 617/426–8700), and, in Cambridge, **Cambridge Taxi** (tel. 617/876–5000).

Guided Tours

When it comes to touring Boston and environs, today's visitor has the same two options the British had when they struck out at the Middlesex hinterland: by land or by sea.

Orientation Tours **Brush Hill Transportation Company** (109 Norfolk St.,
By Land Dorchester, tel. 617/287–1900 or 800/343–1328). Buses leave from several downtown hotels twice daily for 3½ hour "Boston Adventure" tours of Boston and Cambridge, with stops at the USS *Constitution* and the Tea Party Ship. **The Gray Line** (275 Tremont St., tel. 617/426–8805). A three-hour tour of Greater Boston, a three-hour tour of Lexington, Concord, and Cambridge, and a combined seven-hour trip are offered.

By Water **Bay State Spray and Provincetown Steamship Co** (ticket office at 20 Long Wharf, tel. 617/723–7800). The Boston to Provincetown cruise is a three-hour (each way) excursion to the tip of Cape Cod aboard the *Provincetown II*, which departs from Commonwealth Pier. There are weekend sailings from Memorial Day weekend to mid-September and daily sailings from Memorial Day to Labor Day, with one sailing daily in each direction.

Mass Bay Lines (60 Rowes Wharf, tel. 617/542–8000). Harbor sightseeing excursions and trips to Georges Island are scheduled on weekends beginning in June, daily from July 4 through Labor Day weekend.

Special-interest **Whale Watches.** The *Bay State Spray and Provincetown*
Tours *Steamship Company* (ticket office at 20 Long Wharf, tel. 617/723–7800) offers whale-watch cruises Saturday and Sunday from late April to mid-June, Saturday during the summer.

Walking Tours **Freedom Trail.** The 1½-mile Freedom Trail is marked on the sidewalk by a red line that winds its way past 16 of Boston's most important historic sites. The walk begins at the Freedom Trail Information Center on the Tremont Street side of Boston Common, not far from the MBTA Park Street station. Sites along the Freedom Trail include the State House, Park Street Church, Old Granary Burial Ground, King's Chapel and burying ground, Globe Corner Bookstore, Old State House, Boston Massacre Site, Faneuil Hall, Paul Revere House, Old North Church, Copp's Hill Burying Ground, and the USS *Constitution*, with a side trip to the Bunker Hill Monument.

Harborwalk. Maps are available at the Boston Common Information kiosk for a self-guided tour that traces Boston's maritime history. The walk begins at the Old State House (206 Washington St.) and ends on the Congress Street Bridge near the Boston Tea Party ship and museum.

Highlights for First-time Visitors

Faneuil Hall, Tour 3

Freedom Trail, Tours 1–3

Harvard Square, Tour 6

Louisburg Square, Tour 1

Museum of Fine Arts, Tour 5

Public Garden, Tour 4

Tour 1: Boston Common and Beacon Hill

Numbers in the margin correspond with the numbered points of interest on the Boston map.

❶ Nothing is more central to Boston than its **Common,** the oldest public park in the United States and undoubtedly the largset and most famous of the town commons around which all New England settlements were once arranged.

Start your walk at the **Park Street Station,** on the common on the corner of Park and Tremont streets. This is the original eastern terminus of the first subway in America, opened in 1897 against the warnings of those who believed it would make the buildings along Tremont Street collapse. The copper-roof kiosks are National Historic Landmarks. A well-equipped **visitor information booth** is less than 100 yards from here. It serves as the starting point for the Freedom Trail; guide booklets are available at no charge.

❷ The Congregationalist **Park Street Church,** designed by Peter Banner and erected in 1809–1810, occupies the corner of Tremont and Park streets. Here, on July 4, 1831, Samuel Smith's hymn "America" was first sung, and here in 1829 William Lloyd Garrison began his long public campaign for the abolition of slavery. *Open to visitors last week in June–third week in Aug., Tues.–Sat. 9:30–3:30. Closed July 4. Year-round Sun. services 10:30 and 6.*

❸ Next to the church is the **Old Granary Burial Ground.** The most famous individuals interred here are heroes of the Revolution: Samuel Adams, John Hancock (the precise location of his grave is not certain), James Otis, and Paul Revere. Here, too, are the graves of the philanthropist Peter Faneuil, Benjamin Franklin's parents (Franklin is buried in Philadelphia), and the victims of the Boston Massacre. *Open daily 8–4:30.*

❹ At the corner of Park and Beacon streets, at the summit of Beacon Hill, stands Charles Bulfinch's magnificent **State House,** arguably the most architecturally distinguished of American seats of state government. The design is neoclassical, poised between Georgian and Federal; its finest features are the delicate Corinthian columns of the portico, the graceful pediment and window arches, and the vast yet visually weightless golden dome. The dome is sheathed in copper from the foundry of Paul Revere. During World War II, the entire dome was painted gray so that it would not reflect moonlight during blackouts. *Tel. 617/727–3676. Admission free. Open weekdays 10–4. Research library (free) open weekdays 9–5.*

Beacon Hill is the area bounded by Cambridge Street on the north, Beacon Street on the south, the Charles River Esplanade on the west, and Bowdoin Street on the east. The highest of three summits, Beacon Hill was named for the warning light (at first an iron skillet filled with tallow and suspended from a mast) set on its peak in 1634.

No sooner do you put the State House behind you than you encounter the classic face of Beacon Hill: brick row houses, nearly all built between 1800 and 1850 in a style never far divergent from the early Federal norm. Even the sidewalks are brick, and they shall remain so; in the 1940s residents staged a sit-in to prevent conventional paving. Since then, public law, the Beacon Hill Civic Association, and the Beacon Hill Architectural Commission have maintained tight controls over everything from the gas lamps to the color of front doors.

Chestnut and **Mt. Vernon,** two of the loveliest streets in America, are distinguished not only for the history and style of their individual houses but for their general atmosphere and character as well. **Mt. Vernon Street** is the grander of the two, its houses set back farther and rising taller; it even has a freestanding mansion, the Second Otis House. Mt. Vernon opens **⑤** out on **Louisburg Square,** an 1840s model for town-house development that was never repeated on the Hill because of space restrictions. The little green belongs collectively to the owners of the homes facing it.

Chestnut Street is more modest than Mt. Vernon, yet in its trimness and minuteness of detail it is perhaps even more fine.

Delicacy and grace characterize virtually every structure, from the fanlights above the entryways to the wrought-iron boot scrapers on the steps.

Running parallel to Chestnut and Mt. Vernon streets, half a block down Willow Street from Louisburg Square, is **Acorn Street,** a narrow span of cobblestones lined on one side with almost toylike row houses and on the other with the doors to Mt. Vernon's hidden gardens. These were once the houses of artisans and small tradesmen; today they are every bit as prestigious as their larger neighbors. Acorn Street may be the most photographed street of its size in Boston.

⑥ On the north slope of Beacon Hill is the **African Meeting House** at 8 Smith Court (near Joy and Myrtle), built in 1806, the oldest black church building still standing in the United States. It was constructed almost entirely with black labor, using funds raised in both the white and the black communities. In 1832 the New England Anti-Slavery Society was formed here under the leadership of William Lloyd Garrison.

Opposite the Meeting House is the home (1799) of **William Nell,** a black crusader for school integration active in Garrison's circle. These sites and others are part of a **Black Heritage Trail,** a walking tour that explores the history of the city's black community during the 19th century. The recently established **⑦ Museum of Afro-American History** provides information on the trail and on black history throughout Boston. *46 Joy St., tel. 617/742–1854. Admission free. Open Tues.–Fri. 10–4. Information on the Trail can also be obtained from the National Park Service Visitor Center, 15 State St., tel. 617/742–5415. Admission free. Open weekdays 9–5.*

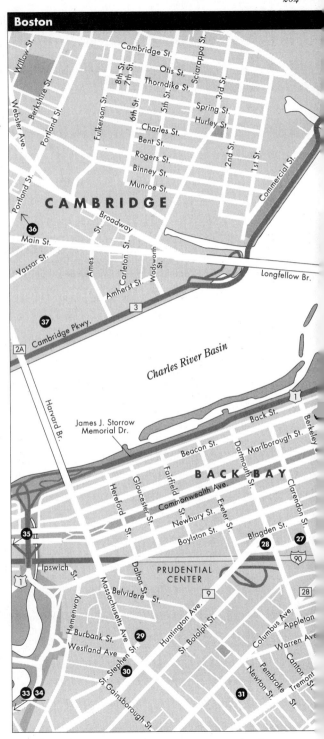

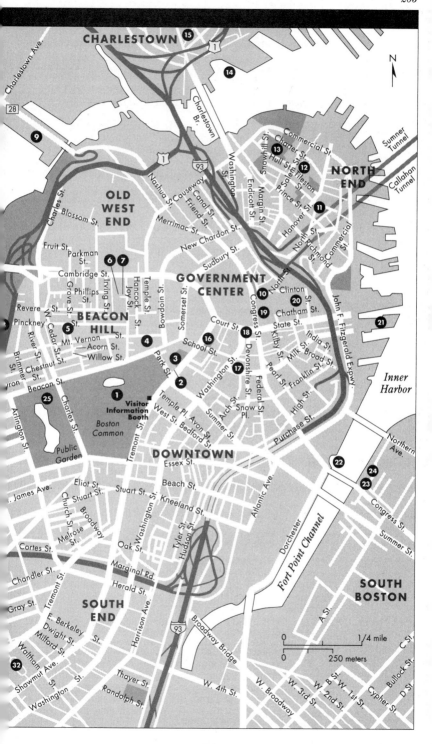

CHARLESTOWN 15
14

9

N

OLD WEST END

Commercial St.
Charter St.
Snowhill St.
Hull St. Fileston
Salem St. 13
Prince St. 12
NORTH END

Sumner Tunnel
Callahan Tunnel

Nashua St.
Causeway St.
Friend St.
Canal St.
Merrimac St.
New Chardon St.
Sudbury St.

Washington St.
Endicott St.
Margin St.
Hanover
North St.
Richmond
Commercial St.
11

Charles St.
Blossom St.
Fruit St.
Parkman St.
Cambridge St. 6 7
Phillips St.
Grove St.
Irving St.
Hancock St.
Joy St.
Temple St.
Bowdoin St.
Somerset St.

GOVERNMENT CENTER
10 Clinton
North St. 20 Chatham St.
19 Court St. State St.
18 Kilby St. India St.
Milk St. Broad St.

John F. Fitzgerald Expwy.

21

Revere St.
Pinckney St. 5
Cedar St.
Mt. Vernon
Acorn St.
Willow St.
Brimmer St.
Chestnut St.
Beacon St.
River St.

4
Park St.
16 School St.
3
2 Washington St.
17 Devonshire St.
Federal St.
Pearl St.
Franklin St.
Snow Pl.
Arch
High St.
Purchase St.

Inner Harbor

Arlington St.
25
Charles St.

1 **Visitor Information Booth**
Boston Common
Temple Pl. Avon St.
West St. Bedford St.
Summer St.

Northern Ave.

Public Garden

DOWNTOWN
Essex St.

James Ave.
Eliot St.
Stuart St.
Church St.
Broadway
Melrose St.
Cortes St.
Beach St.
Kneeland St.
Stuart St.
Washington St.
Tyler St.
Hudson St.
Oak St.

Atlantic Ave.

22
24
23
Congress St.
Summer St.

Fort Point Channel
Dorchester

SOUTH BOSTON

Chandler St.
Tremont St.
Marginal Rd.
Herald St.
Gray St.
E. Berkeley St.
Dwight St.
Milford St.
SOUTH END
32
Waltham St.
Shawmut Ave.
Washington St.
Thayer St.
Randolph St.

Harrison Ave.
I-93
Broadway Bridge

W. 4th St.
W. 3rd St.
W. 2nd St.
W. 1st St.
W. Broadway
A St.
B St.
C St.
Bullock St.
Cypher St.
D St.

0 ___ 1/4 mile
0 ___ 250 meters

Charles Street, on the flat part of Beacon Hill, is home to Boston's antiques district and an assortment of bookstores, leather stores, small restaurants, and vintage-clothing boutiques.

Time Out **Il Dolce Momento** (30 Charles St.), with its homemade gelato and pastries and freshly made gourmet sandwiches, is a perfect stop for a meal, a light snack, or a late-night espresso.

If you head east toward the river, you can cross over to the **❽ Esplanade** on the Arthur Fiedler Footbridge, named for the late maestro who conducted the Boston Pops for 50 years. Many of his concerts were given right here, in the **Hatch Memorial Shell,** where the Pops plays each summer.

Across the Charles River, and a short walk away, Boston's **❾ Museum of Science** has more than 400 exhibits covering astronomy, anthropology, progress in medicine, computers, the organic and inorganic earth sciences, and much more. Many exhibits invite the participation of children and adults. The Transparent Woman's organs light up as their functions are described, and a powerful generator produces controlled indoor lightning flashes. The museum has three restaurants and a gift shop. *Tel. 617/723–2500 (for recorded information, tel. 617/523–6664). Admission: $6 adults, $4 children 4–14, free under 4 and senior citizens. Open Tues.–Sun. 9–5, Fri. until 9. Closed Thanksgiving, Christmas, and Mon. except May 1–Labor Day and Mon. holidays.*

The **Hayden Planetarium,** located in the Museum of Science, features a planetarium projector and sophisticated multi-image system that combine to produce exciting programs on astronomical discoveries. Laser light shows, using a new visual technology complete with brilliant laser graphics and computer animation, are scheduled Thursday–Sunday evenings. *Tel. 617/589–0270. Admission for each: $5 adults, $3.50 children and senior citizens.*

The **Mugar Omni Theater** in the Museum of Science features a 76-foot, four-story domed screen, which wraps around and over you; 27,000 watts of power drive the sound system's 84 loudspeakers. *Tel. 617/523–6664. Admission: $6 adults, $4 senior citizens and children 4–14, under 4 not admitted. Afternoon shows weekdays, evening shows Tues.–Fri.*

Tour 2: The North End and Charlestown

From **Government Center** walk northeast toward the raised central artery (the Fitzgerald Expressway) and you'll soon come upon the oldest commercial block in Boston, the Black-**❿** stone Block. In this block Boston's oldest restaurant, the **Union Oyster House,** has been operating since 1826. Around the corner on Friday and Saturday, come rain or sleet, Haymarket vendors hawk fruit, vegetables, meat, and fish.

Opposite the pedestrian tunnel beneath the expressway is the oldest neighborhood in Boston and one of the oldest in the New World. Men and women walked the narrow streets of the **North End** when Shakespeare was not yet 20 years dead and Louis XIV was new to the throne of France. The town of Boston bustled and grew rich here for a century and a half before American independence. In the 17th century the North End *was* Boston, for much of the rest of the peninsula was still under water or had yet to be cleared of brush.

The North End visible to us today is almost entirely a creature of the late 19th century, when brick tenements began to fill with European immigrants. The Irish and the Jews both had their day here, but the Italians, more recent arrivals, have stayed. For more than 60 years the North End has been Italian Boston. This is not only a district of Italian restaurants (there are dozens) but of Italian groceries, bakeries, churches, social clubs, cafés, festivals honoring saints and food, street-corner debates over soccer games, and encroaching gentrification.

A right turn on Prince Street will take you to Hanover Street and North Square. Here is the oldest house in Boston, the **Paul Revere House,** built nearly a hundred years before Revere's 1775 midnight ride through Middlesex County. He owned it from 1770 until 1800, although he and his wife Rachel rented it out during the later part of that period. Attendants are available to answer questions. *19 North Sq., tel. 617/523–1676. Admission: $2 adults, 50¢ children 5–17, $1.50 senior citizens and college students. Open Apr. 15–Oct. 31, daily 9:30–5:15; other times until 4:15. Closed holidays and Mon. Jan.–March.*

Time Out The **Caffe Vittoria** (296 Hanover St.) serves cappuccino and special coffee drinks in an Old World café ambience. Next door, **Mike's Pastry** (300 Hanover St.) is the place for ricotta cannoli.

Past North Square on Hanover Street is **St. Stephen's,** the only one of architect Charles Bulfinch's churches still standing in Boston. At Hanover and Tileston streets, the **Prado,** or **Paul Revere Mall,** is lined with bronze plaques that tell the stories of famous North Enders. The centerpiece is Cyrus Dallin's equestrian statue of Paul Revere.

Continue on Tileston Street to Salem Street to see the church steeple where the two lanterns were hung as a signal to Paul Revere on the night of April 18, 1775. Christ Church, the **Old North Church** (1723), the oldest church building in Boston, was designed by William Price from a study of Christopher Wren's London churches. *Tel. 617/523–6676. Open daily 9–5. Sun. services at 9, 11, and 4. Closed Thanksgiving.*

Walk uphill on Hull Street to reach the **Copp's Hill Burying Ground,** which incorporates four cemeteries established between 1660 and 1819. Many headstones were chipped by practice shots fired by British soldiers during the occupation of Boston, and a number of the musketball pockmarks can still be seen. Of all Boston's early cemeteries, Copp's Hill seems most to preserve an ancient and melancholic air. *Open daily 9–4.*

The view from Copp's Hill to the north encompasses the mouth of the Charles and much of Charlestown. The USS *Constitution* can be reached via the Charlestown Bridge visible to the northwest.

The USS *Constitution,* nicknamed Old Ironsides for the strength of its oaken hull, not because of any iron plating, is the oldest commissioned ship in the U.S. Navy. She is moored at a national historic site, the **Charlestown Navy Yard,** one of six established to build warships.

14 The USS *Constitution* was launched in Boston, where Constitution Wharf now stands, in 1797. Her principal service was during Thomas Jefferson's campaign against the Barbary pirates, off the coast of North Africa, and in the War of 1812. She never lost an engagement. Sailors show visitors around the ship, taking them below decks to see the impossibly cramped living quarters and the places at the guns where the desperate and difficult work of naval warfare under sail was carried out. *Tel. 617/426–1812. Admission free. Open daily 9:30–3:50.*

The phrase "Battle of Bunker Hill" is one of America's most famous misnomers. The battle was fought on Breed's Hill, and that is where Solomon Willard's 220-foot shaft of Quincy granite stands. The monument, for which the Marquis de Lafayette laid the cornerstone in 1825, rises from the spot where, on June 17, 1775, a citizen's militia, commanded not to fire "till you see the whites of their eyes," inflicted more than 1,100 casualties on the British regulars (who eventually seized the hill).

15 Ascend the **Bunker Hill Monument** (Main Street to Monument Street, then straight uphill) by a flight of 295 steps. There is no elevator, but the views from the observatory are worth the climb. At the base, four dioramas tell the story of the battle; ranger programs are given hourly. If you are in Boston on June 17, go to the hill to see a full-scale historical demonstration. *Admission free. Lodge open daily 9–5, monument until 4:30. Closed Thanksgiving, Christmas, New Year's Day.*

Tour 3: Downtown Boston

The financial district—what Bostonians usually refer to as "downtown"—is off the beaten track for visitors who are concentrating on following the Freedom Trail, yet there is much to see in a walk of an hour or two. There is little logic to the streets here; they are, after all, village lanes that only happen to be lined with 40-story office towers.

The area may be confusing, but it is mercifully small.

Just south of Government Center, at the corner of Tremont and **16** School Streets, stands **King's Chapel,** built in 1754 and never topped with the steeple that the architect Peter Harrison had planned. It took five years to build the solid Quincy granite structure. As construction proceeded, the old church continued to stand within the walls of the new, to be removed in pieces when the stone chapel was completed. The chapel's bell is Paul Revere's largest and, in his opinion, his sweetest-sounding. *Open Tues.–Sun. 10–4. Sun. service at 11. Music program Tues. 12:15–12:45.*

The adjacent **King's Chapel Burying Ground,** the oldest in the city, contains the remains of the first Massachusetts governor, John Winthrop, and several generations of his descendants. Here, too, are many other tombs of Boston worthies of three centuries ago.

Follow School Street down from King's Chapel and pass the **old City Hall,** with Richard S. Greenough's bronze statue of **Benjamin Franklin** (1855), which was Boston's first portrait sculpture. Franklin was born (1706) a few blocks from here on Milk Street and attended the Boston Latin School.

At the Washington Street corner of School Street stands the **Globe Corner Bookstore**, until recently a museum of old editions and now once again a working bookstore, thanks to the good offices of the *Boston Globe*. It was built in 1718, and throughout most of the 19th century it counted among its clientele the leading lights of literary society—Emerson, Holmes, Longfellow, Lowell.

Time Out **Rebecca's** (56 High St.), with an array of fresh salads, sandwiches, and homemade pastries, is a comfortable place to stop for a casual lunch.

⏧ The **Old South Meeting House** is a short block to the right down Washington Street, at the corner of Milk. Built in 1729, it is Boston's second oldest church. Unlike the older Old North, the Old South is no longer the seat of an active congregation. And its principal associations have always been more secular than religious. Some of the fieriest of the town meetings that led to the Revolution were held here, including the one Samuel Adams called concerning some dutiable tea that activists wanted returned to England.

Washington Street is the main commercial street of downtown Boston. You'll pass many of the area's major retail establishments (don't overlook the side streets) and the two venerable anchors of Boston's mercantile district, Filene's and Jordan Marsh.

The **Combat Zone** of lower Washington Street, a two-block area of nude-dancing bars, peep shows, "adult" bookstores, and "adult" movie houses, occasionally lives up to its name. While it is not particularly dangerous during the daytime, it is not to be recommended to the casual stroller at night.

⏨ Retracing your steps on Washington Street to its intersection with Court Street, you'll come to a brightly colored lion and unicorn, symbols of British imperial power, on the facade of the **Old State House.** The Old State House was the seat of the Colonial government from 1713 until the Revolution, and after the evacuation of the British from Boston in 1776 it served the independent Commonwealth until the new State House on Beacon Hill was completed. John Hancock was inaugurated here as the first governor under the new state constitution. *206 Washington St., tel. 617/720–3290. Admission: $1.25 adults, 50¢ children 6–16, 75¢ senior students and college students, free to Massachusetts schoolchildren. Open Apr. 1–Nov. 1, daily 9:30–5; Nov. 1–Mar. 31, daily 10–4.*

Turning left onto Congress Street, we encounter, first, an historic marketplace of ideas and, second, an old provisions market reborn as the emblem of downtown revitalization. Faneuil Hall ("the Cradle of Liberty") and the Quincy Market (also known as Faneuil Hall Marketplace) face each other across a small square thronged with people at all but the smallest hours.

⏩ **Faneuil Hall** (pronounced "Fan'l") was erected in 1742 to serve as both a place for town meetings and a public market. Though it has been rebuilt, enlarged, and remodeled over the years, the great balconied hall is still made available to citizen's groups.

⏪ **Quincy Market** consists of three structures and has served its purpose as a retail and wholesale distribution center for meat and produce for a century and a half. By the 1970s, though, the market area had become seedy. Some of the old tenants—the famous Durgin Park restaurant and a few butchers and grocers in the central building—had hung on through the years, but the old vitality had disappeared.

Thanks to a creative and tasteful urban-renewal project, the north and south market buildings, separated from the central market by attractive pedestrian malls with trees and benches, house retail establishments, offices, and restaurants. There may be more restaurants in Quincy Market than existed in all of downtown Boston before World War II. Abundance and variety, albeit of an ephemeral sort, have been the watchwords of Quincy Market since its reopening in 1976. Some people consider it all hopelessly trendy; 50,000 visitors a day rather enjoy the extravaganza. You'll want to decide for yourself. *Open Mon.–Sat. 10–9, Sun. noon–6. Restaurants and bars generally open daily 11 AM–2 AM.*

At the end of Quincy Market opposite Faneuil Hall is Columbus Park, bordering on the harbor and on several of Boston's restored wharves. **Central Wharf,** immediately to the right of Long Wharf as you face the harbor, is the home of one of Boston's most popular attractions, the **New England Aquarium.** Here you'll find seals, penguins, a variety of sharks and other sea creatures—more than 2,000 species in all, some of which make their home in the aquarium's four-story, 187,000-gallon observation tank. *Tel. 617/973–5200 (whale-watch information, 617/973–5277). Admission: $7 adults, $3.50 children 3–15, $6 senior citizens. Open Mon., Wed., Fri. 9–5, Thurs. until 8, weekends and holidays until 6. Closed Thanksgiving, Christmas, New Year's Day.*

Along Atlantic Avenue, at the foot of Pearl Street, a plaque set into the wall of a commercial building marks the site of the **Boston Tea Party.** When you cross Fort Point Channel on the Congress Street Bridge, you encounter the *Beaver II,* a faithful replica of one of the Tea Party ships that was forcibly boarded and unloaded on the night Boston Harbor became a teapot. Visitors receive a complimentary cup of tea. *Admission: $5 adults, $3 children 5–14, 20% discount senior citizens and college students. Open daily 9–dusk.*

At the opposite end of the bridge is Museum Wharf, home of the popular **Boston Children's Museum.** The multitude of hands-on exhibits designed with kids in mind includes a petting zoo, computers, video cameras, and an assembly line where children "work" and learn how a factory operates. *300 Congress St., tel. 617/426–6500 (617/426–8855 for recorded information). Admission: $6 adults, $5 children 2–15 and senior citizens, free under 1. Open Tues.–Sun. 10–5, Fri. until 9 (admission $1 after 5). Closed Mon. except during Boston school vacations and holidays.*

Museum Wharf is also the home of the new **Computer Museum,** housing exhibits chronicling the spectacular development of machines that calculate and process information. *300 Congress St., tel. 617/426–2800. Admission: $5 adults, $4 children, senior citizens, and students; free under 5; ½ price Fri. evening. Open summer, Sat.–Thurs. 10–5, Fri. 10–9; winter, Tues.–Thurs., Sat.–Sun. 10–5, Fri. 10–9.*

Back across the channel and south along Atlantic Avenue brings you to Boston's **Chinatown,** with one of the larger concentrations of Chinese-Americans in the United States. Most Chinese restaurants, food stores, and retail businesses are located along Beach and Tyler Streets and Harrison Avenue. The area around the intersection of Kneeland Street and Harrison Avenue is the center of Boston's textile and garment industry.

Time Out It's a special treat to sample the Chinese baked goods in shops along Beacon Street. Many visitors familiar with Cantonese and even Szechuan cookery will still be surprised and delighted with moon cakes, steamed cakes made with rice flour, and other sweets that seldom turn up on restaurant menus.

Tour 4: The Back Bay and the South End

The Back Bay once was a bay, a tidal flat that formed the south bank of a distended Charles River in the 1850s. Beacon Street was built in 1814 to separate the Back Bay from the Charles River. At the rate of 3,500 railroad carloads of gravel a day, it took 30 years to complete the filling as far as the Fens. When the work was finished, the 783-acre peninsula of Boston had been expanded by approximately 450 acres. By 1900 the area was the smartest and most desirable in all Boston.

㉕ A walk through the Back Bay properly begins with the **Public Garden,** the oldest botanical garden in the United States. Its establishment marked the first phase of the Back Bay reclamation project, occupying what had been salt marshes on the edge of the Common's dry land. Its pond has been famous since 1877 for its **swan boats,** which make leisurely cruises during the warm months of the year.

The best place to begin exploring the streets of the Back Bay is at the corner of Commonwealth Avenue and Arlington Street, with Washington and his horse looking over your shoulder. The planners of the Back Bay were able to do something that had never before been possible in Boston: to lay out an entire neighborhood of arrow-straight streets. While other parts of Boston may be reminiscent of the mews and squares of London, the main thoroughfares of the Back Bay (especially Commonwealth Avenue) resemble nothing so much as they do Parisian boulevards.

Beginning at the Charles, the main east-west streets are bisected by eight streets named in alphabetical order from Arlington to Hereford, with three-syllable street names alternating with two-syllable names. Service alleys run behind the main streets; they were built so that delivery wagons could be driven up to basement kitchens. That's how thorough the planning was.

Back Bay is a living museum of urban Victorian residential architecture. The **Gibson House** offers a representative look at how life was arranged in—and by—these tall, narrow, formal buildings. One of the first Back Bay residences (1859), the Gibson House is relatively modest in comparison with some of the grand mansions built during the decades that followed. Unlike other Back Bay houses, the Gibson family home has been preserved with all its Victorian fixtures and furniture intact—not restored, but preserved: A conservative family scion lived here until the 1950s and left things as they were. Here you will understand why a squad of servants was a necessity in the old Back Bay. *137 Beacon St., tel. 617/267–6338. Admission: $3. Tours weekends at 2, 3, 4; also Wed.–Fri., May 1–Nov. 1.*

The Great Depression brought an end to the old Back Bay style of living, and today only a few of the houses serve as single-family residences. Most have been cut up into apartments and, more recently, expensive condominiums.

Newbury Street is Boston's Fifth Avenue, with dozens of specialty shops offering fashion clothing, china, antiques, paintings and prints. It is also a street of beauty salons and sidewalk cafés. Boylston Street, similarly busy but a little less posh, boasts elegant apparel shops.

Time Out   The **Harvard Book Store Café** (190 Newbury St.) serves meals or coffee and pastry—outdoors in nice weather. Since it's a real bookstore, you can browse to your heart's content.

Boylston Street, the southern commercial spine of the Back Bay, separates the sedate old district (some say not effectively enough) from the most ambitious developments this side of downtown. One block south of Boylston, on the corner of St. James Avenue and Clarendon Street, stands the tallest building in New England: the 62-story **John Hancock Tower,** built in the early 1970s and notorious in its early years as the building whose windows fell out. The 60th-floor observatory is one of the three best vantage points in the city, and the "Boston 1775" exhibit shows what the city looked like before the great hill-leveling and landfill operations commenced. *Observatory ticket office, Trinity Pl. and St. James Ave., tel. 617/247–1977. Admission: $2.75 adults, $2 children 5–15 and senior citizens. Open Mon.–Sat. 9 AM–10:15 PM, Sun. noon–10:15. Closed Thanksgiving, Christmas.*

The **Hancock Tower** stands at the edge of **Copley Square,** a civic space that is defined by three monumental older buildings. One is the stately, bowfronted **Copley Plaza Hotel,** which faces the square on St. James Avenue and serves as a dignified foil to two of the most important works of architecture in Boston, if not in the United States. At the left is **Trinity Church,** Henry Hobson Richardson's masterwork of 1877. In this church Richardson brought his Romanesque revival to maturity.

Across the street from Copley Square stands the **Boston Public Library.** When this building was opened in 1895, it confirmed the status of McKim, Mead, and White as apostles of the Renaissance Revival and reinforced a Boston commitment to the enlightenment of the citizenry that goes back 350 years to the founding of the Public Latin School. In the older part of the building is a quiet courtyard with chairs around a flower garden, and a sumptuous main reference reading room. *Tel. 617/536–5400. Open Mon.–Thurs. 9–9, Fri.–Sat. 9–5.*

With a modern assertive presence, **Copley Place** comprises two major hotels (the high-rise Westin and the Marriott) and dozens of shops and restaurants, attractively grouped on several levels around bright, open indoor spaces. The scale of the project bothers some people, as does the fact that so vast a complex of buildings effectively isolates the South End from the Back

Bay. *Shopping galleries generally open weekdays 10–7, Sat. 10–7, Sun. noon–5.*

Down Huntington Avenue is the headquarters complex of the **29** **Christian Science Church.** Mary Baker Eddy's original granite First Church of Christ, Scientist (1894) has since been enveloped by the domed Renaissance basilica added to the site in 1906, and both church buildings are now surrounded by the offices of the *Christian Science Monitor* and by I. M. Pei's complex of church administration structures completed in 1973. The 670-foot reflecting pool is a pleasant spot to stroll around. *175 Huntington Ave., tel. 617/450–3790. Open Mon.– Sat. 9:30–3:30, Sun. 11:15–2. Tours on the hour. Services Sun. at 10 and 7, Wed. at 7:30* PM.

The best views of the pool and the precise, abstract geometry of the entire complex are from the **Prudential Center Skywalk,** a 52nd-floor observatory that offers fine views of Boston, Cambridge, and the suburbs to the west and south. *800 Boylston St., tel. 617/236–3318. Admission: $2.50 adults, $1.50 children 5–15 and senior citizens. Skywalk open Mon.–Sat. 10–10, Sun. noon–10.*

30 **Symphony Hall,** since 1900 the home of the Boston Symphony Orchestra, stands at the corner of Huntington and Massachusetts Avenues, another contribution of McKim, Mead, and White to the Boston landscape. Acoustics, rather than exterior design, make this a special place. Not one of the 2,500 seats can be said to be a bad one. *Tel. 617/266–1492. Tours by appointment with the volunteer office.*

From here you can walk southeast on Massachusetts Avenue to explore the South End or southwest on Huntington Avenue to the Fens and the Museum of Fine Arts. This tour finishes with a visit to the **South End,** a neighborhood eclipsed by the Back Bay more than a century ago but now solidly back in fashion, with galleries and restaurants on Tremont Street catering to young urban professionals. The observation is usually made that while the Back Bay is French-inspired, the South End is English. The houses, too, are different. In one sense they continue the pattern established on Beacon Hill (in a uniformly bowfronted style), yet they also aspire to a much more florid standard of decoration. Although it would take years to understand the place fully, you can capture something of the flavor of the South End with a short walk. To see elegant house restora-
31 tions, go to **Rutland Square** (between Columbus Avenue and
32 Tremont Street) or **Union Park** (between Tremont Street and Shawmut Avenue). These oases seem miles distant from the city around them.

There is a substantial black presence in the South End, particularly along Columbus Avenue and Massachusetts Avenue, which marks the beginning of the predominantly black neighborhood of Roxbury. The early integration of the South End set the stage for its eventual transformation into a remarkable polyglot of ethnic groups. You are likely to hear Spanish spoken along Tremont Street, and there are Middle Eastern groceries along Shawmut Avenue. At the northeastern extreme of the South End, Harrison Avenue and Washington Street connect the area with Chinatown, and consequently there is a growing Asian influence. Still another minority presence among the neighborhood's ethnic groups, and sometimes belonging to one or more of them, is Boston's largest gay population.

Time Out For a cross-section of personalities and conversation (and good sweet-potato pie), have breakfast or lunch at **Charlie's Sandwich Shoppe** (429 Columbus Ave.), a family-run institution for more than 50 years.

Tour 5: The Fens

The Back Bay Fens mark the beginning of Boston's Emerald Necklace, a loosely connected chain of parks designed by Frederick Law Olmsted that extends along the Fenway, Riverway, and Jamaicaway to Jamaica Pond, the 265-acre Arnold Arboretum, and the zoo at Franklin Park. The Fens park consists of still, irregular reedbound pools surrounded by broad meadows, trees, and flower gardens.

㉝ The **Museum of Fine Arts,** the MFA, between Huntington Avenue and the Fenway, has holdings of American art that surpass those of all but two or three U.S. museums. The MFA boasts the most extensive collection of Asiatic art gathered under one roof, and European art is represented by works of the 11th through the 20th centuries. It has strong collections of textiles and costumes and an impressive collection of antique musical instruments. The museum's new West Wing, designed by I. M. Pei, is used primarily for traveling exhibitions and special showings of the museum's permanent collection. The museum has a good restaurant and a less formal cafeteria serving light snacks; both are in the West Wing. *465 Huntington Ave., tel. 617/267–9300 (617/267–9377 for recorded schedule and events information). Admission: $6 adults, $5 senior citizens, free under 16; free to all Sat. 10–noon. Open Tues.–Sun. 10–5, Wed. until 10. West Wing open Thurs. and Fri. until 10. 1 hr. tours available.*

On the Fenway Park side of the Museum of Fine Arts, the newly constructed **Tenshin Garden,** the "garden at the heart of heaven," allows visitors to experience landscape as a work of art.

Two blocks west of the MFA, on the Fenway, stands the
㉞ **Isabella Stewart Gardner Museum,** a monument to one woman's taste—and despite the loss of a few masterpieces in a daring 1990 robbery, still a trove of spectacular paintings, sculpture, furniture, and textiles. There is much to see: *The Rape of Europa,* the most important of Titian's works in an American collection; paintings and drawings by Matisse, Whistler, Bellini, Van Dyck, Botticelli, and Rubens; John Singer Sargent's oil portrait of Mrs. Gardner herself, in the Gothic Room. At the center of the building is the magnificent courtyard, fully enclosed beneath a glass room. *280 The Fenway, tel. 617/566–1401 (617/ 734–1359 for recorded concert information). Admission: $5 adults, $2.50 children under 12, students, and senior citizens. Open Tues. noon–6:30, Wed.–Sun. noon–5. Concerts Sept.–June, Tues. at 6, Thurs. at 12:15, Sun. at 3.*

㉟ The Boston shrine known as **Fenway Park** is one of the smallest baseball parks in the major leagues and one of the oldest. It was built in 1912, when the grass on the field was real—and it still is today. Babe Ruth pitched here when the place was new; Ted

Williams and Carl Yastrzemski slugged out their entire careers here.

Kenmore Square, home to fast-food parlors, new wave rock clubs, and an enormous neon sign advertising gasoline, is two blocks north of Fenway Park. The neon sign is so thoroughly identified with the area that historic preservationists have fought successfully to save it—proof that Bostonians are an open-minded lot who do not require that their landmarks be identified with the American Revolution.

Tour 6: Cambridge

Cambridge is an independent city faced with the difficult task of living in the shadow of its larger neighbor, Boston, while being overshadowed as well by the giant educational institutions within its own borders. It provides the brains and the technical know-how that, combined with Boston's financial prowess, has created the vibrant high-tech economy of which Massachusetts is so proud. Cambridge also continues to function as the conscience of the greater Boston area; when a new social experiment or progressive legislation appears on the local scene, chances are it came out of the crucible of Cambridge political activism.

Cambridge, just minutes from Boston by MBTA, is commonly
36 reached on the Red Line train to **Harvard Square.**

A good place to begin a tour is the **Cambridge Discovery** information booth near the MBTA station entrance, where you will find maps, brochures, and information about the entire city. The walking tour brochures cover Old Cambridge, East Cambridge, and Revolutionary Cambridge. Cambridge Discovery also gives a rewarding tour of Old Cambridge conducted by a corps of well-trained high school students. *Cambridge Discovery, Inc., Box 1987, Cambridge 02238, tel. 617/497-1630. Open in winter, Mon.-Sat. 9-5, Sun. 1-5; in summer, Mon.-Sat. 9-6, Sun. 1-5.*

In 1636 the country's first college was established here. Named in 1638 for a young Charlestown clergyman who died that year, leaving the college his entire library and half his estate, Harvard remained the only college in the New World until 1693, by which time it was firmly established as a respected center of learning.

The Harvard University information office on the ground floor of Holyoke Center (1350 Massachusetts Ave.), run by students, offers a free hour-long tour of Harvard Yard and maps of the university area. The tour does not include visits to museums, but it provides a fine orientation and will give you ideas for further sightseeing.

Harvard has two celebrated art museums, each a treasure in itself. The most famous is the **Fogg Art Museum,** behind Harvard Yard on Quincy Street, between Broadway and Harvard Street. Founded in 1895, it now owns 80,000 works of art from every major period and from every corner of the world. Its focus is primarily on European, American, and Far Eastern works; it has notable collections of 19th-century French Impressionist and medieval Italian paintings. Special exhibits change monthly. *32 Quincy St., tel. 617/495-5573. Admission:*

$4 adults, $2.50 senior citizens and students, free under 18. Open Tues.–Sun. 10–5.

When you purchase a ticket to the Fogg, you are entitled to tour the **Arthur M. Sackler Museum** (tel. 617/495–9400) across the street. It exhibits Chinese, Japanese, ancient Greek, Egyptian, Roman, Buddhist, and Islamic works. The Sackler keeps the same hours as the Fogg.

Harvard also maintains the **Harvard University Museums of Natural History,** north of the main campus on Oxford Street. It contains four distinct collections: comparative zoology, archaeology, botany, and minerals. The most famous exhibit here is the display of glass flowers in the **Botanical Museum.** The **Peabody Museum of Archaeology and Ethnology** holds one of the world's outstanding anthropological collections; exhibits focus on American Indian and Central and South American cultures. *26 Oxford St., tel. 617/495–3045 for general information. Admission: $3 adults, $2 children 5–15, $2 students and senior citizens. Open Mon.–Sat. 9–4:30, Sun. 1–4:30.*

Across Massachusetts Avenue, at the north end of the Cambridge Common, go down Appian Way through a small garden to the heart of **Radcliffe College.** Founded in 1897 "to furnish instruction and the opportunities of collegiate life to women and to promote their higher education," it is an independent corporation within Harvard University.

From Harvard Square, follow elegant **Brattle Street** out to the **Longfellow National Historic Site.** George Washington lived here throughout the siege of Boston. The poet Henry Wadsworth Longfellow received the house as a wedding gift and filled it with the exuberant spirit of his own work and that of his literary circle, which included Emerson, Thoreau, Holmes, Dana, and Parkman. *105 Brattle St., tel. 617/876–4491. Admission: $2 adults, free under 16. Open daily 10–4:30.*

37 An exploration of Cambridge would not be complete without a visit to the **Massachusetts Institute of Technology.** The 135-acre campus of MIT borders the Charles River, 1½ miles south of Harvard Square. Obviously designed by and for scientists, the MIT campus is divided by Massachusetts Avenue into the West Campus, which is devoted to student leisure life, and the East Campus, where the heavy work is done. The West Campus has some extraordinary buildings. The **Kresge Auditorium,** designed by Eero Saarinen with a curving roof and unusual thrust, rests on three instead of four points. The **MIT Chapel,** another Saarinen design, is lit primarily by a roof oculus that focuses light on the altar, as well as by reflections from the water in a small moat surrounding it, and it is topped by an aluminum sculpture by Theodore Roszak. **Baker House** was designed in 1947 by the Finnish architect Alvar Aaltoa in such a way as to give every room a view of the Charles River. MIT's East Campus buildings are connected by a 5-mile "infinite corridor," touted as the second-longest corridor in the country.

The Institute maintains an Information Center and offers free tours of the campus Monday–Friday at 10 and 2. *Building Seven, 77 Massachusetts Ave., tel. 617/253–4795. Open weekdays 9–5.*

Boston for Free

Boston's Weekend Events and Package Guide is available free *(tel. 617/536–4100)*.

The **Hatch Shell** on the bank of the Charles River is the site of numerous concerts during the summer months, and the Boston Pops and the Boston Ballet are among the performers.

While most museums charge admission, several museums schedule a period when admission is free to all: **the Museum of Fine Arts,** Saturday 10–noon; **the Children's Museum,** Friday 5–9. In Cambridge, the **Harvard University Museums of Natural History, the Fogg Art Museum,** and the **Arthur M. Sackler Museum** are free on Saturday morning.

What to See and Do with Children

Kids who are interested in history will find much to enjoy in Boston. The city's historical legacy is vivid and accessible: Youngsters can see just where Paul Revere's lanterns were hung, and they can walk the decks of an undefeated man-of-war.

Boston Children's Museum (Tour 3. Downtown Boston) *T stop, South Station.*

The *Boston Parents Paper* (tel. 617/522–1515), published monthly and distributed free throughout the city, is an excellent resource for finding out what's happening.

Off the Beaten Track

A stark white prowlike building at the tip of Columbia Point south of Boston proper pays homage to one of Washington's successors as president, a native Irish Bostonian named John F. Kennedy. The **Kennedy Library** is the official repository of his presidential papers, his desk, and other personal belongings, and there are screenings of a film on his life. The harborfront site alone is worth a visit, even without the library's interpretive displays and trove of Kennedy memorabilia. *Columbia Point, tel. 617/929–4523. Admission: $3.50 adults, $2 senior citizens, free under 16. Open daily 9–5. Accessible on the Red Line.*

Shopping

Boston's shops and stores are generally open Monday through Saturday from 9 or 9:30 until 6 or 7; many stay open until 8 late in the week. Some stores, particularly those in malls or tourist areas, are open Sunday from noon until 5. Boston's two daily newspapers, the *Globe* and the *Herald*, are the best places to learn about sales; Sunday's *Globe* often announces sales for later in the week.

Shopping Districts Most of Boston's stores and shops are located in an area bounded by Quincy Market, the Back Bay, downtown, and

Copley Square. There are few outlet stores in the area, but there are plenty of bargains, particularly in the world-famous Filene's Basement and Chinatown's fabric district.

Copley Place, an indoor shopping mall connecting the Westin and Marriott hotels, has 87 stores, restaurants, and cinemas that blend the elegant, the glitzy, and the overpriced.

Downtown Crossing, Boston's traditional downtown shopping area at Summer and Washington Streets, has been tarted up: It's now a pedestrian mall with outdoor food and merchandise kiosks, street performers, and benches for people watchers. Here are the city's two largest department stores, Jordan Marsh and Filene's.

Faneuil Hall Marketplace has small shops, kiosks of every description, street performers, and one of the great food experiences, Quincy Market. The intrepid shopper must cope with crowds of people, particularly on weekends. Nearby Dock Square is a great place to hunt for bargains in restaurant supply houses.

Harvard Square in Cambridge has more than 150 stores within a few blocks. In addition to the surprising range of items sold in the square, Cambridge is a book-lover's paradise.

Newbury Street is Boston's version of New York's Fifth Avenue, where the trendy gives way to the chic and the expensive.

Department Stores   **Filene's** (426 Washington St., tel. 617/357–2978). This full-service department store's most outstanding feature is its two-level bargain basement, where items are automatically reduced in price according to the number of days they've been on the rack. The competition can be stiff for the great values on discontinued, overstocked, or slightly irregular items.
Harvard Coop Society (1400 Massachusetts Ave., tel. 617/492–1000; at MIT, 3 Cambridge Center, tel. 617/491–4230). Begun in 1882 as a nonprofit service for students and faculty, the Coop is now a full department store known for its extensive selection of records and books.

Food Markets   Every Friday and Saturday, **Haymarket** (near Faneuil Hall Marketplace) is a crowded jumble of outdoor fruit and vegetable vendors, meat markets, and fishmongers. Don't even think of choosing your own fruit!

Specialty Stores   **Charles Street** in Beacon Hill is a mecca for antiques lovers.
Antiques

Baked Goods   **Montilio's** (549 Boylston St., tel. 617/267–4700, and Faneuil Hall Marketplace, tel. 617/367–2371). Fabulously rich rum cakes, strawberry shortcake, ice-cream cakes, cookies, and pastries.

Books   **Barnes and Noble** (395 Washington St., tel. 617/426–5502, and 607 Boylston St., tel. 617/236–1308). Boston's biggest discount bookseller specializes in reduced prices on recent best-sellers and tables heaped with remainders at bargain prices.

Clothing for Men   **Ann Taylor** (18 Newbury St., tel. 617/262–0763, and Faneuil
and Women   Hall Marketplace, tel. 617/742–0031). High-quality fashions for both classic and trendy dressers. Shoes and accessories.

Bonwit Teller (500 Boylston St., tel. 617/267–1200). Imported and American designer clothing and accessories, and an International Boutique and Designer Salon.

Brooks Brothers (46 Newbury St., tel. 617/267–2600). Traditional formal and casual clothing. The styling is somewhat more contemporary in the third-floor Brooksgate shop, but basically Brooks is Brooks: correct and durable down through the ages.

Louis (234 Berkeley St., tel. 617/965–6100). Now located in the former Bonwit Teller building, Louis carries elegantly tailored designs and a wide selection of imported clothing and accessories, including many of the more daring Italian styles. They also have subtly updated classics in everything from linen to tweed.

Ice Cream **Steve's** (31 Church St., tel. 617/354–9106; 95 Massachusetts Ave., tel. 617/247–9401). The original Steve's, which started out in Somerville, was one of the first homemade ice-cream parlors to offer "mix-ins." Some say this is *the best* ice cream.

Jewelry **Shreve, Crump & Low** (330 Boylston St., tel. 617/267–9100). A complete line of the finest jewelry, china, crystal, and silver. A beautiful collection of Steuben glass on the second floor. Also an extensive collection of clocks and watches. Shreve's, one of Boston's oldest and most respected stores, is where generations of Brahmin brides have registered their china selections.

Sports Equipment **Eastern Mountain Sports** (1041 Commonwealth Ave., Brighton, tel. 617/254–4250). New England's best selection of gear for the backpacker, camper, climber, skier, or all-round outdoors person.

Tobacconists **L. J. Peretti Company** (2½ Park Square, tel. 617/482–0218). A Boston institution since 1870, this is one of the few places that still makes pipes. Peretti sells its own blends of tobacco, a large selection of others, and handmade imported cigars.

Toys **F.A.O. Schwarz** (338 Boylston St., tel. 617/266–5101). This branch of the famed New York toy emporium offers the highest quality (and the highest priced) toys.

Participant Sports and Fitness

The mania for physical fitness is big in Boston. Most public recreational facilities, including skating rinks and tennis courts, are operated by the Metropolitan District Commission (MDC) (tel. 617/727–5215).

Bicycling A free pamphlet showing bike paths in Massachusetts and the greater Boston area is available from the Department of Public Works (tel. 617/973–8000).

The **Dr. Paul Dudley White Bikeway,** approximately 18 miles long, runs along both sides of the Charles River.

Jogging Both sides of the Charles River are popular with joggers. Many hotels have printed maps of nearby routes.

Physical Fitness The **Westin Hotel** (Copley Place, Back Bay, tel. 617/262–9600) has complete health club facilities. Nonguests are welcome to use the facilities for a $7 fee.

Spectator Sports

Sports are as much a part of Boston as are codfish and Democrats. Everything you may have heard about the zeal of Boston fans is true, and out-of-towners wishing to experience it firsthand have these choices:

Baseball: The **Boston Red Sox,** American League (tel. 617/267–8661 or 617/267–1700 for tickets), play at Fenway Park.

Basketball: The **Boston Celtics,** NBA (tel. 617/523–3030 or 617/720–3434 for tickets), shoot hoops at Boston Garden on Causeway Street.

Football: The **New England Patriots,** NFL (tel. 800/543–1776), play football at Sullivan Stadium in Foxboro, 45 minutes south of the city.

Hockey: The **Boston Bruins,** NHL (tel. 617/227–3223), are on the ice at Boston Garden.

Dining

The main ingredient in Boston restaurant fare is still the bounty of the North Atlantic, the daily catch of fish and shellfish that appears somewhere on virtually every menu, whether the cuisine be new French, traditional American, Oriental, or simply seafood.

Seafood or no, the choice of dining experience in Boston is unusually wide. At one extreme, respected young chefs emphasize the freshest ingredients and the menu reflects the morning's shopping; at the other, the tradition of decades mandates recipes older than the nation and the menu seems forever unchanged. Between the extremes lies an extensive range of American, French, Italian, and other national and ethnic cuisines, their variety ample enough to create difficult decisions at mealtime.

Bostonians are not traditionally late diners. Many of the city's finest restaurants are busy by 7 PM, and those near the theater district begin filling up earlier. (Advise your waiter when you sit down if you plan to attend an after-dinner performance.)

As a general rule, you can expect to tip about 15% on a check of less than $60, about 20% on a check larger than $60.

Back Bay
★ **L'Espalier.** The simpler, lighter preparations and larger portions that characterize contemporary French and American cuisine are created here by Frank McClelland. The fixed-price, three-course dinner might include roast native partridge with chanterelles, salmon steak with mint and wild onion butter and a salad of peas and radishes, and for dessert a luscious but low-calorie arrangement of figs and peaches with wild strawberry sauce and mascarpone cheese. A *menu dégustation*, which provides a sampling of many items, is available on request Monday through Friday. There is an excellent wine list of 150 choices and the decor of the three dining rooms is intimate but elegant. *30 Gloucester Street, tel. 617/262–3023. Reservations required. Jacket and tie advised. Dinner only. AE, MC, V. Closed Sun. Very Expensive.*

★ **Le Marquis de Lafayette.** One of the city's newest hotel dining rooms is also one of its grandest, with candlelight dining accompanied by harp music. In this French restaurant, the execution of the menu by chef Urs Balmer approaches perfection in dish after dish. Dining is on the highest, most creative level, yet the food doesn't sacrifice flavor for mere innovation. This is a classically based kitchen at the cutting edge of what is new. The menu changes seasonally. *Lafayette Hotel, 1 Ave. de Lafayette, tel. 617/451–2600. Reservations required, especially for weekend. Jacket and tie required. Valet parking after 5*

PM. AE, CB, DC, MC, V. No lunch. Closed Sun. Very Expensive.

Suntory. Opened by the giant Japanese distillery Suntory, this elegant new Japanese restaurant offers a variety of dining experiences—all of them first class—in three dining rooms. A bustling sushi bar dominates the first floor; *shabu shabu* (Japanese hot pot) is served on the second floor; and steaks are cooked on your table by swashbuckling chefs at the *teppan yaki* steak house on the third floor. *212 Stuart St., tel. 617/338–2111. Reservations advised. Jacket and tie advised. AE, DC, MC, V. No lunch Sun. Expensive–Very Expensive.*

Boodle's. This London-style chophouse is one of the Back Bay's best kept restaurant secrets. Bible-thick steaks and fresh local fish, along with a variety of vegetables, are expertly grilled over hickory, cherry, and other woods. There are dozens of sauces to choose from, and guests are encouraged to share larger cuts of meat. The split-level dining room is furnished like a 19th-century club. *40 Dalton St. in the Back Bay Hilton, tel. 617/236–1100. Reservations advised. Dress: casual. AE, CB, DC, MC, V. Expensive.*

Legal Sea Foods. What began as a tiny adjunct to a fish market has grown to important status, with additional locations in Cambridge, Chestnut Hill, and Worcester. Always busy, Legal still does things its own way. Dishes are not allowed to stand until the orders for a table are completed but are brought individually to insure freshness. The style of food preparation is, as always, simple: Seafood is raw, broiled, fried, steamed, or baked; fancy sauces and elaborate presentations are eschewed. You can have a baked stuffed lobster or mussels au gratin, but otherwise your choice lies among the range of sea creatures available that day. The wine list is carefully selected, the house wine equally so. *64 Arlington St., Park Sq., in the Boston Park Plaza Hotel, tel. 617/426–4444. No reservations; expect to wait. Dress: casual. AE, DC, MC, V. Moderate.*

Bnu. Conveniently located in the heart of the theater district, this tiny Italian cafe specializes in pizzas, pasta dishes, and salads. The goat cheese calzone, lobster cannoli, and grilled vegetable and polenta salad are enthusiastically recommended. The decorator borrowed design elements from 2,000 years of Mediterranean architecture: faux marble columns, art deco chairs, neon, and Regency fabrics. *123 Stuart St., Transportation Bldg., tel. 617/367–8405. Reservations accepted only for 5:45 and 6 PM pre-theater sittings. Dress: casual. MC, V. Inexpensive–Moderate.*

Thai Cuisine. Those who have tickets for a Symphony Hall event or simply an adventurous palate will welcome the Thai Cuisine. The food is not merely exotica for the uninitiated; it is well cooked, and the kitchen uses first-rate ingredients. A main course of half a duck is the only sizable entree on the menu; the rest are the kind you order and share, Oriental fashion, with two or three. *14A Westland Ave., tel. 617/262–1485. Dress: informal. No reservations. No lunch Sun. AE, DC, MC, V. Inexpensive.*

Cambridge **The Harvest.** A very popular dining room with a distinctly ★ French decor and a pleasant courtyard for outdoor dining. The Harvest features nouvelle French dishes. The wine list is extensive, the desserts homemade. A portion of the restaurant is given over to the more casual Ben's Cafe, which has its own menu of regional American specialties. *44 Brattle St., tel. 617/*

Dining

Bartley's Burger
Cottage, **8**
Blue Diner, **30**
Bnu, **27**
Boodle's, **16**
Daily Catch, **41**
Durgin-Park, **38**
East Coast Grill, **2**
Grendel's Den, **12**
Hamersley's Bistro, **22**
The Harvest, **6**
Ho Yuen Ting, **29**
Iruna, **7**
Jimmy's
Harborside, **31**
Joyce Chen
Restaurant, **3**
Legal Sea Foods, **24**
Le Marquis de
Lafayette, **32**
L'Espalier, **15**
Michela's, **13**
Rarities, **11**
Restaurant Jasper, **40**
Ristorante Lucia, **42**
Seasons, **39**
Suntory, **25**
Thai Cuisine, **17**
Union Oyster
House, **36**

Lodging

Boston Harbor Hotel
at Rowes Wharf, **35**
Boston International
Hostel, **18**
Boston Park Plaza
Hotel & Towers, **24**
Bostonian, **37**
Cambridge House, **10**
The Charles Hotel, **4**
Copley Plaza, **21**
Copley Square
Hotel, **20**
Eliot Hotel, **14**
Four Seasons, **26**
Harvard Motor
House, **9**
Hilton (at Logan
Airport), **43**
Hotel Meridien, **34**
Lenox Hotel, **19**
Omni Parker
House, **33**
Ritz-Carlton, **23**
Sheraton
Commander, **5**
Susse Chalet Inn, **1**
Tremont House, **28**

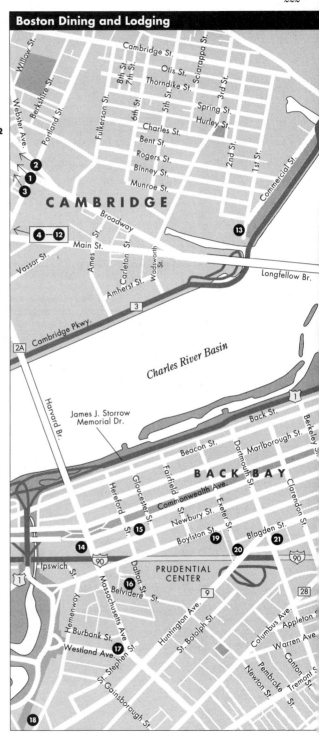

Boston Dining and Lodging

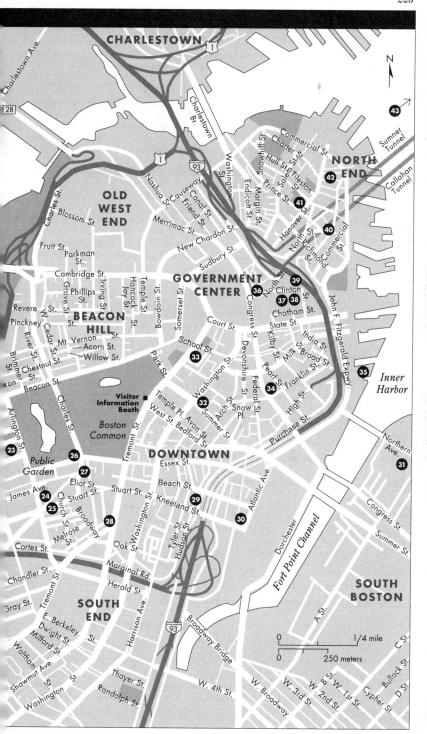

492–1115. Jacket and tie optional. Reservations for the dining room only. AE, CB, DC, MC, V. Expensive.

Michela's. One of the city's most popular restaurants, Michela's boasts a menu that changes every eight weeks or so. It promises imaginative Italian dishes such as pizza *vongole* (with clams and fresh oregano), *petti di anitra e confitura d'aglio* (grilled duck breast with roasted-garlic jam), and *zafferano con cozze* (saffron pasta with mussels, tomatoes, and garlic). All sauces and pastas are made fresh daily. Reflecting the building's former use, the decor is industrial chic with pink walls and exposed heating ducts. An atrium cafe serves a lighter menu, with all dishes under $10 Monday–Friday. *1 Atheneum St. (lobby of the former Carter Ink Bldg.), tel. 617/ 225–2121. Jacket and tie optional. Reservations advised. No lunch Sat. Closed Sun. AE, CB, DC, MC, V. Expensive.*

Rarities. The subdued contemporary decor complements a "New American" cuisine based on regional cooking and seasonal ingredients. The à la carte menu includes porterhouse of veal with vegetable strudel and a Rhode Island wine-based sauce. *Hotel Charles, 1 Bennett St., tel. 617/864–1200. Jacket and tie suggested. Reservations advised. No lunch. Closed Sun. AE, CB, DC, MC, V. Expensive.*

East Coast Grill. The chef calls his food "equator cuisine" to acknowledge the hot pepper and spices. The specialty is New American and American (in particular, North Carolina) barbecue, with a number of ethnic dishes such as grilled tuna with West Indies sofrito, grilled sweetbreads, jerk chicken, and "pasta from Hell"—a pasta livened with inner beauty hot sauce. The dining room is small, bright, and very busy. *1271 Cambridge St., tel. 617/491–6568. Dress: informal. No reservations; go early or late to avoid a long wait. No lunch. MC, V. Moderate.*

Iruna. This Spanish restaurant, popular with students for years, specializes in paellas and seafoods and has great salads. Outdoor dining is possible in warm weather. Wine and beer only. *56 John F. Kennedy St., tel. 617/868–5633. Dress: informal. Reservations accepted. Closed Sun. No credit cards. Moderate.*

Joyce Chen Restaurant. Joyce Chen offers a gracious setting and an extensive menu of Mandarin, Shanghai, and Szechuan food. Specialties include hot and cold soups, Szechuan scallops, and moo shu dishes. The lunch buffet is weekdays and the all-you-can-eat buffet is on Tuesday and Wednesday 6–8:30. *390 Rindge Ave., tel. 617/492–7373. Dress: informal. Reservations suggested for large parties. AE, MC, V. Moderate.*

Grendel's Den. Housed in a former Harvard College fraternity building, Grendel's has an unusually warm, clubby atmosphere, a downstairs bar, and an eclectic assortment of cuisines, including Middle Eastern, Greek, Indian, Italian, and French. Diners are welcome to mix and match small-portion dishes, which generally include such diverse items as shish kebab, fettuccine, spareribs, moussaka, hummus, and broiled fish. And there's a large salad bar. *89 Winthrop St., tel. 617/491–1160. Dress: informal. Reservations accepted, recommended on weekends. AE, CB, DC, MC, V. Moderate–Inexpensive.*

Bartley's Burger Cottage. Famed for its burgers and fried onion rings, Bartley's is good, too, for salads and sandwiches. And it's popular with students. *1246 Massachusetts Ave., tel. 617/ 354–6559. Dress: informal. No reservations. Closed Sun. No credit cards. Inexpensive.*

Downtown **Blue Diner.** Don't let the fresh flowers, cloth napkins, and fancy wine list fool you; this is a genuine diner with genuine diner food (as well as more sophisticated offerings). Since it was refurbished and reopened in July 1986, the diner has been getting rave reviews for such original creations as grilled swordfish with melon chutney and down-home favorites like fresh roasted turkey with old-fashioned gravy, homemade cranberry sauce, and mashed potatoes. *178 Kneeland St., tel. 617/338–4639. Dress: informal. No reservations. AE, DC, MC, V. Inexpensive–Moderate.*

★ **Ho Yuen Ting.** Every night a waiting line forms outside this Chinatown hole-in-the-wall. The reason is simple: Ho Yuen Ting serves some of the best seafood in town. The house specialty is a sole and vegetable stir-fry served in a spectacular whole, crisply fried fish. Come with friends so you can also enjoy the clams with black bean sauce, lobster with ginger and scallion, and whole steamed bass. *13A Hudson St., tel. 617/426 –2316. Dress: informal. Reservations accepted. No credit cards. Inexpensive–Moderate.*

Faneuil Hall **Seasons.** At this solarium-like restaurant overlooking Faneuil
★ Hall, the cuisine of chef William Poirier is American with international influences and changes seasonally. Selections from a summer menu included grilled lamb sausage with feta and calamata olives as an appetizer; veal ribeye with avocado, crab cakes, and lime; and, for dessert, poppy Madeira cake with fresh peaches and cream or an unusual creation of watermelon and root beer sorbets served on a thin slice of watermelon and called Coney Island Ices. The wine list is exclusively American. *Bostonian Hotel, North and Blackstone Sts., tel. 617/523–3600. Jacket required. Reservations suggested. AE, DC, MC, V. Expensive–Very Expensive.*

Union Oyster House. Established in 1826, the Union Oyster House is Boston's oldest restaurant. For nearly two decades its best feature has been a first-floor shellfish bar where the oysters and clams are fresh and well chilled—a handy place to stop for a dozen oysters or cherrystone clams on the halfshell. There have been signs of inner stirrings (a new Union Bar was recently added); perhaps the restaurant can regain some of its former glory. *41 Union St., tel. 617/227–2750. Dress: informal. Reservations accepted. AE, DC, MC, V. Expensive–Moderate.*

Durgin Park. When it opened in the 1830s, Durgin Park was a simple upstairs dining hall with a bar on the first floor that catered to the wholesale meat and produce district. Today the main reason for going to this legendary eatery is its rough and ready atmosphere. Here you still sit family style, elbow to elbow with your neighbor—friend or stranger. The floor is worn plank, the waitresses act tough and gruff, the ceiling is still embossed tin, and redcheckered cloths cover the long tables. The prime rib, pot roast, and baked beans are traditional New England fare served in generous portions; the strawberry shortcake (in season) is mountainous; the fish chowder and broiled scallops are good buys. *340 Faneuil Hall Marketplace (North Market Bldg.), tel. 617/227–2038. Dress: informal. No reservations; expect to wait at prime dining hours. No credit cards. Inexpensive–Moderate.*

North End **Restaurant Jasper.** Jasper White, a young chef with an impres-
★ sive record in the establishments of others, opened his own restaurant on the city's waterfront and soon acquired a national reputation for his stunning new American cuisine. Low-key

decor, spacious seating, and good service complement a respectable wine list and superb food. There is adequate choice of seafood, meat, and fowl, and there is a five-course tasting menu. *240 Commercial St., tel. 617/523–1126. Jacket and tie required. Reservations required. Lunch Fri. only. Closed Sun. AE, CB, DC, MC, V. Expensive.*

Ristorante Lucia. Some aficionados consider Lucia's the best Italian restaurant in the North End. Its specialties from the Abruzzi region include batter-fried artichoke hearts or mozzarella in carrozza as appetizer and the chicken alla Lucia or *pollo arrabiatta.* Check out the upstairs bar, with its pink marble and its takeoff on the Sistine Chapel ceiling. *415 Hanover St., tel. 617/523–9148. Dress: informal. Reservations recommended. No lunch Mon.–Thurs. AE, MC, V. Expensive–Moderate.*

Daily Catch. Shoulder-crowding small, with an informal oyster bar, this storefront restaurant specializes in calamari dishes, lobster *fra diavolo,* linguini with clam sauce—and extremely low prices. A second restaurant has opened at 261 Northern Avenue, across from Jimmy's Harborside, and a third just opened in Kendall Square. Hours of operation vary greatly; call for times. *323 Hanover St., tel. 617/523–8567. Dress: informal. No reservations. No credit cards. Inexpensive.*

South End **Hamersley's Bistro.** Fiona and Gordon Hamersley opened their
★ French-American bistro in July 1987 and have gotten rave reviews. The black and white decor in both dining rooms is accented by a fire-engine-red bar and maître d'station. Specialties that have a permanent place on the daily menu include a garlic and mushroom sandwich served as an appetizer (the mushrooms change seasonally), a bouillabaisse (whose ingredients change with the season), and roast chicken with garlic, lemon, and parsley. *578 Tremont St., tel. 617/267–6068. Dress: informal. Reservations accepted, recommended Fri. and Sat. nights. AE, MC, V. Expensive.*

Waterfront **Jimmy's Harborside.** This exceedingly popular seafood establishment enjoys a solid reputation. The bright, three-tiered main dining room was designed to ensure that every table has an unobstructed view of the harbor. In addition to the many fresh seafood preparations that have long been standard fare, the menu now offers such specials as pasta primavera with a medley of sautéed shrimp, veal, and pork tenderloin. As a change from chowder or traditional bouillabaisse, try the scampi Luciano, a bouillabaisse made with white wine, cream, and a variety of fresh fish and shrimp. The wine list showcases American wines. The Boat Bar, the scene of high-spirited camaraderie, is a favorite watering hole of politicians, among them Tip O'Neill. *242 Northern Ave., tel. 617/423–1000. Jacket preferred after 6 PM. Limited reservations Mon.–Sat. Closed Sun. AE, CB, DC, MC, V. Moderate–Expensive.*

Lodging

Many of the city's most costly lodging places offer attractively priced weekend packages. These weekend rates (and their availability) will vary; for a free copy of the *Boston Travel Planner,* contact the **Greater Boston Convention and Visitors Bureau** (Box 490, Boston, MA 02199, tel. 617/536–4100).

While Boston does not have a large number of bed-and-breakfasts, there are several, and they are usually very reasonable, with daily rates in the $45–$100 per room range. Reservations may be made through **Bed and Breakfast Cambridge and Greater Boston** (Box 665, Cambridge 02140, tel. 617/576–1492), or **Host Homes of Boston** (Box 117, Boston 02168, tel. 617/244–1308).

Back Bay **Copley Plaza.** The stately, bowfronted classic among Boston
★ hotels, built in 1912, was completely refurbished in 1989. Guest rooms have carpeting from England, customized furniture from Italy, and new bathroom fixtures surrounded by marble tile. The Plaza Bar has seating to accommodate a program of cabaret performances; Copley's Bar has just been renovated. A separate concierge area has been created. The hotel staff is multilingual, children under 18 stay free in their parents' room, and pets are welcome. *138 St. James Ave., 02116, tel. 617/267–5300 or 800/826–7539. 396 rooms, 49 suites. Facilities: 2 restaurants, 2 bars, beauty and barber salons. AE, CB, DC, MC, V. Very Expensive.*

★ **Four Seasons.** The only hotel (other than the Ritz) to overlook the Public Garden, the 15-story Four Seasons specializes in luxurious personal service, Old World elegance, and comfort. The rooms have king-size beds, individual climate control, minibars, fresh flowers daily, cable movies, and 24-hour room service. A room overlooking the Garden is worth the extra money. The antique-filled public rooms include a relaxed piano lounge, and Aujourd'hui, a fine restaurant serving American cuisine. Small pets are welcome. *200 Boylston St., 02116, tel. 617/338–4400 or 800/332–3442. 288 rooms and suites. Facilities: lounge, concierge, heated indoor pool, sauna, exercise machines, whirlpool, valet parking. AE, CB, DC, MC, V. Very Expensive.*

★ **Ritz-Carlton.** Since 1927 this hotel overlooking the Public Garden has been one of the most luxurious and elegant places to stay in Boston, and many people consider it the only place in town. Its reputation for quality and service (there are two staff members for every guest) continues. All the rooms are traditionally furnished and equipped with bathroom phones, and some rooms have refrigerators. The most coveted rooms remain the suites in the older section, which have working fireplaces and the best views of the Public Garden. Public rooms include the elegant café, with a window on chic Newbury Street; the sumptuous second-floor main dining room; and the sedate Ritz Bar. Small pets welcome. *Arlington and Newbury Sts., tel. 617/536–5700 or 800/241–3333. 247 rooms, 48 suites. Facilities: affiliated with spa a block away, exercise room, valet parking, concierge, laundry service, beauty and barber salons, multilingual staff, baby-sitting. AE, CB, DC, MC, V. Very Expensive.*

Boston Park Plaza Hotel & Towers. Built in 1927 as flagship for the Statler hotels, the Plaza has had extensive renovations and is an excellent choice for those who want to be at the heart of the action. The hotel is just a block away from the Public Garden (of which some rooms on the top floor have a fine view) and a short walk from Newbury and Boylston streets, Copley Square, and downtown. The rooms vary in size, but all are equipped with direct-dial phones, air-conditioning, and in-room movies. Unless you want to look out on a brick courtyard, ask for an outside room. The lobby is spacious, elegant, and welcoming, with plants, crystal chandeliers, and comfortable couches. High tea is served weekdays and Saturday afternoon. The popular Legal Sea Foods is one of three restaurants; there are two lounges, and the Terrace Room has live shows and entertainment. Children stay free in their parents' room. *One Park Plaza at Arlington St., 02117, tel. 617/426–2000 or 800/ 225–2008. 966 rooms and suites. Facilities: health club, 24-hr room service, overnight laundry and dry-cleaning, foreign currency exchange, specialty shops, garage parking available, travel agency, hairstylist, all major airline ticket offices. AE, CB, DC, MC, V. Expensive.*

Copley Square Hotel. One of Boston's oldest hotels (1891), the Copley Square is still one of the best values in the city. The hotel is popular with Europeans and is European in flavor. The rooms, which are set off long, circuitous hallways, vary tremendously in size from very small to spacious. All rooms have direct-dial phones, air conditioners, windows you can open, color TV, and automatic coffee makers with the necessary materials. The economy rooms, with the toilet and bath down the hall (and sinks in the rooms) remain one of the city's great bargains. If you want a quiet room, ask for one on the courtyard. The popular Café Budapest is downstairs. Children under 12 stay free in their parents' room. *47 Huntington Ave., 02116, tel. 617/536–9000 or 800/225–7062. 150 rooms, 121 with bath. Facilities: use of Westin Hotel's Health Club and Back Bay Raquet Club for a small fee, family suites, airport limousine service, coffee shop, overnight parking across the street. AE, CB, DC, MC, V. Expensive.*

Lenox Hotel. Constructed in 1900, the Lenox has long been a comfortable—if unexciting—hotel, but extensive renovations are under way. The soundproofed guest rooms have spacious walk-in closets, color TV, AM/FM radio, and air-conditioning. Bathrooms come equipped with hair dryers, shaving mirrors, and amenities. The decor is Early American or Chinese on the lower floors, French Provincial on the top floor. The lobby is ornate and handsome, trimmed in blues and golds and set off by a large, welcoming fireplace that evokes the ambience of a country inn. Diamond Jim's Piano Bar, with its loyal local clientele, is a popular spot for joining in on sing-alongs. Children under 18 stay free in their parents' room. *710 Boylston St., 02116, tel. 617/536–5300 or 800/225–7676. 222 rooms. Facilities: 2 restaurants, valet service, valet pay parking, baby-sitting service, shuttle service to airport. AE, CB, DC, MC, V. Expensive.*

Eliot Hotel. An ambitious renovation is bringing a new elegance and lots of marble to a formerly modest nine-floor, European-style, family-run hotel. The upper four floors, all suites, got marble baths and new period furnishings in 1990, and the lower five floors are to be redone by mid-1991, when a newly marble-clad lobby will be ready. One-bedroom and two-bedroom suites are available. The quietest rooms are those that do not face Commonwealth Avenue and those on the higher floors. All rooms have air-conditioning and color cable TV. There is no restaurant; the popular bar next door is not owned by the hotel; parking is at a nearby garage. *370 Commonwealth Ave., 02215, tel. 617/267–1607. 12 rooms, 81 suites. Facilities: laundry room. AE, CB, DC, MC, V. Rates include Continental breakfast. Moderate.*

Boston International Hostel is a youth-oriented hostel near the Museum of Fine Arts and Symphony Hall. Guests sleep in dormitories accommodating four to six persons and must provide their own linens or sleep sacks (sleeping bags are not permitted). The maximum stay is three nights in summer, six nights off season. Reservations are highly recommended. Doors close at midnight. *12 Hemenway St., 02115, tel. 617/536–9455. Capacity 220 in summer, 100 in winter. Cash or traveler's check with proper ID. Inexpensive.*

Cambridge **The Charles Hotel.** The 300-room Charles anchors one end of
★ the Charles Square development, which is set around a brick plaza facing the Charles River. The architecture is sparse and modern, softened by New England antiques and paintings by local artists. Guest rooms have quilts, TV in the bathroom, and an honor bar. The dining room, Rarities, serves New American cuisine. A Sunday buffet brunch is served in the Bennett Street Cafe. The Regattabar is one of the city's hottest spots for jazz. Children under 18 stay free in their parents' room. Small pets allowed. *1 Bennett St., 02138, tel. 617/864–1200 or 800/882–1818. 300 rooms. Facilities: full spa services, indoor pool, paid parking. AE, CB, DC, MC, V. Very Expensive.*

★ **Sheraton Commander.** A nicely maintained older hotel on Cambridge Common, its rooms are furnished with Boston rockers and four-posters. All rooms have color TV and air-conditioning, and some have kitchenettes. *16 Garden St., 02138, tel. 617/ 547–4800 or 800/325–3535. 175 rooms. Facilities: restaurant, lounge, fitness room with rowing machines and exercise cycles, multilingual staff, valet service, free parking. AE, CB, DC, MC, V. Very Expensive.*

★ **Harvard Motor House.** This modern five-story motel in Brattle Square is the nearest lodging to Harvard Square shops, restaurants, and tourist sites. All rooms have color TV and air-conditioning, and the rate includes a complimentary Continental breakfast. Children under 16 stay free in their parents' room. *110 Mt. Auburn St., 02138, tel. 617/864–5200. 72 rooms. Facilities: free parking. AE, DC, MC, V. Expensive.*

Cambridge House. A gracious old home listed on the National Register of Historic Places, Cambridge House offers seven guest rooms, 10 rooms in a house across the street, and five more in its Carriage House. The site is convenient to the T and buses; there is also a reservations center here for host homes throughout New England. *2218 Massachusetts Ave., 02140, tel. 617/491–6300 or 800/232–9989. Facilities: free parking. MC, V. Moderate.*

Susse Chalet Inn. This is a typical Susse Chalet: clean, economical, and sparse. It's isolated from most shopping or sites, a 10-minute drive from Harvard Square, but it is within walking distance of the Red Line terminus, offering T access to Boston and Harvard Square. All rooms have color TV, air-conditioning, and direct-dial phones. *211 Concord Tpk., 02140, tel. 617/ 661–7800 or 800/258–1980. 79 rooms. Facilities: free parking. AE, DC, MC, V. Inexpensive.*

★ **Boston Harbor Hotel at Rowes Wharf.** Boston's newest and one of its most elegant luxury hotels has opened right on the water, providing a dramatic new entryway to the city for travelers arriving from Logan Airport via the water shuttle that docks at the hotel. The hotel is within walking distance of Faneuil Hall, downtown, the New England Aquarium, and the North End. The guest rooms begin at the eighth floor, and each has either a city view or a water view; the decor has hints of mauve or green and cream, and the traditional furnishings include a king-size bed, sitting area, minibar, and remote control TV. The bathrooms have phones, guest bathrobes, hair dryers, and amenity kits. Some rooms have balconies. The elegant and comfortable Rowes Wharf Restaurant offers seafood and American regional cuisine as well as sweeping harbor views. The spectacular Sunday buffet is expensive at $26 per person but worthwhile for those with healthy appetites. There are also an outdoor café and a bar. Small pets accepted. *70 Rowes Wharf, 02110, tel. 617/439–7000 or 800/752–7077. 230 rooms, including 26 suites. Facilities: concierge, health club and spa with 60-foot lap pool, whirlpool, sauna, steam and massage rooms; gift shop, marina, commuter boat to the South Shore, water shuttle, valet parking. AE, CB, DC, MC, V. Very Expensive.*

Bostonian. One of the city's smallest hotels and one of its most charming, the Bostonian epitomizes European-style elegance in the fresh flowers in its rooms, the private balconies, and the French windows. The Harkness Wing, constructed originally in 1824, has rooms with working fireplaces, exposed beamed ceilings, and brick walls. The rooms tend to be a bit small but are extremely comfortable. The service is attentive, and the highly regarded Seasons Restaurant has a glass-enclosed rooftop overlooking the marketplace. Children under 12 stay free in their parents' room. *Faneuil Hall Marketplace, 02109, tel. 617/523–3600 or 800/343–0922. 152 rooms. Facilities: concierge, Jacuzzi in some suites, room service, valet parking. AE, CB, DC, MC, V. Very Expensive.*

★ **Hotel Meridien.** The respected French chain refurbished the old downtown Federal Reserve Building, a landmark Renaissance-Revival building erected in 1922. The rooms, including some cleverly designed loft suites, are airy and naturally lighted, and all have been redecorated recently. Most rooms have queen-size or king-size beds; all rooms have a small sitting area with a writing desk, a minibar, modern furnishings, in-room movies, and two phones, one of them in the bathroom. Julien, one of the city's finest restaurants, is here, as is the Café Fleuri, which serves an elegant Sunday brunch. There are two lounges. Some pets permitted. *250 Franklin St., 02110, tel. 617/451–1900 or 800/543–4300. 326 rooms, including several bilevel suites. Facilities: health club with whirlpool, dry sauna, and exercise equipment; indoor pool, concierge, 24-hr room service, nonsmoking floor, valet parking. AE, CB, DC, MC, V. Very Expensive.*

Omni Parker House. Said to be the oldest continuously operating hotel in America, though its present building dates only from 1927 (and has had extensive renovations), the Parker House is centrally located, one block from the Common and practically in the central business district. All rooms have color TV, some have refrigerators; some rooms have showers only. Parker House rolls, invented here, are still a feature in the main dining room, where Sunday brunch is an extravaganza. Children under 16 stay free in their parents' room. There are special rates for students. *60 School St., 02108, tel. 617/227–8600 or 800/843–6664. 546 rooms. Facilities: 2 restaurants, 2 bars, complimentary use of nearby Fitcorp Health and Fitness Center, valet and room service, barber and beauty salons, multilingual staff, baby-sitting service. AE, CB, DC, MC, V. Very Expensive.*

Logan Airport **Hilton.** The Hilton is the only hotel at the airport (though a Ramada Inn is just 1½ miles and a half down the road), and the airport's proximity to downtown means that the Hilton is close to the action, too. The rooms are modern, soundproofed, air-conditioned; each has color TV with in-room movies. There's a restaurant and lounge, and pets are allowed. Children stay free in their parents' room. *75 Service Rd., Logan International Airport, East Boston 02128, tel. 617/569–9300 or 800/445–8667. 542 rooms. Facilities: outdoor pool, free parking, valet, baby-sitting service, free 24-hr shuttle service to airlines. AE, CB, DC, MC, V. Very Expensive.*

Theater District **Tremont House.** Because the Tremont House was built as national headquarters for the Elks Club in 1925, when things were done on a grand scale, its spacious lobby has high ceilings, marble columns, a marble stairway, lots of gold leaf and a 16-foot, four-tiered crystal chandelier. The guest rooms tend to be small; they are furnished in 18th-century Thomasville reproductions and decorated with prints from the Museum of Fine Arts. The double rooms have queen-size beds, but two double beds are available. The bathrooms also tend to be small; all have tub-and-shower combinations. All rooms have color cable TV. The Roxy, a dance club, is popular, as is the Stage Delicatessen. *275 Tremont St., 02116, tel. 617/426–1400 or 800/228–5151. 281 rooms. Facilities: room and laundry service, concierge, nonsmoking floor, handicapped accessible, valet parkings. AE, CB, DC, MC, V. Expensive.*

The Arts

Boston is a paradise for patrons of all the arts, from the symphony orchestra to experimental theater and dance to Orson Welles film festivals. One source of information and schedules is the daily newspaper. Thursday's *Boston Globe* Calendar and the weekly *Boston Phoenix* provide comprehensive listings of events for the coming week.

Bostix is Boston's official entertainment information center and the largest ticket agency in the city. Half-price tickets are sold here for the same day's performances. *Faneuil Hall Marketplace, tel. 617/723–5181. Open Tues.–Sat. 11–6, Sun. 11–4. Cash only for same-day ticket purchases. Closed major holidays.*

Concert Charge (tel. 617/497–1118) and **Teletron** (tel. 617/720–3434 or 800/382–8080) are ticket brokers for telephone purchases.

Theater First-rate Broadway tryout theaters are clustered in the theater district (near the intersection of Tremont and Stuart Streets) and include the Colonial, the Shubert, the Wang Center, and the Wilbur. Local theater companies all over the city thrive as well.

American Repertory Theatre (Loeb Drama Center, Harvard University, 64 Brattle St., Cambridge, tel. 617/547–8300). Associated with Harvard University, the ART produces both classic and experimental works in the flexible theater at Harvard.

The Huntington Theatre Company (264 Huntington Ave., tel. 617/266–3913). Under the auspices of Boston University, Boston's largest professional resident theater company performs five plays annually, a mix of established 20th-century plays and classics.

New Ehrlich Theater (541 Tremont St., tel. 617/482–6316). In the Cyclorama Building, this theater originates its own productions—classic and modern plays and new works.

Music For its size, Boston is the most musical city in America. Boston is unsurpassed in the variety and caliber of its musical life. Of the many contributing factors, perhaps the most significant is the abundance of universities and other institutions of learning. Boston's churches offer outstanding, often free music programs; check the Saturday listings in the *Boston Globe.* Early music, choral groups, and chamber music also thrive.

Symphony Hall (301 Massachusetts Ave., tel. 617/266–1492). One of the world's most perfect acoustical settings, Symphony Hall is home to the Boston Symphony Orchestra and the Boston Pops.

Dance **Dance Umbrella** (tel. 617/492–7578) is one of New England's largest presenters of contemporary dance. Performances are scheduled in theaters throughout Boston. The Umbrella also offers information on all dance performances in the Boston area.

Boston Ballet (42 Vernon St., tel. 617/964–4070 or 617/931–2000 for tickets). The city's premier dance company performs at the Wang Center for the Performing Arts.

Film Cambridge is the best place in New England for finding classic, foreign, and nostalgia films.

The Brattle Theater (40 Brattle St., Cambridge, tel. 617/876–6837) is a landmark cinema for classic-movie buffs.
Nickelodeon Cinema (606 Commonwealth Ave., tel. 617/424–1500) is one of the few theaters in the city that shows first-run independent and foreign films as well as revivals.

Opera **Opera Company of Boston** (539 Washington St., tel. 617/426–5300). The celebrated Opera Company of Boston, under the brilliant direction of Sarah Caldwell, has established itself as a world force in opera.

Nightlife

Boston restaurants, clubs, and bars, often clustered in distinctive areas in various parts of the city, offer a broad spectrum of evening and late-night entertainment.

The Quincy Market area may be the center of the city's nightlife; it has been thronged with visitors from the day the restoration opened in 1976. Here in the shadow of historic Faneuil Hall you'll find international cuisine and singles bars among the specialty shops and boutiques.

Copley Square is the hub of another major entertainment area, and Kenmore Square, near the Boston University campus, has clubs and discos devoted to rock and new wave groups.

The breathtaking views of the city at night are from the Top of the Hub Restaurant, 60 stories up atop the Prudential Center, and the Bay Tower Room at 60 State Street. Both have convivial bars and live music.

Thursday's *Boston Globe* Calendar, a schedule of events for the upcoming week, includes an extensive listing of live entertainment under *Nightlife*. The weekly *Boston Phoenix* has another excellent listing. The monthly *Boston* magazine, while a bit less current, is a good source of information.

Bar and Lounge **Bull and Finch Pub.** The original Bull and Finch was dismantled in England, shipped to Boston, and reassembled here, an obvious success. This was the setting for the TV series *Cheers*. *84 Beacon St., tel. 617/227-9605. Open daily 11 AM-1:30 AM. No cover. Dancing Thurs.-Sat. AE, DC, MC, V.*

Cafés and **Au Bon Pain** is a true café almost in the center of Harvard
Coffeehouses Square. Some tables are reserved for chess players who challenge all comers. *1360 Massachusetts Ave., tel. 617/497-9797. Open Sun.-Thurs. 7 AM-midnight, Fri.-Sat. 7 AM-1 AM. No credit cards.*

Passim's. One of the country's first and most famous venues for live folk music, Passim's by day is a quiet basement setting for a light lunch or a coffee break. By night it's a gathering place for folk and bluegrass music or poetry readings. *47 Palmer St., tel. 617/492-7679. Tues.-Sat. noon-11. No credit cards.*

Comedy **Comedy Connection.** Boston's top comedians perform in this popular cabaret-style club in the heart of the theater district. *Charles Playhouse, 76 Warrenton St., tel. 617/426-6339. Shows Sun.-Thurs. at 8:30, Fri. at 8:30 and 10:30, Sat. at 7, 9, and 11:15. MC, V. Tickets can also be purchased at BOSTIX.*

Disco **Le Papillon.** One of the city's newest and most fashionable night spots is an upscale disco with an international flair in an Art Deco setting. *Back Bay Hilton Hotel, 40 Dalton St., tel. 617/236-1100. Open Fri.-Sat. 9 PM-2 AM. No sneakers, jeans, or sweaters. Cover charge varies. AE, DC, MC, V.*

Jazz **Regattabar.** Some top names in jazz perform at this spacious and elegant club in the Charles Hotel. *Bennett & Eliot Sts., tel. 617/864-1200. Shows Wed.-Thurs. at 9, Fri.-Sat. at 9 and 11. Proper dress required. No cover charge before 8 PM. AE, MC, V.*

The **Boston Jazz Line** (tel. 617/262-1300) reports jazz happenings.

Rock **The Channel.** A huge, noisy club featuring rock, reggae, and new wave music performed by local as well as national and international bands, The Channel has two dance floors, four bars, and a game room. The crowd is mostly in their early 20s (you must be 21 to get in). Tickets from Teletron or at the box office. *25 Necco St. (near South Station), tel. 617/451-1050 or 617/451-1905 (recorded information). Open daily 8 PM-1 or 2 AM. No credit cards.*

Singles **Cityside Bar.** A well-known singles haven, Cityside offers live entertainment nightly by local rock groups. It's a good spot, but it can be crowded and noisy. *262 Faneuil Hall Marketplace, tel. 617/742-7390. Open daily 9:30 PM-2 AM. Cover charge Thurs.-Sat. AE, DC, MC, V.*

Excursion: Lexington and Concord

The events of April 19, 1775, the first military encounters of the American Revolution, are very much a part of present-day Lexington and Concord. In these two quintessential New England towns, rich in literary and political history, one finds the true beginning of America's Freedom Trail on the very sites where a Colonial people began their fight for freedom and a new nation.

Lexington To reach Lexington by car from Boston, cross the Charles River at the Massachusetts Avenue Bridge and proceed through Cambridge, bearing right for Arlington at Harvard Square. Continue through Arlington Center on Massachusetts Avenue to the first traffic light, turn left into Jason Street, and begin your tour. Travel time is 25 minutes one-way. The **MBTA** (tel. 617/722–3200) operates buses to Lexington and Boston's western suburbs from Alewife Station in Cambridge. Travel time is about one hour one-way.

As the Redcoats retreated from Concord on April 19, 1775, the Minutemen peppered the British with musket fire from behind low stone walls and tall pine trees before marching to the safety of Charlestown's hills. "The bloodiest half mile of Battle Road," now Massachusetts Avenue in Arlington, began in front of the **Jason Russell House.** Bullet holes are still visible in the house. *7 Jason St., Arlington, tel. 617/648–4300. Admission: $2 adults, 50¢ children over 12. Open Apr. 19–Nov. 1, Tues.–Sat. 2–5. 30-min tours.*

Continuing west on Massachusetts Avenue, you'll pass the **Old Schwamb Mill,** the **Museum of Our National Heritage,** and the **Munroe Tavern** (a pub of 1635 now open to the public) before coming to **Lexington Green.** On this two-acre, triangular piece of land, the Minuteman Captain John Parker assembled his men to await the arrival of the British, who marched from Boston to Concord to "teach rebels a lesson" on the morning of April 19. Henry Hudson Kitson's renowned statue of Parker, the **Minuteman Statue,** stands at the tip of the Green, facing downtown Lexington. *Visitors Center (Lexington Chamber of Commerce), 1875 Massachusetts Ave., tel. 617/862–1450. Open June 1–Oct. 31, daily 9–5; Nov. 1–May 31, daily 10–4.*

On the right side of the Green is **Buckman Tavern,** built in 1690, where the Minutemen gathered initially to wait for the British on April 19. A 30-minute tour visits the tavern's seven rooms. *1 Bedford St., tel. 617/862–5598. Admission: $2 adults, 50¢ children 6–16. Open weekend nearest Apr. 19–Oct. 31, Mon.–Sat. 10–5, Sun. 1–5.*

A quarter-mile north of the Green stands the eight-room **Hancock-Clarke House,** built in 1698. Here the patriots John Hancock and Sam Adams were roused from their sleep by Paul Revere, who had ridden out from Boston to "spread the alarm through every Middlesex village and farm" that the British were marching to Concord. A 20-minute tour is offered. *35 Hancock St., tel. 617/861–0928. Admission: $2 adults, 50¢ children 6–16. Open weekend nearest Apr. 19–Oct. 31, Mon.–Sat. 10–5, Sun. 1–5.*

The town of Lexington comes alive each *Patriot's Day* (the Monday nearest April 19) to celebrate and recreate the events of April 19, 1775, beginning at 6 AM, when "Paul Revere" rides down Massachusetts Avenue shouting "The British are coming! The British are coming!" "Minutemen" groups in costume participate in events throughout the day.

Concord To reach Concord from Lexington, take Routes 4/225 through Bedford and Route 62 west to Concord; or Route 2A west, which splits from Routes 4/225 at the Museum of Our National

Heritage. The latter route will take you through parts of **Minute Man National Historical Park,** whose more than 750 acres commemorate the events of April 19; it includes Fiske Hill and the **Battle Road Visitors Center,** approximately 1 mile from the Battle Green on the right off Route 2A. *Tel. 508/862–7753. Admission free. Open Apr.–Dec., daily 8:30–5. Audiovisual programs, printed material, lectures in summer.*

A short drive from Monument Square on Main Street to Thoreau Street, then left onto Belknap Street, takes you to the **Thoreau Lyceum,** where the writer and naturalist's survey maps, letters, and other memorabilia are housed. A replica of his Walden Pond cabin is here. *156 Belknap St., tel. 508/369–5912. Admission: $2 adults, $1 students, 50¢ children under 12. Open Mar.–Dec., Mon.–Sat. 10–5, Sun. 2–5. Closed holidays.*

At the **Old North Bridge** Minutemen from Concord and surrounding towns fired "the shot heard round the world," signaling the start of the American Revolution. The National Historical Park's North Bridge Visitors Center is ½ mile down Monument Street. *174 Liberty St., tel. 508/369–6993. Open daily 8:30–5. Audiovisual programs Jan.–Mar., printed material, lectures in summer.*

Next door is the **Old Manse** where Nathaniel Hawthorne and Ralph Waldo Emerson lived at different times. When Hawthorne returned to Concord in 1852, he bought a rambling structure called **The Wayside,** where visitors can now see his tower study. *455 Lexington Rd. (Rte. 2A), tel. 508/369–6975. Admission: $1 adults, free under 16 and over 62. Open mid-Apr.–Oct. 31, Fri.–Tues. 9:30–5:30 (last tour leaves promptly at 5).*

On the other side of The Wayside is Louisa May Alcott's family home, the **Orchard House,** where she wrote *Little Women.* Next door to The Wayside, the yard of **Grapevine Cottage** (491 Lexington Rd; not open to the public) has the original Concord grapevine, the grape that the Welch's jams and jellies company made famous.

After leaving the Old Manse, Emerson moved to what we know as the **Ralph Waldo Emerson House** at 28 Cambridge Turnpike. Here he wrote the famous *Essays* ("To be great is to be misunderstood"; "A foolish consistency is the hobgoblin of little minds, adored by little statesmen and philosophers and divines"). Furnishings are pretty much as Emerson left them, even down to his hat on the banister newel post. *28 Cambridge Turnpike, on Route 2A, tel. 508/369–2236. Admission: $3 adults, $1.50 children 6–17. Open the weekend nearest Apr. 19–Oct., Thurs.–Sat. 10–4:30, Sun. and holidays 2–4:30. 30-min tours.*

The original contents of Emerson's study are in the **Concord Museum,** ½ mile southeast on Route 2A heading into Concord. *200 Lexington Rd., tel. 508/369–9609. Admission: $4 adults, $1.50 children under 15, $3 senior citizens. Open Mon.–Sat. 10–3:30, Sun. 1–4.*

Dining **Colonial Inn.** Traditional fare—from prime rib to scallops—is served in the gracious dining room of an inn of 1718. Overnight accommodations are available in 57 rooms. *48 Monument Sq., Concord, tel. 508/369–9200. Reservations advised for dinner.*

Jacket and tie advised at night. AE, CB, DC, MC, V. Moderate.

Versailles. An intimate French restaurant, the Versailles serves such specialties as cold poached salmon and quiche Lorraine for lunch, rack of lamb and veal Oscar for dinner. *1777 Massachusetts Ave., Lexington, tel. 617/861–1711. Reservations advised. Jacket and tie optional. AE, DC, MC, V. Moderate.*

Different Drummer. Shrimp scampi, baked stuffed shrimp, soft-shell crabs, fresh veal, and pasta are the highlights of the menu of a restaurant located inside the B&M train station. *86 Thoreau St., Concord, tel. 508/369–8700. Reservations advised. Dress: casual. AE, MC, V. Inexpensive–Moderate.*

The Coast:
The South Shore

Following the northward sweep of the New England coast, many travelers stay on I-95 as it makes its inland shortcut from Providence directly to Boston. In doing so, they bypass a large southeastern chunk of the state, sandwiched in between the Cape and the Boston suburbs. While it may not be as prosperous or as picturesque as other areas of Massachusetts, this is a region with its own strong historical associations—notably the great seafaring towns of Fall River and New Bedford, and the Pilgrims' colony at Plymouth. Even vacationers heading for the Cape all too often barrel past these towns, thus missing an important dimension of New England's past.

Important Addresses and Numbers

Visitor Information   **Bristol County Development Council** (70 N. 2nd St., New Bedford 02740, tel. 508/997–1250).

Fall River Office of Recreation and Tourism (72 Bank St., Fall River 02720, tel. 508/679–0922).

New Bedford Office of Tourism (47 N. 2nd St., New Bedford 02740, tel. 508/991–6200).

Plymouth County Development Council (Box 1620, Pembroke 02359, tel. 617/826–3136).

Emergencies   Dial 911 for **police** and **ambulance** in an emergency.

To dial the local **police** or **ambulance** in New Bedford dial 508/999–1212. For the **fire department,** call 508/997–9431.

Getting Around the South Shore

By Car   Fall River and New Bedford are connected by I–195, and from both cities the most direct road to Boston is Route 24 north. I–93 connects Boston with Quincy; from there Route 3 is the quickest way to reach Plymouth.

By Bus   Quincy is easily reached by the Boston subway (the "T"), and (**MBTA**, tel. 617/722–3200) buses serve both Quincy and Braintree. The **American Eagle** bus line (tel. 508/993–5040) provides service between Boston and New Bedford; **H&L Bloom Bus** (tel. 508/822–1991) serves Fall River from Boston; and **Plym-**

outh and Brockton Street Railway Co. (tel. 617/773-9400) calls at Plymouth en route to Cape Cod.

Special-interest Tours

The most popular special-interest tours in this region are on board ship. **Captain John Boats** operates whale-watch cruises from Plymouth in spring, summer, and early fall; the same organization also runs daily 45-minute tours of Plymouth Harbor, June through September. All tours depart from either State Pier or the nearby Town Wharf. *117 Standish Ave., Plymouth, tel. 508/746-2643 or 800/242-2469.*

Exploring the South Shore

Numbers in the margin correspond with the numbered points of interest on the South Shore map.

❶ East of Rhode Island, as I-195 swings towards the Cape, the first Massachusetts city of interest is **Fall River.** It's hardly an inspiring town in terms of scenery—industrial docks and enormous factories recall the city's past as a major textile center in the 19th and 20th centuries. It also served as a port, however, and today the most interesting site is **Battleship Cove,** down beside the Taunton River in the shadow of the I-195 bridge. The cove harbors several museums and the 35,000-ton battleship USS *Massachusetts*, the battleship USS *Joseph P. Kennedy, Jr.*, and a World War II attack sub, the USS *Lionfish*. *Battleship Cove, tel. 508/678-1905. Admission: $7 adults, $3.50 children 6-14, $5.50 senior citizens. Open daily 9-5. Closed Thanksgiving, Christmas, New Year's Day.*

Near the ships, the **Marine Museum at Fall River** celebrates the age of sail and steamship travel, especially the lavishly fitted ships of the Old Fall River Line, which operated until 1937 between New England and New York City. *70 Water St., tel. 508/674-3533. Admission: $3 adults, $2 senior citizens and children 6-14. Open daily 9-4:30. Closed Thanksgiving, Christmas, New Year's Day.*

In the same riverside location, the **Fall River Heritage State Park** tells the story of Fall River's industrial past, focusing on the city's textile mills and their workers. *200 Davol St. W., tel. 508/675-5759. Admission free. Open early May-early Oct., daily 9-8; Nov.-May, Tues.-Sun. 9-4:30. Closed Thanksgiving, Christmas, New Year's Day.*

Time Out A cheerful establishment at the 187 Plymouth Street factory-outlet complex is **Paul's Millside Restaurant** (313 Pleasant St., tel. 508/672-4211). Serving generous breakfasts and lunches daily except Sunday, the restaurant is on the ground floor of a large stone mill.

❷ Route I-195 links Fall River to **New Bedford,** home of the largest fishing fleet on the East Coast. The historic district near the water is a delight; it was here that Herman Melville set his famous whaling novel, *Moby-Dick*. The **New Bedford Whaling Museum,** established in 1902, is the largest American museum devoted to the history of the whaling era, which lasted some 200 years in New Bedford. A 22-minute film depicting an actual whaling chase is shown twice daily July-August, once on week-

The South Shore

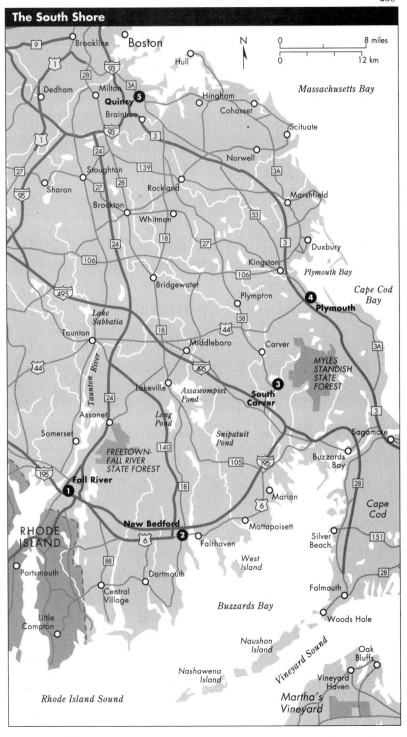

N

0 ——— 8 miles
0 ——— 12 km

Brookline
Boston
9
1
Hull
28
Dedham
Milton
3A
Quincy **5**
Braintree
Hingham
Massachusetts Bay
Cohasset
Scituate
93
93
3
27
24
Stoughton
139
Norwell
27
28
Rockland
3A
95
Sharon
Brockton
Marshfield
Whitman
53
24
18
3
Duxbury
106
27
Kingston
Plymouth Bay
Bridgewater
106
Cape Cod Bay
495
Lake Sabbatia
Plympton
Plymouth **4**
44
58
Taunton
18
Middleboro
Carver
3A
44
495
MYLES STANDISH STATE FOREST
Lakeville
Assawompset Pond
South Carver **3**
24
Long Pond
3
Assonet
Snipatuit Pond
Sagamore
140
Somerset
FREETOWN-FALL RIVER STATE FOREST
105
195
Buzzards Bay
195
18
28
Fall River **1**
Marion
Cape Cod
RHODE ISLAND
New Bedford **2**
6
Mattapoisett
151
6
Fairhaven
Silver Beach
Portsmouth
88
West Island
28
Dartmouth
Falmouth
Central Village
Buzzards Bay
Woods Hole
Little Compton
Naushon Island
Vineyard Sound
Oak Bluffs
Nashawena Island
Vineyard Haven
Rhode Island Sound
Martha's Vineyard

ends the rest of the year. *18 Johnny Cake Hill, tel. 508/997–0046. Admission: $3.50 adults, $2.50 children 6–14, $3 senior citizens. Open Sept.–June, Mon.–Sat. 9–5, Sun. 1–5; July–Aug., Mon.–Sat. 9–5, Sun. 11–5. Closed Thanksgiving, Christmas, New Year's Day.*

In the 1880s New Bedford was also an international leader in the art-glass movement. The **New Bedford Glass Museum** contains a collection of 2,000 objects of glass, silver, and porcelain —most of them made locally. *50 N. 2nd St., tel. 508/994–0115. Admission: $2 adults, 50¢ children 6–12, $1.50 senior citizens. Open mid-Apr.–Dec. 1, Mon.–Sat. 10–5; Dec. 2–mid-Apr., Tues.–Sat. 10–4.*

The **New Bedford Preservation Society** publishes a series of excellent walking tours of the city's restored area. These and other brochures are available at the Visitor's Center (47 N. 2nd St., tel. 508/991–6200).

East of New Bedford, where I–195 intersects with I–495, you may elect to head on southeast to Cape Cod (*see* The Coast: Cape Cod, below) or follow I–495 toward Boston for one exit to ❸ Route 58, which will take you to **South Carver.** Here, in the heart of the cranberry-growing region, the antique steam engine of the 5½-mile **Edaville Railroad** pulls wooden passenger cars through the crimson cranberry bogs. You'll also find a working paddlewheel steamboat, a museum, and children's amusements. *Rte. 58, tel. 508/866–4526. Admission: $12.50 adults, $7.50 children, $8.50 senior citizens. Open Apr.–June 1, weekends noon–5; early June–Labor Day, daily 10–5:30; day after Labor Day–Oct., weekdays 10–3, weekends 10–5:30; Nov.–Dec., weekdays 4–9, weekends 2–9. Closed Thanksgiving, Christmas.*

A 20-minute drive northeast (continue on Route 58 to pick up ❹ Route 44) will take you to **Plymouth,** self-styled as "America's hometown," where 102 weary Pilgrims disembarked in December 1620. At **Plimoth Plantation,** a reconstruction of the original settlement, actors in period costume speak Jacobean English and carry on the daily life of the 17th century. In the furnished homes, "residents" demonstrate household skills such as soap-making; a meetinghouse and the vegetable gardens can also be toured. *Warren Ave. (Rte. 3A), tel. 508/746–1622. Admission: $12 adults, $8 children 5–12. Open Apr.–Nov., daily 9–5.*

At the Plymouth waterfront is moored the ***Mayflower II,*** an exact replica of the 1620 *Mayflower.* The second version was built in England and sailed across the Atlantic in 1957; it, too, is staffed by costumed "Pilgrims" who tell about their hard journey. *State Pier, tel. 508/746–1622. Admission: $5.50 adults, $3.75 children 5–12. Open Apr.–Nov., daily 9–5; July–Aug., daily 9–7.*

Close by the *Mayflower,* on the shore you'll find **Plymouth Rock,** popularly believed to have been the Pilgrims' stepping stone when they left the ship. Across the street is **Cole's Hill,** where the company buried their dead—at night, so the Indians could not count the dwindling numbers of survivors.

On top of Cole's Hill now stands the **Plymouth Wax Museum,** containing 26 scenes with life-size models that tell the Pilgrims' story. *16 Carver St., tel. 508/746–6468. Admission: $4 adults, $2 children 5–12. Open Apr.–Nov., daily 9–5.*

Away from the waterfront, the **Pilgrim Hall Museum** contains a sizeable collection of household goods, books, weapons, and furniture used by the Pilgrims. *75 Court St. (Rte. 3A), tel. 508/746–1620. Admission: $4 adults, $1.50 children 6–15, $3.50 senior citizens. Open daily 9:30–4:30. Closed Thanksgiving, Christmas, New Year's Day.*

Cranberry World, operated by Ocean Spray, tells the story of the one local crop and includes displays on harvesting, an outdoor working cranberry bog, and information about the natural inhabitants of the wetlands. *225 Water St., tel. 508/747–2350. Admission free. Open Apr.–Nov., daily 9:30–5; July–Aug., daily 9:30–9.*

❺ Take scenic Route 3A along the coast north to **Quincy,** the only city in the United States with the birthplaces, homes, and final resting places of two U.S. presidents. The **Adams National Historic Site** comprises the Adams Mansion, residence of the Adams family for four generations; a short distance away, the birthplace of John Adams, second U.S. president; and the neighboring house where his son, John Quincy Adams, sixth U.S. president, was born. A guided tour of all three houses lasts about 1½ hours. *135 Adams St., tel. 617/773–1177. Admission: $2 adults, children under 12 free. Open mid-Apr.–mid-Nov., daily 9–5.*

The South Shore for Free

Cranberry World, Plymouth

Fall River Heritage State Park, Fall River

Seaman's Bethel (15 Johnny Cake Hill, New Bedford, tel. 508/992–3295) is a small chapel featured in *Moby-Dick.*

What to See and Do with Children

Battleship Cove, Fall River

Children's Museum, Dartmouth. This museum contains many hands-on exhibits, including building blocks, bubbles, and a spaceship. Outside are 60 acres of land with nature trails and picnic areas. *276 Gulf Rd., South Dartmouth 02748, tel. 508/993–3361. Admission: $3. Open Tues.–Sat. 10–5; Sun. 1–5; Mon. 10–5 (school vacations only). Closed July 4, Thanksgiving, Christmas, New Year's Day.*

Edaville Railway, South Carver

Mayflower II, Plymouth

Plimoth Plantation, Plymouth

A & D Toy-Train Village, Middleboro (*see* Off the Beaten Track, below)

Whaling Museum, New Bedford

Off the Beaten Track

A 20-minute drive west of Plymouth on Route 44, then north on Route 18, will bring you to the **A&D Toy-Train Village** at

Middleboro. A former supermarket holds the vast collection of toy trains and train memorabilia amassed by Adolf Arnold, who is now the museum curator. The main attraction is a 34-foot, computer-controlled master layout on six levels, but the museum is also crammed with all kinds of toy trains, ranging from antique models to foreign collections. *49 Plymouth St., Middleboro 02346, tel. 508/947–5303. Admission: $4 adults, $3.50 senior citizens; $2.50 children 4–12. Open Memorial Day–Labor Day and Nov. 23–Jan. 7, daily 10–6; Sept.–June, weekends 10–6. Closed Easter, July 4, Thanksgiving, Christmas, New Year's Day.*

Shopping

Antiques A few antiques stores are located on the South Shore, especially in the vicinity of Plymouth, but it is not a prime antiques-hunting area like the Berkshires or the North Shore. A brochure listing some of these shops can be obtained from the **Southeastern New England Antiques Dealers Association** (Box 4416, East Providence, RI 02914, tel. 401/781–7222 or 508/993–8558).

Outlet Stores Fall River is a haven for those who enjoy the bargain hunt of outlet stores. More than 100 small outlets are housed in several old mills in the district north of downtown. Most are listed in a brochure available from the **Fall River Factory Outlet District Association** (Box 2877, 02722, tel. 508/678–6033).

In Plymouth a restored 19th-century rope mill is the site of a large shopping center: **Cordage Park** (Court St., Rte. 3A, 02160, tel. 508/746–7707) has 70 stores; 35 are factory outlets.

Dining and Lodging

Braintree Lodging **Sheraton Tara.** Brass statues of knights stand guard in the lobby of this huge, castle-fronted building. Room size and decor vary in the different wings, but all feature traditional furnishings, recliner chairs, and fanlight-shaped headboards. The hotel lives up to the usual high standards of a Sheraton business hotel and is convenient to both Boston and the South Shore. *Rte. 128, exit 6, 02184, tel. 617/848–0600. 377 rooms, 5 suites. Facilities: 2 restaurants, lounge, bar, health club, sauna, Jacuzzi, indoor pool, outdoor pool, room service, conference facilities. AE, CB, D, DC, MC, V. Expensive–Very Expensive.*

Fall River Dining **Leone's.** Conveniently close to Battleship Cove on the waterfront, Leone's provides free docking space for customers in the summer months. Huge fish tanks, brass railings, and potted plants decorate all three levels of the carpeted dining room, which is candlelit at night. Tables on three decks overlook the river. Specialties include lobster, prime rib, pasta dishes, and chicken. *4 Davol St., Battleship Cove, tel. 508/679–8158. Reservations advised. Dress: casual. AE, CB, DC, MC, V. Moderate.*

T.A. Restaurant. This Portuguese-American restaurant is a friendly place in the center of Fall River. Spot lighting shows up light-pine wall panels hung with wicker decorations and plants. The menu—available in English or Portuguese—lists such specialties as tuna steaks, red snapper, grilled *chaureo* (sausage), stewed octopus with potatoes in wine sauce, chicken, and steaks. *408 S. Main St., tel. 508/673–5890. No reservations. Dress: casual. AE, CB, DC, MC, V. Moderate.*

Fall River Lodging

Days Inn. The only motel within the city limits is this chain inn, just a couple of minutes' walk from Main Street and up the hill from Battleship Cove. Fairly spacious guest rooms have modern, comfortable furnishings in browns and greens, but views from the windows are generally grim. *332 Miliken Blvd., 02721, tel. 508/676–1991. 102 rooms. Facilities: lounge, bar, outdoor pool, health club, conference rooms. AE, CB, D, DC, MC, V. Rates include Continental breakfast. Moderate–Expensive.*

Best Western Airport Inn. This pleasant motel is situated 2 miles north of downtown Fall River, near the airport. The contemporary rooms, decorated in mauve and beige, have mahogany furniture, and executive one-room suites feature an added sitting area. There is a restaurant located next door. *360 Airport Rd., 02720, tel. 508/672–0011. 86 rooms, 1 suite. Facilities: indoor pool, sauna, Jacuzzi, health club, tanning booth. AE, CB, D, DC, MC, V. Rates include Continental breakfast. Moderate.*

New Bedford Dining

Candleworks Café. Housed on the first floor of a restored, Federal-style candle factory, the restaurant has a pink stucco exterior. The glassed-in porch has undesirable views of the interstate highway, but the interior is pretty with lots of exposed wood. The menu features such specialties as seafood Candleworks (tri-color pasta with shrimp, scallops, fish, and lobster in basil cream sauce). *72 N. Water St., tel. 508/992–1635. Reservations advised. Dress: neat but casual. No lunch Sat. Closed Sun. AE, MC, V. Expensive.*

★ **Freestones.** Located in the middle of the restored historic downtown area, this large, attractive restaurant is set in a refurbished bank, originally built in 1877. The interior is a strange but successful mix of marble floors, mahogany paneling, old church furniture (the front desk was once a pulpit), and modern curios. Entrées include Black Angus sirloin, broiled swordfish, lime barbecued chicken, and pasta dishes, as well as sandwiches and salads. *41 William St., tel. 508/993–7477. No reservations. Dress: casual. AE, CB, DC, MC, V. Moderate.*

★ **Penabranca.** In 1990 this fine restaurant moved from the fourth floor to the first floor of the Durant Sail Loft Inn, in an effort to increase trade, although the fourth floor definitely has the better view. The decor is "fishing boat" style, with nets hanging from the ceiling and ship's-wheel chandeliers. The dining room is glassed-in, but most of the windows overlook the parking lot, and you have to crane your neck to see the fishing boats farther down the wharf. The Continental cuisine is excellent, especially the *zuppa de pesce*, which contains generous servings of lobster and shrimp. *1 Merrill's Wharf, tel. 508/999–4444. Dress: casual. AE, CB, DC, MC, V. Moderate.*

New Bedford Lodging

★ **Durant Sail Loft Inn.** This is the best place to stay in New Bedford—it's convenient to the museums in the restored downtown area, comfortable, and right beside the water. Having said that, it must be admitted that the competition is not fierce, as accommodations in New Bedford are few and far between, especially in the historic district. The massive granite block structure, which was restored and converted into a hotel in the late 1970s, occupies the old Bourne Counting House at the end of Merrill's Wharf. Jonathan Bourne, one of the most successful whaling merchants of the 19th century, would stand in the tall bay window on the second floor (now part of the inn's Jonathan Bourne guest room) to watch his ships sail into harbor. Today the New Bedford fishing fleet is moored all around the wharf. Inside, the rooms have modern furnishings, of a category somewhere between top-quality motel style and the small business hotel. Service is friendly. Besides two restaurants, the inn has an authentic (noisy) Portuguese-style first-floor café, with a regular flow of anglers and sailors as clientele. *1 Merrill's Wharf, 02740, tel. 508/999–2700. 18 rooms. Facilities: 2 restaurants, café, hair salon, room service, conference rooms. AE, CB, DC, MC, V. Moderate.*

Skipper Inn and Conference Center. Just across the river from New Bedford, this low modern building is being redesigned to add a marina, conference rooms, and even a beach. The guest quarters that have been upgraded to executive rooms are indeed a welcome contrast to the unattractive exterior: They're small but luxuriously furnished with white couches and bedspreads, brass candlesticks, and thick carpets. Standard rooms are also small, with good-quality motel-style furnishings. Sand is being specially imported for the riverside beach, though it's for sunbathing only: You'd be ill-advised to bathe in the grimy harborside waters. *110 Middle St., Fairhaven 02719, tel. 508/ 997–1281. 130 rooms. Facilities: restaurant, lounge, bar, marina, indoor pool, Jacuzzi, health club, laundry room, ballroom. AE, CB, DC, MC, V. Moderate.*

Plymouth Dining

★ **Station One.** Converted from the city's central fire station, this lofty restaurant is dominated by a huge wooden staircase leading to three levels of dining. The roof is of beautifully carved wooden panels, and large windows at the front overlook Plymouth's main street. The widely varied menu includes lobster-salad roll, grilled swordfish topped with a lobster tail, Cajun dishes, veal Nantucket (with shrimp, mushrooms, and lemon in Marsala wine), and lamb Dijon. Sunday brunch is a specialty here. *51 Main St., tel. 508/746–6001. Dress: casual. AE, DC, MC, V. Expensive.*

The Inn for All Seasons. Away from Route 3A up a long winding drive, this restaurant backs onto pleasant gardens and has the charm of a faded country mansion: It was formerly the private summer residence of a wealthy coal magnate from Pennsylvania. Three small dining rooms have large windows, frilled curtains, and decorative plates on racks. The food is well prepared and the service friendly. Seafood is the specialty, including baked scallops *en casserole*, shrimp Louisiana with Cajun seasonings, and Seafood Citron. *97 Warren Ave., tel. 508/746–8823. Dress: casual. Closed Mon., lunch Tues.–Sat. AE, DC, MC, V. Moderate–Expensive.*

McGrath's Restaurant. This is a seafood restaurant, with seafaring decor—the lights are either ship's-wheel chandeliers or have lobster-pot shades. A porch on the sea side of the restaurant provides outdoor dining with an ocean view. The menu features deep-fried oysters, Ipswich clams, lobster cooked in five different styles, and chicken and steak entrées. *Water St. at Town Wharf, tel. 508/746–9751. Dress: casual. Closed Mon. AE, MC, V. Moderate.*

★ **The Lobster Hut.** The dining at this casual restaurant on the ocean means great value. You can eat in the wood-paneled dining room inside or at stone picnic tables on a deck overlooking the harbor. Specialties, of course, are seafood: fried lobster, clam chowder, fish and chips, fried clams. Chicken and burgers are also available. *Town Wharf, tel. 508/746–2270. No reservations. Dress: casual. Closed Jan. No credit cards. Inexpensive.*

Plymouth Lodging **Sheraton Plymouth at Village Landing.** This is an uncharacteristic Sheraton in many ways: The business atmosphere has been toned down, the location (in a modern shopping complex) is unremarkable, and the exterior resembles a modern condominium block. Still, inside it retains all the reliable, high-quality features of the top-class chain hotel. Most of the guest rooms, all furnished with reproduction antiques, surround the pool in a three-story atrium formation, with overlooking balconies. The lobby is also a three-story atrium. The hotel is just 1 block from the ocean and convenient to all Plymouth's major attractions. *180 Water St., 02360, tel. 508/747–4900 or 800/325–3535. 175 rooms. Facilities: restaurant, lounge, bar, indoor pool, Jacuzzi, sauna, exercise room, room service, conference rooms, ballroom. AE, CB, D, DC, MC, V. Expensive–Very Expensive.*

John Carver Inn. It would be hard for any inn to live up to the expectations raised by the massive pillared facade of this red-brick building, and the John Carver only just manages to do so. Although the public rooms and dining rooms are lavish, with period furnishings and stylish drapes, the bedrooms reveal that the place was built in 1969: They are square and fairly small, with generally modern furnishings and a few shiny reproductions. New managers, however, have worked hard on those beautiful public rooms and intend to turn their attention next to the guest rooms. *125 Summer St., 02360, tel. 508/746–7100. 79 rooms. Facilities: restaurant, lounge, outdoor pool. AE, CB, DC, MC, V. Moderate–Expensive.*

★ **Pilgrim Sands Motel.** Although it's a couple of miles south of downtown Plymouth, on Route 3A, this top-of-the-line motel is opposite the Plimoth Plantation and has its own private beach. Try to reserve a room with an ocean view—the sea practically laps against the building, and the sound of breaking waves will be with you all night long. On the second floor, ocean-view rooms have a balcony and deck chairs. Inside, the light, airy accommodations have pleasant furnishings; some contain refrigerators. Friendly management adds to the motel's quality, as do a large indoor pool, a comfortable lounge with open fireplace, and a wide deck overlooking the sea. *150 Warren Ave., 02360, tel. 508/747–0900. 64 rooms. Facilities: coffee shop, lounge, private beach, indoor pool, Jacuzzi, deck. AE, CB, DC, MC, V. Moderate–Expensive.*

Blue Spruce Motel. This motel was completely rebuilt in the late 1980s, and is well managed and friendly. Its modern rooms have oak furniture, mauve drapes and bedspreads, and ceramic-tiled bathrooms. Each room is equipped with a refrigerator, as well as a private deck with a table and chairs. Sun umbrellas, lounge chairs, and grassy areas surround the pool. It's about 6 miles south of town, but rates are reasonable and the standard is high. *710 State Rd. (Rte. 3A), 02360, tel. 508/224–3990. 25 rooms with bath, 1 cottage, 2 efficiencies. Facilities: outdoor pool, shuffleboard. AE, DC, MC, V. Moderate.*

The Arts

Theater The Zeiterion Theatre in New Bedford is the only year-round performing arts center in southern Massachusetts. It draws a regular flow of well-known artists and attractions to the historic downtown location. *Box J-4084, 684 Purchase St., New Bedford 02741, tel. 508/994-2900.*

The Coast: Cape Cod

Separated from the Massachusetts "mainland" by the 17.4-mile Cape Cod Canal, the Cape is always likened in shape to an outstretched arm bent at the elbow, its fist turned back at Provincetown toward the mainland. It's 90 miles from end to end, with 15 towns, each broken up into villages. The term *Upper Cape* refers to the towns of Bourne, Falmouth, Mashpee, and Sandwich; *Mid-Cape*, to Barnstable, Yarmouth, and Dennis; and *Lower Cape*, to Harwich, Chatham, Brewster, Orleans, Eastham, Wellfleet, Truro, and Provincetown.

The Cape is for relaxing—swimming and sunning, fishing and boating, playing golf and tennis, attending the theater and hunting antiques. Despite summer crowds and overdevelopment, much remains unspoiled. Visitors continue to enjoy the Cape's charming old New England villages of weathered shingle houses and white steepled churches as well as its pine woods, grassy marshes, and rolling dunes.

Important Addresses and Numbers

Visitor Information The main source of information on all of Cape Cod is the **Cape Cod Chamber of Commerce** (Jct. Rtes. 6 and 132, Hyannis 02601, tel. 508/362-3225), open weekdays 8:30-5 year-round, also weekends 9-4 July to Labor Day. It has information booths, open Memorial Day to Labor Day, in Bourne at the Sagamore Rotary (tel. 508/888-2438) and on MacArthur Boulevard (tel. 508/759-3814) heading toward Falmouth.

Emergencies **Police** (tel. 911); **fire, ambulance** (tel. 800/352-7141); **Cape Cod Hospital** (27 Park St., Hyannis, tel. 508/771-1800); **Falmouth Hospital** (100 Ter Heun Dr., Falmouth, tel. 508/548-5300).

Late-night Pharmacies Most of the Cape's nine **CVS** stores, such as the one in the Cape Cod Mall in Hyannis (tel. 508/771-1774), are open until 9 PM Monday through Saturday, until 6 on Sunday.

Getting Around Cape Cod

By Car From Boston take Route 3 south to the Sagamore Bridge. From New York take I-95 north to Providence; change to I-195 and follow signs to the Cape. Both roads connect to Route 6, the main road running the length of the Cape. In summer, try to avoid arriving at the bridges in late afternoon, especially on holidays: All the major roads are heavily congested eastbound on Friday nights and westbound on Sunday afternoons.

If you fly into the area, you can rent a car at the airport—**Avis** (tel. 508/775-2888), **Hertz** (tel. 508/775-5825), and **National** (tel. 508/771-4353)—or through **Thrifty** (tel. 508/771-0450) and **Budget** (tel. 508/775-3832).

By Bus The **Cape Cod Regional Transit Authority** (tel. 800/352-7155) provides bus service between Hyannis and Woods Hole. **Plymouth & Brockton Street Railway** (tel. 508/775-5524 or in MA 800/328-9997) has service from Boston and Logan Airport, as well as between Sagamore and Provincetown, with stops at many towns in between. **Bonanza** (tel. 508/548–7588) serves Bourne, Falmouth, Woods Hole, and Hyannis. All service is year-round.

By Bike Bicycling is a very satisfying way of getting around the Cape, for the terrain is fairly flat and there are several bike trails. Rentals are available at **All Cape Sales** (mopeds also; 627 Main St., West Yarmouth, tel. 508/771–8100), **Arnold's** (329 Commercial St., Provincetown, tel. 508/487–0844), **Bill's Bike Shop** (847 E. Main St., Falmouth, tel. 508/548–7979), **Cascade Motor Lodge** (201 Main St., Hyannis, tel. 508/775–9717), **P&M Cycles** (29 Main St., Buzzards Bay, tel. 508/759–2830), **Rail Trail Bike Rentals** (302 Underpass Rd., Brewster, tel. 508/896–2361), and **The Little Capistrano** (across from Salt Pond Visitor Center, Eastham, tel. 508/255–6515).

Guided Tours

Orientation **Croll Travel** (Box 2070, Orleans 02653, tel. 508/240–1317) offers guided day tours of the Cape, with Martha's Vineyard or Nantucket segments available, in a luxury van (June–Oct.).

Cruises **Captain John Boats** operates cruises to Provincetown from Plymouth. *117 Standish Ave., Plymouth, tel. 508/746–2400 or 800/242–2469. Cost: $17 adults, $13 children under 12. Tours late June–Labor Day.*

One-hour tours of Hyannis Port Harbor, including a view of the Kennedy compound, are offered by **Hy-Line**; sunset cruises also available. *Ocean St. Dock, Pier 1, Hyannis, tel. 508/778–2600. Cost: $7 adults, $2 children under 13 with adult. Tours mid-May–mid-Oct.*

Cape Cod Canal Cruises (two or three hours, narrated) leave from Onset, just east of the bridges onto the Cape. A Sunday jazz cruise, sunset cocktail cruises, and evening dance cruises are available. *Onset Bay Town Pier, tel. 508/295–3883. Cost: $6–$8 adults, $3–$4 children 6–12; $1 senior citizen discount Mon. and Fri. Tours May–mid-Oct.*

Train Tours **Cape Cod Scenic Railroad** runs 1¾-hour excursions between Sagamore and Hyannis with stops at Sandwich and the Canal. The train passes ponds, cranberry bogs, and marshes. *Main and Center Sts., Hyannis, tel. 508/866–4526. Several departures a day (no service Mon. or Fri.) in each direction mid-June–Columbus Day. Cost: $10.50 adults, $6.50 children 3–12.*

Nature Tours From June to mid-December, the **Massachusetts Audubon Society** (contact Wellfleet Bay Wildlife Sanctuary, Box 236, South Wellfleet 02663, tel. 508/349–2615) sponsors naturalist-led wildlife tours of Nauset Marsh and half- or full-day tours to Monomoy Island, plus canoe trips, bird and insect walks, hikes, and more.

Plane Tours Sightseeing by air is offered by **Hyannis Aviation** (tel. 508/775–8171), **Cape Cod Airport** (1000 Race Lane, Marstons Mills, tel. 508/428–8732), **Cape Cod Air** (tel. 508/945–9000 or in MA 800/553–2376), and **Ocean Air** (seaplanes; tel. 508/771–1231).

Dune Tours **Art's Dune Tours** (tel. 508/487–1950 or 1050) has been offering narrated tours through the National Seashore and dunes around Provincetown since 1946. **Mitch's Dune Tours** (tel. 508/487–9500) also operates in the Provincetown area.

Whale-Watching Provincetown is the main center on the Cape for whale-watching because it is closest to the feeding grounds at Stellwagen Bank, a few miles to the north. Several operators offer whale-watch tours from April through October, with morning, afternoon, or sunset sailings lasting three to four hours. The cost is about $15 for adults, $10 for children. Tickets are available at booths on MacMillan Pier.

Dolphin Fleet (tel. 508/255–3857 or in MA 800/826–9300, open 7 AM–9 PM) tours are accompanied by scientists who provide commentary while collecting data on the whale population they've been monitoring for years.

Out of Barnstable Harbor, there's **Hyannis Whale Watcher Cruises** (tel. 508/775–1622 or 508/362–6088, open 7 AM–9 PM; tours Apr.–Nov.). A naturalist narrates and gives commentary on Cape Cod Bay.

Exploring Cape Cod

Numbers in the margin correspond with the numbered points of interest on the Cape Cod map.

Route 6, the Mid-Cape Highway, passes through the relatively unpopulated center of the Cape, characterized by a landscape of scrub pine and oak. Paralleling Route 6 but following the north coast is Route 6A, the Old King's Highway, in most sections a winding country road that passes through some of the Cape's best-preserved old New England towns. The south shore of the Cape, traced by Route 28, is heavily populated and the major center for tourism, encompassing Falmouth, Hyannis, and Chatham.

❶ At the Cape's extreme southwest corner is **Woods Hole,** where ferries depart for Martha's Vineyard. An international center for marine research, it is home to the Woods Hole Oceanographic Institute (WHOI), whose staff led the successful search for the *Titanic* in 1986; the Marine Biological Laboratories (MBL); and the National Marine Fisheries Service, among other scientific institutions.

The Fisheries Service has a public **Aquarium** with two harbor seals, tanks displaying regional fish and shellfish, plus hands-on tanks and microscopes for kids. *Corner Albatross and Water Sts., tel. 508/548–7684. Admission free. Open mid-June–mid-Sept., daily 10–4:30; mid-Sept.–mid-June, weekdays 9–4:30.*

The **Marine Biological Laboratory** (tel. 508/548–3705, ext. 423; call for reservations and meeting instructions) offers 1½-hour tours of its facilities, led by retired scientists, on weekdays from late June through August.

A guided walking tour of the one-street village is conducted in July and August by the **Woods Hole Historical Collection** (Bradley House Museum, 573 Woods Hole Rd., tel. 508/548–7270). Before leaving Woods Hole, stop at **Nobska Light** for a great view out to sea.

❷ The village green in **Falmouth** was used as a military training field in the 18th century. Today it is the center of a considerable shopping district, flanked by attractive old homes, some fine inns, and the **Congregational Church,** with a bell made by Paul Revere.

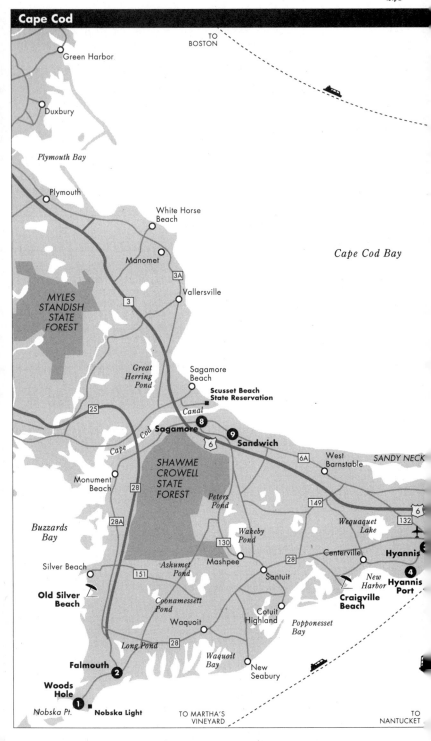

Cape Cod

TO BOSTON

Green Harbor

Duxbury

Plymouth Bay

Plymouth

White Horse Beach

Cape Cod Bay

Manomet

3A

Vallersville

3

MYLES STANDISH STATE FOREST

Great Herring Pond

Sagamore Beach

Scusset Beach State Reservation

25

Canal

Cod

Sagamore 8

6

9 **Sandwich**

Cape

6A

West Barnstable

SANDY NECK

Monument Beach

SHAWME CROWELL STATE FOREST

Peters Pond

149

6

132

28

28A

Buzzards Bay

Wakeby Pond

130

Wequaquet Lake

Centerville

Hyannis

Silver Beach

151

Ashumet Pond

Mashpee

28

Santuit

New Harbor

4 **Hyannis Port**

Old Silver Beach

Coonamessett Pond

Craigville Beach

Cotuit Highland

Popponesset Bay

Waquoit

28

Long Pond

Falmouth 2

Waquoit Bay

New Seabury

Woods Hole

Nobska Pt. 1 ■ **Nobska Light**

TO MARTHA'S VINEYARD

TO NANTUCKET

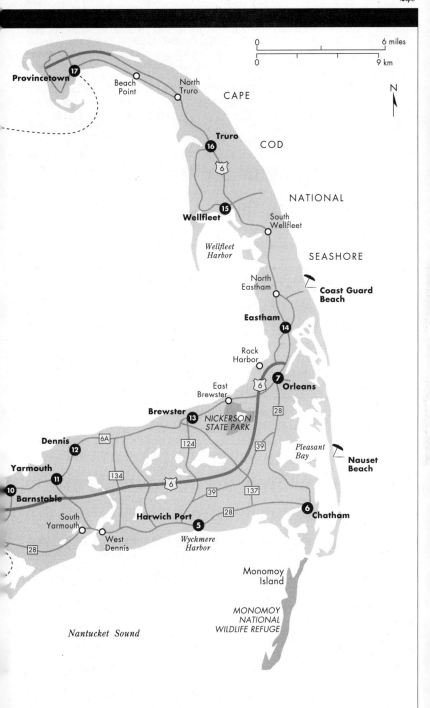

The Falmouth Historical Society conducts free, docent-guided walking tours of the town in season. It also maintains two museums. The 1790 **Julia Wood House** has fascinating architectural details (wide-board floors, leaded-glass windows, Colonial kitchen with wide hearth), plus embroideries, baby shoes and clothes, toys and furniture. The **Conant House** next door, a 1794 half-Cape, has military memorabilia, whaling items, scrimshaw, sailors' valentines, silver, glass, and china. *Palmer Ave. at the Village Green, tel. 508/548–4857. Admission: $2 adults, 50¢ children. Open mid-June–mid-Sept., weekdays 2–5; other times by appointment.*

Also in Falmouth is the **Ashumet Holly Reservation,** a 45-acre tract of woods, ponds, meadows, and hiking trails supervised by the Audubon Society. The 1,000 holly trees include American, Oriental, and European varieties. *Ashumet Rd., off Rte. 151, tel. 508/563–6390. Admission: $3 adults, $2 children, senior citizens. Open daily sunrise–sunset.*

❸ **Hyannis,** with its busy downtown, is the Cape's year-round commercial hub. The **John F. Kennedy Memorial,** on Ocean Street overlooking Lewis Bay, is a plaque and fountain pool in memory of the president who spent his summers nearby.

❹ **Hyannis Port** is the site of the **Kennedy family compound;** although tourists are not allowed onto the compound, sightseeing buses often tie up traffic in the area.

The proliferation of motels, restaurants, and antiques shops continues past Hyannis on the south shore but thins out some-
❺ what as you go east. At **Harwich Port,** a right turn onto Harbor Road will take you past scenic **Wychmere Harbor.**

❻ **Chatham** is a seaside town that is relatively free of the development and commercialism found elsewhere on the Cape. Its attractive Main Street, lined with boutiques and crafts and antiques shops, is a pleasure to wander.

The view from **Chatham Light** is spectacular—a great vantage point to view the "Chatham Break" of 1987, when a fierce storm blasted a channel through a barrier beach off the coast. South of Chatham lies **Monomoy Island,** which was split in two by a similar break in 1958. A fragile barrier-beach area with dunes, it is protected as the **Monomoy National Wildlife Refuge.** The island provides nesting grounds and resting places for 285 bird species.

From Chatham, Route 28 curves north and joins Routes 6 and
❼ 6A at **Orleans,** the busy commercial center of the Lower Cape. A left turn at the Main Street traffic light will take you to Rock Harbor Road, a winding street lined with gray-shingled Cape houses, white picket fences, and neat gardens; at the end is the harbor.

❽ The north-shore segment of this tour begins at **Sagamore,** where you'll find a large Christmas Tree Shop and a factory-outlet mall. At **Pairpont Glass** you can watch richly colored lead crystal being hand-blown in the factory, as it has been for 150 years. The shop sells finished wares, including ornamental cup plates. *Rte. 6A, Sagamore, tel. 508/888–2344. Open daily 9–6; demonstrations weekdays 10–4.*

❾ **Sandwich** is the oldest town on the Cape and one of the most charming. It remains famous for the striking colored glass that was produced here from 1825 until 1888, when competition with glassmakers in the Midwest closed the factory. The **Sandwich Glass Museum** contains relics of the early history of the town, as well as an outstanding collection of pressed and lacy glass. *129 Main St., tel. 508/888-0251. Admission: $2.50 adults, 50¢ children over 6. Open Apr.–Oct., daily 9:30–4:30; Nov., Dec., Feb., Mar., Wed.–Sun. 9:30–4. Closed Jan.*

Nearby is the **Hoxie House,** a restored 1637 shingled saltbox that is the Cape's oldest house. Overlooking Shawme Pond, it has been furnished authentically in period and features a collection of antique textile machines. *Rte. 130, tel. 508/888-1173. Admission: $1.50 adults, 75¢ children. Open Mon.–Sat. 10–5, Sun. 1–5. Closed mid-Oct.–May.*

Heritage Plantation, set on 76 beautifully landscaped acres, is a complex of several museum buildings and gardens, including an extensive collection of rhododendrons. Its Shaker Round Barn showcases classic and historic cars; the Military Museum houses a collection of miniature soldiers and antique firearms; and the Art Museum exhibits a Currier & Ives collection and a working 1912 carousel. *Grove and Pine Sts., tel. 508/888-3300. Admission: $7 adults, $3 children 6–12, $6 senior citizens. Open daily 10–5. Closed Nov.–mid-May.*

As you continue east on Route 6A, past fine views of meadows ⑩ and the bay, you will come to **Barnstable,** a lovely town of large ⑪ old homes. In **Yarmouth, Hallet's Store,** a country drugstore and soda fountain, is preserved as it was 100 years ago. At Centre Street, take a left and follow signs to Gray's Beach, where you'll find the **Bass Hole Boardwalk,** extending out over a ⑫ marshy creek and providing good views of marsh life. In **Dennis** is **Scargo Hill,** offering a spectacular view of Scargo Lake and Cape Cod Bay.

⑬ **Brewster,** in the early 1800s the terminus of a packet cargo service from Boston, was home to many seafaring families. A large number of mansions built for sea captains remain today, and quite a few have been turned into bed-and-breakfasts.

The **Cape Cod Museum of Natural History** has environmental and marine exhibits, guided field walks, and self-guided trails through 80 acres rich in wildlife. *Rte. 6A, Brewster, tel. 508/896-3867. Admission: $2.50 adults, $1.50 children 6–14. Open May–mid-Oct., Mon.–Sat. 9:30–4:30, Sun. 12:30–4:30. Closed Mon. mid-Oct.–Apr.*

At **Orleans,** Main Street leads east to **Nauset Beach,** which begins a 40-mile stretch of barrier beach extending to Provincetown. This is the Cape Cod Beach of which Thoreau wrote in his 1865 classic *Cape Cod.*

⑭ Three miles north on Route 6 is **Eastham.** Just beyond the village is the headquarters of the **Cape Cod National Seashore,** established in 1961 to preserve the Lower Cape's natural and historic resources. Within the Seashore are superb ocean beaches; great rolling, lonely dunes; swamps, marshes, and wetlands; scrub and grasslands; and all kinds of wildlife.

The **Salt Pond Visitor Center** in Eastham has displays, literature racks, and an auditorium for nature films. *Off Rte. 6, tel. 508/255-3421. Open Mar.–Sept. daily 9–4:30; July–Aug. daily 9–6.*

Roads and bicycle trails lead to the **Coast Guard Beach** area and the **Nauset Beach Lighthouse.** During the season, park guides lead daily nature walks and lectures.

Five miles farther on Route 6 is the **Marconi Station,** with a model of the first transatlantic wireless station erected on the U.S. mainland. From here, Guglielmo Marconi sent an early wireless message to Europe on January 18, 1903. *South Wellfleet, tel. 508/349-3785. Open year-round, weekdays 9–4:30; Jan.–Feb., weekends 9–4:30.*

⑮ Wellfleet was once the location of a large oyster industry and, along with Truro to the north, a Colonial whaling and codfishing port. It is one of the more tastefully developed Cape resort towns, with a number of fine restaurants, historic homes, and art galleries.

⑯ Truro is popular with artists and writers. The most prominent painter to have lived here was Edward Hopper, who found the Cape light ideal for his austere brand of realism. About 4 miles up Route 6, follow signs to the **Pilgrim Heights Area.** The early history of the region—which the *Mayflower* explored for weeks before settling in Plymouth—is shown in displays at the shelter. A walking trail leads to the spring where the Pilgrims stopped to refill their casks.

Continue on Route 6 to reach the National Seashore's **Province Lands Area.** This area comprises Race Point and Herring Cove beaches; bike, horse, and nature trails; and a picnic area. *Visitor Center, tel. 508/487-1256. Open Apr.–Nov., daily 9–4:30; July–Aug., daily 9–6.*

⑰ Provincetown, called P-town locally, offers spectacular beaches and dunes, first-rate shops and galleries. Portuguese and American fishermen mix with painters, poets, writers, whale-watchers from Boston or the Midwest, and, in high season, flamboyant gays and cross-dressers from everywhere. During the early 1900s Provincetown became known as Greenwich Village North, and long before the 1960s, local Bohemians were shocking the more staid members of Provincetown society. Inexpensive summer lodgings close to the beaches attracted young rebels and artists, including John Reed, Mabel Dodge, Sinclair Lewis, and Eugene O'Neill. Some of O'Neill's early plays were presented first in Provincetown.

The Historical Society puts out a series of walking-tour pamphlets, available for less than $1 each at many shops in town, with maps and information on the history of many buildings and the famous folk who have occupied them.

Provincetown's main tourist attraction is the **Pilgrim Monument,** on a hill above the town center, commemorating the landing of the Pilgrims in 1620. From atop the 252-foot-high granite tower there's a panoramic view of the entire Cape. At the base a historical museum has a diorama of the *Mayflower* and exhibits on whaling, shipwrecks, scrimshaw, and more. *Tel. 508/487-1310. Admission: $3 adults, $1 children. Open July–Sept., daily 9–9; Oct.–June, daily 9–4.*

What to See and Do with Children

Aqua Circus of Cape Cod offers dolphin and sea lion shows, a petting zoo, pony rides, wandering roosters and peacocks, a large seashell collection, aquariums, and more. *Rte. 28, West Yarmouth, tel. 508/775–8883. Admission: $7 adults, $4 children 2–9. Open daily 9:30–5. Closed late Nov.–mid-Feb.*

Cape Cod Aquarium has harbor seals, sea lions, marine mammal shows, four buildings with sea creatures, and outdoor pools with otters, turtles, birds, and snakes. *Rte. 6A, West Brewster, tel. 508/385–9252. Admission: $7 adults, $4.50 children 5–11. Open daily 10–4.*

GreenBriar Nature Center (off Rte. 6A, East Sandwich, tel. 508/888–6870) has a full summer program of nature walks and slide presentations.

Pirate's Cove is the most elaborate of the Cape's many miniature-golf emporiums, with a hill, waterfall, and stream. *728 Main St. (Rte. 28), South Yarmouth, tel. 508/394–6200. Admission: $5 adults, $4 children under 13. Open daily 9 AM–11 PM in season, 9:30 or 10–7:30 or 10 off-season.*

Water Wizz Water Park has a 50-foot-high water slide with tunnels and dips, a river ride, a six-story tube ride, and minigolf. *Rtes. 6 and 28, Wareham (near Buzzards Bay, over the bridge), tel. 508/295/3255. Admission: $14. Open daily 10–8 mid-June–Labor Day, weekends only Memorial Day–mid-June.*

Four Seas (360 S. Main St., Centerville, tel. 508/775–1394) is a longtime favorite for ice cream. Around the corner is what would once have been called the penny-candy store, now stocked with nickel-and-dime candy.

Off the Beaten Track

New Alchemy Institute is an experimental farm and research center devoted to finding and demonstrating ecologically safe methods of food production and heating. Guided tours explore its 12 acres of organic gardens and solar and composting greenhouses (Sat. at 1 PM year-round; also Sun. at 1 mid-June–mid-Sept.); self-guided tours can be taken at any time. Children's programs in gardening and nature study are offered in July and August. *237 Hatchville Rd., East Falmouth, tel. 508/564–6301 or 2219. Admission: $3 adults, children under 12 free. Open daily 10–4.*

Shopping

Shopping Districts   **Provincetown** has a long history as an art colony and remains an important art center, with many fine galleries and exhibitions of Cape and non-Cape artists. Write for a free "Provincetown Gallery Guide" (Provincetown Gallery Guild, Box 242, Provincetown 02657).

Wellfleet has emerged as a vibrant center for art and crafts as well, without Provincetown's crowds. Write for a free walking map of Wellfleet's art galleries and restaurants (Wellfleet Art Galleries Assn., Box 916, Wellfleet 02667).

Hyannis's Main Street—the Cape's largest—is lined with book shops, gift shops, jewelers, clothing stores, summer wear and T-shirt shops, and ice-cream and candy stores, plus minigolf courses and fun eating places. The orientation is youthful, but everyone enjoys watching the summer parade.

Chatham's Main Street is a pretty shopping area, with generally more upscale and conservative merchandise than Hyannis offers. Here you'll find galleries, crafts and clothing stores, and a few good antiques shops.

Falmouth and **Orleans** also have a large number of shops.

Shopping Malls **Cape Cod Factory Outlet Mall** (Factory Outlet Rd., Exit 1 off Rte. 6, Sagamore, tel. 508/888–8417) has more than 20 outlets.

Cape Cod Mall (Rtes. 132 & 28, Hyannis, tel. 508/771–0200), the Cape's largest, is where everyone congregates on rainy days. Its 90 shops include Jordan Marsh, Filene's, Woolworth, four restaurants, and many food shops.

Falmouth Mall (Rte. 28, Falmouth, tel. 508/540–8329) has Bradlees, T. J. Maxx, and 30 other shops.

Flea Market **The Wellfleet Drive-In Theatre** (Rte. 6, Eastham-Wellfleet line, tel. 508/349–2520) is the site of a giant flea market (mid-Apr.–fall, 8–4 weekends and Mon. holidays; July–Aug., also Wed. and Thurs.). There's a snack bar and playground.

Pick-Your-Own **Tony Andrews Farm and Produce Stand** (398 Old Meeting House
Farm Rd., East Falmouth, tel. 508/548–5257) lets you pick your own strawberries (mornings from mid-June), as well as peas, beans, and tomatoes (late June–late Aug.).

Specialty Stores **Carriage House Antiques** (3425 Rte. 6A, Brewster, tel. 508/896–
Antiques 6570) has museum-quality 18th- and 19th-century marine antiques and American furniture, country pine, pottery, china, botanical prints, paintings, antique toy soldiers, and guns.

Eldred's (Rte. 6A, Box 796, East Dennis 02641, tel. 508/385–3116) has auctions throughout the summer, featuring top-quality antiques such as marine art; Oriental, American, and European art; Americana; and estate jewelry.

Eldred Wheeler (866 Main St., Box 90, Osterville 02655, tel. 508/428–9049 or 508/428–7093) is well known for handcrafting fine 18th-century furniture reproductions.

H. Richard Strand (Town Hall Sq., Sandwich, tel. 508/888–3230), in an 1800 home, displays an eclectic collection of very fine pre-1840 and Victorian antique furniture, paintings, American glass, and more.

Kingsland Manor (Rte. 6A, West Brewster, tel. 508/385–9741) is like a fairyland, with ivy covering the facade, fountains in the courtyard, and everything "from tin to Tiffany" from end to end.

Remembrances of Things Past (376 Commercial St., Provincetown, tel. 508/487–9443) deals in jewelry, photographs, neon, and other articles from the 1920s to the 1960s.

Art **Blue Heron Gallery** (Bank St., Wellfleet, tel. 508/349–6724) is one of the Cape's best, with representational contemporary art by regional and nationally recognized artists.

Cummaquid Fine Arts (4275 Rte. 6A, Cummaquid, tel. 508/362–2593) has works by Cape Cod and New England artists, plus decorative antiques, beautifully displayed in an old home.

Long Point Gallery (492 Commercial St., Provincetown, tel. 508/487–1795) is a collective of several well-established artists, including Robert Motherwell.

Sweetgrass Gallery (445 Commercial St., Provincetown, tel. 508/487–2352) features Native American art.

Books **Kings Way Books and Collectibles** (774 Rte. 6A, Brewster, tel. 508/896–3639) has out-of-print and rare books, including a large medieval section, plus small antiques.

Provincetown Bookshop (246 Commercial St., tel. 508/487–0964) has just about every book ever written on Provincetown, as well as many Cape Cod titles.

Titcomb's Bookshop (432 Rte. 6A, East Sandwich, tel. 508/888–2331) has used, rare, and new books, including a large collection of Cape-related titles and hundreds on fishing.

Clothing **Hannah** (47 Main St., Orleans, tel. 508/255–8234; Main St., Wellfleet, tel. 508/349–9884) has high-end women's fashions in unusual styles.

Laguna Sport (1600 Rte. 28, Bell Tower Mall, Centerville, tel. 508/778–5003) has a full complement of California and Hawaii surf-type beachwear in fluorescent (and quieter) tones.

Northern Lights Leather (361 Commercial St., Provincetown, tel. 508/487–9376) has high-fashion clothing and accessories of very fine, soft leather.

Crafts **The Blacks Handweaving Shop** (597 Rte. 6A, West Barnstable, tel. 508/362–3955), in an old barn with the looms upstairs, makes and sells beautiful shawls, scarfs, throws, and more in traditional and jacquard weaves.

Scargo Pottery (off Rte 6A, Dennis, tel. 508/385–3894) is a 35-year Cape favorite. The setting is a pine forest, where the potter Harry Holl's unusual wares—such as his signature castle birdfeeders—are displayed on tree stumps and hanging from branches. More pottery and the workshop and kiln are indoors.

The Spectrum (Rte. 6A, Brewster, tel. 508/385–3322; 342 Main St., Hyannis, tel. 508/771–4554; W. Main St., Wellfleet, tel. 508/349–1962) showcases imaginative American arts and crafts, including pottery, stained glass, art glass, and more.

Sydenstricker Galleries (Rte. 6A, Brewster, tel. 508/385–3272) features glassware handcrafted by a unique process, which you can watch in progress at the studio on the premises.

Tree's Place (Rte. 6A at Rte. 28, Orleans, tel. 508/255–1330), one of the Cape's most original shops, has handcrafted kaleidoscopes, art glass, hand-painted porcelain and pottery, hand-blown stemware, wooden boxes, Russian lacquer boxes, and jewelry.

Jewelry **September Morn** (385 Commercial St., Provincetown, tel. 508/487–9092) sells fine estate jewelry, plus art glass and antique Oriental art.

Sports and Outdoor Activities

Biking **Cape Cod Rail Trail,** the paved right-of-way of the old Penn Central Railroad, is the Cape's premier bike path. Running 20 miles, from Dennis to Eastham, it passes salt marshes, cranberry bogs, and ponds, and cuts through Nickerson State Park. The terrain is easy to moderate. The Butterworth Company (476 Main St., Harwich Port 02646, tel. 508/432–8200) sells a guide to the trail for $2.50.

On either side of the **Cape Cod Canal** is an easy 7-mile straight trail, offering a view of the bridges and canal traffic.

The **Shining Sea Bikepath** is a nice-and-easy 5-mile coastal route between Locust Street, Falmouth, and the Woods Hole ferry parking lot.

The Cape Cod National Seashore maintains three bicycle trails. (A brochure with maps is available at visitor centers.) **Nauset Trail** is 1.6 miles, from Salt Pond Visitor Center in Eastham to Coast Guard Beach. **Head of the Meadow Trail** is 2 miles of easy cycling between sand dunes and salt marshes from High Head Road, off Route 6A in North Truro, to the Head of the Meadow Beach parking lot. **Province Lands Trail** is a 5¼-mile loop off the Beech Forest parking lot on Race Point Road in Provincetown, with spurs to Herring Cove, Race Point, and Bennett Pond.

Camping There are many private campgrounds throughout the Cape, except within the National Seashore, where camping is not permitted. **Nickerson State Park** is a favorite tenting spot for its setting and wildlife. **Shawme Crowell State Forest** has tent, trailer, and motor home sites on 1,200 acres (*see* National and State Parks, below).

Fishing Charter boats and party boats (per-head fees, rather than charters' group rates) take you offshore for tuna, mako and blue sharks, swordfish, and marlin. There are also hundreds of freshwater ponds, including Mare's Pond in Falmouth and Mashpee-Wakeby Pond in Mashpee. A license is needed for freshwater fishing and is available at tackle shops, such as **Eastman's Sport & Tackle** (145 Main St., Falmouth, tel. 508/548-6900) and **Truman's** (Rte. 28 at railroad crossing, Hyannis, tel. 508/771-3470), which rent gear.

Rental boats (and usually gear) are available from **Flyer's** (131A Commercial St., Provincetown, tel. 508/487-0898), **Goose Hummock** (Rte. 6A, Orleans, tel. 508/255-2262), and **Cape Cod Boats** (power and sail boats and canoes; Rte. 28 at Bass River Bridge, West Dennis, tel. 508/394-9268).

Deep-sea fishing trips are operated on a walk-on basis by **Hy-Line** (Ocean St. Dock, Hyannis, tel. 508/778-2600); **Cap'n Bill & Cee Jay** (MacMillan Pier, Provincetown, tel. 508/487-4330 or 2353); and ***Patriot Too*** (Falmouth Harbor, tel. 508/548-2626).

Golf The Cape's mild climate makes golf possible year-round on most of its 20 public courses, though January and February do get nippy. **Ocean Edge Golf Course** (1 Villagers Rd., Rte. 6A, Brewster, tel. 508/896-6157) is the top championship course, 18 holes. The semiprivate **Country Club of New Seabury** (Great Neck Rd., Mashpee, tel. 508/477-9110) has 36 excellent holes. Other fine courses: **Captain's Course** (1000 Freeman's Way, Brewster, tel. 508/896-5100), 18 holes; **Cranberry Valley Golf Course** (Oak St., Harwich, tel. 508/432-6300), 18 holes; and **Chatham Bars Inn** (Chatham, tel. 508/945-0096), 9 holes—a good beginner's course.

Horseback Riding **Nelson's Riding Stable** (Race Point Rd., Provincetown, tel. 508/487-0034) is located by the **Province Lands Horse Trails,** three 2-hour trails to the beaches through or past dunes, cranberries, forests, and ponds. Other stables: **Deer Meadow Riding Stables** (rides through conservation land; Rte. 137, East Harwich, tel. 508/432-6580), **Provincetown Horse and Carriage**

(dune and beach rides; tel. 508/487–1112), and **Haland Stables** (Rte. 28A, West Falmouth, tel. 508/540–2552).

Sailing and Water Sports **Arey's Pond Boat Yard** (off Rte. 28, Orleans, tel. 508/255–0994) has a sailing school with individual and class lessons. **Flyer's** in Provincetown (*see* Fishing, above) rents sailboats, sailboards, Sunfish, outboards, and rowboats, and teaches sailing. **Club Watersports** (tel. 508/432–7079) has locations on several beaches for sailboat and sailboard rentals and lessons.

Tennis **Bissell's Tennis Courts** (Bradford St. at Herring Cove Beach Rd., tel. 508/487–9512) has five clay courts and offers lessons. **Mid-Cape Racquet Club** (193 White's Path, South Yarmouth, tel. 508/394–3511) has one outdoor and nine indoor tennis courts, three racquetball, and two squash; plus whirlpool, steam, and sauna. **Manning's Tennis** (292 Rte. 28, West Harwich, tel. 508/432–3958) has four championship all-weather courts in a pine grove, and gives lessons. High schools and towns have public courts.

Beaches

Beaches fronting on Cape Cod Bay generally have colder water, carried down from Maine and Canada, and gentle waves. Southside beaches, on Nantucket Sound, have rolling surf and are warmer, because of the Gulf Stream. Open-ocean beaches on the Cape Cod National Seashore have serious surf. Parking lots fill up by 10 AM or so. Those beaches not restricted to residents charge (sometimes hefty) parking-lot fees; for weekly or seasonal passes, contact the local town hall.

All of the Atlantic Ocean beaches on the National Seashore are superior—wide, long, sandy, dune-backed, with great views. They're also contiguous: you can walk from Eastham to Provincetown almost without leaving sand. All have lifeguards and restrooms; none has food.

Craigville Beach, a long, wide strip of beach near Hyannis, is extremely popular, especially with the roving and volleyball-playing young (hence the nickname "Muscle Beach"). It has lifeguards and a bathhouse, and food shops across the road.

Old Silver Beach in North Falmouth is especially good for small children because a sandbar keeps it shallow at one end and makes tidal pools with crabs and minnows. There are restrooms, a snack bar, and showers.

Sandy Neck Beach (tel. 508/362–8300) in West Barnstable, a 6-mile barrier beach between the bay and marshland, is one of the Cape's most beautiful, a wide swath of pebbly sand backed by grassy dunes extending forever in both directions.

National and State Parks

Cape Cod National Seashore (*see* Exploring Cape Cod, above).

Nickerson State Park (Rte. 6A, Box 787, Brewster 02631, tel. 508/896–3491; map available on-site) has more than 1,700 acres of forest with eight freshwater kettle ponds. Higgins Pond is stocked year-round with trout for fishing; other recreational options are biking, canoeing, sailing, motorboating, bird-watching, and ice-fishing, skating, and cross-country skiing in winter.

Scusset Beach Reservation (Scusset Beach Rd., off Rte. 3, Sandwich 02563, tel. 508/888–0859) comprises 450 acres near the canal, with a beach on the bay. Its pier is a popular fishing spot; other activities include biking, hiking, picnicking, swimming, and camping on its 98 sites.

Shawme Crowell State Forest (Rte. 130, Sandwich, tel. 508/888–0351) is 742 acres near the canal. Activities include camping, biking, hiking, and horseback riding.

Monomoy National Wildlife Refuge (*see* Guided Tours, above).

Dining

Malcolm Wilson, dining critic for the Cape Cod Times, *wrote the restaurant reviews of Cape Cod and Nantucket.*

Hearty New England cooking—meat-and-potatoes fare—is the overwhelming cuisine of choice on the Cape, along with the ubiquitous New England clam chowder and fresh fish and seafood. Extraordinary gourmet restaurants can be found, along with occasional ethnic specialties such as the Portuguese kale soup or linguica. In the off season many Cape restaurants advertise early-bird specials (reduced prices in the early evening), and Sunday brunch often has musical accompaniment.

Upper Cape

Coonamessett Inn. Built in 1796, this elegant inn has lots of old-fashioned charm. The theme of the main dining room is the paintings by Ralph Cahoon; his signature hot-air balloons recreated in copper and enamel add a touch of whimsy to an otherwise subdued and romantic room. The regional American menu focuses on fresh fish and seafood, such as lobster pie—crunchy chunks baked with a light breading and cream, butter, and sherry. *Jones Rd., Falmouth, tel. 508/548–2300. Reservations advised. Dress: neat but casual. AE, CB, DC, MC, V. Closed Mon. Jan.–Mar. Moderate–Expensive.*

★ **Dan'l Webster Inn.** The Colonial New England patina of this inn belies its construction in 1971. The glassed-in conservatory features luxuriant greenery; the main dining room has a traditional Colonial look. The mostly regional American menu emphasizes seafood, such as lobster meat sautéed with chanterelle mushrooms in Fontina sauce on pasta. Hearty and elegant breakfasts and Sunday brunches are served. *149 Main St., Sandwich, tel. 508/888–3622. Reservations advised. Dress: neat but casual. AE, MC, V. Moderate–Expensive.*

Amigo's. This busy restaurant, its rough barn-board and plaster walls brightened with Mexican art and Tiffany lamps, serves good traditional Mexican fare as well as "gringo food" and such nightly specials as Cajun or blackened fish. *Tataket Sq., Rte. 28, Falmouth, tel. 508/548–8510. Reservations required for 6 or more. Dress: casual. MC, V. Moderate.*

★ **The Bridge.** The several small dining rooms have recessed lighting, art on the walls, and linen tablecloths. The Yankee pot roast is the star of the eclectic menu, which also features *bijoux de la mer* (lobster, scallops, and shrimp with lemon and tarragon on spinach pasta with a smoky mushroom-cream sauce). *Rte. 6A, Sagamore, tel. 508/888–8144. Weekend reservations advised in season. Dress: casual. MC, V. Moderate.*

The Flume. This clean, plain fish house, decorated only with a few Indian artifacts and crafts (the owner is a Wampanoag chief), offers a small menu of straightforward food guaranteed to satisfy. The chowder is outstanding, perhaps the Cape's best. Other specialties are fried smelts, fried clams, Indian pudding, and in summer, fresh broiled fish. *Lake Ave. (Rte. 130), Mashpee, tel. 508/477–1456. Reservations advised weekends. Dress: casual. MC, V. June–Aug. closed Tues.; Sept.– May closed Mon., Tues., weekday lunch. Closed Thanksgiving–Jan. 1. Moderate.*

Mid-Cape **Anthony's Cummaquid Inn.** The main dining room is spacious
★ and genteel, with huge windows that reveal a water view of great beauty. Complemented by an impressive wine list, the traditional New England menu features an exceptional roast beef *au jus* and a baked fillet of sole rolled and stuffed with bread crumbs and lobster and topped with Newburg sauce. *Rte. 6A, Yarmouth Port, tel. 508/362–4501. Reservations advised. Jacket advised. AE, MC, V. No lunch. Expensive–Very Expensive.*

Cranberry Moose. Past the landscaped courtyard of this 18th-century cottage is a series of attractive dining rooms in different styles, accented with large floral displays. The new American cuisine emphasizes a clean taste, with light use of cream and butter, as in medallions of duck breast on a bed of wild mushrooms with blackberry sauce. The wine list features more than 125 choices. *43 Main St., Yarmouth Port, tel. 508/362–3501. Reservations advised. Jacket advised at dinner. AE, CB, DC, MC, V. Closed Mon.–Tues. Jan.–Mar. Expensive.*

★ **The Paddock.** Long the benchmark of consistent quality dining, this formal restaurant is decorated in Victorian style—from the dark, clubby bar to the airy summer-porch area filled with green wicker and potted plants. The main dining room blends dark beams, frosted-glass dividers, sporting art, and banquettes. The wine list is extensive. The Continental-American menu emphasizes seafood and beef. Steak *au poivre* is popular. *W. Main St. Rotary (next to Melody Tent), Hyannis, tel. 508/775–7677. Reservations advised. Jacket advised. AE, CB, DC, MC, V. Closed mid-Nov.–Apr. Expensive.*

Three Thirty One Main. Also called Penguins Go Pasta—note the penguins in the bar—this sophisticated Northern Italian restaurant focuses on seafood and homemade pastas. A signature dish is the veal chops Pasetto, stuffed with prosciutto and Fontina, lightly breaded, pan-fried, and served with a sauce of shallots, capers, prosciutto, and fresh tomatoes. On the walls, mirrors alternate with warm wood paneling and exposed brick. *331 Main St., Hyannis, tel. 508/775–2023. Reservations advised for large parties. Dress: neat but casual. AE, CB, DC, MC, V. No lunch. Expensive.*

Il Maestro. Behind the brick-and-glass front is regional Italian cuisine as good as you'll find on the Cape. The specialty of the house is veal, such as *braciolettine*—rolled veal stuffed with prosciutto and imported cheeses, sautéed in lemon and wine, and topped with mushroom Marsala sauce. The interior is spare, with dark green walls and paintings of Tuscan villas. *1870 W. Main St., Hyannis, tel. 508/775–1168. Reservations required. Dress: casual. AE, MC, V. No lunch. Moderate–Expensive.*

★ **Red Pheasant Inn.** The main dining room is pleasantly intimate and rustic, with stripped pine floors, exposed beams, and two fireplaces. The cuisine is American regional, with a French twist in the sauces. The large menu always features lamb, plus seafood and sweetbreads, duck, venison, or pheasant. *905 Main St. (Rte. 6A), Dennis, tel. 508/385–2133. Reservations*

advised. Dress: neat but casual. AE, MC, V. No lunch.
Moderate–Expensive.

★ **The Regatta of Cotuit.** A sister restaurant to the Regatta in Falmouth, the Cotuit Regatta is set in a restored 18th-century
home. Its intimate dining rooms—dressed in Venetian mirrors,
Chippendale furniture, Oriental carpeting—are romantically
lighted. A specialty of the Continental and American menu is
grilled foods, as well as pâtés of rabbit, veal, or venison. Boneless sliced rack of lamb with Cabernet sauce is outstanding.
Rte. 28, Cotuit, tel. 508/428–5715. Reservations advised.
Dress: neat but casual. MC, V. No lunch. Closed Mon.–Wed.
Dec.–Apr. Moderate–Expensive.

Fiddlebee's. At this casual eating place, three levels of dining
areas are arranged around a central well that, on the first floor,
opens on a dance floor that's well patronized at night. The preparation is rather uneven, but the menu does have something for
everyone: blackened chicken breast, Rio Grande Tex-Mex chili
(a special), quiche, and basic burgers. *North St., Hyannis, tel.*
508/771–6032. No reservations. Dress: casual. AE, MC, V.
Moderate.

Inaho. A welcome addition to the ethnic diversity of restaurants on the Cape is this little storefront place done up with
such authentic details as screens and a sushi bar. Traditional
Japanese fare, such as tempura, teriyaki, and *shabu-shabu*—
beef cooked at table in hot broth—is served. *569 Main St.,*
Hyannis Oaks Village, Hyannis, tel. 508/771–9255. No
reservations. Dress: casual. AE, MC, V. No lunch. Mod-
erate.

★ **Up the Creek.** This casual spot with a busy hum about it serves
fine food at very good prices. House specialties include seafood strudel—two pastries filled with lobster, shrimp, crab,
cheese—and baked stuffed lobster. *36 Old Colony Rd., Hyan-*
nis, tel. 508/771–7866. Reservations advised. Dress: casual.
AE, CB, DC, MC, V. Moderate.

Baxter's Fish N' Chips. On busy Lewis Bay, Baxter's gets a lot
of back-in boaters at its picnic tables for possibly the best fried
clams on the Cape, as well as other fried, baked, and broiled
fresh fish and seafood (plus burgers, chicken, and Cajun steak).
Pleasant St., Hyannis, tel. 508/775–4490. No reservations.
Dress: casual. No credit cards. Closed Mon.; Oct.–Apr. Inex-
pensive.

Lower Cape **Chillingsworth.** The Cape's best restaurant, this elegant spot,
★ decorated in Louis XV furnishings, offers award-winning
French and nouvelle cuisine and an outstanding wine cellar.
The frequently changing dinner menu is a five-course prix-fixe
and features such entrées as venison with celery root purée and
fried pumpkin; or sweetbreads and foie gras with wild mushrooms and ham, asparagus, and smoky sauce. *Rte. 6A,*
Brewster, tel. 508/896–3640. Reservations required at dinner
(seatings), advised at lunch. Jacket and tie required at dinner.
AE, MC, V. Closed Mon. Memorial Day–Nov.; Mon.–Thurs.
off-season. Very Expensive.

Captain Linnell House. Framed by huge trees, this neoclassic
structure looks like an antebellum mansion. Inside are small
dining rooms: one with a Normandy fireplace, exposed beams,
and white plaster; another with a pecan-paneled fireplace, oil
lamps, Aubusson rug, and rosette ceiling. Wild mushroom sauté is a striking dish with wine, butter, carrots, celery, and
tomato topped with watercress, croutons, and puff pastry. *137*

Skaket Rd., Orleans, tel. 508/255–3400. Reservations required in season. Dress: casual. MC, V. No lunch Sat. Expensive.

High Brewster. A romantic country inn overlooking a pond, this restored sea captain's house offers seasonal four-course prix-fixe menus; a fall menu might include pumpkin-and-sage bisque and tenderloin medallions with chives and cheese glaze. In winter à-la-carte ordering is possible from the American regional menu. *964 Satucket Rd., Brewster, tel. 508/896–3636. Reservations required. Jacket advised. MC, V. No lunch. Often closed Mon.–Wed. mid-Sept.–mid-June. Expensive.*

★ **Ciro and Sal's.** After 30 years, this stage-set Italian restaurant —raffia-covered Chianti bottles hanging from the rafters, walls of plaster and brick, strains of Italian opera in the air— plays out its role with the confidence of years on the boards. Scampi alla Griglia is grilled shrimp in lemon, parsley, garlic, butter, leeks, and shallots; veal and pasta dishes are specialties. *4 Kiley Court, Provincetown, tel. 508/487–0049. Reservations required summer, Sat. nights. Dress: casual. MC, V. Closed Mon.–Thurs. Christmas–Memorial Day. Moderate-Expensive.*

Land Ho. Walk in, grab a newspaper from the lending rack, take a seat, and relax—for 20 years Land Ho has been making sure folks feel right at home. This casual spot serves kale soup that has been noted by *Gourmet* magazine, plus burgers, hearty sandwiches, grilled fish in summer, and very good chicken wings, chowder, and fish and chips. *Rte. 6A, Orleans, tel. 508/255–5165. No reservations. Dress: casual. MC, V. Moderate.*

Lodging

In summer lodgings should be booked as far in advance as possible—several months for the most popular cottages and bed-and-breakfasts. Assistance with last-minute reservations is available at the **Cape Cod Chamber of Commerce information booths** at Bourne, Sagamore, and West Barnstable. Off-season rates are much reduced, and service may be more personalized.

B&B reservations services include **House Guests Cape Cod** (Box 1881, Orleans 02653, tel. 800/666–4678) and **Bed and Breakfast Cape Cod** (Box 341, West Hyannis Port 02672, tel. 508/775–2772). **Provincetown Reservations System** (tel. 508/487 –2400 or 800/648–0364) makes reservations year-round for accommodations, shows, restaurants, transportation, and more.

Upper Cape   **Admiralty Resort.** Suites in this large facility are mostly rooms with a Murphy bed and a sofabed. Every unit has cable TV, a wet bar, a minirefrigerator, and a coffee maker, and is furnished in pastel Formica and wood. Townhouse suites have cathedral ceilings with skylights, a king-bedded loft, a living room with Murphy or king-size bed and sofabed, and a Jacuzzi. The building down the hill is a bit in disrepair but cheaper. *51 Teaticket Hwy. (Rte. 28), Falmouth 02540, tel. 508/548–4240 or 800/341–5700; in MA 800/352–7153. 100 suites. Facilities: restaurant, lounge with dancing, outdoor and indoor pools, 2 saunas. AE, MC, V. Expensive.*

★ **Coonamessett Inn.** This classic inn provides fine dining and gracious accommodations in a tranquil country setting. One- or two-bedroom suites are located in five buildings arranged around a landscaped lawn that spills down to a scenic wooded pond. Rooms are casually decorated, with bleached wood or pine paneling, New England antiques or reproductions, upholstered chairs, couches, color TV, and phones. *Jones Rd. and Gifford St., Box 707, Falmouth 02541, tel. 508/548–2300. 24 suites, 1 cottage. Facilities: 2 restaurants, clothing shop. AE, CB, DC, MC, V. Expensive.*

★ **Mostly Hall.** Set in a landscaped park far back from the street, this 1849 house is imposing, with a wraparound porch and a dramatic cupola. Accommodations are in large corner rooms, with large shuttered windows giving leafy views, reading areas, antique pieces and reproduction canopied queen beds, pretty floral wallpapers, and Oriental accent rugs. *27 Main St., Falmouth 02540, tel. 508/548–3786. 6 rooms. Facilities: bicycles, central phone and TV, lending library, lawn games. No smoking. No credit cards. Closed Jan.–mid-Feb. Rates include full breakfast. Moderate.*

Earl of Sandwich Motor Manor. Single-story Tudor-style buildings form a U around a wooded lawn, with areas for croquet and horseshoes. The newer buildings (1981–1983) have air-conditioning, unlike the main building (1963). The rooms are rather somber—dark, exposed beams on white ceilings, dark paneled walls, Oriental throw rugs, olive leatherette wing chairs—but a good size, with large Tudor-style windows and small tiled baths. *378 Rte. 6A, East Sandwich 02537, tel. 508/888–1415. 24 rooms. Facilities: minirefrigerators. AE, MC, V. Inexpensive– Moderate.*

Mid-Cape
★ **Tara Hyannis Hotel & Resort.** For its central-Cape location, beautiful landscaping, extensive services, and superior resort facilities, it's hard to beat the Tara. The lobby area is elegant, but room decor is a bit dull, with pale colors and standard contemporary hotel-style furnishings; a revamp is in the works. Rooms overlooking the golf greens or the courtyard garden have the best views. *West End Circle, Hyannis 02601, tel. 508/ 775–7775 or 800/843–8272. 216 rooms, 8 suites. Facilities: restaurant, lounge, golf course, 2 putting greens, 2 lighted tennis courts, indoor and outdoor pools, health club, hair salon, gift shop, business services, room service until midnight, full children's program. AE, CB, D, DC, MC, V. Very Expensive.*

★ **Liberty Hill.** An elegant country inn, this 1825 Greek Revival mansion stands on a rise set back from Route 6A, in an attractive setting of trees and flower-edged lawns. Rooms are large, with tall windows and high ceilings, and romantically but unfussily decorated with fine antiques, upholstered chairs, and thick carpets. The Waterford room has the entire third floor, a king-size bed, an oversize bath, and bay views. *77 Main St. (Rte. 6A), Yarmouth Port 02675, tel. 508/362–3976. 5 rooms. Facilities: afternoon tea or iced tea, central TV and phone, guest refrigerator with ice and mixers. MC, V. Rates include Continental or full breakfast. Moderate.*

Capt. Gosnold Village. An easy walk to the beach and town, this colony of motel rooms and cottages is ideal for families. Walls are attractively paneled in knotty pine; floors are carpeted; furnishings are Colonial style, simple and pleasant. All units have TVs and heat; most have decks. Motel rooms have fridges and coffee makers. *Gosnold St., Box 544, Hyannis 02601, tel. 508/ 775–9111. 8 motel rooms, 12 efficiencies. Facilities: outdoor pool, basketball area, game nets, picnic areas, hibachis. AE, MC, V. Closed Nov.–mid-May. Inexpensive–Moderate.*

★ **Inn on Sea Street.** This is a charming, relaxed bed-and-breakfast a walk from the beach and downtown Hyannis. The

Victorian home (1849) has been completely restored and furnished with country antiques and lacy fabrics. A quirky favorite guest room is a glassed-in sun porch. Delicious breakfasts are beautifully served with china, silver, and crystal in a dining room of antiques and lace. *358 Sea St., Hyannis 02601, tel. 508/775–8030. 6 rooms, 3 with private bath. Facilities: central phone and TV. Smoking discouraged. AE, MC, V. Closed Nov.–Mar. Rates include full breakfast. Inexpensive–Moderate.*

Lower Cape **Augustus Snow House.** Luxury is the operative word at this inn, a Princess Anne Victorian with gabled dormers and wraparound veranda. Early evening wine and hot hors d'oeuvres are served in silver and crystal, accompanied by quiet classical music. The rooms are done up in Victorian style, with reproduction furnishings and wallpapers and authentic period brass bathroom fixtures. All rooms have phone and TV. *528 Main St., Harwich Port 02646, tel. 508/430–0528. 5 rooms. AE, MC, V. Rates include full breakfast. Very Expensive.*

★ **Chatham Bars Inn.** An oceanfront resort in the old style, this Chatham landmark comprises the main building—with its grand lobby—and 26 one- to eight-bedroom cottages on 80 beautifully landscaped acres. The entire inn has been renovated. Some cottage rooms have working fireplaces. Many rooms have private ocean-view porches; all have phones and TVs, Colonial reproduction furnishings, upholstered armchairs, and wall-to-wall carpeting. Service is attentive and extensive. *Shore Rd., Chatham 02633, tel. 508/945–0096 or 800/527–4884. 152 rooms. Facilities: restaurant, lounge, bar, beach grill, private beach, 5 tennis courts, 9-hole golf course, heated outdoor pool, shuffleboard court, launch service to North Beach, children's programs (July and Aug.). AE, DC, MC, V. Rates are MAP in season. Very Expensive.*

Bradford Inn and Motel. Just off Main Street are the cheery yellow awnings and colorful gardens of the Bradford. Five buildings, ranging from the main house (1860) to the motel section (1978), accommodate rooms that run the gamut from small and basic to luxurious and spacious with fireplaces and canopy beds. *26 Cross St., Box 750, Chatham 02633, tel. 508/945–1030. 25 rooms. Facilities: lounge, heated outdoor pool, library. AE, D, MC, V. Rates include full breakfast. Expensive–Very Expensive.*

★ **Captain's House Inn.** Finely preserved architectural details, superb taste in decorating, opulent home-baked goods, and an overall feeling of warmth and quiet comfort are just part of what makes this possibly the finest small inn on Cape Cod. Each room in the three inn buildings has its own personality. Some have fireplaces. The decor is mostly Williamsburg; rooms in the Carriage House have a more spare, modern look. *371 Old Harbor Rd., Chatham 02633, tel. 508/945–0127. 12 rooms, 2 suites. AE, MC, V. Rates include Continental breakfast, afternoon tea. No smoking in public areas. Closed mid-Nov.–mid-Feb. Expensive.*

Hargood House. This apartment complex on the water is a great option for longer stays and families. Most of the individually decorated units have decks and large water-view windows; all have kitchens and modern baths. Apartment 8 is on the water, with three glass walls, cathedral ceilings, and private deck. Rental is mostly by the week in season; nightly available off-season. *439 Commercial St., Provincetown 02657, tel. 508/*

487–1324. 20 apartments. Facilities: private beach, maid service in season, barbecue grills. AE, MC, V. Moderate–Expensive.

Provincetown Inn. A Provincetown landmark, the inn is rather the worse for wear. Waterfront rooms are by far the nicest, with wide decks, picture windows looking out to sea, and better furnishings; bay-view rooms look out over the marshes to the dunes; motel rooms are just that. *1 Commercial St., Provincetown 02657, tel. 508/487–1225 or 800/942–5388. 100 rooms. Facilities: restaurant, bar, coffee shop, indoor pool (all in-season only); private beach. MC, V. Rates include full breakfast in season. Moderate–Expensive.*

Nauset Knoll Motor Lodge. On a low rise overlooking Nauset Beach, two minutes' walk away, this row of adjoining Cape houses offers basic, ground-level motel rooms. Each is sparsely furnished but light and bright, with six-foot picture windows facing the ocean, tiled baths, and color TV. Book well in advance. *Nauset Beach, East Orleans 02643, tel. 508/255–2364. 12 rooms. Closed late-Oct.–mid-Apr. MC, V. Moderate.*

★ **Old Sea Pines Inn.** Fronted by a wraparound veranda overlooking a broad lawn, this inn evokes the feel of a summer estate. Guest rooms are decorated with antiques; many are very large. Some fireplaces are available—one in the best room, with an enclosed sun porch. Rooms in a newer building are spare, with bright modern baths, and have TVs. *2553 Main St. (Rte. 6A), Brewster 02631, tel. 508/896–6114. 19 rooms (5 share baths), 2 suites. Smoking discouraged. AE, CB, DC, MC, V. Rates include full breakfast. Inexpensive–Moderate.*

The Arts

Theater Summer stock theater is popular throughout the Cape. The top venues are the **Cape Playhouse** (Rte. 6A, Dennis, tel. 508/385–3911), with a nine-week season of Broadway shows often featuring star performers; and the **Falmouth Playhouse** (off Rte. 151, North Falmouth, tel. 508/563–5922; June–early Oct.), offering Broadway shows and children's plays.

The **College Light Opera Company** (Highfield Theatre, Depot Ave. Ext., Falmouth, tel. 508/548–0668) features college music majors performing operetta and musical comedy late June through August.

Wellfleet Harbor Actors Theatre (Wellfleet, tel. 508/349–6835) offers a May-to-October season with more serious fare, from drama to satire.

Music The 90-member **Cape Cod Symphony** (Mattacheese Middle School, West Yarmouth, tel. 508/428–3577) gives regular and children's concerts, with guest artists, October through May.

The **Cape & Islands Chamber Music Festival** (Box 72, Yarmouth Port 02675, tel. 508/778–5277) presents three weeks of top-caliber performances and master classes in August.

Melody Tent (W. Main St., Hyannis, tel. 508/775–9100; through Ticketron or Teletron tel. 800/382–8080) presents top performers such as Kenny Rogers and the Glenn Miller Orchestra in theater-in-the-round under a tent, July to Labor Day.

Nightlife

Bars and Lounges **Oliver's** restaurant (Rte. 6A, Yarmouth Port, tel. 508/362–6062) has live guitar music weekends in its lounge. **Guido Murphy's Café** (615 Main St., Hyannis, tel. 508/775–7242) and the **Chatham Squire** (487 Main St., Chatham, tel. 508/945–0942), with four bars, are rollicking places drawing a young crowd.

Jazz The **Asa Bearse House** restaurant (415 Main St., Hyannis, tel. 508/771–4131) has dancing under the stars in a glass-topped atrium, to a jazz quartet, most evenings.

Rock **Kasbar** (Rte. 28, South Yarmouth, tel. 508/760–1616) is a large nightclub with dancing to mostly DJ music, plus nightly laser light shows. **Sundancer's** (116 Rte. 28, West Dennis, tel. 508/394–1600) offers dancing to some reggae and Motown, mostly DJ. The **Mill Hill Club** (164 Rte. 28, West Yarmouth, tel. 508/775–2580) has more live entertainment and some DJ, plus large-screen videos. **Fiddlebee's** (North St., Hyannis, tel. 508/771–6032) has dancing to live rock, jazz, and blues.

The Laurels, at the Tara Hyannis Hotel & Resort (West End Circle, Hyannis, tel. 508/775–7775), has dancing to DJs or live music from big band to jazz to rock most nights.

Oldies **Admiralty Resort** (Rte. 28, Falmouth, tel. 508/548–4240) has dancing to '50s and '60s music in its lounge most nights. **T-Birds** (at Dorsie's, 325 Rte. 28, West Yarmouth, tel. 508/771–5898; at King's Ransom, 425 Rte. 28, Dennisport, tel. 508/394–5533) is a '50s and '60s dance emporium, with '50s decor and DJ music.

Country and Western **Bud's Country Lounge** (Bearses Way and Rte. 132, Hyannis, tel. 508/771–2505) has live entertainment most nights; **The Good Times** (Rte. 130, Sandwich, tel. 508/888–6655) and **Sou'wester** (Rte. 28, West Chatham, tel. 508/945–9705), on weekends.

Martha's Vineyard

Much less developed than Cape Cod, yet more diverse and cosmopolitan than neighboring Nantucket, Martha's Vineyard has a split personality. From Memorial Day through Labor Day this island 5 miles southeast of Woods Hole is a vibrant, star-studded event. Seekers of chic descend in droves on the boutiques of Edgartown and the main port of Vineyard Haven. Summer regulars return, including such celebrities as William Styron, Art Buchwald, Walter Cronkite, Jacqueline Onassis, and Carly Simon.

But in the off-season the island becomes a place of peace and simple beauty. Fall covers the moors with a mantle of purple and brown and gold. On drives along country lanes you can linger, free from a throng of other cars, bikes, and mopeds. Though the pace is slower, cultural and recreational events continue, and a number of inns, shops, and restaurants remain open.

Important Addresses and Numbers

Visitor Information The **Martha's Vineyard Chamber of Commerce** publishes an excellent annual guidebook. *Box 1698, Beach Rd., Vineyard*

Haven 02568, tel. 508/693–0085. Open weekdays 9–5, also Sat. 10–2 Memorial Day–Labor Day.

Emergencies Police, fire, or medical emergencies: tel. 911.

Island Medical Services (261 Main St., Edgartown, tel. 508/627–5181) and Vineyard Medical Services (State Rd., Vineyard Haven, tel. 508/693–6933) provide walk-in care.

Late-night Leslie Drug Store (Main St., Vineyard Haven, tel. 508/693–
Pharmacy 1010) has pharmacists on 24-hour call.

Arriving and Departing by Ferry

If you plan to take a car to the island in summer or fine week-ends anytime, you *must* reserve as far ahead as possible; spaces are often sold out months in advance. If you're without a reservation, get there very early, prepared to wait.

From Woods Hole The Steamship Authority (tel. 508/540–2022; on the Vineyard 508/693–9130) operates the only car ferries, which make the 45-minute trip to Vineyard Haven year-round, and to Oak Bluffs from late May through mid-September. (Guaranteed standby service for vehicles may be available in summer.) Cost one-way: $4 adults, $2 children 5–12; cars, $30 mid-May–mid-Oct., $15.25 off-season; bicycles $2.75.

From Hyannis Hy-Line Cruises (Ocean St. Dock, tel. 508/778–2600, 508/778–2602 for reservations; on the Vineyard tel. 508/693–0112) makes the 1¾-hour run to Oak Bluffs from late May through October. Cost one-way: $10 adults, $5 children 4–12, $4 bicycles.

From Falmouth The Island Queen (Falmouth Harbor, tel. 508/548–4800) makes the 40-minute trip to Oak Bluffs from late May through Columbus Day. Cost one-way: $5 adults, $2.50 children under 13, $3 bicycles.

From New Bedford Cape Island Express Lines's ferry (tel. 508/997–1688; on the Vineyard tel. 508/693–2088) makes the 1½-hour trip from Billy Wood's Wharf to Vineyard Haven from mid-May through Columbus Day. Cost one-way: $7.50 adults, $4.50 children, $2 bicycles.

From Nantucket Hy-Line (on Nantucket 508/228–3949, on the Vineyard tel. 508/693–0112) makes 2¼-hour runs to and from Oak Bluffs daily mid-June–mid-September. Cost one-way: $10 adults, $5 children 4–12, $4 bicycles.

Getting Around Martha's Vineyard

By Car Rentals can be booked through a courtesy phone at Woods Hole ferry terminal, or at the airport desks of Budget (tel. 508/693–7322), Hertz (tel. 508/627–4727), National (tel. 508/693–6454), and others. Adventure Rentals (Beach Rd., Vineyard Haven, tel. 508/693–1959) also rents mopeds and dune buggies.

By Bus Late May through mid-October, shuttles (tel. 508/627–7448) operate between Vineyard Haven, Oak Bluffs, and Edgartown daily 8 AM–midnight in high season, 8–7 other times. Cost one-way: $1.25–$3. Buses from Edgartown to Gay Head run frequently in July and August. Cost one-way: $1–$3. A lift vehicle for the disabled is available (tel. 508/693–4633).

By Bicycle and Moped The Vineyard is great for bicycling. For details on rentals and trails, *see* Biking in Sports and Outdoor Activities, below. Most of the bike-rental shops also rent mopeds, as does **Ride-On Mopeds** (Hy-Line Dock, Oak Bluffs, tel. 508/693–2076). A license is required. Be careful: skids on sand cause accidents.

By Ferry The **On Time** ferry (Dock St., Edgartown, tel. 508/627–9794) makes the five-minute run to Chappaquiddick Island every day, 7 AM–midnight June–mid-October, less frequently off-season. Cost one-way: $1.75 car and driver, $1 bicycle and rider, $1.50 moped or motorcycle and rider, 35¢ individual.

By Taxi Companies serving the island include **All Island** (tel. 508/693–3705), **Marlene's** (tel. 508/693–0037), and **Up Island** (tel. 508/693–5454).

Guided Tours

Orientation Three bus companies (tel. 508/693–1555, 508/693–4681, or 508/693–0058) offer two-hour narrated tours of the island, with a stop at Gay Head Cliffs. Buses meet ferries in season; call at other times.

Special-interest Tours Sailplane tours are given in summer by **Soaring Adventures of America** (Edgartown Airpark, Herring Creek Rd., tel. 508/627–3833).

Day, sunset, and overnight sails to Nantucket or Cuttyhunk on the 54-foot ketch **Laissez Faire** (tel. 508/693–1646) are offered in season out of Vineyard Haven. Sunset cruises on the motor tour boat **Skipper** (tel. 508/693–1238), out of Oak Bluffs, promise glimpses of celebrities' homes (weather permitting).

Exploring Martha's Vineyard

Numbers in the margin correspond with the numbered points of interest on the Martha's Vineyard map.

The island is roughly triangular, with maximum distances of about 20 miles east to west and 10 miles north to south. Much of its 130 square miles is undeveloped. Because most visitors arrive by ferry at **Vineyard Haven** (officially Tisbury), we begin there.

Directly across from the steamship terminal is the **Seaman's Bethel,** built in 1892 as a chapel and place of lodging and entertainment for sailors. Today it is a museum and chapel, with photographs, scrimshaw, and other exhibits on the island's history. *Union St., tel. 508/693–9317. Open daily 10–4.*

A short walk along Water Street and a right on Beach Road takes you to the Federal-style **Jirah Luce House,** built in 1804 and now a historical museum. Exhibits in eight rooms—including marine artifacts, clothing, and dolls—depict life in 19th-century Tisbury. *Beach Rd., tel. 508/693–5353. Admission: $2 adults, 50¢ children under 16. Open mid-June–mid-Sept., Tues.–Sat. 10–4:30.*

A block up from Main Street, with lots of shops and cafés, **William Street** has Greek Revival sea captains' houses that were spared during the Great Fire of 1883 that claimed most of the old whaling and fishing town.

Martha's Vineyard

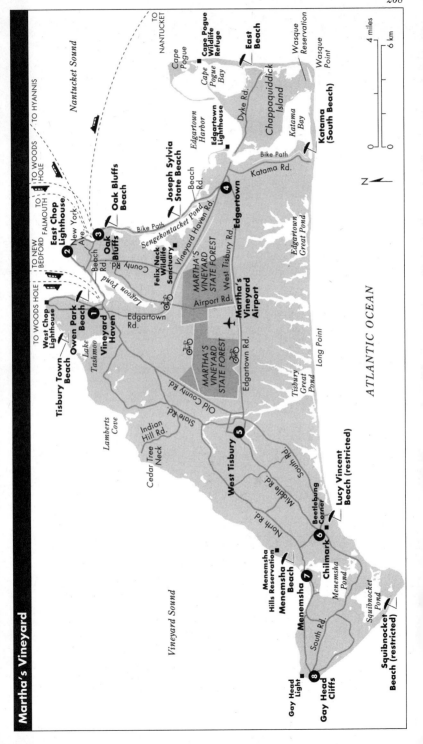

TO WOODS HOLE

West Chop Lighthouse

Tisbury Town Beach

Owen Park Beach

1 Vineyard Haven

Lake Tashmo

Edgartown Rd.

Lagoon Pond

TO WOODS HOLE

TO NEW BEDFORD FALMOUTH

TO FALMOUTH

TO WOODS HOLE

New York Ave.

2

Beach Rd.

County Rd.

3 Oak Bluffs

East Chop Lighthouse

Oak Bluffs Beach

Nantucket Sound

TO HYANNIS

TO NANTUCKET

Cape Pogue

Cape Pogue Wildlife Refuge

East Beach

Cape Pogue Bay

Wasque Reservation

Felix Neck Wildlife Sanctuary

Sengekontacket Pond

Joseph Sylvia State Beach

Bike Path

Beach Rd.

Edgartown Harbor

Edgartown Lighthouse

Dyke Rd.

Chappaquiddick Island

Katama Bay

Wasque Point

Bike Path

Katama Rd.

Katama (South Beach)

4 Edgartown

MARTHA'S VINEYARD STATE FOREST

Vineyard Haven Rd.

West Tisbury Rd.

Airport Rd.

Martha's Vineyard Airport

Edgartown Rd.

Edgartown Great Pond

Long Point

Edgartown Rd.

MARTHA'S VINEYARD STATE FOREST

Tisbury Great Pond

ATLANTIC OCEAN

Vineyard Sound

Lamberts Cove

Cedar Tree Neck

Indian Hill Rd.

State Rd.

Old County Rd.

5 West Tisbury

South Rd.

Middle Rd.

North Rd.

Lucy Vincent Beach (restricted)

Beetlebung Corner

6 Chilmark

Menemsha Hills Reservation

Menemsha Beach

7 Menemsha

Menemsha Pond

Squibnocket Pond

Squibnocket Beach (restricted)

Gay Head Light

8 Gay Head Cliffs

South Rd.

N

0   4 miles
0   6 km

Following Beach Road east, either veer off onto East Chop
Drive toward the 1877 **East Chop Lighthouse** for spectacular
views of Nantucket Sound, or turn right onto New York Avenue, which turns into Lake Avenue and brings you to the heart
of **Oak Bluffs.**

Once the setting for a number of grand hotels—the **Wesley Hotel** (1879) on Lake Avenue is the last of them—the still colorful
Oak Bluffs harbor now specializes in guest houses and minimalls hawking fast food and souvenirs. On Oak Bluffs Avenue is
the **Flying Horses,** the nation's oldest carousel and a National
Historic Landmark. *Tel. 508/693–9481. Rides cost $1; $8 for a
book of 10. Open mid-June–Labor Day, daily 10–10; spring
and fall, weekends only. Closed in winter.*

Circuit Avenue is the center of action, with most of the town's
shops, bars, and restaurants. Here you'll find the entrance to
the **Oak Bluffs Camp Ground,** a warren of streets tightly
packed with Carpenter Gothic Victorian cottages, gaily
painted in pastels and trimmed in lacy filigree. Methodist summer camp meetings have been held here since 1835; as the site's
popularity grew, the original nine tents gave way to hundreds
of cottages by the Victorian era, when the town became a resort known as Cottage City. Visitors are invited to a community sing held Wednesday at 8 PM, in season, at the **Tabernacle,** an impressive open-air structure of iron at the center of the
camp ground.

The island's third main town is about 5 miles from Oak Bluffs
via narrow, scenic Beach Road. **Edgartown** is tidy and polished,
with upscale boutiques, elegant sea-captains' houses, well-
manicured lawns, and photogenic flower gardens. Two of the
finest examples of Greek Revival architecture are on Main
Street, between Pease's Point Way and Church Street: the **Old
Whaling Church,** built in 1843 and now an arts center, with a
92-foot clock tower; and the **Dr. Daniel Fisher House** (1840) next
door, now housing offices.

In back of the Fisher House is the oldest dwelling on the island:
the 1672 **Vincent House,** a full-Cape farmhouse maintained as
an architectural museum. Most of the original glass, brick, and
hardware remain. *Main St., tel. 508/627–8017. Open June–
Sept., weekdays 10–3.*

Head back toward the harbor, then right onto School Street; at
the corner of Cooke Street (Edgartown's oldest) is a complex of
buildings belonging to the Dukes County Historical Society.
Built in 1765, the **Thomas Cooke House** is a museum document-
ing the island's history through furniture, tools, costumes, and
more. It is open in summer only. Open year-round are a small
museum and library and the 1,000-prism, 1854 Fresnel lens
from the Gay Head Lighthouse. *Cooke St., tel. 508/627–4441.
Admission: mid-June–mid-Sept., $2 adults, 50¢ children un-
der 16; free off-season. Open mid-June–mid-Sept., Tues.–Sat.
10–4:30; off-season, Wed.–Fri. 1–4, Sat. 10–4.*

The west end of the Vineyard—known as Up Island, from the
nautical expression of going "up" in degrees of longitude as you
sail west—is more rural than the east. **West Tisbury** occupies
the center of the island, including most of the 4,000-acre **State
Forest,** several farms, and a small New England village, complete with general store and agricultural hall. **Alley's General**

Store (State Rd., tel. 508/693–0088) sells everything from hammers to dill pickles to art.

❻ About 4 miles past West Tisbury center is **Chilmark,** a rustic wooded area with scenic ocean-view roads and two beautiful (residents-only) beaches. At the crossroads called Beetlebung

❼ Corner, head toward the little fishing village of **Menemsha.** Along with the fishing shacks you'll find a few boutiques, a beach, a seafood restaurant, and good fishing from the jetties.

❽ Continue west for the **Gay Head Cliffs.** These dramatically striated walls of red clay are the island's major tourist site. The approach to the overlook—you can see the Elizabeth Islands across Vineyard Sound—is lined with Indian crafts and food shops, for Gay Head is a Wampanoag Indian township.

Time Out The **Aquinnah** (tel. 508/645–9654), at the end of the row of shops, perched over the cliffs, is an Indian-owned family-style restaurant with a wonderful view and great sunsets. The simple menu features burgers and sandwiches, homemade chowder and pies.

Martha's Vineyard for Free

The Winery at Chicama Vineyards (Stoney Hill Rd., off State Rd., West Tisbury, tel. 508/693–0309) offers tours and wine tastings May through October, tastings only January through April.

Vineyard Haven Town Band concerts take place on alternate Sunday evenings in summer at Owen Park in Vineyard Haven and at the gazebo on Beach Road in Oak Bluffs.

What to See and Do with Children

Flying Horses Carousel, Oak Bluffs (*see* Exploring Martha's Vineyard, above).

Children's Theatre, Oak Bluffs (at the high school, Edgartown–Vineyard Haven Rd., tel. 508/693–4060), has performances by and for children daily 9–1 in season.

Windfarm Museum is an unusual introduction to nonpolluting sources of energy, with working windmills and a lived-in solar-heated, energy–self-sufficient house. Daily programs (1½ hours) end for children with a ride in a donkey cart; they can also pet the farm animals. *Edgartown Rd., 2 mi south of Vineyard Haven, tel. 508/693–3658. Admission: $4 adults, $3 children. Open only for programs: July–Labor Day, Mon.– Sat. 10 AM and 2:30 PM, Sun. 2:30; late May–June 30 and Sept., daily at 2:30; Oct., weekends at 2:30. Closed Nov.–late May.*

Shopping

Department Store **The Fligors** (27 N. Water St., Edgartown, tel. 508/627–8811) has everything, including preppy clothing and a bargain basement.

Food and Flea A **flea market** is held on the grounds of the Chilmark Communi-
Markets ty Center (Beetlebung Corner, tel. 508/645–9484) Wednesday and Saturday mornings in season until 2:30 or 3 PM. From spring into September **farmer's markets** are held at the Agri-

cultural Hall on South Road in West Tisbury Saturday 9–noon and at Waban Park in Oak Bluffs on Wednesday 4–6 PM.

Specialty Stores

Antiques **Auntie's Attic** (Edgartown, tel. 508/627–9833) sells mostly New England furniture, clothing, lace, quilts, collectibles, jewelry, and gourmet items.

Soulagnet Collection (Colonial Inn Shops, Edgartown, tel. 508/ 627–7759; Basin Rd., Menemsha, tel. 508/645–3735) has antiques from high-end to Fiestaware, folk art, and clocks.

Art **Edgartown Art Gallery** (Summer St., Edgartown, tel. 508/627– 5991), in the Charlotte Inn, has 19th- and 20th-century oils and watercolors, plus English antiques.

Granary Gallery at the Red Barn Emporium (Old County Rd., West Tisbury, tel. 508/693–0455 or 800/343–0471) has an excellent collection of antiques, as well as a gallery showcasing island artists and the photographs of Alfred Eisenstaedt.

Hermine Merel Smith Gallery (Edgartown Rd., West Tisbury, tel. 508/693–7719) specializes in contemporary American impressionists.

Books **Bickerton & Ripley Books** (Main St., Edgartown, tel. 508/627– 8463) and the **Bunch of Grapes Bookstore** (Main St., Vineyard Haven, tel. 508/693–2291) carry a wide selection of new books, including many island-related titles.

Book Den East (Vineyard Haven Rd., Oak Bluffs, tel. 508/693– 3946) sells out-of-print, antiquarian, and paperback books in an old barn.

Clothing **Bramhall & Dunn** (Main St., Vineyard Haven, tel. 508/693– 6437) has superb hand-knit sweaters and English pine antiques.

Laughing Bear (154 Circuit Ave., Oak Bluffs, tel. 508/693– 9342) sells fun children's and women's wear made of Balinese or Indian batiks and other unusual materials.

Murray's of the Vineyard (Main St., Vineyard Haven, tel. 508/ 693–2640) offers classic designer fashions and accessories.

Crafts **Handworks** (Nevin Square Shops, Winter St., Edgartown, tel. 508/627–8402) showcases jewelry, pottery, toys, dollhouses, and more.

Michaela Gallery of American Crafts (Towanticut Ave., Oak Bluffs, tel. 508/693–8408) has pottery, glass, and jewelry.

Sioux Eagle Designs (Main St., Vineyard Haven, tel. 508/693– 6537) features handcrafted jewelry in exotic designs, the work of Native Americans.

Gifts **The Secret Garden** (148 Circuit Ave., Oak Bluffs, tel. 508/693– 4759) has linens, lace, quilts, wicker furniture, island watercolors, and more.

Tashtego (29 Main St., Edgartown, tel. 508/627–4300) is one of the island's most interesting shops, with antiques and home furnishings.

Sporting Goods The two **Wind's Up!** shops (Tisbury Market Place, Beach Rd., Vineyard Haven, tel. 508/693–4340; Dock St., Edgartown, tel. 508/627–5886, open June–Sept.) sell swimwear, windsurfing and sailing equipment, and other outdoor gear, as does

Brickman's (Main St., Vineyard Haven, tel. 508/693–0047; Main St., Edgartown, tel. 508/627–4700).

Sports and Outdoor Activities

Biking Paths run along the coast road from Oak Bluffs to Edgartown, inland from Vineyard Haven to Edgartown, and from Edgartown to South Beach. Any of these connect with scenic paths that weave through the State Forest. Rent bikes in Vineyard Haven at **Brickman's** (Main St., tel. 508/693–0047), in Oak Bluffs at **De Bettencourt's** (Circuit Ave. Ext., tel. 508/693–0011), and in Edgartown at **R.W. Cutler Bike** (1 Main St., tel. 508/627–4052).

Fishing Party boats, such as the *Skipper* (tel. 508/693–1238), leave from Oak Bluffs Harbor in season. Striped bass and bluefish are the star catches. Rent rods at **Larry's Tackle Shop** (25 Dock St., Edgartown, tel. 508/627–5088) or **Dick's Bait and Tackle** (New York Ave., Oak Bluffs, tel. 508/693–7669).

Golf **Farm Neck Golf Club** (Farm Neck Rd., Oak Bluffs, tel. 508/693–2504), a semiprivate club on Sengekontacket Pond, has 18 holes. The public **Mink Meadows Golf Course** (Franklin St., Vineyard Haven, tel. 508/693–0600), on elite West Chop, has nine.

Horseback Riding **Misty Meadows Horse Farm** (Old County Rd., West Tisbury, tel. 508/693–1870) has a large indoor riding area and offers trail rides and lessons. **Eastover Farms** (across from the airport, tel. 508/693–3770) offers English and Western lessons, indoor and outdoor rings, and beach and other trails. Reservations are necessary.

Sailing Lessons and rentals are available at the **Harborside Inn** in Edgartown (South Water St., tel. 508/627–4321), and the **Selfin Sailing Center** in Vineyard Haven (Beach Rd., tel. 508/693–4252).

Shellfishing Each town hall issues shellfish licenses for the waters under town jurisdiction and will give information on good spots.

Water Sports **Wind's Up!** provides windsurfing and sailing lessons and rentals, plus an invaluable brochure on windsurfing, including best locations and safety tips. In season, it has a shop on the lagoon in Vineyard Haven (tel. 508/693–4252). **Vineyard Boat Rentals** (Dockside Marina, Oak Bluffs, tel. 508/693–8476) offers Boston Whalers, Jet Skis, and parasailing.

Beaches

East Beach, on Chappaquiddick, is accessible only by foot from the Wasque Reservation entrance or by boat; it offers heavy surf, good bird-watching, and relative isolation in a lovely setting.

Joseph Sylvia State Beach, between Oak Bluffs and Edgartown, is a mile-long sandy beach popular with families for its calm, warm water and view of Cape Cod across Nantucket Sound.

Menemsha Public Beach is a sandy beach with gentle surf on Vineyard Sound, backed by tall dunes. Located on the western side of the island, it is a great place to catch the sunset.

Owen Park Beach, a harbor beach on Main Street in Vineyard Haven, is a convenient if unexciting spot, with the plus of a children's play area and lifeguards.

South Beach, the island's largest and most popular, is a 3-mile ribbon of sand on the Atlantic, with strong surf and sometimes riptides. From Edgartown, take the bike path to Katama or catch the trolley at Main and Church streets on the hour or the half-hour.

Nature Areas

Cape Poge Wildlife Refuge and Wasque Reservation on Chappaquiddick Island is a 689-acre wilderness of dunes, woods, salt marshes, ponds, and barrier beach that is an important migration stopover or nesting area for many bird species. You'll find good swimming at East Beach and good surf casting at Wasque Point. *Tel. 508/693–7662. Admission: $4 cars, $2 individuals in season.*

Cedar Tree Neck, more than 250 hilly acres of unspoiled woods, has wildlife, freshwater ponds, brooks, low stone walls, and wooded trails ending at a stony but secluded North Shore beach where swimming is prohibited. *Indian Hill Rd. to left-hand curve; dirt road downhill to right for 1 mi to parking lot. Tel. 508/693–7233. Admission free. Open daily 8:30–5.*

Felix Neck Wildlife Sanctuary comprises 350 acres, including 6 miles of trails traversing marshland, fields, woods, seashore, and a pond rich in wildfowl. It offers a full schedule of events, all led by naturalists. *Edgartown-Vineyard Haven Rd., tel. 508/627–4850. Admission: $2 adults, $1 children. Open daily 8–4.*

Long Point offers 580 acres of grassland, dense heath, grassy dunes, freshwater and saltwater ponds, and a half mile of South Beach, with swimming, surf fishing, and picnicking. *Follow unpaved Deep Bottom Rd. (¾ mi west of airport on Edgartown-West Tisbury Rd.) for 2 mi to Long Point parking lot. Tel. 508/693–7233. Admission: $6 car, $3 adults.*

Dining

Only Edgartown and Oak Bluffs allow the sale of liquor. In the "dry" towns restaurants are glad to provide setups.

Edgartown **L'étoile.** The nouvelle French menu at the Charlotte Inn's popular restaurant highlights imaginative native seafood and shellfish as well as game. Characteristic dishes from the four-course prix-fixe menu include grilled sweetbreads with sorrel in puff pastry with shallot-and-endive cream sauce; and sautéed lobster and scallops with grilled polenta and lobster-champagne beurre blanc. The wine list is extensive. *27 S. Summer St., tel. 508/627–5187. Reservations required. Jacket advised. AE, MC, V. No lunch. Closed Jan.–mid-Feb., weekdays off-season. Very Expensive.*

★ **Andrea's.** Served amid unpretentious surroundings are excellent classic northern Italian and Continental dishes such as lobster *fra diavolo* (in the shell, served with mussels, clams, scallops, and shrimp on a bed of linguine with a spicy marinara sauce) and sirloin Lattenzi (sautéed in cognac with mushroom, truffle, and Madeira sauce; named after the chef). Choose from a seat in the main room, the glassed-in porch, semiprivate rooms, or (in season) the rose garden, weather permitting. *Upper Main St., tel. 508/627–5850. Reservations advised. Dress: casual. AE, MC, V. No lunch. Closed mid-Feb.–Mar.; Sun.–Tues. Nov.–mid-Feb., Apr.–May. Expensive.*

Lawry's Seafood Market & Restaurant. The fish—fried, broiled, or baked—comes from the family's own boats. The chowder is very good, as are the Black Diamond steaks. Don't come for atmosphere, unless your taste runs to orange vinyl, rustic wood booths, lots of kids, and a high decibel level. In 1990 Lawry's changed to self-service, lowered all prices, and added an elaborate sundae-and-dessert hall. *Upper Main St., tel. 508/ 627–8857. No reservations. Dress: casual. No credit cards. Closed Nov.–late Apr. Inexpensive–Moderate.*

Menemsha **Home Port.** Here you'll find very fresh fish and seafood pre-
★ pared in a no-nonsense manner—simply baked, broiled, or fried. The decor, too, is no-nonsense, with plain wood tables and a family atmosphere; window walls overlooking the harbor provide more than enough visual pleasure. The wait is often long, especially around sunset; take a seat outside and order from the raw bar, or wander around the fishing village. *North Rd., tel. 508/645–2679. Reservations required. Dress: casual. MC, V. No lunch. Closed Nov.–Apr. Moderate.*

Oak Bluffs **Oyster Bar.** Subtitled "An American Bistro," the Oyster Bar (named for its 35-foot mahogany raw bar) has a sophisticated art-deco look, with faux-marble columns, tropical greenery, and a line of pink neon along the walls. Though the extensive menu includes pastas, pizzas, soups, and specials, the stars are the 20 or so varieties of fish available each night—including such exotic choices as bonita and mahi-mahi—cooked any way you like: broiled, sautéed, grilled, or steamed. *162 Circuit Ave., tel. 508/693–3300. Reservations advised. Dress: casual. AE, DC, MC, V. No lunch. Closed mid-Oct.–mid-May. Expensive.*

Zapotec. Serving authentic and creative Mexican dishes with "serious salsa," Zapotec is an intimate place with heart and style. "Chef Heather's favorite" dish is the *suiza:* chicken, vegetables, or shrimp served with a *mole* sauce of tomatillas, pumpkin seeds, sour cream, and cheese. *10 Kennebec Ave., tel. 508/693–6800. No reservations. Dress: casual. AE, MC, V (surcharge). Closed Mon.–Wed. Apr.–June, Columbus Day–Thanksgiving; Thanksgiving–Easter. Moderate.*

★ **Giordano's.** Bountiful portions of simply prepared Italian food (pizzas, pastas, cacciatores, cutlets) and fried fish and seafood at excellent prices keep Giordano's—run by the Giordano clan since 1930—a family favorite. Eight different children's meals are available for under $5 (including milk and Jell-O). The ambience suits the clientele—hearty, noisy, and cheerful—with sturdy booths, bright green-topped wood tables, and hanging greenery. Lines wrap around the corner in season. *107 Circuit Ave., tel. 508/693–0184. No reservations. Dress: casual. No credit cards. Closed late Sept.–May. Inexpensive.*

Vineyard Haven **Black Dog Tavern.** An island landmark, the Black Dog serves basic chowders, pastas, fish, and steak, along with such dishes as grilled tuna with lime, garlic, and jalapeño; and rack of lamb with rosemary, mustard, and garlic. The Black Dog Bakery (on Water St., across from the A&P) provides breads and a large daily selection of desserts. The glassed-in porch, lighted by ship's lanterns, looks directly out on the harbor. The wait for a table is often long; put your name on the list and walk around the harbor area to pass the time. *Beach St. Ext., tel. 508/693–9223. No reservations. Dress: casual. AE, MC, V. Expensive.*

West Tisbury **Lambert's Cove Country Inn.** The country inn setting (*see* ★ Lodging, below), soft lighting and music, and fine Continental cuisine make this the coziest, most romantic dining spot on the island. The daily selection of six or seven entrées may include cioppino; scallops of veal with a chanterelle Dijon sauce; or filet mignon with béarnaise sauce. In summer a lavish Sunday brunch is served outdoors in the orchard. *Off Lambert's Cove Rd., tel. 508/693–2298. Reservations required. Dress: casual. No lunch. Closed Jan.; weekdays in winter. Expensive.*

Lodging

Martha's Vineyard and Nantucket Reservations (Box 1322, Lagoon Pond Rd., Vineyard Haven, 02568, tel. 508/693–7200) and **Accommodations Plus** (RFD 273, Edgartown 02539, tel. 508/627–8590) book B&B, hotels, and cottages..

Edgartown **Charlotte Inn.** Built as a whaling-company owner's home in the ★ 1860s, the Charlotte has grown into a five-building complex of meticulously decorated and maintained guest accommodations and is considered one of the finest inns in New England. The rooms are elegantly furnished with antiques and reproductions; some have fireplaces. *27 S. Summer St., 02539, tel. 508/627–4751. 23 rooms (2 with shared bath), 2 suites. Facilities: restaurant, art gallery. AE, MC, V. Rates include Continental breakfast. Very Expensive.*

Harbor View Hotel. A $7 million renovation of this full-service resort hotel was completed in 1990. The historic architecture of the main building (1891) was maintained, but the entire infrastructure and the room decor are new. To the wraparound veranda was added a gazebo looking out across landscaped lawns to the harbor, Edgartown Lighthouse, and the ocean. For the 1991 season, new landscaping, a pool area with gardens and fountains, and renovation of the seven cottages are scheduled. In the Governor Mayhew House the spacious rooms have private decks. Townhouses have cathedral ceilings, decks, kitchens, and large living areas. All rooms have similar decor: pale pink carpeting and light walls, painted wicker, pickled armoires, pastel floral drapes tied with silver braided cord, plus phones, air-conditioning, cable TV with VCR, and a wall safe. Suites have a fax machine and full stereo. The hotel is in a residential neighborhood just minutes from town. A beach good for walking stretches ¾ mile from the jetty, from which there's good blues fishing; children enjoy the sheltered bay. Many packages are available, including a November murder-mystery weekend. *131 N. Water St., 02539, tel. 508/627-4333 or 800/225-6005. 129 rooms. Facilities: restaurant, heated outdoor pool, 2 tennis courts, privileges at golf club, pool bar and café, lounge with entertainment, concierge, room service, business services, children's program, daily newspaper; boat slips, child care, laundry service, nonsmokers' rooms. AE, DC, MC, V. Closed Jan.–Feb. Very Expensive.*

The Victorian Inn. An 1857 whaling captain's home, listed on the National Register of Historic Places, the Victorian (a third floor in the Victorian style was added in the 1970s) is less formal than the Charlotte but also elegantly furnished with antiques. Several of the large rooms, many with comfortable sofas, have porches with a view of the nearby harbor. *S. Water St., Box 947, 02539, tel. 508/627–4784. 14 rooms. MC, V. Rates include full breakfast. Expensive.*

Daggett House. The flower-bordered lawn that separates the main house (1750) from the harbor makes a great retreat after a day of exploring town, a minute away. The breakfast room preserves much of the tavern that it once was, including a secret stairway (it is now a private entrance to an upstairs guest room, but the innkeeper may let you peek in if the room is unoccupied). This and two other buildings are decorated with fine wallpapers, antiques, and reproductions. *59 N. Water St., Box 1333, 02539, tel. 508/627–4600. 22 rooms, 4 suites. Facilities: central TV. MC, V. Rates include Continental breakfast. Moderate–Expensive.*

Menemsha **Beach Plum Inn and Cottages.** The main draws of this 10-acre retreat are the woodland setting, the panoramic view of the ocean and the Menemsha harbor, and the romantic gourmet restaurant that overlooks spectacular sunsets. Cottages (one with Jacuzzi) are decorated in casual beach style. Inn rooms—two with decks offering great views—have modern furnishings and small baths. *North Rd., 02552, tel. 508/645–9454. 5 inn rooms, 3 cottages. Facilities: restaurant, tennis court, fishing pond. AE, MC, V. Closed mid-Oct.–late May. Rates include full breakfast. Very Expensive.*

Oak Bluffs **Oak House.** The wraparound veranda of this pastel-front Vic-
★ torian (1872) looks across a busy street to a wide strand of beach. Several rooms have private terraces; if you're bothered by noise, you might ask for a room at the back. The decor centers on well-preserved woods—some rooms have oak wainscoting from top to bottom—choice antique furniture, and nautical-theme accessories. *Sea View Ave., Box 299, 02557, tel. 508/693–4187. 8 rooms, 2 suites. Facilities: some rooms with TV. MC, V. Closed mid-Oct.–Apr. Rates include Continental breakfast. Expensive.*

Attleboro House. This mom-and-pop guest house across from the bustling Oak Bluffs harbor is a big gingerbread Victorian with wraparound verandas on two floors. It offers small, comfortable, clean rooms, some with sinks and antiques. Linen exchanges but no chambermaid service is provided during a stay. The shared baths are rustic and old, but clean. *11 Lake Ave., 02557, tel. 508/693–4346. 9 rooms share 3½ baths. No credit cards. Closed Oct.–mid-May. Rates include Continental breakfast. Inexpensive.*

Vineyard Haven **Thorncroft Inn.** Set on 3½ acres of woods about a mile from the ferry, the 1918 Craftsman bungalow is furnished with very fine Colonial and richly carved Renaissance Revival antiques and tasteful reproductions. The atmosphere is somewhat formal but not fussy. In addition to the bungalow, the inn comprises three other buildings, two closer to town. Breakfast is a gourmet, sit-down affair conducive to meeting and chatting. *Main St., Box 1022, 02568, tel. 508/693–3333 or 800/332–1236. 17 rooms, 2 suites. Facilities: air-conditioning, phones, wiring for computers, turndown service, complimentary newspaper; deluxe rooms have cable TV and minirefrigerator, 3 have Jacuzzi. No smoking. AE, MC, V. Rates include full breakfast. Very Expensive.*

West Tisbury **Lambert's Cove Country Inn.** The 1790 farmhouse is ap-
★ proached through pine woods and set in an apple orchard. It has
elegance, with rich woodwork and large floral displays, yet
makes you feel at home with firm beds, electric blankets, and
unpretentious furnishings in comfortably sized guest rooms.
*Lambert's Cove Rd., West Tisbury (Box 422, RFD, Vineyard
Haven 02568), tel. 508/693–2298. 15 rooms. Facilities: restaurant, tennis court. AE, MC, V. Closed Jan. Rates include
Continental breakfast. Expensive.*

The Arts

Music A summer music program is held at the **Tabernacle** (tel. 508/693–
0525) in Oak Bluffs. Past highlights have included jazz trum-
peter Wynton Marsalis and a Gilbert and Sullivan show.

Theater The **Vineyard Playhouse** (10 Church St., Vineyard Haven, tel.
508/693–8720) offers a summer season of vintage Broadway
plays.

Nightlife

Bars and Lounges The **Ritz Café** (Circuit Ave., Oak Bluffs, tel. 508/693–9851) has
live blues and jazz on weekends in season; the rest of the year
it's a popular bar, with a pool table and a jukebox.

At **David's Island House** restaurant (Circuit Ave., Oak Bluffs,
tel. 508/693–4516), pianist David Crohan entertains dinner and
lounge patrons with popular and classical music.

Discos The two major clubs offer a mix of live rock and reggae and DJ-
spun dance music: the **Hot Tin Roof** (at the airport, tel. 508/693–
0320; May through Sept.) and the **Atlantic Connection** (124 Circuit Ave., Oak Bluffs, tel. 508/693–7129; year-round).

Nantucket

Thirty miles southeast of Hyannis, in the open Atlantic Ocean,
lies Nantucket. Settled in the mid-17th century by Quakers and
others retreating from the repressive religious authorities of
mainland Massachusetts, this 12-by-3-mile island became the
foremost whaling port in the world during the golden age of
whaling, in the early to mid-19th century. Shipowners and sea
captains built elegant mansions that today remain remarkably
unchanged, thanks to a very strict code regulating any changes
to structures within the town of Nantucket, an official National
Historic District. In addition, more than a third of the island's
acreage is under protection from development.

Visitors on a day trip usually browse in the downtown's many
art galleries, crafts shops, and boutiques, enjoy the architecture and historical museums, and sample the wealth of gourmet
restaurants. Those who stay longer appreciate the breezy
openness of the island. Its moors—swept with fresh salt
breezes and scented with bayberry, wild roses, and
cranberries—and its miles of clean, white-sand beaches make
Nantucket a respite from the rush and regimentation of life
elsewhere.

Important Addresses and Numbers

Visitor Information **Chamber of Commerce** (Pacific Club Bldg., Main St., tel. 508/228–1700; open weekdays 9–5; send $3 for guidebook). **Nantucket Information Bureau** (25 Federal St., tel. 508/228–0925; open daily 9–6 in summer, Mon.–Sat. 10–3 off-season).

Emergencies Police or fire: tel. 911.

Nantucket Cottage Hospital (South Prospect St., tel. 508/228–1200) has a 24-hour emergency room.

Arriving and Departing by Ferry

If you plan to take a car to the island in summer or fine weekends anytime, you *must* reserve as far ahead as possible; spaces are often sold out months in advance.

The **Steamship Authority** (on Nantucket tel. 508/228–3274; on the Cape 508/540–2022) runs car-and-passenger ferries to the island from Hyannis year-round (cars by reservation only). The trip takes 2¼ hours. Cost one-way: $9 adults, $4.50 children 5–12; cars, $71 mid-May–mid-Oct., $43 off-season; bicycles $4.50.

Hy-Line (on Nantucket tel. 508/228–3949; in Hyannis 508/778–2600) carries passengers from Hyannis from mid-May through October. The trip takes 1¾ to 2 hours. Cost one-way: $10 adults, $5 children 3–12, $4 bicycles. There is also service from Oak Bluffs on Martha's Vineyard mid-June to mid-September; that trip takes 2½ hours and the cost is the same.

Getting Around Nantucket

By Car Rent cars and Jeeps at the airport desks of **Avis** (tel. 508/228–1211), **Budget** (tel. 508/228–5666), and **Hertz** (tel. 508/228–9421), at **Ford Rent-a-Car** (Steamboat Wharf, tel. 508/228–1151), or through the free phone at Woods Hole ferry.

By Bus In season **Barrett's Tours** (20 Federal St., tel. 508/228–0174) runs shuttles to 'Sconset, Surfside, and Jetties beaches.

By Taxi Year-round taxi companies include **A-1 Taxi** (tel. 508/228–3330 or 4084), **All Points Taxi** (tel. 508/228–5779), and **Atlantic Cab** (tel. 508/228–1112).

By Bicycle or Moped Bikes and mopeds can be rented on Steamboat Wharf from **Young's Bicycle Shop** (tel. 508/228–1151; also cars and Jeeps) or **Nantucket Bike Shop** (tel. 508/228–1999; in season).

Guided Tours

Orientation Tours **Barrett's Tours** (20 Federal St., tel. 508/228–0174) and **Nantucket Island Tours** (Straight Wharf, tel. 508/228–0334) give 1- to 1½-hour narrated bus tours of the island, spring through fall; buses meet ferries.

Native Scenic Rides (tel. 508/257–6557 before 8 AM or after 6 PM; Apr.–Dec.) offers a lively, intimate 1¾-hour van tour narrated by a native, Gail Johnson.

Special-interest Tours **Roger Young's historic walking tours** (tel. 508/228–1062; in season) of the town center are entertaining and leisurely.

Nantucket Whalewatch (Hy-Line dock, Straight Wharf, tel. 508/283–0313; in MA 800/322–0013; other East Coast states 800/942–5464) runs naturalist-led excursions in season.

Jeep Excursions Ltd. (1 Old North Wharf, tel. 508/228–3728) offers Jeep fishing, beach, and other tours to Great Point.

Exploring Nantucket

Numbers in the margin correspond with the numbered points of interest on the Nantucket map.

❶ In **Nantucket town** the **Museum of Nantucket History,** in the old Thomas Macy Warehouse, gives an overview of the town from its beginnings. It is run by the Nantucket Historical Association (NHA; a visitor's pass allowing a single visit to all 13 NHA properties is available at any of the sites for $6 adults, $2.50 children 5–14). Audio and visual displays include photographs, ship models, 19th-century stereopticon slides, and a 13-foot diorama of the waterfront before the Great Fire of 1846, when hundreds of buildings were lost. *Straight Wharf, tel. 508/228–3889. Admission free. Open daily 10–9 in season, 11–3 off-season. Closed mid-Oct.–mid-Apr.*

The **Whaling Museum** is a short walk away along South Water Street. Set in an 1846 factory for refining spermaceti and making candles, it traces Nantucket's whaling past through such exhibits as a fully rigged whale boat, harpoons and other implements, portraits of sea captains, a large scrimshaw collection, the skeleton of a 43-foot finback whale, and the original 16-foot-high glass prism light from the Sankaty Lighthouse. *Broad St., tel. 508/228–1736. Admission: $3 adults, $1 children; or NHA Visitor's Pass. Open daily 10–5 in season, 11–3 off-season. Closed Nov.–mid-Apr.*

Time Out At lunch and dinner the **Atlantic Café** (S. Water St., tel. 508/228–0570) offers a varied, inexpensive menu. Appetizers are great, including the quahog chowder and zucchini sticks sprinkled with cheese and served with a dipping sauce. Portions are huge.

Work your way eventually to Main Street. A walk up Main past the **Pacific National Bank,** at the corner of Fair Street, takes you out of the business district and past the mansions. At 93–97 Main Street are the well-known **"Three Bricks,"** identical red-brick mansions with columned, Greek Revival porches at the front entrance. They were built between 1836 and 1838 by whaling merchant Joseph Starbuck for his three sons.

Across the street are two white, porticoed Greek Revival mansions built in 1844 by factory owner William Hadwen, the son-in-law of Joseph Starbuck, for himself and for the niece he and his wife adopted. One, called the **Hadwen House,** is now a house museum. A guided tour points out the grand circular staircase, fine plasterwork, carved Italian marble fireplace mantels, and Regency, Empire, and Victorian furnishings. *96 Main St., tel. 508/228–1894. Admission: $1.50 adults, 50¢ children 5–14; or NHA Visitor's Pass. Open daily 10–5 in season, 11–3 off-season. Closed mid-Oct.–late May.*

Turn up Vestal Street and walk past Bloom Street; a sign on the right points the way to the **Old Gaol,** a New England jailhouse

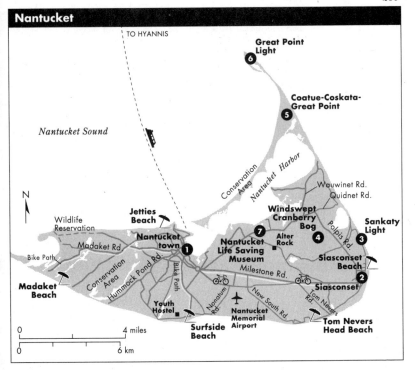

Nantucket

of 1805. Walls, ceilings, and floors are bolted with iron; furnishings consist of rough plank bunks and open privies. Don't feel too sympathetic, though: most prisoners were allowed out at night to sleep in their own beds. *15R Vestal St., tel. 508/228–1894. Admission free. Open daily 10–5. Closed mid-Oct.–late May.*

Return to the beginning of Vestal Street and turn down New Dollar Street, then turn left onto Mill Street. At No. 10 is the furnished **1800 House** museum, representative of an average Nantucketer's home of that time, including a backyard pump and a six-flue chimney with beehive oven. *Tel. 508/228–1894. Admission: $1 adults, 50¢ children 5–14; or NHA Visitor's Pass. Open daily 10–5. Closed mid-Oct.–late May.*

Take a right onto Pleasant Street and another right onto South Mill Street for the **Old Mill**, a 1746 Dutch-style windmill built with lumber from shipwrecks and still worked with wood gears and wind power to grind cornmeal in season. *Tel. 508/228–1894. Admission: $1 adults, 50¢ children 5–14; or NHA Visitor's Pass. Open daily 10–5. Closed mid-Oct.–late May.*

Other in-town sites not on this route are worth particular mention. The tower of the **First Congregational Church** provides the best view of Nantucket—for those who climb the 92 steps. Peek in at the church's trompe-l'oeil ceiling. *62 Centre St. Admission: $1.50 adults, 50¢ children. Open Mon.–Sat. 10–4, Wed. and Thurs. 6–8 PM also. Closed Oct.–mid-June.*

The **Oldest House,** also called the Jethro Coffin House, was severely damaged by lightning in 1987. After extensive renovations, the 1686 saltbox—the oldest house on the island—reopened in 1990. The most striking feature is the massive central brick chimney with a giant brick horseshoe adornment. *Sunset Hill, tel. 508/228–1894. Admission: $1 adults, 50¢ children 5–14; or NHA Visitor's Pass. Closed mid-Oct.–late May.*

2 A lovely day trip from town by bike is the village of **Siasconset** (called 'Sconset). This beach community began as an artists' colony and today offers a peaceful, unhurried lifestyle in elementally beautiful surroundings. Here you'll find pretty little streets with rose-covered cottages, a post office, a general store, a few restaurants, and a beach.

If you return to town via Polpis Road, rather than the 'Sconset
3 bike path, you'll pass **Sankaty Light**—one of three Coast Guard–operated lighthouses on Nantucket—and large areas of
4 open moorland. The entrance to the 205-acre **Windswept Cranberry Bog,** open to walkers and bike riders, is also on Polpis, between Quidnet Road and Wauwinet Road.

5 Wauwinet Road takes you to the gateway of **Coatue-Coskata-Great Point,** an unpopulated spit of sand comprising three cooperatively managed wildlife refuges and entered only by foot or four-wheel-drive over-sand vehicle (tel. 508/228–2884 for information about permits, etc.). Its beaches, dunes, salt marshes, and stands of oak and cedar provide a major habitat for such birds as marsh hawks, oystercatchers, terns, and herring gulls. Because of frequent dangerous currents and riptides and the lack of lifeguards, swimming is strongly
6 discouraged, especially around the **Great Point Light.**

7 A bit farther along on Polpis Road is the **Nantucket Life Saving Museum,** housed in a re-creation of an 1874 Life Saving Service station. It honors the men who valiantly lived by the service's motto: "You have to go out, but you don't have to come back." Exhibits include original rescue equipment and boats, photos and accounts of daring rescues, and more. *Polpis Rd., tel. 508/ 228–1885. Admission: $1 donation. Open Tues.–Sun. 10–5. Closed mid-Oct.–mid-June.*

What to See and Do with Children

Actors Theatre of Nantucket (*see* The Arts, below) has storytelling, music, and more for children in July and August.

Maria Mitchell Aquarium displays local marine life in saltwater and freshwater tanks. *29 Washington St., near Commercial Wharf, tel. 508/228–5387. Admission: $1. Open Tues.–Sat. 10–4. Closed Sept.–mid-June.*

J. J. Clammp's (Nobadeer Farm and Sun Island Rds., off Milestone Rd., tel. 508/228–8977) is an 18-hole miniature-golf course.

Shopping

The island specialty is Nantucket lightship baskets—woven baskets, their covers adorned with scrimshaw or rosewood, that were first made on lightships by crew members between chores and are now used as chic purses. Shops below are open year-round unless otherwise specified.

Food Markets Monday through Saturday in season, colorful farm stands are set up on Main Street to sell local produce and flowers.

Specialty Stores **Nina Hellman Antiques** (22 Broad St., tel. 508/228–4677; closed
Antiques Jan.–Apr.) carries scrimshaw, ship models, nautical instruments, and other marine antiques and Nantucket memorabilia.

Tonkin of Nantucket (33 Main St., tel. 508/228–9697) has two floors of fine English antiques, including furniture, china, art, and marine and scientific instruments.

Art **Janis Aldridge** (7 Centre St., tel. 508/228–6673; closed Dec.–Apr.) sells beautifully framed antique prints, including many botanicals.

The Main Street Gallery (50 Main St., tel. 508/228–2252; closed early Sept.–late June) has changing exhibits.

Paul La Paglia (38 Centre St., tel. 508/228–8760) has less expensive antique prints, including Nantucket scenes and fish.

Sailor's Valentine Gallery (38–40 Centre St., tel. 508/228–2011) features folk art in one building, contemporary art and exquisite sailor's valentines (intricate shell designs in glass boxes) next door.

Books **Mitchell's Book Corner** (54 Main St., tel. 508/228–1080) offers the best selection of books on Nantucket; write for a brochure.

Clothing **Murray's Toggery Shop** (62 Main St., tel. 508/228–0437) carries top-name traditional clothing and footwear for all.

The Peanut Gallery (31 Centre St., tel. 508/228–2010) has a discriminating collection of children's clothing.

Zero Main (Main St., tel. 508/228–4401; closed Jan.–Mar.) stocks stylishly classic women's clothing, shoes, and accessories.

Crafts **Artisans' Cooperative** (58 Main St., tel. 508/228–4631) sells Amish, Appalachian, and other American crafts, such as quilts, jewelry (including miniature lightship baskets), and sweaters.

Four Winds Craft Guild (6 Straight Wharf, tel. 508/228–9623) carries a large selection of antique and new scrimshaw and lightship baskets as well as ship models and duck decoys.

Gifts **Museum Shop** (Broad St., tel. 508/228–5785; closed mid-Dec.–late Apr.) has island-related books, antique whaling tools, toys, spermaceti candles, reproduction furniture, and local jellies.

Nantucket Vineyard (3 Bartlett Farm Rd., tel. 508/228–9235) is the only place on the island for buying local wine.

Seven Seas Gifts (46 Centre St., tel. 508/228–0958; closed Jan.–Mar.) is a fun shop selling paper dolls, kitchen gadgets, shells, rocks and minerals, T-shirts, beach gear, and much more.

Jewelry **The Golden Basket** (44 Main St., tel. 508/228–4344) sells miniature lightship baskets in gold or silver, some with precious stones and pearls, as well as other fine jewelry.

Sports and Outdoor Activities

Biking Scenic and well-maintained bike paths lead to the most popular areas of the island. **Nantucket Cycling Club** (tel. 508/228–2904 or 8480) holds open races in season, including a triathlon in June and a biathlon in September.

Fishing Bluefish and bass are the main catches. **Barry Thurston's Fishing Tackle** (Harbor Sq., tel. 508/228–9595) and **Bill Fisher Tackle** (New Lane, tel. 508/228–2261) rent equipment. Charters sail out of Straight Wharf every day in season. For guided four-wheel-drive trips to remote areas for surf casting, contact **Whitney Mitchell** (tel. 508/228–2331) or **Jeep Excursions** (tel. 508/228–3728).

Golf **Miacomet Golf Club** (off Somerset Rd., tel. 508/228–9764) and **Siasconset Golf Club** (Milestone Rd., tel. 508/257–6596) are public nine-hole courses.

Health and Fitness Clubs **Nantucket Health & Fitness Center** (45 Surfside Rd., tel. 508/228–3945) offers aerobics classes and rowing and other exercise machines, steamrooms and whirlpool.

Tennis **Town courts** (tel. 508/228–3028; closed Labor Day–mid-June) are at Jetties Beach. **Sea Cliff Tennis Club** (N. Beach St., tel. 508/228–0030; closed mid-Oct.–mid-May) has nine clay courts.

Water Sports **Indian Summer Sports** (Jetties Beach, tel. 508/228–9401; Steamboat Wharf, tel. 508/228–3632) and **Force 5** (Jetties Beach, tel. 508/228–5358; Main St., tel. 508/228–0700) rent all kinds of water-sports equipment as well as Sunfish, and give lessons. **The Sunken Ship** (corner of Broad and S. Water Sts., tel. 508/228–9226) offers scuba lessons and equipment rentals.

Beaches

Jetties, a short bike ride from town, is the most popular beach for families because of its calm surf, lifeguards, bathhouse, rest rooms, snack bar, and water-sports rentals.

Children's Beach, a calm north-shore beach, is an easy walk from town and good for small children. It offers a park and playground, lifeguard, food service, and restrooms.

Surfside is 3 miles from town on a bike path. It is the premier surf beach, with lifeguard, bathhouse, restroom, and snack bar.

Madaket is known for great sunsets. Reached by a 6-mile bike path, Madaket offers heavy surf, a lifeguard, and food nearby. **Siasconset Beach,** at the end of a 7-mile bike path, is an uncrowded sandy beach with surf, lifeguard, and playground.

Dining

★ **Chanticleer.** Within a rose-covered cottage is what many consider the island's finest restaurant. The owner and chef Jean-Charles Berruet has for two decades created sumptuous classic French fare using fresh island ingredients. A prix-fixe menu ($50) is offered at dinner (à la carte also available), which is served in the formal, fireplaced main dining room or in the more intimate upstairs room. The wine cellar is legendary, with hundreds of choices. *9 New St., Siasconset, tel. 508/257–6231. Reservations required well in advance. Jacket and tie required at dinner. AE, MC, V. Closed Wed.; mid-Oct.–late May. Very Expensive.*

Topper's. Far from town at the exclusive Wauwinet resort, Topper's serves new American cuisine, including such choices as sautéed lobster with citrus, wild mushrooms, and roasted peppers in a Chardonnay beurre blanc. The interior reflects the inn's casual sophistication: hand-painted floors, fine wood paneling, oil paintings. The patio overlooking the water is a pleasant place for lunch or drinks, especially at sunset. *Wauwinet Rd., tel. 508/228–8768. Reservations required. Dress: casual. AE, DC, MC, V. Closed Nov.–Mar. Expensive–Very Expensive.*

★ **Boarding House.** One of the island's finest restaurants, the Boarding House offers a changing menu of such new American dishes as swordfish with toasted pecans and a shallot-and-parsley béarnaise sauce, or the roast rack of lamb with shoestring potatoes. Appetizers are available in the bar, an airy room with marble-top tables. The dining room is intimate, with low ceilings, soft lighting, muted music, salmon-color upholstery and napkins, and white linen tablecloths. *12 Federal St., tel. 508/228–9622. Reservations required in season. Jacket advised. AE, CB, DC, MC, V. Closed mid-Jan.–mid-Feb. Expensive.*

Jared's. The formal restaurant of the Jared Coffin House is a large, elegant room, with salmon walls, pale green table linens and swag drapes, and Federal-period antique furnishings. The American fare is equally elegant; try grilled breast of duck with honey-plum glaze, or chicken breast stuffed with rock shrimp and baked in pastry. Introduced in 1990 was a menu of $25 prix-fixe meals. *29 Broad St., tel. 508/228–2400. Reservations advised. Jacket required. AE, DC, MC, V. No lunch. Breakfast only Jan.–Apr. Expensive.*

★ **American Seasons.** Chefs-proprietors Everett and Stuart Reid have created an exemplary provincial American menu with offerings such as duckling with maple-cranberry sauce and a pilaf of wild rice and pecans; grilled calf's liver with smoked bacon and applejack-onion jam; and New York sirloin with bourbon gravy and straw potatoes. The creative cuisine is not matched by the interior, which lacks intimacy despite the low ceiling, Colonial wall sconces, and hurricane globes on tables draped in white linen. *80 Centre St., tel. 508/228–7111. Reservations advised. Dress: casual. AE, MC, V. No lunch. Closed Jan.–Mar. Moderate–Expensive.*

★ **The Brotherhood of Thieves.** Long queues are a fixture outside this very old-English pub restaurant. Inside is a dark, cozy room with low ceilings and exposed brick and beams; much of the seating is at long, tightly packed tables. Dine happily on good chowder and soups, fried fish and seafood, burgers, jumbo sandwiches, and shoestring fries (the house specialty: long curls with the skins on). A convivial atmosphere prevails. *23 Broad St. No reservations. Dress: casual. No credit cards. Moderate.*

Quaker House. This storefront restaurant—two small rooms whose lace-curtained small-pane windows look out onto busy Centre Street—is one of the best bargains on the island. Prix-fixe four-course dinners feature such entrées as Bombay chicken, a curry with apple, raisins, and coconut; swordfish with béarnaise sauce; and beef and pasta dishes. The owners take pride in the quality of their ingredients: All meats are raised humanely and without chemicals and hormones. *5 Chestnut St., tel. 508/228–9156. No reservations. Dress: casual. MC, V. No lunch. Closed mid-Oct.–Memorial Day. Moderate.*

Lodging

Lodging, like dining, is an expensive proposition on Nantucket in season. In the off-season those establishments that remain open drop their prices dramatically, by as much as 50%. The **Star of the Sea AYH–Hostel** (Surfside, Nantucket 02554, tel. 508/228–0433; mid-Apr.–Oct.), a 72-bed facility in a former lifesaving station, is a 3-mile ride on a bike path from town, at Surfside Beach. No camping is allowed on Nantucket.

Summer House. Here, across from 'Sconset beach, are the rose-trellised cottages most often associated with Nantucket summers. Each one- or two-bedroom cottage is furnished in a blend of unfussy, breezy beach style and romantic English country, and has a new marble bath with Jacuzzi. Some cottages have fireplaces or kitchens. *Ocean Ave., Box 313, Siasconset 02564, tel. 508/257–9976. 8 cottages. Facilities: restaurant, outdoor pool. AE, MC, V. Closed mid-Oct.–mid-May. Rates include Continental breakfast. Very Expensive.*

★ **Wauwinet.** An exquisite location 8 miles from town, impeccable furnishings, and extensive services and amenities make this recently renovated mid-19th-century property arguably Nantucket's most luxurious accommodation. Each guest room —individually decorated in country style, with pine antiques —has a phone, air-conditioning, and color TV with VCR (tapes free from videocassette library); the most expensive have spectacular views of the sunset over the water. *Wauwinet Rd., Box 2580, 02584, tel. 508/228–0145 or 800/426–8718, fax 508/228–6712. 29 rooms, 5 cottages. Facilities: restaurant, bar, 2 clay tennis courts, Windsurfer and Sunfish rental and lessons, harbor sails, croquet, turndown service, room service, concierge, business services, jitney service. AE, DC, MC, V. Closed Dec.–Mar. Rates include Continental breakfast. Very Expensive.*

Seven Sea Street. This inn on a quiet side street in the center of town was built in 1987 in Colonial style but with modern amenities and all-new furnishings. Rooms have an almost Scandinavian look: white walls, exposed beams, highly polished wood floor with braided rug, queen pencil-post bed with fishnet canopy and quilt, rocking chair, modern bath with large stall shower, and a phone, color TV, refrigerator, and desk area. *7 Sea St., 02554, tel. 508/228–3577. 8 rooms. Facilities: Jacuzzi. AE, MC, V. Rates include Continental breakfast. Expensive–Very Expensive.*

Jared Coffin House. A complex of six buildings, the Jared Coffin is well-loved by many visitors to Nantucket. The main building—a three-story, cupola-topped brick mansion built in 1845—has a historic feel that the others, pleasant as they are, don't have. The main house's public and guest rooms are beautifully furnished with Oriental carpets, lace curtains, and period antiques (the other buildings, with reproductions); the second-floor corner rooms are the nicest, with more windows. All rooms have color TV (except in the main house) and phones. Small, inexpensive single rooms are available. *29 Broad St., 02554, tel. 508/228–2405. 58 rooms. Facilities: restaurant, tavern, outdoor café, concierge. AE, DC, MC, V. Expensive–Very Expensive.*

★ **76 Main Street.** Built in 1883 and now a bed-and-breakfast inn on a quiet part of Main Street, 76 Main carefully blends antiques and reproductions, Oriental rugs, handmade quilts, and lots of fine woods. Room No. 3, originally the dining room, has wonderful woodwork, a carved-wood armoire, and twin canopy four-posters; No. 1, considered the best room, has three large windows, a high ceiling, and a canopy bed with eyelet spread and canopy. Both are on the first floor. The motel-like annex rooms (available in season only) have low ceilings and are a bit dark but are large and good for families, with color TV and refrigerator. *76 Main St., 02554, tel. 508/228–2533. 18 rooms. Facilities: central refrigerator. No smoking. AE, MC, V. Rates include Continental breakfast. Moderate–Expensive.*

Wade Cottages. On a bluff overlooking the ocean, this complex of guest rooms, apartments, and cottages in 'Sconset couldn't be better located for beach lovers. The buildings—most from the 1800s and furnished in casual, somewhat worn beach style —are arranged around a central lawn with a great ocean view; a newer cottage is nearer the water, at beach level. Most inn rooms and cottages have sea views. Inn rooms include Continental breakfast. *Shell St., Siasconset 02564, tel. 508/257–6308 or 6383; 212/989–6423 off-season. 8 rooms, 3 with bath; 5 apartments; 3 cottages. Facilities: ping-pong, badminton, central refrigerator, laundry, beach. No credit cards. Closed mid-Oct.– late May. Moderate–Expensive.*

★ **Hawthorn House.** An 1850 house in the center of town, the Hawthorn offers small, lovely rooms. The owners-innkeepers have created a homey atmosphere with antiques and pretty wallpapers, and art, hooked rugs, and stained glass made by talented family members. A dark but conveniently located cottage sleeps two. *2 Chestnut St., 02554, tel. 508/228–1468. 7 rooms, 5 with bath; 1 cottage. Facilities: morning coffee, central TV, refrigerators. MC, V. Moderate.*

The Arts

Concerts   **Nantucket Chamber Music Center** (Coffin School, Winter St., tel. 508/228–3352) offers year-round choral and instrumental concerts as well as instruction.

In July and August the **Nantucket Musical Arts Society** (tel. 508/228–3735) offers Tuesday-evening concerts featuring internationally acclaimed musicians at the First Congregational Church (62 Centre St.), and **Noonday Concerts** are held at the Unitarian Church (11 Orange St., tel. 508/228–0738 or 5466) Thursdays at noon on an 1831 Goodrich organ.

Theater   The much-praised **Actors Theatre of Nantucket** (Folger Hotel, 89 Easton St., tel. 508/228–6325) presents five plays each season (May–Oct.), plus a guest-artist series and children's matinees.

Theatre Workshop of Nantucket (Little Theatre, Bennett Hall, 62 Centre St., tel. 508/228–4305), a community theater, offers year-round performances.

Nightlife

Piano Lounges   **The Hearth** (5 Beach St., tel. 508/228–1500), the Harbor House hotel's restaurant, has dancing to Top 40 tunes by a piano-and-vocals duo.

The Regatta at the White Elephant (Easton St., tel. 508/228–2500) has the most formal hotel restaurant lounge—proper dress required—with a pianist playing show tunes.

Rock   The island's two rock clubs, open year-round, are **The Box** (6 Daves St., tel. 508/228–9717) and **The Muse** (44 Atlantic Ave., tel. 508/228–6873 or 8801). All ages dance to rock, reggae, and other music, live or recorded, or enjoy the comedy nights.

The Coast:
The North Shore

The slice of Atlantic coast known as the North Shore extends from Boston's well-to-do northern suburbs, past grimy docklands to the picturesque Cape Ann region, and beyond the Cape to Newburyport, just south of the New Hampshire border. It takes in historic Salem, which thrives on a history of witches, millionaires, and maritime trade; quaint little Rockport, crammed with crafts shops and artists' studios; Gloucester, the oldest seaport in America; and Newburyport with its red-brick center and rows of clapboard Federal mansions. Bright and busy in the short summer season, the North Shore is a tranquil area between November and June, when the holiday-making facilities have closed down.

Important Addresses and Numbers

Visitor   The umbrella organization for the whole region is the **North Of**
Information   **Boston Visitors and Convention Bureau** (Box 3031, Peabody, 01961, tel. 508/532–1449). The following cover more specific areas:

Cape Ann Chamber of Commerce (33 Commercial St., Gloucester 01930, tel. 508/283–1601).

Essex North Chamber of Commerce (29 State St., Newburyport 01950, tel. 508/462–6680).

Rockport Chamber of Commerce Visitor's Booth (Upper Main St., Rockport 01966, tel. 508/546–6575).

Salem Chamber of Commerce and Visitor Information (32 Derby Sq., Salem 01970, tel. 508/744–0004).

Emergencies   **Beverly Hospital** (Herrick St., Beverly, tel. 508/922–3000).

Getting Around the North Shore

By Car   The primary link between Boston and the North Shore is Route 128, which follows the line of the coast just inland, as far north as Gloucester. To reach Newburyport directly from Boston, take I–95. The more scenic coastal road (it doesn't become scenic until you're north of Lynn) is Route 1A, which leaves Boston via the Callahan Tunnel. Beyond Beverly Route 1A goes inland, and the new coastal route connecting Beverly, Gloucester, and Rockport is Route 127.

By Bus   Buses between Boston and the North Shore are less frequent than the trains, but **McGregor Smith** Bus Lines (tel. 800/874–3377) operates an express commuter service between Boston and Newburyport, and **Hudson Bus Lines** (tel. 617/395–8083) provides a limited North Shore link.

On the Cape the **Cape Ann Transportation Authority** (CATA) (tel. 508/283–7916) covers the Gloucester/Rockport region and will pick up and drop off passengers anywhere on designated routes.

By Train Massachusetts Bay Transportation Authority (MBTA) trains leave North Station, Boston, for Salem, Beverly, Gloucester, Rockport, and Ipswich. Call 617/227–5070 for schedules.

By Boat A boat leaves Boston daily for Gloucester between May 30 and Labor Day, at 10 AM. The journey lasts three hours, and fares are $20 for adults, and $12 for children under 12. For information, call **A.C. Cruise Lines** (28 Northern Ave. Bridge, Pier 1, Boston, tel. 617/426–8419 or 800/422–8419).

Guided Tours

The **Gray Line** (275 Tremont St., Boston, 02116, tel. 617/426–8805) offers a 4½-hour tour of Salem, including Marblehead, and an 8-hour seacoast tour that takes in Newburyport; Portsmouth, New Hampshire; and York, Maine. All tours begin in Boston.

Special-Interest The most popular special-interest tours on the North Shore are
Tours whale-watching excursions. Four breeds of whale feed in the
Whale-Watching area between May and October, and whales are so thick in the sea that you're practically guaranteed to see at least half a dozen—on "good" days you may see 40 or more. Some of the more reputable whale watch operations include **Cape Ann Whale Watch** (12 Clarendon St., Gloucester, tel. 508/283–5110), **Captain Bill's Whale Watch** (9 Traverse St., Gloucester, tel. 508/283–6995), **New England Whale Watch** (54 Merrimac St., Newburyport, tel. 508/465–9885 or 800/848–1111), and **Yankee Fleet/Gloucester Whale Watch** (75 Essex Ave., Gloucester, tel. 508/283–0313).

Exploring the North Shore

Numbers in the margin correspond with the numbered points of interest on the North Shore map.

Not exactly on the North Shore but north of Boston (take
❶ Route 1) and just inland from Lynn, **Saugus** is worth a visit because of the **Saugus Iron Works** National Historic Site. The foundry on the Saugus River was the first in America when it was begun in 1646 by John Winthrop, son of the governor of Massachusetts. Reconstruction of the site began in the 1950s, and today the restored ironworks has all the appearance of a country village, with stone buildings, waterwheels, and the nearby river. The furnace and the rolling and slitting mills operate by water power, and blacksmiths hammer nails in the forge fires. *224 Central St., tel. 617/233–0500. Admission free. Open Apr. 1–Nov. 1, daily 9–5; Nov. 1–Apr. 1, daily 9–4. Closed Thanksgiving, Christmas, New Year's Day.*

Heading north, branch off Route 1A onto scenic Route 129 and
❷ on to **Marblehead.** Founded by fishermen from Cornwall in 1629, the town is reminiscent of Cornish fishing villages. Now it's also one of the major yachting centers on the East Coast, and Marblehead's Race Week, usually the last week of July, attracts participants from all over the eastern seaboard.

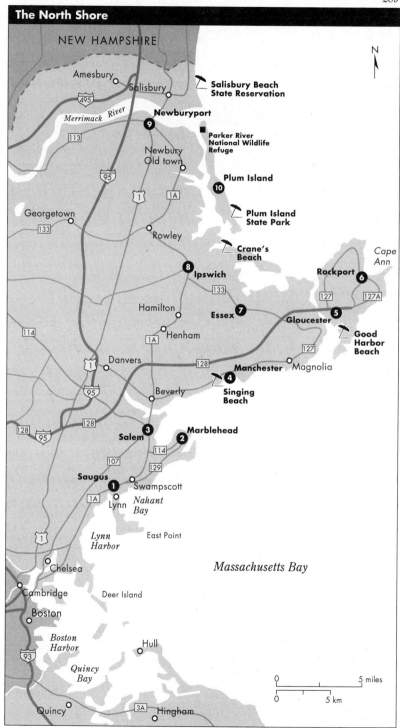

The North Shore

NEW HAMPSHIRE

N

Amesbury

Salisbury

Salisbury Beach State Reservation

Merrimack River

Newburyport 9

113

Newbury Old town

Parker River National Wildlife Refuge

95

1

1A

Plum Island 10

Plum Island State Park

Georgetown

133

Rowley

Crane's Beach

8 **Ipswich**

Cape Ann

Rockport 6

133

127

127A

Hamilton

Essex 7

5

Gloucester

114

1A

Henham

Good Harbor Beach

Danvers

128

Manchester

Magnolia

95

128

Beverly

4

127

Singing Beach

128

95

128

3 **Salem**

2 **Marblehead**

107

114

129

Saugus

1 Swampscott

1A

Lynn

Nahant Bay

Lynn Harbor

East Point

Massachusetts Bay

Chelsea

Cambridge

Deer Island

Boston

93

Boston Harbor

Hull

Quincy Bay

0 — 5 miles

0 — 5 km

Quincy

3A

Hingham

Time Out To experience the fisherman's Marblehead, visit the **Driftwood** (tel. 617/631–1145), a simple, red-clapboard restaurant by the harbor on Front Street. Fishnets hang from the ceiling and excellent, inexpensive breakfasts and lunches are served from 5:30 AM until 2 PM.

The patriotic work of art *The Spirit of '76,* painted by A. M. Willard to celebrate the nation's centenary in 1876, hangs in Marblehead's redbrick town hall. *Washington St., tel. 617/631–0528. Admission free. Open weekday business hours; Memorial Day–Nov., Sat. 9–6, Sun. 11–6.*

Follow Route 114 out of Marblehead, turn right onto Route 1A, and drive the short distance to **Salem,** the most compelling town on the North Shore. Park in the central car park at Riley Plaza by the visitor information booth, and begin your exploration by following the Heritage Trail (painted on the sidewalk) around the town. If you prefer not to walk, the **Sightseeing Trolley and Shuttle Service** leaves from the same booth on narrated tours of the city, every hour from 10–4, April through November.

Salem unabashedly calls itself "Witch City." Witches astride broomsticks enhance the police cars; witchcraft shops, a local witch, and more recall the city's infamous connection with the witchcraft trials of 1692. Sites commemorating the witch hysteria, which resulted in the hangings of 19 innocent people, are numerous. The **Salem Witch Museum** offers a multisensory presentation re-creating the events with 13 stage sets and life-size models. *Washington Square North, tel. 508/744–1692. Admission: $3.50 adults, $2 children 6–14, $3 senior citizens. Open July–Aug. daily 10–7, Sept.–June daily 10–5. Closed Thanksgiving, Christmas, New Year's Day.*

A more sensational version of the same events is presented at the **Witch Dungeon Museum** (16 Lynde St., tel. 508/744–9812). After witnessing the live re-creation of the trials, you can visit the "witches and warlocks" in the dungeon below, daily May through November.

No witch ever lived at **Witch House,** but more than 200 accused witches were questioned there. The decor is authentic late-17th century, reflecting the era when the trials were held. *310½ Essex St., tel. 508/744–0180. Admission: $2.50. Open daily mid-Mar.–June and Labor Day–Dec. 1, 10–4:30; July–Aug. 10–6.*

Salem went on to become a major seaport, with a thriving overseas trade. **Salem Maritime,** a National Historic Site operated by the National Trust, is situated right beside Derby Wharf, opposite the Customs House. Tours take in the Custom's House, Government Warehouse, and historic shipowners' homes. *174 Derby Rd., tel. 508/744–4323. Admission free. Open daily 8:30–5. Closed Thanksgiving, Christmas, New Year's Day.*

The oldest continuously operating museum in America, the **Peabody Museum** houses a fine collection of exotic items brought back by Salem's merchant ships. *East India Sq., tel. 508/745–1876. Admission: $4 adults, $1.50 children 6–16, $3 senior citizens and students. Open Mon.–Sat. 10–5 (Thurs. to*

9), Sun. noon–5. Closed Thanksgiving, Christmas, New Year's Day.

Many historic mansions that belonged to shipowners and other rich merchants are open to the public, several of them overseen by the **Essex Institute Museum Neighborhood,** headquartered in a group of buildings on Essex Street. Additional exhibits in five galleries explain three centuries of Essex County history and culture. *132 Essex St., tel. 508/744–3390. Admission: $5 adults, $4 senior citizens, $2.50 children 6–16. Open June–Oct., Mon.–Sat. 9–5, Sun. and holidays 1–5; Nov.–May, Tues.–Sat. 9–5, Sun. and holidays 1–5. Closed Thanksgiving, Christmas, New Year's Day.*

The **House of the Seven Gables,** immortalized by Nathaniel Hawthorne in his book of the same name, should not be missed. Interesting points on the tour are period furnishings, a secret staircase discovered during 1886 renovations, and the garret with its model of the house. *54 Turner St., tel. 508/744–0991. Admission: $5 adults, $2.50 children 6–16. Open daily July–Labor Day, 9:30–5:30; Labor Day–June, 10–4:30. Closed Thanksgiving, Christmas, New Year's Day.*

Just south of Salem on Route 1A, costumed "interpreters" at the **Pioneer Village and Forest River Park** re-create Salem of the 1630s, when it was the state capital. Replicas of thatched cottages, dugout homes, and wigwams have been constructed at the site. *Jct. Rtes. 1A and 129, tel. 508/745–0525. Admission: $3 adults, $2 senior citizens and children under 12. Open June–Sept., daily 10–5.*

❹ North of Salem, pass through Beverly on Route 127 and on to the small seaside town of **Manchester,** with its excellent Singing Beach, so-called because of the noise of the wind against the sand. Head down Hesperus Avenue in the village of Magnolia to see "Norman's Woe Rock," made famous by Longfellow in his poem *The Wreck of the Hesperus.*

The rock can also be viewed from **Hammond Castle Museum,** a stone building inspired by the castles of the Middle Ages and built in 1926 by the inventor John Hays Hammond Jr. It contains medieval furnishings and paintings, and the Great Hall houses an impressive organ with 8,600 pipes and 126 stops. *80 Hesperus Ave., tel. 508/283–2080. Admission: $3.50. Open daily 9–5. Closed Thanksgiving, Christmas, New Year's Day.*

❺ As the road continues along the coast, you enter **Gloucester** along a fine seaside promenade. The first sight you'll see is the famous statue of a man at a ship's wheel, eyes on the horizon, dedicated to those "who go down to the sea in ships." Gloucester, the oldest seaport in the nation, is still a major fishing port. Another personality of the town is illustrated by **Rocky Neck,** the oldest working artists' colony in America.

❻ **Rockport,** at the very tip of Cape Ann, is reached via the scenic coastal Route 127A, or more quickly by cutting inland on Route 127. Originally a fishing port that developed into an artists' colony in the 1920s, it's a cultured if touristy town that holds firmly to its refined character. Along **Bearskin Neck,** a promontory in the town center, is a concentration of art galleries, crafts stores, and cafés. Walk out to the end for an excellent view of the Atlantic and the red lobster shack affectionately known as Motif #1 because of its favor as a subject for amateur artists.

A curious site to visit is **Paper House,** its walls and furnishings constructed almost entirely of rolled-up newspapers. *Pigeon Hill, tel. 508/546-2629. Admission: $1 adults, 50¢ children. Open July 4–Labor Day, daily 10–5, and by appointment.*

❼ Head west out of Cape Ann on Route 128 and then turn north on Route 133 for the village of **Essex.** Surrounded by salt marshes, the town has more than 15 seafood restaurants. The **Essex Shipbuilding Museum** displays exhibits from the 19th century, when the town was an important shipbuilding center. *Rte. 133, tel. 508/768-7541. Admission: $2. Open Thurs.–Sun. 2–5.*

Time Out   **Woodman's of Essex** (Rte. 133, tel. 508/768-6451) claims to have fried the first clams in town back in 1916. Today, this large wooden shack with unpretentious booths is *the* place for "seafood in the rough," and the menu includes lobster, a raw bar, clam chowder, and, of course, fried clams.

❽ Four miles north of Essex, **Ipswich** is a small historic town with a few mills beside the river. Its best feature is nearby **Crane's Beach** (off Argilla Rd.), part of the privately owned Crane Reservation, where upkeep costs mean a hefty $8 parking fee in summer. The white-sand beach is more than 5 miles long; the refuge covers 735 acres.

❾ Route 1A continues north and eventually becomes the main street through historic **Newburyport,** lined with some of the finest Federal mansions in New England. The granite **Customs House** on the waterfront has been restored, and houses the **Maritime Museum** with shipbuilding and Coast Guard exhibits. *25 Water St., tel. 508/462-8681. Admission: $2 adults, $1 children 6–16, $1.50 senior citizens. Open Apr.–Dec., Mon.–Sat. 10–4; Jan.–Mar., weekdays 10–4.*

❿ A causeway connects Newburyport with **Plum Island,** which has a long, broad, sandy beach and a wildlife refuge at one end. The beaches are open to swimmers and anglers; self-guided trails provide excellent bird-watching opportunities. *Plum Island, tel. 508/462-4481. Admission free. Open daily dawn–dusk.*

What to See and Do with Children

House of the Seven Gables, Salem

Pioneer Village and Forest River Park, Salem

Plum Island, Newburyport

Salem Willows Park (at the eastern end of Derby St., Salem) has picnic grounds, beaches, food stands, amusements, games, boat rentals, and fishing bait.

Salem Witch Museum, Salem

Salisbury Beach, Salisbury, has a number of honky-tonk family amusement parks, water slides, food stalls, and amusement arcades.

Off the Beaten Track

Although Salem is world-famous as the witch hunt city, **Danvers** (Old Salem) is virtually unknown. Yet here are the real relics of the witchcraft episode. The house where the black slave Tituba told stories to two impressionable girls and began the whole business has been demolished, but the foundations were excavated in 1970, and can be viewed—they're located behind 67 Center Street.

The **Rebecca Nurse Homestead** was the home of aged, pious Rebecca, a regular churchgoer whose accusation caused shock waves, whose trial was a mockery (she was pronounced innocent, but the jury was urged to change its verdict), and who was hanged as a witch in 1692. Her family took her body afterward and buried her in secret on the grounds of this house. It has period furnishings and is gradually being developed as a model 18th-century farm. *149 Pine St., tel. 508/774–8799. Admission: $1.50 adults, 75¢ children under 16. Open June 15–Oct. 15, Tues.–Sat. 1–4:30, Sun. 2–4:30, and by appointment.*

Shopping

Antiques
The greatest concentration of antiques stores on the North Shore is around **Essex,** but there are plenty sprinkled throughout **Salem** and **Cape Ann** as well. Members of the North Shore Antique Dealers Association guarantee the authenticity of their merchandise, and a leaflet listing their shops can be obtained from participating stores. Try the **Pickering Wharf Antique Gallery** in Salem, where five shops house 50 dealers.

Art Galleries
As an artist's colony, **Rockport** has a tremendous concentration of artists' studios and galleries selling work by local painters. Most are located on Main Street near the harbor, and on Bearskin Neck. The Rocky Neck Arts Colony east of **Gloucester** is another good place to browse and buy.

Specialty Stores
Salem is the center for a number of offbeat shops that have a distinct relationship to the city's witchcraft history. **Pyramid Books** (214 Derby St., tel. 508/745–7171) stocks New Age books and music, tarot decks, incense, quartz crystals, and healing stones, as well as "power wands" and "metaphysical jewelry." **Gornigo** on Pickering Wharf (tel. 508/745–9552), complete with a black shop cat, sells a marvelous array of scented herbs, herbal teas, potion perfumes, runes, spirit lamps, and crystals. Crystals are a specialty at **The Crystal Chamber** (1 Hawthorne Blvd., tel. 508/745–9400).

Sports and Outdoor Activities

Boating
Marblehead is the pleasure-sailing capital of the North Shore, but here and elsewhere it's not easy to find mooring space for your private yacht; many towns have waiting lists of several years. Town harbormasters will be able to inform you of nightly fees at public docks, when space is available.

Canoeing is less complicated; the best areas are on the Ipswich and Parker rivers. For saltwater canoeing and kayaking, the waters of the Essex River Estuary are generally calm and protected. The **Harold Parker State Forest** in North Andover and the **Willowdale State Forest** in Ipswich also permit canoeing.

Camping Campsites are scarcer in this area than in other parts of Massachusetts, but there's the **Cape Ann Campsite** (80 Atlantic St., West Gloucester, tel. 508/283–8683) open May through October, and a couple of places near Salisbury: the **Black Bear Campground** (116 Main St., Salisbury, tel. 508/462–3183) with many facilities, and the **Rusnik Campground** (Box 5441, Newburyport, tel. 508/462–9551), both open May 15 through October 1. Just two of the region's state parks permit camping —**Harold Parker State Forest** and the **Salisbury Beach State Reservation** (*see* National and State Parks, below).

Fishing Deep-sea fishing excursions are offered at various North Shore ports. In Gloucester try **Captain Bill's Deep Sea Fishing** (9 Traverse St., tel. 508/283–6995), and in Newburyport try **Captain's Fishing Parties** (Plum Island Point, tel. 508/462–3141).

Surf casting is even more popular—bluefish, pollock, and striped bass can be taken from the ocean shores of Plum Island; permits to remain on the beach after dark are obtainable free of charge by anyone entering the refuge with fishing equipment in the daylight. You don't need a permit to fish from the public beach at Plum Island, and the best spot to choose is around the mouth of the Merrimac River.

For freshwater fishing, the Parker and Ipswich rivers are both stocked with trout each spring, and many state parks permit fishing.

Golf The **Sun N' Air** driving range in Danvers (Conant St., tel. 508/774–8180) is open seven days a week. These courses also permit guests: **Salem Country Club** (Peabody, tel. 508/532–2540), **Middleton Golf Course** (Rte. 114, Middleton, tel. 508/774–4075), **Rowley Country Club** (Dodge Rd., Rowley, tel. 508/948–2731).

Spectator Sports

The one spectator sport of note on the North Shore is polo. The **Myopia Hunt Club** (Polo Promotions, Box 2103, South Hamilton 01928, tel. 508/468–4433) stages polo matches on Sundays between late May and October at its grounds along Route 1A in Hamilton.

Beaches

Here are some of the best beaches on the North Shore: **Crane's Beach** (Ipswich), **Parker River Refuge** (Newbury), **Plum Island** (Newburyport), **Salisbury State Reservation** (Salisbury), **Singing Beach** (Manchester), **Wingaersheek Beach** and **Good Harbor Beach** (Gloucester).

National and State Parks

Of the numerous parks in the area, the following have particularly varied facilities: **Halibut Point State Park** (Rte. 127 to Gott Ave., Rockport, tel. 508/546–2997), the 3,000-acre **Harold Parker State Forest** (Rte. 114, North Andover, tel. 508/686–3391), **Plum Island State Reservation** (off Rte. 1A, Newburyport, tel. 508/462–4481), **Salisbury Beach State Reservation** (Rte. 1A, Salisbury, tel. 508/462–4481), and the **Willowdale State Forest** (Linebrook Rd., Ipswich, tel. 508/887–5931).

Dining and Lodging

Danvers Lodging **King's Grant Inn.** This modern building has tastefully appointed guest rooms with some reproduction antiques, and suites with whirlpool baths. Live entertainment is provided in the British Colony lounge, and the dining room re-creates 19th-century England. There's also an atrium with fish in the "brook," parrots in the air, and paths among the palms. *Box 274 (Rte. 128, exit 21N), 01923, tel. 508/774–6800. 125 rooms, 2 suites. Facilities: restaurant, lounge, indoor pool, Jacuzzi. AE, D, DC, MC, V. Expensive.*

Essex Dining **Dexter's Hearthside.** This 250-year-old converted farmhouse is the epitome of coziness. Four small dining rooms have open fireplaces and exposed beams: The first is low-ceilinged with stencils on the walls; the others have cathedral ceilings with rough-paneled walls and small windows. The newest eating area is in the loft. Entrées include baked stuffed haddock, seafood casserole, sirloin steak, lobster, and chicken. *Rte. 133, tel. 508/768–6002 or 6003. Dress: casual. AE, MC, V. Closed lunch Sun. Moderate.*

Tom Shea's. Picture windows in this single-story, cedar-shingled restaurant overlook the salt marsh. Inside, walls are white, and the room has mismatched wooden furniture, with many hanging plants. Seafood is the main fare, including shrimp in coconut beer batter, scallop-stuffed sole, Boston scrod, lobster, and, of course, the fried clams for which Essex is famous. *122 Main St., Rte. 133, tel. 508/768–6931. Dress: casual. AE, DC, MC, V. Closed lunch weekdays. Moderate.*

Gloucester Dining **White Rainbow.** The dining room in this excellent restaurant is
★   in the basement of a west-end store downtown, and candlelight gives a romantic atmosphere. Specialties include Maui onion soup, grilled beef with a Zinfandel wine sauce, lobster *estancia* (lobster sautéed with tomatoes, artichoke hearts, olives, scallions, wine, and herb butter), and fresh fish of the day. *65 Main St., tel. 508/281–0017. Dress: casual. AE, CB, DC, MC, V. Closed lunch; Mon. Expensive.*

★ **The Rhumb Line.** Despite its unimpressive location, this restaurant is worth the three-minute drive from the town center. The skillful decoration of the upstairs dining room gives customers the impression of sitting on a ship's deck, with the wheel and compass at one end, rigging overhead, captain's chairs at the tables, and seascapes on the walls. The selections include seafood casserole of shrimp, crabmeat, and scallops in garlic-lemon butter and white wine; roast duckling glazed with Grand Marnier, honey, and marmalade sauce; and charbroiled steaks. *Railroad Ave., tel. 508/283–9732. Dress: casual. AE, MC, V. Moderate–Expensive.*

Captain Courageous. The most recent owner of this ideally situated restaurant has created a seafaring atmosphere with nets, rigging, and paintings of old ships. In summer dining is on the outside deck above the water. Seafood is the main fare, and daily specials include sautéed scallops, lobster, and scrod. *25 Rogers St., tel. 508/283–0007. Reservations advised. Dress: casual. AE, D, MC, V. Moderate.*

Gloucester House. The large white-clapboard building is located on the historic Seven Seas Wharf, which has been in continuous use for more than 350 years. Inside it's simply furnished with imitation leather booth seating and wood-paneled walls decorated with fishing boat paraphernalia. Lobster is the specialty; the menu also offers fisherman's stew, seafood cakes, shrimp casserole, and chowders. *Seven Seas Wharf, off Rte. 127, tel. 508/283–1812. Dress: casual. CB, D, DC, MC, V. Moderate.*

Gloucester Lodging

Best Western Twin Light Manor. This is not your characteristic chain hotel—it was a manor first, a Best Western second. The English Tudor mansion was built in 1905 as a private home, complete with elevator, children's playhouse, and seven-car garage equipped with a turntable! Newer buildings nearby offer different styles of accommodations, and the complex is set on 7 acres of ground, overlooking the ocean. The most interesting guest rooms are those in the manor itself; some are enormous and have working fireplaces. Golf is free on the local course, and the hotel is affiliated with a Gloucester health club. *Atlantic Rd., 01930, tel. 508/283–7500 or 800/528–1234. 63 rooms. Facilities: dining room, golf, health club, 2 outdoor pools, game room, bicycles, badminton, volleyball, croquet, shuffleboard, baby-sitters, gardens. AE, CB, D, DC, MC, V. Closed Dec.–early Feb. Very Expensive.*

Vista Motel. The name describes it well, because every room in this excellently situated motel overlooks the sea and Good Harbor Beach, just a few minutes' walk away. The rooms, perched atop a small, steep hill, vary in quality depending on price, but all are basically well-furnished and spacious. Some have decks, and some have refrigerators. *22 Thatcher Rd., 01930, tel. 508/281–3410. 40 rooms. Facilities: outdoor pool. AE, MC, V. Expensive.*

Back Shore Motor Lodge. This lodge in East Gloucester overlooks the ocean from a rocky headland. All guest rooms have sea views, and some have sliding doors onto decks at the front of the building. Furnishings are good-quality motor-lodge style, with some reproductions, and the color scheme is sea green. Breakfast, lunch, and dinner are served in summer. *85 Atlantic Rd., 01930, tel. 508/283–1198. 23 rooms. Facilities: dining room, outdoor pool. No credit cards. Moderate–Expensive.*

Marblehead Dining

The Landing. Right on the Marblehead harbor and still in the historic district, this pleasant, small restaurant offers outdoor dining on a balcony over the sea. Inside are wooden chairs and tables, with lots of hanging plants. The chef prepares lobster, swordfish provençale, Oriental red snapper in soy-ginger-lime marinade, Atlantic sole florentine, Ipswich clams, and seafood kabob. A limited choice of steak and chicken are also available. *Clark's Landing off Front St., tel. 617/631–6268. Dress: casual. AE, D, DC, MC, V. Expensive.*

Marblehead Lodging ★

Harbor Light Inn. This is the best place to stay in Marblehead and competes with the Clark Currier Inn in Newburyport as one of the most comfortable and authentic inns on the North Shore. Special features include some in-room Jacuzzis, skylights, rooftop decks, and spacious, modern bathrooms; traditional touches are found in the four-poster and canopy beds, carved arched doorways, sliding (original) Indian shutters, wide-board floors, and antique mahogany furnishings. A generous Continental breakfast is served daily in the first-floor guest parlor with its wingback chairs and fireplace. *58 Washington St., tel. 617/631–2186. 12 rooms, 1 suite. Facilities:*

lounge. No pets. AE, MC, V. Rates include Continental breakfast. Expensive.

10 Mugford St. This large bed-and-breakfast in the historic old town is just one block from the harbor. Rooms of varying sizes are furnished with antiques and four-posters, and suites with private porches and a yard are available in a recently renovated house across the street. *10 Mugford St., 01945, tel. 617/639–5642. 4 rooms share 3 baths, 5 suites with bath. Facilities: dining room, garden. No pets. MC, V. Rates include Continental breakfast. Moderate–Expensive.*

Newburyport Dining ★ **Scandia.** The restaurant is well known locally for its fine cuisine, and house specialties are veal and lobster sauté, and seafood linguine. The dining room is small and narrow, and dimly lighted with candles on the tables and "candle" chandeliers. *25 State St., tel. 508/462–6271. Reservations advised. Dress: casual. CB, D, DC, MC, V. Expensive.*

The Garrison. The dining room at this four-story redbrick inn is formal, with a big brick fireplace and Chinese prints on the walls. Specialties include sirloin and baked haddock, chicken tarragon in sweet cream, and veal piccata in vermouth with butter and lemon. The Pub downstairs serves lighter meals. *Brown Square, tel. 508/465–0910. Dress: casual. AE, CB, DC, MC, V. Moderate.*

East End Seafood Restaurant. For a true dining "in the rough" experience, visit this restaurant just south of Newburyport in the village of Rowley. The exterior is somewhat shabby, but inside, the shedlike building is pleasantly airy, with wood paneling, cathedral ceilings, and rustic beams. Dining is at wooden picnic tables, and the fare is deep-fried seafood. Note that the place closes around 8 PM. *Corner Rte. 1A and Railroad Ave., Rowley, tel. 508/948–7227. No reservations. Dress: casual. No credit cards. Closed Mon. Nov.–April. Inexpensive.*

Newburyport Lodging **Garrison Inn.** This four-story Georgian redbrick building is set back from the main road on a small square. Inside, the atmosphere is impersonal. An elegant lounge and a formal dining room are furnished with smart reproductions; the basement tavern is more casual, with exposed brick arches and wood stoves in open fireplaces. Guest rooms vary in size; all have handsome replicas. The best rooms are definitely the top-floor suites, set on two levels: Spiral or Colonial staircases lead up from the sitting room to the sleeping area above. Suites have working fireplaces. *11 Brown Sq., 01950, tel. 508/465–0910. 24 rooms, 6 suites. Facilities: dining room, lounge, tavern, room service. No pets. AE, CB, DC, MC, V. Expensive.*

★ **Clark Currier Inn.** Opened in 1989, this is one of the newest inns in town, and perhaps the best. The innkeepers have renovated this 1803 Federal mansion with care, taste, imagination, and enthusiasm. Guest rooms are spacious and furnished with antiques: Some have pencil four-posters, one has a reproduction sea captain's bed complete with drawers below, and another contains a glorious sleigh bed dating from the late-19th century. Rooms also have fireplaces, but they are not useable. There's a Federalist "good morning" staircase (so-called because two small staircases join at the head of a large one, permitting family members to greet each other on their way down to breakfast). *45 Green St., 01950, tel. 508/465–8363. 8 rooms. Facilities: TV lounge. AE, MC, V. Moderate.*

Rockport Dining **The Hungry Wolf.** This inconspicuous restaurant outside the
★ town center has been receiving rave reviews ever since the
owners (Charlie and Laura Wolf) moved here from Gloucester's
Rocky Neck in 1988. The small, rather cutesy dining room has
no views—the windows are high up on the clapboard walls—
and some may wonder why the "candles" on the tables are electric. But few will question the quality of the food, which is first
class. Specialties include the French onion soup gratinée, and
the scrod florentine. Steak, chops, and chicken are also available, and meals come with large salads topped by homemade
dressing. *43 South St., tel. 508/546-2100. Reservations advised. Dress: casual. No credit cards. BYOB. Closed lunch;
Sun.; Mon. Oct.–Apr. Moderate.*

My Place by the Sea. By the sea it is—this tiny restaurant is
perched at the very end of Bearskin Neck. Inside, the small
dining area has white wicker chairs and rustic beams. The restaurant serves mainly seafood, including baked scrod,
swordfish steak, seafood fettuccine, and sandwiches. *Bearskin
Neck, tel. 508/546-9667. Dress: casual. AE, DC, MC, V.
BYOB. Closed Wed., Oct. 31–May 14. Moderate.*

Rockport Lodging **Yankee Clipper Inn.** The imposing Georgian mansion that forms
★ the main part of this impressive, perfectly located inn sits
surrounded by gardens on a rocky point jutting into the sea. It
was built as a private home in the 1930s, but has been managed
as an inn by one family for more than 40 years. Guest rooms
vary in size, but most are spacious. Furnished with antiques,
they contain four-posters or canopy beds, and all but one has an
ocean view. In the Quarterdeck, a newer building across the
lawn, all rooms have fabulous sea views; the decor here is more
modern, and rooms are again spacious with big picture windows. The Bullfinch House across the street is an 1840 Greek
Revival house, appointed with tasteful antique furnishings,
but with less of a view. *96 Granite St., 01966, tel. 508/546-3407.
27 rooms, 6 suites. Facilities: restaurant, lounge, outdoor
pool, gardens. Rates include full breakfast. No pets. AE, D,
MC, V. Very Expensive.*

Seacrest Manor. The distinctive inn, surrounded by large gardens, sits on top of a hill overlooking the sea. Two elegant
sitting rooms with floral-print wallpaper have antiques and
leather chairs. The hall and staircase are hung with paintings
—some of which depict the inn—by local artists. Guest rooms
vary in size and character: In the new wing they have more
modern furnishings; upstairs, two have large private decks
with sea views. Special touches are everywhere: complimentary morning newspapers, shoe shining, custom soap and
shampoos, a nightly turndown service, and mints on the pillow
accompanied by a Shakespearean motto. *131 Marmion Way,
01966, tel. 508/546-2211. 8 rooms, 2 with shared bath. Facilities: dining room, 2 lounges, gardens. No pets. Rates include
full breakfast. No credit cards. 2-night minimum stay weekends. Closed mid-Dec.–mid-Feb. Expensive.*

Seaward Inn. This cedar-shingled inn is situated on a quiet
promontory less than a mile south of Rockport, right across a
narrow lane from the sea. Rooms in the inn have Colonial furnishings; those at the front with an ocean view are the best.
Clothespins are used as napkin holders in the dining room, and
guests write their name on the peg—when they return to the
inn at a later date, their clothespin will be waiting for them on a
string alongside thousands of others. Cottages with wood pan-

eling and working fireplaces are available. *62 Marmion Way, 01966, tel. 508/546–3471. 38 rooms, 10 suites, 7 cottages. Facilities: 3 dining rooms, lounge, outdoor pool, gardens, putting green, bicycles, playground. No pets. No credit cards. Expensive.*

Bearskin Neck Motor Lodge. Set almost at the end of Bearskin Neck, the guest-room balconies here overhang the water. From the windows all you see is sea, and at night you can hear it lapping—or thundering—against the rocks below. Rooms are simply appointed with white and wooden furniture and paneled walls. The exterior is gray cedar shingles, and a large deck over the sea at one end of the building can also be used by guests. *Bearskin Neck, 01966, tel. 508/546–6677. 8 rooms. No pets. No credit cards. Closed Dec. 30–Mar. 30. Moderate–Expensive.*

Seven South Street. The white clapboard house on the hill dates back to 1750. It operates as a cozy bed-and-breakfast inn, and each curiously shaped, prettily decorated guest room has a distinct character. All rooms are cheerful, if on the small side: Samplers hang on the walls, some have brass beds or four-posters, and some beds have quilts. Breakfast is served in the dining room with its heavy beams, open fireplace, pewter chandeliers, and wood paneling. It's just a five-minute walk across the property to the beach. *7 South St., 01966, tel. 508/546–6708. 6 rooms, (3 with shared bath), 1 suite, 1 cottage. Facilities: dining room, lounge, outdoor pool, central refrigerator, gardens. No pets. No credit cards. Rates include Continental breakfast. Closed weekdays Nov. 1–Mar. 31. Moderate.*

Salem Dining **Nathaniel's.** This formal restaurant at the Hawthorne Hotel on Salem Common is hung with chandeliers, and diners are soothed by live music from the grand piano in one corner. The menu includes lobster, swordfish in mustard cream, prime rib, and poached sole on spinach with champagne cream sauce. *On-the-Common, tel. 508/744–4080. Dress: casual. AE, CB, D, DC, MC, V. Expensive.*

Chase House. This restaurant is extremely busy in summer, ideally located as it is on Pickering Wharf, with outside dining overlooking the harbor. A giant swordfish hangs beside the chimney in the saloon, and the main dining room has low ceilings and walls of exposed brick. The menu offers steak, squid, flounder, and "old-fashioned seafood dinners" of clams, scallops, shrimp, fish, and lobster with onion rings. *Pickering Wharf, tel. 508/744–0000. Dress: casual. AE, CB, D, DC, MC, V. Moderate.*

Lyceum. This popular restaurant reopened under new management in 1990 after extensive restoration to re-create the '40s look, with paneled ceilings, wooden bar, fans, and old photographs. Food is available in the bar; a more formal dining room has an open fireplace and exposed brick walls. Cuisine is contemporary American with an emphasis on seafood. *43 Church St., tel. 508/745–7665. Reservations advised. Dress: casual. AE, D, MC, V. Moderate.*

Oh Calcutta! This Indian restaurant, part of a Boston-based chain, opened in Salem in 1989. The decor is, of course, Indian, and the spicy menu includes a large variety of lamb, chicken, beef, shrimp, and vegetarian dishes. *6 Hawthorne Blvd. (Rte. 1A), tel. 508/744–6570. Dress: casual. MC, V. Inexpensive.*

Salem Lodging **Hawthorne Hotel.** The former Hawthorn Inn changed its name and its character after a $4 million restoration project back in 1986. The imposing redbrick structure is now the only full-service hotel in Salem—conveniently situated on the green just a short walk from the commercial center and most attractions. Guest rooms in brown and beige are appointed with reproduction antiques, armchairs, and desks (because business clients are numerous). *On-the-Common, 01970, tel. 508/744–4080. 83 rooms, 6 suites. Facilities: restaurant, lounge, tavern, exercise room, meeting rooms, ballroom, baby-sitting. AE, CB, D, DC, MC, V. Expensive.*

The Arts

Music **Castle Hill** (Argilla Rd., Ipswich, tel. 508/356–7774) holds an annual festival, July 4 through mid-August, of pop, folk, and classical music, plus a jazz ball.

The magnificent organ at the **Hammond Castle Museum** (80 Hesperus Ave., Magnolia, tel. 508/283–2080) is used for organ concerts year-round, and in summer pops concerts are added to the schedule.

Theater The **North Shore Music Theatre** (62 Dunham Rd., Beverly, tel. 508/922–8500) is a professional company that, from April through December, performs popular and modern musicals as well as children's theater. On Cape Ann the **Gloucester Stage Company** (267 E. Main St., Gloucester, tel. 508/281–4099) is a nonprofit professional group staging new plays and revivals year-round.

Nightlife

A selection of popular local spots includes: **The Grog** (13 Middle St., Newburyport, tel. 508/465–8008), which hosts live entertainment downstairs Thursday–Sunday nights and features a wide variety of blues and rock bands; **Blue Star Lounge** (Rtes. 1/99, Saugus, tel. 617/233–8027), a rockabilly roadhouse on a busy strip, playing country music Tuesday–Sunday evenings; and in Marblehead **Frankie's Place** (12 School St., tel. 617/631–9894), which features rock bands.

The Pioneer Valley

The Pioneer Valley, a string of historic settlements along the Connecticut River from Springfield in the south up to the Vermont border, formed the western frontier of New England from the early 1600s until the late-18th century. The fertile banks of the river (called Quinnitukut, or "long tidal river," by the Indians) first attracted farmers and traders; later it became a source of power and transport for the earliest industrial cities in America.

Today, the northern regions of the Pioneer Valley remain rural and tranquil, supporting farms and small towns with typical New England architecture. Farther south, the cities of Holyoke and Springfield are more industrial.

Educational pioneers came to this region as well—to form America's first college for women and four other major colleges, as well as several well-known prep schools.

Important Addresses and Numbers

Visitor Information
The **Greater Springfield Convention and Visitors Bureau** (56 Dwight St., Springfield, 01103, tel. 413/787–1548) provides information about the entire Pioneer Valley area.

Getting Around the Pioneer Valley

By Car
I–91 runs north–south the entire length of the Pioneer Valley, from Greenfield to Springfield; I–90 links Springfield to Boston; and Route 2 connects Boston with Greenfield in the north.

By Train
From New York City, **Amtrak** service (tel. 800/872–7245) to Springfield calls at New Haven and Hartford, Connecticut; and the *Montrealer* from Washington, DC, stops at Amherst. The *Lake Shore Limited* between Boston and Chicago calls at Springfield once daily in each direction, and two more trains run between Boston and Springfield every day.

By Bus
Peter Pan Bus Lines (tel. 413/781–2900) links Springfield, Holyoke, Northampton, Amherst, South Hadley, and Deerfield. Local bus companies with regular service are the **Pioneer Valley Transit Authority** (tel. 413/781–7882), and **Greenfield Montague Transit Area** (tel. 413/773–9478).

Guided Tours

Sightseeing tours of the Pioneer Valley, along a 12-mile stretch of the Connecticut River between Northfield and Gill, are available on the *Quinnetukut II* riverboat. Excursions last 1½ hours, and commentary covers geographical, natural, and historical features of the region. *Northfield Mountain Recreation Center, R.R. 2, Box 117, 01360, tel. 413/659–3714. Cost: $6 adults, $5 senior citizens, $2.50 children under 14. Operates June 1–early Oct., Wed.–Sun.*

Exploring the Pioneer Valley

Numbers in the margin correspond with the numbered points of interest on the Pioneer Valley map.

❶ Off scenic Route 2 (the Mohawk Trail) 10 miles west of Deerfield, the village of **Shelburne Falls,** a nearly perfect example of small-town Americana, straddles the Deerfield River. The **Bridge of Flowers** (tel. 413/773–5463), a 40-foot former trolley bridge that was taken over by the Shelburne Women's Club in 1929, has been covered with plants to produce a riot of color in spring, summer, and early fall, when you can walk across it. In the riverbed just downstream are 50 immense **glacial potholes** ground out of the granite during the last ice age.

❷ Once a hardy pioneer outpost and the site of a bloody massacre, **Historic Deerfield** now basks in a far more genteel aura as the site of the prestigious Deerfield Academy preparatory school. Half the village is in fact a museum site, consisting of 13 18th-century houses along "The Street." Some, as period homes, contain antique furnishings and decorative arts; others exhibit collections of textiles, silver, pewter, or ceramics. The **Barnard Tavern** has a ballroom with fiddlers' gallery and several hands-on displays. The whole village is an impressive historical site. *The Street, tel. 413/774–5581. Two-day admission: $7.50 ad-*

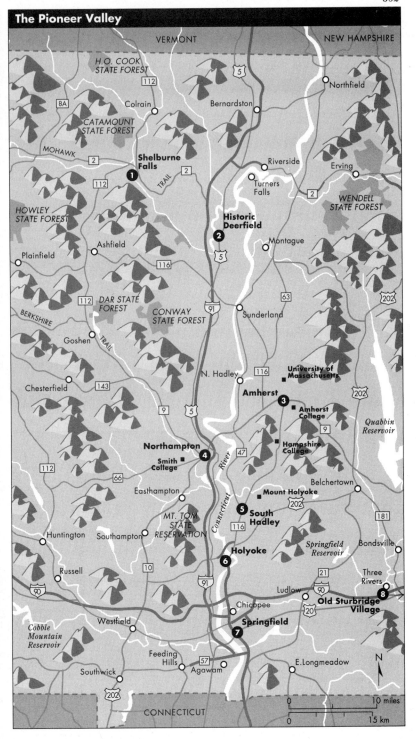

The Pioneer Valley

*ults, $4 children 6–17. Open daily 9:30–4:30. Closed Thanks-
giving, Christmas Eve, Christmas Day.*

❸ Head south of Deerfield on Route 5, then southeast along Route 116, to come upon the college town of **Amherst.** Three of the valley's five major colleges—the University of Massachusetts (UMass), Amherst College, and Hampshire College—are here. Not surprisingly, the area has a youthful bias, reflected in its numerous bookstores, bars, and cafés.

The poet Emily Dickinson was born and spent most of her life here, and the **Emily Dickinson Homestead** (280 Main St., tel. 413/542–8161), now owned by Amherst College, offers afternoon guided tours by appointment.

❹ Eight miles west on Route 9 is **Northampton,** home of Smith College, founded in 1871; it currently enrolls almost 3,000 women undergraduates. Visit the Lyman Plant House and botanic gardens. The **College Art Museum** (Rte. 9, tel. 413/584–2700), which has more than 18,000 paintings, was scheduled to reopen early in 1991 following a reorganization of its galleries.

Time Out The **Albion Bookshop Café** (68 Green St., beside Smith College) is a pleasant spot to relax with coffee and homemade cookies, cakes, or brownies. Tables and chairs of various shapes and sizes are set among the book shelves.

Northampton was also the Massachusetts home of the 30th U.S. President, Calvin Coolidge. He practiced law here, served as mayor from 1910–1911, and returned to town after his presidential term. The **Coolidge Room** at the Forbes Library (20 West St., tel. 413/586–2954) contains a collection of papers and memorabilia.

❺ **South Hadley** is a small village best known for its college, **Mount Holyoke,** founded in 1837 as the first women's college in the United States. Among its famous alumnae is Emily Dickinson. The handsome wooded campus was landscaped by Frederick Law Olmsted. The **College Art Museum** (tel. 413/538–2245) has exhibits of Asian, Egyptian, and classical art.

Time Out **Woodbridge's** (tel. 413/536–7341), on the common at South Hadley, was the village meetinghouse between 1733 and 1764. Now it is a restaurant that serves sandwiches, burgers, and more all day long.

❻ Head south on I–91 for **Holyoke,** a city of red-brick factories and canals. The **Wistariahurst Museum** (238 Cabot St., tel. 413/534–2216) shows how wealthy manufacturers lived; **Heritage State Park** tells the story of this so-called "Paper City" and is the starting point for the **Heritage Park Railroad** (June–Oct.) —three antique railroad cars that make 45-minute excursions to nearby Westwood. *221 Appleton St., tel. 413/534–1723. Admission free. Train ride: $6 adults, $3 children, $5 senior citizens. Open 9–4:30. Closed Mon.*

Right beside Heritage Park is the **Children's Museum,** housed in a converted mill by the canal. Packed with hands-on games and educational toys, the museum features a TV weather station, water guns, and a sand pendulum. *444 Dwight St., tel. 413/536–5437. Admission: $2.50. Open Wed.–Sat. 10–5, Sun. noon–5.*

The **Volleyball Hall of Fame** is a one-room tribute to the sport and to William Morgan, who invented it here in 1895. *444 Dwight St., tel. 413/536-0926. Admission free. Open Tues.– Fri. 10–5, Sat.–Sun. noon–5.*

❼ South of Holyoke is **Springfield,** the largest city in the Pioneer Valley—a sprawling industrial town where modern skyscrapers rise between grand historic buildings. The city owed much of its early development to the establishment in 1794 of the **Springfield Armory,** which made small arms for the U.S. military until it closed in 1968. It still holds one of the most extensive firearms collections in the world. *1 Armory Sq. (off State St.), tel. 413/734-8551. Admission free. Open daily 8:30– 4:30. Closed Thanksgiving, Christmas, New Year's Day.*

Perhaps the city's greatest claim to fame, however, is that Dr. James Naismith invented basketball here in 1891. The **Naismith Memorial Basketball Hall of Fame** features a cinema, basketball fountain, and a moving walkway from which visitors can shoot baskets. *W. Columbus Ave. at Union St., tel. 413/781– 6500. Admission: $5 adults, $3 senior citizens and children 9– 15. Open July–Labor Day, daily 9–6; Sept.–June, daily 9–5. Closed Thanksgiving, Christmas, New Year's Day.*

Four more conventional museums are situated at the museum quadrangle near downtown. The **Connecticut Valley Historical Museum** (tel. 413/732–3080) commemorates the history of the Pioneer Valley. The **George Walter Vincent Smith Art Museum** (tel. 413/733–4214) contains a private collection of Japanese armor, ceramics, and textiles. The **Museum of Fine Arts** (tel. 413/ 732–6092) has paintings by Gauguin, Renoir, Degas, and Monet. The **Springfield Science Museum** (tel. 413/733–1194) contains an "Exploration Center" of touchable displays, a planetarium, and dinosaur exhibits. All four museums have free admission.

If you drive about 30 miles east out of Springfield on scenic Route 20, you'll reach the star attraction of central Mass-
❽ achusetts—**Old Sturbridge Village,** one of the country's finest period restorations. Though technically out of the Pioneer Valley, Old Sturbridge is worth the detour. The village is a living, working model of an early 1800s New England town with more than 40 buildings on a 200-acre site. Working exhibits include a 200-year-old newspaper printing press, a blacksmith and forge, and a sawmill. Inside the houses, interpreters in period costume demonstrate home-based crafts such as spinning, weaving, and cooking. *1 Old Sturbridge Village Rd., 01566, tel. 508/347-3362. Admission: $12 adults, $6 children 6–15. Open late-Apr.–late-Oct., daily 9–5; off-season, Tues.–Sun. 10–5. Closed Christmas, New Year's Day.*

What to See and Do with Children

Barnard Tavern, Deerfield

Children's Museum, Holyoke

Forest Park, Springfield (413/733–2251) has many recreational facilities, including paddleboats and a children's zoo.

Heritage State Railway, Holyoke

Look Memorial Park (300 N. Main St., Florence, tel. 413/584–

5457) maintains a small zoo, wading and swimming pools, and children's playgrounds.

Naismith Memorial Basketball Hall of Fame, Springfield

Old Sturbridge Village, Sturbridge

Quinnetukut II riverboat tours

Riverside Park, the largest amusement park in New England, features a giant roller coaster and many other rides; there are picnic facilities as well. *1623 Main St., Agawam, tel. 413/786–9300. Admission: $17 adults, $8.50 senior citizens; $13 children under 48″ tall. Open weekends Mar. 31–Memorial Day and Labor Day–Sept. 30; daily Memorial Day–Labor Day.*

Off the Beaten Track

The reopening of the Connecticut River to salmon and shad began with the construction of the **Robert Barrett Fishway** at the Holyoke Dam (tel. 413/536–5520) in 1955. Two elevators lift more than 500,000 migrating fish over the dam each year, and the operation can be seen through viewing windows mid-April to the end of June.

Mattoon Street in Springfield consists of picturesque red-brick Victorian rowhouses that call to mind the Brahmin-built Back Bay neighborhood of Boston. Gaslight-style street lamps add atmosphere, and a two-day arts festival takes place here each September.

Although few people have heard of Dr. Sylvester Graham, a onetime Northampton resident, most Americans are familiar with the graham cracker, which was named after him. Graham believed in eating natural foods and exercising, unpopular ideas in the 1830s: Emerson called him "the poet of bran bread and pumpkins." His home at 111 Pleasant St. is now **Sylvester's Restaurant** (tel. 413/586–5343), offering homemade breads and healthy soups.

Shopping

Shopping Malls Try **The Mall at Center Square** in downtown Springfield, with Steiger's department store, or the **Holyoke Mall** at Ingleside (Exit 15 off I–91), with 150 stores including JCPenney, Sears, and Steiger's.

Outlet Stores Factory stores and mill shops are concentrated in Holyoke. The **Becker Jean Factory** (323 Main St., tel. 413/532–5797) carries Becker as well as Lee and Levi jeans for men, women, and children. The **Ekco Factory Store** (191½ Appleton St., tel. 413/532–3219) sells seconds, overruns, and closeouts of cookware, cutlery, and kitchen gadgets. Of course, paper products and furniture are widely available: The **City Paper Co.** (390–394 Main St., tel. 413/532–1352) offers wholesale and retail paper and plastic disposables; **Deerfield Woodworking** (420 Dwight St., tel. 413/532–2377) and **Riverbends Woodworks** (111 High St., tel. 413/532–3227) sell firsts and seconds of wood furnishings.

Farm Stands The area around Shelburne Falls is rich with maple-syrup operations; for a complete list, write to the **Massachusetts Maple Producers Association** (Box 377, Ashfield 01330).

For lists of pick-your-own orchards, contact the **Massachusetts Association of Roadside Stands and Pick Your Own Stands** (721 Parker St., East Longmeadow 01028, tel. 413/525–4147).

Specialty Stores
Antiques   For a list of members of the **Pioneer Valley Antique Dealers Association,** which guarantees the honest representation of merchandise, write to Maggie Herbert (Secretary), 201 N. Elm St., Northampton 01060. The **Antique Center of Northampton** (9½ Market St.) covers 8,000 square feet and houses a number of dealers; the **Hadley Antique Center** (Rte. 9, tel. 413/586–4093) contains 35 different stores.

Books   Amherst has dozens of bookstores, as do the other collegiate centers. The **Odyssey Bookstore** (29 College Street, South Hadley) is outstanding. **L.B.C. Books** (185 Main St., Holyoke) specializes in children's and discount books.

Crafts   Among the larger, permanent crafts stores are the **Leverette Crafts and Arts Center** (Montague Rd., Leverett, tel. 413/548–9070), housing 15 resident artists in jewelry, ceramics, glass and fibers; the **Salmon Falls Artisans Showroom** (Ashfield St., tel. 413/625–9833) at Shelburne Falls; the **Ferrin Gallery at Pinch Pottery** (179 Main St., Northampton, tel. 413/586–4509) with exhibits of contemporary ceramics, jewelry, glass and wood; and the **Avis Neigher Gallery** (Baystate West, Springfield, tel. 413/734–1844).

Sports and Outdoor Activities

Boating and Canoeing   The Connecticut River is navigable by all types of craft between the Turners Falls Dam, just north of Greenfield, and the Holyoke Dam. Canoes can also travel north of Turners Falls to beyond the Vermont border. The large dams control the water level daily, so you will notice a tidal effect, and those with larger craft should beware of sandbanks.

Canoes can be rented during summer and early fall from **Sportsman's Marina** (Rte. 9, Hadley, tel. 413/584–7141). The **Northfield Mountain Recreation Center** (*see* Guided Tours, above) rents out canoes and rowboats at Barton Cove, from where you can paddle to the Munn's Ferry campground, accessible only by canoe.

Further south at the wide place in the river known as the Oxbow, the Massachusetts Audubon Society's **Arcadia Wildlife Sanctuary** (Fort Hill Rd., Easthampton, tel. 413/584–3009) organizes canoe trips and maintains hiking and nature trails.

Camping   A list of private campgrounds throughout Massachusetts can be obtained free from the **Commonwealth of Massachusetts Office of Tourism** (100 Cambridge St., Boston 02202, tel. 617/727–3201). The following regional parks also have camping facilities: **Chicopee Memorial State Park, D.A.R. State Forest, Erving State Forest, Granville State Forest,** and **Mohawk Trail State Forest** (*see* State Parks, below).

Fishing   A massive cleanup program of the Connecticut River has resulted in the return of shad and even salmon to the purer waters, and in fact the river now supports 63 species of fish.

The privately owned **Red-Wing Meadow Farm** raises trout; for a fee visitors may fish in the ponds, paying for fish they catch. *500 Sunderland Rd., Sunderland, 01375, tel. 413/549–4118. Admission: $2, $5 family.*

Hiking   The abundance of state parks and forests in this region makes for an equal abundance of well-maintained hiking trails. Recommended parks include: **Erving State Forest, D.A.R. State Forest,** and **Mount Tom State Reservation** (*see* State Parks, below). The Audubon Society's **Arcadia Wildlife Sanctuary,** the Pioneer Valley, also encompasses nature trails around The Oxbow; **Northfield Mountain Recreation Center** (*see* Guided Tours, above) has 29 miles of hiking trails.

State Parks

Of the 29 state parks and forests in the Pioneer Valley, the following have a wide variety of facilities for outdoor recreation: **Chicopee Memorial State Park** (Burnett Rd., Chicopee), **D.A.R. State Forest** (Rte. 9, Goshen), **Erving State Forest** (Rte. 2A, Erving), **Granville State Forest** (S. Hartland Rd., Granby), **Hampton Ponds State Park** (Rte. 202, Westfield), **Mohawk Trail State Forest** (Rte. 2, Charlemont), **Mount Sugarloaf State Reservation** (Deerfield), **Mount Tom State Reservation** (Rte. 5, Holyoke), and **Wendell State Forest** (Wendell Rd., Wendell).

Dining and Lodging

Amherst Dining   **Lord Jeffrey Inn.** The large, elegant dining room has an open fireplace, chandeliers, heavy drapes, and white-painted wooden beams. The menu offers such fish dishes as seafood ravioli (shrimp and scallops in pasta with lobster sauce) as well as chicken and steaks. *30 Boltwood Ave., 01002, tel. 413/253–2576. Reservations advised. Dress: neat but casual. AE, DC, MC, V. Expensive.*

Judie's. A glassed-in porch where students crowd around small round tables creates the atmosphere of a cheerful street café. Cuisine is Continental and imaginative American; specialties are paella, maple lemon chicken, and a selection of gourmet chocolate cakes. Judie's sells cookery books as well as apple butter and bottles of house dressing. *51 N. Pleasant St., tel. 413/253–3491. No reservations. Dress: casual. AE, D, MC, V. Moderate.*

Amherst Lodging   **Lord Jeffrey Inn.** This gabled brick inn with green shutters sits right on the green between the town center and the Amherst College campus. Colonial furnishings and the lounge's open fire make for an innlike atmosphere, although the smart reproduction antiques and light, floral decor in the bedrooms breathe formality more than real character. The best rooms either open onto the garden courtyard or have a balcony that overlooks it. *30 Boltwood Ave., 01002, tel. 413/253–2576. 49 rooms, 6 suites. Facilities: restaurant, lounge, tavern, garden courtyard. AE, DC, MC, V. Expensive.*

Campus Center Hotel. Literally on top of the UMass campus, the spacious rooms of this modern hotel have large windows with excellent views over campus and countryside. The decor is exposed cinderblock, with simple, convenient furnishings. Guests can use university exercise facilities with prior reservation, and the campus status means no tax is charged for accommodations. *Murray D. Lincoln Tower, Univ. of Mass., 01003, tel. 413/549–6000. 116 rooms, 2 suites. Facilities: 2 indoor pools, 3 tennis courts, gym. AE, MC, V. Moderate.*

Deerfield Dining ★   **Deerfield Inn.** The large, sunny dining room is elegantly decorated with antiques, and tables are candlelit in the evening.

Specialties include saddle of venison sautéed with chestnuts in black currant sauce, rack of lamb with Dijon mustard and garlic, and caviar pie with buttered pumpernickel. Many recipes are taken from old cookery books in the village museum. *The Street, tel. 413/774–5587. Reservations advised. Jacket and tie advised. AE, DC, MC, V. Expensive.*

The Whately Inn. A vast dining room with exposed beams has tables on a raised stage at one end and some booths. The room is dimly lighted, with candles on the tables. Roast duck, baked lobster with shrimp stuffing, and crab meat casserole all come with salad, appetizer, and dessert. The restaurant is very busy on weekends. *Chestnut Plain Rd., Whately Center 01093, tel. 413/665–3044 or 800/635–3055. Reservations advised. Dress: casual. MC, V. Closed lunch Mon.–Sat. Moderate.*

Deerfield Lodging
★

Deerfield Inn. This inn is perfectly located in the center of Historic Deerfield. Guest rooms have recently been redecorated with period wallpapers designed for the inn, which was built in 1884. It was substantially modernized after a fire in 1981 and a new wing was added. Rooms have antiques and replicas, sofas and bureaus; some have four-posters or canopied beds. One bed is so high that a ladder is provided! The porch has rocking chairs, and it is said a ghost wanders the hallways. *The Street, 01342, tel. 413/774–5587. 23 rooms. Facilities: dining room, lounge, coffee shop. Rates include full breakfast. AE, DC, MC, V. Very Expensive.*

Sunnyside Farm Bed and Breakfast. Country-style guest rooms of varying sizes are appointed with maple antiques and family heirlooms. All rooms, which are hung with fine art reproductions, have views across the fields, and some overlook the large strawberry farm next door. Guests share a small library. Breakfast is served family-style in the dining room, which has a wood-burning stove. The farm is about 8 miles south of Deerfield. *11 River Rd., Whately (Box 486, S. Deerfield 01373), tel. 413/665–3113. 5 rooms share 2 baths. Facilities: outdoor pool. No pets. No credit cards. Rates include full breakfast. Moderate.*

The Whately Inn. Guest rooms with sloping old wooden floors are furnished simply with antiques and four-posters. Two are located over the dining room, which can be noisy. *Chestnut Plain Rd., Whately Center 01093, tel. 413/665–3044 or 800/635–3055. 4 rooms. MC, V. Moderate.*

Greenfield Dining

Brickers. Right beside Route 91, this restaurant is set in a converted ice-cream factory. Decor is country style, in a large room with exposed brick walls and a high ceiling supported by metal beams and pillars. The sunny porch at one end is a pleasant place to eat lunch. Entrées include Cajun chicken, pan-fried sole, and pasta dishes; burgers and sandwiches are also available. *Shelburne Rd., tel. 413/774–2857. Dress: casual. MC, V. Closed lunch Sun. Moderate.*

Riverside. The restaurant is perched between the Bridge of Flowers, which it overlooks, and Shelburne Falls's main street. Long tables, square tables, benches, chairs, and customers are crammed into a small, bright room, and there is often a wait. The menu includes Cornish game hen with fresh cranberry and chestnut sauce; cauliflower crêpes Florentine; and "Udon, the floating meal"—tofu, scallions, and stir-fry vegetables in tamari-ginger broth. Riverside also serves soups, sandwiches, and home-baked pies. *4 State St., Shelburne Falls, tel. 413/*

625–2570. No reservations. Dress: casual. MC, V. Closed Mon. Moderate.

Greenfield Lodging **Northfield Country House.** Truly remote, this big English man-
★ or house is set amid thick woodlands on a small hill that
overlooks Northfield's Main Street. A wide staircase leads to
the bedrooms, some of which have working fireplaces. The
smallest rooms are in the former servants' quarters; larger
rooms are furnished with antiques, and several have brass
beds. The present owner has considerably renovated this 100-
year-old house, and has planted hundreds of tulip and daffodil
bulbs in the gardens. *School St., RR 1, Box 617, Northfield
01360. tel. 413/498–2692. 7 rooms share 4 baths. Facilities:
lounge, outdoor pool. No pets. MC, V. Rates include full breakfast. Moderate.*

1797 House. Built almost 200 years ago, this white clapboard
house stands on the green in tiny, quiet Buckland Village.
Guest rooms are furnished with antiques, and the beds—one
brass, one iron, and one four-poster—have quilts. In summer,
breakfast is served on the large screened porch overlooking the
woods; in winter it's in the dining room with an open fireplace.
*Charlemont Rd., Buckland 01338, tel. 413/625–2975. 3 rooms.
Facilities: TV lounge. No credit cards. Rates include full
breakfast. Moderate.*

Holyoke Dining **Yankee Pedlar Inn.** Most rooms in this superbly furnished inn
and Lodging have antiques, with four-posters or canopied beds, and each is
★ uniquely styled. Victorian guest rooms are elaborate and heavily curtained, with lots of lace, while the carriage house has
beams and rustic furnishings, with simple canopied beds.
Suites are spacious and definitely worth the small price difference. The dining room has exposed beams and antique wood
paneling, much of it taken from a nearby castle that was demolished; "candle" chandeliers provide the lighting, and
waitresses wear Victorian dress. In summer the herb garden—
with its orange trees, herbs, fountain, and gazebo—is a lovely
spot to dine in. The Sand Dollar Scallops are scallops sautéed in
white bread crumbs with garlic, green onion, and lemon butter; Currier and Ives is a filet mignon with béarnaise sauce,
jumbo shrimps, and scallops on a skewer. *1866 Northampton
St., 01040, tel. 413/532–9494. 47 rooms, 16 suites. Facilities: 4
dining rooms, 4 banquet rooms, oyster bar, live entertainment.
Dining room reservations required for Sun. brunch, advised
other times. Dress: casual. AE, CB, D, DC, MC, V. Hotel rates
include Continental breakfast. Moderate.*

Northampton **Beardsley's.** The intimate aura of the first- and second-floor
Dining dining rooms in this fine French restaurant is created by dark
wood paneling, candlelight, and shining silverware. Windows
overlooking the street make the second floor a little lighter.
The menu includes chicken roulade stuffed with spinach and
proscuitto mousse; sirloin steak; and pheasant roasted with
hazelnuts. *140 Main St., tel. 413/586–2699. Reservations advised. Dress: casual. AE, CB, MC. Expensive.*

Wiggins Tavern. Part of the Hotel Northampton, the Tavern
specializes in such New England dishes as Yankee cider pot
roast, chicken potpie, and Boston scrod; Indian pudding,
peppermint-stick ice cream, and apple pie follow. Open fires
burn in three dimly lighted, "olde worlde" dining rooms, where
heavy exposed beams support low ceilings and antique kitchen
appliances decorate every available space. Eleanor Roosevelt

and John F. Kennedy ate here. *36 King St., tel. 413/584–3100. Reservations advised. Dress: casual. AE, CB, D, DC, MC, V. Closed lunch weekends. Expensive.*

Paul and Elizabeth's. This natural-foods restaurant serves seasonal specials such as butternut-squash soup, home-baked corn muffins, and Indian pudding. The restaurant is airy with lots of plants and trellis work, and fans hang from the high ceiling. *150 Main St., tel. 413/584–4832. Reservations advised. Dress: casual. MC, V. Closed Sun. Moderate.*

Northampton Lodging

Hotel Northampton. Located in the town center, the hotel was built in 1916 and completely refurbished in 1987. Antique and reproduction furnishings combine with open fires in the parlor, lounge, and dining rooms to give the atmosphere of a cozy inn. The porch has a piano and wicker chairs. Guest rooms are appointed with Colonial reproductions, heavy curtains, and four-posters. Some rooms come with balconies that overlook a busy street. *36 King St., 01060, tel. 413/584–3100. 72 rooms, 5 suites. Facilities: restaurant, café, bar, lounge, ballroom, room service. AE, CB, D, DC, MC, V. Expensive.*

The Knoll Bed and Breakfast. A spacious private home, this B&B sits well away from the busy road and backs onto steep woodlands. There's a sweeping staircase and Oriental rugs on polished wood floors; guest rooms are furnished with a mixture of antiques and hand-me-downs, and some have high four-posters. *230 N. Main St., Florence 01060, tel. 413/584–8164. 5 rooms share 2 baths. Facilities: lounge, library. No smoking. No pets. No credit cards. Rates include full breakfast. Moderate.*

Twin Maples Bed and Breakfast. Seven miles northwest of Northampton near the village of Williamsburg, this 200-year-old, fully restored farmhouse is surrounded by fields and woods. Inside are exposed beams, wide brick fireplaces, and wood stoves. Colonial-style antique and reproduction furnishings decorate the rather small guest rooms, which have restored brass beds and quilts. *106 South St., Williamsburg 01096, tel. 413/268–7925. 3 rooms share one bath. Facilities: TV lounge, No smoking. No pets. No credit cards. Rates include full breakfast. Moderate.*

Springfield Dining

Springfield's on the Park. A full menu is available upstairs; lighter snacks are at the bar downstairs. The walls are exposed brick, one of them decorated with a gigantic mural depicting the town and local culture. Service downstairs can be slow. The restaurant offers daily stir-fry and pasta specials, as well as seafood and steaks. *232 Worthington St., tel. 413/787–1522. Reservations advised. Dress: casual. AE, MC, V. Closed Sun. Expensive.*

T.D. Smith's. This trendy new restaurant is located on the first floor of one of Springfield's characteristic old brick buildings—an early Duryea automobile factory. Modern furnishings include plants and booths, and the place is popular at lunchtime. The menu features clam chowder, bluefish, Caribbean swordfish, chicken, and steaks. *Duryea Square, off Worthington St., tel. 413/737–5317. Dress: casual. AE, MC, V. Moderate.*

Theodore's. There's saloon-style dining at booths near the bar or in a small adjacent dining room. The 1930s are re-created with period furniture and framed advertisements for such curious products as foot soap. Brass lights date from 1897. Theodore's serves burgers, sandwiches, some Mexican dishes, chicken, and seafood. Thursday through Saturday, there is live entertainment in the evenings. *201 Worthington St., tel. 413/ 739–7637. Dress: casual. AE, DC, MC, V. Moderate.*

Springfield Lodging

Marriott Hotel. Conveniently located in the middle of downtown, this newly renovated hotel opens onto the large Baystate West shopping mall. The lobby features green marble, brass chandeliers, and Oriental rugs. Rooms at the front overlook the river, and all are comfortably decorated with oak furniture, Impressionist prints, and mauve or sea-foam green color schemes. *1500 Main St., 01104, tel. 413/781–7111 or 800/228– 9290. 264 rooms, 1 suite. Facilities: restaurant, lounge, bar, indoor–outdoor pool, 2 saunas, whirlpool, fitness center, room service, meeting rooms. AE, CB, D, DC, MC, V. Very Expensive.*

Sheraton Tara. This hotel, in the middle of downtown, was built in 1987. Guest rooms have reproduction antiques and are plush, with heavy drapes and thick carpets; they surround an impressive 14-story atrium. Hotel staff wear the distinctive red-and-gold Beefeater costume. *1 Monarch Place, 01144, tel. 413/781– 1010 or 800/325–3535. 303 rooms, 7 suites. Facilities: 2 restaurants, lounge, health club, exercise room, 4 racquetball courts, 2 saunas, steam room, whirlpool, indoor pool, room service, conference rooms, ballroom. AE, D, DC, MC, V. Very Expensive.*

Holiday Inn. Half a mile north of downtown, beside I–91, this hotel offers a relaxed atmosphere and a touch of old New England in the reproduction antique furnishings of the bedrooms (some have four-posters). All rooms were renovated in 1987; the Presidential Suite is enormous. Upper stories and the top-floor bar-lounge afford panoramic views of Springfield, the river, and the surrounding countryside. *711 Dwight St., 01104, tel. 413/781–0900 or 800/465–4329. 250 rooms, 12 suites. Facilities: restaurant, lounge, bar, indoor pool, whirlpool, room service, meeting rooms. AE, CB, D, DC, MC, V. Expensive.*

Cityspace. In 1989 the Springfield YMCA renovated its standard accommodations into small, attractive pastel-tone rooms with gray cinderblock walls, modern paintings, large lamps, and large windows. Each has a private bath. The big advantage over other budget motels is that visitors can use all the sports and fitness facilities at the Y for free. Cityspace is close to I–91, near downtown, and a five-minute walk from the Amtrak station. *275 Chestnut St., 01104, tel. 413/739–6951. 91 rooms. Facilities: restaurant, indoor pool, 4 racquetball courts, 2 squash courts, 2 tracks, fitness center, gym, whirlpool, steam room, sauna, massage. MC, V. Inexpensive.*

Sturbridge Dining

Publick House. This popular restaurant is big, bustling, and very busy at weekends. The high cathedral ceilings in the main dining room are supported by wooden beams and hung with enormous period chandeliers. The menu advertises "hearty gourmet meals and hefty desserts," which translates into individually baked lobster pies, double-thick loin lamb chops, duckling, and a turkey dinner served on Sunday. Desserts include Indian pudding, pecan bread pudding, and apple pie. *Rte. 131, tel. 508/347–3313. Reservations advised. Dress: casual. AE, CB, D, DC, MC, V. Expensive.*

The Whistling Swan. There are two separate eating areas here; the loft serves lighter meals than the main dining room. The ambience in both is fairly formal, with matching floral-print drapes and wallpaper and pink tablecloths. Specialties include rack of lamb, veal, Madeira chicken, and catch of the day. *502*

Main St., tel. 508/347–2321. Reservations advised. Dress: casual. AE, CB, DC, MC, V. Closed Mon., Easter, Mother's Day, Thanksgiving, Christmas, New Year's Day. Moderate–Expensive.

Rom's. This has become something of a local institution—after humble beginnings as a sandwich stand, the restaurant was extended to seat about 700 people. The six dining rooms have an Early American decor, with wood panelling and beamed ceilings. Now serving Italian and American cuisine ranging from pizza to roast beef, Rom's attracts the crowds with a classic formula: good food at low prices. The veal parmesan is very popular. *Rte. 131, tel. 508/347–3349. Dress: casual. AE, V. Closed lunch weekdays. Inexpensive.*

Sturbridge Lodging   **Sheraton Sturbridge Inn.** The Sheraton is ideally located just across the street from Old Sturbridge Village on Cedar Lake. Luxuriously appointed bedrooms have Colonial decor and reproduction furnishings, and the lakeside location enhances the recreational offerings. *Rte. 20, 01566, tel. 508/347–7393. 241 rooms, 9 suites. Facilities: 2 dining rooms, 2 lounges, indoor pool, health club, exercise room, minigolf, 2 tennis courts, racquetball, basketball, sauna, canoes, rowboats, fishing, room service, meeting rooms. AE, CB, D, DC, MC, V. Very Expensive.*

★ **Sturbridge Country Inn.** This imposing Greek Revival–facade inn on Sturbridge's busy Main Street was once a farmhouse. After a period as an apartment building, it reopened in 1989 as a luxury hotel. If it lives up to its promise, this will be one of the best accommodations in the region. Guest rooms—all have working fireplaces—are superbly furnished, with reproduction antiques and a Jacuzzi in every room. The best is the top floor suite, with a cathedral ceiling, a large Jacuzzi in the living room, and big windows. The public TV lounge, with roaring fire, also manages to mix old furnishings with modern comforts. *530 Main St. (Box 60), 01566. 9 rooms, 1 suite. Facilities: lounge, in-room Jacuzzi. AE, D, MC, V. Rates include Continental breakfast. Expensive–Very Expensive.*

Publick House and Col. Ebenezer Crafts Inn. The Publick House dates to 1771 and is now surrounded by a "complex" of different styles of lodging. Rooms in the Publick House itself are Colonial in design, with uneven wide-board floors; some have canopy beds. The neighboring Chamberlain House consists of larger suites, and the Country Motor Lodge has more modern appointments with comfortable, updated rooms. The Col. Ebenezer Crafts Inn, named for the man who built the Publick House, is a restored Colonial farmhouse dating from 1786. Located just over a mile away from the Publick House, it has a library and sun porch and Colonial furnishings. Considering the bustle that dominates the Publick House, especially on weekends, the Crafts Inn is a pleasantly tranquil alternative. *Rte. 131, On-the-Common, 01566, tel. 508/347–3313. 118 rooms, 12 suites. Facilities: 2 dining rooms, bar, outdoor pool, tennis court, track, shuffleboard, playground, conference rooms. Rates include Continental breakfast. AE, D, DC, CB, MC, V. Moderate–Expensive.*

The Arts

Dance   The **Berkshire Ballet** performs twice a year at Springfield's American International College—usually in fall and spring.

Call the college (tel. 413/737–7000) and ask for the Performing Arts Center for details. Other major ballet and modern dance companies appear in season at the UMass Fine Arts Center in Amherst (tel. 413/545–2511).

Music The **Springfield Symphony Orchestra** performs October through May at Symphony Hall, and mounts a summer program of free concerts in Springfield's parks. *31 Elm St., Suite 210, 01103, tel. 413/733–2291.*

Other concerts are hosted at the **Paramount Performing Arts Center** (1700 Main St., 01103, tel. 413/734–5706) and the **Springfield Civic Center** (127 Main St., 01103, tel. 413/787–6610.)

Theater Springfield is the home of **StageWest,** the only resident professional theater company in western Massachusetts. The schedule includes a series of plays and musicals October through May. *1 Columbus Ctr., 01103, tel. 413/781–2340.*

The **Children's Theatre** of **Massachusetts** (tel. 413/788–0705), based at the Springfield Symphony Hall, performs a series of family-oriented performances.

Nightlife

The collegiate population ensures a lively club and nightlife scene in the valley. Popular spots include: **Iron Horse** (20 Center St., Northampton, tel. 413/584–0610) with a variety of folk, blues, jazz, Celtic, and new wave music seven nights a week; **Jazzberries** (406 Dwight St., Springfield, tel. 413/732–4606) presenting jazz and comedy acts; **Katina's** (Rte. 9, Hadley, tel. 413/586–4463) specializing in rock and blues; **Sheehan's Café** (24 Pleasant St., Northampton, tel. 413/586–4258) featuring rock 'n' roll and blues six nights a week; and **Theodore's** (201 Worthington St., Springfield, tel. 413/739–7637), with comedians and live music Thursday through Saturday evenings.

The Berkshires

More than a century ago, wealthy families from New York and Boston built "summer cottages" in western Massachusetts' Berkshire hills—great country estates that earned Berkshire County the nickname "inland Newport." Although most of those grand houses have since been converted into schools or hotels, the region is still popular, for obvious reasons. Occupying the entire far western end of the state, it's only about a 2½-hour drive directly west from Boston or north from New York City, yet it lives up to the storybook image of rural New England, with its wooded hills, narrow winding roads, and compact charming villages. Summer offers an astonishing variety of cultural events, not the least of which is the Tanglewood festival in Lenox; fall brings a blaze of brilliant foliage; in winter, it's a popular ski area; and springtime visitors can enjoy maple-sugaring. Keep in mind, however, that the Berkshire's popularity often goes hand-in-hand with high prices and crowds, especially on weekends.

Important Addresses and Numbers

Visitor Information **Berkshire Visitor's Bureau** (Box SGB, Berkshire Common, Pittsfield 01201, tel. 413/443–9186 or 800/237–5747).

Lenox Chamber of Commerce (Lenox Academy Building, 75 Main St., 01240, tel. 413/637–3646).

Mohawk Trail Association (Box 7, North Adams 01247, tel. 413/664–6256).

Emergencies **Police** or **fire** (tel. 911). **Hillcrest Hospital** (165 Tor Ct., Pittsfield, tel. 413/443–4761). **North Adams Regional Hospital** (Hospital Ave., North Adams, tel. 413/663–3701).

Getting Around the Berkshires

By Car The Massachusetts Turnpike (I–90) connects Boston with Lee and Stockbridge, continuing into New York, where it becomes the New York Thruway. The Thruway passes just south of Albany. To reach the Berkshires from New York City, take either the Thruway (I–87) or the Taconic State Parkway.

Within the Berkshires the main north-south road is Route 7. The scenic Mohawk Trail (Route 2) runs from the northern Berkshires to Greenfield at the head of the Pioneer Valley, and continues across Massachusetts into Boston.

By Bus **Peter Pan Bus Lines** (tel. 413/442–4451) serves Lee and Pittsfield from Boston and Albany. **Bonanza Bus Lines** (tel. 413/781–3320) connects points throughout the Berkshires with Albany; New York City; and Providence, Rhode Island.

Guided Tours

Willa Tours offers a wide range of Berkshire tours, including walks through Williamstown, trips to Lenox and Stockbridge, country-mansion visits, and antiques-hunting tours. *53 Belden St., Williamstown 01267, tel. 413/458–9503.*

Balloon tours over the Berkshires are offered twice daily throughout the summer, on weekends during the off-season (weather permitting) by **American Balloon Works, Inc.** (East Nassau, NY 12062, tel. 518/766–5111).

Berkshire Cottage Tours covers 20 of the summer mansions constructed at the end of the last century in the Lenox–Stockbridge region. The 3½-hour tour costs $17. *Edith Wharton Restoration, Box 974, Lenox 01240, tel. 413/637–1899. Operates late-July–early Sept., Thurs.–Sun.; mid-Sept.–mid-Oct., weekends.*

New England Hiking Holidays organizes guided hiking vacations through the Berkshires, with overnight stays at a country inn. Hikes vary from 5 to 9 miles per day. *Box 1648, North Conway, NH 03860, tel. 603/356–9696.*

Exploring the Berkshires

Numbers in the margin correspond with the numbered points of interest on the Berkshires map.

❶ **Williamstown** is the northernmost Berkshire town, at the junction of Routes 2 and 7. When Col. Ephraim Williams left money to found a free school in what was then known as West Hooskuk, he stipulated that the name be changed to Williamstown. Williams College opened in 1793, and even today the town revolves around it. Gracious campus buildings line the wide main street and are open to visitors. Highlights include the **Gothic cathedral,** built in 1904, and the **Williams College Museum of Art,** with works emphasizing American, modern, and contemporary art. *Main St., tel. 413/597–2429. Admission free. Open Mon.–Sat. 10–5, Sun. 1–5.*

Formerly a private collection, the **Sterling and Francine Clark Art Institute** is now one of the nation's outstanding small art museums. Its famous works include paintings by Renoir, Monet, Pissaro, and Degas. *225 South St., tel. 413/458–9545. Admission free. Open Tues.–Sun. 10–5. Closed Thanksgiving, Christmas, New Year's Day.*

Travelers looking for a fine scenic drive may head east on the **Mohawk Trail,** a 67-mile stretch of Route 2 that follows a former Indian path from Williamstown. The first stop is **North Adams.** Despite the proximity of the two towns, they are utterly different in character. North Adams, once a railroad boomtown and a thriving industrial city, is still industrial but no longer thriving —the dilapidated mills and row houses are reminiscent of northern industrial England. The **Western Gateway Heritage State Park** (tel. 413/663–6312), housed in the restored freight-yard district, is open daily and tells the story of the town's past successes. The freight-yard district also contains a number of specialty stores and restaurants.

From North Adams the road begins a steep ascent, complete with hairpin turns, to the Western Summit, with excellent views of North Adams and Williamstown. It continues to Whitcomb Summit, the highest point on the trail, with more spectacular views.

Heading downhill, you can reach the entrance to the **Hoosac Tunnel** by turning left off Route 2 beyond Florida, on the road toward Monroe Bridge. The 4.7-mile tunnel took 24 years to build and was the longest in the nation when it was completed in 1875.

Back on the Mohawk Trail, just before the town of Charlemont, off to the right stands **Hail to the Sunrise,** a monument to the Native American. This 900-pound bronze statue facing east, with arms uplifted, is dedicated to the five Indian nations who lived along the Mohawk Trail. A handful of somewhat kitschy "Indian trading posts" along this highway carry out the Mohawk theme.

Other travelers may want to head straight for the heart of the Berkshires by taking scenic Route 7 south from Williamstown to the pretty lakeside village of Lanesborough. Signs will direct you to the top of **Mt. Greylock,** at 3,491 feet the highest point in Massachusetts. The 10,327-acre **Mount Greylock State Reservation** (*see* National and State Parks, below) provides facilities for cycling, fishing, hiking, horseback riding, hunting, and snowmobiling.

Continuing south on Route 7 will bring you to the busy town of **Pittsfield,** county seat and geographic center of the region. Though not particularly attractive, the town has a lively small-town atmosphere. The **Berkshire Museum** especially appeals to

The Berkshires

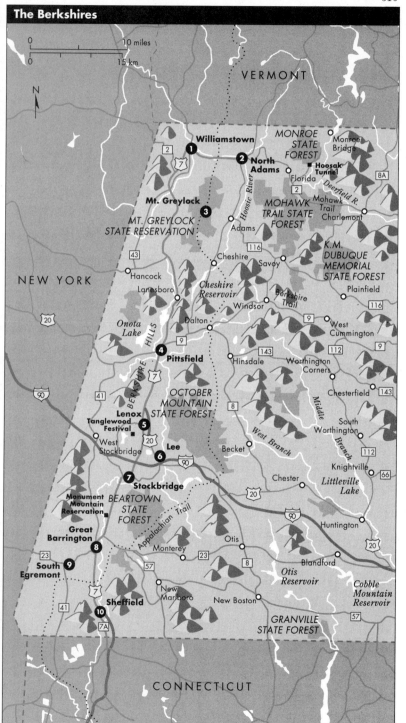

0
10 miles
0
15 km

N

VERMONT

MONROE STATE FOREST

Monroe Bridge

Williamstown ①

② **North Adams**

Hoosak Tunnel

Florida

2

8A

Mt. Greylock ③

MT. GREYLOCK STATE RESERVATION

Hoosic River

MOHAWK TRAIL STATE FOREST

Mohawk Trail

Charlemont

Deerfield R.

Adams

NEW YORK

43

Hancock

Lanesboro

Cheshire

116

Savoy

Berkshire Trail

K.M. DUBUQUE MEMORIAL STATE FOREST

Plainfield

116

20

Onota Lake

Cheshire Reservoir

Windsor

9

West Cummington

112

9

BERKSHIRE HILLS

Dalton

9

Pittsfield ④

143

Hinsdale

Worthington Corners

Chesterfield

143

41

OCTOBER MOUNTAIN STATE FOREST

8

112

South Worthington

7

I-90

Lenox
Tanglewood Festival ⑤

20

West Stockbridge

Lee ⑥

90

West Branch

Becket

Middle Branch

Knightville

66

Littleville Lake

① **Stockbridge** ⑦

BEARTOWN STATE FOREST

Monument Mountain Reservation

Appalachian Trail

20

Chester

I-90

Huntington

20

Great Barrington ⑧

Monterey

23

Otis

Blandford

South Egremont ⑨

23

57

8

Otis Reservoir

Cobble Mountain Reservoir

41

New Marlboro

New Boston

GRANVILLE STATE FOREST

57

Sheffield ⑩

7A

CONNECTICUT

children, with its aquarium, animal exhibits, and glowing rocks. A local repository with a "bit of everything," the museum also contains works of art and historical relics. *39 South St., tel. 413/443–7171. Admission free. Open Tues.–Sat. 10–5, Sun. 1–5. Closed Thanksgiving, Christmas, New Year's Day.*

At the **Berkshire Athenaeum** (Berkshire Public Library, 1 Wendell Ave.), the **Herman Melville Memorial Room** (tel. 413/499–9486) houses a collection of books, letters, and memorabilia of the author of *Moby-Dick*. **Arrowhead,** the house Melville purchased in 1850, is just outside Pittsfield; tours include the study in which *Moby-Dick* was written. *780 Holmes Rd., tel. 413/442–1793. Admission: $3.50 adults, $2 children 6–16, $3 senior citizens. Open Memorial Day–Labor Day, Mon.–Sat. 10–4:15, Sun. 11–3:15; Labor Day–late-Oct., Thurs.–Mon. 10–4:15, Sun. 11–3.*

Take Route 20 west out of the center of Pittsfield to discover the town's star attraction—**Hancock Shaker Village.** Founded in the 1790s, Hancock was the third Shaker community in America. At its peak in the 1840s, the village had almost 300 inhabitants, who made their living from farming, selling seeds and herbs, making medicines, and producing crafts. The religious community officially closed in 1960; in 1961 the site opened as a museum. Many examples of the famous Shaker ingenuity are visible at Hancock today: the **Round Stone Barn** with its labor-saving devices and the **Laundry and Machine Shop** with its water-powered instruments are two of the best buildings to visit. *Rte. 20, 5 mi west of Pittsfield, tel. 413/443–0188. Admission: $7.50 adults, $3 children 6–16, $6.75 senior citizens and students. Open late-May–late-Oct. daily 9:30–5; Apr. 1–late May and Nov. 1–30, daily 10–3.*

⑤ Five miles south of Pittsfield on Route 7, the village of **Lenox** epitomizes the Berkshires for many visitors. In the thick of the "summer cottage" region, it's rich with old inns and majestic buildings. One of the most interesting to visit is **The Mount,** former summer home of novelist Edith Wharton. The house and grounds were designed and built under Wharton's direction in 1901 and 1902. An expert in the field of design, Wharton used the principles set forth in her book *The Decoration of Houses* (1897) to plan The Mount for a calm, well-ordered lifestyle. *Plunkett St., tel. 413/637–1899. Admission: $3.50 adults, $2 children 13–18, $3 senior citizens. Open late May–early Sept., Tues.–Sun 10–5; early Sept.–late Oct., Thurs.–Sun. 10–5.*

Lenox is the nearest Berkshire village to **Tanglewood,** summer home of the Boston Symphony. The 200-acre estate attracts thousands every summer to hear concerts featuring world-famous performers. One of the most popular ways to experience Tanglewood is to take a blanket and picnic on the grounds and watch the performance from the lawn. (*See* The Arts, below, for information.)

In the village center Lenox Station is the starting point for the **Berkshire Scenic Railway,** which operates vintage railroad cars over a portion of the historic New Haven Railway's Housatonic Valley Line. The route takes in Lee and Stockbridge, and an open ticket allows passengers to alight at different stations and rejoin a later train. *Willow Creek Rd., tel. 413/637–2210. Fares vary according to destination. Open late May–late Oct., weekends and holidays only.*

❻ South on Route 7, past the busy crossroads of **Lee,** where there are dining and lodging opportunities, you'll find the archetypal
❼ New England small town of **Stockbridge,** with its history of literary and artistic inhabitants. The painter Norman Rockwell, the sculptor Daniel Chester French, and the writers Norman Mailer and Robert Sherwood lived here. For the moment the **Norman Rockwell Museum** stands in the center of town, but a larger museum being constructed on Route 183 has a proposed opening date of 1992. Rockwell lived in Stockbridge between 1953 and his death in 1978; the museum owns the largest collection of Rockwell originals in the world. *Main St., tel. 413/298–3822. Admission: $4 adults, $1 children 6–18. Open Apr. 1–Dec. 31, daily 10–5; Jan. 2–Mar. 31, daily 11–4. Closed Jan. 15–31, Thanksgiving, Christmas, New Year's Day.*

Time Out **Chez Vous** (tel. 413/298–4278), signposted off Main Street in the town center, was originally Alice's Restaurant, made famous by Arlo Guthrie's comic protest song of the same name. This quirky establishment serves gourmet food to stay or to go; try the baby eggplant stuffed with curried lamb or feast on sinful chocolate cake and coffee.

Several historic houses in this area are worth seeing, especially **Chesterwood,** for 33 years the summer home of Daniel Chester French, best known for his statues of the Minute Man in Concord and of Abraham Lincoln at the Lincoln Memorial in Washington, DC. *Williamsville Rd. (off Rte. 183), tel. 413/298–3579. Admission: $4.50 adults, $1 children 7–18. Open May 1–Oct. 31, daily 10–5.*

❽ Heading south on Route 7 toward **Great Barrington** takes you past **Monument Mountain;** two trails here lead to the summit at Squaw Peak, named for an Indian maiden, suffering from unrequited love, who hurled herself to her death. Great Barrington itself is the largest town in the southern Berkshires and a mec-
❾ ca for antiques hunters (as are the nearby villages of **South**
❿ **Egremont** and **Sheffield).**

Those in search of nature may want to make two excursions into the southernmost reaches of the Berkshire countryside from Great Barrington. **Bartholomew's Cobble** (Rte. 7A, tel. 413/229–8600), 11 miles from town, is a natural rock garden beside the Housatonic River. The 277-acre reservation is filled with trees, ferns, wild flowers, and hiking trails.

At **Bash Bish Falls** (Rte. 23, tel. 413/528–0330), 16 miles southwest of Great Barrington on the New York State border, Bash Bish brook flows through a gorge and over a 50-foot waterfall into a clear natural pool.

What to See and Do with Children

Berkshire Museum, Pittsfield

Hancock Shaker Village. Besides its inherent attractions, the village organizes special programs for children.

Jiminy Peak. (tel. 413/738–5500). The ski resort at Hancock offers an alpine slide, putting course, and bicycle rentals in summer.

Pleasant Valley Wildlife Sanctuary, Pittsfield

The Robbins-Zust Family Marionettes have been performing puppet shows for children and families in Pittsfield and Great Barrington since 1971. Each year they mount a varied program, which always includes the old favorite—Punch and Judy. *East Rd., Richmond 01254, tel. 413/698–2591. Tickets: $3. late June–late Aug. Call for performance schedule.*

Off the Beaten Track

The **Chapin Library of Rare Books and Manuscripts** at Williams College contains the Four Founding Documents of the United States, as well as 35,000 other books, manuscripts, and illustrations dating from the 9th to the 20th century. In 1983 it purchased a recently discovered copy of the Declaration of Independence that had been owned by one of the signers. *Stetson Hall, Main St., Williamstown, tel. 413/587–2462. Admission free. Open Mon.–Fri. 9–12 and 1–5.*

Dalton is the home of paper manufacturers Crane and Co., a business started by Zenas Crane in 1801 and now the major employer in town. The **Crane Museum of Paper Making,** housed in the Old Stone Mill (1844), has been beautifully restored with oak beams, Colonial chandeliers, and wide oak floorboards. Exhibits trace the history of American paper making from Revolutionary times to the present day. *Off Rte. 9, Dalton, tel. 413/684–2600. Admission free. Open June–mid-Oct., Mon.–Fri. 2–5.*

The only natural bridge in North America caused by water erosion is the marble arch at **Natural Bridge State Park.** It stands above a narrow 500-foot chasm; look for the numerous potholes, faults, and fractures in its walls. *Rte. 8 N., North Adams, tel. 413/663–6392. Admission: $3 per car. Open May–Oct., Mon.–Fri. 10–6, weekends 10–8.*

Shopping

Shopping Districts   The only enclosed shopping mall in the region is the **Berkshire Mall,** on Route 8 east of Lanesborough. The mall consists of 65 specialty stores and contains Hill's, JCPenney, Sears, Steiger's, several food stores, and a cinema complex.

Outlet Stores   Along Route 7 just north of Lenox are two factory-outlet malls, **Lenox House Country Shops** and **Brushwood Farms.**

A number of outlet stores are concentrated at **The Buggy Whip Factory,** some distance from the main tourist routes, on Route 272 in Southfield. Stores include **Dudley's Clothing Factory Outlet** (shirts, sweaters, and jackets for men); **Devoted to Children** (children's toys and clothing); and the **Neuma Sweater Factory Outlet** (New England–made cotton sweaters). The building also contains 58 **antiques dealers** and 15 **craft stalls.**

Antiques   There are hundreds of antiques stores throughout the Berkshires, but the greatest concentration is around Great Barrington, South Egremont, and Sheffield. For a list of storekeepers who belong to the **Berkshire County Antiques Dealers Association** and guarantee the authenticity of their merchandise, send a self-addressed, stamped envelope to RD 1, Box 1, Sheffield 01257.

Great Barrington   **Corashire Antiques** (Rtes. 23 and 7 at Belcher Square, tel. 413/528–0014), a shop in a red barn, carries American country furniture and accessories, including the occasional rare Shaker piece.

Mullin-Jones Antiquities (525 S. Main St., Rte. 7, tel. 413/528–4871) has 18th- and 19th-century country French antiques: armoires, buffets, tables, chairs, architectural elements, fabrics, and lace.

Lanesborough   **Amber Springs Antiques** (29 S. Main St., Rte. 7, tel. 413/442–1237), in a shop behind a fine old white-clapboard house, shows an eclectic assortment of American furnishings from the late-18th to early 20th centuries. Tools, pottery, and country store items are the house specialties.

Sheffield   **Bradford Galleries** (Rte. 7, tel. 413/229–6667) holds monthly auctions of furniture, paintings and prints, china, glass, and silver. A tag sale of household items is open daily.

Darr Antiques and Interiors (S. Main St., Rte. 7, tel. 413/229–7773) displays elegant 18th- and 19th-century American, English, Continental, and Oriental furniture and accessories in impressive, formal room settings in a fine Colonial house. The wall coverings and draperies are reproductions of period furnishings.

Dovetail Antiques (Rte. 7, tel. 413/229–2628) shows American clocks and country furniture in a small, friendly shop.

Good & Hutchinson Associates (Rte. 7, tel. 413/229–8832) specializes in American, English, and Continental furniture, paintings, fine pottery, and china "for museums and antiquarians."

South Egremont   **Red Barn Antiques** (Rte. 23, tel. 413/528–3230) has a wide selection of antique lamps and 19th-century American and English furniture, glass, and accessories.

The Splendid Peasant (Rte. 23 and Old Sheffield Rd., tel. 413/528–5755) concentrates on 18th- and 19th-century American and European country-primitive furnishings, including painted chests and other notable folk art.

Southfield   **Antiques at the Buggy Whip Factory** (Main St., Rte. 272, tel. 413/229–8280), located in a former buggy whip factory restored as a crafts, food, and antiques market, provides space for 38 dealers to show American country antiques.

West Stockbridge   **Sawyer Antiques** (Depot St., tel. 413/232–7062) offers early American furniture and accessories in a large, spare, clapboard structure that was once a Shaker mill.

Sports and Outdoor Activities

Biking   Bikes can be rented from **Plaine's Cycling Center** (55 W. Housatonic St., Pittsfield, tel. 413/499–0294).

Boating and   The **Housatonic River** (the Indian name means "river beyond
Canoeing   the mountains") flows south from Pittsfield between the Berkshire Hills and the Taconic Range toward Connecticut. Suggested canoe trips in the Berkshires include Dalton–Lenox (19 miles), Lenox–Stockbridge (12 miles), Stockbridge–Great Barrington (13 miles) and, for the experts, Great Barrington–Falls Village—a total of 25 miles. Information about these and other trips can be found in the *AMC River Guide–Central/ Southern New England* (AMC, 5 Joy St., Boston, 02198). Ca-

noes and small motorboats can be rented from the **Onota Boat Livery** (455 Pecks Rd., Pittsfield, tel. 413/442–1724) on Onota Lake.

Fishing The rivers, lakes, and streams of Berkshire County abound with fish—bass, pike, and perch, to name but a few. Stocked trout waters include the Hoosic River (south branch) near Cheshire; Green River, Great Barrington; Notch Brook and Hoosic River (north branch), North Adams; Goose Pond and Hop Brook, Lee; and Williams River, West Stockbridge. **Points North Fishing and Hunting Outfitters** (Rte. 8, Adams, tel. 413/743–4030) organizes fly-fishing schools May through September at Jiminy Peak, which include instruction in knot tying, fly casting, and fishing in a trout pond. **Onota Boat Livery** (455 Pecks Rd., Pittsfield, tel. 413/442–1724) sells fishing tackle and live bait.

Golf The following Berkshires golf clubs welcome guests: **Bas Ridge Country Club** (9 holes; Plunkett St., Hinsdale, tel. 413/655–2605); **Forest Park Country Club** (9 holes; Forest Park Ave., Adams, tel. 413/743–3311); **Greenock Country Club** (9 holes; W. Park St., Lee, tel. 413/243–3323); **General Electric Athletic Association** (9 holes; 303 Crane Ave., Pittsfield, tel. 413/442–3585); **Pontoosuc Lake Country Club** (18 holes; Ridge Ave., Pittsfield, tel. 413/445–5584); **Waconah Country Club** (18 holes; Orchard Rd., Dalton, tel. 413/684–1333); and **Waubeeka Golf Links** (18 holes; Rte. 7, Williamstown, tel. 413/458–5869).

Hiking The **Appalachian Trail** goes right through Berkshire County, and attracts many walkers. Hiking is encouraged in most state parks, and is particularly rewarding in the higher elevations of the **Mount Greylock State Reservation** (*see* National and State Parks, below), where the views are excellent. **New England Hiking Holidays** operates guided hiking vacations in the region (*see* Guided Tours, above).

Rafting Rafting takes place at just one location in the Berkshires— along the Deerfield River at Charlemont, on the Mohawk Trail. One-day raft tours over 10 miles of class II–III rapids take place daily April through October. *Zoar Outdoor, Mohawk Trail, Charlemont 01339, tel. 413/339–4010.*

National and State Parks

There are 19 state parks and forests in the Berkshires. Those with particularly varied facilities—most with camping— include: **Beartown State Forest** (Blue Hill Rd., Monterey, tel. 413/528–0904), **Clarksburg State Forest** (Middle Rd., Clarksburg, tel. 413/664–8345), **Mount Greylock State Reservation** (Rockwell Rd., Lanesborough, tel. 413/499–4262/3), **October Mountain State Forest** (Woodland Rd., Lee, tel. 413/243–1778), **Otis State Forest** (Rte. 23, Otis, tel. 413/528–0904), **Pittsfield State Forest** (Cascade St., Pittsfield, tel. 413/442–8992), **Sandisfield State Forest** (West St., Sandisfield, tel. 413/258–4774), **Savoy Mountain State Forest** (Rte. 2, Florida; Rte. 116, Savoy, tel. 413/663–8469), **Tolland State Forest** (Rte. 8, Otis, tel. 413/269–6002), **Windsor State Forest** (Windsor, tel. 413/684–9760).

Dining and Lodging

Great Barrington **The Egremont Inn.** This venerable inn's sunny dining room,
Dining with its open fireplace and uneven floor, is decorated in blue
and white. Entrées include sautéed trout; sole with pecan butter; smoked pork chop; and chicken breast with goat cheese and
herbs. *Old Sheffield Rd., South Egremont, tel. 413/528–2111.
Reservations required weekends in season. Dress: casual. AE,
D, DC, MC, Moderate–Expensive.*

Whole Wheat 'N Wild Berries. The original branch of this restaurant is in Greenwich Village, New York City. This one
opened in 1988, specializing in gourmet natural foods, and vegetarian and fish dishes, such as sautéed tofu, ratatouille, and
fresh tuna. The setting is "country-kitchen," with flowered
curtains and pine tables and chairs. *293 Main St., tel. 413/528–
1586. Dress: casual. No credit cards. Closed Mon.; Tues. Nov.
–Apr. Moderate.*

20 Railroad St. The exposed brick and subdued lighting lend atmosphere to this bustling restaurant, which features a 28-foot
mahogany bar taken from the Commodore Hotel in New York
City in 1919. Small wooden tables are packed together in the
long, narrow room, but despite the crowd, service is speedy.
Specialties include sausage pie, burgers, and sandwiches. *20
Railroad St., tel. 413/528–9345. Dress: casual. MC, V. Inexpensive.*

Great Barrington **Windflower Inn.** A comfortable, casual atmosphere prevails at
Lodging the family-run Windflower. Everything is homemade, and
many vegetables and herbs come from the inn garden. The dining room is sunny, and in summer food is served on the screened
porch. Bedrooms of varying sizes—mostly spacious—have
four-posters and are filled with antiques. Several rooms contain working fireplaces: The most impressive has a stone
surround that covers most of the wall. *Rte. 23 (Egremont Star
Rte., Box 25), 01230, tel. 413/528–2720. 13 rooms with bath. Facilities: restaurant, outdoor pool, gardens. No pets. No credit
cards. Rates include full breakfast, dinner. Very Expensive.*

The Egremont Inn. The public rooms in this 1780 inn are
enormous—the main lounge, with its vast open fireplace and
coffee table made from an old door, is worth a visit in itself. The
bedrooms, by contrast, are small, with wide-board floors, uneven ceilings, four-posters, and clawfoot baths. A wraparound
porch is furnished with white wicker chairs. *Old Sheffield Rd.
(Box 418), South Egremont 01258, tel. 413/528–2111. 22 rooms
with bath. Facilities: dining room, lounge, bar, outdoor pool, 2
tennis courts. AE, D, DC, MC, V. Rates include Continental
breakfast. Moderate–Expensive.*

Hancock Dining **Drummond's Restaurant.** At the Jiminy Peak ski resort, this
restaurant is designed like a ski lodge, with cathedral ceilings,
lots of wood, and a stone chimney with wood-burning stove. Tables at the back overlook the slopes, which are lit for night
skiing in season. Entrées include fresh salmon, roast duck, and
pasta Jericho, with scallops, shrimp, crab meat, and clams in
sherry-cream sauce. *Corey Rd., tel. 413/445–5500. Reservations advised. Dress: casual. AE, D, DC, MC, V. Moderate.*

The Springs. This restaurant sits in the shadow of Brodie Mountain and its ski resort. A fireplace in the lobby, exposed-brick
walls, and wooden ceiling (from which hangs the biggest chandelier in the Berkshires) make for a country-lodge atmosphere.

The menu offers lobster blended with mushrooms in cream sauce, duckling flambé in cherry sauce, chicken livers, and veal dishes. *Rte. 7, New Ashford, tel. 413/458–3465. Dress: casual. AE, CB, D, DC, MC, V. Moderate.*

Lee Dining **Cork 'n Hearth.** A large stone fireplace separates the long dining room into two: On one side wooden beams show off all kinds of brassware; on the other, they are hung with bundles of dried herbs. Picture windows look onto Laurel Lake, which practically laps against the side of the building. The menu is traditional, offering steak, seafood, chicken Kiev, and veal cordon bleu. *Rte. 20, tel. 413/243–0535. Reservations advised. Dress: casual. AE, CB, D, DC, MC, V. Closed lunch; Mon. Nov. 1–May 1. Expensive.*

Lee Lodging **Oak n' Spruce Resort.** Rooms in the main lodge are like high-quality motel rooms; large rooms in the building next door have modern furniture, kitchen units, and sliding doors onto the spacious grounds surrounding this former farm. The lodge lounge is a converted cow barn built around the original brick silo. An excellent children's program makes this a great place for kids. *Meadow St. (Box 237), South Lee 01260, tel. 413/243–3500 or 800/341–5700, in MA 800/352–7153. 17 rooms, 26 suites, 107 condos. Facilities: restaurant, lounge, live entertainment, indoor and outdoor pool, Jacuzzi, sauna, health club, cross-country ski trails, shuffleboard, basketball, 2 tennis courts, badminton, horseshoes, volleyball, central VCR, children's program, hiking trails. AE, MC, V. Moderate.*

The Pilgrim Motel. This motel is well furnished with gleaming reproduction antiques and color coordinated drapes, but even so the rates during the Tanglewood season are high. The location in the very center of Lee is busy but convenient. *127 Housatonic St., tel. 413/243–1328. 24 rooms with bath. Facilities: outdoor pool, laundry. AE, CB, DC, MC, V. Moderate (Very Expensive in Tanglewood season).*

The Morgan House. Most guest rooms in this inn, which dates to 1817, are small, but the rates reflect that. Some are so narrow they resemble servants' quarters, with their scrubbed boards and brightly painted wooden furniture; others have four-posters, stenciled walls, and well-used antiques. The lobby is papered with the pages from old guest registers; among the signatures are those of George Bernard Shaw and Ulysses S. Grant. Mrs. Nat King Cole owned the inn until 1981. *31 Main St., 01238, tel. 413/243–0181. 12 rooms share 5 baths, 1 suite. Facilities: 3 dining rooms, bar. AE, D, MC, V. Rates include Continental breakfast. Inexpensive (Moderate–Expensive in Tanglewood season).*

Lenox Dining **Gateways Inn.** Four dining rooms are hung with chandeliers and tapestries; working fireplaces soften the otherwise formal tone. The Rockwell Room is small and sunny. Continental and American cuisine includes veal, pheasant, salmon, and rack of lamb. *71 Walker St., tel. 413/637–2532. Reservations required. Jacket and tie advised. AE, DC, MC, V. Closed Sun.; lunch Nov.–Apr. Very Expensive.*

Lenox House Restaurant. Continental cuisine is served in a large, bright dining room with country-style furniture, floral-print drapes, and flowers on the tables. Entrées include king crab *fra diavolo* (crab legs, clams, and mussels in a spicy marinara sauce), bouillabaisse, veal, steaks, and chicken. *339*

*Pittsfield–Lenox Rd. (Rtes. 7 and 20), tel. 413/637–1341.
Dress: casual. AE, CB, DC, MC, V. Expensive.*

Sophia's Restaurant and Pizza. This unpretentious establishment serves up pizza, generous Greek salads, pasta dishes, and grinders (the Massachusetts equivalent of a submarine sandwich). Seating is in booths with imitation-leather seats. *Rtes. 7/20, tel. 413/499–1101. Dress: casual. AE, MC, V. Closed Mon. Inexpensive.*

Lenox Lodging
★

Gateways Inn. This formal and elegant mansion was built as a summer home in 1912 by Harley Proctor of Proctor and Gamble. From the large entrance hall, a grand open staircase lit by a skylight leads to the second-floor guest rooms. The huge Fiedler Suite (Tanglewood conductor Arthur Fiedler stayed here and gave his name to it) has two working fireplaces and a dressing room. All rooms have light, period wallpapers; antiques; and Oriental rugs. *71 Walker St., 01240, tel. 413/637–2532. 8 rooms. Facilities: 4 dining rooms, TV lounge. No pets. AE, DC, MC, V. Rates include Continental breakfast. Very Expensive.*

The Candlelight Inn. Attractive, spacious bedrooms have floral-print wallpapers and antiques; those on the top floor are especially charming, with sloping ceilings and skylights. The inn is located right in the middle of Lenox village and has a popular Continental restaurant. Although elegant, this inn is less formal than the nearby Gateways. *53 Walker St., 01240, tel. 413/637–1555. 8 rooms. Facilities: 4 dining rooms, bar. No pets. AE, MC, V. Rates include Continental breakfast. Expensive (Very Expensive in Tanglewood season).*

★ **Rookwood Inn.** This "painted lady" was restored to her original grandeur in 1985, exactly 100 years after being built as a summer cottage for a wealthy New York family. Guest rooms are generally roomy and some have working fireplaces; the Victorian era is perfectly re-created with period wallpapers, matching linen, and English and American antiques. Some rooms have balconies. The elegant lounge has reading material, an open fire, and a screened porch with wicker furniture. The inn is on a quiet street, two minutes' walk from the center of Lenox. *19 Old Stockbridge Rd. (Box 1717), 01240, tel. 413/637–9750. 17 rooms. Facilities: breakfast room. lounge. No smoking. No pets. Rates include full breakfast, afternoon tea. Expensive.*

★ **Whistler's Inn.** The antiques decorating the parlor of this English Tudor mansion are ornate with a touch of the exotic—some are in the Louis XVI style, others the innkeepers brought back from various travels abroad. Bedrooms are more conventionally decorated with Laura Ashley drapes and bedspreads. Some rooms have working fireplaces, and most have great views across the valley. *5 Greenwood St., 01240, tel. 413/637–0975. 11 rooms with bath. Facilities: lounge, library, badminton, croquet. AE, MC, V. Rates include full breakfast. Expensive.*

Eastover. An antidote to the posh atmosphere prevailing in most of Lenox, this resort was opened by an ex–circus roustabout, and the tradition of noisy fun and informality continues with gusto. Guest rooms are functional and vary from dormitory to motel-style: Although the period wallpapers are stylish, some rooms with four or more beds resemble hospital wards with their metal rails and white bedspreads. Dining rooms are vast and very noisy, but period decor and furnishings temper the absolute informality to some extent. The grounds are huge, and wandered by buffalo; facilities are extensive. *East St. (off Rte. 7), Box 2160, 01240, tel. 413/637-0625. 195 rooms, 120 with bath. Facilities: 6 tennis courts, indoor and outdoor pools, golf driving range, softball, volleyball, archery, skeet shooting, cross-country and downhill skiing, tobogganing, exercise room, sauna, ice-skating, canoeing, shuffleboard, badminton, live music, dancing, free local transport, horseback riding. Rates include tax, service charges, three meals a day, and most facilities. AE, DC, MC, V. Moderate.*

Pittsfield Dining **La Cocina.** This restaurant offers a selection of typical Mexican dishes such as burritos, flautas, and fajitas. The decor is exposed brick with Mexican rug hangings; seating is at dimly lit booths. Live guitar music adds to a cozy atmosphere. *140 Wahconah St., tel. 413/499-4027. No reservations. Dress: casual. AE, CB, DC, MC, V. Closed dinner Sun. Moderate.*

Dakota. Moose and elk heads watch over diners at this large restaurant decorated like a rustic hunting lodge. A canoe swings overhead, and Indian artifacts hang on the walls. A broiler stocked with Texan mesquite wood is used for specialties, which include swordfish steaks, shrimp, sirloin, and grilled chicken. *Rtes. 7 & 20, tel. 413/499-7900. Dress: casual. AE, CB, DC, MC, V. Closed lunch Mon.-Sat. Moderate.*

Pittsfield Lodging **Berkshire Hilton Inn.** This is a typically comfortable, sophisticated Hilton with a spacious hall featuring wingback chairs, glass, and brass. Guest rooms have new reproductions and floral-print drapes. Upgraded rooms on the two top floors have the best views over the town and surrounding mountains. *Berkshire Common, South St., 01201, tel. 413/499-2000 or 800/445-8667. 175 rooms. Facilities: restaurant, lounge, bar, live entertainment, indoor pool, sauna, Jacuzzi, meeting rooms. AE, CB, DC, MC, V. Very Expensive.*

Sheffield Dining **Stagecoach Hill Inn.** Constructed in the early 1800s as a stagecoach stop, the restaurant offers a character inspired by England—there are numerous pictures of the British royal family and several hunting scenes, as well as steak and kidney pie, roast beef and Yorkshire pudding, and British ale on tap. Other menu items include pasta dishes, steak au poivre, and chicken al forno. *Rte. 41, tel. 413/229-8585. Dress: casual. AE, DC, MC, V. Closed Tues.-Wed. and Mar. Expensive.*

Sheffield Lodging **Ivanhoe Country House.** The Appalachian Trail runs right across the property of this bed-and-breakfast. The house was originally built in 1780, but various wings were added later. The antique-furnished guest rooms are generally spacious; several have private porches or balconies, and all have excellent country views. The large sitting room has antique desks, a piano, and comfortable couches. *Undermountain Rd., Rte. 41, 01257, tel. 413/258-4453. 9 rooms, 1 suite with kitchen. Facilities: lounge, outdoor pool, refrigerators. No credit cards. Rates include Continental breakfast. $10 fee for dogs. Expensive.*

Stockbridge Dining **The Red Lion Inn.** The dining rooms at this distinguished inn are filled with antiques, and tables are set with pewter plates. New England specialties include oyster pie, broiled scallops prepared with sherry, lemon, and paprika, and steamed or stuffed lobster. *Main St., tel. 413/298-5545. Reservations advised. Jacket and tie advised. AE, CB, D, DC, MC, V. Expensive.*

Hoplands. Located about a mile north of Stockbridge center, this restaurant has two dining rooms—downstairs around the bar or upstairs in a simply furnished room with polished wood floors and no tablecloths (somewhat reminiscent of an old-fashioned schoolroom). The menu features chicken pie, stir-fry, burgers, and sandwiches. *Rte. 102, tel. 413/243–4414. Reservations required for parties of more than 6. Dress: casual. AE, MC, V. Closed Mon.; Tues. Nov.–May. Moderate.*

Stockbridge Lodging

The Red Lion Inn. An inn since 1773, and rebuilt after a fire in 1896, the Red Lion is now a massive place, with guest rooms situated both in the main building and in several annexes on the property. It's a well-known landmark, but it *is* old, and many of the guest rooms are small. In general, the annex houses are more appealing. Rooms are individually decorated with floral-print wallpapers and country curtains (from the mail-order store Country Curtains owned by the innkeepers and operated out of the inn). All are furnished with antiques, and hung with Rockwell prints; some have Oriental rugs. *Main St., 02162, tel. 413/298–5545. 108 rooms, 75 with bath, 10 suites. Facilities: dining room, lounge, bar, outdoor pool, exercise room, meeting rooms. AE, CB, D, DC, MC, V. Expensive (Very Expensive in Tanglewood season).*

The Golden Goose. This friendly, informal place 5 miles south of Lee is cluttered with antiques, bric-a-brac, and dozens of geese in various shapes and sizes (many were donated by guests). Bedrooms are Victorian in style; some have brass beds and quilts, and the walls are stenciled. Guests' names are chalked up on the little welcome board on each door. *Main Rd. (Box 336), Tyringham 01264, tel. 413/243–3008. 5 rooms, 2 with bath. Facilities: dining room, lounge. No smoking. No pets. No credit cards. Rates include Continental breakfast. Moderate–Expensive.*

★ **Merrell Tavern Inn.** If you are looking for a genuine old New England inn, this is it. It was built in 1800, and is listed in the National Register of Historic Places; despite its age, it has good-size bedrooms, several with working fireplaces. The style is simple: polished wide-board floors, cream-painted plaster walls with Shaker pegs, and plain wooden antiques. Guest rooms have pencil four-posters with unfussy canopies. The breakfast room has an open fireplace and contains the only complete "birdcage" Colonial bar in America. *Rte. 102, South Lee 01260, tel. 413/243–1794. 7 rooms. Facilities: breakfast room, lounge, gardens. No pets. AE, MC, V. Rates include full breakfast. Moderate–Expensive.*

West Stockbridge Dining

The Williamsville Inn. The main dining room is decorated with period wallpaper and has a large fireplace. Lamps burn on the table in the evening, and the windows look onto the surrounding woodlands. Entrées include broiled yellowfin tuna marinated in soy sauce, lime juice, and sesame oil; pan-seared loin veal chop with Dijon mustard and tarragon glaze; and roast duckling with brandied apricot sauce. *Rte. 41, tel. 413/274–6118. Dress: casual. AE, MC, V. Expensive.*

Shaker Mill Tavern. The only concession to Shakers here is a row of Shaker pegs on the wall, but the restaurant is located just down the street from the Shaker mill, hence its name. In summer dining can be outside on the "deck café," otherwise it's in the large modern dining room with wood floors and ceilings and lots of plants. American dishes include burgers, fried chicken, buffalo wings, pizza, and pasta dishes. *Rte. 102, tel.*

413/232–8565. Dress: casual. AE, MC, V. Closed Wed. Jan.–May. Moderate.

West Stockbridge **The Williamsville Inn.** A couple of miles south of West Stock-
Lodging bridge, this inn has been carefully renovated to re-create the
late 1700s, when it was built. Guest rooms have wide-board
floors, embroidered chairs, four-posters, and canopied beds;
several have working fireplaces. The halls and the bar are decorated with stencils, and four dining rooms with fireplaces (*see
West Stockbridge Dining,* above) look onto the woods. *Rte. 41,
Williamsville 01266, tel. 413/274–6118. 15 rooms, 1 suite. Facilities: 4 dining rooms, bar, croquet, outdoor pool, tennis
court, horseshoes, badminton, volleyball, boccie. No pets. AE,
MC, V. Rates include Continental breakfast. Very Expensive.*

Williamstown **Le Jardin.** Set on a hillock above the road just west of
Dining Williamstown, this French restaurant has the feel of a small inn
(there are guest rooms on the upper floor). The two dining
rooms are paneled and candlelit, and a fire burns in the hall in
season. The menu offers snails in garlic butter, oysters baked
with spinach and Pernod, sole florentine, filet mignon, and rack
of lamb. *777 Cold Spring Rd. (Rte. 7), tel. 413/458–8032. Reservations advised. Dress: casual. AE, MC, V. Closed Tues.;
Jan.–Feb. Expensive.*

Four Acres. Located on the commercial strip of Route 2 just
east of Williamstown, this pleasant restaurant has two dining
rooms: One is casual, decorated with street signs, paneling,
and mirrors; the other is more formal, with collegiate insignia
and modern paintings on the walls. American and Continental
cuisine includes sautéed calf's liver glazed in applejack; veal
cutlet sautéed in butter and topped with a Newburg of lobster
and asparagus; and pork tenderloin with cognac and walnut
sauce. *Rte. 2, tel. 413/458–5436. Reservations advised. Dress:
casual. AE, MC, V. Closed Sun. Moderate.*

Williamstown **The Orchards.** After seeing the pale-orange stucco exterior,
Lodging and perhaps wondering about the location on a commercial
strip of Route 2 east of town, it's a pleasant surprise to enter
the quiet, tasteful interior of this small luxury hotel built in
1985. Church pews and a heavy pulpit adorn the corridors, the
cozy lounge has wall cases of silverware and an open fireplace,
and guest rooms are furnished with elegant four-posters, antiques, and reproductions. Ask for a room with a view of the
hills or the small modern courtyard and its lily pond. *Main St.
(Rte. 2), tel. 413/458–9611. 49 rooms. Facilities: restaurant,
lounge, tavern, outdoor pool, sauna, Jacuzzi, room service.
AE, DC, MC, V. Very Expensive.*

Williams Inn. The spacious guest rooms in this new inn have
good-quality, modern furnishings, with floral-print drapes and
bedspreads. The lounge has an open fireplace and is
comfortable—the atmosphere is collegiate. The inn allows pets
for a $5 fee; children under 14 stay free in their parents' room.
*On-the-Green at Williams College, 01267, tel. 413/458–9371.
105 rooms. Facilities: dining room, lounge, coffee shop, live entertainment, indoor pool, sauna, Jacuzzi. AE, CB, D, DC,
MC, V. Expensive.*

Berkshire Hills Motel. This excellent motel is housed in a two-
story brick-and-clapboard building about 3 miles south of
Williamstown. All guest rooms were recently refurbished in
Colonial style—each with a rocking chair and good-quality reproduction furniture. The lounge, complete with a teddy-bear

collection, has an open fireplace and a piano. Outside, the pool is located across a brook amid 2½ acres of woodland and landscaped garden. *Rte. 7, 01267, tel. 413/458–3950. 20 rooms with bath. Facilities: lounge, outdoor pool. AE, MC, V. Rates include Continental breakfast. Moderate.*

The Arts

Tickets for most events may be purchased through individual offices, but last-minute reservations can be made, in person only, at the **Berkshire Ticket Booth** in the Lenox Chamber of Commerce Information Center, 75 Main St., between 1 PM and 5:30 PM, seven days a week. Tickets are for same-day performances, and after 3 PM, discount tickets are available.

Listings are published weekly in the *Berkshire Week* and the *Williamstown Advocate;* major concert listings are published Thursdays in the *Boston Globe.* The quarterly *Berkshire Magazine* contains "The Berkshire Guide," a comprehensive listing of local events ranging from theater to sports.

Dance The **Berkshire Ballet** (Koussevitzky Arts Center, Berkshire Community College, West St., Pittsfield, tel. 413/445–5382) performs classical and contemporary works for seven weeks during July and August.

Jacob's Pillow Dance Festival, the oldest in the nation, mounts a 10-week summer program every year. Performers vary from well-known classical ballet companies to Native American dance groups and contemporary choreographers. Before the main events, free showings of works-in-progress are staged outdoors. Visitors can picnic on the grounds or eat at the Pillow Café. *Rte. 20, Becket (mailing address: Box 287, Lee, 01238), tel. 413/243–0745. Open June–Sept.*

Music The best-known music festival in New England is the **Tanglewood** concert series near Lenox between June and September. The main shed seats 6,000; the Chamber Music Hall holds 300 for smaller concerts. *Lenox, tel. 617/266–1492 Oct.–June; 413/637–1940 June–Sept. Ticket prices $10–$50.*

The **Berkshire Performing Arts Center** (Kemble St., Lenox, tel. 413/637–4718), the newest arts center in the county, attracts top-name artists in jazz, folk, and blues.

Opera The **Berkshire Opera Company** (17 Main St., Lee, tel. 413/243–1343) performs two operas in English from the Baroque repertoire during July and August at different Pittsfield and Lenox venues.

Theater The **Berkshire Theatre Festival** stages nightly performances in summer at the century-old theater in Stockbridge. A series of children's plays, usually written by local schoolchildren, are performed weekends during the day. *Box 797 (Rte. 102), Stockbridge, tel. 413/298–5576 or 413/298–5536.*

The **Williamstown Theatre Festival** presents well-known theatrical works on the Main Stage, and contemporary works on the Other Stage. *Adams Memorial Theatre, Williams College Campus, tel. 413/597–3400. July–Aug.*

The **Music-Theatre** (tel. 413/298–5122) at Lenox Arts Center presents new music-theater works, July through August.

The **Berkshire Ensemble for Theatre Arts** (Williamstown venues, tel. 413/458–9441) also produces a program of original music-theater with professional ensemble cabarets during July and August.

Shakespeare and Company (tel. 413/637–3353) performs Shakespeare and Edith Wharton's works throughout the summer at The Mount (Plunkett St., Lenox).

Berkshire Public Theatre (30 Union St., Pittsfield, tel. 413/445–4634), the county's only year-round repertory company, performs a variety of modern and traditional pieces.

Nightlife

The emphasis in the Berkshires is definitely on classical entertainment. However, **The Lion's Den** (tel. 413/298–5545) downstairs at the Red Lion Inn in Stockbridge has nightly folk music and some contemporary local bands every evening throughout the year. **The Night Spot** (tel. 413/637–0060), at Seven Hills Inn in Lenox, stages a program of jazz and blues music on Friday and Saturday evenings between July 4 and Labor Day.

6 Vermont

by Mary H. Frakes, with an introduction by William G. Scheller

A restaurant columnist for the Boston Phoenix, *Mary Frakes also writes on travel, business, and contemporary art and crafts.*

Everywhere you look around Vermont, the evidence is clear: This is not the state it was 25 years ago.

That may be true for the rest of New England as well, but the contrasts between present and recent past seem all the more sharply drawn in the Green Mountain State, if only because an aura of timelessness has always been at the heart of the Vermont image. Vermont was where all the quirks and virtues outsiders associate with upcountry New England were supposed to reside. It was where the Yankees were Yankee-est and where there were more cows than people.

Not that you should be alarmed, if you haven't been here in a while; Vermont hasn't become southern California, or even, for that matter, southern New Hampshire. This is still the most rural state in the Union (meaning that it has the smallest percentage of citizens living in statistically defined metropolitan areas), even if there are, finally, more people than cows. It's still a place where cars occasionally have to stop while a dairyman walks his cows across a secondary road; and up in Essex County, in what George Aiken dubbed the Northeast Kingdom, there are townships with zero population. And the kind of scrupulous, straightforward, plainspoken politics practiced by Governor (later Senator) Aiken for 50 years has not become outmoded in a state that still turns out on town meeting day.

How has Vermont changed? In strictly physical terms, the most obvious transformations have taken place in and around the two major cities, Burlington and Rutland, and near the larger ski resorts such as Stowe, Killington, Stratton, and Mt. Snow. Burlington's Church Street, once a paradigm of all the sleepy redbrick shopping thoroughfares in northern New England, is now a pedestrian mall complete with chic bistros; outside the city, suburban development has supplanted dairy farms in towns where someone's trip to Burlington might once have been an item in a weekly newspaper. As for the ski areas, it's no longer enough simply to boast the latest in chairlift technology. Stratton has an entire "Austrian Village" of restaurants and shops, while a hillside adjacent to Bromley's slopes has sprouted instant replica Victorians for the second-home market. The town of Manchester, convenient to both resorts, is awash in designer fashion discount outlets.

But the real metamorphosis in the Green Mountains has to do more with style, with the personality of the place, than with the mere substance of development. The past couple of decades have seen a tremendous influx of outsiders—not just skiers and "leaf peekers," but people who've come to stay year-round— and many of them are determined either to freshen the local scene with their own idiosyncrasies or to make Vermont even more like Vermont than they found it. On the one hand, this translates into the fact that the most popular restaurant in Hinesburg, Kali-Yuga, has a name drawn from Hindu mythology; on the other, it means that sheep farming has been reintroduced into the state, largely to provide a high-quality product for the hand-weaving industry.

This ties in with another local phenomenon, one best described as Made in Vermont. Once upon a time, maple syrup and sharp cheddar cheese were the products that carried Vermont's name to the world. The market niche that they created has since been widened by Vermonters—a great many of them refugees from

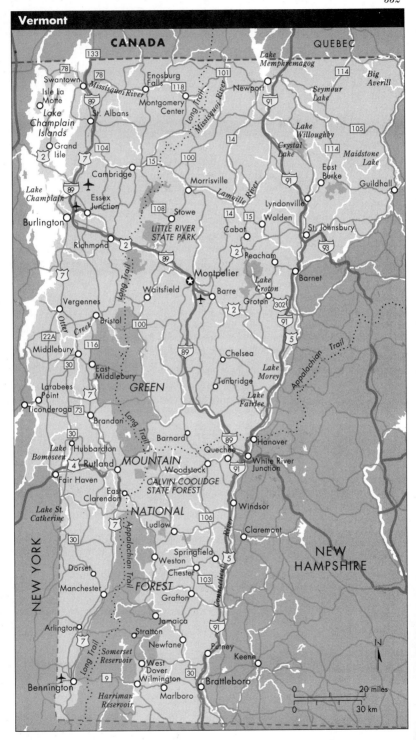

Vermont

more hectic arenas of commerce in places like Massachusetts and New York—offering a dizzying variety of goods with the ineffable cachet of Vermont manufacture. There are Vermont wooden toys, Vermont apple wines, Vermont chocolates, even Vermont gin. All of it is marketed with the tacit suggestion that it was made by Yankee elves in a shed out back on a bright autumn morning.

As the 1990s begin, the most successful Made in Vermont product is the renowned Ben & Jerry's ice cream. Neither Ben nor Jerry come from old Green Mountain stock, but their product has benefited immensely from the magical reputation of the place where it is made. Along the way, the company (which started in Burlington under the most modest circumstances a little more than a decade ago) has become the largest single purchaser of Vermont's still considerable dairy output. Thus the modern dovetails with the traditional in a small state where it's best that they get along.

Yet tradition, wearing a red plaid cap and a Johnson Woolen Mills hunting jacket, still gets along very nicely by itself here. One of the state's smaller milk purchasers is the cheese factory in Plymouth, which is still owned by the family of Vermont's own Calvin Coolidge.

Essential Information

Visitor Information

Vermont Travel Division (134 State St., Montpelier 05602, tel. 802/828–3236).

Vermont Chamber of Commerce, Department of Travel and Tourism (Box 37, Montpelier 05602, tel. 802/223–3443).

Tour Groups

General-Interest **New England Vacation Tours** (Box 947, West Dover 05356, tel.
Tours 802/464–2076 or 800/742–7669).

Special-Interest **Vermont Travel Information Service** (Pond Village, Brookfield
Tours 05036, tel. 802/276–3120) offers a maple-sugaring weekend, a visit to several cheese factories, a family vacation package, an antiques and crafts tour, and programs for fishing, golfing, and bicycling.

Bicycling **Vermont Bicycle Touring** (Box 711, Bristol 05443, tel. 802/453–4811), the first bike tour operator in the United States and one of the most respected, operates a 10-day Grand Tour of Vermont that covers 25–40 or 45–65 miles each day. Vermont is a leading state for bicycle touring; a number of companies offer weekend tours and weeklong trips that range throughout the state. The state travel division has prepared an information sheet on biking, and many bookstores have *25 Bicycle Tours in Vermont* by John Freidin, the founder of Vermont Bicycle Touring.

Canoeing **Canoe Vermont** (Box 610, Waitsfield 05673, tel. 802/496–2409) sponsors two-day and five-day inn-to-inn canoe trips throughout the state.

Hiking **Vermont Hiking Holidays** (Box 845, Waitsfield 05673, tel. 802/495–2219) leads guided hikes and walks from May to October, with lodging in country inns.

Outdoor Recreation **Vermont Voyageur Expeditions** (Box 101S, Montgomery Center 05471, tel. 802/326–4789) conducts canoeing, kayaking, hiking, walking, backpacking, snowshoeing and cross-country skiing tours.

Package Deals for Independent Travelers

Vermont Houseboat Vacations (90 Forbes St., Riverside, RI 02915, tel. 401/437–1377) has a variety of houseboat vacations.

Country Inns Along the Trail (Churchill House Inn, RD 3, Box VTG, Brandon 05733, tel. 802/247–3300) organizes inn-to-inn vacations for independent travelers.

When to Go

The peak tourist season in Vermont runs from mid-September to mid-October, when the fall foliage is most colorful. Lodging reservations are important then, especially if you want to stay at a particular inn; rooms are often booked a year in advance. In many areas the other peak time comes in February, the height of the ski season that begins around Thanksgiving and runs through March, weather permitting; Christmas week, too, is popular with skiers. Many visitors avoid "mud season" in late April, when melting snows soften dirt roads and hiking trails. In early May the blackflies are usually rampant in heavily forested areas. November is generally a slow month, one when many inns and tourist attractions are closed. Maple sugaring occurs in March–April, depending on weather conditions.

Festivals and Seasonal Events

Mid-Jan.: Stowe Winter Carnival, among the country's oldest such celebrations, features winter sports competitions. *Tel. 802/253–7326.*

Late Jan.: Brookfield Ice Harvest Festival is one of New England's last ice harvest festivals. *Tel. 802/276–3352.*

Mid-Feb.: Newport Winterfest's week of winter activities includes curling, dogsled races, hockey, and cross-country skiing. *Tel. 802/334–7782.*

Late Feb.: Benson Fishing Derby hosts ice-fishing competitions. *Tel. 802/773–2747.*

Early–mid-Apr.: Vermont Maple Festival, St. Albans, celebrates the end of the spring sugaring. *Tel. 802/524–4966.*

Late Apr.: St. Johnsbury Maple Sugar Festival comes at the close of the sugaring season. *Tel. 802/748–3678.*

Early May: Whitewater canoe races are held on the Passumpsic River near East Burke. *Tel. 802/748–3678.*

Mid-May: The Festival of Traditional Crafts at the Fairbanks Museum in St. Johnsbury demonstrates such old Vermont skills as blacksmithing. *Tel. 802/748–3678.*

Late May–early June: Vermont Dairy Festival at Enosburg Falls celebrates the products of all those Holsteins you see in the fields alongside the roads. *Tel. 802/933–2513.*

Memorial Day: State parks open for the summer season. *Tel. 802/828–3375.*

Late June: The Quechee Balloon Festival sponsors a regional hot-air balloon competition. *Tel. 802/295–7900.*

July 4: Burlington's month-long **Lake Champlain Discovery Festival** ends with a large-scale version of the July 4 celebrations held throughout the state. *Tel. 802/863–3489.*

July: One of the state's largest **antiques festivals** takes place in Dorset in odd-numbered years, in Manchester in even-numbered years. *Tel. 802/362–2100.*

Mid-July: Vermont Quilt Festival in Northfield draws visitors and exhibitors from throughout New England. *Tel. 802/485–7092.*

July–Aug.: Marlboro College hosts the celebrated Marlboro Music Festival of classical music. *Tel. 802/254–8163.*

Early Aug.: Art on the Mountain, a weeklong show at Haystack Mountain, presents the work of Vermont artists and craftspeople. *Tel. 802/464–5321.*

Early Aug.: The Southern Vermont Crafts Fair in Manchester has juried exhibits of contemporary crafts. *Tel. 802/362–2100.*

Mid-Aug.: Bennington Battle Days commemorates the state's most important conflict of the Revolutionary era. *Tel. 802/447–3311.*

Late Aug.: The Domestic Resurrection Day Circus of the Bread and Puppet Theater, an outdoor pageant on social and political themes, draws thousands to Glover. *Tel. 802/525–3031.*

Early Sept.: The Vermont State Fair, held in Rutland over the

Labor Day weekend, has agricultural exhibits, a midway, and entertainment. *Tel. 802/775-5200.*

Early Sept.: Burlington's **Champlain Valley Exposition** has all the attributes of a large county fair. *Tel. 802/878-5545.*

Early Sept.: Tunbridge World's Fair, a large agricultural fair, has rides and farm horse competitions. *Tel. 802/889-3458.*

Mid-Sept.: Stratton Arts Festival, Stratton Mountain, brings together artists and well-known performers in various media. *Tel. 802/297-2200.*

Late Sept.–early Oct.: The **Northeast Kingdom Fall Foliage Festival** is a weeklong affair hosted by six small towns—Walden, Cabot, Plainfield, Peacham, Barnet, and Groton. *Tel. 802/563-2472.*

Late Sept.: The **National Traditional Old-Time Fiddler's Contest** in Barre celebrates folk music. *Tel. 802/229-5711.*

Late Oct.: Montpelier's **Festival of Vermont Crafts** focuses on traditional and contemporary crafts. *Tel. 802/229-5711.*

Mid-Nov.: Vermont Hand Crafters Crafts Fair, Burlington. *Tel. 802/453-4240.*

Late Nov.: Thanksgiving Weekend Crafts Show takes place in Killington. *Tel. 802/422-3783.*

Late Nov.: The **Bradford Wild Game Supper** draws thousands to sample a variety of large and small game animals and birds. *Tel. 802/222-4670.*

Late Dec.: Hildene in Manchester holds candlelight tours of this historic home. *Tel. 802/362-1788.*

Dec. 31: The **First Night celebration** sees downtown Burlington transformed by musical and theatrical performances, street happenings, a parade, and fireworks. *Tel. 802/863-6005.*

What to Pack

Because Vermont is basically a rural state, casual clothing is the norm; jacket and tie are required only at the most elegant restaurants. Comfortable walking shoes are essential for exploring back roads and small-town centers. Because Vermont evenings can be quite chilly even in summer, it's helpful to have layers of clothing that can be removed during the day. Winter requires heavy clothing, gloves, a hat, and warm socks.

Bug repellent can be a lifesaver when you plan a walk in the woods. A hamper, a corkscrew, and a small knife are good for impromptu picnics, and a detailed road map will show which roads are closed in winter.

Traveling with Children

Many country inns, especially those furnished with antiques, are wary of children as guests. Nor should you expect innkeepers to baby-sit, though they will usually be happy to help you find a baby-sitter. Major hotel chains gladly accept children, and hotel concierges can arrange baby-sitting services.

Renting a vacation home can be the least expensive way to house a family. The publication *Four Seasons Vacation Rentals*, a guide to rental cottages, is available from the Vermont Travel Division (134 State St., Montpelier 05602, tel. 802/828-3236).

Hints for Disabled Travelers

A recent Vermont law requires that new construction include facilities for the handicapped, so the newer hotels and those that have added new sections are the most likely to have handicapped access and handicapped-equipped rooms. A list of facilities is available from the Vermont Travel Division.

The official state map indicates public recreation areas at state parks that are handicapped accessible.

Hints for Older Travelers

Many country inns are happy to accommodate a request for a room on the ground floor, but it should be made when booking the reservation. Older visitors may want to make sure they reserve a room with a shower—or at least a room without a Victorian clawfoot tub that requires climbing in and out.

Arriving and Departing

By Plane **Burlington International Airport** (tel. 802/863–2874) has scheduled daily flights by six major U.S. airlines. West of Bennington and convenient to southern Vermont, **Albany–Schenectady County Airport** in New York State is served by 10 major U.S. carriers.

By Car Interstate 91, from Connecticut and Massachusetts in the south and Quebec (highway 55) in the north, reaches most points along Vermont's eastern border. I–89, from New Hampshire to the east and Quebec (highway 133) in the north, crosses central Vermont to and from Burlington. Southwestern Vermont can be reached by Route 7 from Massachusetts and Route 4 from New York.

By Train **Amtrak**'s (tel. 800/872–7245) *Montrealer*, an overnight train linking New York City and Montreal, stops at Brattleboro, Bellows Falls, Claremont, White River Junction, Montpelier, Waterbury, Essex Junction, and St. Albans. Service to Albany and Glens Falls, New York, is convenient to western Vermont.

By Bus A subsidiary of Greyhound Lines, **Vermont Transit Lines** (135 St. Paul St., Burlington 05401, tel. 802/864–6811 or 800/451–3292) connects Bennington, Brattleboro, Burlington, Rutland, and other cities with Boston, Springfield, Albany, New York, Montreal, and cities in New Hampshire.

Getting Around Vermont

By Plane Aircraft charters are available at Burlington International Airport from **Montair** (tel. 802/862–2246), **Mansfield Heliflight** (tel. 802/864–3954), **Northern Airways** (tel. 802/658–2204), and **Valley Air Services** (tel. 802/863–3626).

Southern Vermont Helicopter (Box 15G, West Brattleboro 05301, tel. 802/257–4354) provides helicopter transportation throughout New England.

By Car The official state map, available free from the Vermont Travel Division, is helpful for most driving in the state; a table shows the mileage between principal towns, and there are enlarged maps of major downtown areas. *The Vermont Atlas and Gazet-*

teer, sold in many bookstores, has more detail on the smaller roads. Information centers are located on the Massachusetts border at I–91, the New Hampshire border at I–89, the New York border at Route 4A, and the Canadian border at I–89.

By Bus **Vermont Transit** (tel. 802/864–6811 or 800/451–3292) links Bennington, Brattleboro, Bellows Falls, Rutland, White River Junction, Middlebury, Montpelier, Burlington, St. Johnsbury, and Newport, with intermediate stops at smaller towns.

Shopping

Most shopping is to be had in small shops; the few large department stores are located in Burlington and other cities. Some small stores specialize in goods made in Vermont, while others mix Vermont products with imports domestic and foreign. Maple syrup is available in different grades; light amber is the most refined, yet many Vermonters prefer grade C, the richest in flavor and the one most often used in cooking. A sugarhouse can be the most or the least expensive place to shop, depending on how tourist-oriented it is. Small grocery stores are often a good bet.

Vermont is heavily populated with craftspeople whose work ranges from the rustic and strictly functional to the quaint and decorative to the sophisticated and contemporary. Many craftspeople sell from their studios; a directory of the members of **Vermont Hand Crafters** (Box 9385, South Burlington 05403) is available for a stamped, self-addressed envelope. The two state crafts centers at Windsor and Middlebury display juried work from throughout the state. Among the most popular items are functional stoneware, quilts, handmade wooden toys, handknit and handwoven items, and dried herbs and flowers.

Factory outlet stores—those of national chains as well as local manufacturers—can be found throughout the state. With its designer name outlets, Manchester has become to Vermont what Freeport is to Maine. A guide to Vermont factory outlets is available from the Vermont Chamber of Commerce.

The **Vermont Antiques Dealers' Association** will mail a directory of its members to anyone who sends a stamped, self-addressed envelope to Muriel McKirryher, 55 Allen St., Rutland 05701.

A directory of the 45 members of the **Vermont Antiquarian Booksellers' Association** (Box 23, North Pomfret 05053, tel. 802/457–2608) is available on request.

Sports and Outdoor Activities

Biking On almost any summer day in Vermont you'll see bikers on the roads, for the many back roads and attractive scenery of the state make it a natural for bike touring. Numerous tour operators run inn-to-inn trips (luggage is carried in a van) or take bikers on guided trips that return at night to the same inn. Among the most picturesque areas for biking are those around Manchester and Dorset; the small towns near Randolph, Chelsea, and Tunbridge; Stowe, which has a recreational path; the Champlain Valley; and the southeast, near Grafton and Chester.

Boating and The principal center for water activities in Vermont is the nar-
Sailing row 120-mile stretch of Lake Champlain. Boat rentals and

charters are available in or near Vergennes, Burlington, and the Lake Champlain islands. Remember that the lake is notorious for its unpredictable and rapidly changing conditions.

Mountain lakes and reservoirs, too, are good for boating; some of the most popular lakes are Bomoseen, Memphremagog, Willoughby, Seymour, and Crystal. Canoeists and rafters also head for the thousands of miles of navigable rivers and streams. Some of the easiest stretches are on the Connecticut River and the Battenkill. Several companies organize group tours, and rentals are often available from outdoors stores in cities along the rivers.

Among tour organizers are **Canoe Vermont** (Box 610, Waitsfield 05673, tel. 802/496–2409), **Connecticut River Safari** (3A Putney Rd., Brattleboro 05301, tel. 802/257–5008), **Vermont Canoe Trippers/Battenkill Canoe, Ltd.** (Box 65, Arlington 05250, tel. 802/375–9559), and **Vermont Voyager Expeditions** (Box 101S, Montgomery Center 05471, tel. 802/326–4789). The Vermont Travel Division publishes a list of suggested summer canoe trips.

Camping The largest single wilderness area is the 275,000-acre Green Mountain National Forest, with 95 campsites that should be reserved in advance. Information is available from the **Forest Supervisor, Green Mountain National Forest** (Box 519, Rutland 05701). The **Green Mountain Club** (Box 889, 43 State St., Montpelier 05602, tel. 802/223–3463) publishes a number of helpful maps and guides.

In addition, the state operates nearly 40 campgrounds with more than 2,000 campsites in state parks. However, because both visitors and natives tend to take every opportunity to be outdoors during the short summer season, camping areas can be crowded, so it's wise to call individual parks in advance for reservations for stays of a week or more. Especially popular are the Champlain islands sites: Burton Island, Kill Kare, and Sand Bar. The **Department of Forests, Parks, and Recreation** (103 S. Main St., Waterbury 05676, tel. 802/828–3375) can provide information. The **Vermont Association of Private Campground Owners and Operators** (Char-Bo Campground, Box 54, Derby 05829) has a listing of the private campgrounds that are members of the association.

Hiking Most people who hike Vermont head for the 255-mile **Long Trail** that runs north–south through the center of the state. (The southern half of this trail is part of the Appalachian Trail.) The Green Mountain Club and the Forest Supervisor, Green Mountain National Forest can provide hiking guidance, including planning tips and news of trail conditions. The Department of Forests, Parks, and Recreation publishes a guide to hiking trails in state parks; parks with nature or wilderness trails are designated on the official state map.

Skiing *The skiing facilities of Vermont are reviewed in Chapter 2, Skiing New England.*

Tennis The **Stowe Area Association** (tel. 802/253–7321) hosts a grand prix tennis tournament in early August.

Water Sports White-water rafting has become popular in the Green Mountain State; the season begins in mid-April, and guided trips are available from **Vermont Whitewater** (Box 800, Norwich 05055, tel. 802/649–2998).

Sailboard enthusiasts and waterskiers favor Lake Champlain, the Harriman reservoir in southern Vermont, Lake Bomoseen, and Lake Memphremagog. The official state map lists the facilities of the 35 state parks and dam sites, including boat launches.

Beaches

Lake Champlain is the major center for beaches. The most popular are the beaches just north of Burlington and at the island state parks: North Hero, Knight Point, Grand Isle, Sand Bar, Kamp Kill Kare, and Burton Island. Most state parks provide changing facilities; the official state map has a complete list. Towns near major lakes often have town recreation areas as well.

National and State Parks

National Park The Green Mountain National Forest's 275,000 acres of recreational opportunity extend south from Bristol in the center of the state to the Massachusetts border. Hikers treasure the miles of hiking trails, especially the Long Trail; canoeists work its white-water streams; and campers and anglers abound. Among the most popular spots are the Falls of Lana near Middlebury; Hapgood Pond between Manchester and Peru, the first section of the forest to be acquired by the federal government; Silver Lake near Middlebury; and Chittenden Brook near Rochester. There are six wilderness areas. The Forest Supervisor has topographic maps and other information.

State Parks The 40 parks owned and maintained by the state contain 45 recreational areas that may include hiking trails, campsites, swimming, boating facilities, nature trails (some have an on-site naturalist), and fishing. The official state map details the facilities available at each. The Department of Forests, Parks, and Recreation provides park information.

Dining

Vermont restaurants have not escaped recent efforts to adapt traditional New England fare to offset its reputation for blandness. The New England Culinary Institute, based in Montpelier, has trained a number of Vermont chefs who have now turned their attention to such native New England foods as fiddlehead ferns (available only for a short time in the spring); maple syrup (Vermont is the largest producer in the United States); dairy products, especially cheese; native fruits and berries that are often transformed into sauces, jams, jellies, and preserves; "new Vermont" products such as salsa; and venison, quail, pheasant, and other game.

Your chances of finding a table for dinner will vary dramatically with the season: Many restaurants have lengthy waits during peak seasons (when it's always a good idea to call about reservations) and then shut down during the slow months of April and November. Some of the best dining will be found in country inns. Casual dress is the general rule in Vermont restaurants; the formal dining rooms of a few upscale country inns are the dressiest places, but even there you'll rarely need a tie—though you'll often find a jacket useful on nippy Vermont evenings.

Highly recommended restaurants in each price category are indicated by a star ★ .

Category	Cost*
Very Expensive	over $35
Expensive	$25–$35
Moderate	$15–$25
Inexpensive	under $15

average cost of a three-course dinner, per person, excluding drinks, service, and 6% sales tax

Lodging

The large hotels of Vermont are in Rutland and in the vicinity of the major ski resorts. Elsewhere throughout the state travelers will find a variety of inns, bed-and-breakfasts, and small motels. Rates are generally highest during foliage season, from late September to mid-October, and lowest in late spring and November, when many properties close. It makes sense to inquire about package rates if you plan a stay of several days, especially at the larger hotels. Some inns whose furnishings are largely antiques may not welcome children as guests; if you are traveling with kids, you will want to discuss this question in advance.

The **Vermont Travel Information Service** (tel. 802/276–3120) operates a centralized referral service for lodging. Other organizations provide referral services for bed-and-breakfasts throughout Vermont; they include **American Country Collection of Bed and Breakfast** (984 Gloucester Place, Schenectady, NY 12309; tel. 518/370–4948) and **American–Vermont Bed and Breakfast Reservation Service** (Box 1, E. Fairfield 05448, tel. 802/827–3827). In addition, many ski resort areas operate lodging referral services.

The Vermont Chamber of Commerce publishes the *Vermont Travelers' Guidebook*, which is an extensive list of lodgings, and additional guides to country inns and vacation rentals. The Vermont Travel Division (*see* Visitor Information, above) has a brochure that lists lodgings at working farms.

Highly recommended lodgings in each price category are indicated by a star ★ .

Category	Cost*
Very Expensive	over $150
Expensive	$100–$150
Moderate	$60–$100
Inexpensive	under $60

All prices are for a standard double room during peak season, with no meals unless noted, and excluding service charge.

Southern Vermont

The Vermont tradition of independence and rebellion began in southern Vermont. Many towns founded in the early 18th century as frontier outposts or fortifications were later important as trading centers. In the western region the Green Mountain Boys fought off both the British and the claims of land-hungry New Yorkers—and some say their descendants are still fighting. In the 19th century, as many towns turned to manufacturing, the eastern part of the state preserved much of its rich farming and orchard areas. Many of the people who have moved to Vermont in the last 20 years have settled in the southern part of the state.

Important Addresses and Numbers

Weather (tel. 802/464–2111).

Visitor Information   **Brattleboro Chamber of Commerce** (180 Main St., Brattleboro 05301, tel. 802/254–4565).

Great Falls Regional Chamber of Commerce (Box 554, Bellows Falls 05101, tel. 802/463–4280).

Bennington Area Chamber of Commerce (Veterans Memorial Dr., Bennington 05201, tel. 802/447–3311).

Chamber of Commerce, Manchester and the Mountains (Adams Park Green, Box 928, Manchester 05255, tel. 802/362–2100).

Mt. Snow/Haystack Region Chamber of Commerce (Box 3, Wilmington 05363, tel. 802/464–8092).

Windsor Area Chamber of Commerce (Box 5, Windsor 05089, tel. 802/672–5910).

Emergencies   Vermont's Medical Health Care Information Center has a **24-hour line** (tel. 802/864–0454).

Brattleboro Memorial Hospital (9 Belmont Ave., tel. 802/257–0341) is the largest in the region.

Telecommunications Device for the Deaf (TDD) has a 24-hour emergency hotline (tel. 802/254–3929).

Getting Around Southern Vermont

By Car   In the south the principal east–west highway is Route 9, the Molly Stark Trail, from Brattleboro to Bennington. The most important north–south roads are Route 7, the more scenic Route 7A to the west, and I–91 and Route 5 on the east. Route 100, which runs north–south through the state's center; and Rte. 30 from Brattleboro to Manchester are scenic drives. All routes may be heavily traveled during peak tourist seasons.

By Bus   **Vermont Transit Lines** (tel. 802/864–6811 or 800/451–3292) links Bennington, Manchester, Brattleboro, and Bellows Falls.

Guided Tours

Back Road Country Tours (tel. 802/442–3876) sponsors daily jeep tours on the back roads of Bennington County.

Exploring Southern Vermont

Numbers in the margin correspond with the numbered points of interest on the Southern Vermont map.

Travelers in southern Vermont will see verdant farmland, posh ski resorts, newly rejuvenated towns, tourist-clogged highways, and quiet back roads. Our tour begins in the east, south of the junction of I–91 and Route 9.

❶ Brattleboro, a town of about 12,000, originated as a frontier scouting post and became a thriving industrial center and resort town in the 1800s. More recently, such institutions as the Experiment in International Living (which trains Peace Corps volunteers) have left indelible traces of the back-to-the-land movement.

The **Brattleboro Museum and Art Center** selects an annual theme and gears each exhibit to it. The converted railroad station displays historical photos and an Estey organ from the days when the city was home to one of the world's largest organ companies. *Canal and Bridge Sts., tel. 802/257–0124. Admission free. Open May–Oct., Tues.–Fri. noon–4, weekends 1–4.*

Take Route 142 a mile south of Brattleboro, watch for the sign announcing the Erving Paper Co. access road, and turn toward the river to reach the *Belle of Brattleboro.* The elegance of a Mississippi riverboat may be lacking—it has no paddlewheel, and there's a canopy roof rather than multiple levels—but the passenger craft provides a unique look at the Connecticut River on its daily two-hour foliage, sunset, moonlight, dinner, and Sunday brunch cruises. *91 Chestnut St., tel. 802/254–8080. Cruise fares: $6 adults, $4 children under 12; meal cruises higher.*

Larkin G. Mead Jr., a Brattleboro resident, stirred 19th-century America's imagination with an 8-foot snow angel he built at the intersection of Routes 30 and 5. **Brooks Memorial Library** has a replica of the angel as well as art exhibits that change frequently. *224 Main St., tel. 802/254–5290. Open Mon.–Thurs. 9–9, Fri. 9–6, Sat. 9–5.*

Time Out | **Hamelmann's Bakery** on Elliot Street in Brattleboro has crusty country breads in hand-shaped loaves, thick Napoleans, and delicate fruit and almond tarts.

From Brattleboro one can head north along the eastern edge of the state to Putney, where **Harlow's Sugar House** (Rte. 5, 2 mi north of Putney, tel. 802/387–5852) has maple sugaring in spring, berry picking in summer, and sleigh rides in winter.

❷ Nearly 10 miles west of Brattleboro on Route 9 (the Molly Stark Trail) is **Marlboro,** a tiny town that draws musicians and audiences from around the world each summer to the Marlboro Music Festival, founded by Rudolf Serkin and led for many years by Pablo Casals. Marlboro is also home to the New England Bach Festival in the fall.

Perched high on a hill just off Route 9, **Marlboro College** is the center of the musical activity. The demure white frame buildings have an outstanding view of the valley below, and the campus is studded with apple trees.

Southern Vermont

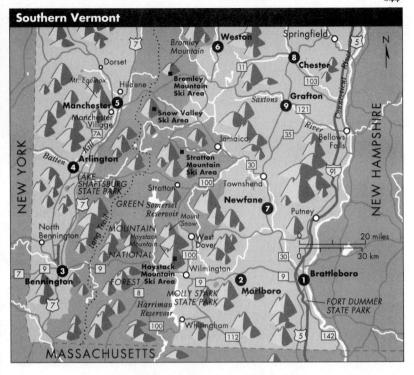

The **Luman Nelson New England Wildlife Museum** (tel. 802/464–5494), housed in a gift shop on Route 9 opposite the Skyline Restaurant, is taxidermy heaven. The display of large animals includes majestic deer heads, a bobcat eyeing a couple of concerned-looking squirrels, and a wild boar who seems surprised to be there. The large room downstairs is filled with stuffed bird species in cages with hand-lettered signs.

Wilmington, the shopping and dining center for the Mount Snow and Haystack Mountain ski areas to the north, lies 8 miles west of Marlboro on Route 9. Here you can take one of Vermont's most scenic drives, a 35-mile circular tour: Drive west on Route 9 to the intersection with Route 8, turn south and continue to the junction with Route 100, follow Route 100 through Whitingham (the birthplace of the Mormon prophet Brigham Young), and stay with the road as it turns north again and takes you back to Route 9.

③ Bennington, founded in 1749 when the New Hampshire governor made an early land grant, is the focus of Vermont's southwest corner. Here, at the Catamount Tavern, Ethan Allen organized the Green Mountain Boys, who helped capture Fort Ticonderoga in 1775. Here in 1777 the American general John Stark urged his militia to attack the Hessians across the New York border: "There are the Redcoats; they will be ours or tonight Molly Stark sleeps a widow!" Now the state's third-largest city, Bennington has retained much of the industrial character it developed in the 19th century, when paper mills, grist mills, and potteries formed the city's economic base.

A Chamber of Commerce brochure describes two self-guided walking tours; the more interesting is the tour of **Old Bennington,** a National Register Historic District just west of downtown, where impressive white-column Greek Revival and sturdy brick Federal homes stand around a village green. In the graveyard of the Old First Church, at the corner of Church Street and Monument Avenue, the tombstone of the poet Robert Frost proclaims, "I had a lover's quarrel with the world."

The **Bennington Battle Monument,** a 306-foot stone obelisk with an elevator to the top, commemorates General Stark's victory over the British, who attempted to capture Bennington's stockpile of supplies. The battle, which took place near Walloomsac Heights in New York State, helped bring about the surrender two months later of the British commander, "Gentleman Johnny" Burgoyne. *15 Monument Ave., tel. 802/447-0550. Admission: $1 adults, 50¢ children 6–11. Open Apr.–Oct., daily 9–5.*

The **Bennington Museum's** rich collections of early Americana include artifacts of rural life piled higgledy-piggledy in large cases. The decorative arts are well represented; one room is devoted to early Bennington pottery, then known as Norton pottery, the product of one of the first ceramic makers in the country. Another room covers the history of American glass and contains fine Tiffany specimens. Devotees of folk art will want to see the exhibit of the work of Grandma Moses, who lived and painted in the area. *W. Main St. (Rte. 9), tel. 802/447-1571. Admission: $4.50 adults, $3.50 senior citizens and children 12–18, $10 family. Open Mar.–Dec., daily 9–5.*

The **Park-McCullough House,** a 35-room restored mansion in North Bennington, shows what the forty-niners did with the money they made in the California gold rush. The elaborately carved Second Empire mahogany furnishings, massive oak staircase, and etched glass doors are original. Guided tours begin on the hour. *Rte. 67A, North Bennington, tel. 802/442-5441. Admission: $3 adults, $1.50 children 12–17. Open weekdays 9–4.*

Bennington College's placid campus features green meadows punctuated with contemporary stone sculpture, white frame neo-Colonial dorms, and acres of cornfields. The small coeducational liberal arts college, one of the most exclusive in the country, is noted for its progressive program in the arts. To reach the campus, take Route 67A off Route 7 and look for the stone entrance gate.

❹ Don't be surprised to see familiar-looking faces among the roughly 2,200 people of **Arlington,** about 15 miles north of Bennington on Route 7A. The illustrator Norman Rockwell lived here for 14 years, and many of the models for his portraits of small-town life were his neighbors. Settled first in 1763, Arlington was called Tory Hollow for its Loyalist sympathies—even though a number of the Green Mountain Boys lived here as well. Smaller than Bennington and less sophisticated than Manchester to the north, Arlington displays a certain Rockwellian folksiness. It's also known as the home of Dorothy Canfield Fisher, a novelist popular in the 1930s and 1940s.

Don't expect to find original paintings at the **Norman Rockwell Exhibition;** it has none. The rooms of reproductions are arranged in every way conceivable: chronologically, by subject matter, and juxtaposed with photos of the models, some of whom work at the exhibition. In the white church building (ca. 1875) that houses the exhibition is a gift shop that sells still more reproductions. *Rte. 7A, Arlington, tel. 802/375–6423. Admission: $1, children under 6 free. Open daily 9–7.*

⑤ Manchester, where Ira Allen proposed financing Vermont's participation in the American Revolution by confiscating Tory estates, has been a popular summer retreat since the mid-19th century, when Mary Todd Lincoln visited. Manchester Village's tree-shaded marble sidewalks and stately old homes converted to bed-and-breakfasts reflect the luxurious resort lifestyle of a century ago, while Manchester Center's upscale factory outlet stores appeal to the 20th-century's affluent ski crowd drawn by nearby Bromley and Stratton mountains.

Time Out | At the **Gourmet Deli** in Factory Point Square, Route 7A, Manchester, you'll find homemade soups, sandwiches, baked goods, and outdoor tables with umbrellas in summer.

Hildene, the summer home of Abraham Lincoln's son Robert, on Route 7A, 2 miles south of the intersection with Route 11/30, is situated on a 412-acre estate that the former chairman of the board of the Pullman Company built for his family and their descendants, who lived here as recently as 1975. With its Georgian Revival symmetry, gracious central hallway, and grand curved staircase, the 24-room mansion is unusual in that its rooms are not roped off. When "The Ride of the Valkyries" is played on the 1,000-pipe Aeolian organ, the music comes out of the mansion's very bones. Tours include a short film on the owner's life and a walk through the elaborate formal gardens. *Rte. 7A, Manchester, tel. 802/362–1788. Admission: $5 adults, $2 children 6–15. Open mid-May–Oct., daily 9:30–4.*

For fly-fishing devotees, the **American Museum of Fly Fishing** displays more than 1,000 rods, 400 reels, 40,000 flies, and the tackle of such celebrities as General George Patton, Daniel Webster, and Winslow Homer. Its 2,200 books on angling comprise the largest public library devoted to fishing. Only the fish are missing here. *Rte. 7A, Manchester, tel. 802/362–3300. Admission: $2 adults, children under 12 free. Open May–Oct., daily 10–4; Nov.–Apr., weekdays 10–4.*

The **Southern Vermont Art Center's** 10 rooms are set on 375 acres dotted with contemporary sculpture. Here are a permanent collection, changing exhibits, and a serene botany trail; the graceful Georgian mansion is also the site of concerts, dramatic performances, and films. *West Rd., Box 617, Manchester, tel. 802/362–1405. Admission: $3 adults, 50¢ students. Open Memorial Day–Oct. 15, Tues.–Sat. 10–5, Sun. noon–5.*

Time Out | **Mother Myrick's** on Route 7A offers sugar in all its forms: ice cream sundaes, cakes, cookies, handmade chocolates, fudge. The waiting lines even in winter attest to its popularity.

You may be tempted to keep your eye on the temperature gauge of your car as you drive the 5.2 miles to the top of 3,825-foot **Mount Equinox.** Remember to look out the window periodically for views of the Battenkill trout stream and the surrounding Vermont countryside. Picnic tables line the drive, and there's an outstanding view down both sides of the mountain from what is called the Saddle. *Rte. 7A, Manchester, tel. 802/362–1114. Admission: $4.50 car. Open May–Oct., daily 8 AM-10 PM.*

Head east on Route 11 and then north on Route 100 to reach
❻ **Weston,** perhaps best known for the Vermont Country Store (Rte. 100, tel. 802/824–3184), which may be more a way of life than a shop. For years the retail store and mail-order catalogue have carried such nearly forgotten items from the past as Lilac Vegetal aftershave, Monkey Brand black tooth powder, Flexible Flyer sleds, pickles in a barrel, and tiny wax bottles of colored syrup. In the store, nostalgia-laden implements dangle from walls and ceiling.

Weston Priory, a Benedictine monastery just north of the junction of routes 100 and 155, is a tranquil spot in a pretty quiet state. Guests are welcome to join in services (evening vespers is the most impressive), walk by the pond, picnic under the trees, and visit the gift shop, which has records of the well-known monastery choir. *½o mi north of junction of Rtes. 100 and 155.*

From Weston you might head south on Route 100 and then down Route 30 through Jamaica, Townshend, and Newfane,
❼ hamlets typical of small-town Vermont. **Newfane** is especially attractive for its crisp white buildings surrounding the village green. Just south of Townshend, near the Townshend Dam on Route 30, is the state's longest single-span bridge, which is closed to traffic.

Another option is to travel east to Route 11, which will take you
❽ to **Chester.** There, on North Street, Stone Village is two rows of buildings constructed from quarried stone, all built by two brothers and said to have been used during the Civil War as stations on the Underground Railroad.

To examine the oldest one-room schoolhouse in the state, take Route 11 east almost to I–91. Completed in 1790, the **Eureka Schoolhouse** has a collection of 19th-century primers and other education materials. *Rte. 11, off I–91, tel. 802/828–3226. Admission free. Open Memorial Day–mid-Oct., daily 9–4.*

❾ It's 8 miles south on Route 35 from Chester to **Grafton,** the picturesque village that got a second lease on life when the Windham Foundation provided funds for the restoration of most of the town, now one of the best-kept in the state. The Grafton Historical Society documents the change and shows other exhibits. *Townshend Rd., tel. 802/843–2388. Admission free. Open Memorial Day–Columbus Day, Sat. 2:30–4:40; also, July–Aug. Sun. 2:30–4:40.*

Southern Vermont for Free

Brattleboro Museum and Art Center, Brattleboro

Weston Priory, Weston

Stone Village, Chester

Grafton Historical Society, Grafton

What to See and Do with Children

Harlow's Sugar House, Putney

Battle Monument and Museum, Bennington

Mt. Equinox, Arlington

Luman Nelson New England Wildlife Museum, Marlboro

Off the Beaten Track

In Bellows Falls, on the Connecticut River at the eastern edge of the state, about 12 miles east of Grafton, you can board the ***Green Mountain Flyer*** for a 26-mile round-trip to Chester and Ludlow in cars that date from the golden age of railroading. The journey takes you through scenic countryside that includes the Brockway Mills gorge. *Island St. off Bridge St. (Rte. 12), tel. 802/463–3069. Round-trip fare: $7–$21 adults, $4–$14 children 5–12, depending on destination. Open July–early Sept., late Sept.–early Oct., daily 11–4.*

Indian petroglyphs can be found on the banks of the Connecticut River in Bellows Falls, but you'll have to scramble down the side of the riverbank to examine the carvings in stone made by Native Americans. The Bellows Falls Chamber of Commerce (tel. 802/463–4280) has a map showing the site; follow the small sign off Bridge Street near the river.

The **Alpine Slide** at Bromley Mountain was the first in the country; here you can ride small motorized sleds down any of three twisting, turning tracks, each ⅔ mile long. *Rte. 11, Bromley Village, tel. 802/324–5522. Admission: $4.50. Open May–Sept., daily 9:30–6; early Oct., daily 9:30–5.*

Shopping

Shopping Districts **Manchester Commons** (tel. 802/661–5428), at the intersection of Routes 7 and 11/30, the largest and spiffiest of three large factory-direct shopping minimalls, has such big-city names as Joan and David, Coach, Boston Trader, Ralph Lauren, Hickey-Freeman, and Cole-Haan. Not far off are Factory Point Square on Route 7 and Battenkill Place on Rte. 11.

Candle Mill Village (tel. 802/375–6068), on Old Mill Road, off Route 7A in East Arlington, offers shops that specialize in community cookbooks from around the country, bears in all forms, and music boxes. A waterfall makes a pleasant backdrop for a picnic.

Flea Market **Wilmington Flea Market** (Junction Rtes. 9 and 100 South, tel. 802/464–3345), a cornucopia of leftovers and never-solds, operates weekends and holidays from Memorial Day to mid-October.

Food and Drink **Allen Bros.** (Rte. 5 south of Bellows Falls, tel. 802/722–3395), offers its own apple pies, cider doughnuts, other baked goods, and a selection of Vermont food products and produce.

Equinox Nursery (Rte. 7A, between Arlington and Manchester, tel. 802/362–2610) carries a wide selection of Vermont-made food and produce, including locally manufactured ice cream.

H & M Orchard (Dummerston Center, tel. 802/254–8100) lets you watch sugaring in spring and pick your own fruit in other seasons.

North River Winery, which occupies a converted farmhouse and barn, produces such fruit wines as Green Mountain Apple and offers tours and tastings. *Rte. 112, 6 mi south of Wilmington, tel. 802/368-7557. Open May-Dec., daily 10-5; Jan.-Apr., Fri.-Sun. 11-5.*

Vermont Country Store (Rte, 100, Weston, tel. 802/824-3184) sets aside one room of its old-fashioned emporium for Vermont Common Crackers and bins of fudge and other candy.

Specialty Stores

Antiques

Carriage Trade (tel. 802/362-1125) and **1812 House** (tel. 802/362-1189) are two antiques centers just north of Manchester Center on Route 7. They hold room after room of early American antiques gathered by many dealers; Carriage Trade has especially fine collections of clocks and ceramics.

Danby Antiques Center (⅛ mi off Rte. 7, 13 mi north of Manchester, tel. 802/293-9984) has 11 rooms and a barn filled with furniture and accessories, folk art, textiles, and stoneware.

Four Corners East (307 North St., Bennington, tel. 802/442-2612) has a selection of early American antiques.

Newfane Antiques Center (Rte. 30, south of Newfane, tel. 802/365-4482) displays antiques from 20 dealers on three floors.

Books

The Book Cellar (120 Main St., Brattleboro, tel. 802/254-6026), with three floors of books, is strong on Vermont and New England.

Johnny Appleseed (tel. 802/362-2458), next to the Equinox Hotel in Manchester Village, specializes in Vermont lore and the hard-to-find.

Northshire Bookstore (Main St., Manchester, tel. 802/362-2200) has excellent selections of travel and children's books in a large inventory.

Crafts

Basketville (Rte. 5, Putney, tel. 802/362-1609), as its name suggests, is an immense space filled with baskets from around the world.

Bennington Potters Yard (324 County St., tel. 802/447-7531) has seconds from the famed Bennington Potters. Prepare to get dusty digging through the bad stuff to find an almost-perfect piece at a modest discount. The complex of buildings also houses a glass factory outlet and John McLeod woodenware.

Carol Brown (Westminster West Rd., Putney, tel. 802/387-5875) imports quality natural-fiber fabrics such as Irish linen and tweed, Dutch and African batik, and Chinese and Indian silks.

Green Mountain Spinnery offers yarns, knit items, and tours of its yarn factory at 1:30 on the first and third Tuesdays each month. *Exit 4, I-91, Putney, tel. 802/387-4528. Tour: $1 adults, 50¢ children.*

Handworks on the Green (Rte. 7, Manchester, tel. 802/362-5033) deals in contemporary crafts—ceramics, jewelry, glass —of high quality, with an emphasis on sophisticated, brightly colored decorative work.

Newfane Country Store (Rte. 30, Newfane, tel. 802/365-7916) has an immense selection of quilts—they can be custom ordered as well—and homemade fudge.

Vermont Artisan Design (115 Main St., Brattleboro, tel. 802/257-7044) displays contemporary ceramics, glass, wood, and clothing from Vermont.

Men's Clothing　**Orvis Retail Store** (Rte. 7A, Manchester, tel. 802/362-3750) carries the outdoorsman's clothing and home furnishings featured in its mail order catalog (don't overlook the bargain basement), and the company offers three-day fly fishing courses nearby.

Women's Clothing　**Anne Klein, Liz Claiborne, Jones New York, London Fog,** and **Coach** are among the shops on routes 11/30 and 7 South in Manchester—a center for women's designer factory stores.

The Silver Forest (Westminster West Rd., Putney, tel. 802/387-4149) carries natural-fiber clothing and jewelry reminiscent of the 1960s.

Sports and Outdoor Activities

Biking　A Dorset–Manchester trail of about 20 miles runs from Manchester Village north on West Street to Route 30, turns west at the Dorset village green to West Road, and heads back south to Manchester. **Battenkill Sports** (Rte. 7, at Rtes. 11/30, tel. 802/362-2634) has bike rentals and information.

Chester is the start of a 26-mile round-trip beside the Williams River along Route 103 to Pleasant Valley Road north of Bellows Falls. Pleasant Valley Road meets Route 121 at Saxtons River; turn west on Route 121 as it runs beside Saxtons River, to connect with Route 35. When the two routes separate, follow Route 35 north back to Chester. **Neal's Wheels** (Rte. 11, tel. 802/875-3627) has rentals.

Canoeing　The stretch of the Connecticut River between Bellows Falls and the Massachusetts border, interrupted by one dam at Vernon, is relatively easy. A good resource is *The Complete Boating Guide to the Connecticut River*, available from CRWC Headquarters (125 Combs Rd., Easthampton, MA 01027, tel. 413/584-0057). **Connecticut River Safari** (Rte. 5, Brattleboro 05301, tel. 802/257-5008) has guided and self-guided tours.

Battenkill Canoe (River Rd., Box 65, Arlington 05250, tel. 802/375-9559) offers day trips and rentals on the Batten Kill and can arrange custom tours, inn-to-inn.

Fishing　**The Orvis Co.** (Manchester Center, tel. 802/362-3900) hosts a nationally known fly-fishing school on the Batten Kill, the state's most famous trout stream, with three-day courses given weekly, April–October. The Connecticut River contains smallmouth bass, walleye, and perch; and shad are beginning to return via the fish ladders at Vernon and Bellows Falls. Harriman and Somerset reservoirs in the central part of the state offer both warm and coldwater species; Harriman has a greater variety.

Strictly Trout (Box 930, Westminster West 05346, tel. 802/496-6572) will arrange a fly-fishing trip on any Vermont stream or river.

Hiking　One of the most popular segments of the Long Trail starts at Route 11/30 west of Peru Notch and goes to the top of Bromley Mountain (four hours). About 4 miles east of Bennington, the Long Trail crosses Route 9 and runs south to the summit of

Harmon Hill (two–three hours). On Route 30 about 1 mile south of Townshend is Townshend State Park; from here the hiking trail runs to the top of Bald Mountain, passing an alder swamp, a brook, and a hemlock forest (two hours).

Water Sports **Lake Front Restaurant** (Harriman Reservoir, tel. 802/464–5838) rents sailboats, canoes, and rowboats by the hour or day.

West River Canoe (Rte. 100, off Rte. 30, Townshend, tel. 802/896–6209) has sailboard rentals and lessons.

National and State Parks

The 275,000 acres of Green Mountain National Forest extend down the center of the state, providing scenic drives, picnic areas, campsites, lakes, and hiking and cross-country ski trails. The waterfalls at the **Lye Brook Wilderness Area** are a popular attraction. Maps and information are available at the U.S. Forest Service Office. *Rte. 11/30, east of Manchester, tel. 802/362–2307. Open weekdays 8–4:30.*

Emerald Lake State Park has a marked nature trail and an on-site naturalist. *Rte. 7, 9 mi north of Manchester, tel. 802/362–1655. 430 acres. Facilities: 105 campsites (no hookups), toilets, showers, picnic tables, fireplaces, phone, boat and canoe rentals, snack bar.*

Fort Dummer State Park's hiking trails afford views of the Connecticut River Valley. *S. Main St., 2 mi south of Brattleboro, tel. 802/254–2610. 217 acres. Facilities: 61 campsites (no hookups), toilets, showers, picnic tables, fireplaces, phone.*

Lake Shaftsbury State Park is one of the few in Vermont with a group camping area. *Rte. 7A, 10½ mi north of Bennington, tel. 802/375–9978. 101 acres. Facilities: group camping area (with hookups), picnic tables and shelter, swimming beach, bathhouse, self-guided nature trails, boat and canoe rentals, phone.*

Molly Stark State Park has a hiking trail to a vista from a fire tower on Mt. Olga. *Rte. 9, east of Wilmington, tel. 802/464–5460. 158 acres. Facilities: 34 campsites (no hookups), toilets, showers, picnic tables and shelter, fireplaces, phone.*

Townshend State Park, the largest in southern Vermont, is popular for the swimming at Townshend Dam and the stiff hiking trail to the top of Bald Mountaif. *3 ma north of Rte. 30, between Newfane and Townshend, tel. 802/365–7500. 856 acres. Facilities: 34 campsites (no hookups), toilets, showers, picnic tables and shelter, fireplaces.*

Woodford State Park activities center on Adams Reservoir, though there are also marked nature trails. *Rte. 9, east of Bennington, tel. 802/447–4169. 400 acres. Facilities: 102 campsites (no hookups), toilets, showers, picnic tables, fireplaces, phone, playground, boat and canoe rentals.*

Dining and Lodging

The large hotels of southern Vermont are the ski lodges around Stratton, Bromley, Mount Snow, and Haystack. The Manchester area has a lodging referral service (tel. 802/824–6915). In the restaurants, dress is casual and reservations are unnecessary except where noted.

Arlington Dining — **West Mountain Inn.** A low-beamed, paneled, candlelit room is the setting for such specialties as veal chops topped with sun-dried tomatoes and Asiago cheese. Aunt Min's Swedish rye and other toothsome breads, as well as desserts, are all made on the premises. Tables by the windows allow a glorious view of the mountains. *Rte. 313, tel. 802/375–6516. Reservations advised. AE, MC, V. Moderate–Expensive.*

★ **Arlington Inn.** Paul Kruzel, an award-winning chef, has one of the most respected restaurants in the state. The seasonal menu offers inventive nouvelle American dishes such as veal scallopini with strawberries in a dill beurre blanc; and shrimp wrapped in paper-thin slices of grilled zucchini with a light to-mato sauce. Polished hardwood floors, mauve napkins and walls, candlelight, and soft piano music complement the food. *Rte. 7A, tel. 802/375–6532. Reservations advised. AE, MC, V. Closed Dec. 25, Jan. 1. Expensive.*

Arlington Lodging — **Arlington Inn.** The Greek Revival columns at the entrance to this railroad magnate's home of 1848 give it an imposing pres-ence, yet the rooms are welcoming. Their cozy charm is created by clawfoot tubs in some bathrooms, linens that coordinate with the Victorian-style wallpaper, and the house's original moldings and wainscoting. The carriage house, built at the turn of the century and renovated in 1985, has country French and Queen Anne furnishings. *Rte. 7, 05250, tel. 802/375–6532. 13 rooms with bath, 5 suites. Facilities: cable TV and VCR in public area, bar, tennis court. AE, MC, V. Closed Dec. 25, Jan. 1. Rates include Continental breakfast. Moderate.*

★ **West Mountain Inn.** A llama ranch on the property, African vio-lets and chocolate bars in the rooms, quilted bedspreads, and a front lawn with a spectacular view of the countryside were ele-ments in Michael J. Fox's decision to be married here. This former farmhouse of the 1840s, restored over the last 13 years, sits on 5 acres and seems to be a world apart. Rooms 2, 3, and 4 in the front of the house overlook the front-lawn view; the three small nooks of Room 11 resemble railroad sleeper berths and are perfect for kids. Plush carpeting, complimentary hors d'oeuvres (chicken fingers, fruit), and copies of the books of Dorothy Canfield Fisher adorn the rooms. *Rte. 313, 05250, tel. 802/375–6516. 13 rooms with bath, 3 suites. Facilities: bar, walking and ski trails, handicapped-access room. AE, MC, V. Rates are MAP. Expensive.*

Hill Farm Inn. This homey inn still has the feel of the country farmhouse it used to be: The mix of sturdy antiques and hand-me-downs, the spinning wheel in a corner of the living room, the paintings by a family member, the ducks that roam the 50 acres, the jars of homemade jam that visitors may take away— all convey the relaxed, friendly personalities of the owners, George and Joanne Hardy. Room 7, the newest, has a beamed cathedral ceiling and a porch with a view of Mount Equinox; the rooms in the guest house of 1790 are very private. *Rte. 7, Box 2015, 05250, tel. 802/375–2269. 17 rooms, 11 with bath; 2 suites; 4 cabins in summer. Facilities: restaurant, cable TV in public area. AE, D, MC, V. Rates include full breakfast. Moderate.*

Bennington Dining — **Four Chimneys.** Those who seek classic French cuisine in Ben-nington will come here. Heavy silverware, crisply starched linens, candlelight, and the delicately rose-colored walls com-plement a menu that recently included steak flambéed in cognac with green peppercorns. *21 West Rd., tel. 802/447–*

3500. Reservations advised. Jacket and tie advised. AE, CB, DC, MC, V. Closed Mon. and Jan. 2–Feb. 14. Expensive.

Main Street Cafe. Since it opened in 1989, this small storefront with the polished hardwood floors, candlelit tables, and fresh flowers has drawn raves, its Northern Italian cuisine judged well worth the few minutes' drive from downtown Bennington. The rigatoni tossed with Romano, Parmesan, broccoli, and sausage in a cream sauce; and the chicken stuffed with ham, provolone, and fresh spinach and served in a marsala-onion sauce are favorites. The look is casual chic, like that of a New York loft transplanted to a small town. *Rte. 67A, North Bennington, tel. 802/442–3210. Reservations advised. AE, MC, V. Dinner only. Closed Mon.–Tues.; Thanksgiving, Dec. 25. Expensive.*

★ **Alldays and Onions.** It may look like a deli—it *is* a deli during the day—yet its dinner menus (changed weekly) have featured such creative dishes as sautéed scallops and fettuccine in a jalapeño-ginger sauce; and rack of lamb with a honey-thyme sauce. Desserts are baked on the premises. *519 Main St., tel. 802/447–0043. MC, V. Closed Sun. Moderate.*

The Brasserie. The Brasserie's fare is some of the city's most creative. A mozzarella loaf swirls cheese through bread topped with anchovy-herb butter, and the soups are filling enough for a meal. The decor is as clean-lined and contemporary as the Bennington pottery for sale in the same complex of buildings. *324 County St., tel. 802/447–7922. MC, V. Closed Tues. Moderate.*

★ **Blue Benn Diner.** Breakfast is served all day in this authentic diner, and the eats are as down-home as turkey hash and as off-the-wall as tabbouleh or breakfast burritos that wrap scrambled eggs, sausage, and chiles in a tortilla. There can be a long wait. *Rte. 7 North, tel. 802/442–8977. No credit cards. No dinner Sun.–Tues. Inexpensive.*

Bennington Lodging
★

South Shire Inn. Canopy beds in lushly carpeted rooms, ornate plaster moldings, and a dark mahogany fireplace in the library create turn-of-the-century grandeur. The inn is in a quiet residential neighborhood within walking distance of the bus depot and downtown stores. Furnishings are antique except for reproduction beds that provide contemporary comfort. Breakfast is served in the peach-and-white wedding cake of a dining room. *124 Elm St., 05201, tel. 802/447–3839. 9 rooms with bath. Facilities: fireplaces in 7 rooms. No smoking. AE, MC, V. Rates include full breakfast. Expensive.*

Molly Stark Inn. Tidy blue plaid wallpaper, gleaming hardwood floors, antique furnishings, and a wood-burning stove in a brick alcove of the sitting room give a country charm to this recently renovated inn of 1860 on the main road to Brattleboro. The Rockwell Room on the first floor is spacious but opens onto the sitting room; Molly's Room at the back of the building gets less noise from the highway. *1067 E. Main St., 05201, tel. 802/442–9631. 6 rooms, 2 with bath. Facilities: cable TV in public area. No smoking. MC, V. Rates include Continental breakfast. Moderate.*

Brattleboro Dining
Peter Havens. Eclectic specialties such as shrimp curry or tortellini alfredo with smoked mussels and cappicola complement the mix of cane Breuer chairs, folk art, and Warholesque prints. Yes, there are ferns. *32 Elliot St., tel. 802/257–3333. MC, V. Closed Sun. Expensive.*

Whetstone Cafe. The table with seating on a sofa gives a relaxed feel to this tiny find west of town that opens for breakfast. The cooks in the deli-style front section serve up home cooking: Yankee pot roast, baked honey chicken, stuffed pork chops with fried apples, and braised beef with vegetables. The clay masks on the walls lend a city touch to the down-home character of chairs around a woodstove. *414 Western Ave., tel. 802/254–5533. MC, V. Closed Tues. Moderate.*

Common Ground. The political posters and concert fliers that line the staircase may lead you to think you're back in the 1960s. Owned cooperatively by the staff, this vegetarian restaurant serves the likes of cashew burgers and the "humble bowl of brown rice." A chocolate cake with peanut butter frosting and other desserts will lure confirmed meat-eaters. *25 Elliot St., tel. 802/257–0855. No credit cards. Closed Tues. Inexpensive–Moderate.*

Brattleboro Lodging
Latchis Hotel. Restoration of the downtown landmark's Art Deco grandeur was completed in 1989, and everything old is new again: black-and-white-check bathroom tiles, painted geometric borders along the ceiling, multicolored swirls of terrazzo on the lobby floor. Three suites have refrigerator, complimentary Continental breakfast, movie passes, and shopping discounts at Brattleboro stores. Odd-numbered rooms offer a view of the Connecticut River or Main Street. *50 Main St., 05301, tel. 802/254–6300. 35 rooms with bath. Facilities: cable TV, use of health club. AE, MC, V. Inexpensive–Moderate.*

Grafton Dining
The Old Tavern at Grafton. Two dining rooms, one with formal Georgian furniture and oil portraits, the other with rustic paneling and low beams, serve hearty traditional New England dishes such as venison stew or grilled quail; some offerings feature cheeses made just down the road. *Rte. 35, tel. 802/843–2231. AE, MC, V. Closed Apr., Dec. 24–25. Expensive.*

Grafton Lodging
★
The Old Tavern at Grafton. The white-column porches on both stories of the main building wrap around a structure that dates to 1788 and has hosted Daniel Webster and Nathaniel Hawthorne. Carefully restored by the private foundation that has been at work throughout Grafton, the inn has 14 rooms in the main building and 21 rooms in two structures across the street. Individually decorated, all rooms have private bath; rooms in the older part of the inn are furnished in antiques, and some have crocheted canopies or four-posters. Homes in town can also be rented through the inn. *Rte. 35, 05146, tel. 802/843–2231. 35 rooms with bath. Facilities: restaurant, lounge, swimming pond, 2 tennis courts, platform tennis in winter, game room. AE, MC, V. Closed Apr., Dec. 24–25. Moderate–Expensive.*

Manchester Dining
Chantecleer. Five miles north of Manchester, intimate dining rooms have been created in a converted dairy barn with a large fieldstone fireplace. The menu reflects the chef's Swiss background: The appetizers include *Bündnerfleisch* (air-dried Swiss beef), and recent entrées were Wiener schnitzel; and frogs' legs in garlic butter. *Rte. 7, East Dorset, tel. 802/362–1616. Reservations required. DC, MC, V. Dinner only. Closed Mon.–Tues. Expensive–Very Expensive.*

Wildflowers. As the dining room of the Reluctant Panther, Wildflowers has long been known for elegant cuisine, and the new owner, Robert Bachofen, former director of food and beverage at New York's Plaza Hotel, is upholding that tradition. A huge fieldstone fireplace dominates the larger of the two dining rooms; the other is a small greenhouse with five tables. Glasses and silver sparkle in the candlelight, the service is impeccable, and the menu, which changes daily, might include boneless stuffed chicken with spinach, Gruyère, and Chardonnay-thyme sauce; or stuffed rainbow trout with scallops and chive butter. *West Rd. at Rte. 7A, tel. 802/362–3568. Reservations required. AE, MC, V. Closed Wed. Expensive.*

Garden Cafe. This sunny room with hanging plants has a terrific view of the spacious Southern Vermont Art Center grounds and an outdoor terrace; the menu includes such fare as sautéed trout with almonds; ragout of mushrooms in puff pastry; and home-baked fruit tart. *West Rd., tel. 802/362–4220. No credit cards. Closed mid-Oct.–Memorial Day. Moderate.*

Garlic John's. Italian specialties such as veal (piccata, marsala, saltimbocca, parmigiana) and calamari fra diavolo; red sauce and lots of it; and a dangling thicket of straw-covered Chianti bottles give this large and popular family-oriented restaurant the feel of a busy trattoria. *Rte. 11/30, tel. 802/362–9843. MC, V. Dinner only. Moderate.*

Quality Restaurant. Gentrification has reached the down-home neighborhood place that was the model for Norman Rockwell's *War News* painting. The Quality now has Provençal wallpaper and polished wooden booths, and the sturdy New England standbys of grilled meatloaf and hot roast beef or turkey sandwiches have been joined by tortellini Alfredo with shrimp and smoked salmon. *Main St., tel. 802/362–9839. AE, MC, V. Inexpensive–Moderate.*

Manchester Lodging

The Equinox. This white-column resort was a fixture on the tourism scene even before the family of Abraham Lincoln began spending summers here. A complete overhaul in 1985 restored all 154 rooms to color-coordinated comfort. The relatively simple rooms are furnished in Vermont pine, while floor-to-ceiling white lace curtains give the public areas a Victorian air. The front porch is perfect for watching the world go by. Six suites in the old section, including the Mary Todd Lincoln room, are furnished completely in antiques. Unusual for a Vermont inn are the spa programs in the hotel's fitness center, which have medical supervision and are tailored to the needs of the individual. The resort is often the site of large conferences. *Rte. 7A, Manchester Village 05254, tel. 802/362–4700 or 800/ 362–4747. 154 rooms with bath, 10 3-bedroom condos. Facilities: restaurant, lounge, cable TV, 24-hour room service, 3 tennis courts, 18-hole golf course, health club with sauna, steamroom, indoor and outdoor pools, fitness classes, exercise equipment. AE, D, DC, MC, V. Rates include afternoon tea. Expensive–Very Expensive.*

Reluctant Panther. The spacious rooms each have goosedown duvets, linens by Pierre Deux, and a complimentary half-bottle of wine. New owners have softened the decor with grays and peaches, while the furnishings are an eclectic mix of antique and contemporary. Nine rooms have fireplaces—the Mary Porter suite has two—and another suite has a woodburning stove; all suites have whirlpools. The best views are from rooms B and D. *West Rd., Box 678, 05254, tel. 802/362–2568. 14 rooms with bath, 3 suites. Facilities: restaurant, lounge, conference room. AE, MC, V. Rates include Continental breakfast. Expensive– Very Expensive.*

★ **1811 House.** The atmosphere of an elegant English country home can be enjoyed without crossing the Atlantic. A tiny pub-style bar decorated with horse brasses, the Waterford crystal and ornately carved chairs in the dining room, equestrian paintings, and the English floral landscaping of three acres of lawn all contribute to an inn worthy of Princess Di. The rooms contain period antiques; six have fireplaces, and many have four-posters. Bathrooms are old-fashioned but serviceable, particularly the Robinson Room's marble-enclosed tub. *Rte. 7A, 05254, tel. 802/362–1811. 14 rooms with bath. Facilities: lounge, air conditioning. No smoking. AE, MC, V. Rates include full breakfast. Expensive.*

Village Country Inn. Here the decor is for romance-novel fans: ruffled table skirts, ruffled pillowcases, canopy beds draped in swags of lace, white wicker—and roses, roses, roses. Rooms on the north face the pool, those on the south get the parking lot; rooms at the back of the inn are farthest from the staircase and road and are quieter. Bathrooms carved out of a house dating from 1889 can be small and oddly shaped, but five suites on the top floor are newly renovated. The front porch with its rocking chairs looks onto Route 7A and the mountains. *Rte. 7A, Box 408, 05254, tel. 802/362–1792. 30 rooms with bath. Facilities: cable TV in some rooms, tennis court. AE, MC, V. Rates are MAP. Expensive.*

Wilburton Inn. The stone-wall Tudor estate sits atop 20 acres of manicured grounds enhanced with sculpture, and the dining room and outdoor terrace overlook the Battenkill Valley. Rooms are spacious, especially those on the second floor, but the chenille-covered beds date to the home's conversion to an inn in 1946 (decor in the six outlying cottages is a bit newer). The public areas—with an ornately carved mantel on the first floor, mahogany paneling and stained glass door in one of the small dining rooms, a sweeping stone staircase to the lawn, and Oriental rugs on stone floors—are as elaborate as a railroad magnate's fortune could make them. *River Rd., 05254, tel. 802/362–2500 or 800/648–4944. 32 rooms with bath. Facilities: restaurant, lounge, outdoor pool, 3 tennis courts. AE, MC, V. Rates include full breakfast and afternoon tea. Expensive.*

Barnstead Innstead. A barn of the 1830s was transformed in 1968 into a handful of rooms that combine the rustic charm of exposed beams and barnboard walls with modern plumbing and cheerful wallpaper. *Rte. 30, 05255, tel. 802/362–1619. 12 rooms with bath, 1 suite. Facilities: cable TV, outdoor pool. MC, V. Moderate.*

Aspen Motel. Set well back from busy Route 7A, this family-owned motel has clean rooms with standardized motel furnishings. *Box 548, 05255, tel. 802/362–2450. 24 rooms with bath. Facilities: cable TV, outdoor pool, shuffleboard courts. AE, D, MC, V. Inexpensive–Moderate.*

Marlboro Dining   **Longwood Inn.** A former chef at the Commander's Palace in New Orleans has added such fare as blackened Florida angelfish to an often-changing menu of nouvelle Vermont specialties that might include roast duckling with cranberry glaze; and curried rabbit with sun-dried tomatoes over pasta. Diners have a view of the inn's rolling lawn, and an antique leaded glass cabinet with spice tins, salt dishes, and painted fans adds elegance. *Rte. 9, tel. 802/257–1545. Reservations advised. AE, MC, V. Closed Mon.–Tues. and early Apr. Expensive.*

Marlboro Lodging   **Longwood Inn.** Originally a farmhouse built in 1790, the inn has hand-stenciled willows in the halls, gleaming pine floors, and country antiques mixed with the occasional vinyl chair. The carriage house has four efficiency apartments that sleep three to six people. The newer rooms have larger windows and carpeting; one has a Jacuzzi. *Rte. 9, Box 86A, 05344, tel. 802/257–1545. 15 rooms, 13 with bath. Facilities: restaurant, trout pond. AE, MC, V. Closed Mon.–Tues. and early Apr. Rates include full breakfast. Moderate–Expensive.*

Whetstone Inn. A favorite of visitors to the Marlboro Music Festival, the 200-year-old farmhouse mixes authentic Colonial architecture and furnishings with pottery lamps, stenciled curtains, Scandinavian-style wall hangings, and a library filled with the works of Thoreau, Tolstoy, Zola, Hugo, and Proust. Three rooms have kitchenettes, and two can be joined to form a suite. During the music festival, early July through mid-August, a one-week minimum stay is required. *Marlboro 05344, tel. 802/254–2500. 12 rooms, 8 with bath. Facilities: restaurant, skating pond. No credit cards. Inexpensive–Moderate.*

Newfane Dining
★

The Four Columns. The restaurant made its reputation with a former White House chef, Rene Chardain. His successor, Greg Parks, has introduced nouvelle American dishes such as mixed grilled game sausages, jumbo shrimp with poblano butter and tapenade toast, and grilled marinated quail with pesto couscous. The Colonial-style dining room is decorated with antique tools and copper pots, and the tables sport Towle place settings and Limoges china. *West St. on the village green, tel. 802/365–7713. Reservations advised. Jacket and tie advised. AE, MC, V. Closed Tues.; weekdays Apr.; early Dec. Expensive–Very Expensive.*

Newfane Lodging

The Four Columns. Erected 150 years ago for a homesick Southern bride, the majestic white columns of the Greek Revival mansion are more intimidating than the Colonial-style rooms inside. Room 1 in the older section has an enclosed porch overlooking the town common; three rooms and a suite were added in an annex eight years ago. All rooms have antiques, brass beds, and quilts; some have fireplaces. The third-floor room in the old section, with the most privacy, is frequently requested by honeymooners. *West St., Box 278, 05345, tel. 802/365–7713. 17 rooms with bath. Facilities: restaurant, cable TV in public area, hiking trails. AE, MC, V. Rates are MAP in foliage season. Very Expensive.*

Weston Dining

The Inn at Weston. The food served in the large candlelit room —entrées such as lamb sautéed with mushrooms and Dijon mustard sauce; grilled chicken breast marinated in olive oil and lemon and served with raspberry sauce—has been praised by gourmet magazines. Breads and desserts are made on the premises. *Main St., tel. 802/824–5804. Reservations advised. No credit cards. Dinner only. Closed Wed. in winter, Mon. in summer. Moderate–Expensive.*

Weston Lodging

Darling Family Inn. The rooms in this renovated farmhouse of 1830 have baskets of apples and hand-stenciling by Joan Darling, and some rooms have folk art or an antique silver pitcher. Two cottages in back are less meticulously furnished, with twin beds, refrigerator, and shower stall. *Rte. 100, 05161, tel. 802/824–3223. 5 rooms with bath, 2 cottages. Facilities: outdoor pool, cable TV in public area. No pets. No credit cards. Rates include full breakfast. Moderate.*

The Arts

Music   **Marlboro Music Festival** (Marlboro Music Center, tel. 802/257–4333) presents a broad range of classical and contemporary music in weekend concerts during July and August.

New England Bach Festival (Brattleboro Music Center, tel. 802/257–4523), with a chorus under the direction of Blanche Moyse, is held in the fall.

Vermont Symphony Orchestra (tel. 802/864–5741) performs in Bennington and Arlington in winter, in Manchester and Brattleboro in summer.

Opera   **Brattleboro Opera Theatre** (tel. 802/254–6649) stages a complete opera once a year and holds an opera workshop.

Theater   **Dorset Playhouse** (north of Manchester, tel. 802/867–2223) hosts performances by a community group in winter and a resident professional troupe in the summer months.

Oldcastle Theatre Co. (Southern Vermont College, Bennington, (tel. 802/447–0564) performs from April to October.

Whetstone Theatre (River Valley Playhouse, Putney, tel. 802/387–5678) stages six productions from April to December.

Nightlife

Southern Vermont nightlife centers on Wilmington and other ski areas. In ski season you can expect to find live entertainment most nights; during the slower summer months it will be limited to weekends—or nonexistent. Most of the larger ski resorts have live entertainment. Performers may be listed in local newspapers.

Bars and Lounges   **Avalanche.** The Saturday night program features a little of everything—country, blues, soft rock. *Rte. 11/30, Manchester, tel. 802/362–2622.*

Marsh Tavern. The lounge in the Equinox Hotel programs individual performers Tuesday to Saturday in summer. *Rte. 7A, Manchester, tel. 802/362–4700.*

Mole's Eye Cafe. This basement room offers Mexican food, burgers, and live bands: perhaps acoustic or folk on Wednesday, danceable R&B, blues, or reggae on the weekend. *High St., Brattleboro, tel. 802/257–0771. Cover charge, Fri.–Sat.*

Poncho's Wreck. Acoustic jazz or mellow rock is the rule here. *S. Main St., south of Rte. 9, tel. 802/464–9320.*

Nightclubs   **Colors** has a DJ Thursday–Saturday; Thursday is ladies' night, Friday belongs to the guys. *20 Elliot St., Brattleboro, tel. 802/254–8646. Cover charge.*

Flat Street Night Club has a DJ on the weekend, an oldies band Thursday, and a 10- by 12-foot video screen. *17 Flat St., Brattleboro, tel. 802/254–8257. Cover charge.*

Central Vermont

Manufacturing has dwindled in central Vermont even as strip development and the creation of service jobs in tourism and recreation have increased along Route 4. Some manufacturing is still to be seen, particularly in the west, where Rutland is the state's second-largest city. The southern tip of Lake Champlain and a major ski resort make the area an economically diverse section of the state. Freshwater lakes are here, as are the state's famed marble industry and large dairy herds. The Green Mountains at the center of the area gave the state its nickname.

Important Addresses and Numbers

Weather (tel. 802/773–8056).

Visitor Information
Addison County Chamber of Commerce (2 Court St., Middlebury 05753, tel. 802/388–7951).

Quechee Chamber of Commerce (Box 757, Quechee 05059, tel. 802/295–7900).

Rutland Region Chamber of Commerce, Convention and Visitors Division (Box 67, Rutland 05701, tel. 802/773–2747).

Windsor Area Chamber of Commerce (Box 5, Windsor 05089, tel. 802/674–5910).

Woodstock Area Chamber of Commerce (4 Central St., Woodstock 05091, tel. 802/457–3555 or 802/457–1042 in summer).

Emergencies
Vermont's Medical Health Care Information Center has a **24-hour line** (tel. 802/864–0454).

Telecommunications Device for the Deaf (TDD) has a 24-hour emergency hotline (tel. 802/254–3929).

Getting Around Central Vermont

By Car
The major east–west road is Route 4, from White River Junction in the east to Fair Haven in the west. I–91 and the parallel Route 5 follow the eastern border; routes 7 and 30 are the north–south highways in the west. I–89 links White River Junction with Montpelier to the north, and Route 100 splits the region in half along the eastern edge of the Green Mountains.

By Bus
Vermont Transit Lines (tel. 802/864–6811 or 800/451–3292) links Rutland, White River Junction, Burlington, and many smaller towns.

Guided Tours

Land o' Goshen Farm raises llamas for sale and offers guided day or overnight trips in which llamas carry the luggage. *Rte. 73, Brandon, tel. 802/247–6015. Fares: day trip $75 per person (2-person minimum), overnight $210–$250 (6-person minimum). Treks mid-May–mid-Oct.*

Exploring Central Vermont

Numbers in the margin correspond with the numbered points of interest on the Central Vermont map.

Mountains, freshwater lakes, dairy herds, and ski resort activities await visitors to central Vermont. Our tour begins in Windsor, on Route 5 near I–91, at the eastern edge of the state.

① **Windsor** was the delivery room for the birth of Vermont. The **Old Constitution House,** where in 1777 grantholders declared Vermont an independent republic, was originally a tavern that was moved to the present site. It now holds 18th- and 19th-century furnishings, American paintings and prints; and tools, toys, and kitchenware from Vermont. *Rte. 5, tel. 802/828–3226. Admission free. Open mid-May–mid-Oct., daily 9:30–5:30.*

The firm of Robbins & Lawrence became famous for applying the "American system"—the use of interchangeable parts—to the manufacture of rifles. Although the company no longer exists, one of its factories houses the **American Precision Museum,** whose displays extol the Yankee ingenuity that created a major machine-tool industry here in the 19th century. *Rte. 5, tel. 802/674–5781. Admission: $2 adults, 75¢ children 6–12, $6 family. Open May 20–Oct. 1, weekdays 9–5, weekends 10–4.*

The **covered bridge** just off Route 5 that spans the Connecticut River between Windsor and Cornish, New Hampshire, is the longest in the state; it was reopened to traffic in 1990 after having been closed for two years for repairs.

② **White River Junction,** on the Connecticut River 14 miles north of Windsor, is the home of the **Catamount Brewery,** which makes the state beer. A relatively new brewery, Catamount produces a golden ale, a British-style amber, and a dark porter. If you can handle the smell of fermenting malt, you'll want to take the brewery tour (limited to 20 people at a time). Samples are available at the conclusion, and there's a company store. *58 S. Main St., tel. 802/296–2248. Open mid-June–mid-Oct., Mon.–Sat. 9–5. Brewery tour Tues. 11 AM, Fri. 1 PM, Sat. 11 and 1.*

③ The village of **Quechee,** 6 miles west of White River Junction, is perched astride the Ottauquechee River, where the 165-foot drop to the bottom of **Quechee Gorge** is an impressive sight. The mile-long gorge, carved by a glacier and the river, is visible from Route 4; many visitors spend time picnicking nearby or scrambling down one of the several descents. A decade ago **Simon Pearce** set up a glassblowing factory by the bank of a waterfall here, using the water power to drive his furnace. The glass studio is now a complex that also houses a pottery workshop, a retail shop, and a restaurant; visitors can watch both potters and glassblowers at work. *Main St., tel. 802/295–2711. Workshops open weekdays 10–5.*

④ Four miles east of Quechee on Route 4, **Woodstock** fulfills virtually every expectation most people have of a quiet New England town. The tree-lined village green is surrounded by exquisitely preserved Federal houses, streams flow around the center of town, and there's a covered bridge at the center. The interest of Rockefeller family members in historic preservation and land conservation is in part responsible for the town's pristine appearance.

The **Billings Farm and Museum** is one example of Rockefeller money at work (Billings's granddaughter married Laurance Rockefeller). The exhibits in the reconstructed farmhouse,

Central Vermont

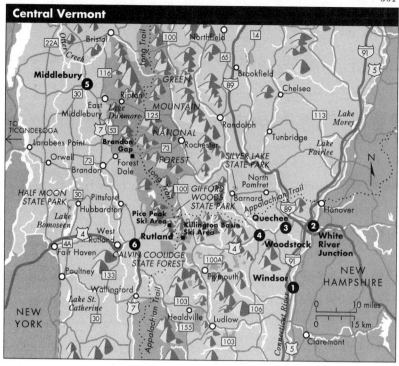

school, general store, and workshop demonstrate the daily activities and skills of early Vermont. Splitting logs doesn't seem nearly so quaint when you've watched the effort that goes into it! Visitors can contrast the older methods with those of a contemporary working dairy farm on the site. *Rte. 12, ½ mile north of Woodstock, tel. 802/457–2355. Admission: $4 adults, $2 children. Open early May–late Oct., daily 10–5.*

The Woodstock Historical Society has filled the rooms of the white clapboard **Dana House,** built in 1807, with its collection of period furnishings from the 18th and 19th centuries. Exhibits on the first floor include the town charter, furniture, maps, and locally minted silver. The elaborate sleigh owned by Frederick Billings, displayed in the barn, conjures up visions of romantic sleigh rides at the turn of the century. *26 Elm St., tel. 802/457–1822. Admission: $2.50 adults, $1 senior citizens, 50¢ children. Open May–late Oct., Mon.–Sat. 10–5, Sun. 2–5.*

Near Woodstock, the **Raptor Center** of the **Vermont Institute of Natural Science** houses 26 species of birds of prey, among them a bald eagle, a peregrine falcon, and the 3-ounce saw-whet owl. All the caged birds have been found injured and unable to survive in the wild. Nature trails wind over the institute's 77 acres. *Church Hill Rd., tel. 802/457–2779. Admission: $3.50 adults, $1 children 5–15. Open May–Oct., Wed.–Sun. 10–4; Nov.–Apr., Mon., Wed.–Sat. 11–4.*

Time Out The **Marketplace at Bridgewater Mills** on Route 4 has baked goods and sandwiches in its third-floor café and public restrooms.

The intersection of routes 4 and 100 presents two options for scenic drives in the **Green Mountain National Forest.** You can continue west on Route 4 along the Killington and Pico ski areas, which is the most heavily developed route; or you can head north on Route 100 toward Rochester and then go east on Route 73 through the Brandon Gap, where there are terrific views of Mount Horrid (much lovelier than the name suggests) and Lake Champlain, and several recreation areas and picnic spots.

Paralleling Route 73 about 5 miles to the north, Route 125 passes a waterfall at the Texas Falls Recreation area. This is Robert Frost country; Vermont's late poet laureate spent 23 summers at a farm just east of Ripton. The farm isn't open to the public, but 2 miles east of Ripton and 12 miles east of Middlebury, the **Robert Frost Wayside Trail** is an easy ¾-mile gravel path that winds through quiet woodland. Plaques along the way bear quotations from Frost's poems. A picnic area is ¼ mile to the east.

❺ In the late 1800s **Middlebury** was the largest community in the state west of the Green Mountains; it was at one time an industrial center, with wool, grain, and marble mills powered by the river that runs through the town. **Middlebury College,** founded in 1800, was conceived as an alternative to the more worldly University of Vermont, and its white stone buildings give a unified look to the campus, located in the center of town. Middlebury's Johnson Memorial Art Gallery, located in the Fine Arts Building, has a permanent collection of paintings and sculpture that includes work by Rodin and Hiram Powers. *Fine Arts Bldg., tel. 802/388–3711. Open weekdays, Sun. noon–5; Sat. 9–noon, 1–5.*

The **Vermont Folk Life Center** is housed in the basement of the restored 1801 home of Gamaliel Painter, the founder of Middlebury College. The rotating exhibits relate to early Vermont life, which could mean antiques, paintings by folk artists, or manuscripts. *2 Court St., tel. 802/388–4964. Open weekdays, Sun. noon–5, Sat. 9–noon, 1–5.*

At the **Sheldon Museum** a guide walks groups through period rooms that range from Colonial to turn-of-the-century and hold not only furniture but toys, clothes, kitchen tools, and paintings. The museum archives contain 30,000 letters, account books, ledgers, manuscripts, and photos. *1 Park St., tel. 802/ 388–2117. Admission: $2.50 adults, $2 senior citizens and students, 50¢ children under 12. Open June–Oct., Mon.–Sat. 10–5; Nov.–May, Wed., Fri. 1–4.*

Time Out Sandwiches, a marble-counter soda fountain, and an extensive menu of ice-cream dishes (including "girls' dishes") are the attractions at **Calvi's** on Merchants Row in Middlebury.

More than a crafts store, the **Vermont State Craft Center** at Frog Hollow is a juried display of the work of more than 250 Vermont artisans. The center sponsors classes with some of those artists. *Park St., tel. 802/388–3177. Open Mon.–Sat. 9:30–5; also Sun. noon–5 June–Oct.*

The Morgan horse—the official state animal—is known for its even temper and stamina even though its legs are a bit truncated in proportion to its body. The University of Vermont's **Morgan Horse Farm,** about 2½ miles from Middlebury, is a breeding and training farm where visitors may tour the stables and paddocks. *Rte. 23, tel. 802/388–2011. Admission: $2.50 adults, 75¢ children. Open daily 9–4. Tours May–Oct.*

❻ Rutland, the principal city of central Vermont, is at the heart of marble country, though the homes of blue-collar workers vastly outnumber the mansions of the marble magnates. Founded in the late 1700s, its traditional economic ties to railroading and marble are rapidly being displaced by the growth of the Pico and Killington ski areas to the east.

At the **Vermont Marble Exhibit,** 4 miles north of Rutland, visitors can see the transformation of the rough stone into slabs, blocks, and gift items. The artistic potential of the material is pursued by a full-time sculptor-in-residence, while a walkway above the production floor lets visitors watch the industrial applications. A hall has marble bas-reliefs of all the U.S. presidents, and a film explains the quarrying and production processes. A gift shop carries factory seconds and marble items both foreign and domestic. Expect crowds here; this is one of the state's most popular tourist attractions. Take Route 3 north from Route 4, turn left after 4.4 miles, and follow the signs. *Tel. 802/459–3311. Admission: $1.50 adults, 50¢ children 6–12. Open Memorial Day–mid-Oct., daily 9–5:30.*

Just what goes into producing all those jugs of maple syrup? The **New England Maple Museum** in Rutland gives the historical perspective (the process originated with Native Americans, who cooked the sap over an open fire) and shows antique sugaring implements, folk murals, and a film. When your sweet tooth is aching, you'll find that the gift shop has all syrup grades for sale. *Rte. 7, Pittsford, tel. 802/482–9414. Admission: $1 adults, 50¢ children 6–12. Open mid-Mar.–late May, daily 10–4; late May–Oct., daily 8:30–5:30; Nov.–Dec. 23, daily 10–4.*

The **Chaffee Art Gallery** is housed in a former Victorian mansion complete with parquet floors and grand staircase. The 200 artists work in a variety of media, and the gallery contains both abstract and representational pieces. Most of the work is for sale. The gallery's rotating exhibits may deal with such subjects as trains, folk art, and airplanes. *16 S. Main St., tel. 802/775–0356. Contribution. Open weekdays 10–5.*

Wilson Castle, a tribute to 19th-century America's infatuation with European culture, is a 32-room Romanesque mansion complete with turrets, stone portico, and frescoed ceilings. Furnished with a potpourri of Oriental and European furniture and objets d'art, it represents the Gilded Age at its most extravagant. *West Proctor Rd., tel. 802/773–3284. Admission: $4 adults, $1 children. Open mid-May–Oct., daily 9–6.*

Central Vermont for Free

Catamount Brewery, White River Junction

Johnson Art Gallery, Middlebury

Simon Pearce Glass Studio, Quechee

Vermont State Craft Center, Middlebury

What to See and Do with Children

Billings Farm and Museum, Woodstock
Morgan Horse Farm, Middlebury

New England Maple Museum, Rutland

Raptor Center, Woodstock

Off the Beaten Track

At the **Crowley Cheese Factory's** converted barn, visitors can watch the process that turns milk into cheese. What's different here is that the curds are manipulated by hand rather than by a machine. Turn south from Route 103 about 5 miles west of Ludlow (at the sign for Healdville) and continue 1 mile to the factory. *Tel. 802/259–2340. Open Mon.–Sat. 8–4, Sun. 11–5.*

Crossing the **floating bridge at Brookfield** feels like driving on water. The bridge, supported by almost 400 barrels, sits at water level and is the scene of the annual ice harvest festival in January (the bridge is closed in winter). Take Route 65 off I–89 to Brookfield and follow the signs.

Plymouth Notch, where Calvin Coolidge was born, inaugurated president of the United States, and buried, has the character of the man himself: low-key and quiet. Now owned by the state, the small cluster of buildings looks more like a large farm than a town; in addition to the homestead itself there's a facsimile of the general store run by Coolidge's father, a visitor center, and a film about Coolidge's life. Coolidge is buried in the cemetery on the other side of Route 100A. *Rte. 100A, 6 mi south of Rte. 4, east of Rte. 100, tel. 802/672–3650. Admission: $2 adults, children under 12 free. Open Memorial Day–mid-Oct., daily 9:30–5:30.*

Shopping

Shopping Districts **The Marketplace at Bridgewater Mills** (Rte. 4, west of Woodstock, tel. 802/672–3332) is a converted mill that houses factory stores (Van Heusen, Dunham, Manhattan, and others) and three stories of boutiques with Vermont crafts, including Vermont Clock Craft, Vermont Marble, and the Vermont Country Gourmet.

Waterman Place on Route 4, Quechee, is a trendy shopping center that caters to the affluent with second homes in the area. Shops include Leslie's Loft (women's apparel) and Trends (hairdressing and "creative nail design").

Food and Drink **Vermont Country Gourmet** (The Marketplace, Bridgewater Mills, tel. 802/672–3870) is an emporium for Vermont comestibles.

Specialty Stores **Antiques Center at Hartland** (Rte. 5, Hartland, tel. 802/436–
Art and Antiques 2441), one of the best known in Vermont, displays, in two 18th-century houses, inventory from 50 dealers around the state.

Foundation Antiques (148 N. Main St., Fair Haven, tel. 802/265–4544) has a strong selection of Quimper china, graniteware, art pottery, lighting, and ephemera.

Gallery 2 (43 Central St. and 6 Elm St., Woodstock, tel. 802/ 457–1171) showcases the best of Vermont's artists working in many media.

Park Antiques (75 Woodstock Ave., Rutland, tel. 802/775–4184) has furniture, folk art, glass, china, jewelry, paintings, and quilts.

Timber Rail Village (Rte. 4, Quechee, tel. 802/295–1550) bills itself as an antiques mall and stocks inventory from 225 dealers in its immense reconstructed barn. If you enjoy antiques, allow plenty of time; many people stay an entire afternoon. A small-scale working railroad will take the kids for a ride while Mom and Dad browse.

Windsor Antiques Market (53 N. Main St., Windsor, tel. 802/ 674–9336) occupies a Gothic Revival church and features Oriental, Native American, and military items in addition to American furniture, folk art, and accessories.

Books **Charles E. Tuttle** (28 S. Main St., Rutland, tel. 802/773–8930) is a major publisher of books on Oriental subjects, particularly art. In addition to its own publications, Tuttle has rare and out-of-print books, genealogies, and local histories.

Crafts **East Meets West** (Rte. 7 at Sangamon Rd., north of Rutland, tel. 802/443–2242) shows carvings, masks, statues, textiles, pottery, and baskets from the Third World, the American Southwest, the Pacific Northwest, and the Arctic.

Log Cabin Quilts (9 Central St., Woodstock, tel. 802/457–2725) has an outstanding collection of quilts in traditional designs and quilting supplies for the do-it-yourself enthusiast.

Minerva (61 Central St., Woodstock, tel. 802/457–1940) is a cooperative of eight artisans whose work includes stoneware and porcelain, jewelry, and handwoven clothing, rugs, and blankets.

North Wind Artisans' Gallery (81 Central St., Woodstock, tel. 802/457–4587) has contemporary crafts of sleeker, jazzier design.

Women's Clothing **Scotland by the Yard** (Rte. 4, Quechee, tel. 802/295–5351) has authentic Scottish kilts, kilt pins in imaginative designs, and jewelry bearing traditional Scottish emblems and symbols.

Sports and Outdoor Activities

Biking A bike trail runs alongside Route 106 south of Woodstock. **Four Seasons Sports** (Clubhouse Rd., Woodstock, tel. 802/295–7527) rents equipment and schedules daily bike trips.

Canoeing **Four Seasons Sports** rents equipment for canoeing on Dewey's Lake.

North Star Canoes in Cornish, New Hampshire, rents canoes for half-day, full-day, and overnight trips on the Connecticut River.

Fishing Central Vermont is the heart of the state's warm-water lake and pond fishing. **Lake Dunmore** produced the state record rainbow trout; **Lakes Bomoseen** and **St. Catherine** are good for rainbows and largemouth bass. In the east, **Lakes Fairlee** and **Morey** feature bass, perch, and chain pickerel, while the lower part of the **Connecticut River** has bass, pickerel, walleye, and perch.

Yankee Charters (20 S. Pleasant St., Middlebury 05753, tel. 802/388–7365) arranges sport fishing trips on Lake Champlain and provides equipment.

Golf Robert Trent Jones designed the 18-hole championship course of the **Woodstock Country Club** (Woodstock, tel. 802/457–2112), which is operated by the Woodstock Inn and Resort and is open to the public.

Health and Fitness Clubs The **Woodstock Sports Center** (Woodstock, tel. 802/457–1160), operated by the Woodstock Inn and Resort, has an indoor pool and tennis courts, whirlpool, exercise equipment, racquetball and squash courts, and sauna.

Hiking Several day hikes in the vicinity of Middlebury take in the scenery of the Green Mountains. About 8 miles east of Brandon on Route 73, one trail starts at Brandon Gap and climbs steeply up **Mount Horrid** (one hour). On Route 116, about 5½ miles north of East Middlebury, a U.S. Forest Service sign marks a dirt road that forks to the right and leads to the start of the hike to **Abbey Pond,** which has a view of Robert Frost Mountain (two–three hours).

About 5½ miles north of Forest Dale on Route 53, a large turnout marks a trail to the **Falls of Lana** (two hours). Three other trails—two short ones of less than a mile each and one of 2½ miles—lead to the old abandoned fortifications at **Mount Independence;** to reach them, take Route 22A west of Orwell for 3½ miles and continue on the right fork almost 2 miles to a parking area.

Polo **Quechee Polo Club** draws several hundred spectators every Saturday afternoon in summer to its matches with visiting teams on a field near the Quechee Gorge. *Deweys' Mills Rd., ½ mile off Rte. 4, Quechee, tel. 802/295–7152. Admission: $2 adults, $1 children, or $5 car.*

Water Sports Boat rentals are available at **Chipman Point Marina,** (Rte. 73A, Middlebury, tel. 401/948–2288), where there is dock space for 60 boats. This is also headquarters for **Vermont Houseboat Vacations** (90 Forbes St., Riverside, RI 02915, tel. 401/437–1277), which operates from May to August and rents houseboats that sleep six to eight persons.

State Parks

Ascutney State Park has a scenic mountain toll road and snowmobile trails. *Rte. 5, 2 mi north of Exit 8 from I–91, tel. 802/674–2060. 1,984 acres. Facilities: 49 campsites (no hookups), toilets, showers, picnic tables, fireplaces.*

Coolidge State Park, part of Calvin Coolidge National Forest, which also includes the village where Calvin Coolidge was born. *Rte. 100A, 2 mi north of junction with Rte. 100, tel. 802/672–3612. 500 acres. Facilities: 60 campsites (no hookups), toilets, showers, picnic tables, fireplaces, phone, snowmobile trails.*

Gifford Woods State Park, between Woodstock and Rutland, includes Kent Pond, a popular spot for fishing. *Rte. 100, ½ mi north of junction with Rte. 4, tel. 802/775–5354. 114 acres. Fa-*

cilities: 47 campsites (no hookups), toilets, showers, picnic tables and shelter, fireplaces, phone.

Half Moon State Park's principal attraction is Half Moon Pond, which has approach trails, nature trails, and a naturalist on duty. *Town Rd., 3½ mi off Rte. 30 from Hubbardton, tel. 802/273–2848. Facilities: 69 campsites (no hookups), toilets, showers, picnic tables, fireplaces, phone, boat and canoe rentals.*

Lake Bomoseen, a medium-size state park, has a naturalist on duty who explains the park's marked nature trails. Campers, swimmers, anglers, picnickers, boaters, and hikers use the park. *West Shore Rd., 4 mi north from Rte. 4, tel. 802/265–4242. 2,739 acres. Facilities: 66 campsites (no hookups), toilets, showers, picnic tables and shelter, fireplaces, phone, snack bar.*

Quechee Gorge State Park has the 165-foot Quechee Gorge with the Ottauquechee River at the bottom. *Rte. 4, 6 mi west of White River Junction, tel. 802/295–2990. 612 acres. Facilities: 30 campsites (no hookups), toilets, showers, picnic tables, fireplaces.*

Silver Lake State Park has swimming, canoe and boat rentals, and fishing. *Town Rd., ¼ mi north of Barnard, tel. 802/234–9451. 34 acres. Facilities: 46 campsites (no hookups), phone, toilets, showers, picnic tables and shelter, fireplaces, playground.*

Dining and Lodging

The large hotels are in Rutland and near the Killington ski area just to the east; elsewhere, travelers stay at inns, bed-and-breakfasts, or small motels. The **Woodstock Area Chamber of Commerce** provides a lodging referral service (tel. 802/457–2389). In the restaurants, dress is casual and reservations are unnecessary except where noted.

Middlebury Dining
★ **Woody's.** The peach walls with diner-Deco fixtures, the abstract paintings, and the cool jazz create a setting where assistant professors celebrate special occasions. Of the three levels, the lowest has the best view of Otter Creek. The nightly specials might include a homemade soup of roast pheasant broth with barley; a dinner entrée could be charbroiled strip steak with smoked cheddar nachos and salsa butter; and there's usually a Vermont lamb offering. *5 Bakery La., tel. 802/388–3603. Reservations advised. AE, CB, DC, MC, V. Moderate–Expensive.*

Middlebury Inn. At lunchtime the big bay window of the blue and white Colonial dining room lets in lots of light, and in the evening the candles above the fireplace give the pristine white columns, curtains, and lace tablecloths a romantic glow. The specialty here is the all-you-can-eat buffet, with (for example) roast top sirloin; a chicken dish; salmon, haddock, or seafood Newburg; and popovers. *Court House Sq., tel. 802/388–4961. Reservations advised. AE, MC, V. Moderate.*

Middlebury Lodging
Waybury Inn. The Waybury Inn may look familiar; it appeared as the "Stratford Inn" on television's "Newhart." Guest rooms, some of which have the awkward configuration that can result from the conversion of a building of the early 1800s, have original wall stenciling, quilted pillows, antique furnishings, and middle-aged plumbing; the Robert Frost Room has a canopy

four-poster. Comfortable sofas around the fireplace create a homey living room. *Rte. 125, 05740, tel. 802/388–4015. 14 rooms with bath. Facilities: restaurant, lounge, cable TV in public area. AE, MC, V. Expensive.*

Middlebury Inn. Queen Anne furniture, white fluted columns, a baby grand piano, and a black marble fireplace in the lobby reflect the heritage of Middlebury's foremost lodging place since 1827. The Otis elevator dates from 1926. Rooms in the main building mix the formal with country antiques: Reproduction mahogany cabinets house television sets. Bathrooms are early 20th-century, with more contemporary hairdryers, scales, and a phone. The 20 motel rooms have newer plumbing, sofa beds for a third person, quilt hangings, and floor-to-ceiling windows. *Court House Sq., 05753, tel. 802/388–4961 or 800/842–4666. 75 rooms with bath. Facilities: restaurant, lounge. AE, MC, V. Rates include afternoon tea. Moderate–Expensive.*

★ **Swift House Inn.** The white paneled wainscoting, elaborately carved mahogany and marble fireplaces, and cherry paneling in the dining room give this Georgian home of a 19th-century governor and his philanthropist daughter a formal elegance. Rooms, each with Oriental rugs, are decorated with antique reproductions that might include canopy beds, swag curtains, or a clawfoot Victorian tub. Bathrooms have Crabtree and Evelyn amenities, bath pillows, and guest robes. *25 Stewart La., 05753, tel. 802/388–9925. 19 rooms with bath. Facilities: restaurant, lounge, cable TV in public area, handicapped-access room. AE, MC, V. Rates include full breakfast. Moderate–Expensive.*

Quechee Dining   **Parker House.** The elegant Parker House is high ceilings and high-back chairs, starched burgundy and cream table linens that match the wallpaper in three intimate dining rooms, and, in summer and fall, a terrace with a spectacular river view. The atmosphere is one in which diners automatically lower their voices to a refined murmur. The menu, which might include a plate of charcuterie or milk-fed veal with morels and cream, is noted for an emphasis on game birds, such as pheasant braised with marsala and cabbage. *Main St., tel. 802/295–6077. Reservations advised. MC, V. Dinner only. Closed Mon.–Tues. (except summer); Mar.; early Nov. Expensive.*

Quechee Inn at Marshland Farm. This low-ceiling Colonial room manages to be both elegant and rustic at the same time, with brass wall sconces, candlelight, and crisp napery. The menu, which changes with the seasons, might include roast lamb in a cabernet sauce or duck breast with orange slices, lingonberries, and Cointreau. *Clubhouse Rd., tel. 802/295–3133. Reservations required. Jacket advised. AE, DC, MC, V. Moderate–Expensive.*

Simon Pearce. Candlelight and fresh flowers, sparkling glassware from the studio downstairs, contemporary dinnerware, and large windows that overlook the banks of the Ottauquechee River all contribute to a romantic setting. Beef and Guinness stew, (which reflects the owner's Irish background) and roast duck with mango chutney sauce are specialties of the house. *Main St., tel. 802/295–1470. Reservations advised. AE, MC, V. Moderate–Expensive.*

Rosalita's. *Ay yi yi yi*—who would expect Mexican cuisine in the heart of Yankeedom? This casual place has the right decorative touches—cacti, stucco, clay tiles—and the standard burritos, nachos, and fajitas, plus such entrées as grilled chicken breast with green chiles, tomatoes, and Jack cheese; and steak rolled in pepper and flamed with tequila. *Waterman Pl., Rte. 4, tel. 802/295-1600. AE, MC, V. Inexpensive–Moderate.*

Quechee Lodging **Quechee Inn at Marshland Farm.** The home of Vermont's first lieutenant governor, this 1793 building has Queen Anne furniture and wide-plank pine floors. Two sofas face the enormous fireplace in the public area; a harp stands in one corner and a 5-foot teddy bear looks comfy sitting at a table in another. *Clubhouse Rd., 05059, tel. 802/295-3133. 24 rooms with bath. Facilities: restaurant, lounge, cable TV, air-conditioning, conference rooms, ski center, fly-fishing school, bike and canoe rentals. AE, DC, MC, V. Rates are MAP. Expensive–Very Expensive.*

Parker House. The spacious peach and blue rooms of this renovated Victorian mansion of 1857 are named for former residents. Emily boasts a marble fireplace and an iron and brass bed. The armoire and dressing table in Rebecca have delicate faux inlays. Walter is the smallest room. Joseph has a spectacular view of the Ottauquechee River. *Main St., Box 0780, 05059, tel. 802/295-6077. 4 rooms with bath. Facilities: restaurant. MC, V. Closed Mar., early Nov. Expensive.*

★ **Quechee Bed and Breakfast.** Dried herbs hang from the beams in the living room, where a wood settee sits before a floor-to-ceiling fireplace that dates to the original structure of 1795. In the guest rooms, handwoven throws cover the beds and soft pastels coordinate linens and decor. Jessica's Room is the smallest; the Bird Room with its exposed beams is one of four that overlook the Ottauquechee River. Rooms at the back are farther from busy Route 4. Luminarias or cornstalks decorate the wide front porch seasonally, and the inn is within walking distance of Quechee Gorge. *Rte. 4, 05059, tel. 802/295-1776. 8 rooms with bath. Facilities: cable TV in public area, air-conditioning. MC, V. Rates include full breakfast. Moderate–Expensive.*

Rutland Dining **Vermont Marble Inn.** The dining room, with nine tables, is inti-
★ mate enough to allow diners to make new friends. Anything less than the classical music, crystal chandelier, candlelight, and antique Victorian sideboard would scarcely do justice to a meal that might include veal loin sautéed in saffron oil with sweet peppers and olives in a chive pesto; or braised duckling in port and raspberry sauce with wild rice. A vegetarian plate may offer lentil-and-vegetable-stuffed zucchini and grilled polenta, and there's a selection of home-baked desserts. All food is prepared to order, and special diets can be accommodated. *Fair Haven, tel. 802/265-8383. AE, MC, V. Moderate–Expensive.*

Ernie's Hearthside. Known also as Royal's Hearthside, Royal's Grill and Bar, and Ernie's Grill and Bar, the Rutland institution features an open hearth with hand-painted tiles, behind which the staff prepares mesquite-grilled chicken with basil, tomato, and mushrooms; roast prime rib; and lamb chops grilled with ginger and rosemary. Dinner includes a bit of cheddar spread and crackers, crudités, popovers, a vegetable, and salad. *37 N. Main St., tel. 802/775-0856. Reservations advised. AE, CB, DC, MC, V. Moderate.*

121 West. The menu features Wiener schnitzel and other Continental entrees as well as New England standbys—broiled fish; and lobster and shrimp casserole. The decor is as middle-of-the-road as the menu: red tablecloths, white stucco walls. Portions are ample, and the restaurant is popular locally. *121 W. Central St., tel. 802/773–7148. Reservations advised. AE, MC, V. Closed Sun. Moderate.*

★ **Back Home Cafe.** Wood booths, black and white linoleum tile, and exposed brick give this second-story cafe the air of a hole-in-the-wall in New York City—where the owners come from. Dinner might be baked stuffed fillet of sole with spinach, mushrooms, feta cheese, and tarragon sauce; or any of a number of Italian specialties. Daily lunch specials offer soup, entrée, and dessert for less than $5. *21 Center St., tel. 802/775–2104. AE, MC, V. Inexpensive–Moderate.*

Rutland Lodging **Holiday Inn.** Big, bland, and businesslike, this complex is placed to attract travelers on Routes 7 and 4. The hotel has the familiar Holiday Inn accoutrements, with a banquet and conference center geared to handle large groups. *Rte. 7, 05701, tel. 802/774–1911 or 800/465–4329. 150 rooms with bath. Facilities: restaurant, lounge, indoor pool, sauna, hot tubs, tanning and exercise equipment. AE, D, DC, MC, V. Very Expensive.*

★ **Vermont Marble Inn.** The innkeepers are the sort of people who beg you to put on your coat so you don't catch cold and later present an elaborate afternoon tea on a sterling silver service. Two ornate Carrara marble living room fireplaces look and feel as though they were carved from solid cream, and the crystal chandeliers in the dining room, the plush settees, Oriental rugs, and etched glass front doors may make you think of Lillie Langtry or Diamond Jim Brady. Guest rooms are named for authors (Byron, Elizabeth Barrett Browning) whose works are placed beside the bed. The antique furnishings may include a canopy bed, a working fireplace, an antique trunk; the bathrooms are large enough to have accommodated the full, flowing dresses of 1867, when the inn was built as a private home. Eight baths have shower stall only. *Fair Haven, 05743, tel. 802/ 265–8383. 13 rooms with bath. Facilities: restaurant, lounge. AE, MC, V. Rates include 5-course breakfast, afternoon tea, dinner. Very Expensive.*

Comfort Inn. This hotel intended for business travelers is just in back of the Trolley Barn shops. Guest room decor is a cut above the hotel chain standard, with upholstered wing chairs and blond furnishings, though the bathrooms are a bit small. Rooms with even numbers face away from the parking lot. *170 S. Main St., 05701, tel. 802/775–2200. 103 rooms with bath. Facilities: restaurant, lounge, indoor pool, racquetball and tennis courts, sauna, whirlpool, exercise equipment, cable TV, phones. AE, CB, D, DC, MC, V. Expensive.*

The Inn at Rutland. Mary and Michael Clark gave Rutland an alternative to motel and hotel chain accommodations when they renovated a Victorian mansion in 1988. The ornate oak staircase lined with heavy embossed metallic paper wainscoting leads to rooms that blend modern bathrooms with turn-of-the-century touches: botanical prints, elaborate ceiling moldings, frosted glass, pictures of ladies in long white dresses. Rooms on the second floor are larger than those on the third (once the servants' quarters). *70 N. Main St., 05701, tel. 802/773–0575. 12 rooms with bath. Facilities: phones, cable TV. AE, MC, V. Rates include Continental breakfast. Expensive.*

Windsor Dining **Windsor Station.** Yet another converted mainline railroad station serves mainline entrées such as chicken Kiev or filet mignon (prime rib on Saturday night). The booths with their curtained brass railings were created from the high-back railroad benches in the depot. *Depot Ave., tel. 802/674–2052. AE, MC, V. Closed early Nov. Moderate.*

Windsor Lodging **Juniper Hill Inn.** An expanse of green lawn with Adirondack chairs and a small pond sweeps up to the portico of this Greek Revival mansion, built at the turn of the century and now a National Historic Landmark. The central living room with its hardwood floors, oak paneling, Oriental carpets, and thickly upholstered wing chairs and sofas has a stately feel. The spacious rooms are furnished with some antiques, and some have fireplaces. The four-course dinners served in the candlelit dining room may include roast pork glazed with mustard and brandy. *Juniper Hill Rd., Box 79, 05069, tel. 802/674–5273. 14 rooms with bath. Facilities: restaurant, pool, walking trails. AE, MC, V. Rates include full breakfast. Moderate.*

Woodstock Dining **Woodstock Inn.** The dinner fare is nouvelle New England in this large dining room with several dozen tables: Vermont apple fritter with papaya and raspberry purée; smoked pheasant and chestnut pâté; sautéed venison marinated with brandy and peppercorns and served with braised endive; baked quail with wild rice, steamed artichoke hearts, and lentil purée. The wall of windows affords diners a view over the inn's putting green. *Rte. 4, tel. 802/457–1100. Reservations advised. Jacket required after 6 PM. AE, MC, V. Expensive–Very Expensive.*

Kedron Valley Inn. The chef trained at La Varenne cooking school in Paris, and that means classical French dishes such as filet of Norwegian salmon stuffed with herb seafood mousse in puff pastry; and shrimp, scallops, and lobster with wild mushrooms sautéed in shallots and white wine and served with a Fra Angelico cream sauce. The decor, too, is striking; antique linens are displayed in frames like works of art, and a terrace looking onto the grounds is open in summer. *Rte. 106, tel. 802/ 457–1473. AE, MC, V. Closed Apr. Expensive.*

★ **The Prince and the Pauper.** Here is a romantically candlelit Colonial setting, a prix fixe menu, and nouvelle French fare with a Vermont accent. The roast duckling might be served with a black cherry or Cointreau glaze; escalopes de veau could have a madeira demiglace or creamed onions with tarragon vinegar. Homemade lamb and pork sausage in puff pastry with a honey-mustard sauce is another possibility. *24 Elm St., tel. 802/457– 1818. Reservations advised. D, MC, V. Dinner only. Closed Mon. some seasons. Expensive.*

Bentley's. The decor here is tongue-in-cheek Victorian: antique silk-fringed lampshades, long lace curtains, a life-size carved kneeling winged knight. In addition to the standards—burgers, chili, homemade soups, omelets, croissants with various fillings—entrées include duck in raspberry purée, almonds, and Chambord; and tournedos with red zinfandel sauce. Remy rum raisin ice cream is one of the tempting desserts. *3 Elm St., tel. 802/457–3232. AE, MC, V. Moderate.*

Woodstock Lodging **Kedron Valley Inn.** The inn is imbued with the personalities of
★ its owners, Max and Merrily Comins; in 1985 they began the renovation of what in the 1840s had been the National Hotel, one of the state's oldest. Mannequins in the entry wear the wedding dresses of Merrily and her grandmother, a collection of family quilts is displayed throughout the inn (with a handwritten history of each one), and framed antique linens deck the walls. Many rooms have either a fireplace or a Franklin stove, and each is decorated with a quilt. Two rooms have pri-

vate decks, another has a private veranda, and a fourth has a private terrace overlooking the stream that runs through the inn's 15 acres. The exposed log walls in the motel units in back are more rustic than the rooms in the main inn, but they're decorated in similar fashion, with a mix of antiques and reproductions. *Rte. 106, 05071, tel. 802/457–1473. 28 rooms with bath. Facilities: restaurant, lounge, 1½-acre pond with sand beach, riding center. AE, MC, V. Closed Apr. Rates include full breakfast. Expensive.*

Village Inn at Woodstock. This renovated Victorian mansion features oak wainscoting, ornate pressed-tin ceilings, and a front porch perfect for studying the passersby on the sidewalks of Main Street; it's also convenient to downtown. Rooms are decorated simply with country antiques, chenille bedspreads, and dried flowers. *Rte. 4, 05091, tel. 802/457–1255. 8 rooms, 6 with bath. Facilities: restaurant, lounge, cable TV in public area. MC, V. Closed early Nov., Thanksgiving. Moderate.*

★ **Pond Ridge Motel.** The strip of rooms was renovated in 1989, so the furnishings are simple but fresh and tidy. Unlike many motels, it's set far enough back from Route 4 to mute the noise of the traffic. The big surprise here is the spacious back lawn that runs down to the Ottauquechee River. Many visitors choose one of the two-bedroom apartments with refrigerator, table, and stove. *Rte. 4, 05091, tel. 802/456–1667. 21 rooms, 20 with bath. Facilities: air-conditioning. AE, MC, V. Inexpensive–Moderate.*

The Arts

Middlebury College (tel. 802/388–3711) sponsors music, theater, and dance performances throughout the year at Wright Memorial Theatre.

The **Pentangle Council on the Arts** in Woodstock organizes performances of music and dance at the Town Hall Theater (tel. 802/457–398).

In Rutland, the **Crossroads Arts Council** (tel. 802/775–5413) presents music, opera, dance, jazz, and theater events.

Music **Point-Counterpoint Chamber Players** (tel. 802/247–8467) gives a summer series of concerts.

Vermont Symphony Orchestra (tel. 802/864–5741) performs in Rutland and (during the summer) in Woodstock.

Opera **Opera North** (Norwich, tel. 802/649–1060) does three opera productions annually at locations throughout the state.

Theater **Vermont Ensemble Theater** (tel. 802/388–2676 or 802/388–3001) has a three-week summer season in a tent on the Middlebury College campus.

Nightlife

Most of the nighttime activity of central Vermont takes place around the ski resorts of Killington, Pico, and Sugarbush.

Bars and Lounges **Centre Stage Lounge** (Holiday Inn, Rte. 7, Rutland, tel. 802/775–1911) has live entertainment and dancing Tuesday–Saturday.

Northern Vermont

Northern Vermont, where much of the state's logging and dairying takes place, is a land of contrasts: It has the state's largest city, some of New England's most rural areas, and many rare species of wildlife. With Montreal only an hour from the border, the Canadian influence can be felt and Canadian accents and currency encountered. On the west, Lake Champlain and the islands are the closest Vermont comes to having a seacoast.

Important Addresses and Numbers

Weather (tel. 802/862–2375).

Visitor Information **Central Vermont Chamber of Commerce** (Box 336, Barre 05641, tel. 802/229–5711).

Lake Champlain Regional Chamber of Commerce (Box 453, Burlington 05402, tel. 802/863–3489).

Greater Newport Area Chamber of Commerce (The Causeway, Newport 05855, tel. 802/334–7782).

St. Johnsbury Chamber of Commerce (30 Western Ave., St. Johnsbury 05819, tel. 802/748–3678).

Smugglers' Notch Area Chamber of Commerce (Box 3264, Jeffersonville 05464, tel. 802/644–5195).

Stowe Area Association (Box 1230, Stowe 05672, tel. 802/253–7321).

Emergencies Vermont's Medical Health Care Information Center has a 24-hour line (tel. 802/864–0454).

Telecommunications Device for the Deaf (TDD) has a 24-hour emergency hotline (tel. 802/254–3929).

Getting Around Northern Vermont

By Car In north central Vermont, I–89 heads west from Montpelier to Burlington and continues north to Canada. I–91 is the principal north–south route in the east, and Route 100 runs north–south through the middle of Vermont. North of I–89, routes 15 and 104 provide a major east–west transverse.

By Bus **Vermont Transit Lines** (tel. 802/864–6811 or 800/451–3292) links Burlington, Stowe, Montpelier, Barre, St. Johnsbury, and Newport.

Guided Tours

A replica of an old Champlain paddlewheeler, ***The Spirit of Ethan Allen*** hosts narrated cruises on Lake Champlain and, in the evening, dinner and moonlight dance sailings that drift by the Adirondacks and the Green Mountains. *Perkins Pier, tel. 802/862–9685. Cruises June–mid-Oct., daily at 10, noon, 2, 4.*

The **Lamoille Valley Railroad,** a working line, augments its income by carrying passengers on two-hour, 40-mile excursions along the Lamoille River, where the green and gold cars crisscross the water and pass through one of the rare covered railroad bridges in the country. *Stafford Ave., Morrisville 05661, tel. 802/888–4255. Reservations advised. Fare: $15 ad-*

ults, $7 children; children under 5, when held, free. MC, V. July–Aug., Tues.–Fri. at 10, 1; mid-Sept.–mid-Oct., weekends at 10, 1.

Easy Street Limousine (tel. 802/425–3912) has package and individualized tours of antiques shops from Salisbury to Burlington in air-conditioned limousines.

Exploring Northern Vermont

Numbers in the margin correspond with the numbered points of interest on the Northern Vermont map.

Visitors to northern Vermont find activity in the busy ski area at Stowe; in Burlington, the state capital; and in rural and even remote areas in the Lake Champlain islands and the Northeast Kingdom. We begin at Barre, 3 miles east of I–89.

● **Barre** has been famous as the source of Vermont granite ever since two men began working the quarries in the early 1800s, and the large number of immigrant laborers attracted to the industry made the city prominent in the early years of the American labor movement.

The attractions of the **Rock of Ages granite quarry** (take Exit 6 from I–89 and follow Route 63) range from the awe-inspiring—the quarry resembles a man-made miniature of the Grand Canyon—to the absurd: The company invites you to consult a directory of tombstone dealers throughout the United States. Trains carry visitors closer to the working area of the quarry, but from the visitor center you can easily see the sheer faces marked off in blocks. At the craftsman center, which you pass on the drive to the visitor center, the view from the elevated platform at one end seems to take in a scene out of Dante's *Inferno:* A dusty, smoky haze hangs above the acres of men at work, with machines screaming as they bite into the rock. The process that transfers designs to the smooth stone and etches them into it is fascinating. *Rte. 63, tel. 802/476–3115. Quarry and visitor center open May–mid-Oct., daily 8:30–5. Train tour weekdays 9:30–3:30; admission: $2 adults, $1 children 5–12. Craftsman center open weekdays 8–3:30.*

Hope Cemetery on Route 14, 2 miles north of Barre, has one of the largest displays of the quarry's product. Here are the monuments the stonecutters carved for themselves and one another, taking the opportunity to show what they could do.

❷ In **Montpelier,** the larger city 5 miles northwest of Barre, the **Vermont State House** with its gold dome and granite columns 6 feet in diameter has an impressive scale. Inside, the relatively intimate House chamber conjures up visions of *Mr. Smith Goes to Montpelier,* and the even smaller Senate chamber looks like a rather grand committee room. The center hall is decorated with quotations reflecting on the nature of Vermont. *State St., tel. 802/828–2228. Open weekdays 8–4.*

Are you wondering what the last panther shot in Vermont looked like? why New England bridges are covered? what a niddy-noddy is? or what Christmas was like for a Bethel boy in 1879? ("I skated on my new skates. In the morning Papa and I set up a stove for Gramper.") The **Vermont Museum,** on the ground floor of the Vermont Historical Society offices in Montpelier, has the answers. *109 State St., tel. 802/828–3391.*

Northern Vermont

QUEBEC

CANADA

NEW HAMPSHIRE

NEW YORK

QUEBEC

Lake Memphremagog

Big Averill

Maidstone Lake

Seymour Lake

Lake Willoughby

Crystal Lake

Guildhall

Missisquoi R.

Missisquoi River

Lamoille River

Lake Champlain

Lake Groton

Newport **7**

Barnet

St. Johnsbury **8**

East Burke

Lyndonville

Walden

Cabot

Peacham

Groton

Plainfield

Barre **1**

Northfield

Montpelier

Waitsfield

Hardwick

Morrisville

Stowe **3**

Smugglers' Notch

Mt. Mansfield Ski Area **4**

LITTLE RIVER STATE PARK

Waterbury

Winooski R.

Jeffersonville

Cambridge

Essex Junction

Richmond

Hinesburg

South Burlington

Burlington **5**

Shelburne

Vergennes

Bristol

North Hero **6**

Lake Champlain Islands

Kill Kare State Park

Burton Island State Park

Knight Point State Park

Sand Bar Wildlife Area

St. Albans

Grand Isle

South Hero

Aburg Center

Isle La Motte

Swanton

East Berkshire

Enosburg Falls

Montgomery Center

Long Trail

Long Trail

Lamoille River

N

14 miles

21 km

302

Suggested contribution: $2. Open weekdays 8–4:30; also July–Aug., weekends 10–5.

The **T. W. Wood Art Gallery** is named for a Barre artist, a prominent painter of the Academy school of realism, who endowed this facility with his collection of his own work and that of his peers. Changing exhibits feature contemporary work. *Vermont College Arts Center, E. State St., tel. 802/223–8743. Admission free. Open Tues.–Sun. noon–4.*

Northwest of Montpelier, one of Vermont's best-loved attractions is **Ben and Jerry's Ice Cream Factory,** a mecca, nirvana, and Valhalla for ice cream lovers. Jerry and Ben began selling homemade ice cream from a bus in the 1960s, and the company reflects its heritage with corporate grants and a "1 Percent for Peace" program that benefits from the admission fee for tours. *Rte. 100, 1 mi north of I–89, tel. 802/244–5641. Admission: $1, children under 12 free. Open Mon.–Sat. 9–4. Tour every ½ hour.*

❸ For more than a century the history of **Stowe**—northwest of Montpelier on Route 100, 10 miles north of I–89—has been determined by the town's proximity to Mt. Mansfield, the highest elevation in the state. As early as 1858 visitors were trooping to the area to view the mountain whose shape suggests the profile of the face of a man lying on his back. Popular at first as a summer resort, Stowe has been a major ski center for 60 years.

The Mount Mansfield Co., formed in 1951, operates the ski facilities at Stowe (*see* Chapter 2). In summer, visitors can take the 4½-mile **toll road** to the top for a short scenic walk and a magnificent view. *Mountain Rd., 7 mi from Rte. 100. Admission: $8 car, $5 motorcycle. Open late May–early Oct., daily 10–5.*

An alternative means of reaching the Mt. Mansfield summit is the four-seat **gondola** that shuttles continuously up 4,393 feet to the area of "the Chin," which has a small restaurant (dinner reservations required). *Mountain Rd., 7 mi from Rte. 100. Admission: $8 adults, $4 children, under 5 free. Open late June–early Oct., daily 10–5; Oct.–late June, weekends 10–5.*

Time Out | **The Whip,** on Main Street at Mountain Road in Stowe, got its name from the buggy whips everywhere. Here are hearty bowls of chili, sandwiches, a few low-fat dishes, and specials at lunch.

The Mount Mansfield Co. also operates a 2,300-foot **Alpine slide** on Spruce Peak. *Spruce Peak Lodge, Mountain Lodge. Admission: single ride $5 adults, $3.50 children; unlimited rides $15 adults, $12 children. Open late June–early Sept., daily 10–5; early Sept.–early Oct., weekends 10–5.*

❹ Northwest of Stowe lies a scenic but not very direct route to Burlington: **Smugglers' Notch,** the narrow pass over Mt. Mansfield that is said to have given shelter to 18th-century outlaws in its rugged, bouldered terrain. There are picnic tables and places to park at roadside and, as you begin the descent on the western side of the mountain, a spectacular waterfall to your left, though you may have to look over your shoulder to see it. Follow Route 108 to Route 15, which turns west and south at Jeffersonville.

Time Out **Windridge Bakery and Cafe** on Route 15 in Jeffersonville prepares positively incredible breads, pies, and other pastries.
Their simple ingredients would make for dull sandwiches if
their quality weren't so high.

⑤ Vermont's largest population center, **Burlington** was founded
in 1763 and had a long history as a trade center following the
growth of the shipping industry on Lake Champlain during the
18th century.

The city is energized by the roughly 10,000 students at the University of Vermont, whose campus is in the heart of the city.
The **Robert Hull Fleming Museum,** with its collections of primitive masks, archaeological artifacts, natural history holdings,
and art from pre-Columbian to modern times is the largest in
the state. *Colchester Ave., tel. 802/656-0750. Admission free.
Open Sept.–June, Tues.–Fri. 10–5, weekends 1–5; July–
Aug., Wed.–Sat. 11–4.*

One could trace all New England history simply by wandering
the 100 acres of the **Shelburne Museum,** whose 35 buildings
seem a collection of individual museums. The large collection of
Americana contains 18th- and 19th-century period homes and
furniture, fine and folk art, farm tools, more than 140 carriages
and sleighs, Audubon prints, even a private railroad car from
the days of steam. And an old-fashioned jail. And an assortment of duck decoys. And an old stone cottage. And a display of
early toys. And the *Ticonderoga,* an old sidewheel steamship.
*Rte. 7, 5 mi south of Burlington, tel. 802/985-3346. Admission:
$9.50 adults, $4 children 6-17. Open mid-May–mid-Oct., daily 9-5.*

Shelburne Farms, 5 miles south of Burlington, has a history of
improving the farmer's lot by developing new agricultural
methods. Founded in the 1880s as the private estate of a gentleman farmer, the 1,000-acre property is now an educational and
cultural resource center. Visitors can see a working dairy farm,
listen to nature lectures, or simply stroll the immaculate
grounds on a scenic stretch of Lake Champlain waterfront. The
original landscaping, designed by Frederick Law Olmsted, the
creator of Central Park and Boston's Emerald Necklace, gently
channels the eye to expansive vistas and aesthetically satisfying views of such buildings as the five-story, 2-acre Farm Barn.
*East of Rte. 7, 3 mi south of I-89, tel. 802/985-8686. Admis-
sion: $2 adults, $1 senior citizens; walking trail $1; guided tour
$2.50. Visitor center and shop open daily 9:30-5, last tour at
3:30; farm closed mid-Oct.–late May.*

At the six-acre **Vermont Wildflower Farm,** the display along the
flowering pathways changes constantly: violets in the spring,
daisies and black-eyed Susans for summer, and fall colors that
rival the foliage. A brief slide show treats those who prefer a
darkened theater to the real thing, and the gift shop has seeds,
gifts, and books. *Rte. 7, 5 mi south of the Shelburne Museum,
tel. 802/425-3500. Admission: $2 adults, $1.50 senior citizens.
Open May–mid-Oct., daily 10-5.*

Time Out The food and ambience of **Leunig's Cafe,** at Church and College
streets in Burlington, recall a European bistro. In summer
there is an outdoor café that looks onto the Church Street Marketplace parade.

The **Old Round Church** of Richmond, 14 miles east of Burlington, is a 16-sided structure built in the early 19th century as a place of worship for five denominations. *Rte. 2, Richmond. Contribution: $1. Open July–Labor Day, weekends 10–4.*

Ethan Allen, Vermont's famous early settler, is a figure of some mystery. The visitor center at his **homestead** by the Winooski River both answers and raises questions about his flamboyant life. The house, about 70% original, has such frontier hallmarks as nails pointing through the roof on the top floor, rough saw-cut boards, and an open hearth for cooking. The Ethan Allen commemorative tower within walking distance of the homestead has been restored by a private organization. *North Ave., north of Burlington, tel. 802/865–4556. Admission: $3 adults, $2 students and senior citizens, children under 6 free, $10 family. Open mid-Apr.–June, Wed.–Sun. 1–5; July–Aug., Tues.–Sat. 10–5, Sun. noon–5; Sept.–Oct., Tues.–Sun. 1–5.*

❻ The **Lake Champlain islands** lie between the Adirondacks to the west and the Green Mountains to the east. Their great moment in history was their discovery by Samuel de Champlain, represented on Isle La Motte by a granite statue that looks south to the shrine to St. Anne on the site of the first French settlement. Today the islands are a center of water recreation in summer, ice fishing in winter. North of Burlington, the scenic drive through the islands on Route 2 begins at I–89 and travels north through South Hero, Grand Isle, and Isle La Motte to Alburg Center, 5 miles from the Canadian border. Here Route 78 will take you east to the mainland.

To cross northern Vermont, take Route 78 east to Route 105, continue to Route 118 in East Berkshire, and follow that to Route 242 in the Jay Peak area. From the 3,860-foot pass can be seen not only Canada but the expanse of relatively undeveloped land to the east called the **Northeast Kingdom**—a rugged expanse of timber and agriculture that calls on hardihood for survival.

❼ The descent from Jay Peak on Route 101 leads to Route 100, which takes us east to the city of **Newport** on Lake Memphremagog (accent on *gog*). The waterfront is the dominant view of the city, which is built on a peninsula. The grand hotels of the last century are gone, yet the buildings still drape themselves along the lake's edge and climb the hills behind.

❽ The drive south from Newport on I–91 encounters some of the most unspoiled areas in all Vermont. This is the Northeast Kingdom, named for the remoteness that has helped to preserve its rural nature. Its chief city is **St. Johnsbury,** the southern gateway, on I–91.

St. J still displays the influence of the Fairbanks family, whose fortune was derived from the invention of the platform scale, and the **Fairbanks Museum and Planetarium** attests to the family inquisitiveness about all things scientific. The redbrick building in the squat Romanesque architectural style of H. H. Richardson houses collections of plants and animals, Vermont items, and an intimate 50-seat planetarium. *Main and Prospect Sts., tel. 802/748–2372. Admission: $2.50 adults, $1.25 children, $5.50 family; planetarium $1. Open Sept.–June,*

Mon.–Sat. 10–4, Sun. 1–5; July–Aug., Mon.–Sat. 10–6, Sun. 1–5.

The **St. Johnsbury Athenaeum,** with its dark rich paneling, polished Victorian woodwork, and ornate circular staircases that rise to the gallery around the perimeter, is a tiny gem. The gallery at the back of the building has the overwhelming *Domes of Yosemite* by Albert Bierstadt and a lot of sentimental 19th-century material. *30 Main St., tel. 802/748–8291. Admission free. Open Tues., Thurs.–Sat. 9:30–5; Mon., Wed. 9–8; in summer, Sat. 9:30–2.*

Northern Vermont for Free

Vermont State House, Montpelier

T. W. Wood Art Gallery, Montpelier

Robert Hull Fleming Museum, Burlington

St. Johnsbury Athenaeum, St. Johnsbury

What to See and Do with Children

The **Discovery Museum,** northeast of Burlington in Essex Junction, is a cornucopia of hands-on natural science, art, and history, with changing exhibits and an outdoor area where injured animals are cared for and children can pet healthy ones. *51 Park St., Essex Junction, tel. 802/878–8687. Admission: $2.50 adults, $2 children. Open July–Aug., Tues.–Sat. 10–4:30, Sun. 1–4:30; Sept.–June, Tues.–Fri., Sun. 1–4:30, Sat. 10–4:30.*

The Spirit of Ethan Allen, Burlington

Lamoille Valley Railroad, Morrisville

Ben and Jerry's Ice Cream Factory, Waterbury

Shelburne Museum, Shelburne

Off the Beaten Track

The **Lake Champlain Maritime Museum** commemorates the days when steamships sailed along the coast of northern Vermont carrying logs, livestock, and merchandise bound for New York City. The exhibits housed here in a one-room stone schoolhouse 25 miles south of Burlington include historic maps and nautical prints, paintings and archaeology. *Basin Harbor Rd., 5 mi west of Vergennes, tel. 802/475–2317. Admission: $2 adults. Open Memorial Day–mid-Oct., Wed.–Sun. 10–5.*

North of Rte. 2, midway between Barre and St. Johnsbury, the biggest cheese producer in the state, the **Cabot Creamery,** has a visitor center with an audiovisual presentation about the state's dairy and cheese industry, tours of the plant, and—best of all—samples. *Cabot, 3 mi north of Rte. 2, tel. 802/563–2231. Admission: $1. Open Mon.–Sat. 8–4:30.*

Shopping

Shopping Districts **Church Street Marketplace** (tel. 802/863–1648), a pedestrian thoroughfare that runs from Main Street to Pearl Street in downtown Burlington, is lined with boutiques, cafés, and street vendors.

Burlington Square Mall (tel. 802/863–3311), entered from Church Street Marketplace, has Porteous (the city's major department store) and some 60 shops.

The Champlain Mill (tel. 802/655–9477), a former woolen mill on the banks of the Winooski River on Route 2/7 northeast of Burlington, has three floors of stores.

The **Outlet Center** on Route 7 at I–89 in South Burlington has both full-price and discount retailers.

Food and Drink **Champlain Chocolates** (431 Pine St., Burlington, tel. 802/864–1807), a factory store, discounts maple crunch and other candy.

The Cheese Outlet Shop (400 Pine St., Burlington, tel. 802/863–3698) has Vermont and imported cheeses, its own cheesecake, imported crackers and cookies, and wines.

Cold Hollow Cider Mill (Rte. 100, Stowe, tel. 802/244–8771) offers cider, baked goods, Vermont produce, and free samples at the pressing machine.

Harrington's (Rte. 7 opposite Shelburne Museum, south of Burlington, tel. 802/985–2000) cob-smoked hams, bacon, turkey, and summer sausage will generate thoughts of lunch at any hour, and the store has cheese, syrup, and other New England specialties as well.

Morse Farm (County Rd., Montpelier, tel. 802/223–2740) has been producing maple syrup for three generations; the sugar house is open for viewing in spring when the syrup is being made.

Specialty Stores **English Country at Stowe** (1 Pond St., Stowe, tel. 802/253–4420)
Antiques offers English country antiques.

Ethan Allen Antique Shop (1 mi east of Exit 14E from I–89, Burlington, tel. 802/863–3764) has a large stock of early American and period country furniture and accessories.

Great American Salvage (3 Main St., Montpelier, tel. 802/223–7711) supplies architectural detailing: moldings, brackets, stained glass and leaded windows, doors, and trim retrieved from old homes.

Sign of the Dial Clock Shop (63 Eastern Ave., St. Johnsbury, tel. 802/748–5044) specializes in antique clock sales, repairs, and restorations.

Tailor's Antiques (68 Pearl St., Burlington, tel. 802/862–8156) carries small primitive paintings, glass, and china for collectors.

Books **Chassman & Bem Booksellers** (1 Church St., Burlington, tel. 802/862–4332), voted best bookstore in Vermont, has more than 20,000 titles, with a discriminating selection of children's books and a large magazine rack.

Crafts **Bennington Potters North** (127 College St., Burlington, tel. 802/863–2221) has glassware, baskets, small household items, and a seconds outlet downstairs.

The Christmas Place (Mountain Rd., Stowe, tel. 802/253–8767) has imported nativity scenes, nutcracker dolls, 12 lords a'leaping, wreaths, and other decorations.

Designers' Circle (21 Church St., Burlington, tel. 802/864–4238) stocks wovens, ceramics, wood, and jewelry crafts.

Men's and Women's **Moriarty Hat and Sweater Shop** (Mountain Rd., Stowe, tel. 802/
Clothing 253–4052) is the home of the original ski hat with the funny peak on top; the assortment is mind-boggling, and you can order a custom knit.

Sports and Outdoor Activities

Biking South of Burlington, a moderately easy 18½-mile trail begins at the blinker on Route 7, Shelburne, and follows Mt. Philo Road, Hinesburg Road, Route 116, and Irish Hill Road. The **Ski Rack** (81 Main St., tel. 802/858–3313) rents equipment and has maps. In Burlington a recreational path runs 9 miles along the waterfront.

Stowe's recreational trail begins behind the Community Church on Main Street and meanders for 2.7 miles behind the strip development that lines Mountain Road. The intersection of Routes 100 and 108 is the start of a 21-mile tour with scenic views of Mt. Mansfield; the route takes you along Route 100 to Stagecoach Road, to Morristown, over to Morrisville, and south on Randolph Road. **Mountain Bike** (Mountain Rd., tel. 802/253–7919) supplies equipment and information.

Canoeing **Sailworks** (176 Battery St., Burlington, tel. 802/864–0111) rents canoes and gives lessons at Sand Bar State Park in summer.

The upper Winooski River offers good short canoe trips. The **Fly Rod Shop** (Rte. 100, 3 mi south of Stowe, tel. 802/253–7346) rents canoes.

The **Village Sport Shop** (Lyndonville, tel. 802/626–8448) has canoes for use on the Connecticut River.

Fishing Lake Champlain, stocked annually with salmon and lake trout, has become the state's ice-fishing capital; walleye, bass, pike, pickerel, muskellunge, yellow perch, steelhead, and channel catfish are also taken. Rainbow trout can be found on the Missisquoi, Lamoille, Winooski, and Willoughby rivers, and there's warm-water fishing at many smaller lakes and ponds in the region. Lakes Seymour, Willoughby, and Memphremagog and Big Averill in the Northeast Kingdom are good for salmon and lake trout. Ice fishing is also popular on Lake Memphremagog.

Marina services are available north and south of Burlington. **Malletts Bay Marina** (228 Lakeshore Dr., Colchester, tel. 802/862–4077) and **Point Bay Marina** (Thompson's Point, Charlotte, tel. 802/425–2431) both provide full service and repairs.

Groton Pond (Rte. 302, off I–91, 20 mi south of St. Johnsbury, tel. 802/584–3829) is popular for trout fishing; boat rentals are available at the site.

Health and Fitness **The Fitness Advantage** (137 Iroquois Ave., Essex Junction, tel.
Clubs 802/878–6568), a co-ed center, offers spa and fitness equipment, a licensed day-care center, massage therapy, nutritional and lifestyle counseling, and image consultation.

Hiking **Mount Mansfield State Forest** and **Little River State Park** (Rte. 2, 1½ mi west of Waterbury) provide an extensive trail system, including one that reaches the site of the Civilian Conservation Corps unit that was here in the 1930s.

For the climb to Stowe Pinnacle, go 1½ miles south of Stowe on Route 100 and turn east on Gold Brook Road opposite the Nichols Farm Lodge; bear left at the first fork, continue through an intersection at a covered bridge, turn right after 1.8 miles, and travel 2.3 miles to a parking lot on the left. The trail crosses an abandoned pasture and takes a short, steep climb to views of the Green Mountains and Stowe Valley (two hours).

Water Sports **Burlington Community Boathouse** (foot of College St., Burlington Harbor, tel. 802/865–3377) has sailboard and boat rentals (some captained) and lessons.

International Yacht Sales (Colchester, tel. 802/864–6800) makes the yacht *Intrepid,* an America's Cup winner, available for charter.

Sailworks (176 Battery St., Burlington, tel. 802/864–0111) rents rowing shells, sailboats, and sailboards at Sand Bar State Park.

Beaches

Some of the most scenic Lake Champlain beaches are on the Champlain islands. **North Hero State Park** (tel. 802/372–8727) has a children's play area nearby, **Knight Point State Park** (tel. 802/372–8389) is the reputed home of "Champ," Lake Champlain's answer to the Loch Ness monster, and **Sand Bar State Park** (tel. 802/372–8240) is near a waterfowl preserve. Summer crowds make it wise to arrive early. *Admission: $1 adults, 50¢ children. Open mid-May–Oct.*

The **North Beaches** are on the northern edge of Burlington: North Beach Park (North Ave., tel. 802/864–0123), Bayside Beach (Rte. 127 near Malletts Bay), and Leddy Beach, which is popular for sailboarding.

State Parks

Burton Island State Park is accessible only by passenger ferry or boat; at the nature center a naturalist discusses the island habitat. *Rte. 105, 2 mi east of Island Pond, then south on marked local road, tel. 802/524–6353. 253 acres. Facilities: 42 campsites (no hookups), 100-slip marina with power hookups and 20 moorings, toilets, showers, picnic tables, fireplaces, phone, playground, snack bar.*

Grand Isle State Park has a fitness trail and a naturalist. *Rte. 2, 1 mi south of Grand Isle, tel. 802/372–4300. 226 acres. Facilities: 155 campsites (no hookups), toilets, showers, picnic tables, fireplaces, recreation building, phone.*

Kamp Kill Kare State Park is popular for sailboarding, and it provides ferry access to Burton Island. *Rte. 36, 4½ mi west of St. Albans Bay, then south on town road 3½ mi, tel. 802/524–6021. 17.7 acres. Facilities: 60 campsites (no hookups), toilets, showers, picnic shelter, fireplaces, phone, boat rentals and ramp.*

Little River State Park features hiking on Mount Mansfield and Camel's Hump and marked nature trails. *Little River Rd., 3½ mi north of junction with Rte. 2, 2 mi east of Rte. 100, tel. 802/*

244–7103. 12,000 acres. Facilities: 101 campsites (no hook-ups), toilets, showers, picnic tables, fireplaces, boat rentals and ramp, phone.

North Hero State Park, oriented around Lake Champlain, is popular with camping groups. *Rte. 2, 6 mi southwest of Alburg, tel. 802/372–8727. 399 acres. Facilities: 60 campsites (no hook-ups), toilets, showers, picnic tables, fireplaces, phone, rowboat rentals, boat ramp.*

Sand Bar State Park has a swimming beach and is heavily used by sailboarders. *Rte. 2, 4 mi north of Exit 17 on I–89, tel. 802/ 372–8240. 20 acres. Facilities: picnic area, bathhouse, boat rentals, snack bar.*

Smugglers' Notch State Park is good for picnicking and hiking on wild terrain among large boulders. *Rte. 108, 10 mi north of Mt. Mansfield, tel. 802/253–4014. 25 acres. Facilities: 38 campsites (no hookups), toilets, showers, picnic tables, fire-places, phone.*

Dining and Lodging

Burlington and Stowe have the large resort hotels; the rest of the region offers inns, bed-and-breakfasts, and small motels. The Stowe area has a **lodging referral service** (tel. 800/247–8693). In the restaurants, dress is casual and reservations may be helpful in the peak season.

Barre Dining   **Green Mountain Diner.** The daily fare is hearty macaroni and cheese, meat loaf, and pork chops at prices that let you enjoy your dinner. Fresh grated coconut is sprinkled on the home-made coconut pie on serving. *240 N. Main St., tel. 802/476–6292. No credit cards. Inexpensive.*

Barre Lodging   **Pierre Motel.** The headboards may be Formica, but the furnishings are neat and clean; rooms with one double bed have a recliner chair. *362 N. Main St., 05641, tel. 802/476–3188. 20 rooms with bath. Facilities: cable TV, some refrigerators, phone, radio. AE, D, MC, V. Moderate.*

Burlington Dining   **Butler's.** At Butler's—one of two restaurants at the Inn at
★   Essex—the food is prepared by an outpost of the New England Culinary Institute, and the style is updated New England: pan-seared salmon fillet with pistachio pesto; lobster in yellow corn sauce with spinach pasta. *70 Essex Way, Essex Junction, tel. 802/878–1100. Reservations advised. AE, CB, D, DC, MC, V. Expensive.*

★   **Deja Vu.** High Gothic booths made from ornately carved church pews, fringed silk lampshades, soft New Age or classical music, and brass accents that gleam in the candlelight create a lushly romantic yet informal dining room. Dinner entrées might be smoked duck breast and confit leg with a Concord grape demiglace; or Vermont pheasant stuffed with apples, cranber-ries, and pecans. Sandwiches and crepes are available, too. *185 Pearl St., tel. 802/864–7917. AE, CB, DC, MC, V. Moderate–Expensive.*

The Ice House. For a great view of Lake Champlain, the out-door terrace is the place to be in summer; in winter the picture windows are almost as good. The menu is mainstream: grilled swordfish, boiled lobster, steak, a seafood combination plate that changes daily. *171 Battery St., tel. 802/864–1800. Reserva-tions advised. AE, DC, MC, V. Moderate–Expensive.*

The Daily Planet. Contemporary plaid oilcloth, an old jukebox playing Aretha Franklin, a solarium, and a turn-of-the-century bar add up to Burlington's hippest restaurant. This is Marco Polo cuisine—basically Mediterranean with Oriental influences: lobster risotto with peas; braised lamb loin with polenta and chutney; various stir-frys. *15 Center St., tel. 802/862–9647. Reservations advised. AE, DC, MC, V. Moderate.*

Sakura. The serene Japanese setting has *samisen* music in the background and tatami seating for up to 15. On the menu are a popular combination platter, à la carte items, tempura, and other Japanese specialties. *2 Church St., tel. 802/863–1988. AE, DC, MC, V. Closed Mon. Moderate.*

★ **Five Spice Cafe.** This tiny spot has only a dozen tables set against whitewashed barnboard walls enlivened with framed sheet music or perhaps a drawing of Laurel and Hardy. The chef toys with Asian cuisines to create such specialties as the searing Thai Fire Shrimp and a more traditional Kung Pao chicken. The menu has an extensive selection of vegetarian dishes, and there's a dim sum brunch on Sunday. *175 Church St., tel. 802/864–4045. AE, CB, DC, MC, V. Inexpensive–Moderate.*

Burlington Lodging

Radisson. This sleek corporate giant is the hotel closest to downtown shopping, and it faces the lakefront. Odd-numbered rooms have the view; rooms whose number end in 1 look onto both lake and city. *60 Battery St., 05401, tel. 802/658–6500 or 800/333–3333. 256 rooms with bath. Facilities: restaurant, indoor pool, whirlpool, indoor garage, complimentary airport shuttle. AE, CB, D, DC, MC, V. Expensive.*

The Inn at Essex. This new Georgian-style facility about 10 miles from downtown is a hotel and conference center in country-inn clothing. Flowered wallpaper and matching dust ruffles, working fireplaces in some rooms, and library books on the reproduction desks give innlike touches to spacious rooms. Room service and the restaurants are run by the New England Culinary Institute. *70 Essex Way, off Rte. 15, Essex Junction 05452, tel. 802/878–1100 or 800/288–7613. 97 rooms with bath. Facilities: 2 restaurants, pool, health club with Jacuzzi. AE, CB, D, DC, MC, V. Moderate–Very Expensive.*

Sheraton–Burlington. Now the biggest hotel in the city (90% of the rooms and the health club were added in 1989) and the closest to the airport, the Sheraton accommodates large groups as well as individuals. Upholstered wing chairs and dust ruffles give a New England touch to the upscale mauve and burgundy decor of the rooms. On the concierge level are a cocktail bar, complimentary hors d'oeuvres, and Continental breakfast. *870 Williston Rd., 05403, tel. 802/862–6576 or 800/325–3535. 309 rooms with bath, 30 handicapped-equipped rooms. Facilities: conference center, health club, pool with retractable roof, complimentary airport shuttle, in-room modems, corporate business center with clerical services. AE, CB, D, DC, MC, V. Moderate–Expensive.*

★ **Queen City Inn and Motel.** This Victorian home of 1881 was meticulously restored in 1989 and its 12 rooms individually decorated; rich architectural details include a magnificent mahogany staircase and (in room 24, for example) polished oak arches that frame a bay window alcove. Although it's on a busy main road, the back rooms get little traffic noise. Motel accommodations, while simple, include Continental breakfast in a sunny sitting room with white wicker and a red marble fireplace. The inn will add a conference center in the basement. *428 Shelburne Rd., South Burlington 05403, tel. 802/864–4220. 25 rooms with bath. Facilities: cable TV, phones, complimentary use of nearby gym and pool. AE, MC, V. Inexpensive–Expensive.*

Montpelier Dining **Tubb's.** Waiters and waitresses are students at the New England Culinary Institute, and this is their training ground. Yet the quality and inventiveness are anything but beginner's luck; while the menu changes daily, it runs along the lines of swordfish with spinach and cherry tomatoes. The atmosphere is more formal than that of the Elm Street Cafe, the sister operation down the block. *24 Elm St., tel. 802/229–9202. Reservations advised. MC, V. Closed Sun. Moderate–Expensive.*

Horn of the Moon. Bowls of honey, battered wooden chairs and tables, and the bulletin board of political notices at the entrance proclaim that the 1960s live on here. This vegetarian restaurant has attracted a following for an inventive cuisine that includes a little Mexican, a little Thai, a lot of flavor, and not too much tofu. *8 Langdon St., tel. 802/223–2895. No credit cards. No dinner Sun., Mon. Inexpensive–Moderate.*

Montpelier Lodging ★ **The Inn at Montpelier.** This spacious home of the early 1800s was renovated in 1988 with the business traveler in mind, yet the architectural detailing, antique four-posters, Windsor chairs, and stately upholstered wing chairs and the classical guitar on the stereo attract casual visitors as well. Maureen's Room has a private sundeck, and the wide wraparound Colonial Revival porch is conducive to relaxing. The rooms in the annex across the street are equally elegant. *147 Main St., 05602, tel. 802/223–2727. 19 rooms with bath, 2 suites. Facilities: conference rooms, phones, cable TV. AE, MC, V. Rates include Continental breakfast. Moderate–Expensive.*

Treadway Tavern. Located across the street from the state capitol, this is a home away from home and watering hole for legislators. Built in 1896, it is now part of the Treadway chain, which means a mix of Colonial-style headboards and such institutional touches as plastic-wrapped glasses and black metal doors. The rooms in the older section are larger than those in the 1960s addition. *100 State St., 05602, tel. 802/223–5252. 79 rooms with bath. Facilities: restaurant, lounge, indoor pool, cable TV, discount at fitness club. AE, CB, DC, MC, V. Moderate.*

Newport Dining **East Side Restaurant and Lounge.** The green napkins match the green padded booths, which match the green lampshades, which match the plants. This is the sort of family restaurant that will comply with customers' pleas to keep the fried chicken livers on the menu along with burgers, sandwiches, soups, and bar food. *E. Main St., tel. 802/334–2340. MC, V. Closed Mon. Inexpensive–Moderate.*

Newport Lodging **Top of the Hills Motel.** The motel rooms are attached to a small inn whose Victorian architectural detailing is meticulous and well cared for. One of the four rooms in the inn has a kitchenette, another a private bath. *Rtes. 5 and 105, 05855, tel. 802/334–6748. 10 rooms, 8 with bath. Facilities: picnic area, gas grill, cable TV, phones, snowmobile trail. D, MC, V. Rates include Continental breakfast. Inexpensive.*

St. Johnsbury Dining **Tucci's Bistro.** Veal topped with crisp fried eggplant, mozzarella, and ham; and beef scallopini sautéed with capers and anchovies go beyond the standard red-sauce recipes. The whitewashed barnboard trim and kelly green tablecloths complete the simple but tasteful decor. *41 Eastern Ave., tel. 802/ 748-4778. AE, MC, V. Moderate.*

St. Johnsbury Lodging

Fairbanks Motor Inn. A location convenient to I-89, a putting green, a view that makes visitors want to sit for hours on the balcony, and a honeymoon suite with whirlpool and wet bar make this more than the average Holiday Inn clone. *Rte. 2 East, 05819, tel. 802/748-5666. 45 rooms with bath. Facilities: cable TV, phones, pool, nonsmoking rooms. AE, MC, V. Moderate.*

Stowe Dining

Number One Main Street. The low-ceiling Colonial room with subdued watercolors and a small dining area in the bar livens cuisine basics with a hint of creativity: broiled swordfish with garlic butter and Pernod in a cream sauce; roast pork with red currant and crème de cassis sauce. *1 Main St., tel. 802/253-7301. Reservations advised. AE, MC, V. Moderate-Expensive.*

Stubb's. Jim Dinan is one of those New England chefs who are rethinking such traditional dishes as calves' liver—he prepares it with a balsamic vinegar shallot sauce—and Vermont ham, which he combines with veal ribs, sage, and apples. The marbleized walls and pink-on-burgundy linens add a sophisticated note to the rustic beams and fireplaces at either end of the two rooms. *Mountain Rd., tel. 802/253-7110. Reservations advised. AE, DC, MC, V. Moderate-Expensive.*

★ **Villa Tragara.** A converted farmhouse has been carved into intimate dining nooks where romance reigns over such specialties as ravioli filled with four cheeses and served with half-tomato, half-cream sauce. The tasting menu is a five-course dinner for $35 (plus $15 for coordinating wines). *Rte. 100, south of Stowe, tel. 802/244-5288. Reservations advised. AE, MC, V. Moderate-Expensive.*

★ **Hapleton's West Branch Cafe.** Tucked below a group of shops, this cozy, barnboard-paneled spot is good for lunch, dinner, or a late-night snack with cider before the fireplace. Entrées are simple—rib-eye steak; barbecued baby back ribs; pasta with a creamy cheese sauce, tomatoes, and bacon—and portions are generous for the price. The staff is friendly enough to bring extra anchovies for a Caesar salad. *Main St., Stowe, tel. 802/253-4653. AE, DC, MC, V. Moderate.*

Stowe Lodging

Trapp Family Lodge. Rebuilt in 1981 after a fire destroyed the ski lodge built by the Baroness von Trapp of *Sound of Music* fame, this Stowe institution caters to an older clientele that prefers the comforts of padded leather sofas and private modern bathrooms. *Luce Hill Rd., 05672, tel. 802/253-8511 or 800/ 826-7000. 73 rooms with bath. Facilities: 4 tennis courts, sauna, indoor and outdoor pools, cable TV, Jacuzzis, fitness room. AE, CB, D, DC, MC, V. Rates are MAP. Very Expensive.*

10 Acres Lodge. The 10 rooms in the main inn are smaller than those in the new building high on the hill, but all have decorator furnishings. Contemporary pottery or low-key abstract art complement the antique horse brasses over the fireplace in the living room. This is truly in the country; the cows are just across the road. *Luce Hill Rd., Box 3220, 05672, tel. 802/253-7638 or 800/327-7357. 18 rooms, 16 with bath; 2 cottages. Facilities: restaurant, lounge, phones, cable TV in some rooms,* *outdoor pool, tennis court. AE, MC, V. Rates include full breakfast. Moderate–Very Expensive.*

★ **The Inn at the Brass Lantern.** Home-baked cookies in the afternoon, a basket of logs by your fireplace, and stenciled hearts along the wainscoting reflect the care taken in turning this 18th-century farmhouse into a place of welcome. All rooms have quilts and country antiques; most are oversize. The honeymoon suite has a brass and iron bed with a heart-shaped headboard; the breakfast room (like some guest rooms) has a terrific view of Mt. Mansfield. *Rte. 100, 1 mi north of Stowe, 05672, tel. 802/253–2229. 9 rooms with bath. Facilities: some fireplaces, cable TV in public area. AE, MC, V. Rates include full breakfast. Moderate.*

The Arts

Barre Opera House (City Hall, Main St., Barre, tel. 802/476–8188) hosts music, opera, theater, and dance performances.

Flynn Theatre for the Performing Arts, a grandiose old structure, is the cultural heart of Burlington; it schedules the Vermont Symphony Orchestra, theater, dance, and lectures. The box office also has tickets for other performances and festivals in the area. *153 Main St., Burlington, tel. 802/864–8778 for theater information, 802/863–5966 for ticket information.*

Music **Stowe Performing Arts** (tel. 802/253–7321) sponsors a series of classical and jazz concerts during July and August in a meadow high above the village, next to the Trapp Family Lodge.

Vermont Symphony Orchestra (tel. 802/864–5741) performs at the Flynn Theatre in Burlington in winter and outdoors at Shelburne Farms in summer.

Theater **Champlain Shakespeare Festival** performs each summer at the Royall Tyler Theater (tel. 802/656–0090) at the University of Vermont.

Stowe Stage Co. does musical comedy, July to early October. *Stowe Playhouse, Mountain Rd., Stowe, tel. 802/253–7944.*

Vermont Repertory Theater (tel. 802/655–9620) mounts five productions in a season from September to May.

Nightlife

Nighttime activities are centered in Burlington, with its business travelers and college students, and in the ski areas. Many resort hotels have après-ski entertainment.

Bars and lounges **Vermont Pub and Brewery** (College and St. Paul Sts., Burlington, tel. 802/865–0500) is the only pub in Vermont that makes its own beers and fruit seltzers. It also serves a full lunch and dinner menu and late-night snacks.

The Butter Tub at Topnotch (Mountain Rd., Stowe, tel. 802/253–8585) has live entertainment most nights in ski season.

Comedy **Club New England**'s Saturday dinner show features comedy and a buffet dinner. *Rte. 7, South Burlington, tel. 802/658–1421. Reservations advised.*

Country and **Club New England**'s Sunday dinner is a barbecue on country
Western and western night. *Reservations advised..*

Disco **Club New England**'s Metro Disco features New England rock bands Wednesday, Friday, and Saturday at 8.

Rock **Sha-na-na** plays music from the 1950s and 1960s. Wednesday night is singles night. *101 Main St., Burlington, tel. 802/864-2496.*

7 New Hampshire

*by Betty Lowry,
with an
introduction by
William G.
Scheller*

*A freelance travel
correspondent,
Betty Lowry has
written extensively
on New England,
the Caribbean,
and Europe for
magazines and
newspapers
throughout the
United States.*

When General John Stark coined the expression Live Free or
Die, he knew what he was talking about. Stark had been
through the Revolutionary War battles of Bunker Hill and
Bennington—where he was victorious—and was clearly entitled to state the choice as he saw it. It was, after all, a choice he
was willing to make. But Stark could never have imagined that
hundreds of thousands of his fellow New Hampshire men and
women would one day display the same fierce sentiment as they
traveled the streets and roads of the state: Live Free or Die is
the legend of the New Hampshire license plate, the only state
license plate in the Union to adopt a sociopolitical ultimatum instead of a tribute to scenic beauty or native produce.

In a column in *New England Monthly*, the editor maintained
that bumper stickers (and aren't license plates a form of state-
sponsored bumper sticker?) are intended not to reflect the be-
liefs of the automobile's driver but to suggest that others do not
measure up to his or her standards. According to this line of
reasoning, a driver who announces that "War is not healthy for
children and other living things" is implying that others believe
that war is salutary. Can this be the attitude of New Hampshire? Is it telling us that other citizens appear to value their
lives more than their liberty?

One might be tempted to answer in the affirmative after browsing through a few issues of the reactionary *Manchester Union
Leader*. However, the fact remains that the citizens of New
Hampshire are a diverse lot who cannot be tucked neatly into
any sociopolitical pigeonhole. To be sure, a white-collar worker
in one of the high-tech industries that have sprung up around
Nashua or Manchester is no mountaineer defending his homestead with a muzzle-loader, no matter what it says on his
license plates.

Yet there is a strong civic tradition in New Hampshire that has
variously been described as individualistic, mistrustful of government, even libertarian. This tradition manifests itself most
prominently in the state's long-standing aversion to any form of
broad-based tax: There is no New Hampshire earned-income
tax, nor is there a retail sales tax. Instead, the government re-
lies for its revenue on property taxes, sales of liquor and lottery
tickets, and levies on restaurant meals and lodgings—the same
measures that other states use to varying degrees. Nor are
candidates for state office likely to be successful unless they de-
clare themselves opposed to sales and income taxes.

Another aspect of New Hampshire's suspiciousness of government is its limitation of the gubernatorial term of service to two
years: With the running of the reelection gauntlet ever immi-
nent, no incumbent is likely to take the risk of being identified
as a proponent of an income or a sales tax—or any other similarly unpopular measure.

And then there's the New Hampshire House of Representa-
tives. With no fewer than 400 members, it is the most populous
state assembly in the nation and one of the largest deliberative
bodies in the world. Each town with sufficient population sends
at least one representative to the House, and he or she had better be able to give straight answers on being greeted—on a
first-name basis—at the town hardware store on Saturday.

Yankee individualism, a regional cliché, may or may not be the
appropriate description here, but New Hampshire does carry

New Hampshire

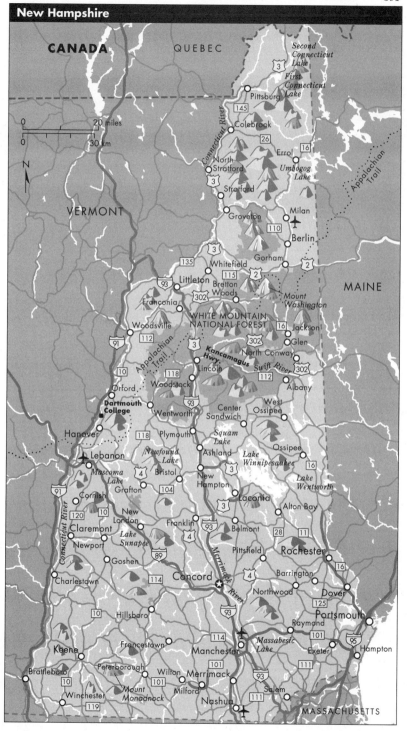

CANADA

QUEBEC

Second Connecticut Lake

First Connecticut Lake

Pittsburg

145

Colebrook

26

Errol

16

North Stratford

Umbogog Lake

Stratford

Appalachian Trail

Milan

Groveton

110

Berlin

Gorham

3

2

2

MAINE

135

Whitefield

Littleton

115

2

93

Bretton Woods

Franconia

302

Mount Washington

Woodsville

WHITE MOUNTAIN NATIONAL FOREST

16

Jackson

91

112

3

302

Glen

Appalachian Trail

Kancamagus Hwy.

118

Lincoln

North Conway

112

Swift River

302

Orford

Woodstock

Albany

10

93

West Ossipee

Dartmouth College

Wentworth

Center Sandwich

Hanover

118

Plymouth

Squam Lake

Ossipee

Lebanon

Newfound Lake

Ashland

Lake Winnipesaukee

16

Mascoma Lake

Bristol

New Hampton

Lake Wentworth

91

Cornish

4

104

3

Grafton

Laconia

120

10

New London

Franklin

Alton Bay

Claremont

93

28

11

Newport

4

Belmont

Rochester

Lake Sunapee

Goshen

89

Pittsfield

16

Charlestown

114

Concord

Barrington

10

Hillsboro

Northwood

Dover

125

Portsmouth

Francestown

Raymond

101

95

Keene

114

Massabesic Lake

Exeter

Hampton

Peterborough

Manchester

111

Brattleboro

Wilton

101

Milford

Merrimack

93

Salem

10

Mount Monadnock

101

Nashua

111

119

Winchester

MASSACHUSETTS

Connecticut River

Merrimack River

VERMONT

0   20 miles
0   30 km

N

on with a quirky, flinty interpretation of the Jeffersonian credo that that government governs best that governs least. Meanwhile, visitors to New Hampshire see all those license plates and wonder whether they're being told that they've betrayed General Stark's maxim by paying an income tax or a deposit on soda bottles—still another indignity the folks in the Granite State have spared themselves.

Essential Information

Visitor Information

New Hampshire Office of Vacation Travel (Box 856, Concord 03301, tel. 603/271–2666 or 800/441–5370).

New Hampshire Council on the Arts (40 N. Main St., Concord 03301, tel. 603/271–2789).

When to Go

Although New Hampshire has outdoor activities and scenic pleasures in all four seasons, country museums and attractions are open only from Memorial Day to mid-October. Out-of-the-way antiques stores close for the winter and may be open only by appointment until June. Late March to mid-April is mud season, the time of maple sugaring and waiting for the daffodils of April and the lilacs of May. Summer begins with a bang on July 4, when festivals and concerts take place on town commons throughout the state. August and September see serious crafts shows and country fairs. Autumn color begins to move through the state as early as September 1, reaching its peak in the southern sections during the second week of October. In the north country, snow and winter sports are expected by Thanksgiving, and at the higher elevations they will continue through March.

Festivals and Seasonal Events

Early Mar.: Sugaring Off goes public as many sugar houses demonstrate procedures from maple-tree tapping to sap boiling and offer tastings of grades of syrup, sugar-on-snow, traditional unsweetened doughnuts, and pickles. Bascom's (Alstead, tel. 603/835–2230), Clark's (Alstead, tel. 603/835–6863), Parker's (Mason, tel. 603/878–2308), Great Hills (Newmarket, tel. 603/659–3736), Stuart & John's (Westmoreland, tel. 603/399–4486).
Mid-May: New Hampshire Sheep and Wool Festival, New Boston, demonstrates shearing, carding, and spinning. *Tel. 603/763–5859.*
Late May: Lilac festivals involve variety shows, parades, and flea markets in Lisbon. *Tel. 603/838–6336.*
Late May: The **Spring 3-Day Sale** at the Town Hall in Weare offers furniture, dolls, braided rugs, and food. *Tel. 603/529–7262.*
Mid-June: Market Square Day Weekend features a street fair with some 300 exhibitors, a road race, a concert, historic house tours, and fireworks in Portsmouth. *Tel. 603/431–5388.*
Early July: Independence Day weekend sees parades, flea markets, music, and fireworks in many towns across the state.
Late July: Wolfeboro Antiques Fair has been a perennial for nearly 40 years. *Tel. 603/539–5126.*
Late July: Bean Hole Bash Weekend sees food, games, a flea market, and a pancake breakfast in Northwood. *Tel. 603/942–5586.*
Early Aug.: Pittsfield's Hot Air Balloon Rally floats balloons, entertainment, and arts and crafts. *Tel. 603/478–5666.*
Mid-Aug.: Fair of the League of New Hampshire Craftsmen Foundation, the nation's oldest crafts fair, schedules special

events daily along with exhibits, sales, and demos at Mt. Sunapee State Park, Newbury. *Tel. 603/224–1471.*

Mid-Aug.: Children's Week in Hampton Beach State Park involves games, prizes, and clowns. *Tel. 603/926–8717.*

Mid-Sept.: Squam Lakes Apple Festival picks a peak foliage date for its bake-off, sale, auction, crafts bazaar, and pony ride spectacular on Golden Pond in Holderness. *Tel. 603/968–4494.*

Mid-Sept.: Highland Games brings pipe bands, athletics, music, and dance to Lincoln. *Tel. 603/745–6621.*

What to Pack

Casual clothing (but not swimwear away from the beach) is appropriate dress throughout New Hampshire except at a few inns that insist on jacket and tie. A sweater will be welcome in the evening, even in summertime; winter requires heavy clothing, gloves, a hat, and warm socks.

Arriving and Departing

By Plane **Manchester Airport** (tel. 603/624–6556), south of the city, has scheduled flights by Continental, Delta, Northwest, USAir.

West Lebanon Municipal Airport (tel. 603/198–8878), near Dartmouth College, is served by Northwest.

By Car I–95 becomes the New Hampshire Turnpike as it passes through the coastal area between southern Maine and eastern Massachusetts. I–93, the principal north–south route through Manchester, Concord, and central New Hampshire, joins eastern Massachusetts in the south with Vermont in the north. I–89 links Concord with central Vermont.

By Train **Amtrak's** (tel. 800/872–7245) *Montrealer* stops at Claremont on its Washington, DC–Montreal runs—New Hampshire's only rail service.

By Bus **Greyhound Lines** (tel. 603/436–0163) and its subsidiary **Vermont Transit Lines** (tel. 603/228–3300) link the cities of New Hampshire with major cities of the eastern United States.

Getting Around New Hampshire

By Plane Small local airports that handle charters and private planes are **Berlin Airport** in Milan (tel. 603/485–9526), **Concord Airport** (tel. 603/224–4033), **Jaffrey Municipal Airport** (tel. 603/532–7763), **Laconia Airport** (tel. 603/524–5003), **Nashua Municipal Airport** (tel. 603/882–0661), and **Sky Haven Airport** in Rochester (tel. 603/332–9299).

By Car The official state map, available free from the Office of Vacation Travel, has directories for each of the tourist areas and is useful for most driving in the state. It gives the locations of the 17 safety rest areas throughout the state that provide rest rooms, picnic facilities, public phones, and vacation information; those at Hooksett (I–93 northbound and southbound) and Seabrook (I–95 northbound) are open 24 hours.

By Bus **Coast** (Durham, tel. 603/862–1931 or 800/862–9909), **C&J** (tel. 603/742–5111), and **Peter Pan Bus Lines** (tel. 603/889–2121) provide bus service between the cities and towns of the state.

Shopping

That traffic can slow to a crawl on Route 16 in North Conway
testifies to the popularity of the factory outlet stores bunched
together in the area. Handcrafts are the specialty of the state,
and artists' studios that open to the public exist in every region.
New Hampshire has no sales tax.

Sports and Outdoor Activities

Biking The Connecticut River and southern New Hampshire provide
the best biking opportunities; traffic around the lakes and
along the seacoast can be dense midsummer. **The Biking Expedition** (Box 547, Henniker 03242, tel. 603/428–7500), **Granite
State Wheelmen** (various locations, Apr.–Oct., tel. 603/898–
9926), and **Bike Vermont** (Box 207, Woodstock, VT 05091, tel.
802/457–3553) organize bike tours.

Boating and Deep-sea fishing and whale watches on the seacoast, lake
Sailing tours, scuba and windsurfing, and canoe rentals are the principal water recreation of New Hampshire. The **Office of Vacation
Travel** (tel. 603/271–2666) has a list of boating-service providers.

Camping A national forest, state parks, and more than 65 private camp-
grounds offer campers lake, stream, and mountain settings.
New Hampshire Campground Owners Association (Box 141,
Twin Mountain 13595, tel. 603/846–5511) and the **U.S. Forest
Service** (Box 638, Laconia 03246, tel. 603/524–6450) have infor-
mation.

Fishing Fishing licenses are required for nonresidents of the state. Licenses cost from $18 (three days) to $35 (season)—$4.50 for the
season for ages 12–15—and are available from most town
clerks, sporting goods stores, and general stores.

Hiking In addition to hiking trails in the national forest and state
parks, the 2,000-mile, Maine-to-Georgia **Appalachian Trail** bisects New Hampshire. Information on facilities and resources
is available from the **Appalachian Mountain Club** (Box 298,
Pinkham Notch, Gorham 03581, tel. 603/466–2725); **White
Mountain National Forest** (U.S. Forest Service, Box 638, Laconia 03246, tel. 603/524–6450); **AMC Hut System** (Box 298,
Gorham 03581, tel. 603/466–2721); and **Road's End Farm Hiking Center** (Jackson Hill Rd., Chesterfield 03443, May–Dec.,
tel. 603/363–4703). **Audubon Society of New Hampshire** (Box
528B, Concord 03302, tel. 603/224–9909) maintains marked
trails.

Skiing *The skiing facilities of New Hampshire are reviewed in Chapter 2, Skiing New England.*

Beaches

Seven freshwater and five ocean beaches are maintained by the
Division of Parks and Recreation, and there are municipal and
privately owned beaches. State beaches have lifeguards on
duty during peak hours; many have bathhouses and lunch and
picnic facilities. The Atlantic beaches vary widely in character
—from swinging Seashell at Hampton Beach to the family-
oriented Jenness at Rye—and all are well attended in summer.
Local beaches on Winnipesaukee, Forest, Silver, Kezar, New-

found, and Wentworth lakes are good for picnicking and swimming. Pollution is uncommon; Lake Little Sunapee's water is so pure it is used as town drinking water.

State Parks

New Hampshire parklands vary widely, even within a region. Major recreation parks are at Franconia Notch, Crawford Notch, and Mt. Sunapee. Rhododendron Park (Monadnock) has a singular collection of wild rhododendrons; Mt. Washington Park (White Mountains) is on top of the highest mountain in the northeast. In addition to the state parks and White Mountain National Forest, 23 state recreation areas provide vacation facilities that include camping, picnicking, hiking, boating, fishing, swimming, bike trails, winter sports, and food services. **Division of Parks and Recreation** (Box 856, Concord 03301, tel. 603/271–3254) provides information.

Dining

New Hampshire cuisine ranges in character from down-home Yankee to classic French, and ethnic and vegetarian menus are well represented. Seafood is plentiful and prepared in a variety of ways. Numerous country inns are known for the quality of their dining rooms, and the diner is an institution, a place where young professionals lunch on spinach pie and herbal tea and families dine on pot roast, mashed potatoes, and apple or blueberry pie. Ice-cream parlors, too, flourish here, especially in college towns; Knights ice-cream is favored for such old-fashioned flavors as grapenut pudding. Restaurants and/or specialty food shops are often associated with nearby small farms that operate orchards or maple sugar groves.

Highly recommended restaurants in each price category are indicated by a star ★.

Category	Cost*
Very Expensive	Over $35
Expensive	$25–$35
Moderate	$15–$25
Inexpensive	Under $15

*average cost of a three-course dinner, per person, excluding drinks, service, and 8% meals tax

Lodging

While the hotel chains are well represented in and around the major cities, and there are notable resort complexes, the lodging of choice in New Hampshire remains the country inn. Usually a family-owned facility with 10 to 30 rooms, most with private bath, the inn's eclectic furnishings (and often a good restaurant) contribute to the charm of vintage houses.

Highly recommended lodgings in each price category are indicated by a star ★.

Category	Cost*
Very Expensive	Over $150
Expensive	$100–$150
Moderate	$60–$100
Inexpensive	Under $60

All prices are for a standard double room during peak season, with no meals unless noted, and excluding service charge and 8% occupancy tax.

The Coast: New Hampshire

In 1603 the first English explorer sailed into the mouth of the Piscataqua River, and in 1623 the first colonists settled at Odiorne's Point. Yet the New Hampshire coast today is more than 18 miles of Early Americana. Six state parks and beaches provide picnicking space, walking trails, swimming, boating, fishing, and water sports. Hampton Beach has a boardwalk right out of the 1940s—and the coastal area includes a scramble of patchy retail and housing development. Portsmouth's restaurants, galleries, special events, historic houses, and an outdoor museum at Strawbery Banke attract a trendsetting Boston crowd. Inland, Exeter is an important Colonial capital with 18th-century and early 19th-century homes clustered around Phillips Exeter Academy. The crowds are heaviest on summer weekends; weekdays in summer and weekends in June or September are more likely to provide quiet times along the dunes and salt marshes.

Important Addresses and Numbers

Visitor Information
Seacoast Council on Tourism (1000 Market St., Portsmouth 03801, tel. 603/436–7678 or 800/221–5623).

Hampton Beach Area Chamber of Commerce (836 Lafayette Rd., Hampton 03842, tel. 603/926–8717).

Greater Portsmouth Chamber of Commerce (500 Market St., Portsmouth 03801, tel. 603/436–1118).

Dover Chamber of Commerce (299 Central Ave., Dover 03820, tel. 603/742–2218).

Exeter Area Chamber of Commerce (120 Water St., Exeter 03833, tel. 603/772–2411).

Emergencies New Hampshire State Police (tel. 800/525–5555).

Poison Center (tel. 800/562–8236).

Portsmouth Regional Hospital (333 Borthwick Ave., tel. 603/436–4042).

Exeter Hospital (10 Buzzell Ave., tel. 603/778–7311).

Late-night Pharmacy
Rexall (Kingston Plaza, Main St., Kingston, tel. 603/642–3323).

Getting Around the New Hampshire Coast

By Car Route 1 and, along the coast, Route 1A are the principal high-ways through an area where most points are within 30 minutes of Portsmouth, although summer beach traffic in the Hamptons may lengthen driving times considerably along Route 1A.

By Bus Seacoast Trolley (tel. 207/439–1941) operates a trolley that con-nects the beaches in summer.

Guided Tours

Audubon Society of New Hampshire (Box 528B, Concord 03301, tel. 603/224–9909) conducts field trips of the coast.

Olde Port Trolley Company (tel. 603/692–5111) offers a Ports-mouth area tour from June 15 to Labor Day.

Exploring the New Hampshire Coast

Numbers in the margin correspond with the numbered points of interest on the New Hampshire Coast map.

1 Our tour of the coast begins at **Seabrook,** on Route 1 almost 2 miles north of the Massachusetts state line. Seabrook is an old town where whaling boats were once built and residents were known for their Yorkshire accents. Today Seabrook is virtually a one-industry town, and the nuclear power plant, finally granted an operating license early in 1990, is visible from the road.

Two miles farther north, where Route 1 meets Route 88, **2** **Hampton Falls** offers a jogging trail, cross-country skiing in winter, and the **Applecrest Farm Orchards,** a pick-your-own ap-ple grove and berry patch, with a picnic ground, shop, and bakery where you can put together a bread-and-cheese lunch or add fresh fruit and farm apple cider to the contents of your own picnic basket. *Rte. 88, Hampton Falls, tel. 603/926–3721. Open daily 10–dusk.*

Route 88 at Hampton Falls affords the opportunity to visit **3** **Exeter,** the state's Revolutionary capital, 8 miles to the north-west. Today the town is known best for **Phillips Exeter Academy,** one of the nation's oldest prep schools and an assem-bly of Georgian architecture on a verdant campus. Settled in 1638, Exeter was a radical and revolutionary counterpoint to Tory Portsmouth in 1776. Among the handsome Colonial homes is the **Gilman Garrison House** (Water St., Exeter, tel. 603/227–3956), where settlers once fortified themselves against Indians and the Governor's Council met during the American Revolu-tion.

Time Out The **Loaf and Ladle,** at 9 Water Street in Exeter, is a bistro where the chowders, soups, and stews are homemade and even the sandwiches come on homebaked bread. Overlooking the river, the Loaf and Ladle is handy to shops, galleries, and his-toric houses.

Returned to (or continuing on) Route 1 at Hampton Falls, it's 2 miles north to the junction with Route 101, where we turn east **4** to the coastal Route 1A and **Hampton Beach.** Sometimes bawdy, never boring, the two-beach and 3-mile-boardwalk

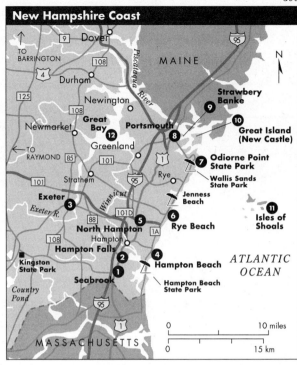

New Hampshire Coast

complex has the look of a location for a movie taking place in the 1940s and 1950s. This is an area of pizza and cotton candy, palm readers and performers, fireworks and fast-talking pitchmen. Young people swarm across Ocean Boulevard, oblivious to honking cars and blaring radios. Bands play swing in the amphitheater on the beach, and big names perform in the club of the 7-acre, multiple-arcade Hampton Beach Casino (tel. 603/ 926–4541).

⑤ Route 1A continues north to North Hampton (west on Route 101D) and Rye Beach. In **North Hampton,** Millionaires' Row sits just beyond the blare of Hampton Beach. At Fuller Gardens are 2 acres of estate flower gardens, circa 1939, where 1,500 rose bushes bloom all summer. *10 Willow Ave., North Hampton, tel. 603/964–5414. Open mid-May–Oct., daily 10–6.*

⑥ At **Rye Beach** the petrified stumps of an Ice Age forest protrude at low tide, and from Rye harbor one can embark on coastline cruises, whale watches, and one-hour lobster trips through the agency of New Hampshire Seacoast Cruises (tel. 603/964–5545), though Portsmouth offers a larger selection of such cruises.

⑦ Jenness Beach and Wallis Sands State Park, north of Rye Beach, have attractive white beaches that can be readily seen; it will take a few hours or more to make the most of **Odiorne Point State Park** and Audubon Nature Center, site of the first New Hampshire settlement (Pannaway Plantation) and now 230 acres of tide pools, nature trails, and bird walks. The museum and visitor center has programs on ecology and the environment, and one can find further information in the book-store. *Rte. 1A, Rye, tel. 603/436–8043. Open June, Sept.–Oct., Tues.–Sun. 10–4; July–Labor Day, weekends 10–4.*

8 Routes 1, 1A, and 1B all converge on **Portsmouth,** the state's principal coastal city, the conclusion of the 18-mile New Hampshire coast, and the launch of I–95 and Route 1 on their long journeys up the coast of Maine.

The shops, galleries, restaurants, and historic houses of Portsmouth recall Colonial times. On entering the city from the south, turn right on Little Harbor Road to visit the **Wentworth-Coolidge Mansion** (tel. 603/446–6607), once the official residence of the Royal Governor. No furnishings are original to the house, but all are of the period. What is said to be the oldest lilac bush in New Hampshire still blooms in the garden.

Time Out | **Ceres Bakery,** at 51 Penhallow, is a bright, simple place to go for an apricot brioche and coffee mid-morning; homemade soup and quiche at lunch; tea and an almond torte mid-afternoon.

The **Portsmouth Historical Society** is located in the **John Paul Jones House** (Middle and State Sts., tel. 603/436–8420), which has been restored and furnished as it might have been when it was the boardinghouse residence of the naval hero. It is now one of six historic houses on the Portsmouth Trail, a historic walking tour. Tickets good for one or all may be purchased at each house and at the Chamber of Commerce (500 Market St., tel. 603/436–1118). Candles light the way on the Portsmouth Trail on evenings in late August.

Along the waterfront, Prescott Park is an ever-blooming retreat between Strawbery Banke and the river, with a fishing pier and two historic warehouses. One of them contains the **Folk Art Museum** (tel. 603/431–8748), with its carved mastheads and ship models.

The **Port of Portsmouth Maritime Museum,** in Albacore Park, has the USS *Albacore,* built here in 1953 as a prototype and testing submarine for the U.S. Navy. A film, followed by a tour, shows visitors how the 55-man crew lived and worked aboard the vessel. A section of Albacore Park has been dedicated as a memorial to submariners. *500 Market St., tel. 603/436–3680. Admission: $4 adults, $3 senior citizens, $2 children, $10 family. Open daily 9:30–5:30. Closed Jan. 1, Dec. 25.*

The **Children's Museum,** a hands-on gallery with both permanent and temporary exhibits, has activities for children of all ages, from toddlers to young teens. Lobstering, art, geography, computers, and space are among the subjects treated. Classes and workshops may require advance notice. *South Meeting House, 280 Marcy St., tel. 603/436–3853. Admission: $3.50 adults and children, $3 senior citizens. Open Tues.–Sat. 10–5, Sun. 1–5.*

9 Portsmouth's ever-changing major attraction is **Strawbery Banke,** a 10-acre outdoor museum with period gardens, monthly activities, and more than 40 original buildings that date from the years 1695 to 1820. The Candlelight Tours in early December are downright romantic. The boyhood home of Thomas Bailey Aldrich (author of *The Story of a Bad Boy*) is the **Nutter House.** The **Wheelwright House** affords a daily demonstration of 18th-century cooking. Snacks and lunch are served in the museum restaurant, the Washington Street Eatery. *Marcy St., tel. 603/433–1100. Admission: $8 adults, $7 senior citizens, $4 children under 17, $22 family. Open May–Oct., daily 10–5; early Dec., weekends 4:30–8:30.*

⑩ Great Island, commonly called New Castle, just east of Portsmouth and overlooking the Piscataqua River, is reached by Route 1B (New Castle Avenue) from Portsmouth. Its attractions are New Castle Path and **Fort Constitution.** The fort, then a British bastion, was raided by rebel patriots in 1774 and the stolen munitions used against the British at the Battle of Bunker Hill four months later. Take the paved walking trail from the fort through the 18th-century town for a close-up look at the former Colonial residences that are now private homes. *Fort Constitution, Great Island. Open mid-June–Labor Day, daily 9–5; Labor Day–mid-June, weekends 9–5.*

Island Excursions **Isles of Shoals** is an archipelago of nine islands (eight at high
⑪ tide) in the Atlantic, one hour from Portsmouth, that was one of the region's major attractions for settlers. The islands were named for the shoals (schools) of fish that supposedly jumped into the nets of fishermen. A dispute between Maine and New Hampshire over the ownership of the islands caused them to be divided between the two states, but the invisible boundary is only of academic interest. In the 19th century the islands were an offshore retreat for the literary and art circle of the poet Celia Thaxter, whose Appledore Island is now used by the Marine Laboratory of Cornell University; Star Island houses a conference center for Unitarian, Universalist, and Congregational church organizations. In summer scheduled cruises take visitors to Star in the morning, leave them long enough for a nonalcoholic picnic and a hike, and return them to the mainland in mid-afternoon (only conference attendees may stay overnight in the rambling hotel and cottages). The Isles of Shoals Steamship Company also runs whale-watch expeditions, and its M/V *Thomas Leighton*, a Victorian-era steamship replica, schedules minivoyages on which ghost and pirate stories—the islands have them in abundance—are told; other excursions include some meals. Light snacks are available on board, or you can bring your own. *Isles of Shoals Steamship Company, Barker Wharf, 315 Market St., Portsmouth, tel. 603/431–5500. Reservations advised. Cruises mid-June–Labor Day; foliage cruises Oct.*

New Hampshire Coast for Free

Boardwalk, Hampton Beach

Fuller Gardens, North Hampton

Fort Constitution, Great Island, Portsmouth

What to See and Do with Children

Casino Cascade Waterslide, Hampton Beach

Hampton Playhouse, Hampton

Children's Museum, Portsmouth

Port of Portsmouth Maritime Museum and Albacore Park, Portsmouth

Off the Beaten Track

⑫ **Great Bay.** The magnificent Great Bay estuary, 4 miles west of
Portsmouth, is the haunt of seabirds, migrating landbirds, her-
ons, and harbor seals. Upland and wetland game-management
areas are kept much as they were when the first visitors ar-
rived, and today's visitors are cautioned to respect the natural
environment. Every species of regional aquatic fowl may be
seen here and, in Great Bay Access on the southeastern shore,
every species of indigenous animal except moose and bear. The
early morning hours are the best time to appreciate the area;
its isolation from populated centers nearby brings out the Thoreau in all of us. Great Bay Access is reached by taking Route
101 to Greenland and turning north on the unmarked road near
Winnicut River; leave your car at the railway track and walk in.
The University of New Hampshire maintains the Jackson
Estuan Laboratory on the western shore, an area that can be
toured on Durham Point Road, which loops east from Route 108
at points south of Durham and north of Newmarket.

Shopping

Portsmouth's harborside district has unusual and high-quality
gift and clothing specialty shops, though you will find art and
craft galleries of particular note in Dover and Exeter as well.
The malls are divided between designer and name-brand outlets and an amalgam of department and big stores where slight
discounts are commonplace. Shopping hours in general are
Monday through Saturday from 10 to 9 and Sunday from 10
to 6.

Antiques stores tend to be scattered; in Portsmouth, look on
Chapel and Market streets. Along Route 4 between Portsmouth and Durham is an antiques row of barns and overflowing
shops. From May to October, street fairs, yard sales, and flea
markets may be found all along the seacoast. Look for posted
notices and in the classified section of the newspapers. There is
a regular Sunday **flea market** in the Star Center (25 Fox Run
Rd., Newington, tel. 603/431–9403).

Country and farm products such as homemade jams and pickles
are available at Applecrest Farm and Raspberry Farm, Hampton Falls; Emery Farm, Durham; and Thornwood Farm, Dover.

Factory Outlets **Artisan Outlet Village,** just off Route 1, offers designer mer-
chandise by names like Ralph Lauren, Liz Claiborne, Perry
Ellis, and Andrew Geller. Also located in the complex are the
Royal Discount Book Store, 3-D Homeworks, and others. *72
Mirona Road, Portsmouth, tel. 603/436–0022.*

Factory Outlet Center promises 20% to 70% savings on brand
names like Clothesworks, Van Heusen, Old Mill, and Aileen.
Shoes are a good value here: Shoe Bazaar Outlet carries over 50
brands, and Bass and Timberland have their own factory outlet
stores. Visit American Tourister for luggage and Toy Liquida-
tors for zillions of nationally advertised toys. *Rte. 1 (Lafayette
Rd.), North Hampton, tel. 603/595–9000.*

Galleries and **A Pictures Worth a Thousand Words** (65 Water St., Exeter, tel.
Craft Shops 603/778–1991) offers two showrooms of pictures (antique and
contemporary prints, old maps) and rare books.

Alie's Fine Jewelry (1 Market St., Portsmouth, tel. 603/436–0531) has gifts as well as gold, silver, and gems.

N.W. Barrett (53 Market St., Portsmouth, tel. 603/431–4262) is a good source for local crafts, especially in wood, leather, and pottery. Silver and gold jewelry are also sold here.

Country Curtains (2299 Woodbury Ave., Newington, tel. 603/431–2315), located on the Old Beane Farm, has fabrics, ready-made as well as custom curtains, bedding, furniture, gifts, and folk art.

Exeter League of New Hampshire Craftsmen (61 Water St., Exeter, tel. 603/778–8282) is the seacoast shop for originals by select, juried members of L.N.H.C. Exhibits feature a different local craftsperson each month.

Guild of Strawbery Banke, Inc.–Kingsbury House (93 State St., Portsmouth, tel. 603/436–8004) stocks books, fine handcrafts, needlework, reproductions, and gifts in an 1815 townhouse. Profits support Strawbery Banke.

Salamandra Glass Studio/Gallery (133 Market St., Portsmouth, tel. 603/431–4511) gives new meaning as well as form to hand-blown glass. Also shown are jewelry and gifts.

Salmon Falls Stoneware (The Engine House on Oak St., Dover, tel. 603/749–1467 or 800/621–2030) is handmade, American salt-glaze ware decorated with traditional, country, and whimsical designs. Potters are on hand if you want to place a special order.

The Square Rigger (143 Market St., Portsmouth, tel. 603/433–2422). The name is the clue here. You'll see everything from scrimshaw to sculpture, decoys to foul-weather gear. There is also a children's corner.

Tulips (19 Market St., Portsmouth, tel. 603/431–9445) was Portsmouth's first craft gallery and is still the city's leading venue for both local and national craftspeople. Wooden crafts and quilts are specialties.

Malls   **Fox Run Mall** (Fox Run Rd., Newington, tel. 603/431–5911) is the largest hereabouts, with Filene's, Jordan Marsh, JC Penney, Sears, and 100 other stores.

Newington Mall (45 Gosling Rd., Newington, tel. 603/431–4104) has Bradlees, Montgomery Ward, and 70 more stores as well as restaurants and a supermarket.

Sports and Outdoor Activities

Biking   The Durham-to-Exeter route is a flat, pleasant roundtrip of about 30 miles. Start off on Route 108/85 and return by crossing Route 101 and taking back roads along and across the Piscassic and Lamprey rivers. Avoid Route 1. A bike trail runs along part of Route 1A, and you can take a break at Odiorne Point. For **group rides** in various locations from April to October, tel. 603/898–9926.

Boating   There are rentals aplenty, along with deep-sea fishing charters, at Hampton, Portsmouth, Rye, and Seabrook piers. For water sports (scuba diving and windsurfing) try **Wet Fun Diving and Windsurfing School** (265 Deer St., Portsmouth, tel. 603/430–8626).

Camping **Len-Kay Camping Area** (Hall Rd., Barrington 03825, tel. 603/664–9333) is on 3½ Mile Lake.

Liberty Hill Campground (Rte. 101, Greenfield 03047, tel. 603/431–6359).

Pine Acres Family Campground (274 Prescott Rd., Raymond 03077, tel. 603/895–2519) has a giant water slide.

Tuxbury Pond Camping Area (W. Whitehall Rd., South Hampton 03842, tel. 603/394–7660) is convenient to the Hampton Casino action.

Hiking There are good short hikes at **Blue Job Mountain** (Crown Point Rd. off Rte. 202A, 1 mi from Rochester) and at the Urban Forestry Center, Portsmouth. Serious hikers should move on to the White Mountains.

Beaches

Swimming beaches on the New Hampshire shore and one inland freshwater pond are maintained and supervised by the Division of Parks and Recreation. You will usually find Jenness, Rye, and Wallis Sands less congested than Hampton, but you can view them and take your choice as you cruise Route 1A. For freshwater swimming, try Kingston State Park at Kingston on Great Pond (not to be confused with Great Bay). In summer a trolley connects the ocean beaches. Beaches outside the state park system include Foss Beach, Rye; New Castle Common, New Castle; and Four Tree Island, Portsmouth.

Dining

Portsmouth has a reputation throughout New England for dining excellence. Because many of its most highly regarded restaurants are small and prepare all dishes to order, reservations are imperative and in some cases should be made several days ahead.

★ **L'Auberge.** Classic French versions of duck l'orange, frogs' legs, veal, and escargots are prepared by the owner and chef. The tarte of the evening is always a surprise. Reserve as far in advance as possible. *96 Bridge St., Portsmouth, tel. 603/436–2377. Reservations required. Jacket advised. AE, DC, MC, V. Dinner only. Very Expensive.*
Strawbery Court Restaurant Français. In spite of the proximity of Strawbery Banke, the cuisine here is classic and nouvelle French, not Early American. The tiny Federal brick town house has been lovingly restored, its twin front rooms each holding a handful of tables. Oyster bisque, white asparagus, and escargots may be on the prix-fixe menu. *20 Atkinson St., Portsmouth, tel. 603/431–7722. Reservations required. Dress: casual but neat. AE, MC, V. Closed Sun., Mon., Thanksgiving, Dec. 25, Jan. 1. Very Expensive.*
Seventy-Two. Getting to church on time has culinary overtones here, for this popular restaurant is located in the shell of a 19th-century Free Will Baptist church. The French chef prepares asparagus and broccoli bisques as well as lobster. Desserts include a chocolate truffle cake. *45 Pearl St., Portsmouth, tel. 603/436–5666. Reservations advised. Dress: casual but neat. MC, V. Expensive.*
Anthony's Al Dente. A busy, noisy restaurant with a loyal fol-

lowing is located in what was once a customs-house cellar on the harbor. Among the attractions of the kitchen are fresh tomato marinara over homemade pasta; a peppery anchovy sauce; and clams served simply with chopped parsley and garlic. A long wine list features hard-to-find Italian vintages. *59 Penhallow, Portsmouth, tel. 603/436–2527. Reservations advised. Dress: casual. DC, MC, V. Closed Mon. Moderate–Expensive.*

Exeter Inn Dining Room. The restaurant on the Phillips Exeter Academy campus serves chateaubriand on a plank that goes miles beyond any student's dream night out with Mom and Dad. On Friday and Saturday night, look for cherries flambé or some equally spectacular flaming dessert. Sunday brunch, with at least 60 savory items, including a variety of omelets, provides a bright start to the day, for the dining room is a circle of windows with a fig tree growing in the center. *90 Front St., Exeter, tel. 603/772–5901. Reservations advised; not accepted for Sunday brunch. Dress: casual but neat. AE, D, DC, MC, V. Moderate–Expensive.*

The Dolphin Striker. The local pols hang out here, but they have to squeeze in past the tourists in high season. Seafood is the specialty (mariner's pie is a fisherman's platter in a crust) but not the only choice; steaks, chops, chicken, and vegetarian selections are on the menu, too. The ambience is what you would expect in a restored warehouse: original beams, low ceilings, a stone-wall tavern downstairs. *15 Bow St., Portsmouth, tel. 603/431–5222. Reservations advised. Dress: casual. AE, DC, MC, V. Closed Thanksgiving, Dec. 25. Moderate.*

Lamie's Tavern. The terrace is open for dining when the weather allows, and the New England cookery has been lightened: Bean soup has fresh tomatoes; lobster comes sautéed as well as stuffed. This is a good place to wind down from the Hampton Beach action. *490 Lafayette Rd. (junction Rtes. 1 and 101C), Hampton, tel. 603/926–0330. Reservations advised. Dress: casual but neat. AE, MC, V. Moderate.*

Luka's Greenhouse Restaurant. A big, fresh, greenery-filled restaurant where, in addition to steak, seafood, and lamb, there are traditional Greek specialties such as moussaka and spinach pie. The contemporary cooking matches the setting. *12 Lafayette Rd., Hampton Falls, tel. 603/926–2107. Reservations advised in summer. Dress: casual. AE, MC, V. Closed Thanksgiving, Dec. 25. Moderate.*

The Woods. On-campus dining at the restaurant of the New England Center Hotel at the University of New Hampshire is a pleasing mix of American and Continental cuisine served by a congenial student-staff. Chicken and veal are lightly sauced; beef comes done to order; and there are vegetarian and low-cal dishes. The attractiveness is enhanced by the pine woods outside and an art gallery upstairs. *15 Strafford Ave., Durham, tel. 603/862–2815. Reservations advised. Dress: casual but neat. MC, V. Closed Dec. 20–Jan. 3. Moderate.*

★ **Newick's Lobster House.** This is a regular stop for many who travel the coast, and, until foul weather drives everyone inside, the dining is outdoors. It's an informal place, with paper napkins and plastic plates and the owner in rubber boots keeping an eye on things. The principal fare is lobster, clams, and oyster stew; slaw and chewy bread are the natural accompaniments. *431 Dover Point Rd. (Rte. 16), Dover, tel. 603/742–3205. No reservations. Dress: casual. MC, V. Closed Mon. and Thanksgiving, Dec. 25. Inexpensive–Moderate.*

★ **State Street Saloon.** It's new on the block, but this small Italian restaurant in the harbor district is known by the line of prospective diners waiting outside every night. An imaginative chef is one reason; another is the price. Consider pork tenderloin marsala; chicken breasts and artichokes over fettuccine; and a true *bruschetta* (toasted bread prepared with garlic and olive oil). With its corrugated tin ceiling and the black-and-white color scheme, only the bill will convince you you're not in Boston's North End. *268 State St., Portsmouth, tel. 603/431–4357. Dress: casual. MC, V. Inexpensive–Moderate.*

Lodging

All the lodgings described here are convenient to both town and shore, and all require advance reservations, at least during the period from mid-June to mid-October.

★ **Sise Inn.** With silks and polished chintz, rubbed woods and armoires, this inn recreates the lifestyle of the affluent of the 1880s. The Queen Anne town house is in Portsmouth's historic district and is ideally located for waterfront strolling and dining. No two rooms are alike. *40 Court St., Portsmouth 03801, tel. 603/433–1200 or 800/232–4667. 34 rooms with bath. Facilities: cable TV, VCR, fitness room, some whirlpool tubs, morning newspaper. No pets. AE, MC, V. Rates include breakfast. Expensive.*

Ashworth by the Sea. Since this centrally located hotel opened, in 1912, it has been renovated, rebuilt, and renovated again and is familiar to generations of beach-goers. Most rooms have decks, and the furnishings are either period or contemporary, depending on the room. Be sure to specify whether you want sea view or quiet, because you can't have it both ways. *295 Ocean Blvd., Hampton Beach 03842, tel. 603/926–6762. 105 rooms with bath. Facilities: 3 restaurants, pool, room service. AE, MC, V. Moderate.*

Best Western Hearthside. Although a designated businessperson's place, the motor inn's well-furnished rooms and good management (the manager has been with the inn in various capacities since high school) recommend it to family travelers as well. *Portsmouth Ave. (Rte. 108), Exeter 03833, tel. 603/772–3794 or 800/528–1234. 33 rooms with bath. Facilities: restaurant, lounge, pool. No pets. AE, CB, D, DC, MC, V. Moderate.*

Exeter Inn. A three-story, Georgian-style inn with handsomely appointed guest rooms is properly set on the campus of the Phillips Exeter Academy, in the heart of Exeter's historic district. This is understated elegance, New England–preppie style. *90 Front St., Exeter 03833, tel. 603/772–5901 or 800/782–8444, fax 603/778–8757. 50 rooms with bath. Facilities: restaurant, cable TV, fitness room. No pets. AE, CB, D, DC, MC, V. Moderate.*

New England Center Hotel. Set in a pine grove on the campus of the University of New Hampshire, this is a quiet spot. The rooms are larger in the new wing, and none are noisy. *15 Strafford Ave., Durham 03824, tel. 603/862–2800. 115 rooms with bath. Facilities: restaurant, lounge, cable TV. No pets. AE, MC, V. Moderate.*

★ **Rock Ledge Manor.** This B&B was once part of a late-19th-century resort colony, and its sun room and white wicker are signs of its past. The owners speak French, and you may well find crepes served one morning in the sunny dining room overlooking the Atlantic. All the bedrooms have sea views. *1413 Ocean Blvd. (Rte. 1A), Rye 03870, tel. 603/431–1413. 4 rooms, 2 with bath. No pets. No smoking. No credit cards. Rates include full breakfast. Moderate.*

Country House Inn. A farmhouse in the 1800s and an inn since 1985, this inn is up-to-date and unusual. How many country inns offer sculling packages, even if they are located near the water? Great Bay and the University of New Hampshire campus are close at hand. The suite has its own woodstove and a private deck. *Stagecoach Rd. and Rte. 108, Durham 03824, tel. 603/659–6565. 20 rooms, 18 with bath. Facilities: restaurant (closed dinner), some cable TV, cross-country skiing, sculling. MC, V. Inexpensive–Moderate.*

Inn at Christian Shore. The inn is owned—and decorated—by former antiques dealers who came to B&B innkeeping after restoring and furnishing houses elsewhere. It is a 10-minute walk from the historic district, the harbor, and shops; and you'll need the walk after breakfasting on fruit, eggs, a meat dish, vegetables, and homemade muffins. *335 Maplewood Ave., Portsmouth 03801, tel. 603/431–6770. 6 rooms, 3 with bath. Facilities: cable TV. No credit cards. Rates include full breakfast. Inexpensive–Moderate.*

The Arts

Music   **Music in Market Square** (tel. 603/436–9109) is a free Friday-afternoon variety show of vocal and instrumental artists in the heart of Portsmouth.

Prescott Park Arts Festival (Marcy St., Portsmouth, tel. 603/436–2848), on the waterfront, provides art, music, theater, and dance for the family, July 4 to mid-August.

Strawbery Banke Chamber Music Festival (Box 1529, Portsmouth, tel. 603/436–3110) schedules performances from October to June.

Theater   **Hampton Playhouse** (357 Winnacunnet Rd., Rte. 101E, Hampton, tel. 603/926–3073) has children's theater and Equity summer theater with familiar TV, Broadway, and Hollywood faces from July to September. Tickets are available at the box office or at the Chamber of Commerce Sea Shell office on Ocean Boulevard.

Theatre by the Sea (125 Bow St., Portsmouth, tel. 603/433–4793) is New England's only year-round Equity theater. The Portsmouth Academy of Performing Arts and the Bow Street Theater combine to bring classical, traditional, musical, and children's presentations to the waterfront.

Nightlife

Club Casino. As many as 2,500 people can crowd the floor on a summer night, and because people have been coming here for 30 years all generations are well represented. As for the nightly show, Tina Turner, The Monkees, Jay Leno, and Loretta Lynn have played here. *Ocean Beach Blvd., Hampton Beach, tel. 603/926–4541. Open Apr.–Oct.*

The Press Room. Media folk come from Boston, Portland, and towns in New Hampshire to hang out in the old three-story, five-fireplace brick building. The shows are good, but the preliminaries are better. From five to nine, it's open-gig for jazz and folk-music makers. Tuesday night is variety; Friday look for sea shanties, pre-1850 Celtic ballads, or maybe just open jams. *77 Daniels St., Portsmouth, tel. 603/431–5186. No reservations. Dress: casual. Name entertainment upstairs, Fri.–Sat. 9–midnight, Sun. 8–midnight. Open gig Tues.–Sat. 5–9. Cover varies.*

Lakes Region

Lake Winnipesaukee ("Smiling Water") is the largest of the dozens of lakes scattered across the eastern half of central New Hampshire; Squam Lake took on a new identity when *On Golden Pond* was filmed here; and Lake Wentworth is named for the first Royal Governor of the state, who in building his country manor here established North America's first summer resort. The lake islands number more than 200, and there are preserved Colonial and 19th-century villages minutes away. Swimming, boating, fishing, and other water recreation abound.

Important Addresses and Numbers

Visitor Information **Lakes Region Chamber of Commerce** (9 Veterans Circle, Laconia 03246, tel. 603/352–1303).

Lakes Region Attractions (Box 300, Wolfeboro 03894, tel. 603/569–1117).

Emergencies **State Police** (tel. 800/852–4311).

Poison Center (tel. 800/562–8236).

Lake Region General Hospital (Highland St., Laconia, tel. 603/524–3211 or 800/852–3311).

Late-night Pharmacy **Laconia Clinic** (720 Main St., Laconia, tel. 603/524–6064).

Getting Around the Lakes Region

By Car Interstate 93, on the western side of the region, is the principal artery, with exits to the lakes. From the coast, Route 11 reaches southwestern Lake Winnipesaukee, and Route 16 stretches to the White Mountains, with roads leading to the lakeside towns.

By Bus **Concord Trailways** (tel. 800/852–3317).

Guided Tours

M/S *Mount Washington's* (Box 5367, Weirs Beach 03246, tel. 603/366–5531) three-hour cruises of Winnipesaukee allow time for breakfast or lunch aboard while touring the lake. Departures are daily from Weirs Beach and Wolfeboro, three times a week from Center Harbor and Alton Bay.

Winnipesaukee Railroad departures are timed to connect with the boat, but rides can be taken independently. Historic equipment carries passengers along the lakeshore for just under two hours; boarding is at Weirs Beach or Meredith. *Box 317, Meredith 03253, tel. 603/528–2330. Fare: $7 adults, $4 children.*

*Season: Memorial Day-late June, late Sept.-mid-Oct, week-
ends.*

Exploring the Lakes Region

*Numbers in the margin correspond with the numbered points
of interest on the New Hampshire Lakes map.*

❶ Each of the more than two dozen major lakes in this region has
its advocates. Our tour will concentrate on **Winnipesaukee,** the
state's largest lake, with a 283-mile shoreline and more than
200 islands. We'll begin at Alton Bay, at the southernmost tip,
and move clockwise around the lake, starting off on Route 11.
Visitors to the lakes region often plan a shopping excursion to
the outlet strip at the southern end of North Conway (*see* The
White Mountains, below).

❷ Two mountain ridges hold 7 miles of Winnipesaukee in a bay. Of
the twin towns at the southern extremity of the lake, Alton is
the quiet village while **Alton Bay** is where the lake cruise boats
dock and you will find a dance pavilion, minigolf, a public
beach, and a Victorian-style bandstand used for summer concerts.

❸ One of the larger public beaches is at **Gilford,** an affluent community that traces its origins to Colonial days. The **Gunstock
Recreation Area** (tel. 603/293–4341), with an Olympic pool, a
children's playground, hiking trails, and a campground, is east
of Gilford on Route 11A.

❹ North of Gilford on Route 11A, **Weirs Beach** provides the
boardwalk atmosphere of the lakes. Fireworks are common
here on summer evenings; cruise ships (M/S *Mount Washington,* M/V *Sophie C.,* and M/V *Doris E.,* tel. 603/366–5531)
depart from its dock; and the **Winnipesaukee Railroad** (tel. 603/
528–2330) picks up passengers here for an hour-long tour of the
shore. You can do crazy water things at Surf Coaster, descend
four giant water slides at Water Slide, or work your way
through the games, minigolf, and 20 lanes of bowling at
Funspot. Weirs are fish traps, and this was once a major Native
American settlement; Endicott Rock on the waterfront marks
the spot where explorers rested in 1682 before proceeding 3
miles north and declaring an invisible line the border of Massachusetts.

Time Out **Kellerhaus,** just north of Weirs Beach and overlooking the lake,
is a candy shop beloved by lake visitors since 1906. At the half-
timbered, Alpine-style building you'll find an ice-cream smor-
gasbord with a variety of toppings to dress as much ice cream
as you can pile in your dish. The price is based on dish size.

❺ At **Meredith,** on Route 3 at the western extremity of
Winnipesaukee, **Annalee's Doll Museum** (tel. 603/279–4144), an
adjunct to a gift shop, has hundreds of felt dolls, and there are
shops and galleries. An information center is located across
from the Town Docks.

❻ The town of **Center Harbor,** set on the middle of three bays at
the northern end of Winnipesaukee, borders on Lakes Squam,
Waukewan, and Winona.

❼ Further north on Route 25, **Moultonborough** has 6.5 miles of
shoreline on Lake Kanasatka as well as a piece of Squam.

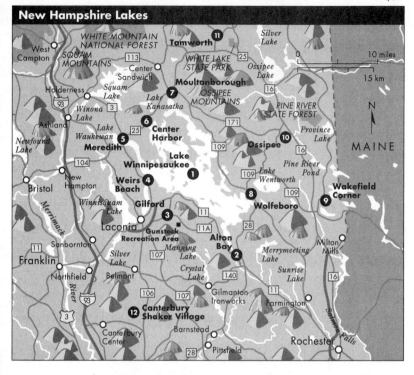

New Hampshire Lakes

Moultonborough, oriented to leisure, has restaurants of good quality.

❽ Wolfeboro has been a resort since John Wentworth built his summer home on the shores of Lake Wentworth in 1763. The original Wentworth house burned down in 1820, but by then summering at the lake was a well-established routine. The sedate village is headquarters of the **Hampshire Pewter Company** (tel. 603/569–4944), where 17th-century techniques are still used to make hollowware and accessories, and there are antiques shows and crafts events all summer.

Between Winnipesaukee and the border of Maine to the east lie several villages with historical districts and considerable charm that differ markedly from the heavily visited lakeside towns. With their own lakes close at hand, and their proximity to Route 16, they are good stopping-off places for those headed to the Mt. Washington valley.

❾ Wakefield Corner is a registered historic district, with church, houses, and inn looking just as they did in the 18th century. The **❿** larger Wakefield encompasses 10 lakes. **Ossipee** consists of three villages around Lake Ossipee and satellite ponds. Good antiques (and other) shops are here for those who don't want to spend all their time fishing, swimming, boating, and hiking.

⓫ Tamworth has a clutch of villages within its borders. The view through the birches of Chocorua Lake has been so often photographed that you may get a sense of having been here before.

Lakes Region for Free

Lakes Region Winery (tours), Belmont

Old Print Barn, Meredith

Old Village Barn, Chocorua

Hampshire Pewter Company (tours), Wolfeboro

What to See and Do with Children

Gunstock Recreation Area, Gilford

Funspot, Surf Coaster, and **Water Slide,** Weirs Beach

Winnipesaukee Railroad, Meredith and Weirs beaches

Annalee's Doll Museum, Meredith

Off the Beaten Track

⑫ **Canterbury Shaker Village.** Established in 1792, the Canterbury community flourished in the 1800s. Shakers were known for fine workmanship and for the simplicity and integrity of their design, especially in household furniture. They were also prolific inventors (of the clothespin, for example). The village is now an outdoor museum with guided tours, craft demonstrations, and a large shop offering books and reproductions. At the heart of the village, the Creamery Restaurant practices the plain cookery of people who made the most of the freshest ingredients; even the butter is home-churned. Authentic Shaker recipes create the raised-squash biscuits, the rose-water apple pie, and everything else on the menu. Consider this a 4-hour stop. From I–93 Exit 18, follow signs; the village is 7 miles from the exit. *288 Shaker Rd., Canterbury, tel. 603/783–9511. Admission: $8 adults, $4 children. Open May–Oct., Mon.–Sat. 10–5.*

Shopping

Crafts shops, galleries, and sportswear boutiques dominate the shopping scene around the lakes. Antiques shops (mostly open by chance or by appointment) are thickest along the eastern side of Winnipesaukee near Wolfeboro and around Ossipee.

Mills Falls Marketplace (tel. 603/279–7006), in Meredith, contains 22 shops and galleries.

A few factory stores—MacKintosh coats; Timberland shoes; Swank leather goods, Bowl & Board wood products—are at **One Gilford Place** (145 Lake St., Gilford, tel. 603/527–0566 or 800/225–1965). Hours are generally 9–5 in summer, though some stores stay open until 9. Most are open Sunday, but the season is short: late May–October.

Pepi Hermann Crystal (Gilford, tel. 603/528–1020). You can buy all your wedding gifts plus stemware and even handcut crystal chandeliers in this famous hand-factory shop. Take a tour of the workshop while you're there.

Annalee's Gift Shop and Museum (Reservoir Rd., off Rte. 3, Meredith, tel. 603/279–6542.) Annalee's whimsical felt dolls are known all over the world. Here you will see hundreds of dolls no longer manufactured that are treasured by collectors. You can also buy the latest.

Meredith-Laconia League of New Hampshire Craftsmen (Rte. 3, ½ mi north of intersection of Rtes. 3 and 104, Meredith, tel. 603/279–7920). Work of juried craftspeople is on display and for sale in all price ranges.

The Old Print Barn (Meredith, tel. 603/279–6479). Hundreds of rare prints from the Middle Ages to modern times are available in this extraordinary barn. It's the largest print gallery in northern New England. From Route 104 in Meredith, follow Winona Road and look for "Lane" on the mailbox.

Sandwich Home Industries. (Rte. 109, Center Sandwich, tel. 603/284–6831). This 65-year-old grandparent of the League of New Hampshire Craftsmen was formed to foster cottage crafts. There are craft demonstrations in July and August and sales of home furnishings and accessories mid-May–October.

League of New Hampshire Craftsmen–Wolfeboro (Wolfeboro, tel. 603/569–3489). This retail craft gallery shows and sells the work of member artisans. Follow Route 28 to downtown Wolfeboro's Central Square. The gallery is on Railroad Avenue, near the station.

Sports and Outdoor Activities

Biking Traffic can be heavy midsummer (particularly between Gilford and Meredith), but it is slow-moving; bikes can follow the exploring route through the region.

Boating **The Lake Region Association** (Wolfeboro, tel. 603/569–1117) can answer questions about boating opportunities. There are Marinas with **boat rentals** at Meredith (tel. 603/2769–7921 or 603/366–4811).

Camping **Gunstock** (Laconia 03246, tel. 603/293–4344) offers multiple sports facilities including an Olympic pool and children's playground.

Yogi Bear's Jellystone Park (Ashland 03217, tel. 603/968–3654) is especially good for families.

Clearwater Campground (New Hampton 03256, tel. 603/279–7761).

Len Kay (Barrington 03825, tel. 603/642–5596).

Twin Tamarack (New Hampton 03256, tel. 603/279–4387) has camping and RV facilities.

White Lake State Park (Tamworth 03886, tel. 603/271–3254), between Tamworth and Ossipee, has two camping areas.

Fishing Lake trout and salmon in Winnipesaukee, trout and bass in the smaller lakes, and trout streams all around make this a fisherman's paradise. Alton Bay has an "Ice Out" salmon derby in spring. During winter, on all the lakes including Winnipesaukee, intrepid ice fishers fish from huts known as "ice bobs."

Hiking There are many trails, but just to get you started: Mt. Major, Alton; Squam Range, Holderness; Red Hill, off Route 25 on Bean Road northeast of Centre Harbor; Pine River State Forest, east of Route 16.

Water Sports The lake is crowded with boats in summer, and waterskiing regulations are posted at every marina. Scuba divers can explore a sunken paddle-wheeler off Wolfeboro. Instruction, rentals, repairs, and sales are available at **North Country Scuba & Windsurfing, Inc.** in both Laconia and Wolfeboro (tel. 603/524–8606).

State Parks

White Lake State Park, between Tamworth and West Ossipee, is the only state park in the lakes region. Picnicking, swimming, camping, and fishing are available.

Beaches

There are many private beaches around the lake. **Ellacoya State Beach,** in Gilford, is 600 feet long and is the major public beach.

Dining

Because restaurants around the lakes serve hundreds of visitors during the summer, grilling is the usual means of preparing meats, and you should be able to find a steak or prime rib in almost any dining room.

Tamworth Inn. Across the street from Barnstormer's, the vintage summer theater of the lakes region, the inn offers dinner in a package with the show. The New American cuisine includes blackened swordfish and veal Picasso (mustard, white wine, onions, and capers over rice or fettuccini). Among the desserts are homebaked pie, carrot cake, and profiterole Tamworth (with the chef's own chocolate sauce). In summer you can dine on the porch, which looks over the back meadow and the river. Burgers and chili are the fare in the pub. *Main St., Tamworth, tel. 603/323–7721. Reservations advised. Dress: casual but neat. MC, V. Closed Mon. (summer), Mon.–Tues. (winter). Moderate–Expensive.*

★ **Le Chalet Rouge.** Located on the west side of Tilton, the modest yellow house with a small, simply decorated dining room is not unlike the country bistros of France. The cuisine offers a remarkable house pâté; frogs' legs; duck with raspberry sauce; and tarte au citron. *321 Main St., Tilton, tel. 603/286–4035. Reservations advised. Dress: casual. AE, MC, V. Closed Nov. Moderate.*

Christopher's. Mesquite grilling and stir-frying are basic to the restaurant's preparation of chicken, scallops, and filet mignon; and the house specialty is veal medallions with herbs, bread crumbs, and a lemon-veal demi-glacé. You can order just a salad or an all-vegetable entrée, and any order can be split between two children. *Rtes. Old 109 & 25, Moultonborough, tel. 603/476–2300. Reservations advised. Dress: casual. AE, MC, V. Moderate.*

Gunstock Inn. The inn's seafood chowder took first prize at the Lakes Region Chowder Festival. The extensive menu includes variations on familiar dishes (two veal Oscars, two pork tenderloins) and vegetarian offerings. Candlelight dining is in a cherry-table, Windsor-chair, country-inn atmosphere. *580 Cherry Valley Rd. (Rte. 11A), Gilford, tel. 603/293–2021. Reservations advised. Dress: casual. AE, DC, MC, V. Moderate.*

★ **Sweetwater Inn.** Pasta made daily is the basis of such dishes as lobster ravioli (with a white-wine-and-tomato sauce) and fettuccine jambalaya (sautéed chicken, scallops, and andouille sausage with garlic, sherry, peppers, and cajun spices). Spanish offerings include paellas and *pollo con gambas* (chicken breast and shrimp sautéed with brandy). Even the butter is home churned, with blackberry honey and fresh orange. Only herbs and spices are used as seasonings; no salt is used. *Rte. 25, Moultonborough, tel. 603/476–5079. Reservations advised. Dress: casual. AE, MC, V. Moderate.*

Wakefield Inn. You dine around a three-sided fireplace in this historic inn and choose from daily specials or such regulars as chicken Wakefield (boneless breast stuffed with lobster and shrimp, baked in light pastry, and topped with hollandaise sauce); seafood; and pasta primavera. Watch for the Inn sign on Route 16 and turn east to Wakefield Corners. *Mt. Laurel Rd., Wakefield, tel. 603/522–8272. Reservations advised. Dress: casual. AE, MC, V. Moderate.*

The Woodshed. Beef and seafood are the basics here, all done to order. Try a New England menu of clam chowder, scrod, and Indian pudding; an alternative is escargots Rockefeller, prime rib, and cheesecake. *Lee's Mill Rd., Moultonborough, tel. 603/476–2311. Reservations advised. Dress: casual. AE, MC, V. Moderate.*

★ **Hickory Stick Farm.** The specialty is roast duckling with country herb stuffing and orange-sherry sauce, and you order by portion—the quarter, half, or whole duck. The entrée price includes salad, orange rolls, vegetable, and potato. Also on the menu are seafood, beef tenderloin, rack of lamb, and a vegetarian casserole. The restaurant is open only in summer; two large, old-fashioned upstairs rooms with bath are available as B&B year-round. The inn is 4 miles from Laconia. Follow signs off Union Road into the woods, all on paved roads. *R.F.D. 2 (Union Rd.), Laconia, tel. 603/524–3333. Reservations required. Dress: casual. AE, CB, D, DC, MC, V. Dinner only. Closed Mon. and Nov.–May. Inexpensive–Moderate.*

Lodging

The Inn at Mill Falls. A large new country-style inn is the lodging part of the Mill Falls Marketplace complex. Restaurants, galleries, and shops are at your door, and Lake Winnipesaukee is just across Route 3. *Rte. 3/25, Meredith 03253, tel. 603/279–7006. 54 rooms with bath. Facilities: 2 restaurants, cable TV, pool, sauna, whirlpool. No pets. AE, CB, D, MC, V. Moderate–Expensive.*

Red Hill Inn. This once-upon-a-time summer mansion overlooks "Golden Pond" from a respectful distance. Furnished with Victorian period pieces, many of the rooms have fireplaces, and some have whirlpool baths. Hiking and ski trails on the inn's 50 acres provide opportunities for activity, though the inn's original occupants probably just looked at the view. *RD 1, Box 99M (Rte. 25B), Center Harbor 03226, tel. 603/279–7001. 13 rooms with bath. Facilities: restaurant. AE, CB, D, MC, V. Rates include full breakfast. Moderate–Expensive.*

★ **Tamworth Inn.** The touch of show-biz sophistication may be the result of sharing the stage with the Barnstormers across the street. Whatever the reason, this friendly country inn has much of the romantic charm of an old movie. Every room is different, and all are comfortably furnished and decorated with

19th-century American pieces. Fresh flowers in your room are the rule in summer, fresh fruit in winter. The field behind the inn slopes to a trout-filled brook. The gazebo has been used for weddings. *Main St., Box 189, Tamworth 03886, tel. 603/323–7721. 14 rooms with bath. Facilities: restaurant, pub, pool, video film library with VCR. No smoking in rooms. MC, V. Rates include breakfast. Moderate–Expensive.*

The Inn on Golden Pond. This country home of 1879 on 55 wooded acres is across the road from Squam Lake. Visitors enjoy the variety of the lake, then take refuge on the screened porch or walk one of the nature trails on the property. The rooms have braided rugs and easy chairs. The rear of the third floor is where it's the most quiet. *Rte. 3, Holderness 03245, tel. 603/968–7269. 9 rooms, 7 with bath. Facilities: cable TV in common room. No pets. No smoking. MC, V. Rates include full breakfast. Moderate.*

Olde Orchard Inn. A restored 1790s farmhouse on 12 acres of fields and orchards, with its own pond and brook, this B&B remains very much in the country. Uncluttered rooms are decorated with needlework. Bricks used in the original construction were made on the property. In winter it's possible to set off on skis from the front door; in summer you can get your exercise walking the mile to the lake. *Box 266 (Lee Rd.), Moultonborough 03254, tel. 603/476–5004. 5 rooms with bath. No smoking. AE, MC, V. Rates include full breakfast. Moderate.*

★ **Wakefield Inn.** The restoration of the house and coaching inn of 1815, located in a historic district, has been done with care. Among the inn's many features is a freestanding spiral staircase that rises three stories. Rooms are named for famous guests, including John Greenleaf Whittier. The weekend Quilting Package could send you home with a finished quilt. *Rte. 1, Box 2165, Wakefield 03872, tel. 603/522–8272. 6 rooms with bath. Facilities: restaurant. No pets. No smoking in rooms. AE, MC, V. Rates include full breakfast. Moderate.*

The Arts

Music   **Arts Council of Tamworth** (tel. 603/323–8693) produces concerts—soloists, string quartets, revues, children's programs—throughout the year in the north lake region.

Theater   **Barnstormers** (Main St., Tamworth, tel. 603/323–8500), an Equity summer theater and New Hampshire's oldest professional theater, performs from mid-July to Labor Day, with dinner-and-theater packages available Tuesday to Friday.

Nightlife

Meredith Station (Rte. 3, Meredith, tel. 603/279–7777), with dining and dancing in a railway station of 1849, provides the nightly entertainment for the under-thirties summering on the lakes. In the newest part of the building, windows overlook Winnipesaukee. The fare is pub-style as well as full-menu, but this is a buffalo-wing, shrimp-stir-fry sort of place.

Funspot (Weirs Beach, tel. 603/366–4377) remains open 24 hours, July to Labor Day. You can bowl, snack, and play the 500 advertised games all night long.

M/S *Mount Washington* (tel. 603/366–5531) has dinner/dance Moonlight Cruises Tuesday-Saturday evenings with a different menu each night and two bands. Departure points vary; ticket prices range from $23 to $30.

Belknap Mill (Mill Plaza, Laconia, tel. 603/524–8813), a brick textile mill built in 1823, is a performing arts site.

The White Mountains

Northern New Hampshire has the highest mountains in New England, the 750,000 acres of White Mountain National Forest, and wilderness that stretches north into Canada. Hikers, climbers, and motorists who seek dramatic vistas are at home here, where gorges slash the mountain range and rivers are born and flow south. Southeast of the national forest, on the eastern side of the state, North Conway's miles of factory outlets and off-price designer boutiques draw heavy shopping traffic throughout the year. Yet the heaviest traffic is seasonal: The two-week autumn explosion of color sees carloads and busloads of people, bumper-to-bumper on the Kancamagus Highway.

Important Addresses and Numbers

Visitor Information **Mt. Washington Valley Chamber of Commerce** (Box 385, North Conway 03860, tel. 603/356–3171).

White Mountains Attractions (Box 10, North Woodstock 03262, tel. 603/745–8720).

Emergencies **State Police** (tel. 800/852–4311).

Poison Center (tel. 800/562–8236).

Memorial Hospital (Intervale Rd., North Conway, tel. 603/356–5461).

Getting Around the White Mountains

By Plane **Berlin Airport** (Milan, tel. 603/485–9526) has facilities for charters and private planes.

By Car You will need a car to see this region if you aren't taking a bus tour during foliage season. I–93 and Route 3 bisect the White Mountain National Forest on their south-north extent between Massachusetts and Quebec. On the eastern side of the area, Route 16 is the main artery from the coast, past the Mt. Washington valley and on toward Maine. The Kancamagus Highway (Route 112) is the east-west thoroughfare through the White Mountain National Forest.

By Bus **Concord Trailways** (tel. 800/852–3317).

Exploring the White Mountains

Numbers in the margin correspond with the numbered points of interest on the White Mountains map.

Our tour begins at the southeastern gateway to the Mt. Washington valley, where the towns are downright sweet and the discount shopping opportunities cause frequent gridlock. We take Route 16/302 through the Conways to Glen and continue west to Bethlehem, then south to Franconia Notch, Lincoln, and the Kancamagus Highway.

① The winter sports area and shopper's world of **North Conway** has a high concentration of lodging and dining facilities. Here the **Conway Scenic Railroad** (Main St., tel. 603/356–5251) operates from May to October out of a railroad station built circa 1874. A steam engine pulls the antique coaches 11 miles in one hour, and it's necessary to make reservations early during foliage season.

Overlooking the valley is **Cathedral Ledge,** a 1,000-foot viewpoint you can reach by following signs after turning left just past the railway station. For yet another bird's-eye view, the **Mt. Cranmore Skimobile** (tel. 603/356–5543), said to be the oldest operating ski lift in the United States, takes visitors to the summit of Mt. Cranmore in August, September, and October.

From Glen, Route 16 continues north to Jackson, Mt. Washington, Pinkham Notch, and the North Country; we follow Route 302 west in the direction of Franconia Notch.

② **Mt. Washington,** at 6,288 feet the highest mountain in the northeastern United States, has measured at its summit the greatest velocity of winds ever recorded—231 miles per hour—and its Antarctic-like temperatures are the ultimate lows broadcast to New Englanders every winter.

The **Mount Washington Auto Road,** a toll road open when weather conditions permit, begins at Glen House, 16 miles north of Glen, and will take at least 2 hours to drive. You use low gear all the way, and there are frequent rests, yet this is a route for the experienced mountain driver only. At the top the Sherman Adams Summit Building has a museum and glassed-in viewing area. Drivers for hire are available at Glen House to take you on a guided tour up the mountain; you can also hike it or take the cog railway at Bretton Woods. *Tel. 603/466–3988. Toll: $10 car and driver, $4 each adult passenger, $3 children 5–12. Open mid-May–mid-Oct.*

③ Few traveling families can resist one or the other of the entertain-ments at **Glen. Storyland** theme park has life-size storybook and nursery-rhyme characters, an African safari, Cinderella's castle, and 16 rides. You can figure on a full day for this one. *Rte. 16, Glen, tel. 603/383–4293. Admission: $11 (free under 4) includes rides and entertainment. Open June–Oct., daily 10–5.*

Heritage New Hampshire, next door to Storyland, offers a simulated journey into the past that begins with a village street in 1634 England. Sights, sounds, and animation usher you aboard the *Reliance* and carry you over tossing seas. You stop at the cabin of a snowbound settler, walk Portsmouth's streets in the late 1700s, applaud George Washington's presidency, and plunge into the dark side of the Industrial Revolution. The trip ends cheerily aboard a train heading through Crawford's Notch during foliage season. *Rte. 16, Glen, tel. 603/383–9776. Admission: $6 adults, $4 children 4–12. Open May–Oct., daily 9–5.*

④ The Bear Notch road south from Route 302 in Bartlett provides the only midpoint access to the Kancamagus Highway. **Bartlett** is primarily a recreation area and a place to pick up picnic ingredients for the drive ahead. The **Attitash Alpine Slide** (Rte.

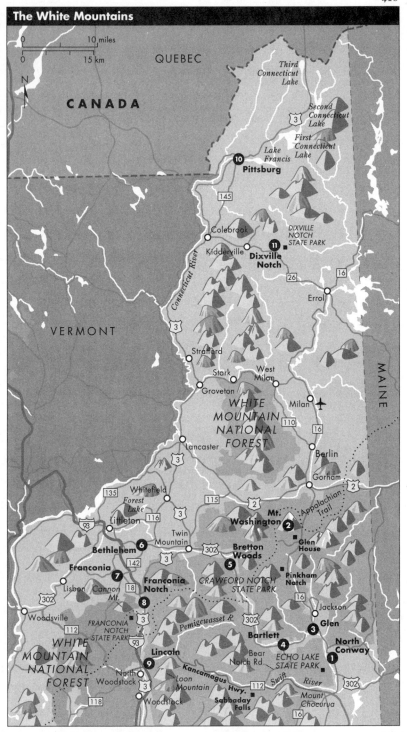

The White Mountains

QUEBEC

CANADA

Third
Connecticut
Lake

Second
Connecticut
Lake

First
Connecticut
Lake

Lake
Francis

3

10 Pittsburg

145

Colebrook

DIXVILLE
NOTCH
STATE PARK

Kidderville

11 **Dixville
Notch**

26

16

Errol

VERMONT

Connecticut River

3

Stratford

Stark

West
Milan

Groveton

WHITE
MOUNTAIN
NATIONAL
FOREST

Milan

110

16

Berlin

Lancaster

3

Gorham

2

MAINE

Whitefield

Forest
Lake

135

116

115

2

93

Littleton

Twin
Mountain

3

302

**Mt.
Washington** **2**

Appalachian Trail

Glen
House

Bethlehem **6**

**Bretton
Woods**

5

142

18

Franconia **7**

**Franconia
Notch**

CRAWFORD NOTCH
STATE PARK

Pinkham
Notch

Lisbon

Cannon
Mt.

8

16

302

FRANCONIA
NOTCH
STATE PARK

3

93

Jackson

Woodsville

112

WHITE
MOUNTAIN
NATIONAL
FOREST

Lincoln **9**

Pemigewasset R.

Bartlett

302

4

Glen **3**

**North
Conway** **1**

ECHO LAKE
STATE PARK

North
Woodstock

Woodstock

Kancamagus

Loon
Mountain

Hwy.

Sabbaday
Falls

112

Bear
Notch Rd.

Swift

River

Mount
Chocorua

302

118

16

302, tel. 603/374–2368) in Bartlett has a water slide and chairlift facility.

At the mountain pass, **Crawford Notch State Park** (tel. 603/374–2272) is a good place for a picnic and a leg-stretching hike along the well-trodden trails to Arethusa Falls or Silver and Flume cascades. A shop sells soft drinks and items made by blind New Hampshire craftspeople.

⑤ Twenty miles north of Bartlett on Route 302 lies the secluded **Bretton Woods.** In the early decades of this century, as many as 50 trains a day brought the private railway cars of the rich and famous from New York and Philadelphia to Mt. Washington Hotel. In July 1944 the World Monetary Fund Conference convened here and established the American dollar as the basic medium of international exchange. The hotel contains a small museum.

The **Mt. Washington Cog Railway** is a steam-powered mountain-climbing railway, operating since 1869, that provides an alternative to driving the corkscrew road up the mountain or climbing it on foot (first accomplished by Darby Field in 1642). To reach the railway from Bretton Woods, take the marked road 6 miles northeast from Route 302; if the weather is poor, forget it. *Rte. 302, Bretton Woods, tel. 603/846 –5404. Round-trip: $32 (ask about discounts). Reservations advised. Operates mid-Apr.–Oct., daily 8:30–5:30, weather conditions permitting.*

⑥ The pure air of **Bethlehem,** where Route 142 meets Route 302 north and west of the national forest, drew hay-fever sufferers to the mountains, where Hasidic Jews established a Kosher resort in the Arlington and Alpine hotels.

⑦ Take Route 142 south to Route 18 to reach **Franconia,** where Route 116 will take you south (follow the signs) to the poet Robert Frost's 1915 home, known as The Frost Place (tel. 603/823–5510). Two rooms contain memorabilia and signed editions of his books, and on summer evenings visiting poets give readings. Behind the house a ½-mile nature trail is posted with lines from Frost's poems.

Franconia is just north of Cannon Mountain, where the **New England Ski Museum** (tel. 603/823–7177) will be found at the foot of the aerial tramway. Slide and film presentations, art, photographs, and ski clothing and equipment are shown. The **Cannon Mountain Aerial Tramway** (tel. 603/823–5563) will lift you 2,022 feet in 5 minutes at any time of year. Foot trails lead from the summit observation platform to other vistas.

⑧ A series of scenic spectacles along a 13-mile stretch of Route 3 in **Franconia Notch** has been stopping travelers for centuries. The granite profile of the **Old Man of the Mountains** is the most famous feature, but the point of greatest viewing advantage remains in dispute. Is it from the shore of Profile Lake or from the highway parking area? At what time of day? P. T. Barnum wanted to buy it; Nathanial Hawthorne told the world about it in his tale "The Great Stone Face." Travelers who saw it in 1805 thought it looked like Thomas Jefferson.

The Flume (tel. 603/823–5563), open from May to October, is an 800-foot-long natural chasm through which you make your way on a series of boardwalks and stairways. **The Basin** is a glacial pothole, 20 feet across, at the base of a waterfall. **Echo Lake** will tempt you to try its acoustics.

North Woodstock and Lincoln, two towns on opposite sides of the Pemigewasset River, anchor the western end of Route 112, the Kancamagus Highway. **Lincoln** is the center for the resort communities; it has shops, restaurants, and an amusement park, the **Whale's Tale** (Rte. 3, tel. 603/745–8810), with flume water-slides, a wave pool, and a kiddie pool.

The **Kancamagus Highway** is the state's most popular single route for viewing the foliage in fall, a 33-mile extent interrupted by only one cutoff, Bear Notch Road to Bartlett. It goes by Loon Mountain, follows the Hancock branch of the Pemigewasset River and the Swift River. The self-guided Rail and River trail begins at the **Passaconaway Information Center** near the Bear Notch road.

Park at the Sabbaday Falls parking lot and follow the trail to **Sabbaday Falls,** a multilevel cascade that plunges through two potholes and a flume. You can also leave the road to climb the Champney Falls and Piper trails to the top of Mount Chocorua. Spectacular views can be had at many points, but it is easy to get lost when you leave the main trail, so keep an eye on the signs.

The eastern terminus of the Kancamagus Highway is Route 16.

The White Mountains for Free

Abenaki Indian Shop, Intervale

Bretzfelder Park, Bethlehem

What to See and Do with Children

Conway Scenic Railroad, North Conway

Storyland, Glen

Attitash Alpine Slide, Bartlett

Mt. Washington Cog Railway, Bretton Woods

Fantasy Farm, Lincoln

Off the Beaten Track

Pittsburg (Indian Stream Republic). Beyond the White Mountains lies the far north of New Hampshire, with many miles of forest and lakes but few roads. Here bubble the springs that become the Connecticut River, and here in 1829 a small band of settlers, disgusted with the slow processes of politics, proclaimed themselves citizens of a separate territory. By 1832 the United States and Canada still had not fixed an international border, and the "Streamers" declared their independence and wrote a constitution providing for an assembly, council, courts, and militia. They called their country Indian Stream Republic, after the river that came down from Quebec and melded into the newborn Connecticut. The republic encompassed 250 square miles between Halls Stream and the brook at the Third Connecticut Lake. The capital was Pittsburg. In 1835 the feisty, 40-man Indian Stream militia invaded Canada, causing the New Hampshire Militia to invade Indian Stream—

which convinced residents they were de facto citizens of the United States after all. The Indian Stream war ended more by common consent than surrender, and in 1842 the Webster-Ashburton Treaty fixed the international boundary. Indian Stream was incorporated as Pittsburg, making that hamlet the largest township in the state. The town of Pittsburg still has the feeling of an outpost, for it serves primarily as a supplier to campers, hunters, anglers, lumbermen, gold miners, and the like. A marker on Highway 3 attests to its former status. Information on the town is available at the Colebrook-Pittsburg Chamber of Commerce (Colebrook 03576, tel. 603/237–8939).

⑪ Dixville Notch. Midway between Errol and Colebrook, Dixville Notch is the home of The Balsams Grand Resort Hotel but is better known nationally for being the election district first in the nation to vote and report its returns in the presidential elections. The polling place where the 34 ballots (more or less) are cast is a small meeting room next to the hotel bar, a location chosen for the convenience of the media. Dixville Notch won its distinction over smaller towns such as Hart's Location (population 9 or 10) because the resort has its own phone company—a convenience journalists appreciate.

Shopping

Custom-made hiking boots are the pride of the valley, but the area is known for good family sportswear, especially ski clothes. Even North Conway—synonymous with designer and factory outlets for good reason—has less-frantic specialty stores in town, where Route 16/302 is known familiarly as Main Street. Among these are **Joe Jones** (tel. 603/356–9411), a sportswear and ski shop; and **Carroll Reed** (tel. 603/356–3122). As for crafts, the local **League of New Hampshire Craftsmen** (tel. 603/356–2441) and **New Hampshire Silver and Leather** (tel. 603/356–5524) in the alley behind the largest brick building downtown, are among the best.

Antiques **Antiques & Collectibles Barn** (Rte. 302, North Conway, tel. 603/356–7118), 1.5 miles north of the village, is a 35-dealer group with everything from furniture and quilts to coins and jewelry.

Richard M. Plusch (Main St., North Conway, tel. 603/356–3333) deals in period furniture, glass, sterling silver, oriental porcelains, rugs, and paintings.

Red Shed Antiques (Rte. 16, Jackson, tel. 603/383–9267) has primitive paintings, tools, kitchenware, and furniture.

Custom-made Hiking Boots Made-to-order **Limmerboots** (Intervale, tel. 603/356–5378) take about a year from measure to wear and cost $220 plus shipping.

Factory Outlets The **National Outlet Hotline** (tel. 800/368–8538) can answer your questions about outlet locations. In North Conway, look for names like Down Outlet, Anne Klein, Dansk, Frye Boots, L.L. Bean, Corning, Barbizon, Reebok, and Ralph Lauren.

Malls **Millfront Marketplace, Mill at Loon Mountain** (tel. 603/745–2245) is a clutch of specialty stores and restaurants at the junction of I–93 and the Kancamagus Highway. Nonshoppers are entertained by horse-drawn sleighs and an ice skating rink.

Sports and Outdoor Activities

Biking There are 86 major mountains in the area, so you may be biking in short stretches, but at least there's a bike path in Franconia Notch State Park, at Lafayette Campground.

Camping **New Hampshire Campground Owners Association** (Box 320, Twin Mountain 03595, tel. 603/846–5511) will send a list of all private, state, and national-forest campgrounds.

White Mountain National Forest (Box 638, Laconia 03247, tel. 603/524–6450) has 20 roadside campgrounds on a no-reserve and 14-day-limit basis.

Appalachian Mountain Club headquarters at Pinkham Notch was built in 1920 and now offers lectures, workshops, slide shows, and movies during the June–October season. The 100-bunk main lodge and six rustic cabins aside, you may also want to look into other programs like AMC–The Friendly Huts and the AMC Backcountry Host Program. *Box 298, Gorham 03581, tel. 603/466–2721. Trail information, tel. 603/466–2725; reservations, tel. 603/466–2727.*

Lafayette Campground (Franconia Notch State Park, 03580) has good hiking and biking, easy access to the Appalachian Trail, and 97 tent sites and showers. Other state parks have camping facilities, too. Reservations are not accepted.

Canoeing Canoe-kayak white-water runs on the Swift River are fast and intricate. If you go with river outfitters **Saco Bound–Northern Waters** (Box 119, Center Conway 03813, tel. 603/447–2177), day's end is the full-facility (Jacuzzi, sauna, pool, racquetball, and more) Mt. Cranmore Racquet Club. Saco Bound handles rentals as well as organized trips April–November.

Fishing For serious trout and salmon fishing, try the Connecticut Lakes (*see* Off the Beaten Track, above) though any clear stream in the White Mountains will do. Many are stocked, and there are 650 miles of them in the national forest alone. Some 45 lakes and ponds contain trout and bass.

Hiking The web of trails through the White Mountains can keep a hiker busy for years. Overnight hiking is a regional specialty, and the Appalachian Trail runs across the state. Short hikes include Artist's Bluff, Lonesome Lake, and Basin-Cascades Trails, Franconia Notch State Park; Boulder Loop and Greely Ponds off the Kancamagus Highway; and Sanguinari Ridge Trail, Dixville Notch.

Appalachian Mountain Club (Box 298, Pinkham Notch, Gorham 03581, tel. 603/466–2725).

AMC Hut System (Box 298, Gorham 03581, tel. 603/466–2721).

White Mountain National Forest (U.S. Forest Service, Box 638, Laconia 03246, tel. 603/524–6450).

New England Hiking Holidays–White Mountains (Box 1648, North Conway 03860, tel. 603/356–9696) offers inn-to-inn, guided hiking tours that include two, three, or five nights in country inns.

Gourmet Hikes **Snowvillage Inn** (Snowville 03849, tel. 603/447–2818) conducts guided mountain hikes complete with an elegant picnic (teriyaki beef on skewers, phyllo stuffed with spinach and feta cheese, wine, and more) on a checkered tablecloth.

Stag Hollow Inn (Jefferson 03583, tel. 603/586–4598) will introduce you to llama trekking. Gourmet picnics, with such delicacies as melon balls in Cointreau and chicken-pear salad, are toted by friendly, sure-footed llamas as you hike.

Recreation Areas

Bretzfelder Park (Bethlehem 03574, tel. 603/869–2683), a 77-acre nature and wildlife park, has a picnic shelter.

Lost River Reservation (North Woodstock 03293, tel. 603/705–8031). From May to October tour the gorge on boardwalks, as the river appears and vanishes.

Loon Mountain Recreation Area, on the western terminus of the Kancamagus Highway, has aerial rides, hiking, picnics, tennis, and a pool, hotel, and restaurant. *Lincoln 03251, tel. 603/745–8111. Open May–Oct.*

Waterville Valley Recreation Area (Waterville Valley 03215, tel. 603/236–8311 or 800/258–8988) is a full-facility complex with hotels, restaurants, pool, tennis, and skiing.

State Parks

Crawford Notch State Park (Harts Location). Six miles of scenic mountain pass with waterfalls, picnic sites, fishing, and hiking.

Dixville Notch State Park (Dixville). This most-northern notch has a waterfall, hiking, and picnic areas.

Echo Lake State Park (Conway). The mountain lake beneath White Horse Ledge has swimming, picnic sites, and a road to Cathedral Ledge.

Franconia Notch State Park (Franconia and Lincoln), has swimming, camping, picnicking, biking, and hiking on a 27-mile network of Appalachian-system trails. The top attraction is the Old Man of the Mountains ("Great Stone Face"), a 40-foot granite profile that is the official symbol of New Hampshire. Also in the park are the Flume, Echo Lake, Liberty Gorge, the Cascades, and the Basin.

White Mountain National Forest is managed by the U.S. Forest Service (tel. 603/524–6450) and covers nearly 763,000 acres. It includes most of New England's highest peaks.

Dining

Places to dine are abundant in the area, and only the very special dining room requires reservations. Innkeepers often choose a slow time to close for renovation or travel.

★ **The Balsams Grand Resort Hotel.** The chef and his staff are culinary award-winners, and they prepare a different menu each evening. On a warm night you might begin with chilled strawberry soup Grand Marnier; go on to poached salmon fillet with golden caviar sauce; and end with chocolate hazelnut cake. Because the dining room is essentially for guests of the resort, reservations are necessary if you are staying elsewhere.

Dixville Notch, tel. 603/255-3400 or 800/255-0600. Reservations required. Jacket required. AE, MC, V. Expensive.

Christmas Farm Inn. The food is straightforward American, and you might start with ravioli of smoked chicken with tomato-basil dressing; poached scallops with diced tomato and fines herbes; or sautéed venison with spinach, wild mushrooms, and dark game sauce. The menu alerts diners to "heart healthy" dinners approved by the American Heart Association. *Jackson Village, tel. 603/383-4313. Reservations advised. Dress: casual. AE, MC, V. Expensive.*

Darby Field Inn. If you call after 4 PM, you will be told the four daily specials, which depend on what was freshest and best in the market. Or choose from menu regulars like chicken marquis (a sautéed breast of chicken with mushrooms, tomatoes, and white wine); or duckling glazed with Chambord or Grand Marnier. The recipe for Darby cream pie may be coaxed from the chef. *Bald Hill, Conway, tel. 603/447-2181. Reservations advised. Dress: casual. AE, MC, V. Expensive.*

The Bernerhof. A Taste of the Mountains Cooking School was founded here, one of its directors the Bernerhof's executive chef, Richard Spence. The cuisine is primarily classic French but perhaps is better described as high Continental. This may be because of the ambience of the Alpine dining room, with its rubbed wood and flowers—too charming to be merely classic. The wine list is heavily French and Austrian, and veal is a specialty. *Rte. 302, Glen, tel. 603/383-4411. Reservations advised. Dress: casual but neat. AE, MC, V. Closed Apr.–mid-May, mid-Nov.–mid-Dec. Moderate–Expensive.*

Franconia Inn. While you dine on medallions of veal with apple-mustard sauce, or filet mignon with sun-dried tomatoes, your child can have "The Young Epicurean Cheeseburger" or a "Petite Breast of Chicken." The two brothers who own and operate Franconia Inn understand how families work. *Easton Rd., Franconia, tel. 603/823-5542. Reservations advised. Dress: casual. AE, MC, V. Closed Apr.–mid-May. Moderate–Expensive.*

Snowvillage Inn. There's a touch of Austria in the cuisine here. Walnut-beer bread? Bourbon in the salad dressing? Is that how they survive in the Tyrolean Alps? Reservations are essential, and you will be told the day's main course and several alternatives when you call. *Snowville, tel. 603/447-2818. Reservations required. Dress: casual. AE, MC, V. Closed Apr. Moderate–Expensive.*

★ **The Scottish Lion.** The dining room overlooks meadows and mountains, and Sunday brunch is a full meal that attracts local residents as well as visitors. Until the inn became a B&B a decade ago, it was solely a restaurant. Now the tartan-papered pub has over 100 varieties of Scotch, and the American-Scottish cuisine includes hot oatcakes in the evening bread basket. *Rte. 16, North Conway, tel. 603/356-6381. Reservations advised. Dress: casual. AE, CB, DC, MC, V. Moderate.*

★ **Margaritaville.** The taste of the authentic Mexican food is enhanced by outdoor dining on the patio in summer. The appropriately named restaurant is family run, with five daughters waiting table. *Rte. 302, Glen, tel. 603/383-6556. Reservations accepted. Dress: casual. MC, V. Inexpensive.*

Rivagale Inn and Restaurant. The Fireside Taverne of the Rivagale Inn serves black-diamond steak, baked stuffed shrimp, and chicken enchiladas, but you can settle for soup and a sandwich if that's all you want. The owner-chefs run a comfortable restaurant in their century-old inn. The dining room has a huge fireplace and overlooks the Gale River. On Supper Club nights, you'll get vintage 1940s entertainment as you dine. *195 Main St., Franconia, tel. 603/823–7044. Reservations accepted. Dress: casual. AE, MC, V. Inexpensive.*

Lodging

Resorts, motels, country inns, and B&Bs are thick as snowflakes, and only during foliage season should you hesitate to travel without reservations. (Getting into a special place requires advance calling in any season.) The **Mt. Washington Valley B&B Reservation Service** (tel. 603/822–5502) will find you a room when you need one.

★ **The Balsams Grand Resort Hotel.** Getting away from it all luxuriously is only part of the appeal of this famous full-service resort. Families can divide according to interest and regroup at meals; couples can find any number of cozy nooks for private conversation. The Tower Suite, with its 20-foot conical ceiling, is located in a Victorian turret; its view is 360 degrees. More-standard accommodations have views, too, as well as all the deluxe amenities. Incidentally, guests wear jackets and ties to dinner. *Dixville Notch 03576, tel. 603/255–3400 or 800/255–0600. 232 rooms with bath. Facilities: restaurant, biking, boating, children's program, dancing, golf, pool, tennis, downhill and cross-country skiing. AE, D, MC, V. Rates include all meals, sports, entertainment. Very Expensive.*

★ **Mount Washington Hotel.** The grand dowager, undergoing a $20 million facelift in 1990, is expected to reopen in 1991 with its stately public rooms and its large, traditionally furnished bedrooms and suites more elegant than ever. The formal atmosphere extends to the dining room, where jacket and tie are expected at dinner. New additions to the 2,600-acre property are to include a recreation center with pool, tennis courts, and spa, and a 36-hole golf course. *Rte. 302, Bretton Woods 03575, tel. 603/278–1000 or 800/258–0330. 200 rooms with bath. Facilities: restaurant, golf, indoor and outdoor pools, sauna, tennis, cross-country ski trails. AE, CB, D, MC, V. Rates are MAP. Very Expensive.*

Darby Field Inn. Every room is different at this inn, but what most have in common—besides all being on the second and third floors—is the spectacular mountain view. A fieldstone fireplace is the centerpiece of the living room; the dining room is panelled in pine; the bar has a wood stove and a piano. *Bald Hill, Conway 03818, tel. 603/447–2181 or 800/426–4147. 16 rooms, 14 with bath. Facilities: restaurant, cross-country trails, pool. No pets. No smoking in rooms. AE, MC, V. Closed Apr., Nov. Rates are MAP. Expensive.*

★ **Inn at Thorn Hill.** The inn was designed and built by Stanford White in 1895, and its rooms are decorated as if White were the expected guest, with polished dark woods and rose-motif papers and fabrics. *Thorn Hill Rd., Jackson 03846, tel. 603/383–4242. 20 rooms with bath. Facilities: restaurant, pub, pool. No pets. AE, MC, V. Closed Apr. Rates are MAP. Expensive.*

Red Jacket Mountain View Inn. How often do you find a motor inn/resort that feels like a country inn? The bedrooms are large and traditionally furnished with all the amenities of a fine hotel. Deep chairs and plants fill the cozy public rooms. The manager has been here for nearly three decades and runs a friendly albeit tight ship. *Rte. 16, North Conway 03860, tel. 603/356–5411 or 800/343–0476. 159 rooms with bath. Facilities: restaurant, cable TV, indoor and outdoor pools, saunas, whirlpool, tennis, playground. No pets. MC, V. Expensive.*

The Bernerhof. This small, Old World hotel, built a century ago, is at home in its Alpine setting. There's a Finnish sauna on the third floor, a coal stove in the living room, and lace curtains in the bedrooms. The inn was completely refurbished in 1988, and four deluxe rooms now have oversize spa tubs. Stay three days in any room, and you are served a champagne breakfast in bed. The owners founded A Taste of the Mountains Cooking School, which convenes at the inn. *Rte. 302, Glen 03838, tel. 603/383–9131 or 800/548–8007. 12 rooms with bath. Facilities: restaurant, playground, sauna. No pets. No smoking in rooms. AE, MC, V. Rates include full breakfast. Moderate–Expensive.*

★ **Christmas Farm Inn.** Despite its name, this 200-year-old village inn is an all-season retreat. Rooms in the main inn and the salt box are decorated with Laura Ashley prints; the cottages, log cabin, and dairy barn suites have beamed ceilings and fireplaces and are better suited to active families. *Box CC, Rte. 16B, Jackson 03846, tel. 603/383–4313 or 800/443–5837, fax 603/383–6495. 38 rooms with bath. Facilities: restaurant, children's play area, game rooms, pool, putting green, sauna, volleyball. No pets. AE, MC, V. Rates are MAP. Moderate–Expensive.*

Franconia Inn. A year-round resort like this one will supply you with anything from a bike to a babysitter. Movies are shown each evening in the lounge, there is croquet in summer and skiing in winter. Greens fees are waived for inn guests at Sunset Hill's nine-hole course. You can play tennis, ride horseback, swim in the pool or swimming hole, order your lunch-to-go for a day of hiking—even try soaring from the inn's own airstrip. The rooms have designer chintzes and canopied beds; some have whirlpools, some have fireplaces. *Easton Rd., Franconia 03580, tel. 603/823–5542. 34 rooms with bath. Facilities: restaurant, pool, bicycles, croquet, golf privileges, hot tub, movies, soaring center, stable, tennis. No pets. Limited smoking. AE, MC, V. Rates include full breakfast or are MAP. Closed Apr.–mid-May. Moderate–Expensive.*

The Glen. A rustic lodge on the First Connecticut Lake, this sportsman's resort has log cabins, boats to rent, and uncomplicated cookery. A stone fireplace in the dining room and wood panelling throughout set the tone. The dining room is open to public by reservation only, so if you are seeing the area and want to stop here for dinner, plan ahead. *Box 77, Pittsburg 03592, tel. 603/538–6500. 18 rooms with bath. Facilities: restaurant, dock. No credit cards. Rates include 3 meals. Closed mid-Oct.–mid-May. Moderate–Expensive.*

★ **Snowvillage Inn.** Cheerful barn-red exteriors and guest rooms filled with such Americana as four-posters and working fireplaces are only part of the scene. The owners/innkeepers are ardent conservationists who can take you on gourmet hikes up the mountains. They are also builders who have added a Tyrolean chalet to their turn-of-the-century farmhouse, converted a 150-year-old barn to guest quarters, and built libraries in each of the inn's three buildings. *Box A–50, Snowville 03849, tel. 603/447–2818. 18 rooms with bath. Facilities: restaurant, cross-country trails, sauna, tennis. AE, MC, V. Closed Apr. Rates include full breakfast or are MAP. Moderate–Expensive.*

Sugar Hill Inn. There's an old carriage on the lawn and wicker chairs on the wraparound porch of this converted 1789 farmhouse. Many rooms are hand-stenciled, and much of the antique furniture came from neighboring farms. Not a single room is square, level, or without at least some rippled window-glass. Climb out of your four poster, canopy, or brass bed, and set foot on braided rugs strategically placed to show off the pumpkin-pine and northern-maple floors. There are ten rooms in the inn and six in three country cottages. Dinner is served to guests and the public by reservation only. *Rte. 117, Sugar Hill 03585, tel. 603/823–5621. 16 rooms with bath. Facilities: dining room. No pets. No smoking. MC, V. Rates include full breakfast (spring–summer) or are MAP (fall–winter). Closed Apr., mid-Nov.–Dec. Cottages closed Nov.–May. Moderate–Expensive.*

Cranmore Inn. This easygoing lodge at the foot of Mt. Cranmore has the atmosphere of an upcountry guest house. High school students serve the meals, and the print of the wallpaper harmonizes with the spreads and curtains in the rooms. The furnishings date from the mid-1800s to the 1930s, in keeping with the history and atmosphere of the inn. *Kearsage St., North Conway 03860, tel. 603/356–5502 or 800/822–5502. 19 rooms, 9 with bath. Facilities: restaurant, pool. No smoking in rooms. AE, MC, V. Closed Apr.–May, Nov.–Dec. Rates include full breakfast. Moderate.*

Ledgeland. The owners are descended from 18th-century Sugar Hill settlers, and the accommodations are best described as homey. Cottages are situated about the grounds, and most have fireplaces and equipped kitchens. *Rte. 117, Sugar Hill 03585, tel. 603/823–5341. 22 rooms with bath. No pets. No credit cards. Closed mid-Oct.–June. Rates include Continental breakfast July–Aug. Moderate.*

Purity Spring Resort. Before the first guests came, in the late 1800s, Purity Spring consisted of a farm, sawmill, and private lake. It is now a four-season, American-plan resort that has been operated by the same family for nearly a century. It's a place to swim, fish, hike, and play tennis or lawn games. There is a supervised program for children, and King Pine Ski Area is on the property. Whether you choose rooms in the main inn, adjacent lodges, or cottages, the decor is sturdy, old-fashioned New England. *Rte. 153, East Madison 03849, tel. 603/367–8896 or 800/367–8897. 45 rooms, 35 with bath. Facilities: restaurant, private lake, tennis, volleyball. No pets. MC, V. Closed Apr.–mid-June, late Oct.–mid-Dec. Rates are MAP (or include 3 meals). Moderate.*

Rivagale Inn. This small village inn, near the town ice rink and the public library, is as down-home as all New Hampshire. Guests eat breakfast in the sunny morning-room overlooking the Gale River. Each room has an antique bed and homemade quilt, and two have working fireplaces. The inn's collection of political cartoons, newspapers, and century-old issues of *Forest & Stream* will give you a glimpse of another era. *195 Main St., Franconia 03850, tel. 603/823–7044. 8 rooms, 6 with bath. Facilities: restaurant, tavern, cable TV, VCR, play area. No pets. No smoking. AE, MC, V. Rates include breakfast. Inexpensive–Moderate.*

Tanglewood Motel & Cottages. Swim or fish in a mountain stream just outside the door of this neat, family-operated, one-floor motel-inn. Some rooms in the motel sleep up to six, and the two-person cottages have fully equipped kitchens, though you provide your own maid service. *Rte. 16, Conway 03818, tel. 603/447–5932. 13 rooms with bath. Facilities: cribs. AE, MC, V. Inexpensive–Moderate.*

The Arts

Theater **Mt. Washington Valley Theater Company** (Eastern Slope Playhouse, North Conway, tel. 603/356–5701) has musicals and Equity summer theater from July to September.

North Country Center for the Arts (Mill at Loon Mountain, Lincoln, tel. 603/745–6032) presents music, concerts, children's theater, and performing and visual arts from July to October.

Nightlife

Mt. Washington Hotel (Bretton Woods, tel. 603/278–1000) has dancing nightly in an atmosphere that requires jacket and tie.

Red Parka Pub (Glen, tel. 603/383–4344) is a hangout for the under-thirties. Barbecued spare ribs are the house specialty.

Thunderbird Lounge (Indian Head Resort, North Lincoln, tel. 603/745–8000) has nightly entertainment year round.

Nereledge Inn and White Horse Pub (River Rd., North Conway, tel. 603/356–2831), an English-style pub, is popular with ages 30–50. The inn is host to the Mountain Guides Alliance climbing school; River Road is off Main Street.

Dartmouth–Lake Sunapee

The Upper Connecticut River means Dartmouth College, great canoeing, and the estate of the sculptor Augustus Saint-Gaudens. Travel inland a few miles, and the hills become mountains, the ponds grow to lakes. Lake Sunapee has its neighboring mountain and state park, a total recreation package. Scattered across the region are villages where summer nights mean band concerts on the green and the quality of life seems to be as carefully preserved as the 18th- and 19th-century houses.

Important Addresses and Numbers

Visitor Information **Lake Sunapee Business Association** (Box 400, Sunapee 03782, tel. 603/763–2495).

Hanover Chamber of Commerce (Box A–105, Hanover 03755, tel. 603/643–3115).

Emergencies **State Police** (tel. 800/852–4311).

Poison Center (tel. 800/562–8236).

Hitchcock Clinic (Hanover, tel. 603/646–5000).

New London Hospital (County Rd., New London, tel. 603/526–2911).

Valley Regional Hospital (Elm St., Claremont, tel. 603/542–7771).

Late-night Pharmacies **Bannon Pharmacy** (109 Pleasant St., Claremont, tel. 603/542–7722).

Eastman's Drug Store (Main St., Hanover, tel. 603/643–4112).

Getting Around Dartmouth–Lake Sunapee

By Car I–89 bisects the region from southeast to northwest and continues into Vermont. North–south I–91 follows the Vermont side of the Connecticut River. On the New Hampshire side, Route 12A is a picturesque but slow back road with frequent speed zones. Route 4 crosses the region, winding between Lebanon and the seacoast. Once you leave I–89 and I–91, all roads are back roads.

By Bus **Concord Trailways** (tel. 800/258–3722).

Advance Transit (tel. 603/448–2815) provides public transportation for the upper valley.

Exploring Dartmouth–Lake Sunapee

Numbers in the margin correspond with the numbered points of interest on the Dartmouth–Lake Sunapee map.

Our tour of the region takes a slow road of particular beauty, Route 4, to a junction with Route 11, which the tour follows west in the direction of Lake Sunapee.

❶ **Andover,** on Route 4, 8 miles west of Franklin and 20 miles northeast of Concord, and the home of Proctor Academy, is a village of early Federal to late-Victorian period homes. Its museum, open weekends from June to October, occupies a railway station built in 1874 in the neighboring hamlet of Potter Place.

❷ Colby-Sawyer College (1837) is the heartbeat of **New London** (on Route 114, 2 miles northwest of its junction with Route 11), but the inn and meeting house on Main Street show the visitor the face of an idealized American town.

Time Out **Peter Christian's Tavern,** in the Edgewood Inn on Main Street, is a hangout for youth where the soups are homemade and the hearty stews are available by the mug. "Peter's Father's Favorite Sandwich" is roast beef, cheese, onion, tomato, spinach, and horseradish; and there are more-basic combos as well.

❸ Beach, mountains, and state parkland set off **Lake Sunapee,** a jewel of water in the western highlands of New Hampshire. You can cruise it on the MV *Mt. Sunapee II* (tel. 603/763–4030), rise above it on chairlift or gondola, or picnic along its beach or in the park. The Craftsmen's Fair, the Antique and Classic Boat Parade, and the Gem and Mineral Festival take place here (Lake Sunapee Association, Box 400, Sunapee 03782, tel. 603/763–2495).

❹ **Dartmouth College,** in **Hanover,** was founded in 1769 to educate "Youth of the Indian Tribes," but local boys could come, too. The handsome campus around the green is the northernmost Ivy League college and the cultural center of the region. Among the buildings to visit are **Hopkins Center for the Creative and Performing Arts** (tel. 603/646–2422), a prototype for the Metropolitan Opera House at Lincoln Center, New York City; and, across the green from the Baker Library, the Hood Museum.

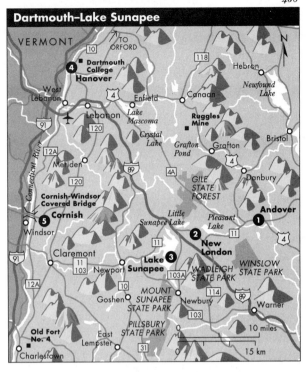

Dartmouth–Lake Sunapee

The 10 permanent galleries of the **Hood Museum of Art** house works from Africa, Asia, Europe, and America. Assyrian reliefs from the 5th century BC and an amphora from ancient Greece are among the most venerable pieces. The American collections include silver by Paul Revere, paintings by Winslow Homer, and works by Native Americans. *Wheelock St., tel. 603/ 646–2808). Admission free. Open Tues.–Fri. 11–5, weekends 9:30–5.*

⑤ The modest village of **Cornish,** with its brace of four covered bridges, was an unlikely host of the 19th-century American Renaissance. Yet the American novelist Winston Churchill and the painter Maxfield Parrish lived and worked in Cornish, and it was here that the sculptor Augustus Saint-Gaudens (1848–1907) set up his studio and created the heroic, sensitive bronzes that would insure his fame. Today you may tour Saint-Gaudens's house, studio, gallery, and gardens. Of particular interest are the full-size copies of the sculptor's famous pieces, as well as sketches and casting molds. At 2 on Sunday afternoons in summer, everyone is invited to bring a picnic lunch and enjoy a free chamber-music concert on the lawn. *Saint-Gaudens National Historic Site, off Rte. 12A, Cornish, tel. 603/675–2175. Admission: $1. Open Mid-May–Oct., daily 8:30–4:30; grounds open until dusk.*

The **Cornish–Windsor covered bridge,** the longest covered bridge in the United States, was built in 1866 and rebuttressed in 1988–89. It spans the Connecticut River, connecting New Hampshire and Vermont.

When the Connecticut River was the Colonial frontier, **Old Fort No. 4** was an outpost. What you see now is a re-creation, a living history museum whose costumed interpreters tell what went on in and outside the stockade in the 1740s. Although there are 13 buildings (where you will see demonstrations of weaving, cooking, and candlemaking) and a small museum, the fort is not comparable to Old Sturbridge Village in Massachusetts or to Old Mystic in Connecticut. During the year there are frequent reenactments of militia musters and training exercises from the French and Indian War era. *Rte. 11, Springfield Rd., Charlestown, tel. 603/826–5700. Admission: $4.75 adults, $3.25 children. Open May–Oct., Wed.–Mon.*

Dartmouth–Lake Sunapee for Free

Hood Museum of Art, Dartmouth College, Hanover

Hopkins Center for Creative and Performing Arts, Dartmouth College, Hanover (free tours)

Sunday Chamber Concerts, Saint-Gaudens National Historic Site, Cornish

What to See and Do with Children

Children's matinees, New London Barn Playhouse

The Ruggles Mine, Grafton

Old Fort No. 4, Charlestown

Off the Beaten Track

The Ruggles Mine. More than 150 minerals are found here on top of Isinglass Mountain in the oldest mica, feldspar, beryl, and uranium mine in the United States. Primarily an open-pit pegmatite mine, now out of use, the space has giant caverns, winding passageways, and arched-ceiling tunnels to explore. The 19th-century owner, Sam Ruggles, was so afraid someone would usurp his claim that he mined only at night and sold his ore secretly in England. Watch for signs directing you from Route 4; the mine is about 2 miles from Grafton Center. Collecting is permitted. *Rte. 4, Grafton, tel. 603/448–6911. Admission: $5.75 adults, $2.50 children. Open May–mid-June, weekends 9–5; July–Aug., daily 9–6; Sept.–mid-Oct., daily 9–5.*

Shopping

There are galleries aplenty in both New London and Hanover, and the open studios of many artisans are marked along the roads by neat New Hampshire state signs. An occasional enclave of shops is the local equivalent of a mall, but don't expect a cluster of large discount or department stores. Hours are generally 10–5:30, and most shops open Sunday as well. Fairs like the League of New Hampshire Craftsmen's at Mt. Sunapee State Park and Hospital Day in New London, offer excellent shopping opportunities. Small-town fairs on church lawns offer bargains and occasional treasures of all kinds. The absence of a state sales tax regularly brings Vermonters across the Connecticut.

Hanover League of New Hampshire Craftsmen (13 Lebanon St., Hanover, tel. 603/643–5050).

Artisan's Workshop. Most of the gifts, jewelry, handblown glass and other handcrafts available here are made by local artists and craftspeople. The workshop is next to Peter Christian's Tavern in the 1847 Edgewood Inn. *Main St., New London, tel. 603/526–4227. Open daily and evenings.*

Dorr Mill Store (Rte. 103, Guild, tel. 603/863–1197). Fabrics, sweaters, yarns, rug wools, and sweaters are sold in this famous store located between Newport and Sunapee. The remnants are especially tempting.

Mouse Menagerie of Fine Crafts (Rte. 120, Cornish, tel. 603/542–9691). If cats could shop, this store would be filled with them. There is pricey collector's series of more than 50 mice, or you can choose more mundane creatures that wouldn't break a kitty's bank.

Designer Gold (68 S. Main St., Hanover, tel. 603/643–3864). Paul Gross, goldsmith, makes one-of-a-kind and limited-edition gold jewelry. You can commission whatever you want but don't see.

The Powerhouse (Rte. 12A, 1 mi n. of I–89 Exit 20, West Lebanon, tel. 603/643–2275). A onetime power station and three adjacent buildings on the riverfront have become a retail complex with 40 stores, boutiques, and restaurants. Free-standing sculpture and windows that overlook the Mascoma River make visiting almost as much fun as shopping.

Antiques Center (Main St., Charlestown, tel. 603/826–3639). This shop has a wide inventory but specializes in fine china, glass, primitives, and fine furniture. It also carries ephemera.

Sports and Outdoor Activities

Biking Low-traffic roads both along the river and elsewhere are ideal for biking. Try Route 12A north from Charlestown to Cornish; Route 4 from West Andover to Enfield; Route 10 from Hanover to Orford; and Routes 11, 103, and 103A around Sunapee Lake. Inn-to-inn bike tours from Hanover north are available through **Bike Vermont** (Box 207, Woodstock, VT 05091, tel. 802/457–3553).

Camping **Crow's Nest Campground** (Rte. 10, Newport 03773, tel. 603/863–6170).

Northstar Campground (278 Coonbrook Rd., Newport 03773, tel. 603/863–4001).

Otter Pond Camping Area (Otterville Rd., New London 03257, tel. 603/763–5800).

Rand's Pond Campground (Rand Pond Rd., Goshen 03752, tel. 603/863–3350).

Canoeing The Connecticut is considered generally safe after June 15, but canoeists should always proceed with caution. The river is not for beginners at any time of year. Canoe rentals are available from May to November at **North Star Canoe & Mountain Bike Rentals** (Rte. 12A, Balloch's Crossing, Cornish, tel. 603/542–5802).

Fishing In Lake Sunapee there are brook and lake trout, salmon, small-mouth bass, and pickerel. Lake Mascoma has rainbow trout, pickerel, and horned pout.

Hiking Hikes in the state parks include a steep, mile-long trail to the summit of Mt. Kearsage in Winslow State Park; a network of trails on Mt. Sunapee; rugged hiking in Pillsbury State Park, a wilderness area in Washington; and trails to the 3,121-foot summit of Mt. Cardigan.

State Parks

Mt. Sunapee State Park is in Newbury; **Wadleigh State Park** is in Sutton, with swimming and picnicking on Kezar Lake; and Winslow State Park in Wilmot affords great views to those who ascend Mt. Kearsage.

Dining

Daniel Webster Room. The classic New England fare of this inn owned and operated by Dartmouth College is appropriate to the setting. An appetizer of house-smoked scallops with a cider-rosemary mayonnaise might be followed by saddle of lamb served with winter squash and celery root. The contemporary Ivy Grill serves lighter, faster food. Both restaurants are in the Hanover Inn, on the College Green. *Main and Wheelock Sts., Hanover, tel. 603/643–4300. Reservations advised. Dress: casual but neat. AE, MC, V. Expensive.*

★ **D'Artagnan.** The food is country-French nouvelle in this 18th-century public house. Summer dining is on a stone terrace overlooking a brook, and the indoor dining area has wide-plank pine floors and exposed beams. A four-course prix-fixe menu may offer pâté of rabbit with hazelnuts on watercress; Scottish smoked salmon; or poached golden bass with mushrooms and leeks in vermouth sauce. The desserts include fresh pear almond cream tartelette; and apricot vacherin with apricot-almond-rum ice cream. The flavors of Cool Moose brand ice cream were devised here by the owner and chef. *13 Dartmouth College Hwy. (Rte. 10), Lyme, tel. 603/795–2137. Reservations required. Dress: casual but neat. AE, MC, V. Closed Mon.–Tues. No dinner Sun. Expensive.*

Home Hill Country Inn. The owner and chef of this nouvelle French restaurant is a native of Brittany. Butternut squash is translated here into a bisque, and the fresh Norwegian salmon is braised with spring vegetables and saffron. Local morels and hydroponic lettuce are basic to the cuisine. For dessert: local berries in pastry shells; and white- and dark-chocolate mousse with raspberry sauce. The prix-fixe menu changes daily. *River Rd., 3½ mi from Rte. 12A, Plainfield, tel. 603/675–6165. Reservations required. Dress: casual but neat. AE, MC, V. Closed Sun. Expensive.*

★ **Millstone.** A country cottage is now a small, homey restaurant serving New American cuisine in the center of New London. There's a variation of roast duckling, a rosemary-chicken sauté, and a special such as veal del sol (sun-dried tomatoes, shallots, garlic, lemon, and wine sauce) every day. *Newport Rd., New London, tel. 603/526–4201. Reservations advised. Dress: casual. AE, DC, MC, V. Moderate.*

New London Inn. The dining room has the look of a traditional country inn; the food is reminiscent of the California coast.

Main St., New London, tel. 603/526-2791. Reservations advised. Dress: casual. AE, MC, V. Closed Mon. No lunch Tues.–Sat. Moderate.

Lodging

The **Lodging Reservation Service, Sunapee Region** (tel. 603/763-2495 or 800/258-3530), will find accommodations for you.

★ **Hanover Inn.** The inn's three stories of Georgian brick trimmed with white are the embodiment of American traditional architecture. This is the oldest continuously operating business in New Hampshire and is now a part of Dartmouth College. The building was converted from home to tavern in 1780, and subsequent additions brought it to its present size in 1924. Recent renovation has reduced the number of rooms to enlarge their space and create 16 junior suites. Furnishings include 19th-century antiques and reproductions. *The Green, Hanover 03755, tel. 603/643-4300 or 800/443-7024, fax 603/643-4300. 92 rooms with bath. Facilities: 2 restaurants. AE, D, MC, V. Rates include full breakfast. Expensive–Very Expensive.*

★ **Home Hill Country Inn.** A restored 1800 mansion set back from the river on 25 acres of meadow and woods, this is a tranquil place. The chef-owner is from Brittany, so there's more than a touch of French in the 19th-century patrician antiques and collectibles. A suite in the guest house is a romantic hideaway. The dining room serves classic and nouvelle French cuisine. *River Rd., Plainfield 03781, tel. 603/675-6165. 5 rooms with bath. Facilities: pool, tennis court, cross-country ski trails. French spoken. No pets. AE, MC, V. Closed early Nov. Rates include Continental breakfast. Expensive.*

Dexter's Inn and Tennis Club. This small resort has a teaching pro as well as all-weather tennis courts. Players can sit on the terrace and drink lemonade between sets. *Box 20, Stagecoach Rd., Sunapee 03782, tel. 603/763-5571 or 800/232-5571. 17 rooms with bath. Facilities: restaurant, pool, 3 tennis courts. MC, V. Rates are MAP. Moderate–Expensive.*

Seven Hearths Inn. Nooks and crannies where guests can visit or just settle with a good book are almost as numerous as working fireplaces. Five of the seven hearths are in the guest rooms, by the way, and there are gardens to stroll in summer. Meals in the restaurant are by reservation only. *Box 712, Old Rte. 11, Sunapee 03782, tel. 603/763-5657. 10 rooms with bath. Facilities: restaurant, pool. MC, V. Rates include full breakfast. Moderate–Expensive.*

★ **Chase House Bed & Breakfast.** This is the former home of Samuel P. Chase, who was Abraham Lincoln's secretary of the treasury, a chief justice of the United States, and the founder of the Republican Party. A few years ago it was rescued from derelict obscurity and restored to 19th-century elegance. Some rooms have settees and canopied beds; some look out onto meadows and others across to the Connecticut River. The B&B is on Route 12A, just north of the Cornish-Windsor covered bridge. *RR 2, Box 909, Cornish 03746, tel. 603/675-5391. 6 rooms, 4 with bath. Facilities: canoes. MC, V. Rates include full breakfast. Moderate.*

English House Bed & Breakfast. An English couple owns this Edwardian-period inn, and guests are naturally served tea and homemade cookies at 4 PM. Large, sunny rooms furnished with English and American antiques are hung with watercolors by the owner's mother and uncle, both well-known British artists. *Main St., Andover 03216, tel. 603/735–5987. 7 rooms with bath. Facilities: Cable TV, cross-country ski trails. No pets. No smoking. MC, V. Rates include full breakfast, afternoon tea. Moderate.*

Inn on Canaan Street. Situated 2½ miles north of Canaan town, the inn is part of the preserved historical district on a street laid out in the 1700s. There is stenciling on the walls, and decorations in each room are based on a different flower. "Forget-me-not" has a working fireplace and can be combined with "Aster" to make a suite. *Box 92, Canaan St., Canaan 03741, tel. 603/523–7310. 5 rooms, 3 with bath. Facilities: Cable TV, canoes. No pets. No smoking. MC, V. Rates include full buffet breakfast. Moderate.*

New London Inn. A rambling 1792 country inn in the center of town has an inviting porch with rocking chairs overseeing Main Street. The owners' son is chef in the dining room. *Main St., New London 03257, tel. 603/526–2791. 30 rooms with bath. Facilities: restaurant. AE, MC, V. Rates include full breakfast. Moderate.*

The Arts

Theater   **Dartmouth Drama Summer Repertory** (Hopkins Center, Hanover, tel. 603/646–2422) performs on the campus.

New London Barn Playhouse. A converted barn on Main Street houses Equity productions of musicals, comedies, and children's theater. *Box 285, New London 03257, tel. 603/526–6570. Season: mid-Jun.–Aug.*

Nightlife

Sheraton North Country Inn Lounge (Airport Rd., West Lebanon, tel. 603/298–5906) hosts dancing on weekend nights, and there is a piano bar daily.

Peter Christian's Tavern (39 S. Main St., Hanover, tel. 603/643–2345) and **Peter Christian's Tavern** at the **Edgewood Inn** (Main St., New London, tel. 603/526–4042) are drop-in spots for the under-30 crowd, where you'll usually find a folksinger and a guitar in performance.

Monadnock Region

The solitary Mt. Monadnock, prominent over many miles of southwestern New Hampshire, is the prototypical New England peak. It presides over a kingdom of calendar-page villages, hardwood forests, small colleges, and more than 200 lakes. The mountain itself attracted Henry David Thoreau, Ralph Waldo Emerson, and Henry James, among others, first to climb, then to enjoy the fellowship before the fire of a coaching inn. Writers and artists still come, some for the retreat at the MacDowell Colony of Peterborough, others to live unpretentiously and practice their craft.

Important Addresses and Numbers

Visitor Information   **Monadnock Travel Council** (8 Central Sq., Keene 03431, tel. 603/352–1303).

Greater Keene Chamber of Commerce (Keene 03431, tel. 603/352–1303).

Hillsboro Chamber of Commerce (Hillsboro 03244, tel. 603/464–5858).

Jaffrey Chamber of Commerce (Jaffrey 03452, tel. 603/532–1303).

Peterborough Chamber of Commerce (Peterborough 03458, tel. 603/924–7234).

Emergencies **State Police** (tel. 800/852–3411).

Poison Center (tel. 800/562–8236).

Cheshire Medical Center (580 Court St., Keene, tel. 603/352–4111).

Monadnock Community Hospital (Old Street Rd., Peterborough, tel. 603/924–7191).

Late-night Pharmacies **Brooks Pharmacy** (Riverside Plaza, Keene, tel. 603/352–6969).

Rite Aid (Peterborough Rd., Jaffrey, tel. 603/532–7905).

Getting Around the Monadnock Region

By Car The roads are good in the region, and a car is essential. From Keene in the southwestern corner, roads radiate through the entire area. Further east, U.S. Route 202 is a major north-south artery. Among a number of pleasant back roads that enter the region from Massachusetts, Route 12 passes through Fitzwilliam and Keene, veers west to the Connecticut River, and continues as Route 12A north to the Dartmouth–Lake Sunapee area.

Guided Tours

Cheshire Transportation Company (Keene, tel. 603/352–2303) provides charter services in the region.

Exploring the Monadnock Region

Numbers in the margin correspond with the numbered points of interest on the Monadnock Region map.

Covered bridges and 18th-century villages give this area a Currier and Ives look, yet there are patches of real forest here, such as the undeveloped Pisgah State Forest, home to wolves, foxes, deer, and moose. We begin our tour at the southeast corner of the region, where Route 119 enters from Massachusetts.

❶ The village of **Rindge** on Route 119, chartered in the middle of the 18th century, is a picturesque spot that becomes busy when the summer people arrive at the nearby lakes. During the academic year there are concerts and lectures at Franklin Pierce College (tel. 603/899–5111).

Cathedral of the Pines, an outdoor hall of worship, has an inspiring view of Mt. Monadnock from its Altar of the Nation. Services are held here by all faiths (no solicitations take place); the simple rectangular altar is composed of rock from every state and territory. Organ meditations can be heard at midday, Monday through Thursday. The Memorial Bell Tower, with its carillon of international bells, is dedicated to the American

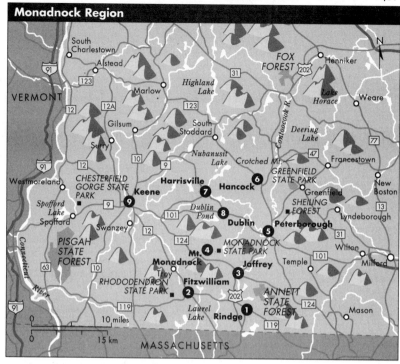

women, military and civilian, who sacrificed their lives in service to their country. The tower is built of native stone; the bronze tablets over the four arches are by Norman Rockwell. A fountain sculpture, *Tree of Life,* stands in the rotunda. Cathedral of the Pines was established by Dr. and Mrs. Douglas Sloane in 1946 to honor their son, Sanderson Sloane, a World War II pilot killed in action. Flower gardens, an indoor chapel, and a museum of military memorabilia share the hilltop. Opposite the entrance, the Wayside Park of Annett State Forest has picnic sites. The turn off Route 119 is well marked. *Rindge 03461, tel. 603/899–3300. Open May–Oct., dawn–sunset.*

A well-preserved historic district set around an oval common has made the town of **Fitzwilliam,** 8 miles west of Rindge on Route 119, a textbook of early American village architecture. The Meeting House (1817) now houses town offices; the **Historical Society** (tel. 603/585–3134) maintains a museum and country store in the Amos J. Blake House, a 19th-century law office. On a hillock at one end of the green is the church, at the other, the Fitzwilliam Inn (1796). Grouped about the common are well-preserved Colonial and Federal houses that are now antiques stores, a clock shop, and the public library.

Rhododendron State Park, 2½ miles northwest of the common, has picnic tables in a pine grove and marked footpaths. Sixteen of its 294 acres are solidly *rhododendron maximum,* the largest concentration north of the Alleghenies and well-worth seeing at their peak, early to mid-July. Just at the entrance to the park is a wildflower trail that blooms somewhat earlier.

Time Out Just off Route 12, on Marlborough Road in Troy, the **Monad-nock Mountainview Restaurant** offers uncomplicated food and a great view of the mountain from the Village Gathering Mall. Soup and half a sandwich (roast beef, tuna, or ham and Swiss cheese) are a bargain, and the children's menu includes peanut butter and jelly sandwiches.

❸ From Troy, take the Jaffrey Road east to **Jaffrey,** which claims Mt. Monadnock as its own. In the hilltop cemetery of Jaffrey Center (the old part of town), the novelist Willa Cather is buried not far from Amos Fortune, the freed slave who became Jaffrey's town philanthropist. Cather, a perennial summer visitor, wrote *My Antonia* in a tent pitched in a local meadow. The **Amos Fortune Forum** (tel. 603/532–1303) brings nationally known speakers to the 1773 Meeting House on summer evenings.

❹ **Mt. Monadnock,** a National Natural Landmark, rises 3,165 feet above the plain. It is the most climbed mountain in America and second in the world only to Japan's Mt. Fuji. More than 20 trails of varying difficulty lead to the bald stone top, and park rangers redirect climbers if one route is overcrowded. The Monadnock Ecocenter has guided walks, a lecture room, and a small museum. Here you can identify the birds and plants you see on your climb. Allow at least three hours to go up and down the mountain. **Monadnock State Park** (tel. 603/532–8035) has picnic grounds and some tent campsites. On a clear day the view from the summit is of three states. The park entrance is 4 miles north of Jaffrey; turn right off Route 124.

The drive north from Jaffrey on Route 202 gives you a momentary sense of an earlier time, when this was virgin territory. ❺ **Peterborough** was the model for Thornton Wilder's *Our Town,* and the play is performed every summer by the Peterborough Players (tel. 603/924–7585), who perform a variety of plays in repertory. Main Street has not been overly updated, yet the town is now known as a publishing center for computer magazines.

Peterborough's Free Public Library was the nation's first, and the Historical Society's **Museum of Americana** (19 Grove St., tel. 603/924–3235) contains a circa-1840 millworker's house, a country store, and a Colonial kitchen, plus changing exhibits.

The MacDowell Colony (tel. 603/924–3886), established by the composer Edward MacDowell in 1907, offers artistic seclusion to painters, writers, sculptors, composers, and filmmakers, among others. Only a small part is open to the public.

Time Out **Peterborough Diner,** at 10 Depot Street, is a hangout for young professionals and anyone else who wants a quick bite to eat or a long dawdle over a cup of coffee. Choose a booth or a counter seat in a railroad-car setting. The spinach pie and occasional quiche are perhaps out of sync with the decor, but you can also have a cheeseburger or even franks and beans.

❻ Just off Route 202, north of Peterborough, **Hancock** was founded (and named for the statesman John Hancock) when George Washington was president. Now preserved in its entirety as an historic district, it has a bandstand on the green and New Hampshire's oldest inn, the Hancock Inn of 1789.

South of town, on Cavender Road, is a covered bridge across the Contoocook River.

❼ **Harrisville,** once called Twitchell Village, is southwest of Hancock on the Old Dublin Road. It, too, is a preserved town (Historic Harrisville, Inc., Church Hill, Harrisville 03450, tel. 603/827–3722) and dates from the early years of the Industrial Revolution. It is perhaps the only mill town in America to have survived in its original form. Here are factories that once produced woodenware and woolens; the **Weaving Center** (tel. 603/827–3996), a shop of yarns and looms on Main Street, will teach you to weave a scarf in a day.

❽ Beyond Harrisville is the prosperous hill town of **Dublin,** the highest town in the state and the longtime home of the *Old Farmer's Almanac.* One of the entrances to Monadnock State Park is here, as well as **Friendly Farm** (tel. 603/563–8444), where children can see chickens hatching and play pat-the-goat.

❾ If Peterborough is "our town," then **Keene,** west of Dublin on Rte. 101, is "our city." The cultural and market center of the Monadnock is an interesting blend of the progressive and the nostalgic. The Center for the Fine and Performing Arts on Brickyard Pond (tel. 603/352–1909) of Keene State College has three theaters, eight art studios, and a dance studio as well as the Thorne-Sagendorph Art Gallery, which regularly exhibits traveling shows from museums around the country and is a showcase for New England artists. Indoor and outdoor concerts are given here by nationally known rock and folk stars as well as local contemporary and chamber groups.

The 900-seat **Colonial Theater** (Main St., tel. 603/352–2033) is a 70-year-old concert house and movie theater where major acts (B. B. King, Taj Mahal, Bonnie Raitt, Judy Collins) appear and new films are shown. The theater has brass ticket-booths, near-perfect acoustics, and an ice cream parlor next door.

Keene has been recognized for its large number of trees and the width of its main street, where stately homes of 19th-century mill owners sit beside still older historic houses. **Horatio Colony House Museum** (199 Main St., tel. 603/352–0460) is a well-furnished homestead of 1806. The **Wyman Tavern** (330 Main St., tel. 603/352–1895), where the first trustees of Dartmouth College met in 1770, is maintained as a period house and museum.

Time Out **Lindy's Diner,** across from the bus station on Gilbo Avenue, is where you'll see the presidential candidates if you're here in February of an election year. The menu is most likely to feature liver and onions, pot roast, or meat loaf.

New Hampshire claims to have more covered bridges than any state in the nation, but the concentration south of Keene may be a record in itself. Each one, of course, is different, and some have stone-arch bridges, hand-cut and fitted without mortar. There is no one, riverside, bridge-to-bridge road, but you can explore by following the Ashuelot River along Route 10, south from Route 9, keeping a sharp eye on the river side for the spurs that lead to the bridges. This route is a tad easier to do by bicycle; automobile traffic is insignificant.

Monadnock Region for Free

Cathedral of the Pines, Rindge

Harris Center for Conservation Education, Hancock

Sharon Arts Center, Peterborough

Thorne-Sagendorph Art Gallery, Keene

What to See and Do with Children

Andy's Summer Playhouse, Wilton Center

Friendly Farm, Dublin

Monadnock Children's Museum, Keene

Covered bridges south of Keene

Maple sugar houses, Alstead and Mason

Off the Beaten Track

Maple sugar houses answer the question "Is there joy in mudtime?" When the days begin to warm, but the nights are still freezing—that is, sometime in late February or early March—the sap starts flowing from the maple trees. Visitors can watch the tapping process, including demonstrations of old methods. Then comes the cooking-down, followed by the reward: tasting the syrup. You can try it with unsweetened doughnuts and maybe a pickle, or taste sugar-on-snow, the confection that results when hot syrup is poured upon snow. Always telephone first to see if the sugaring-off is underway. Open to the public are: **Bacon's Sugar House** (Dublin Rd., Jaffrey Center, tel. 603/532–8836); **Clark's Sugar House** (off Rte. 123A, Alstead, tel. 603/835–6863); **Old Brick Sugar House** (Summit Rd., Keene, tel. 603/352–6812); **Parker's Maple Barn** (Brookline Rd., Mason, tel. 603/878–2308), where a restaurant serves a whole-grain pancake breakfast any time of day along with a regular menu; and **Stuart & John's Sugar House & Pancake Restaurant** (Jct. Rtes. 12 and 63, Westmoreland, tel. 603/399–4486).

Shopping

Western Monadnock and southeastern Vermont share shoppers, since Brattleboro is just across the river. On the New Hampshire side, Keene is the market town for the region, with enormous supermarkets in their own malls and, in its heart, an exceptional upscale mall in a restored mill. Peterborough has the headquarters and retail outlets of two top-of-the-line companies: the national, mostly mail-order **Brookstone** (Rte. 202N, tel. 603/924–7181) for tools and gadgets; and **Eastern Mountain Sports** (Vose Farm Rd., tel. 603/924–7231) known for rugged outdoor sportswear and equipment. There are also fine galleries and craft shops throughout the region.

Antiquing is a major preoccupation for visitors to the Monadnock, and you will find dealers in barns and home-stores that are strung along back roads and "open by chance or by appointment"; in well-stocked shops around village greens; and in clusters of stores along heavily traveled strips. Route 119 from

Fitzwilliam to Hinsdale is a good stretch, as is Route 101 from Marlborough to Wilton.

Shopping hours in Keene are generally Mon.–Sat. 10–9, Sun. 11–6. Small towns are more likely to roll up the sidewalks at 5 and stay closed Sunday.

Antiques **Fitzwilliam Antique Center** (Jct. Rtes. 12 and 119, Fitzwilliam, tel. 603/585–9092).

Peterborough Antiques (76 Grove St., Peterborough, tel. 603/924–7297).

The Antique Shops (Rte. 12, Westmoreland, tel. 603/399–7039).

Galleries **North Gallery at Tewksbury's** (Rte. 101E, Peterborough, tel. 603/924–3224) has a wide selection of gifts and local handcrafts.

Sharon Arts Center (Rte. 123, Sharon, tel. 603/924–7256) is affiliated with the League of New Hampshire Craftsmen. Classes, shows, gallery, and a large shop are located on a pretty back road south of Peterborough.

Mall **Colony Mill Marketplace** (West St., Keene, tel. 603/357–1240) is a warren of boutiques, specialty stores, galleries, and cafés a few steps from the center of town. The shops include **Country Artisans** (tel. 603/352–6980), which carries art and handcrafts including stoneware, textiles, prints, and baskets. **Harrisville Designs** (tel. 603/827–3996) is a branch of the Harrisville weaving center specializing in finished clothing and decorative art; here you can also buy yarns and order looms. **Joe Jones Ski & Sport Shop** (tel. 603/352–5266) has sports gear as well as outdoor sportswear for men and women. **Toadstool Bookshop** (tel. 603/352–8815) has a particularly strong selection of children's books, but offers a variety of good reading material and art books. **Ye Goodie Shoppe** (tel. 603/352–0236) was founded in 1931 and has been handmaking chocolates ever since.

Sports and Outdoor Activities

In addition to the normal outdoor activities in the hills, forests, and mountains, horse-drawn sleigh and hay rides are seasonal pleasures hereabouts. Two providers are **Stonewall Farm** (Keene, tel. 603/357–7278) and **Silver Ranch, Inc.** (Jaffrey, tel. 603/532–7363).

Biking The rolling hills and low-traffic back roads make this an especially good region for bikers. The 45-mile **Covered Bridge Loop** is especially suited to biking. From Keene, follow Route 10 south to Swanzey, then take back roads, seeking out the six covered bridges (*see* Exploring the Monadnock Region, above). For planned routes throughout the Monadnock, contact the **Greater Keene Chamber of Commerce** (8 Central Sq., Keene 03431, tel. 603/352–1303). **The Biking Expedition** (10 Maple St., Box 547, Henniker 03242, tel. 603/428–7500) designs teenage bicycle camping/hosteling trips. For organized bike rides in southern New Hampshire contact the **Granite State Wheelmen** (16 Clinton St., Salem 03079, tel. 603/898–9926).

Camping Greenfield, Mt. Monadnock, and Surry Mountain Dam state parks have campsites, as do **Field 'n Forest Recreation Area** (Rte. 137, RFD 1, Box 750, Hancock 03449, tel. 603/526–3568) and **Forest Lake Campground** (Rte. 10, Winchester, tel. 603/239–4267). A complete list of private, state, and national-forest campgrounds is available from the **New Hampshire Campground Owners Association** (Box 320, Twin Mountain 03595, tel. 603/846–5511).

Fishing There are more than 200 lakes and ponds in the Monadnock. Dublin Pond, Dublin, has lake trout. Goose Pond, West Canaan, has smallmouth bass and white perch. Rainbow and golden trout, pickerel, and horned pout are found in Laurel Lake, Fitzwilliam; and there are rainbow and brown trout in the Ashuelot River. For word on what's biting and where, contact the Department of Fish and Game (2 Hazen Dr., Concord 03301, tel. 603/271–3211).

Hiking Trails may be found at **Crotched Mountain** (Francestown and Greenfield), **Drummer Hill Preserve** (Keene), **Fox State Forest** (Hillsboro), **Horatio Colony Trust** (Keene), **Sheiling Forest** (Peterborough), and **Wapack Reservation** (Greenfield). The **Harris Conservation Center** (Hancock, tel. 603/525–3394) and the **Monadnock Ecocenter** (Jaffrey, tel. 603/525–4073) sponsor guided walks.

Rafting White-water rafting is a springtime thrill, as you chase the runoff of melting snow in a canoe or rubber raft. For the Contoocook River, regular trips start at the **White Birch Community Center** in Henniker.

State Parks

Parks and recreation areas are more varied in the Monadnock than in any other region of New Hampshire. Consider **Bear Den Geological Park** (Gilsum) a 19th-century mining town surrounded by more than 50 abandoned mines; **Chesterfield Gorge**, a wilderness area conveniently located along busy Route 9; **Curtiss Dogwood State Reservation** (Lyndeborough, off Rte. 31), where the blossoms are out in early May; **Pisgah State Park** (off Rte. 63 or Rte. 119), a 13,000-acre wilderness area full of wild game; and **Rhododendron State Park** (north of Fitzwilliam), with the largest stand of *rhododendron maximum* north of the Alleghenies.

Dining

Restaurants are small (many of them no more than cafés) and cookery simple in the Monadnock.

★ **Maitre Jacq.** The building is putty-colored and plain; the food provincial French; and the owner and chef, a native of Brittany, is likely to ask whether you're enjoying your meal. The bouillabaisse contains lobster, monkfish, shrimp, mussels, clams, and more than a dozen other ingredients. Prix-fixe and five-course tasting dinners seem an illusion in an isolated setting where even Francestown is 2 miles away. *Mountain Rd. at Rte. 47, Francestown, tel. 603/588–6655. Reservations advised. Dress: casual but neat. MC, V. Closed Mon. Expensive.*

The Ram in the Thicket. Either of the small, intimate dining areas in this formal Federal house lends romance to the Continental menu. The appetizer-of-the-day might be sautéed olives, onion, and tomatoes. The filet mignon is prepared to order, and the lamb is cooked to a slightly pink, French turn. *Rte. 101 near Wilton, tel. 603/654–6440. Reservations advised. Dress: casual but neat. AE, MC, V. No lunch. Expensive.*

Chesterfield Inn. This upstairs dining room is candlelit and romantic, the fare somewhere between Continental and new American—that is, light. *Rte. 9, West Chesterfield, tel. 603/ 256–3211. Reservations advised. Dress: casual but neat. MC, V. Closed Mon., Tues. Moderate–Expensive.*

Del Rossi's. This is a pasta-plus Italian trattoria, with good bread, salad, ravioli, and fettuccine. Homemade pasta and live entertainment on weekends make this hilltop restaurant irresistible to the thirty- and forty-somethings. *Rtes. 137 and 101, Dublin, tel. 603/563–7195. Reservations advised. Dress: casual but neat. AE, MC, V. Moderate.*

Fitzwilliam Inn. As in any good Yankee household, you will be served a heaping plate and at least two kinds of home-baked bread, along with vegetables, salad, and dessert, all for one price. Black Diamond steaks and roast leg of lamb are typical of the hearty entrées; apple pie or carrot cake top them off. *The Green, Fitzwilliam, tel. 603/585–9000. Reservations advised. Dress: casual but neat. AE, DC, MC, V. Moderate.*

Birchwood Inn. She-crab soup and roast duckling are two Saturday-night specials, and you might be lucky enough to find the cream-cheese pecan pie on the blackboard dessert menu any night at all. Everything is cooked to order, so allow time for lingering. *Rte. 45, Temple, tel. 603/878–3285. Reservations required. Dress: casual. No credit cards. BYOB. No lunch. Closed Sun.–Mon. Inexpensive–Moderate.*

★ **Henry David's.** The restaurant is a tribute to its namesake, Henry David Thoreau, who never dined here but who would have enjoyed the greenery and the simple but well-prepared food. Crab bisque is a frequent soup of the day, and tomato cheddar is a regular. Scrod with lemon-thyme crumbs; baked chicken with apple-brandy sauce; and full-meal-size salads are usually on the menu. Choose from a long list of sandwiches; try a cup of chili served with honey-wheat bread and butter; or sample a boursin cheese and fresh-fruit board with sweet bread and crackers. *81 Main St., Keene, tel. 603/352–0608. Reservations accepted. Dress: casual. MC, V. Inexpensive–Moderate.*

Latacarta. Put a New Age restaurant in an old movie theater and you get the essence of Peterborough. Offered here are chicken, fish, and a pasta of the day in addition to classic vegetarian dishes. A small indoor café serves late lunches, light dinners, and between-meal bites. Everything is fresh and organic; salt-free and reduced-calorie dishes are available on request. You can read the Thoreau quotes on the menu while you wait. *6 School St., Peterborough, tel. 603/924–6878. Reservations advised. Dress: casual but neat. AE, MC, V. Closed Mon. Inexpensive–Moderate.*

Lodging

The basic lodging of the region remains the village inn, and it is often the best place to eat as well. B&Bs in the Monadnock are among the best anywhere. The **Monadnock Bed and Breakfast Association** (Box 236, Jaffrey 03452, tel. 603/585–6540) prepares a brochure describing the facilities of its members, but the association is not a booking agency.

★ **Chesterfield Inn.** The Federal period in American domestic architecture was more than a touch elegant, as this 1781 home well illustrates. The inn sits on a rise above the main Brattleboro–Keene road, surrounded by rose, herb, and wildflower gardens. Rooms have been appropriately furnished with armoires, fine antiques, and period fabrics. You may ask for a fireplace or a balcony and have your wish granted. *Rte. 9, West Chesterfield 03466, tel. 603/256–3211. 7 rooms with bath. Facilities: restaurant, some whirlpool baths. AE, DC, MC, V. Expensive.*

Birchwood Inn. Thoreau slept here, probably on his way to climb Monadnock or to visit Jaffrey or Peterborough. In 1825 Rufus Porter painted the mural in the dining room. Country furniture and handmade quilts outfit the bedrooms, as they did in 1775 when the house was new and no one dreamed it would someday be listed in the National Register of Historic Places. *Rte. 45, Temple 03084, tel. 603/878–3285. 7 rooms with bath. Facilities: restaurant, cable TV in sitting room, piano. No pets. No credit cards. Rates include full breakfast. Moderate.*

Inn at Crotched Mountain. The inn is at the base of the ski area, but outdoor activities are not limited to winter. Hikers, swimmers, tennis players, and even volleyball players are accommodated along with those who want to rest and read. The original farmhouse burned in 1930, but the rebuilding was in the spirit of the old. Ask what rooms are available when you reserve, as they vary in size and location. *Mountain Rd., Francestown 03043, tel. 603/588–6840. 14 rooms with bath. Facilities: restaurant, pool, tennis, volleyball, cross-country skiing. No credit cards. Closed Apr.–mid-May, Nov. Rates include breakfast or are MAP. Moderate.*

Inn at East Hill Farm. It could be called a farm-resort, and it is definitely a family affair. The owners met here as working college students and have owned the 1830 inn for 30 years. Children are not only welcome, they are planned-for; the chef will cook the eggs they gather. Finicky eaters can always order a hamburger or hotdog if they don't like what's on the menu. Hayrides or sleigh rides are offered once a week. Picnic lunches are available on request—or how about a cookout? Almost anything you want in an easygoing family vacation is available here. *Mountain Rd., Troy 03465, tel. 603/242–6495. 23 rooms with bath. Facilities: restaurant, boating, cable TV, farm activities, fishing, pool, sauna, tennis. No credit cards. Rates include 3 meals. Moderate.*

John Hancock Inn. The oldest operating inn in New Hampshire dates from 1789 and is the pride of its historically preserved town. The dining room serves Yankee fare by candlelight, and the rubbed natural woodwork throughout the house is a tribute to centuries past. *Main St., Hancock 03447, tel. 603/525–3318. 10 rooms with bath. Facilities: restaurant, lounge, bicycles. AE, MC, V. Moderate.*

Partridge Brook Inn. Built in 1790, this historic house was once a tavern and a stop on the Underground Railroad. Boating, fishing, golf, hiking, horseback riding, tennis, and skiing are all nearby. Original fireplaces, wide-board floors, and stenciling give you a sense of the past. Rooms have views of the valley and are furnished with country antiques and collectible handwork. *Box 151, Westmoreland 03467, tel. 603/399–4994. 5 rooms with bath. MC, V. Rates include full breakfast. Moderate.*

Salzburg Inn. From schnitzel in the dining room to alpine and cross-country skiing nearby, there's a lot of Austria in this well-named inn. It was once a governor's estate, but motel rooms have long since been added, and you have your choice of old or new sleeping quarters. Whichever you choose, you'll find Tyrolean touches in the rooms and enjoy sweeping views across the 146-acre property. *Steele Rd., Peterborough 03458, tel. 603/ 924–3808. 26 rooms with bath. Facilities: restaurant, pool, cable TV. AE, MC, V. Moderate.*

Thatcher Hill Inn. What began as a farmhouse in 1794, was enlarged between 1890 and 1915 and totally renovated in 1985. Handmade quilts cover the beds, and guests can enjoy the reclining comfort of clawfoot bathtubs and with heated towel bars. Scatter rugs are used because the floors are too beautiful to hide. Large, sunny rooms look beyond the inn's own 60 acres of rolling hills to Mt. Monadnock. *Thatcher Hill Rd., Marlborough 03455, tel. 603/876–3361. 7 rooms with bath. Facilities: wheelchair access. No pets. No smoking. MC, V. Rates include buffet Continental breakfast and all taxes. Moderate.*

★ **Amos Parker House.** The original structure (now the great room and kitchen) must have been one of the earliest in the village, and from the front windows just off the green, the owners could watch Fitzwilliam grow. Now six fireplaces spread warmth in winter; a deck and flower garden make the most of summer. Wide pine-board floors show around the edges of Oriental rugs. *Rte. 119, Box 202, Fitzwilliam 03447, tel. 603/585– 6540. 6 rooms, 4 with bath. No pets. No smoking. No credit cards. Rates include full breakfast and all taxes. Inexpensive– Moderate.*

Carriage Barn Guest House. The location, on Main Street across from Keene State College, puts everything within walking distance. The barn-cum-house is furnished with antiques mostly from this area, and the operational word is "comfortable." *358 Main St., Keene 03431, tel. 603/357–3812. 4 rooms with bath. Facilities: cable TV. No pets. No smoking. No credit cards. Rates include breakfast. Inexpensive.*

★ **Fitzwilliam Inn.** Vermont Transit buses from Boston's Logan Airport stop at the door, just as the stagecoach once did. Indoors, too, much remains as it was in 1796. Local residents dally in the tavern, and the restaurant serves Yankee cooking. Upstairs in the rooms the furniture is a hodgepodge of early and late hand-me-downs. The imperfections suggest that this is how inns really were in bygone times. *The Green, Fitzwilliam 03447, tel. 603/585–9000. 20 rooms, 17 with bath. Facilities: restaurant, bar, pool, cross-country ski trail. AE, DC, MC, V. Inexpensive.*

The Arts

Leisure Weekly, available Thursday at shops and chambers of commerce, has arts listings for southwestern New Hampshire.

The Art Center at Brickyard Pond (Keene, tel. 603/357–4041) is the Monadnock's center for music and dance, with performances year round in a modern facility.

Music **Monadnock Music** (Box 255, Peterborough 03458, tel. 603/924– 7610) produces concerts by the Temple Town Band (founded 1799), the Apple Hill Chamber Players, and other groups in summer.

Theater **Summer Theater at Brickyard Pond** (Keene, tel. 603/357–4041) and the **Peterborough Players** (Stearns Farm, Middle Hancock Rd., Peterborough, tel. 603/924–7585) perform in summer.

Nightlife

Colonial Theater (95 Main St., Keene, tel. 603/352–2033) has folk, rock, and jazz acts.

The Folkway (85 Grove St., Peterborough, tel. 603/924–7484), a small New Age café, offers international folk performances.

8 Maine

by David Laskin, with an introduction by William G. Scheller

The travel writings of David Laskin have appeared in the New York Times and Travel and Leisure, and 1990 saw publication of his book Eastern Islands: Accessible Islands of the East Coast.

If any two individuals can be associated d rectly with the disparate images evoked by the very mention of the state of Maine, they are George Bush and Carolyn Chute.

President Bush is the most famous summer resident of Kennebunkport, where he and his family vacation in his grandfather's rambling seaside mansion. Having a summer White House on the Maine coast reminds Americans that this craggy, wildly irregular stretch of shoreline has long enjoyed an aristocratic cachet: Here Nelson Rockefeller was born in the millionaires' enclave at Bar Harbor; here the Brahmin historian Samuel Eliot Morison sailed the cold waters of Frenchman Bay; and here, at Campobello Island on the Canadian border, Franklin D. Roosevelt spent summers as a young man. In those times, anyone living on the coast of Maine who wasn't rich, famous, or powerful was almost certainly an old-stock yeoman, probably someone with a lobster boat.

Carolyn Chute is the novelist who wrote *The Beans of Egypt, Maine.* Chute's fictional Egypt and its inhabitants are a reminder that Appalachia stretches far to the north of the Cumberland Gap and that not far inland from the famous rockbound coast there are places where rusting house trailers are far more common than white Federalist sea captains' mansions.

In fact, neither stereotype (and both have strong foundations in fact) makes a serious dent in the task of defining or explaining Maine. Reality in most of the state resembles neither a cross between a Ralph Lauren ad and a Winslow Homer painting nor a milieu in which modern history dates from the day they began renting videos at the gas station.

Maine is by far the largest state in New England. At its extremes it measures 300 miles north to south and 200 miles across; Connecticut and Rhode Island together could fit into Aroostook, its northernmost county. There is an expansiveness to Maine, a sense of real distance between places that hardly exists elsewhere in the region, and along with the sheer size and spread of the place there is a tremendous variety of terrain. One speaks of "coastal" Maine and "inland" Maine, as though the state could be summed up under the twin emblems of lobsters and pine trees. Yet the state's topography and character are a good deal more complicated.

Even the coast is several places in one. South of the rapidly gentrifying city of Portland, resort towns such as Ogunquit, Kennebunkport, and Old Orchard Beach (sometimes called the Quebec Riviera because of its popularity with French Canadians) predominate along a reasonably smooth shoreline. Development has been considerable; north of Portland and Casco Bay, secondary roads turn south off Route 1 onto so many oddly chiseled peninsulas that it's possible to drive for days without retracing your route and to conclude that motels, discount outlets, and fried-clam stands are taking over the domain of presidents and lobstermen. Freeport is an entity unto itself, a place where a bewildering assortment of off-price, name-brand outlets has sprung up around the famous outfitter L. L. Bean (no relation to the Egypt clan).

Inland Maine likewise defies characterization. For one thing, a good part of it is virtually uninhabited. This is the land Henry David Thoreau wrote about in *The Maine Woods* nearly 150 years ago; aside from having been logged over several times, much of it hasn't changed since Thoreau and his Indian guides passed through. Ownership of vast portions of northern Maine by forest products corporations has kept out subdivision and development; many of the roads here are private, open to travel only by permit. The north woods' day of reckoning may be coming, however, for the paper companies plan to sell off millions of acres in a forested belt that reaches all the way to the Adirondacks in New York State. In the 1990s state governments and environmental organizations will be working to preserve as much as possible of the great silent expanses of pine.

Logging the north created the culture of the mill towns, the Rumfords, Skowhegans, and Bangors that lay at the end of the old river drives. The logs arrive by truck today, but Maine's harvested wilderness still feeds the mills and the nation's hunger for paper.

Our hunger for potatoes has given rise to an entirely different Maine culture, in one of the most isolated agricultural regions of the country. Northeastern Aroostook County is where the Maine potatoes come from, and this place, too, is changing. In what was once called the Potato Empire, farmers are as pressed between high costs and low prices as any of their counterparts in the Midwest; add to the bleak economic picture a growing national preference for Idaho baking potatoes rather than the traditional small, round Maine boiling potatoes, and Aroostook's troubles are compounded. Some farmers have gone out of business; a few have turned to farming broccoli. Recently the last school board to permit the harvest recess abolished this period during which high school students would help bring in the crop.

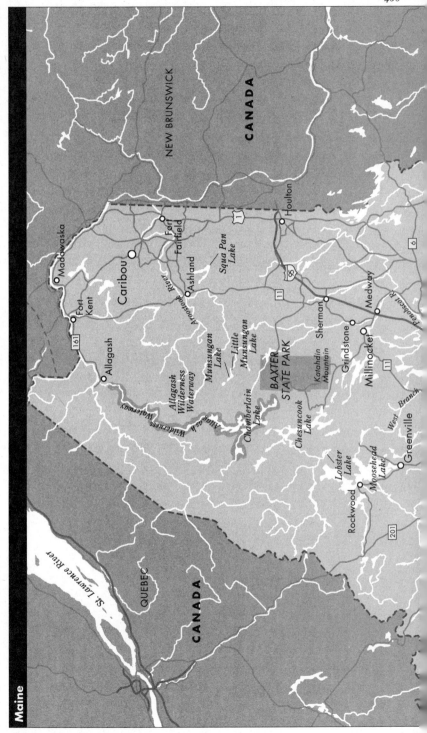

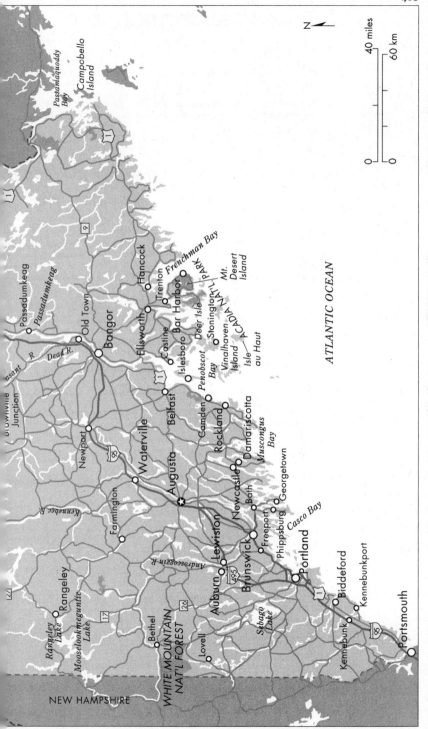

Essential Information

Visitor Information

Maine Publicity Bureau (97 Winthrop St., Hallowell 04347, tel. 207/289–2423 or 800/533–9595).

Maine Innkeepers Association (142 Free St., Portland 04101, tel. 207/773–7670) publishes a statewide lodging and dining guide.

Tour Groups

Beckham Reception Services (587 Washington St., Canton, MA 02021, tel. 617/821–5990 or 800/343–4323) runs a clambake group tour to the Bar Harbor area and other general-interest tours.

Golden Age Festival (5501 New Jersey Ave., Wildwood Crest, NJ 08260, tel. 609/522–6316 or 800/257–8920) offers a four-night bus tour geared to senior citizens, with shopping at Kittery outlets and L. L. Bean, a Boothbay Harbor boat cruise, and stops at Pemaquid Point, Mt. Battie, and Acadia National Park.

Paragon Tours (680 Purchase St., Box B977, New Bedford, MA 02741, tel. 800/999–5050) has three-day and four-day bus tours of the coast that include Camden, Boothbay Harbor, and Acadia National Park; lobster bake and boating cruises are part of the tour.

When to Go

Although July and August are peak season, Maine is at its best after Labor Day: The crowds thin out, foggy days are less common on the coast, and by the end of September the first scarlets and oranges are blazing in the foliage. The coast remains temperate into late October. November and early December are hunting season, and if you're not hunting, you won't want to venture into the woods. The compensation for Maine's long, harsh winters is skiing and endless snowmobiling. Spring, which brings mud to the north and blackflies everywhere, is generally Maine's least appealing season, although it's also a time of solitude, lilacs, and off-season rates.

Festivals and Seasonal Events

Mid-Feb.: Western Mountain Winter Wonderland Week at Sunday River Resort is the second week of the month. *Tel. 207/824–2187.*
Early Mar.: Ice-Fishing Tournament on Moosehead Lake near Rockwood begins the first Sunday. *Tel. 207/534–7300.*
Mid-Mar.: Rangeley Lake Sled Dog Races draws crowds on the second weekend of the month. *Tel. 207/864–5364.*
Late Mar.: On **Maine Maple Sunday,** the third Sunday in March, maple sugarhouses open their doors to visitors. *Tel. 207/289–3491.*
Mid-Apr.: Boothbay Harbor Fishermen's Festival takes place on the second weekend of the month. *Tel. 207/633–4008.*

Mid-June: Old Port Festival sees street performers and sales at Portland's Old Port on the second Saturday. *Tel. 207/772–6828.*

Late June: Maine Storytellers Festival gathers the tallest tale tellers at the Rockport Opera House on the last weekend in June. *Tel. 207/773–4909.*

Early July: The **Great Schooner Regatta** brings sailboats to Penobscot Bay on the Friday after July 4. *Tel. 207/596–0376.*

Mid-July: Boothbay Harbor Windjammer Days, the second week of July, is high season for the boating set. *Tel. 207/633–2353.*

July–Aug.: Bar Harbor Music Festival hosts classical and popular music concerts. *Tel. 212/222–1026.*

Late July: Camden Garden House Tour, on the third Thursday, shows fine houses and gardens in Camden and Rockport. *Tel. 207/236–4404.*

July–Aug.: Bangor State Fair, a true country fair, fills Bass Park from the last weekend in July through the first week in August. *Tel. 207/942–9000.*

Early Aug.: Maine Lobster Festival, Rockland, is a public feast held on the first weekend of the month. *Tel. 207/596–0376.*

Late Aug.: Rangeley Lakes Blueberry Festival takes place on the Rangeley Inn Green on the third Thursday. *Tel. 207/864–3334.*

Early Sept.: Blue Hill Fair—horse races, rides, auctions—is Labor Day weekend at the fairgrounds.

Mid-Sept.: International Seaplane Fly-In Weekend sets Moosehead Lake buzzing on the weekend after Labor Day. *Tel. 207/695–2702.*

Late Sept.: Tour D'Acadia, a 25-mile bike race through the park, begins in Bar Harbor on the last Sunday. *Tel. 207/288–3511.*

Early Oct.: Blue Mountain Arts & Crafts Festival takes place at Sunday River Resort on Columbus Day weekend. *Tel. 207/824–2187.*

Early Oct.: Maine Antiquarian Booksellers Fair fills the Portland Holiday Inn with books on the Sunday of Columbus Day weekend. *Tel. 207/799–1889.*

Early Dec.: Christmas Prelude brings suppers, concerts, and shopping opportunities to Kennebunkport on the first weekend.

What to Pack

Maine nights can be cool even in July and August, so you will always want to have a sweater or a heavy sweatshirt. For summer days, which are usually warm, shorts, bathing suit, and suntan lotion are in order. Rain gear is essential. When you plan a boat ride, be prepared for chilly winds and salt spray: Be sure you have extra shoes, a waterproof windbreaker, a hat, and an extra sweater. If you'll be walking in the woods, bring heavy boots and expect to encounter mud. Wool, which will keep you warm even when it's wet, is best for winter sports, camping, and hunting trips. In remote areas clothing is still hung to dry outdoors; since nothing dries in the fog, and the fog can hang in for days at a stretch, you'll want extra clothing if you plan a long visit. Only the very posh resorts and restaurants expect a jacket at dinner.

Arriving and Departing

By Plane Maine's major airports are **Portland International Jetport** (tel. 207/774–7301) and **Bangor International Airport** (tel. 207/947–0384); each has scheduled daily flights by major U.S. carriers.

Auburn/Lewiston Municipal Airport (tel. 207/786–0631), 5 miles southwest of the city, is the principal airport in that region, with flights by Northeast Express Regional (tel. 800/322–1008).

Bar Harbor Airport (tel. 207/667–7329), 8 miles northwest of the city, is served by Continental Express (tel. 800/525–0280) and Northeast Express Regional.

Knox County Regional Airport (tel. 207/594–4131), 3 miles south of Rockland, has flights by Northeast Express Regional.

By Car Interstate 95 is the fastest route to and through the state from coastal New Hampshire and points south, turning inland at Brunswick and going on to Bangor and the Canadian border. Route 1, more leisurely and more scenic, is the principal coastal highway from New Hampshire to Canada.

By Train Canada's **VIA Rail** (Box 8116, 2 Place Ville-Marie, Montreal, Quebec, tel. 800/361–3677) provides Maine's only passenger rail service. The run between Montreal and Halifax crosses the center of the state, stopping at Jackman, Greenville, Brownville Junction, Mattawamkeag, Danforth, and Vanceboro.

By Bus **Greyhound Lines** (tel. 800/237–8211) and **Vermont Transit** (tel. 207/772–6587) connect towns in southwestern Maine with cities in New England and throughout the United States.

By Boat **Marine Atlantic** (tel. 800/341–7981) operates ferry service between Yarmouth, Nova Scotia, and Bar Harbor; **Prince of Fundy Cruises** (tel. 800/341–7540) operates ferry service between Yarmouth and Portland (May–October only).

Getting Around Maine

By Plane Regional flying services, operating from the regional and municipal airports, provide access to remote lakes and wilderness areas.

By Car In many areas of the state a car is the only practical means of travel. The Maine Map and Guide, available free from offices of the Maine Publicity Bureau, is useful for driving throughout the state; it has directories, mileage charts, and enlarged maps of city areas.

By Boat **Casco Bay Lines** (tel. 207/774–7871) provides ferry service from Portland to the islands of Casco Bay, and **Maine State Ferry Service** (tel. 207/594–5543) provides ferry service from Rockland to Penobscot Bay.

Shopping

The success of L. L. Bean, Maine's retail phenomenon, has fostered the growth of a great retail marketplace in the Freeport area, with scores of factory outlets and specialty stores selling all manner of goods. Kennebunkport, Wells, Searsport, and Bridgton have concentrations of antiques shops. During the

summer months, yard sales and flea markets abound on coastal
Route 1.

Sports and Outdoor Activities

Biking The back roads around the coastal towns are ideal for biking,
and the biking is especially scenic near Kennebunkport and
Camden, on the peninsula where Castine and Blue Hill are situated, and on Deer Isle. The carriage paths in Acadia National
Park make ideal bike routes. Maine Publicity Bureau publishes
a statewide list of bike rentals, and **Maine Coast Cyclers** (Camden, tel. 207/236–8608) can provide further information on
biking in Maine.

Boating and Motorboats and sailboats may be rented at most towns on the
Sailing coast, including Kennebunkport, Boothbay Harbor, Rockland,
Camden, and Bar Harbor. Penobscot Bay has some of the most
splendid cruising grounds on the East Coast, particularly in
Eggemoggin Reach and the waters between Camden and
Islesboro and Castine and Islesboro.

Camping Maine Publicity Bureau and the **Maine Campground Owners
Association** (655 Main St., Lewiston 04240, tel. 207/782–5874)
have information about private campgrounds in Maine.

Fishing and Maine's north woods are a mecca for fisherfolk and hunters,
Hunting with abundant trout and salmon; deer, moose, bear, and game
birds. **Maine Department of Inland Fisheries and Wildlife** (284
State St., Augusta 04333, tel. 207/289–2043) has the latest information on regulations and seasons.

Golf Kennebunkport, Portland, Boothbay, Camden, Castine, Bar
Harbor, Bethel, Rangeley, and Sugarloaf all have fine golf
courses. The Bethel Inn and Country Club, the Samoset Resort
in Rockport, and the Country Club Inn in Rangeley are good
choices for serious golfers, since all have fairway accommodations. Maine Publicity Bureau publishes a guide to the state's
golf courses.

Hiking Acadia National Park and the White Mountains National Forest have the largest variety and the most interesting hiking
trails.

Skiing *The skiing facilities of Maine are reviewed in Chapter 2, Skiing
New England.*

Beaches

Maine's ocean is beautiful to behold, but to swim in it for very
long you'd need the constitution of a polar bear. Water is warmest south of Portland, and the resort towns of York, Ogunquit,
Wells, Kennebunk Beach, and Old Orchard Beach have long
sandy beaches open to the public. Reid and Popham Beach state
parks have fine stretches of sandy beach, and both attract lots
of families. There is a small sand beach in Acadia National Park;
and lake beaches at Sebago Lake State Park and Rangeley
Lake State Park have refreshing swimming, not too cold, in
late July and August.

National and State Parks

National Park **Acadia National Park** (Box 177, Bar Harbor 04609, tel. 207/288–
3338), which preserves fine stretches of shoreline and the high-

est mountains along the East Coast, covers much of Mount Desert Island and more than half of Isle au Haut and Schoodic Point on the mainland. Camping is permitted at designated campgrounds; hiking, biking, and boat cruises are the most popular activities. Isle au Haut, accessible by mailboat, is the least crowded section; the loop road on Mount Desert is the busiest.

State Parks   **Baxter State Park** (64 Balsam Dr., Millinocket 04462, tel. 207/723–5140) comprises more than 200,000 acres of wilderness surrounding Katahdin, Maine's highest mountain. Campgrounds are located both at sites near the park's dirt road and in remote backcountry sections; reservations are strongly recommended. Hiking and moose-watching are major activities at Baxter.

The **Allagash Wilderness Waterway** (Maine Department of Conservation, Bureau of Parks and Recreation, State House Station 22, Augusta 04333, tel. 207/289–3821 May–Oct.; 207/723–8518 Nov.–Apr.) is a 92-mile corridor of lakes and rivers surrounded by vast commercial forest property. Canoeing the Allagash is a highly demanding activity that requires advance planning and the ability to handle white water. Guides are recommended for novice canoers. Reservations are not taken for campsites.

White Mountain National Forest (Evans Notch Ranger District, RFD 2, Box 2270, Bethel 04217, tel. 207/824–2134) has camping areas in rugged mountain locations, hiking trails, and picnic areas.

Other major state parks in Maine include **Camden Hills State Park** (tel. 207/236–3109), with hiking and camping; **Crescent Beach State Park** (Rte. 77, Cape Elizabeth, tel. 207/767–3625), with a good sand beach and picnic area; **Grafton Notch State Park** (north of Bethel), with spectacular White Mountain scenery, hiking, and picnic area; **Lamoine State Park** (Rte. 184, 8 mi from Ellsworth), with camping and swimming on Blue Hill Bay near Acadia; **Lily Bay State Park** (Moosehead Lake, tel. 207/695–2700), with lakeside camping, boat ramps, and a hiking trail; **Popham Beach State Park** (Rte. 209 near Phippsburg, tel. 207/389–1335), with a sand beach and picnic area; **Rangeley Lake State Park** (tel. 207/864–3858), with lakeside camping, boat ramps, showers, and swimming beach; **Reid State Park** (Rte. 127, tel. 207/371–2303), with a large sand swimming beach; and **Sebago Lake State Park** (Rte. 302, Naples, tel. 207/693–6613), with nature trails, boat ramp, sand beach, and camping.

Dining

For most visitors Maine means lobster, and lobster can be found on the menus of a majority of Maine restaurants. As a general rule, the closer you are to a working harbor, the fresher your lobster will be. Aficionados eschew ordering lobster in restaurants, preferring to eat them "in the rough" at classic lobster pounds, where you select your lobster swimming in a pool and enjoy it at a waterside picnic table. Shrimp and crab are also caught in the cold waters off Maine, and the better restaurants in Portland and the coastal resort towns prepare the shellfish in creative combinations with lobster, haddock, salmon, and swordfish. Blueberries are grown commercially in Maine, and Maine cooks use them generously in pancakes, muffins, pies, and cobblers. Full country breakfasts of fruit, eggs, breakfast meats, pancakes, and muffins are commonly served at inns and bed-and-breakfasts.

Highly recommended restaurants in each price category are indicated by a star ★ .

Category	Cost*
Very Expensive	over $35
Expensive	$25–$35
Moderate	$15–$25
Inexpensive	under $15

average cost of a three-course dinner, per person, excluding drinks, service, and 5% sales tax

Lodging

Bed-and-breakfasts and Victorian inns furnished with lace, chintz, and mahogany have joined the family-oriented motels of Ogunquit, Boothbay Harbor, Bar Harbor, and the Camden region. Two world-class resorts with good health club and sports facilities are on the coast near Portland and on Penobscot Bay. Although accommodations tend to be more rustic away from the coast, Bethel, Center Lovell, and Rangeley offer sophisticated hotels and inns. In the far north the best alternative to camping is to stay in a rustic wilderness camp, several of which serve hearty meals.

At many of Maine's larger hotels and inns with restaurants, Modified American Plan (includes breakfast and dinner) is either an option or required during the peak summer season. In general, when MAP is optional, hotels give dinner credits of $20 per guest.

Highly recommended lodgings in each price category are indicated by a star ★ .

Category	Cost*
Very Expensive	over $100
Expensive	$80–$100
Moderate	$60–$80
Inexpensive	under $60

All prices are for a standard double room for two during peak season, with no meals unless noted and excluding 5% sales tax.

The Coast: North from Kittery

Maine's southernmost coastal towns won't give you the rugged, windbitten "downeast" experience, but they offer all the amenities, they are easy to drive to from the south, and most have the sand beaches that all but vanish beyond Portland.

Kittery, which lacks a large sand beach, hosts a complex of factory outlets. North of Kittery the Maine coast has long stretches of hard-packed white-sand beach, closely crowded by nearly unbroken ranks of beach cottages, motels, and ocean-front restaurants. The summer colonies of York Beach, Ogunquit, and Wells Beach have the crowds and the ticky-tack of shorefront overdevelopment. Farther inland, York's historic district is on the National Register.

More than any other region south of Portland, the Kennebunks—and especially Kennebunkport—offer the complete Maine coast experience: classic townscapes where perfectly proportioned white-clapboard houses rise from manicured lawns and gardens; rocky shorelines punctuated by sandy beaches, beach motels, and cottages; quaint downtown districts packed with gift shops, ice-cream stands, and tourists; harbors where lobster boats bob alongside yachts; lobster pounds and well-appointed dining rooms. The range of accommodations includes rambling Victorian-era hotels, beachside family motels, and inns.

Important Addresses and Numbers

Visitor Information **Kennebunk-Kennebunkport Chamber of Commerce** (Cooper's Corner, Rtes. 9 and 35, tel. 207/967–0857).

Kittery Tourist Information Center (Rte. 1 and I–95, tel. 207/439–1319).

Ogunquit Chamber of Commerce (Box 2289, Ogunquit, tel. 207/646–2939).

The Yorks Chamber of Commerce (Box 417, York, tel. 207/363–4422).

Emergencies **Maine State Police** (Scarborough, tel. 207/883–3473).

Kennebunk Walk-in Clinic (Rte. 1 N, tel. 207/985–6027).

Southern Maine Medical Center (1 Mountain Rd., Biddeford, tel. 207/283–3663).

Getting Around North from Kittery

By Car Route 1 from Kittery will take you touring through the area; I–95 should be faster for travelers headed for specific towns: Exit 1 for York, Exit 2 for Wells and Ogunquit, Exit 3 (and Route 35) for Kennebunk and Kennebunkport. Route 9 goes from Kennebunkport to Cape Porpoise and Goose Rocks.

By Trolley A trolley circulates among the Yorks, June to Labor Day. Four trolleys serve the major tourist areas and beaches of Ogunquit, Memorial Day to Columbus Day. The trolley from Dock Square in Kennebunkport to Kennebunk Beach runs from late June to Labor Day.

Exploring North from Kittery

Numbers in the margin correspond with the numbered points of interest on the Southern Maine Coast map.

❶ Our tour of the Maine coast begins at **Kittery,** just across the New Hampshire border, off I–95 on Route 1. Kittery will be of most interest to shoppers headed for its factory outlet stores.

❷ Beyond Kittery, Route 1 heads north to **the Yorks,** and a right
onto Route 1A (York Street) leads to the **York Village Historic
District,** where a number of 18th- and 19th-century buildings
have been restored and maintained by the Old York Historical
Society. Most of the buildings are clustered along York Street
and Lindsay Road, and you can buy an admission ticket for all
the buildings at the Jefferds Tavern (Rte. 1A and Lindsay
Rd.), a restored late-18th-century inn. Other historic buildings
open to the public include the Old York Gaol (1720), once the
King's Prison for the Province of Maine, which has dungeons,
cells, and jailer's quarters; and the Elizabeth Perkins House
(1731), with Victorian-era furniture that reflects the style of its
last occupants, the prominent Perkins family. The district offers tours with guides in period costumes, crafts workshops,
and special programs in summer. *Tel. 207/363–4974. Admission: $6 adults, $2.50 children 6–16, $16 family. Open mid-
June–Sept., Tues.–Sat. 10–4.*

Complete your tour of the Yorks by driving down Nubble Road
(turn right off Route 1A) to the end of Cape Neddick, where
you can park and gaze out at the Nubble Light (1879), which
sits on a tiny island just offshore. The keeper's house is a tidy
Victorian cottage with gingerbread woodwork and red shutters.

Shore Road to Ogunquit passes the 100-foot Bald Head Cliff,
which allows a view up and down the coast; on a stormy day the
surf can be quite wild here. Shore Road will take you right into
❸ **Ogunquit,** a coastal village that became a resort in the 1880s
and gained fame as an artist's colony, though few artists or actors can afford the condos and seaside cottages that now
dominate the Ogunquit seascape.

On Shore Road, the **Museum of Art of Ogunquit,** a low-lying
concrete building overlooking the ocean and set amid a three-
acre sculpture garden, shows works by Henry Strater,
Marsden Hartley, William Bailey, Gaston Lachaise, Walt
Kuhn, and Reginald Marsh. The huge windows of the sculpture
court command a view of cliffs and ocean. *Shore Rd., tel. 207/
646–4909. Admission free. Open June–Labor Day, Mon.–Sat.
10:30–5, Sun. 1–5.*

Perkins Cove, a neck of land connected to the mainland by a pedestrian drawbridge as well as a narrows, is ½ mile from the art
museum. Quaint is the only word for this jumble of sea-beaten
fish houses transformed by the tide of tourism to shops and restaurants. When you've had your fill of browsing and jostling the
crowds at Perkins Cove, stroll out along the Marginal Way, a
mile-long footpath that hugs the shore of a rocky promontory
known as Israel's Head.

❹ Follow Route 1 north through **Wells.** Five miles north of Wells,
Route 1 becomes Main Street in Kennebunk. For a sense of the
area's history and architecture, begin here at the **Brick Store
Museum.** The cornerstone of this block-long preservation of
early 19th-century commercial buildings is William Lord's
Brick Store, built as a dry-goods store in 1825 in the Federal
style, with an open-work balustrade across the roof line, granite lintels over the windows, and paired chimneys. Walking
tours of Kennebunk's National Historic Register District depart from the museum on Friday at 2, June through October.

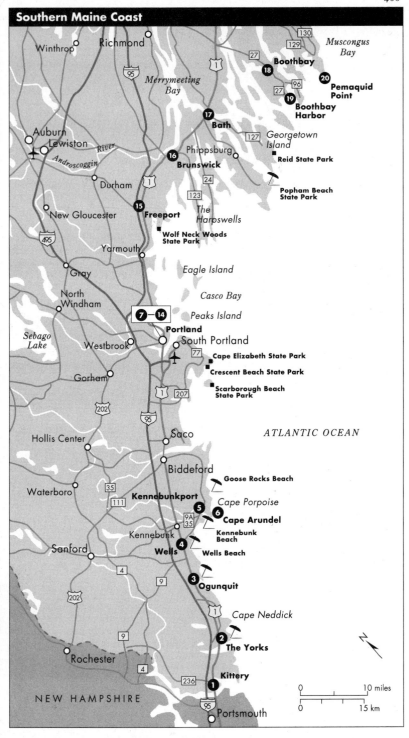

Southern Maine Coast

Winthrop
Richmond
Muscongus Bay
130
129
27
Boothbay 18
20 **Pemaquid Point**
95
Merrymeeting Bay
1
27
96
19 **Boothbay Harbor**
Auburn
Lewiston
Androscoggin River
17 **Bath**
127
Georgetown Island
Durham
Phippsburg
16 **Brunswick**
Reid State Park
1
24
New Gloucester
123
15 **Freeport**
The Harpswells
Popham Beach State Park
495
Yarmouth
■ **Wolf Neck Woods State Park**
Eagle Island
Gray
Casco Bay
North Windham
Peaks Island
7 — 14
Sebago Lake
Westbrook
Portland
■ **South Portland**
77
■ **Cape Elizabeth State Park**
Gorham
1
207
■ **Crescent Beach State Park**
202
■ **Scarborough Beach State Park**
95
Saco
ATLANTIC OCEAN
Hollis Center
Biddeford
Goose Rocks Beach
Waterboro
35
Kennebunkport
Cape Porpoise
111
5
6 **Cape Arundel**
9A 35
Kennebunk
Kennebunk Beach
Sanford
4 **Wells**
Wells Beach
4
9
3 **Ogunquit**
202
1
Cape Neddick
9
2 **The Yorks**
Rochester
4
236
1 **Kittery**
NEW HAMPSHIRE
95
Portsmouth

0   10 miles
0   15 km

117 Main St., tel. 207/985-4802. Admission: $2 adults, $1 children 6-16. Open Tues.-Sat., 10-4:30.

❺ While heading for **Kennebunkport** on Summer Street (Route 35), keep an eye out for the **Wedding Cake House** about a mile along on the left. The legend behind this confection in fancy wood fretwork is that its sea captain builder was forced to set sail in the middle of his wedding, and the house was his bride's consolation for the lack of a wedding cake. The home, built in 1826, is not open to the public.

Route 35 takes you right into Kennebunkport's **Dock Square,** the busy town center, which is lined with shops and galleries and draws crowds in the summer. Parking is tight in Kennebunkport in peak season. One possibility is the municipal lot next to the Congregational Church ($2/hour, May-Oct.); another is the Consolidated School on School Street (free, June 25-Labor Day).

When you stroll the square, walk onto the drawbridge to admire the tidal Kennebunk River. Then turn around and head up Spring Street two blocks to Maine Street and the very grand **Nott House,** known also as the White Columns, an imposing Greek Revival mansion with Doric columns that rise the height of the house. The Nott House is the gathering place for village walking tours on Tuesday and Friday mornings in July and August. *Maine St., tel. 207/967-2751. Admission: $2. Open mid-June-mid-Oct., Tues., Fri., Sat. 1-4.*

A stroll along Maine Street takes you to many fine 19th-century homes. Pearl and Green streets, off Maine Street, also have attractive homes set amid pretty gardens. A few of the grand ship captains' homes have been converted to inns.

Return to your car for a leisurely drive on Ocean Avenue, which follows the Kennebunk River to the sea and then winds around **❻** the peninsula of **Cape Arundel.** Parson's Way, a small and tranquil stretch of rocky shoreline, is open to all. As you round Cape Arundel, look to the right for the entrance to President Bush's summer home at Walker's Point.

The **Seashore Trolley Museum,** on Log Cabin Road about 3 miles from Dock Square, shows transport from classic Victorian-era horsecars to vintage 1960s streetcars and includes exhibits about the Atlantic Shore Railway, which once ran a trolley from Boston to Dock Square. Best of all, you can take a trolley ride for nearly 2 miles through woods and fields and past the museum restoration shop. *Log Cabin Rd., tel. 207/967-2712. Admission: $5.50 adults, $4.50 senior citizens, $3.50 children 6-16. Open mid-June-Labor Day, daily 10-5:30; late Apr.-mid-June, weekends for a trolley ride at 1:30; Labor Day -Oct., weekends noon-5, weekdays for a trolley ride at 1:30.*

North from Kittery for Free

Museum of Art of Ogunquit, Ogunquit.

St. Anthony Monastery and Shrine (Kennebunkport, tel. 207/967-2011), a Tudor-style Franciscan monastery, has gardens and quiet walks along the river.

What to See and Do with Children

Mariner's Playland (Rte. 1, Wells, tel. 207/646–3977) is an amusement park with go-carts, rides, miniature golf, baseball range, and arcades.

Wells Auto Museum. A must for motor fanatics as well as youngsters, the museum has 70 vintage cars, antique coin games, and a restored Model T you can ride in. *Rte. 1, tel. 207/646–9064. Admission: $3 adults, $2 children. Open mid-June–mid-Sept., daily 10–5.*

Maine Aquarium. Live sharks, seals, penguins, a petting zoo, a tide pool, snack bar, and gift shop make a busy stop on a rainy day. *Rte. 1, Saco, tel. 207/284–4511. Open June–mid-Sept., daily 9–9; mid-Sept.–May, daily 9–5.*

Seashore Trolley Museum, Kennebunkport

Shopping

Several factory outlet stores along Route 1 in Kittery and Wells offer clothing, shoes, glassware, and other products from top-of-the-line manufacturers. As an outgrowth of its longestablished art community, Ogunquit has numerous galleries, many on Shore Road. Perkins Cove in Ogunquit and Dock Square in Kennebunkport have seasonal gift shops, boutiques, and galleries.

Antiques
Kennebunk
J. J. Keating (Rte. 1, tel. 207/985–2097) deals in antiques, reproductions, and auctions.

Kennebunkport
Old Fort Inn and Antiques (Old Fort Ave., tel. 207/967–5353) stocks a small but choice selection of primitives, china, and country furniture in a converted barn adjoining an inn.

Saml's Stairs Antiques (27 Western Ave., tel. 207/967–2850) has American furniture of the 18th and early 19th centuries, specializing in tiger maple, and a good selection of Staffordshire.

Wells
Douglas N. Harding Rare Books (Rte. 1, tel. 207/646–8785) has a huge stock of old books, maps, and prints.

Kenneth & Ida Manko (Seabreeze St., tel. 207/646–2595) shows folk art, primitives, paintings, and a large selection of 19th-century weathervanes. (Turn right on Eldridge Rd. off Rte. 1, and after ½ mi turn left on Seabreeze.)

Books
Kennebunkport
Kennebunk Book Port (10 Dock Sq., tel. 207/967–3815), housed in a rum warehouse built in 1775, has a wide selection of titles and specializes in local and maritime subjects.

Crafts
Kennebunk
Marlows Artisans Gallery (109 Lafayette Center, tel. 207/985–2931) features wood, glass, weaving, and pottery crafts.

Kennebunkport
Pascos (Ocean Ave., tel. 207/967–4722) focuses on handweaving and knitting.

Men's and Women's Clothing
Kennebunk
Chadwick's (101 Lafayette Center, tel. 207/985–7042) carries a selection of women's casual clothing, beachwear, and evening gowns.

Kennebunkport
Atlantic Cotton Co. (Dock Sq., tel. 207/967–2855) is a good bet for sweats and T-shirts.

Ogunquit **Dock Square Clothier** (Main St., tel. 207/646–8548) sells casual clothing in natural fibers for men and women.

The Shoe String (Rte. 1, tel. 207/646–3533) has a range of shoes and handbags, from the sporty to the dressy.

Sports and Outdoor Activities

Biking **Cape-Able Bike Shop** (Townhouse Corners, Kennebunkport, tel. 207/967–4382) has bicycles for rent.

Bird-watching **Biddeford Pool East Sanctuary** (Rte. 9, Biddeford) is a nature preserve where shorebirds congregate.

Boat Trips **Finestkind** (Perkins Cove, Ogunquit, tel. 207/646–5227) has cruises to Nubble Lighthouse and lobstering trips.

Sail Me (Perkins Cove, Ogunquit, tel. 207/646–2457) tours the area on the 35-foot sloop *Airborne*.

Deep-Sea Fishing *Porpoise III* (York Harbor, tel. 207/363–5106) is available for full-day or half-day trips.

Elizabeth II (Arundel Shipyard, Kennebunkport, tel. 207/967–5595) carries passengers on 1½-hour narrated cruises down the Kennebunk River and out to Cape Porpoise. The *Nautilus,* run by the same outfit, goes on whale-watching cruises from May through September, daily at 10 AM.

Spectator Sports

Baseball The **Maine Guides** baseball club plays at The Ball Park (Old Orchard Beach, tel. 207/934–4561) from April through September.

Beaches

Maine's sand beaches tend to be rather hard-packed and built up with beach cottages and motels. Yet the water is clean (and cold), the surf usually gentle, and the crowds manageable except on the hottest summer weekends.

Kennebunk Beach. Gooch's Beach, Middle Beach, and Kennebunk Beach (also called Mother's Beach) are the three areas of Kennebunk Beach. Beach Road with its cottages and old Victorian boardinghouses runs right behind them. For parking permits, go to the Kennebunk Town Office (1 Summer St., tel. 207/985–3675). Gooch's and Middle beaches attract lots of teenagers; Mother's Beach, which has a small playground and tidal puddles for splashing, is popular with moms and kids.

Kennebunkport. Goose Rocks, a few minutes' drive north of town, is the largest in the Kennebunk area and the favorite of families with small children. For a parking permit, go to the Kennebunkport Town Office (Elm St., tel. 207/967–4244).

Ogunquit. The 3 miles of sand beach have snack bars, boardwalk, rest rooms, and changing areas at the Beach Street entrance. The section to the north that is accessible by footbridge has rest rooms and is less crowded. The ocean beach is backed by the Ogunquit River, which is ideal for children because it is sheltered and waveless. There is a parking fee.

York. York's Long Sands Beach has free parking and Route 1A running right behind it; the smaller Short Sands beach has meter parking. Both beaches have commercial development.

Dining and Lodging

Kennebunks Dining
★

Cape Arundel Inn. Were it not for the rocky shore beyond the picture windows, the pillared porch with wicker chairs, and the cozy parlor, with fireplace and backgammon boards, which you just passed through, you might well think you were dining at a major Boston restaurant. The lobster bisque is creamy, with just a bit of cognac. Entrées include marlin with sorrel butter; coho salmon with mushrooms, white wine, and lemon; rack of lamb; and pecan chicken with peaches and crème fraîche. The inn has 13 guest rooms, seven in the Victorian-era converted "cottage" and six in a motel facility adjoining. *Ocean Ave., tel. 207/967–2125. Reservations advised. Dress: casual but neat. AE, MC, V. Closed mid-Oct.–mid-May. No lunch. Expensive.*

Olde Grist Mill. The bar and lounge area occupy a restored grist mill, with original equipment and fixtures intact; the dining room is a spare, modern space with white linen, china, and picture windows on the Kennebunk River. The Continental menu features sole in papillote with seafood stuffing; sirloin steak au poivre; and a classic shore dinner. The baked Indian pudding is a local legend. *1 Mill La., Kennebunkport, tel. 207/967–4781. Reservations accepted. Dress: casual but neat. AE, CB, DC, MC, V. Closed Mon. Apr.–Oct. No lunch. Expensive.*

Breakwater Inn. The restaurant of this inn serves baked stuffed scrod; grilled game hen with basil pesto; poached salmon with orange and leeks; and spice-crusted pork tenderloin. The lobster clambake is popular. The intimate dining room has picture windows on the water. *Ocean Ave., tel. 207/967–3118. Reservations advised. Dress: casual but neat. AE, MC, V. Closed Jan.–Apr. Moderate–Expensive.*

★ **Mabel's Lobster Claw.** George and Barbara Bush have been eating here for years; his favorite is said to be the baked lobster stuffed with scallops, hers the eggplant parmigiana. The fisherman's platter includes fried haddock, scallops, shrimp, and onion rings. Mabel's is a homey, birch-paneled, family-style restaurant. *425 Ocean Ave., tel. 207/967–2562. Reservations required in summer. Dress: casual. No credit cards. Closed mid-Oct.–mid-Apr. Moderate.*

Kennebunks Lodging

Breakwater Inn. Kennebunkport has few accommodations that are elegantly old-fashioned in decor, located right on the water, and well suited to families with young children, and this inn is all three. Overlooking Kennebunk Beach from the breakwater, rooms have stained pine four-posters and hand-stenciling or wallpaper. The Riverside building next door offers spacious, airy rooms with sliding glass doors facing the water. *Box 1160, Ocean Ave., Kennebunkport 04046, tel. 207/967–3118. 20 rooms with bath, 2 suites. Facilities: dining room, small playground. AE, MC, V. Closed Dec. 15–Jan. 15. Expensive–Very Expensive.*

The Captain Lord Mansion. A long and distinguished history, a three-story elliptical staircase, and a cupola with widow's walk make this something more than the standard bed-and-breakfast. The rooms, named for clipper ships, are mostly large and stately—11 have a fireplace—though the style relaxes as one ascends from the ground floor rooms (damask and mahogany) to the country-style third floor accommodations (pine furniture and leafy views). *Box 800, Kennebunkport 04046, tel. 207/ 967–3141. 16 rooms with bath. D, MC, V. Expensive–Very Expensive.*

Inn at Harbor Head. The 100-year-old shingled farmhouse on the harbor at Cape Porpoise has become a tiny bed-and-breakfast full of antiques, paintings, and heirlooms. The Harbor Room upstairs has the best water view and murals; the Greenery downstairs boasts a whirlpool tub and a garden view. The grounds are bright with flower beds. *RR 2, Box 1180, Kennebunkport 04046, tel. 207/967–4873. 4 rooms with bath, 1 suite. Facilities: private dock. No smoking. D, MC, V. Expensive–Very Expensive.*

The Seaside. The modern motel units, all with sliding glass doors opening onto private decks or patios, half of them with ocean views, are appropriate for families; so are the cottages, which have from one to four bedrooms, and where well-behaved pets are accepted. The four bedrooms in the inn, furnished with antiques, are more suitable for adults. *Gooch's Beach, Kennebunkport 04046, tel. 207/967–4461 or 207/967–4282. 26 rooms with bath, 10 cottages. Facilities: private beach, laundry, playground. No credit cards. Inn rooms closed Labor Day–June; cottages closed Nov.–Apr. Expensive–Very Expensive.*

Captain Jefferds Inn. The three-story white-clapboard sea captain's home with black shutters, built in 1804, has been restored and filled with the innkeeper's collections of majolica, American art pottery, Venetian glass, and Sienese pottery. Most rooms are done in Laura Ashley fabrics and wallpapers, and many have been furnished with English curly maple chests, marbletop dressers, old books, and paintings. Pets are welcome. *Pearl St., Box 691, Kennebunkport 04046, tel. 207/ 967–2311. 12 rooms with bath; 3 suites in the carriage house. Facilities: croquet. No credit cards. Closed Jan.–Mar., Nov. Moderate–Very Expensive.*

Bufflehead Cove. Situated on the Kennebunk River at the end of a winding dirt road, the friendly gray-shingle bed-and-breakfast affords the quiet of country fields and apple trees only five minutes from Dock Square. The small guest rooms are dollhouse pretty, with white wicker and flowers painted on the walls. *Box 499, 04046, tel. 207/967–0626. 6 rooms with bath, 1 suite, 1 apartment. Facilities: canoe, private dock. No smoking. No credit cards. Closed Mar.–Apr. Moderate–Expensive.*

Beachwood Motel. This motel a mile from Goose Rocks Beach has farm animals, swings and sandbox, indoor and outdoor kiddie pools, basketball and racquetball courts, free porto-cribs, and lots of land. The standard motel rooms have two double beds; half the rooms have kitchenettes. Off-season rates are much lower. *Rte. 9, 04046, tel. 207/967–2483. 112 rooms with bath. Facilities: tennis court; basketball court; indoor, outdoor, and kiddie pools; hot tub. MC, V. Moderate.*

Ogunquit Dining **Old Village Inn.** Each of the five dining rooms has a different character—a mock English pub, a greenhouse dense with foliage, etc.—yet the menu throughout is consistently rich: duck flambéed at tableside; prime rib; shrimp and filet mignon teriyaki kebab. Peach walnut crisp has been a favorite dessert. *30 Main St., tel. 207/646–7088. Reservations advised. Dress: casual but neat. AE, MC, V. Closed Sun. and Mon. Nov.–Mar. No lunch. Expensive.*

Tavern at Clay Hill Farm. The three softly lit dining rooms of the white-clapboard farmhouse seat 200; entrées on recent menus have included sliced breast of duck with orange horse-radish sauce; poached salmon with dill hollandaise; halibut broiled in pecan lobster butter. Cajun crab cakes and stuffed mushrooms are starters. *Agamenticus Rd., tel. 207/646-2272. Reservations advised. Dress: casual. AE, MC, V. No lunch. Expensive.*

Ogunquit Lobster Pound. Select your lobster live, then dine under the trees or in the rustic dining room of the log cabin. The menu includes steamed clams, steak, and chicken; and there is a children's menu. *Rte. 1, tel. 207/646-2516. No reservations. Dress: casual. AE, MC, V. Closed late Oct.–mid-May. Moderate.*

Ogunquit Lodging   **Colonial Inn.** This complex of accommodations in the middle of Ogunquit includes a large white Victorian inn building, modern motel units, and efficiency apartments. Inn rooms have flowered wallpaper, Colonial reproduction furniture, and white ruffle curtains. Efficiencies are popular with families. Two-thirds of the rooms have water views. *Shore Rd., Box 895, 03907, tel. 207/646-5191. 80 units, 78 with bath; 13 suites. Facilities: heated outdoor pool, laundromat, grills, Jacuzzi, playground, shuffleboard. AE, D, MC, V. Closed Nov.–Apr. Moderate–Very Expensive.*

Seafair Inn. A century-old white-clapboard house set back behind shrubs and lawn in the center of town, the Seafair has a homey atmosphere and proximity to the beach. Rooms are furnished with odds and ends of country furniture; the Continental breakfast is served on an enclosed sun porch. *Box 1221, 03907, tel. 207/646-2181. 18 units, 14 with bath; 4 efficiency suites. MC, V. Closed Nov.–Mar. Moderate–Expensive.*

The Yorks Dining   **Cape Neddick Inn.** This restaurant and art gallery has an airy ambience, with tables set well apart, lots of windows, and art everywhere. The New American menu has offered lobster macadamia tart (shelled lobster sautéed with shallots, macadamia nuts, sherry, and cream and served in pastry); breaded pork tenderloin; and such appetizers as spicy sesame chicken dumplings and gravlax with Russian pepper vodka. Duckling flamed in brandy is always on the menu. *Rte. 1, Cape Neddick, tel. 207/363-2899. Reservations advised. Dress: casual. MC, V. Closed Mon. and Tues. Columbus Day–May 31. No lunch. Expensive.*

Dockside Dining Room. The seclusion, the gardens, and the water views are the attractions of the inn dining room on a private island in York Harbor. Entrées may include scallop-stuffed shrimp Casino; broiled Boston scrod; steak au poivre with brandied mushroom sauce; and roast stuffed duckling. *York Harbor off Rte. 103, tel. 207/363-4800. Reservations advised on weekends. Dress: casual but neat. MC, V. Closed Mon. Closed late-Oct.–Memorial Day. Moderate.*

The Yorks Lodging   **Dockside Guest Quarters.** Situated on a private island 8 acres large in the middle of York Harbor, the Dockside promises water views, seclusion, and quiet. Rooms in the Maine house, the oldest structure on the site, are furnished with early American antiques, marine artifacts, and nautical paintings and prints. Four modern cottages tucked among the trees have less character but bigger windows on the water, and many have kitchenettes. *Box 205, York 03909, tel. 207/363-2868. 22* rooms, 20 with bath; 5 suites. Facilities: private dock, dining room, small motorboat, croquet, badminton. MC, V (limit $100). Closed late Oct.–Apr. Moderate–Very Expensive.

The Arts

Theater **Ogunquit Playhouse** (Rte. 1, tel. 207/646–5511), one of America's oldest summer theaters, mounts plays and musicals from late June to Labor Day.

The Coast: Portland to Pemaquid Point

Maine's largest city, yet small enough to be seen with ease in a day or two, Portland is undergoing a cultural and economic renaissance. New hotels and a bright new performing arts center have joined the neighborhoods of historic homes; the Old Port Exchange, perhaps the finest urban renovation project on the East Coast, balances modern commercial enterprise with a salty waterfront character in an area bustling with restaurants, shops, and galleries. The piers of Commercial Street abound with opportunities for water tours of the harbor and excursions to the Calendar Islands.

Freeport, north of Portland, is a town made famous by the L. L. Bean store, whose success led to the opening of scores of other clothing stores and outlets. Brunswick is best known for Bowdoin College; Bath has been a shipbuilding center since 1607, and the Maine Maritime Museum preserves its history.

The Boothbays—the coastal areas of Boothbay Harbor, East Boothbay, Linekin Neck, Southport Island, and the inland town of Boothbay—attract hordes of vacationing families and flotillas of pleasure craft. The Pemaquid peninsula juts into the Atlantic south of Damariscotta and just east of the Boothbays, and near Pemaquid Beach one can view the objects unearthed at the Colonial Pemaquid Restoration.

Important Addresses and Numbers

Visitor **Convention and Visitors Bureau of Greater Portland** (142 Free
Information St., tel. 207/772–4994).

Boothbay Harbor Region Chamber of Commerce (Box 356, Boothbay Harbor, tel. 207/633–2353).

Brunswick Area Chamber of Commerce (59 Pleasant St., Brunswick, tel. 207/725–8797).

Bath Area Chamber of Commerce (45 Front St., Bath, tel. 207/443–9751).

Freeport Merchants Association (Box 452, Freeport, tel. 207/865–1212).

Getting Around Portland to Pemaquid Point

By Car The Congress Street exit from I–295 will take you into the heart of Portland. Numerous city parking lots have hourly rates of 40¢ to 70¢; the Gateway Garage on High Street, off Congress, is a convenient place to leave your car while exploring downtown. North of Portland, I–95 takes you to Exit 20 and Route 1, Freeport's Main Street, which continues on to Brunswick and Bath. East of Wiscasset you can take Route 27 south to the Boothbays, where Route 96 is good for further exploration.

By Bus Portland's **Metro** (tel. 207/774–0351) runs eight bus routes in Portland, South Portland, and Westbrook; the fare is 80¢, exact change only, and buses operate from 5:30 AM to 11:45 PM.

Guided Tours

Greater Portland Landmarks (165 State St., tel. 207/774–5561) has bus and walking tours of historic districts.

Brunswick Transportation/Maineline Tours (184 Main St., South Portland, tel. 207/799–8527) has charter and tour buses.

Exploring Portland

Numbers in the margin correspond with the numbered points of interest on the Portland map.

7 Congress Street, **Portland's** main street, runs the length of the peninsular city from the Western Promenade in the southwest to the Eastern Promenade in the northeast, passing through the small downtown area. A few blocks southeast of downtown, the bustling Old Port Exchange sprawls along the waterfront.

Time Out Those who are making an early start and are ready for a meal will welcome the **Good Egg Cafe** at 705 Congress Street, where imaginative and hearty breakfasts are prepared from 6 AM weekdays, 7 AM Saturday, and 8 AM Sunday. The restaurant closes at lunchtime.

8 One of the notable homes on Congress Street is the **Neal Dow Memorial,** a gray brick mansion built in 1829 in the late Federal style by General Neal Dow, a zealous abolitionist and prohibitionist. The library has fine ornamental ironwork, and the furnishings include the family china, silver, and portraits. Don't miss the grandfather clocks and the original deed granted by James II. *714 Congress St., tel. 207/773–7773. Admission free. Open for tours weekdays 11–4. Closed Thanksgiving, Dec. 25.*

Just off Congress Street, next to the chamber of commerce, the
9 distinguished **Portland Museum of Art** has a strong collection of seascapes and landscapes by such masters as Winslow Homer, John Marin, Andrew Wyeth, and Marsden Hartley. Homer's *Pulling the Dory* and *Weatherbeaten*, two quintessential Maine coast images, are here. A wall of photographs by Paul Strand includes some of his best work. The strikingly modern Charles Shipman Payson wing was designed by I. M. Pei in 1983. Also part of the museum complex is the McLellan Sweat House at 111 High Street, a fine example of the Federal style with a semicircular front portico and openwork balustrade around the roof. *7 Congress Sq., tel. 207/775–6148. Admission: $3.50 adults, $2.50 senior citizens and students, $1 children 6–18, free Thurs. 5–9. Open Tues.–Sat. 10–5, Thurs. 10–9, Sun. noon–5.*

10 Walk east on Congress Street to the **Wadsworth Longfellow House** of 1785, the boyhood home of the poet and the first brick

Portland

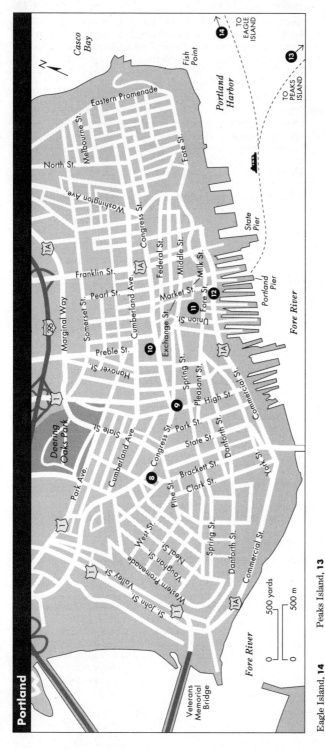

Casco Bay

Eastern Promenade

Fish Point

Portland Harbor

North St.

Melbourne St.

Fore St.

Washington Ave.

State Pier

Congress St.

Federal St.

Middle St.

Franklin St.

Pearl St.

Market St.

Milk St.

Fore St.

Somerset St.

Cumberland Ave.

Marginal Way

Union St.

Exchange St.

Portland Pier

Preble St.

Hanover St.

Spring St.

Pleasant St.

Fore River

Deering Oaks Park

State St.

High St.

Park St.

Congress St.

State St.

Danforth St.

Commercial St.

Cumberland Ave.

Park Ave.

Brackett St.

Clark St.

York St.

Pine St.

Spring St.

West St.

Vaughan St.

Neal St.

Western Promenade

St. John St.

Valley St.

Danforth St.

Commercial St.

Veterans Memorial Bridge

Fore River

TO EAGLE ISLAND

TO PEAKS ISLAND

0 500 yards

0 500 m

Eagle Island, **14**

Mariner's Church, **12**

Neal Dow Memorial, **8**

Old Port Exchange, **11**

Peaks Island, **13**

Portland Museum of Art, **9**

Wadsworth Longfellow House, **10**

house in Portland. The late Colonial-style structure sits well back from the street and has a small portico over its entrance and four chimneys surmounting the hip roof. Most of the furnishings are original to the house. *485 Congress St., tel. 207/ 772–1807 or 207/774–1822. Admission: $2.50 adults, $1 children. Open June–Columbus Day weekend, Tues.–Sat. 10–4. Closed July 4, Labor Day. Garden open daily 9–5.*

⓫ Although you can walk from downtown to the **Old Port Exchange,** you're better off driving and parking your car either at the city garage on Fore Street (between Exchange and Union streets) or opposite the U.S. Customs House at the corner of Fore and Pearl streets. Like the Customs House, the brick buildings and warehouses of the Old Port Exchange were built following the Great Fire of 1866 and were intended to last for ages. When the city's economy slumped in the middle of the present century, however, the Old Port declined and seemed slated for demolition. Then artists and craftspeople began opening shops here in the late 1960s, and in time restaurants, chic boutiques, bookstores, and gift shops followed.

The Old Port is best explored on foot. Allow a couple of hours to wander at leisure on Market, Exchange, Middle, and Fore **⓬** streets. The **Mariner's Church** (376 Fore St.) has a fine facade of granite columns, and the Elias Thomas Block on Commercial Street demonstrates the graceful use of bricks in commercial architecture. Inevitably the salt smell of the sea will draw you to one of the wharves off Commercial Street; Custom House Wharf retains some of the older, rougher waterfront atmosphere.

Time Out **Al's,** at 15 Exchange Street in the middle of the Old Port Exchange, prepares clam chowder, shish kebab, burgers, and sandwiches. Service is prompt, the jukebox loud.

Island Excursions The brightly painted ferries of **Casco Bay Lines** (tel. 207/774–7871) are the lifeline to the Calendar Islands of Casco Bay, which number about 136, depending on the tides and how one defines an island.

⓭ **Peaks Island,** nearest Portland, is the most developed, and some residents commute to work in Portland. Yet you can still commune with the wind and the sea on Peaks, explore an old fort, and ramble along the alternately rocky and sandy shore. A bed-and-breakfast has overnight accommodation (*see* Peaks Island Lodging, below).

⓮ The 17-acre **Eagle Island,** owned by the state of Maine and open to the public for day trips in summer, was the home of Admiral Robert E. Peary, the American explorer of the North Pole. Peary built a stone and wood house on the island as a summer retreat in 1904, then made it his permanent residence. The house remains as it was when Peary was here with his stuffed Arctic birds and the quartz he brought home set into the fieldstone fireplace. The *Kristy K.,* departing from Long Wharf, makes a four-hour narrated tour. *Long Wharf, tel. 207/774–6498. Excursion tour: $15 adults, $12 senior citizens, $9 children 5–9. Departures late May–mid-Sept., daily 10, 2.*

Exploring North of Portland

Numbers in the margin correspond with the numbered points of interest on the Southern Maine Coast map.

⑮ Freeport, on Route 1, 15 miles northeast of Portland, has charming back streets lined with old clapboard houses and even a small harbor on the Harraseeket River, but the overwhelming majority of visitors come to shop, and **L. L. Bean** is the store that put Freeport on the map. Founded in 1912 as a small mail order merchandiser of products for hunters, guides, and fisherfolk, L. L. Bean now attracts some 3.5 million shoppers a year to its giant store in the heart of Freeport's shopping district on Route 1. Here you can still find the original hunting boots, along with cotton, wool, and silk sweaters, camping and ski equipment, comforters, and hundreds of other items for the home, car, boat, or campsite. Across the street from the main store, a Bean factory outlet has seconds and discontinued merchandise at marked-down prices. *Rte. 1, Freeport, tel. 800/341–4341. Open 24 hours.*

All around L. L. Bean, like seedlings under a mighty spruce, some 85 outlets have sprouted, offering designer clothes, shoes, housewares, and toys at marked-down prices (*see* Shopping, below).

⑯ It's 9 miles northeast on Route 1 from Freeport to **Brunswick.** Follow the signs to the Brunswick business district, Pleasant Street, and—at the end of Pleasant Street—Maine Street, which claims to be the widest (198 feet across) in the state. Friday from May to October sees a fine farmer's market on the town mall, between Maine Street and Park Row.

Maine Street takes you to the 110-acre campus of **Bowdoin College,** an enclave of distinguished architecture, gardens, and grassy quadrangles in the middle of the city. Campus tours (tel. 207/725–3000) depart weekdays from Moulton Union. Among the historic buildings are Massachusetts Hall, a stout, sober, hip-roofed brick structure that dates from 1802, and Hubbard Hall, an imposing 1902 neo-Gothic building with a central tower capped by spires. The slender, twin-tower chapel of undressed Brunswick granite dates from the middle of the last century.

Don't miss the **Bowdoin College Museum of Art,** a splendid limestone, brick, and granite structure in a Renaissance Revival style, with three galleries radiating from a central rotunda. Designed in 1894 by Charles F. McKim, the building stands on a rise, its facade adorned with classical statues and the entrance set off by a triumphal arch. The collections encompass Dutch and Italian Old Masters, including Brueghel's *Alpine Landscape;* a superb gathering of Colonial and Federal paintings, notably the Gilbert Stuart portraits of Madison and Jefferson; John Singer Sargent's *Mrs. Nelson Fairchild;* and paintings and drawings by Winslow Homer, Mary Cassatt, John Sloan, and Rockwell Kent. Christo, Jim Dine, and Robert Rauschenberg are also represented, and the museum has a strong photography collection. *Walker Art Bldg., tel. 207/725–8731. Admission free. Open June–Aug., Tues.–Sat. 10–8; Sept.–May, Tues.–Fri. 10–4, Sat. 10–5, Sun. 2–5.*

Before going on to Bath, you may elect to drive down Route 123 or Route 24 to the peninsulas and islands known collectively as the **Harpswells.** The numerous small coves along Harpswell Neck shelter the boats of local lobstermen, and summer cottages are tucked away amid the birch and spruces.

⑰ Bath, 7 miles east of Brunswick on Route 1, has been a shipbuilding center since 1607. Today the Bath Iron Works turns out guided-missile frigates for the U.S. Navy and merchant container ships.

The **Maine Maritime Museum** in South Bath (take the Bath Business District exit from Route 1, turn right on Washington Street, and follow the signs) has ship models, journals, photographs, and other artifacts to stir the nautical dreams of old salts and young. The 142-foot Grand Banks fishing schooner *Sherman Zwicker,* one of the last of its kind, is on display when in port. On clement winter weekdays you can watch apprentice boatbuilders wield their tools on classic Maine boats at the restored Percy & Small Shipyard and Apprentice Shop. *243 Washington St., tel. 207/443–1316. Admission: $5 adults, $4.50 senior citizens, $2.50 children 6–15. Open daily 9:30–5. Closed Thanksgiving, Dec. 25, Jan. 1.*

From Bath it's 10 miles northeast on Route 1 to Wiscasset and, across the river, Route 27. Drive south on Route 27 to reach the **⑱ Boothbay Railway Village,** about a mile north of **Boothbay,** where you can ride 1½ miles on a narrow-gauge steam train through a re-creation of a turn-of-the-century New England village. Among the 24 village buildings is a museum with more than 50 antique automobiles and trucks. *Rte. 27, Boothbay, tel. 207/633–4727. Admission: $5 adults, $2.50 children 2–12. Open mid-June–mid-Oct., daily 9:30–5.*

The **Boothbay Theater Museum,** opposite the post office, contains two centuries of theatrical memorabilia: stage jewelry, costumes, portraits, set models, toy theaters, playbills, photos. *Corey La., Boothbay, tel. 207/633–4536. Admission: $4. Open mid-June–mid-Sept., Mon.–Sat. by appointment only.*

Continue south on Route 27 into Boothbay Harbor, bear right on Oak Street, and follow it to the waterfront parking lots. **⑲ Boothbay Harbor** is a town to wander through: Commercial Street, Wharf Street, the By-Way, and Townsend Avenue are lined with shops, galleries, and ice-cream parlors. Excursion boats (*see* Sports and Outdoor Activities, below) leave from the piers off Commercial Street. Even if you don't plan a voyage, you can hang around the piers and watch the pleasure craft come and go.

Time Out   The **P&P Pastry Shoppe** (6 McKown St.) is a welcome stop for a sandwich or a pastry.

Having explored Boothbay Harbor, return to Route 27 and head north again to Route 1. Proceed north to Business Route 1, and follow it through Damariscotta, an appealing shipbuilding town on the Damariscotta River. Bear right on the Bristol Road (Route 129/130), and when the highway splits, stay on **⑳** Route 130, which leads to Bristol and terminates at **Pemaquid Point.**

About 5 miles south of Bristol you'll come to New Harbor, where a right turn will take you to Pemaquid Beach and the Colonial Pemaquid Restoration. Here, on a small peninsula jutting into the Pemaquid River, English mariners established a fishing and trading settlement in the early 17th century. The excavations at Pemaquid Beach, begun in the mid-1960s, have turned up thousands of artifacts from the Colonial settlement and from even earlier Indian settlements, including the remains of an old customs house, tavern, jail, forge, and homes. The State of Maine operates a museum displaying many of the artifacts. *Rte. 130, Pemaquid Point, tel. 207/677–2423. Admission: $1.50 adults, 50¢ children 6–12. Open Memorial Day–Labor Day, daily 9:30–5.*

Route 130 terminates at the **Pemaquid Point Light,** which looks as though it sprouted from the ragged, tilted chunk of granite that it commands. The former lighthouse keeper's cottage is now the **Fishermen's Museum,** with photos, models, and artifacts that explore commercial fishing in Maine. Here, too, is the Pemaquid Art Gallery, which mounts changing exhibitions from July 1 through Labor Day. *Rte. 130, tel. 207/677–2494. Museum admission by contribution. Open Memorial Day–Columbus Day, Mon.–Sat. 10–5, Sun. 11–5.*

Portland to Pemaquid Point for Free

Neal Dow Memorial, Portland

Bowdoin College Museum of Art, Brunswick

Marine Aquarium. Huge tanks hold lobsters and fish, and harbor seals flop around in the outdoor saltwater pools of the aquarium maintained by the Maine Department of Marine Resources at McKown Point. Outdoor tables permit picnicking by the shore. *West Boothbay Harbor, tel. 207/633–5572. Open Memorial Day–Columbus Day, weekdays 8–5, weekends 9–5.*

What to See and Do with Children

Children's Museum of Maine. Touching is okay at this museum where little ones can pretend they are lobstermen, shopkeepers, computer experts. *746 Stevens Ave. at Westbrook College, tel. 207/797–5483. Admission: $2.50 adults, $1.50 children, ½ price Wed. Open Mon.–Sat. 10–5.*

Maine Maritime Museum, South Bath

Boothbay Railway Village, Boothbay

Off the Beaten Track

Stroudwater Village, 3 miles west of Portland, was spared the devastation of the fire of 1866 and thus contains some of the best examples of 18th- and early 19th-century architecture in the region. Here are the remains of mills, canals, and historic homes, including the Tate House, built in 1755 with paneling from England. It overlooks the old mastyard where George Tate, Mast Agent to the King, prepared tall pines for the ships of the Royal Navy. The furnishings date to the late-18th-century. *Tate House, 1270 Westbrook St., tel. 207/774–9781. Admission: $2.50 adults, $1 children. Open June–Sept. 15, Tues.–Sat. 11–5, Sun. 1:30–5.*

Shopping

The best and most unusual shopping in Portland is at the Old Port Exchange, where many shops are concentrated along Fore and Exchange streets. Freeport's name is almost synonymous with shopping, and shopping in Freeport means L. L. Bean and the 85 factory outlets that opened during the 1980s. Outlet stores are located in the Fashion Outlet Mall (2 Depot St.) and the Freeport Crossing (200 Lower Main St.), and many others crowd Main Street and Bow Street. *The Freeport Visitors Guide* (Freeport Merchants Association, Box 452, Freeport 04032) has a complete listing. Boothbay Harbor, and Commercial Street in particular, is chockablock with gift shops, T-shirt shops, and other seasonal emporia catering to visitors.

Antiques
Portland

E. Klaman, Bottles (428 Fore St., no phone) stocks countless bottles, mostly old and dusty, of every size, shape, and type.

F. O. Bailey Antiquarians (141 Middle St., tel. 207/774–1479), Portland's largest retail showroom, features antique and reproduction furniture; jewelry, paintings, rugs, and china.

West Port Antiques (17 Pleasant St., tel. 207/774–6747) has a pleasing jumble of curios, primitives, textiles, miniatures.

Freeport

The **Freeport Antique Mall** (Rte. 1, tel. 207/865–0607), five minutes south of downtown Freeport, brings together 65 antiques dealers and their goods.

Harrington House Gallery Store (45 Main St., tel. 207/865–0477) is a restored 19th-century merchant's home owned by the Freeport Historical Society; all the period reproductions that furnish the rooms are for sale. In addition, you can buy wallpaper, crafts, Shaker items, toys, and kitchen utensils.

Books and Maps
Portland

Carlson and Turner (241 Congress St., tel. 207/773–4200) is an antiquarian book dealer with an estimated 40,000 titles, including sets of Dickens and Thackeray.

Enchanted Forest (377 Fore St., tel. 207/773–8651) shows a fine selection of children's books in a cheerful, inviting shop.

Raffles Cafe Bookstore (555 Congress St., tel. 207/761–3930) presents an impressive selection of fiction and nonfiction. Coffee and a light lunch are served, and there are frequent readings and literary gatherings.

Freeport

DeLorme's Map Store (Rte. 1, tel. 207/865–4171) carries an exceptional selection of maps and atlases of Maine and New England, nautical charts, and travel books.

Crafts and Art Galleries
Portland

Abacus (44 Exchange St., tel. 207/772–4880) has unusual gift items in glass, wood, and textiles, plus fine modern jewelry.

Barridoff Galleries (26 Free St., tel. 207/772–5011) buys and sells 19th- and 20th-century American paintings; changing shows feature regional painters.

Stein Glass Gallery (20 Milk St., tel. 207/772–9072) specializes in contemporary glass, both decorative and utilitarian.

Wellin Gardiner Fine Arts (4½ Milk St., tel. 207/774–1944) deals in antique prints, with an emphasis on nautical, sporting, and botanical subjects.

Men's and **A. H. Benoit** (188 Middle St., tel. 207/773–8372) sells quality
Women's Clothing men's clothing from sportswear to evening attire.
Portland
Joseph's (410 Fore St., tel. 207/773–1274) has elegant tailored
designer clothing for men and women.

Lucky Strike (345 Fore St., tel. 207/773–7784) is a funky little
boutique with a full line of Kiko washable silks, sportswear,
and Portland's best offering of lingerie.

Sports and Outdoor Activities

Boat Trips For tours of the harbor, Casco Bay, and the nearby islands, try
Portland **Bay View Cruises** (Fisherman's Wharf, tel. 207/883–5456), **The
Buccaneer** (Long Wharf, tel. 207/799–8188), **Casco Bay Lines**
(Custom House Wharf, tel. 207/774–7871), **Eagle Tours** (Long
Wharf, tel. 207/774–6498), **Longfellow Cruise Line**
(Long Wharf, tel. 207/774–3578), or **Old Port Mariner Fleet**
(Long Wharf, tel. 207/775–0727).

Boothbay Harbor ***Appledore*** (tel. 207/633–6598), an 85-foot windjammer, departs
from Pier 6 at 9, noon, 3, and 6 for voyages to the outer islands.

Argo Cruises (tel. 207/633–4925) runs the *Argo III* for morning
cruises, Bath Hellgate cruises, supper sails, and whale watching; the *Linekin II* for 1½-hour trips to Seal Rocks; the *Miss
Boothbay*, a licensed lobster boat, for lobster-trap hauling
trips. Departures are from Pier 6.

Balmy Days II (tel. 207/633–2284) leaves from Pier 8 for its day
trips to Monhegan Island; the ***Maranbo II,*** operated by the
same company, tours the harbor and nearby lighthouses.

Bay Lady (tel. 207/633–3244), a 31-foot Friendship sloop, offers
sailing trips of under two hours from Pier 1.

Breakaway (tel. 207/633–4414, or the Ocean Point Inn, tel. 207/
633–4200) is a motorboat that carries 12 passengers to
Pemaquid Point, South Bristol, Southport Island, or Linekin
Bay. Sunset cruises go to Seal Rocks, and there are sport fishing trips. Departures are from Ocean Point in East Boothbay.

Cap'n Fish's Boat Trips (tel. 207/633–3244) offers sightseeing
cruises throughout the region, including puffin cruises, trips to
Damariscove Harbor, Pemaquid Point, and up the Kennebec
River to Bath, departing from Pier 1.

Eastward (tel. 207/633–4780) is a Friendship sloop with six-
passenger capacity that departs from Ocean Point Road in East
Boothbay for one-day or half-day sailing trips. Itineraries vary
with passengers' desires and the weather.

Deep-Sea Fishing Half-day and full-day fishing charter boats operating out of
Portland include ***Anjin-San*** (tel. 207/772–7168), ***Devils Den***
(DeMillo's Marina, tel. 207/761–4466), and ***Lazy Day*** (tel. 207/
883–3430).

Operating out of Boothbay Harbor, **Cap'n Fish's Deep Sea Fishing** (tel. 207/633–3244) schedules daylong and half-day trips,
departing from Pier 1, and **Lucky Star Charters** (tel. 207/633–
4624) runs full-day and half-day charters for up to six people,
with departures from Pier 8.

Nature Walks **Wolfe's Neck Woods State Park** has self-guided trails along
Casco Bay, the Harraseeket River, and a fringe salt marsh, as
well as walks led by naturalists. Picnic tables and grills are

available, but there's no camping. Follow Bow Street opposite L. L. Bean off Route 1. *Wolfe's Neck Rd., tel. 207/865–4465. Open Memorial Day–Labor Day.*

Spectator Sports

Hockey The **Maine Mariners** (tel. 207/775–3411) play professional hockey at the Cumberland County Civic Center, 1 Civic Center Square, October through April.

Beaches

Crescent Beach State Park (Rte. 77, Cape Elizabeth, tel. 207/767–3625), about 8 miles from Portland, has a sand beach, picnic tables, seasonal snack bar, and bathhouse.

Scarborough Beach State Park (Rte. 207, off Rte. 1 in Scarborough, tel. 207/883–2416) has a small sand beach with dunes and marshes. Parking is limited.

Popham Beach State Park, at the end of Route 209, south of Bath, has a good sand beach, tidal pools, rocky outcrops, a nature area, and picnic tables. *Phippsburg, tel. 207/389–2303. Admission: $1 per person, late Apr.–mid-Oct.*

Reid State Park, on Georgetown Island, off Route 127, has 1½ miles of sand on three beaches. Facilities include bathhouses, picnic tables, fireplaces, and snack bar. Parking lots fill by 11 AM on summer Sundays and holidays. *Georgetown, tel. 207/371–2303. Admission: $1.50 per person, late Apr.–mid-Oct.*

Dining and Lodging

Portland Dining Many of Portland's best restaurants are in the Old Port Exchange district. Casual dress is the rule in restaurants throughout the area except where noted.

Raphael's. The delicate Northern Italian cooking is presented in an airy and stylish dining room done in subdued grays and blues with pale wood accents. Tables set well apart and soft music (often light jazz) allow one to concentrate on such specialties as fettucine with parsley walnut pesto; medallions of veal with sun-dried tomatoes; and *fritto misto di mare* (fried squid, shrimp, and whitefish). The less formal downstairs room, Little Willie's, has a good selection of *crostini* (grilled breads with a variety of toppings). *36 Market St., tel. 207/773–4500. Reservations advised. Dress: casual but neat. AE, D, DC, MC, V. Expensive.*

★ **Alberta's.** Small, bright, casual, and friendly, Alberta's specializes in what one waiter described as "electric American" cuisine, dishes like London broil spiced with garlic, cumin, and lime; pan-blackened rib-eye steak with sour cream and scallions; and Atlantic salmon fillet with orange-ginger sauce, grilled red cabbage, and apple salad. The two-tier dining room has photos mounted on salmon-hued walls, and the music ranges from country to classical. *21 Pleasant St., tel. 207/774–0016. No reservations. AE, CB, DC, MC, V. Beer and wine only. Closed Thanksgiving, Dec. 25. No lunch weekends. Moderate–Expensive.*

Baker's Table. You descend a short flight of stairs and walk through the kitchen area to arrive at a cheerful, lively, informal dining room with oak beam ceilings, hanging plants, and original art work. The bistro-style cuisine features grilled king salmon; sautéed veal medallions with pleurrot mushrooms and shallots; black bean chili; and seafood chowders. *434 Fore St., tel. 207/775–0303. Reservations advised on weekends. Jacket advised. AE, MC, V. Moderate–Expensive.*

F. Parker Reidy's. An old standby in the Old Port, this popular restaurant in a former bank building serves broiled scallops, sirloin and teriyaki steaks, chowders, and sandwiches in a Victorian atmosphere of exposed brick, mahogany, and brass. It's an invigorating place for Sunday brunch and late (for Portland) suppers. *83 Exchange St., tel. 207/773–4731. No reservations. AE, V. Moderate.*

Hu-Shang Exchange. An extensive Chinese menu includes Hunan chicken, lamb with ginger and scallions, and Mandarin moo shu shrimp. The three dining rooms with exposed brick walls, hanging plants, and soft lighting are far more soothing than a standard storefront Chinese restaurant. *29–33 Exchange St., tel. 207/773–0300. Reservations accepted. AE, MC, V. Moderate.*

J's Oyster Bar. Right on the waterfront, J's preserves some of the roughness and grit that renovation has smoothed out elsewhere in the Old Port. Patrons ranging from tourists to blue-collar types to local office workers sit around the central bar and wash down scallops, shrimp, and oysters (raw and nude) with free-flowing beer. *5 Portland Pier, tel. 207/772–4828. No reservations. MC, V. Inexpensive.*

Portland Lodging **Pomegranate Inn.** Clever touches like faux marbling on the moldings and mustard-colored rag-rolling in the hallways give this bed-and-breakfast a bright, postmodern air. Most guest rooms are spacious and bright, accented with original paintings on floral and tropical motifs; the location on a quiet street in the city's Victorian Western Promenade district ensures serenity. Telephones and televisions, rare in an inn, make this a good choice for businesspeople. *49 Neal St., 04102, tel. 207/772–1006 or 800/356–0408. 6 rooms with bath. AE, MC, V. Expensive.*

Portland Regency Inn. The only major hotel in the center of the Old Port Exchange, the Regency building was Portland's armory in the late 19th century. While leaving intact the exterior and the windows, renovation in 1987 transformed the interior into the city's most luxurious, most distinctive hotel. The bright, plush, airy rooms have four-posters, tall standing mirrors, floral curtains, and loveseats. The health club, the best in the city, offers massage and has an aerobics studio, free weights, Nautilus equipment, a large Jacuzzi, dry sauna and steam room. *20 Milk St., 04101, tel. 207/774–4200 or 800/727–3436. 95 rooms with bath, 8 suites. Facilities: restaurant, health club, pub, banquet and convention rooms. AE, D, DC, MC, V. Expensive.*

Sonesta Hotel. Across the street from the art museum and in the heart of the downtown business district, the 12-story brick building, vintage 1927, looks a bit dowdy today. Rooms in the tower section (added in 1961) have floor-to-ceiling windows, and the higher floors have harbor views. The small health club offers Universal gym equipment, rowing machines, stationary bikes, and a sauna. *157 High St., 04101, tel. 207/775–5411 or 800/343–7170. 184 rooms with bath, 6 suites. Facilities: 2 restaurants, 2 bars, health club, banquet and convention facilities. AE, CB, D, DC, MC, V. Moderate–Expensive.*

Bath Dining   **New Meadows Inn.** The restaurant is a bright, airy room with large windows on the New Meadows River (you can dock your boat at the adjacent marina). The cuisine is the standard Maine seafood menu: shore dinners, seafood chowder, a fish platter, baked stuffed lobster—and steak and prime rib. *Bath Rd., West Bath, tel. 207/443–3921. AE, DC, MC, V. Closed Dec. 25. Inexpensive–Moderate.*

Bath Lodging   **Fairhaven Inn.** A cedar-shingle structure of 1790 set on 27 acres of rolling meadows, the inn has lawns sloping down to the Kennebec River and white pine and birch woods. Guest rooms are furnished with handmade quilts and mahogany pineapple four-posters; the Cherry and Apple rooms face the river and get the most light. *N. Bath Rd., 04530, tel. 207/433–4391. 6 rooms, 1 with bath. Facilities: badminton, cross-country skiing. MC, V. Rates include Continental breakfast. Inexpensive–Moderate.*

Boothbay Lodging   **Kenniston Hill Inn.** The white-clapboard house with columned porch offers comfortably old-fashioned accommodations in a country setting only minutes from Boothbay Harbor. Four guest rooms have fireplaces, some have four-posters, rocking chairs, gilt mirrors. Full breakfasts are served family style at a large wood table. *Box 125, Boothbay 04537, tel. 207/633–2159. 10 rooms with bath. No pets. No smoking. MC, V. Closed Dec.– Mar. Moderate.*

Boothbay Harbor Dining   **Black Orchid.** The classic Italian fare includes fettuccine Alfredo with fresh lobster and mushrooms, and *petit filet à la diabolo* (fillets of Angus steak with marsala sauce). The upstairs and downstairs dining rooms sport a Roman-trattoria ambience, with frilly leaves and fruit hanging from the rafters and little else in the way of decor. Summertime allows dining outdoors. *5 By-Way, tel. 207/633–6659. AE, MC, V. Closed Nov.–Apr. No lunch. Expensive.*

Andrew's Harborside. The seafood menu is typical of the area—lobster, fried clams and oysters, haddock with seafood stuffing—but the harbor view makes it memorable. Lunch features lobster and crab rolls; children's and seniors' menus are available. You can dine outdoors on a harborside deck in the summer. *8 Bridge St., tel. 207/633–4074. Reservations for 4 or more only. AE, DC, MC, V. Closed mid-Oct.–mid-May. Moderate.*

Boothbay Harbor Lodging   **Fisherman's Wharf Inn.** All rooms overlook the water at this modern motel-style facility built 200 feet out over the harbor. The large dining room has floor-to-ceiling windows, and several day-trip cruises leave from this location. *40 Commercial St., 04538, tel. 207/633–5090. 54 rooms with bath. Facilities: restaurant. AE, CB, D, DC, MC, V. Closed Nov.–mid-May. Rates include Continental breakfast. Moderate–Very Expensive.*

The Pines. Families seeking a secluded setting with lots of room for little ones to run will be interested in this motel on a hillside a mile from town. Rooms have sliding glass doors opening onto private decks, two double beds, and small refrigerators. Cribs are free. *Sunset Rd., Box 693, 04538, tel. 207/ 633–4555. 29 rooms with bath. Facilities: all-weather tennis court, heated outdoor pool, playground. MC, V. Closed late Oct.–late Apr. Inexpensive–Moderate.*

Brunswick Dining   **Twenty-two Lincoln.** The fare is rich: Maine pheasant with
★   chanterelles and Calvados; lobster with basil and vanilla beans;

Atlantic salmon with mustard mousseline. The furnishings of this gourmet restaurant in a Victorian town house in downtown Brunswick include antique oak chairs, white lace curtains, and works by local artists. The Side Door Cafe, under the same roof and using the same kitchen, serves less elaborate dishes— Maine crab cakes with sweet and piquant peppers; a vegetarian Mexican dish known as *flauta*—in a friendly, publike atmosphere. The award-winning wine list is particularly strong in California wines. *22 Lincoln St., tel. 207/725–5893. Reservations accepted. MC, V. Dinner only. Closed Sun. and Mon. Moderate–Expensive.*

Brunswick Lodging **Stowe House.** The boast of this Federal-style inn built of white clapboards in 1807 is that Henry Wadsworth Longfellow slept here and Harriet Beecher Stowe lived here for two years while she wrote *Uncle Tom's Cabin*. Today's guests are put up in the modern motel to the rear, with accommodations of the standard motel variety; the charm is reserved for the dining room and public rooms of the historic building. *63 Federal St., 04011, tel. 207/725–5543. 48 rooms with bath. Facilities: restaurant, lounge. AE, CB, DC, MC, V. Moderate.*

Freeport Dining **Harraseeket Inn.** The formal dining room upstairs is a simply appointed, light and airy space with picture windows facing the inn's garden courtyard. Specialties include roast duckling with peach glaze; and a Maine seafood medley glacé with lobster, shrimp, crab, and scallops. Waiters prepare fettuccine Alfredo and flaming desserts tableside. Downstairs, the Broad Arrow Tavern appears to have been furnished by L. L. Bean, with fly rods, snowshoes, moose heads, and other hunting-lodge trappings. The fare is hearty, with less formal lunches and snacks and dinners of charbroiled skewered shrimp and scallops, ribs, burgers, pasta, or lobster. *162 Main St., tel. 207/865–9377. Reservations advised. No shorts at dinner. AE, CB, D, DC, MC, V. Expensive.*
Harraseeket Lunch. This no-frills, bare-bones, genuine lobster pound and fried seafood place is located beside the town landing in South Freeport. Seafood baskets and lobster dinners are what it's all about; there are picnic tables outside, a few more tables inside. *Main St., South Freeport, tel. 207/865–4888. No reservations. No credit cards. Inexpensive.*

Freeport Lodging **Harraseeket Inn.** When two white-clapboard houses, one a fine Greek Revival home of 1850, found themselves two blocks from the biggest retailing explosion ever to hit Maine, the innkeepers added a four-story building that looks like an old New England inn—white clapboard with green shutters—and is in fact a steel and concrete structure with elevators and Jacuzzis. The Harraseeket strives to achieve the country inn experience, with afternoon tea in the mahogany drawing room and fireplaces throughout. Guest rooms (vintage 1989) have reproductions of Federal-period canopy beds and bright, coordinated fabrics. The full breakfast is served buffet style in an airy upstairs formal dining room facing the garden. *162 Main St., 04032, tel. 207/865–9377 or 800/342–6423. 54 rooms with bath, 2 suites. Facilities: restaurant, tavern, room service until 11 PM, croquet. AE, CB, D, DC, MC, V. Very Expensive.*

Newcastle Dining **Newcastle Inn.** Served in the small, plain, cheerful dining room of the inn are elaborate gourmet meals using fresh local ingredients and lots of imagination. The five-course, prix fixe dinner, served at 7, has a single entrée, perhaps grilled swordfish with butter diablo; rack of lamb with chive cream sauce and goat cheese lasagne; or grilled pork tenderloin with mustard cream sauce. Dessert might be peach crisp with white chocolate and brandy sauce. *River Rd., tel. 207/563–5685. Reservations required for nonguests. No jeans or shorts. MC, V. Dinner only. Closed Mon. July–Oct., weekdays Nov.–June. Expensive.*

Newcastle Lodging
★

Newcastle Inn. The white-clapboard house, vintage mid-19th century, has a homey living room with a red velvet sofa, books, and family photos on the mantel and a sun porch with white wicker furniture and ice cream parlor chairs. Guest rooms are not large, but they have been carefully appointed with old spool beds, toys, and Victorian velvet sofas, minimizing clutter and maximizing the light and the river views. Guests choose between bed and breakfast (a full gourmet meal, perhaps scrambled eggs with caviar in puff pastry, ricotta cheese pie, or frittata) and Modified American Plan. *River Rd., Newcastle 04553, tel. 207/563–5685. 15 rooms with bath. Facilities: dining room. No smoking. MC, V. Expensive.*

Peaks Island Lodging

The Moonshell Inn. This bed-and-breakfast has six simple, sunny rooms with wood floors, finished pine furniture, and white walls; most rooms have water views. The hearty Continental breakfast menu includes muffins, toast, and cereal. *Peaks Island 04108, tel. 207/766–2331. 6 rooms with bath. No credit cards. Closed Columbus Day–Thanksgiving, Jan.–Apr. Moderate–Inexpensive.*

Prouts Neck Lodging

Black Point Inn. At the tip of the peninsula that juts into the ocean at Prouts Neck, 12 miles south of Portland, stands one of the great oldtime resorts of Maine. The sun porch has wicker and plants, the music room—in the English country house style—has wing chairs, silk flowers, Chinese prints, and a grand piano. In the guest rooms are rock maple bedsteads, Martha Washington bedspreads, and white-ruffle Priscilla curtains. Older guests prefer the main inn; families choose from the three cottages. The extensive grounds offer beaches, hiking, a bird sanctuary, and sports. The dining room, done in pale Renaissance-style wallpaper and water-stained pine paneling, has a menu strong in seafood. *510 Black Point Rd., Scarborough 04074, tel. 207/883–4126, fax 207/883–9976. 80 rooms with bath, 6 suites. Facilities: restaurant, bar, entertainment; 14 tennis courts, 18-hole golf course, outdoor saltwater pool and Jacuzzi, indoor freshwater pool and Jacuzzi, volleyball, putting green, bicycles, sailboats, fishing boats. AE, MC, V. Closed Nov.–Apr. Very Expensive.*

The Arts

Portland Performing Arts Center (25A Forest Ave., Portland, tel. 207/761–0591) hosts music, dance, and theater performances.

Dance

Ram Island Dance Company (25A Forest Ave., Portland, tel. 207/773–2562), the city's resident modern dance troupe, appears at the Portland Performing Arts Center.

Music

Cumberland County Civic Center (1 Civic Center Sq., Portland, tel. 207/775–3458) hosts touring rock groups in a 9,000-seat auditorium.

Portland Symphony Orchestra (30 Myrtle St., Portland, tel. 207/773–8191) gives annual seasons of concerts.

Theater **Mad Horse Theatre Company** (955 Forest Ave., Portland, tel. 207/797–3398) performs contemporary and original works.

Maine State Music Theater (Packard Theater, Bowdoin College, Brunswick, tel. 207/725–8769) stages musicals from the end of June through August.

Portland Stage Company (25A Forest Ave., Portland, tel. 207/774–0465), a producer of national reputation, mounts six productions, from November to April, at the Portland Performing Arts Center.

Theater Project of Brunswick (14 School St., Brunswick, tel. 207/729–8584) performs from late June through August.

Nightlife

Bars and Lounges **Gritty McDuff's Brew Pub** (396 Fore St., Portland, tel. 207/772–2739) attracts the young, the lively, and connoisseurs of the ales and bitters brewed on the premises. Steak and kidney pie and fish and chips are served.

Sullivan's Lounge at Christiana's (Boothbay Harbor Inn, 37 Atlantic Ave., Boothbay Harbor, tel. 207/633–6302) offers a lively bar scene.

Top of the East (Sonesta Hotel, 157 High St., Portland, tel. 207/775–5411) has a view of the city and live entertainment—jazz, piano, and comedy.

Jazz Club **Blue Moon** (425 Fore St., Portland, tel. 207/871–0663), a movie theater-turned-restaurant, features jazz groups on weekends.

Rock Music **McSeagull's Gulf Dock** (Boothbay Harbor, tel. 207/633–4041) draws young singles with live music and a loud bar scene.

The Coast: Penobscot Bay

Purists hold that the Maine coast begins at Penobscot Bay, where the vistas over the water are wider and bluer, the shore a jumble of broken granite boulders, cobblestones, and gravel punctuated by small sand beaches, and the water numbingly cold. Port Clyde in the southwest and Stonington in the southeast are the outer limits of Maine's largest bay, 35 miles apart across the bay waters but separated by a drive of almost 100 miles on scenic but slow two-lane highways.

Rockland, the largest town on the bay, is Maine's major lobster distribution center and the port of departure to several bay islands. The Camden Hills, looming green over Camden's fashionable waterfront, turn bluer and fainter as one moves on to Castine, the elegant small town across the bay. Deer Isle is connected to the mainland by a slender, high-arching bridge, but Isle au Haut, accessible from Deer Isle's fishing town of Stonington, may be reached by passenger ferry only: More than half of this steep, wooded island is wilderness, the most remote section of Acadia National Park.

Important Addresses and Numbers

Visitor Information

Blue Hill Chamber of Commerce (Box 520, Blue Hill).

Castine Town Office (tel. 207/326–4502).

Deer Isle–Stonington Chamber of Commerce (Rte. 15, Little Deer Isle; Box 268, Stonington, tel. 207/348–6124).

Rockland Area Chamber of Commerce (Public Landing, Box 508, Rockland, tel. 207/596–0376).

Rockport–Camden–Lincolnville Chamber of Commerce (Box 919, Camden, tel. 207/236–4404).

Searsport Chamber of Commerce (Searsport, tel. 207/548–6510).

Emergencies

Island Medical Center (Airport Rd., Stonington, tel. 207/367–2311).

Penobscot Bay Medical Center (Rte. 1, Rockland, tel. 207/596–8000).

Arriving and Departing by Plane

Bangor International Airport (tel. 207/947–0384), north of Penobscot Bay, has daily flights by major U.S. carriers.

Knox County Regional Airport (tel. 207/594–4131), 3 miles south of Rockland, has flights by Northeast Express Regional.

Getting Around Penobscot Bay

By Car

Route 1 follows the west coast of Penobscot Bay, linking Rockland, Camden, Belfast, and Searsport. On the east side of the bay, Route 175 (south from Route 1) takes you to Route 166A (for Castine) and Route 15 (for Blue Hill, Deer Isle, and Stonington). A car is essential for exploring the bay area.

Exploring Penobscot Bay

Numbers in the margin correspond with the numbered points of interest on the Penobscot Bay map.

From Pemaquid Point at the western extremity of Muscongus Bay to Port Clyde at its eastern extent, it's less than 15 miles across the water, but it's 50 miles for the motorist who must return north to Route 1 to reach the far shore.

Travelers on Route 1 can make an easy detour south through Tenants Harbor and Port Clyde before reaching Rockland. Turn onto Route 131 at Thomaston, 5 miles west of Rockland, and follow the winding road past waterside fields, spruce woods, ramshackle barns, and trim houses. **Tenants Harbor,** 7 miles from Thomaston, is a quintessential Maine fishing town, its harbor dominated by squat, serviceable lobster boats, its shores rocky and slippery, its town a scattering of clapboard houses, a church, a general store. The fictional Dunnet Landing of Sarah Orne Jewett's classic sketches of Maine coastal life, *The Country of the Pointed Firs*, is based on this region.

Route 131 ends at **Port Clyde,** a fishing town that is the point of departure for the *Laura B.* (tel. 207/372–8848 for schedules),

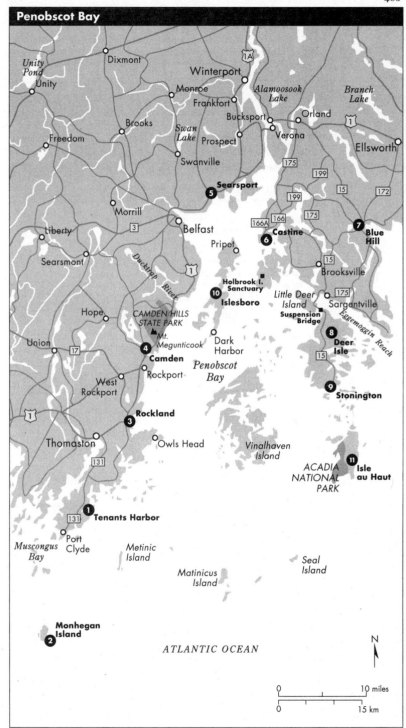

Penobscot Bay

the mailboat that serves Monhegan Island. Tiny, remote
Monhegan Island with its high cliffs fronting the open sea was
known to Basque, Portuguese, and Breton fishermen well before Columbus "discovered" America. About a century ago
Monhegan was discovered again by some of America's finest
painters, including Rockwell Kent, Robert Henri, and Edward
Hopper, who sailed out to paint the savage cliffs, the meadows,
the wild ocean views, and the shacks of fisherfolk. Tourists followed, and today Monhegan is overrun with visitors in
summer.

Monhegan's attractions include the Plantation Gallery in town
and, a short walk inland, the **Monhegan Museum**, housed in the
lighthouse keeper's quarters. Permanent exhibits document
the social and natural history of the island, and the work of a
different local painter is shown each year. *No phone. Admission by contribution. Open July–mid-Sept., daily 11:30–3.*

Nearby, Cathedral Woods is a privately owned nature sanctuary open to the considerate public.

Returning north to Route 1, you have less than 5 miles to go to
Rockland on Penobscot Bay and the **William A. Farnsworth Li-
brary and Art Museum.** Here are oil and watercolor landscapes
of the coastal lands you have just seen, among them Andrew
Wyeth's *Eight Bells* and *Her Room.* Other Wyeths (N. C. and
Jamie) are represented in the collections, as are Winslow Ho-
mer, Rockwell Kent, and the sculptor Louise Nevelson. *19 Elm
St., tel. 207/596–6457. Admission: $3 adults, $2 senior citi-
zens. Open Mon.–Sat. 10–5, Sun. 1–5. (Closed Mon. Oct.–
May.)*

From Rockland it's 8 miles north on Route 1 to **Camden,**
"Where the mountains meet the sea"—an apt description, as
you will discover when you step out of your car and look up from
the harbor. Camden is famous not only for geography but for
the nation's largest windjammer fleet; at just about any hour
during the warmer months you're likely to see at least one
windjammer tied up in the harbor, and windjammer cruises are
a superb way to explore the ports and islands of Penobscot Bay.

Time Out   **Ayer's Fish Market** on Main Street has the best fish chowder in
town; take a cup to the pleasant park at the head of the harbor
when you're ready for a break from the shops on Bayview and
Main streets.

The entrance to the 6,000-acre **Camden Hills State Park** (tel.
207/236–3109) is 2 miles north of Camden on Route 1. If you're
accustomed to the Rockies or the Alps, you may not be impressed with heights of not much more than 1,000 feet, yet the
Camden Hills are landmarks for miles along the vast, flat
reaches of the Maine coast. The park contains 25 miles of trails,
including an easy trail up Mount Megunticook, the highest of
the group. The 112-site camping area, open mid-May to mid-
October, has flush toilets and hot showers.

Farther north on Route 1, **Searsport**—Maine's second largest
deepwater port (after Portland)—claims to be the antiques
capital of Maine. The town's stretch of Route 1 hosts a seasonal
weekend flea market in addition to its antiques shops.

Searsport preserves a rich nautical history at the **Penobscot Marine Museum,** whose seven buildings display portraits of 284 sea captains, artifacts of the whaling industry (lots of scrimshaw), paintings and models of famous ships, navigational instruments, and treasures that seafarers collected. *Church St., tel. 207/548–2529. Admission: $3 adults, $2.50 senior citizens, $1 children 7–15. Open June–mid-Oct., Mon.–Sat. 9:30–5, Sun. 1–5.*

6 Historic **Castine,** over which the French, the British, and the Americans fought from the 17th century to the War of 1812, has two museums and the ruins of a British fort, but the finest thing about Castine is the town itself: the lively, welcoming town landing, the serene Federal and Greek revival houses, and the town common. Castine invites strolling, and you would do well to start at the town landing, where you can park your car, and walk up Main Street past the two inns and on to the white Trinitarian Federated Church with its tapering spire.

Turn right on Court Street and walk to the **town common,** which is ringed by a collection of white-clapboard buildings that includes the Ives House (once the summer home of the poet Robert Lowell), the Abbott School, and the Unitarian Church, capped by a whimsical belfry that suggests a gazebo.

From Castine, take Route 166 north to Route 199 and follow the **7** signs to **Blue Hill.** Castine may have the edge over Blue Hill in charm, for its Main Street is not a major thoroughfare and it claims a more dramatic perch over its harbor, yet Blue Hill is certainly appealing and boasts a better selection of shops and galleries. In fine weather you might wander about the shaded back streets, up Union Street past the inn and private school, and along Maine Street, window-shopping and looking out at the water. Blue Hill is renowned for its pottery, and two good shops are right in town.

Time Out   **Bagaduce Lunch** on Route 175/176 near North Brooksville serves fried fish and clams in summer, to be taken away or eaten at one of the picnic tables on the Bagaduce River.

The scenic Route 15 south from Blue Hill passes through Brooksville and on to the graceful suspension bridge that **8** crosses Eggemoggin Reach to **Deer Isle.** The turnout and picnic area at Caterpillar Hill, 1 mile south of the junction of Routes 15 and 175, commands a fabulous view of Penobscot Bay, the hundreds of dark green islands, and the Camden Hills across the bay, which from this perspective look like a range of mountains dwarfed and faded by an immense distance—yet they are not 25 miles away.

Route 15 continues the length of Deer Isle—a sparsely settled landscape of thick woods opening to tidal coves, shingled houses with lobster traps stacked in the yards, and dirt roads **9** that lead to summer cottages—to **Stonington,** an emphatically ungentrified community that tolerates summer visitors but makes no effort to cater to them. Main Street has gift shops and galleries, but this is a working port town, and the principal activity is at the waterfront, where fishing boats arrive with the day's catch. The high, sloped island that rises beyond the archipelago of Merchants Row is Isle au Haut, accessible by mailboat from Stonington, which contains sections of Acadia National Park.

Island Excursions
⑩ **Islesboro,** accessible by car-and-passenger ferry from Lincolnville Beach north of Rockland (Maine State Ferry Service, tel. 207/789–5611), has been a retreat of wealthy, very private families for more than a century. The long, narrow, mostly wooded island has no real town to speak of; there are scatterings of mansions as well as humbler homes at Dark Harbor and at Pripet near the north end. A good plan is to leave your car on the mainland and bring your bike for a day of cycling the narrow roads that wind past the compounds of the summer folk. Since the amenities on Islesboro are quite spread out, you don't want to come on foot. If you plan to spend the night on Islesboro, you should make a reservation well in advance (*see* Islesboro Lodging, below).

⑪ **Isle au Haut** thrusts its steeply ridged back out of the sea 7 miles south of Stonington. Accessible only by passenger ferry (tel. 207/367–5193), the island is worth visiting for the ferry ride alone, a half-hour cruise amid the tiny, pink-shore islands of Merchants Row, where you may see terns, guillemots, and harbor seals. More than half the island is part of Acadia National Park; 17½ miles of trails extend through quiet spruce and birch woods, along cobble beaches and seaside cliffs, and over the spine of the central mountain ridge. From late June to mid-September, the mailboat docks at Duck Harbor within the park. The small campground there, with five Adirondack-type lean-tos (open mid-May to mid-October), fills up quickly; reservations are essential, and they can be made only by writing to Acadia National Park (Box 177, Bar Harbor 04609).

Penobscot Bay for Free

Maine Coast Artists Gallery (Russell Ave., Rockport, tel. 207/236–2875) shows the work of Maine artists from June through September; lectures and classes are also scheduled.

Shore Village Museum exhibits U.S. Coast Guard memorabilia and artifacts, including lighthouse lenses, lifesaving gear, ship models, Civil War uniforms, and dolls. *104 Limerock St., Rockland, tel. 207/594–4950. Open June–mid-Oct., daily 10–4.*

State of Maine (Castine Harbor, tel. 207/326–4311), a retired troopship now used as a training vessel for the Maine Maritime Academy, can be toured when it's in port.

What to See and Do with Children

Owls Head Transportation Museum, 2 miles south of Rockland on Route 73, shows antique aircraft, cars, and engines and stages weekend air shows. *Rte. 73, Owls Head, tel. 207/594–4418. Admission: $3.50 adults, $2 children 5–12. Open May–Oct., daily 10–5; Nov.–Apr., weekdays 10–5.*

Penobscot Marine Museum, Searsport

Shopping

The most promising shopping streets are Main and Bayview streets in Camden and Main Street in Stonington. Antiques shops are scattered around the outskirts of villages, in farmhouses and barns; yard sales abound in summertime.

Antiques *Brooklin*	**Creative Antiques** (Rte. 175, tel. 207/359–8525) features painted furniture, hooked rugs, and prints.
Castine	**Acadia Book Service** (Main St., tel. 207/326–9332), which sells antiquarian books, prints, and paintings, is a snug place for browsing.

Oakum Bay Ltd. (Main St., tel. 207/326–9690) carries a good selection of New England antique furniture and accessories, plus handcrafted pewter, pottery, baskets, quilts, and paintings.

Deer Isle Village   **Old Deer Isle Parish House** (Rte. 15, tel. 207/367–2455) is a place for poking around in the jumbles of old kitchenware, glassware, books, and linen.

Sargentville   **Old Cove Antiques** (Rte. 15, tel. 207/359–8585) has folk art, quilts, hooked rugs, and folk carvings; hours are by appointment.

Searsport   Billing itself the antiques capital of Maine, Searsport hosts a massive weekend flea market on Route 1 during the summer months. Indoor shops, most of them in old houses and barns, are also located on Route 1, in Lincolnville Beach as well as Searsport. Shops are open daily during the summer months, by chance or by appointment from mid-October through the end of May.

Stonington   **Lavender & Old Lace** (Main St., tel. 207/359–2188) offers vintage clothing, linens, glass, china, and small furniture.

Art Galleries
Blue Hill   **Leighton Gallery** (Parker Point Rd., tel. 207/374–5001) shows oil paintings in the gallery, sculpture in its garden, and fine painted furniture.

Deer Isle Village   **Deer Isle Artist Association** (Rte. 15, tel. 207/348–6864) has group exhibits of prints, drawings, and sculpture from mid-June through September.

Turtle Gallery (tel. 207/348–2538) features one-person shows in a variety of media during the summer months.

Stonington   **Eastern Bay Cooperative Gallery** (Main St., tel. 207/367–5006) shows arts and crafts by numerous area artists.

Books and Gifts
Castine   **Four Flags Ship Chandlery** (Main St., tel. 207/326–8526) sells useful and decorative nautical items, jewelry, cards, candles, and books and maps about Maine.

Stonington   **Dockside** (W. Main St., no phone) carries a pleasing jumble of gifts and souvenirs and a good selection of books.

Crafts and Pottery
Blue Hill   **Rackliffe Pottery** (Rte. 172, tel. 207/374–2297) is famous for its vivid blue pottery: plates, tea and coffee sets, casseroles, canisters.

Rowantrees Pottery (Union St., tel. 207/374–5535) has an extensive selection of styles and patterns in dinnerware, tea sets, vases, and decorative items.

South Penobscot   **North Country Textiles** (Rte. 175, tel. 207/326–4131) is worth the detour for fine woven shawls, placemats, throws, and pillows in subtle patterns and color schemes.

Herbs
Blue Hill   **Meadow House** (Old Cart Rd., tel. 207/374–5043) is a gorgeous herb garden worth visiting for the aromas and colors alone, and you can buy living and dried herbs and related gift items.

Sports and Outdoor Activities

Boat Trips   Windjammers create a stir whenever they sail into Camden harbor, and a voyage around the bay on one of them, whether for an afternoon or a week, is unforgettable. The season for the excursions is June through September.

Camden   ***Angelique*** (Yankee Packet Co., Box 736, tel. 207/236–8873) makes weekly trips.

Appledore (0 Lilly Pond Dr., tel. 207/236–8353) offers day sails as well as private charters.

Maine Windjammer Cruises (Box 617CC, tel. 207/236–2938) has three two-masted schooners making weekly trips along the coast and to the islands.

Mary Day (Coastal Cruises, Box 798C, tel. 207/236–2750) offers weekly cruises departing Monday.

Schooner Roseway (Box 696, tel. 207/236–4449) takes three-day and six-day cruises.

Stephen Taber (70 Elm St., tel. 207/236–3520 or 800/999–7352) schedules weekly cruises.

Rockport   ***Timberwind*** (Box 247, tel. 207/236–9063) sails out of Rockport harbor.

Stonington   ***Palmer Day IV*** (Stonington Harbor, tel. 207/367–2207) cruises Penobscot Bay in July and August, stopping at North Haven and Vinalhaven.

Biking   **Maine Sport** (Main Street, Camden, tel. 207/236–8797) rents bikes, canoes, and kayaks.

Deep-Sea Fishing   **Bay Island Yacht Charters** (Box 639, Camden, tel. 207/236–2776) has charters by the day, week, and month.

Henrietta (Rockland Public Landing, tel. 207/594–5411) takes 30 passengers for fishing and sightseeing on Penobscot Bay.

Union Jack (Box 842, Camden, tel. 207/785–3521) goes out on fishing charters.

Water Sports   Eggemoggin Reach is a famous cruising ground for yachts, as are the coves and inlets around Deer Isle and the Penobscot Bay waters between Castine and Islesboro. For sailboat, kayak, and canoe rentals, try **Eaton's Boatyard** (Sea St., Castine, tel. 207/326–8579), **Indian Island Kayak** (Rockport, tel. 207/236–4088), **Maine Sport** (Main St., Camden, tel. 207/236–8797), or **Sailways** (Goose Cove Lodge, Deer Isle, tel. 207/348–2279).

State Parks

Camden Hills State Park (*see* Exploring Penobscot Bay, above).

Holbrook Island Sanctuary (on Penobscot Bay in Brooksville, tel. 207/326–4012) has a gravelly beach with a splendid view; hiking trails through meadow and forest; no camping facilities.

Dining and Lodging

Camden has the greatest variety of inns and restaurants in the region.

Blue Hill Dining **Jonathan's.** The older downstairs room has captain's chairs, blue tablecloths, and local art; in the post-and-beam upstairs, there's wood everywhere, candles with hurricane globes, and high-back chairs. The menu may include chicken breast in a fennel sauce with peppers, garlic, rosemary, and shallots; shrimp scorpio (shrimp served on linguine with a touch of ouzo and feta cheese); and grilled strip steak. Chocolate bourbon pecan cake makes a compelling finale. The wine list has 250 selections from French and California vineyards. *Main St., tel. 207/374–5226. Reservations advised in summer. Dress: casual. AE, MC, V. Closed Mon. Jan.–Apr. Dinner only. Moderate–Expensive.*

Blue Hill Lodging **Blue Hill Inn.** The dignified white-clapboard building in Blue Hill's historic district celebrated its 150th anniversary as an inn in 1990. Five guest rooms have working fireplaces; all are decorated with Empire or early Victorian pieces, including marble-topped walnut dressers, Oriental rugs on painted wood or pumpkin pine floors, and wing chairs. Guests dine beneath a Persian candle chandelier on elaborate six-course meals that might include lobster bisque, rosemary sorbet, rack of lamb, honey-roasted duck, cod with pecans and black beans, and chocolate mousse with pecan bourbon. Dinner is open to the public on a limited basis by reservation only; and jackets are encouraged. You choose between Modified American Plan and bed-and-breakfast. *Box 403, 04614, tel. 207/374–2844. 11 rooms with bath. MC, V. Expensive–Very Expensive.*

Camden Dining **The Belmont.** Round tables are set well apart in this dining
★ room with smoke-colored walls and soft classical music or jazz. The changing menu of New American cuisine might include sautéed scallops with Pernod leek cream; grilled pheasant with cranberry; chicken with a tomato coconut curry; or braised lamb shanks. *6 Belmont Ave., tel. 207/236–8053. Reservations advised. Dress: casual. MC, V. Closed Jan.–Apr. Closed Mon. May–Columbus Day, closed Mon.–Wed. Columbus Day–Dec. Dinner only. Expensive.*

The Waterfront Restaurant. A ringside seat on Camden Harbor can be had here; the best view is from the outdoor deck, open in warm weather. The fare is seafood: boiled lobster, scallops, bouillabaisse, steamed mussels, Cajun barbecued shrimp. Lunchtime features are lobster salad, crabmeat salad, lobster and crab rolls, tuna niçoise, turkey melt, and burgers. *Bayview St., tel. 207/236–3747. No reservations. Dress: casual. AE, MC, V. Closed Jan.–mid-Feb. Moderate–Expensive.*

★ **Whitehall Inn.** The spacious, red-carpeted, simply furnished dining room of Camden's venerable inn serves creative American fare such as Eastern salmon in puff pastry; scallop brochettes with rice; swordfish grilled with roast red pepper sauce; and more traditional dishes like baked breaded haddock, prime rib, and lamb tenderloin. The pewter Williamsburg chandeliers, ferns, and big windows on a sunny terrace contribute to a stately elegance that stops just short of being formal. *52 High St. (Rte. 1), tel. 207/236–3391. Reservations required. Jacket advised. MC, V. Closed mid-Oct.–mid-June. No lunch. Moderate.*

Village Restaurant. This restaurant recalls the days before gift shops and condos came to Camden. The large, no-frills dining room has windows on the water and nautical pictures; the substantial old-fashioned fare includes New England boiled dinner, chicken pie, steaks, and lobster in summer. Strawberry angel pie heads the dessert menu. *7 Main St., tel. 207/236–3232. No reservations. Dress: casual. MC, V. Closed Tues. Inexpensive–Moderate.*

Camden Lodging **Norumbega.** The stone castle amid Camden's elegant clapboard houses, built in 1886 by Joseph B. Stearns, the inventor of duplex telegraphy, was obviously the fulfillment of a fantasy. The public rooms boast gleaming parquet floors, oak and mahogany paneling, richly carved wood mantels over four fireplaces on the first floor alone, gilt mirrors, and Empire furnishings. At the back of the house, several decks and balconies overlook the garden, the gazebo, and the bay. The view improves as you ascend; the newly completed penthouse suite features a small deck, private bar, and a skylight in the bedroom. *61 High St., 04843, tel. 207/236–4646. 12 rooms with bath. AE, MC, V. Very Expensive.*

Whitehall Inn. Camden's best-known inn, just north of town on Route 1, boasts a central white-clapboard, wide-porch ship captain's home of 1843 connected to a turn-of-the-century wing. Just off the comfortable main lobby with its faded Oriental rugs, the Millay Room preserves memorabilia of the poet Edna St. Vincent Millay, who grew up in Rockland. Loyal adherents cherish the fact that everything looks the same year after year, down to the old-fashioned telephones connected to an ancient switchboard with plugs. Newcomers could be disappointed with the small, sparsely furnished rooms with their dark wood bedsteads, white bedspreads, and clawfoot bathtubs. Rooms in the Victorian Maine and Wicker houses across Route 1 offer greater quiet and king-size beds. The dining room is open to the public for dinner and breakfast. The inn offers Modified American Plan (dinner credit available) from mid-June to mid-October. *Box 558, 04843, tel. 207/236–3391. 50 rooms, 42 with bath. Facilities: restaurants, all-weather tennis court, shuffleboard, motorboat, golf privileges. MC, V. Closed mid-Oct.–mid-May. Rates are MAP. Expensive–Very Expensive.*

Windward House. A choice bed-and-breakfast, this Greek Revival house of 1854, situated at the edge of town, features rooms furnished with fishnet lace canopy beds, cherry highboys, curly maple bedsteads, and clawfoot mahogany dressers. Guests are welcome to use any of three sitting rooms, including the Wicker Room with its glass-topped white wicker table where morning coffee is served. A small deck overlooks the back garden. Breakfasts may include quiche, apple puff pancakes, peaches-and-cream French toast, or soufflés. *6 High St., 04843, tel. 207/236–9656. 5 rooms with bath, 1 efficiency. MC, V. Moderate–Expensive.*

Castine Lodging **The Pentagoet.** A recent renovation of the rambling, pale yellow Pentagoet gave each room a bath, enlarged the dining room, and opened up the public rooms. The porch wraps around three sides of the inn. Guest rooms are warmer, more flowery, more feminine than those of the Castine Inn across the street; they have hooked rugs, a mix of Victorian antiques, and floral wallpapers. Dinner in the deep rose and cream formal dining room (open to the public on a limited basis) is an elaborate affair; you might find such dishes as mushroom streudel, lemon egg drop soup, lobster pie, tournedos of beef, and broiled haddock. *Main St., 04421, tel. 207/326–8616. 17 rooms with bath. MC, V. Closed Dec.–Apr. Rates are MAP. Very Expensive.*

★ **The Castine Inn.** Dark wood pineapple four-posters, white up-holstered easy chairs, and oil paintings are typical of the room furnishings here. The newly renovated third floor has the best views: the harbor over the back garden on one side, Main Street on the other. The dining room, decorated with whimsical murals, is open to the public for breakfast and dinner; the menu features traditional New England fare—Maine lobster, crab-meat cakes with mustard sauce, roast leg of lamb, and chicken and leek pot pie. A snug, old-fashioned pub off the lobby has small tables and antique spirit jars over the mantel. *Main St., 04421, tel. 207/326–4365. 20 rooms with bath, 2 suites. Facilities: restaurant, pub. MC, V. Closed Nov.–mid-Apr. Rates include full breakfast. Moderate–Expensive.*

Deer Isle Lodging **Goose Cove Lodge.** The heavily wooded property at the end of a back road has 2,500 feet of ocean frontage, two sandy beaches, a long sandbar that leads to the Barred Island nature preserve, nature trails, and sailboats for rent nearby. Some cottages and suites are in secluded woodlands, some on the shore, some attached, some with a single large room, others with one or two bedrooms. All but two units have fireplaces. In July and August the minimum stay is one week. *Sunset 04683, tel. 207/348–2508 (summer) or 207/767–3003 (winter). 11 cottages, 10 suites, 1 apartment. Facilities: rowboat, canoe, volleyball, horseshoes. No credit cards. Closed mid-Oct.–Apr. Rates are MAP. Expensive–Very Expensive.*

Pilgrim's Inn. The bright red, four-story, gambrel-roof house dating from about 1793 overlooks a mill pond and harbor at the center of Deer Isle. The library has wing chairs and Oriental rugs; a downstairs taproom has pine furniture, braided rugs, and parson's benches. Guest rooms, each with its own character, sport Laura Ashley fabrics and select antiques. The dining room in the attached barn, an open space both rustic and elegant, has farm implements, French oil lamps, and tiny windows. The single-entrée menu changes nightly; it might include rack of lamb or fresh local seafood; scallop bisque; asparagus and smoked salmon; and poached pear tart for dessert. *Deer Isle 04627, tel. 207/348–6615. 13 rooms, 8 with bath, 1 cottage. Facilities: restaurant. No credit cards. Closed mid-Oct.–mid-May. Expensive–Very Expensive.*

Isle au Haut Lodging **Keeper's House.** The converted lighthouse keeper's house, set on a rock ledge surrounded by thick spruce forest, has no electricity and no access by road; guests dine by candlelight on seafood or chicken and read in the evening by kerosene lantern. Trails link the inn with the park trail network, and you can walk to the village, a collection of simple houses, a church, a tiny school, and a general store. The four guest rooms are spacious, airy, and simply decorated with painted wood furniture and local crafts. A separate cottage, the Oil House, has no indoor plumbing. *Isle au Haut 04645, tel. 207/367–2261. 4 rooms with bath, 1 cottage. Facilities: dock. No credit cards. Closed Nov.–Apr. Rates include 3 meals. Expensive.*

Islesboro Lodging **Dark Harbor House.** The yellow-clapboard, neo-Georgian summer "cottage" of 1896 has a stately portico and a hilltop setting. Inside, an elegant double staircase curves from the ground floor to the bedrooms, which are spacious, some with balconies, one with an 18th-century four-poster. The dining room, open to the public for prix-fixe dinners, features seafood with a West Indian accent. *Box 185, 04848, tel. 207/734–6669. 12 rooms, 4* *with bath. Facilities: restaurant. Closed Nov.–Memorial Day. Very Expensive.*

Islesboro Inn. Built early in the century by summer residents of the island, the inn retains the exclusive air of a posh estate. The terrace, where meals are served in fine weather, gives way to a perfect lawn that extends to the shore. Marble mantels, wood paneling, and Oriental rugs decorate public rooms. The rooms in the front of the house are larger and face the water; those in the back, where servants once slept, are less expensive. *Islesboro 04848, tel. 207/734–2222. 16 rooms with bath. Facilities: sailboat, rowboat, tennis, shuffleboard, croquet. Closed mid-Sept.–May. Expensive–Very Expensive.*

North Brooklin Lodging **The Lookout.** The stately white-clapboard building stands in a wide field at the tip of Flye Point, with a superb view of the water and the mountains of Mount Desert Island. Rustic rooms have country antiques original to the house and newer matching pieces, though the floors show a tendency to slope, and a century of damp has left a certain mustiness. The larger south-facing rooms command the view. Seven cottages have from one to four bedrooms each. With the dining room expanded onto the porch, seven tables enjoy a view of the outdoors. Entrées could include filet mignon, grilled salmon, and shrimp and scallops provençale; the lobster cookout is Wednesday night. *North Brooklin 04661, tel. 207/359–2188. 6 rooms with bath, 7 cottages. Facilities: restaurant. MC, V. Closed mid-Oct.–Memorial Day. Inexpensive–Moderate.*

Spruce Head Dining and Lodging **The Craignair Inn.** Built in the 1930s as a boardinghouse for stonecutters and converted to an inn a decade later, the Craignair commands a coastal view of rocky shore and lobster boats. Inside the three-story gambrel-roof house you'll find country clutter, books, and cut glass in the parlor; braided rugs, brass beds, and dowdy dressers in the guest rooms. A few years ago the owners converted a church dating from the 1890s into another accommodation with six rooms—each with bath—that have a more modern feel. The waterside dining room, decorated with Delft and Staffordshire plates, serves such fare as bouillabaisse; lemon pepper seafood kebab; rabbit with tarragon and wine; and those New England standards: shore dinner, prime rib, and scampi. A bourbon pecan tart and crème brûlée are the dessert headliners. *Clark Island Rd., 04859, tel. 207/594–7644. 21 rooms, 6 with bath. Facilities: restaurant. D, MC, V. Closed Feb. Moderate.*

Stonington Dining ★ **Fisherman's Friend Restaurant.** Fresh salmon, halibut, monkfish, lobster, and even prime rib and chicken are on the menu here. Friday is fish-fry day: free seconds on fried haddock, french fries, and cole slaw for $5.99. *School St., tel. 207/367–2442. Reservations advised. Dress: casual. No credit cards. BYOB. Closed mid-Nov.–mid-Mar.; closed Mon. Labor Day–mid-Nov. Inexpensive.*

Stonington Lodging **Captain's Quarters Inn and Motel.** Accommodations, as plain and unadorned as Stonington itself, are in the middle of town, a two-minute walk from the Isle au Haut mailboat. You have your choice of motel-type rooms and suites or efficiencies, and you can take your breakfast muffins and coffee to the sunny deck on the water. *Main St., Box 83, 04681, tel. 207/367–2420. 13 units, 11 with bath. AE, MC, V. Inexpensive–Moderate.*

Tenants Harbor Dining and Lodging **East Wind Inn & Meeting House.** On Route 131, 10 miles off Route 1 and set on a knob of land overlooking the harbor and the islands, the inn offers simple hospitality, a wraparound porch, and unadorned but comfortable guest rooms furnished with an iron bedstead, flowered wallpaper, and heritage bedspread. The dining room has a rustic decor; the dinner menu features duck with black currant sauce; seafood stew with scallops, shrimp, mussels, and grilled sausage; boiled lobster; and baked stuffed haddock. *Box 149, 04860, tel. 207/372–6366. 26 rooms, 12 with bath. Facilities: sailboat cruises in season. AE, MC, V. No dinner Sun. Inexpensive–Moderate.*

The Arts

Music **Bay Chamber Concerts** (Rockport Opera House, Rockport, tel. 207/236–2823) offers chamber music Thursday and Friday.

Kneisel Hall Chamber Music Festival (Box 648, Blue Hill, tel. 207/374–2811) has concerts Sunday and Friday in summer.

Theater **Camden Civic Theatre** (Camden Opera House, Elm St., tel. 207/594–4982) stages theatrical productions through the year.

Camden Shakespeare Company (Bok Amphitheater, Atlantic Ave., tel. 207/236–8011) produces plays, musicals, and concerts from July to Labor Day.

Cold Comfort Productions (Box 259, Castine, tel. 207/326–9041), a community theater, mounts plays in summer.

Nightlife

Bars and Lounges **Bennett's Wharf** (Sea St., Castine, tel. 207/326–4861) has a long bar that can become rowdy after dark.

Peter Ott's Tavern (Bayview St., Camden, tel. 207/236–4032) is a steakhouse with a lively bar scene.

Thirsty Whale Tavern (Camden Harbour Inn, 83 Bayview St., Camden, tel. 207/236–4200) is a popular local drinking spot.

Comedy Clubs **Trade Winds Comedy Club** (Trade Winds Motor Inn, Rockland, tel. 207/596–6661) features performers who deal with adult themes.

The Coast: Acadia

East of Penobscot Bay, *Acadia* is the informal name for the area that includes Mount Desert Island (pronounced like *dessert*) and its surroundings: Blue Hill Bay, Frenchman Bay, and Ellsworth, Hancock, and other mainland towns. Mount Desert, 13 miles across, is Maine's largest island, and it harbors most of Acadia National Park, Maine's principal tourist attraction with more than 4 million visitors a year. The 34,000 acres of woods and mountains, lake and shore, footpaths, carriage paths, and hiking trails that make up the park extend as well to other islands and some of the mainland. Outside the park, on Mount Desert's east shore, an upper-class resort town of the 19th century has become a busy tourist town of the 20th century in Bar Harbor, which services the park with inns, motels, and restaurants.

Important Addresses and Numbers

Visitor Information   Acadia National Park (Box 177, Bar Harbor 04609, tel. 207/288–3338).

Bar Harbor Chamber of Commerce (Box BC, Cottage St., Bar Harbor 04609, tel. 207/288–3393 or 207/288–5103).

Getting Around Acadia

By Car   North of Bar Harbor the scenic 27-mile Park Loop Road takes leave of Route 3 to circle the eastern quarter of Mount Desert Island, with one-way traffic from Sieur de Monts Spring to Seal Harbor and two-way traffic between Seal Harbor and Hulls Cove. Route 102, which serves the western half of Mount Desert, is reached from Route 3 just after it crosses onto the island or from Route 233 west from Bar Harbor. All these island roads pass in, out, and through the precincts of Acadia National Park.

Guided Tours

Bar Harbor Limousine Servive (tel. 207/288–5398) conducts half-day historic and scenic tours of the area.

National Park Tours (tel. 207/288–3327) 2½-hour bus tour of Acadia National Park, narrated by a park naturalist, departs twice daily from Testa's Restaurant on Main Street in Bar Harbor.

Bar Harbor Trolley (tel. 207/288–5741) makes frequent trips through Bar Harbor and the national park.

Exploring Acadia

Numbers in the margin correspond with the numbered points of interest on the Acadia map.

Coastal Route 1 passes through Ellsworth, where Route 3 turns south to Mount Desert Island and takes you into the busy
❶ town of **Bar Harbor.** Although most of Bar Harbor's grand mansions were destroyed in the fire of 1947 and replaced by modern motels, the town retains the beauty of a commanding location on Frenchman Bay. Shops, restaurants, and hotels are clustered along Main, Mount Desert, and Cottage streets.

❷ The **Hulls Cove** approach to Acadia National Park is 4 miles northwest of Bar Harbor on Route 3. Even though it is often clogged with traffic in summer, the Park Loop Road provides the best introduction to Acadia National Park. At the start of the loop at Hulls Cove, the visitor center shows a free 15-minute orientation film and has maps of the hiking trails and carriage paths in the park.

❸ Follow the road to the parking area for **Sand Beach,** a small stretch of pink sand backed by the mountains of Acadia and the odd lump of rock known as the Beehive. The Ocean Trail, which parallels the Park Loop Road from Sand Beach to the Otter Point parking area, is a popular and easily accessible walk with some of the most spectacular scenery in Maine: huge slabs of pink granite heaped at the ocean's edge, ocean views unob-

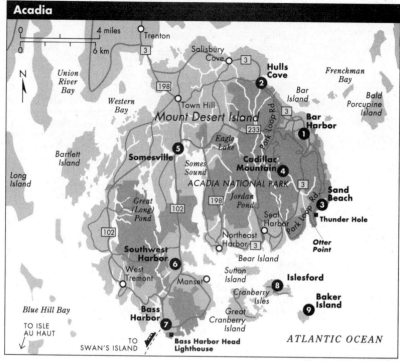

Acadia

structed to the horizon, and Thunder Hole, a natural seaside cave in which the ocean rushes and roars.

④ Those who want a mountaintop experience without the effort of hiking can drive to the summit of **Cadillac Mountain,** at 1,523 feet the highest point along the eastern coast. From the smooth, bald summit you have a 360-degree view of the ocean, the islands, the jagged coast, and the woods and lakes of Acadia.

⑤ On completing the 27-mile Park Loop, you can continue your auto tour of the island by heading west on Route 233 for the villages on Somes Sound, a true fjord—the only one on the East Coast—which almost bisects Mount Desert Island. **Somesville,** the oldest settlement on the island (1621), is a carefully preserved New England village of white-clapboard houses and churches, neat green lawns, and bits of blue water visible behind them.

⑥ Route 102 south from Somesville takes you to **Southwest Harbor,** which combines the rough, salty character of a working port with the refinements of a summer resort community. From the town's Main Street along Route 102, turn left onto Clark Point Road to reach the harbor.

Time Out   At the end of Clark Point Road in Somesville, **Beal's Lobster Pier** serves lobsters, clams, and crab rolls in season at dockside picnic tables.

Those who want to tour more of the island will continue south on Route 102, following Route 102A where the road forks, and passing through the communities of Manset and Seawall. The Bass Harbor Head lighthouse, which clings to a cliff at the eastern entrance to Blue Hill Bay, was built in 1858. The tiny **⑦** lobstering village of **Bass Harbor** has cottages for rent, a gift shop, and a car and passenger ferry to Swans Island.

Island Excursions Situated off the southeast shore of Mount Desert Island at the entrance to Somes Sound, the five Cranberry Isles—Great Cranberry, Islesford (or Little Cranberry), Baker Island, Sutton Island, and Bear Island—escape the hubbub that engulfs Acadia National Park in summer. Great Cranberry and Islesford are served by the Beal & Bunker passenger ferry (tel. 207/244–3575) from Northeast Harbor; Baker Island is reached by the summer cruise boats of the Islesford Ferry Company (tel. 207/276–3717); Sutton and Bear islands are privately owned.

⑧ **Islesford** comes closest to having a village: a collection of houses, a church, a fishermen's co-op, a market, and a post office near the ferry dock. The Islesford Historical Museum, run by the national park, has displays of tools, documents relating to the island's history, and books and manuscripts of the writer Rachel Field (1894–1942), who summered on Sutton Island. Island Bed and Breakfast (tel. 207/244–9283), a short walk from the ferry landing, offers overnight accommodations from mid-June through September. The Islesford Dock restaurant (tel. 207/244–3177) serves three meals a day from June to September.

⑨ The 123-acre **Baker Island,** the most remote of the group, looks almost black from a distance because of its thick spruce forest. The cruise boat from Northeast Harbor makes a 4½-hour narrated tour, in the course of which you are likely to see ospreys nesting on a sea stack off Sutton Island, harbor seals hauled out on ledges, and cormorants flying low over the water. Because Baker Island has no natural harbor, the tour boat ties up offshore and you take a fishing dory to reach the island.

Acadia for Free

Bar Harbor Historical Society Museum displays photos of Bar Harbor from the days when it catered to the very rich. Other exhibits document the great fire of 1947, in which many of the Gilded Age cottages were destroyed. *34 Mt. Desert St., tel. 207/ 288–3838. Admission free. Open mid-June–mid-Sept., Mon.– Sat. 1–4; by appointment at other seasons.*

What to See and Do with Children

Acadia Zoological Park, a 100-acre preserve and petting zoo, has pastures, streams, woods, and wild and domestic animals. *Rte. 3, Trenton, tel. 207/667–3244. Open May–Columbus Day.*

Mount Desert Oceanarium has exhibits on the fishing and sea life of the Gulf of Maine. *Clark Point Rd., Southwest Harbor, tel. 207/244–7330. Admission: $3.50 adults, $2 children. Open mid-May–mid-Oct., Mon.–Sat. 9–5.*

Off the Beaten Track

Jackson Laboratory, a center for research in mammalian genetics, studies cancer, diabetes, and heart disease. *Rte. 3, 3½ mi south of Bar Harbor, tel. 207/288–3371. Audiovisual presentations mid-June–Aug., Mon., Tues., Thurs. at 2.*

Shopping

Bar Harbor is a good place for browsing for gifts, T-shirts, and novelty items; for bargains, head for the outlets that line Route 3 in Ellsworth, which have good discounts on shoes.

Antiques **1895 Shop** (1 Steamboat Wharf Rd., tel. 207/244–7039) has chi-
Bernard na, glassware, jewelry, postcards, and curios. The detour to Bernard—off Route 102 on Mount Desert Island—is worth making.

E. and L. Higgins (tel. 207/244–3983) has a good stock of wicker, along with pine and oak country furniture.

Southwest Harbor **Marianne Clark Fine Antiques** (Main St., tel. 207/244–9247) has an eclectic stock of country furniture and American paintings.

Trenton **Acadia Mews Antique Center** (Bar Harbor Rd., tel. 207/667–7323) is three shops offering folk art and country and formal furniture in mahogany and wicker.

Crafts **Acadia Shops** (inside the park at Cadillac Mountain summit;
Bar Harbor Thunder Hole on Ocean Dr.; Jordan Pond House on Park Loop Rd.; and 85 Main St.) sell crafts and Maine foods.

Island Artisans (99 Main St., tel. 207/288–4214) is a crafts cooperative that shows work in various media and styles.

Willis' Rock Shop (Main St., tel. 207/288–4935) carries gold and semiprecious stones, scrimshaw and stone samples.

Sports and Outdoor Activities

Biking, Jogging, The network of carriage paths that wind through the woods
Cross-Country and fields of Acadia National Park is ideal for biking and jog-
Skiing ging when the ground is dry and for cross-country skiing in winter. Hulls Cove visitor center has a carriage paths map.

Bikes for hire can be found at **Acadia Bike & Canoe** (48 Cottage St., Bar Harbor, tel. 207/288–5483) and **Bar Harbor Bicycle Shop** (141 Cottage St., tel. 207/288–3886).

Boat Trips **Acadia Boat Tours & Charters** (West St., tel. 207/288–9505) em-
Bar Harbor barks on 1½-hour lobster fishing trips in summer.

Acadian Whale Watcher (Golden Anchor Pier, tel. 207/288–9794) runs 2½-hour whale-watching cruises in summer.

Bay Lady (1 West St., tel. 207/288–3322) offers two-hour windjammer cruises on Frenchman Bay during the season.

Natalie Todd (Inn Pier, tel. 207/288–4585) offers weekend windjammer cruises from July through September.

Northeast Harbor *Blackjack* (Town Dock, tel. 207/276–5043 or 207/288–3056), a 33-foot Friendship sloop, makes five trips daily, May to October.

Sunrise (Sea St. Pier, tel. 207/276–5352) does lobster fishing tours in the summer months.

Camping The two campgrounds in Acadia National Park—**Blackwoods** (tel. 207/288–3274), open year-round, and **Seawall** (tel. 207/ 244–3600), open late May to late September—fill up quickly during the summer season. Off Mount Desert Island, but convenient to it, the campground at **Lamoine State Park** (tel. 207/ 667–4778) is open mid-May to mid-October; the 55-acre park has a great location on Frenchman Bay.

Canoeing and Kayaking For canoe and kayak rentals, see **Acadia Bike & Canoe, Life Sports** (34 High St., Ellsworth, tel. 207/667–7819), or **National Park Canoe Rentals** (Rte. 102, 2 mi west of Somesville, at the head of Long Pond, tel. 207/244–5854).

Deep-Sea Fishing
Bar Harbor *Dolphin* (Frenchman Bay Co., 1 West St., tel. 207/288–3322) is available for charter from Memorial Day to Columbus Day.

Southwest Harbor *Masako Queen* (Clark Point Rd., tel. 207/667–3281) offers daily fishing trips in summer.

Hiking Acadia National Park maintains nearly 200 miles of foot and carriage paths, ranging from easy strolls along flatlands to rigorous climbs that involve ladders and handholds on rock faces. Among the more rewarding hikes are the Precipice Trail to Champlain Mountain, the Great Head Loop, the Gorham Mountain Trail, and the path around Eagle Lake. The National Park visitor center has a trail guide and map.

Sailing
Bar Harbor **Harbor Boat Rentals** (Harbor Pl., 1 West St., tel. 207/288– 3757) has 13-foot and 17-foot Boston whalers.

Southwest Harbor **Manset Boat Rental** (Manset Boatyard, just south of Southwest Harbor, tel. 207/244–9233) rents sailboats.

Dining and Lodging

Bar Harbor has the greatest concentration of accommodations on Mount Desert Island and a number of fine restaurants.

Bar Harbor Dining
★ **George's.** Candles, flowers, and linens grace the tables in four small dining rooms in an old house. The menu shows a distinct Mediterranean influence in the lobster streudel wrapped in phyllo, and in the sautéed veal; fresh char-grilled salmon and swordfish stand on their own. Couples tend to linger in the romantic setting. *7 Stephen's La., tel. 207/288–4505. Reservations advised. Dress: casual. AE, CB, DC, MC, V. Closed late Oct.–mid-June. Dinner only. Moderate–Expensive.*

Jordan Pond House. Oversize popovers and tea are a warm tradition at this rustic restaurant in the park, where in fine weather you can sit on the terrace or the lawn and admire the views of Jordan Pond and the mountains. The dinner menu offers lobster stew, seafood thermidor, and fisherman's stew. *Park Loop Rd., tel. 207/276–3316. Reservations one day in advance advised in summer. Dress: casual. AE, D, MC, V. Closed late Oct.–late May. Moderate.*

★ **124 Cottage Street.** The four dining rooms of the cheerful, flower-filled restaurant have the feel of a country inn, and the back room has an extra treat—a sliding glass door to a small garden and woods. The fare is seafood and pasta dishes with an Oriental twist: Szechuan shrimp; pasta primavera with pea pods and broccoli; seafood pasta with mussels, shrimp, and scallops in tomato sauce; broiled swordfish, salmon, haddock.

124 Cottage St., tel. 207/288-4383. Reservations advised. Dress: casual. MC, V. Closed late Oct.–mid-June. Dinner only. Moderate.

Bar Harbor Lodging

Inn at Canoe Point. Seclusion and privacy are bywords of this snug, 100-year-old Tudor-style house on the water at Hulls Cove, 2 miles from Bar Harbor. The Master Suite, a large room with a fireplace, is a favorite for its size and the French doors opening onto a waterside deck. The inn's large living room has huge windows on the water, a fieldstone fireplace, and, just outside, a deck that hangs over the water. *216 Hulls Cove Rd., 04644, tel. 207/288-9511. 6 rooms, 5 with bath. No credit cards. Expensive–Very Expensive.*

Mira Monte. Built as a summer home in 1864, the Mira Monte bespeaks Victorian leisure, with columned verandas, latticed bay windows, and landscaped grounds for strolling and sunning; and the inn is set back far enough from the road to assure quiet and seclusion. The guest rooms have brass beds or four-posters, white wicker, hooked rugs, lace curtains, and oil paintings in gilt frames. The quieter, rear-facing rooms offer sunny garden views. Some rooms have porches, fireplaces, and separate entrances. *69 Mt. Desert St., 04609, tel. 207/288-4263. 11 rooms with bath. AE, MC, V. Closed late Oct.–early May. Moderate–Very Expensive.*

Wonder View Motor Lodge. While the rooms are standard motel accommodations, with two double beds and nondescript furniture, this establishment is distinguished by its extensive grounds, the view of Frenchman Bay, and a location opposite the Bluenose ferry terminal. The woods muffle the sounds of traffic on Route 3. Pets are accepted, and the dining room has picture windows. *Rte. 3, Box 25, 04609, tel. 207/288-3358 or 800/341-1553. 82 rooms with bath. Facilities: dining room, outdoor pool. AE, MC, V. Closed late Oct.–mid-May. Inexpensive–Expensive.*

Hancock Dining ★

Le Domaine. On a rural stretch of Route 1, 9 miles east of Ellsworth, a French chef prepares *lapin pruneaux* (rabbit in a rich brown sauce); sweetbreads with lemon and capers; and coquilles St. Jacques. The elegant but not intimidating dining room has polished wood floors, copper pots hanging from the mantel, and silver, crystal, and linen on the tables. *Rte. 1, Hancock, tel. 207/422-3395. Reservations advised. Dress: casual but neat. Dinner only. Closed Nov.–Apr. Expensive.*

Hancock Lodging

Le Domaine. The seven smallish rooms in the inn are done in French country style, with chintz and wicker, simple desks, and sofas near the windows. Four rooms have balconies or porches over the gardens. The 100-acre property offers paths for walking and badminton on the lawn. *Box 496, 04640, tel. 207/422-3395. 7 rooms with bath. Facilities: restaurant. AE, MC, V. Closed Nov.–Apr. Rates are MAP. Very Expensive.*

Northeast Harbor Dining

Asticou Inn. At night guests of the inn trade topsiders and polo shirt for jacket and tie to dine in the stately formal dining room, which is open to the public for a prix-fixe dinner by reservation only. A recent menu featured swordfish with orange mustard glaze; lobster; seared catfish; and chicken in a lemon cream and mushroom sauce. *Tel. 207/276-3344. Reservations required. Jacket and tie required. Closed mid-Sept.–mid-June. Dinner only. Expensive.*

Northeast Harbor **Lodging**	**Asticou Inn.** This grand turn-of-the-century inn at the head of exclusive Northeast Harbor serves a loyal clientele. Guest rooms in the main building have a country feel, with bright fabrics, white lace curtains, and white painted furniture. The more modern cottages scattered around the grounds afford greater privacy; among them, the decks and picture windows make the Topsider Cottages particularly attractive. A stay at the inn includes breakfast and dinner, but the cottages and the Victorian-style Cranberry Lodge across the street operate on a bed-and-breakfast policy from mid-May to mid-June and from mid-September to January 1. *Northeast Harbor 04662, tel. 207/276–3344. 50 rooms with bath, 23 suites, 6 cottages. Facilities: clay tennis court, heated pool. MC, V. Inn closed mid-Sept.–mid-June; cottages, lodge closed Jan.–mid-May. Rates are MAP. Very Expensive (lodge, Moderate–Expensive).*

Southwest Harbor Dining — **Claremont Hotel.** The large, airy dining room of the inn, open to the public for dinner only, is awash in light streaming through the picture windows. The atmosphere is on the formal side, with crystal, silver, and china service. Rack of lamb, baked stuffed shrimp, coquilles St. Jacques, and tournedos au poivre are specialties. *Tel. 207/244–5036. Reservations required. Jacket required. No credit cards. Closed mid-Sept.–mid-June. Dinner only. Moderate.*

Southwest Harbor Lodging — **Claremont Hotel.** Built in 1884 and operated continuously as an inn, the Claremont calls up memories of long, leisurely vacations of days gone by. The yellow-clapboard structure commands a view of Somes Sound, croquet is played on the lawn, and cocktails are served at the boathouse from mid-July to the end of August. Guest rooms are bright, white, and quite plain; cottages and two guest houses on the grounds are homier and woodsier. Modified American Plan is in effect from mid-June to mid-September. *Box 137, 04679, tel. 207/244–5036. 22 rooms, 20 with bath; 3 suites, 11 cottages, 2 guest houses. Facilities: clay tennis court, croquet, bicycles, private dock and moorings. No credit cards. Hotel closed mid-Sept.–mid-June. Cottages closed mid-Oct.–mid-May. Rates are MAP. Expensive–Very Expensive.*

The Arts

Music — **Arcady Music Festival** (tel. 207/288–3151) schedules concerts around Mount Desert Island from late July through August.

Bar Harbor Festival (36 Mt. Desert St., Bar Harbor, tel. 207/288–5744; 510 5th Ave., New York, NY 10036, tel. 212/222–1026) programs recitals, jazz, chamber music, and pops concerts from mid-July to mid-August.

Domaine School (Hancock, tel. 207/422–6251) presents public concerts by faculty and students at Monteux Memorial Hall.

Theater — **Acadia Repertory Company** (Masonic Hall, Rte. 102, Somesville, tel. 207/244–7260) mounts plays in July and August.

Nightlife

Acadia has little nighttime activity. The lounge at the **Moorings Restaurant** (Manset, tel. 207/244–7070), accessible by boat and car, is open until midnight from May to October, and the company is a lively boating crowd.

Western Lakes and Mountains

Less than 20 miles northwest of Portland and the coast, the lakes and mountains of western Maine begin their stretch north along the New Hampshire border to Quebec. In winter this is ski country; in summer the woods and waters draw vacationers to recreation or seclusion in areas less densely populated than much of Maine's coast.

The Sebago–Long Lake region has antiques stores and lake cruises on a 42-mile waterway. Kezar Lake, tucked away in a fold of the White Mountains, has long been a hideaway of the wealthy. Bethel, in the Androscoggin River valley, is a classic New England town, its town common lined with historic homes. The far more rural Rangeley Lake area brings long stretches of pine, beech, spruce, and sky—and stylish inns and bed-and-breakfasts with easy access to golf, boating, fishing, and hiking.

Important Addresses and Numbers

Visitor Information **Bethel Area Chamber of Commerce** (Box 121, Bethel, tel. 207/824–2282).

Bridgton–Lakes Region Chamber of Commerce (Box 236, Bridgton, tel. 207/647–3472).

Rangeley Lakes Region Chamber of Commerce (Box 317, Rangeley, tel. 207/864–5364).

Emergencies **Bethel Area Medical Center** (tel. 207/824–2193).

Getting Around the Western Lakes and Mountains

By Plane **Mountain Air Service** (Rangeley, tel. 207/864–5307) provides air access to remote areas.

By Car A car is essential to a tour of the western lakes and mountains. Of the variety of routes available, the itinerary that follows takes Route 302, Route 26, Route 2, Route 17, and Route 4/16.

By Bus **Western Maine Transportation Services** (Rumford, tel. 207/364–3969) links Auburn, Rumford, and Farmington.

Guided Tours

Naples Flying Service (Naples Causeway, no phone) offers sightseeing flights over the lakes in summer.

Exploring the Western Lakes and Mountains

Numbers in the margin correspond with numbered points of interest on the Western Maine map.

❶ A tour of the lakes begins at **Sebago Lake,** west of Route 302, less than 20 miles northwest of Portland. At the north end of the lake, the **Songo Lock** (tel. 207/693–6231), which permits the passage of watercraft from Sebago Lake to Long Lake, is the one surviving lock of the Cumberland and Oxford Canal. Built of wood and masonry, the original lock dates from 1830 and was expanded in 1911; today it sees heavy traffic in the summer months.

The 1,300-acre **Sebago Lake State Park** on the north shore of Sebago Lake offers opportunities for swimming, picnicking, boating, and fishing (salmon and togue). *Tel. 207/693–6613, June 20–Labor Day; 207/693–6231, other times.*

Route 302 continues north to Naples, where the Naples Causeway has rental craft for fishing or cruising on Long Lake, and rather drab Bridgton, near Highland Lake, which has antiques shops in and around the town.

The most scenic route to Bethel, 30 miles to the north, follows Route 302 west from Bridgton, across Moose Pond to Knight's Hill Road, turning north to Lovell and Route 5, which will take you on to Bethel. It's a drive that lets you admire the jagged crests of the White Mountains outlined against the sky to the west and the lush, rolling hills that alternate with brooding forests at roadside. At **Center Lovell** you can barely glimpse the secluded Kezar Lake to the west, the retreat of wealthy and very private people; Sabattus Mountain, which rises behind Center Lovell, has a public hiking trail and stupendous views of the Presidential range from the summit.

Bethel is pure New England, a town with white-clapboard houses and white steepled churches and a mountain vista at the end of every street. In the winter this is ski country, and Bethel serves the Sunday River area (*see* Chapter 2). A stroll of Bethel should begin at the town common, where the sprawling Bethel Inn and Country Club has a walking-tour brochure at the main desk.

On Broad Street, opposite the inn, the **Moses Mason House and Museum,** a Federal-period home of 1813, has a fan pattern over the door and black shutters against white clapboards. Inside there are eight period rooms and a front hall and stairway wall decorated with murals by Rufus Porter. *Broad St., tel. 207/ 824–2908. Admission: $1.50 adults, 75¢ children under 12. Open July–Labor Day, Tues.–Sun. 1–4.*

The **Major Gideon Hastings House** nearby on Broad Street has a columned front portico typical of the Greek Revival style. Around the common, on Church Street, stands the severe white **West Parish Congregational Church,** (1847) with its unadorned triangular pediment and steeple supported on open columns. Beyond the church is the campus of **Gould Academy,** a preparatory school chartered in 1835; the dominant style of the school buildings is Georgian, and the tall brick main campus building is surmounted by a white cupola. Main Street will take you from the common past the Town Hall–Cole Block, built in 1891, to the shops.

The routes north from Bethel to the Rangeley district are all scenic, particularly in the autumn when the maples and beeches are aflame. On Route 26 it's about 12 miles to **Grafton Notch State Park,** where you can hike to stunning gorges and waterfalls and into the Baldpate Mountains. Route 26 continues on to Errol, New Hampshire, where Route 16 will return you east around the north shore of Mooselookmeguntic Lake, through Oquossoc, and into Rangeley.

A more direct—if marginally less scenic—tour follows Route 2 north and east from Bethel to the twin towns of Rumford and

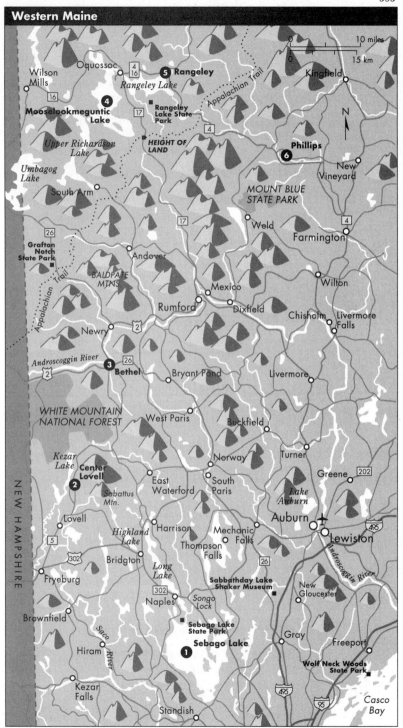

Western Maine

Mexico, where Route 17 continues north to Oquossoc, about an hour's drive. When you've gone about 20 minutes beyond Rumford, the signs of civilization all but vanish and you pass through what seems like virgin territory; in fact, the lumber companies have long since tackled the virgin forests, and sporting camps and cottages are tucked away here and there. The high point of this route is **Height of Land,** about 30 miles north of Rumford, with its unforgettable views of range after range of mountains and the huge, island-studded blue mass of Mooselookmeguntic Lake directly below. Turnouts on both sides of the highway allow you to pull over for a long look.

❹ Route 4 ends at Haines Landing on **Mooselookmeguntic Lake,** 7 miles west of Rangeley. Here you can stand at 1,400 feet above sea level and face the same magnificent scenery you admired at 2,400 feet from Height of Land on Route 17. Boat and canoe rentals are available at Mooselookmeguntic House.

❺ **Rangeley,** north of Rangeley Lake on Route 4/16, has lured fisherfolk, hunters, and winter-sports enthusiasts for a century to its more than 40 lakes and ponds within a 20-mile radius and 450 square miles of woodlands. Rangeley makes only a mediocre first impression, for the town has a rough, wilderness feel to it, and its best parts—including the choice lodgings—are tucked away in the woods, around the lake, and along the golf course.

❻ In **Phillips,** 14 miles southeast of Rangeley on Route 4, the Sandy River & Rangeley Lakes Railroad, a restored narrow-gauge railroad, has a mile of track through the woods, where you can board a century-old train drawn by a replica of the Sandy River #4 locomotive. *Tel. 207/639–3001. Admission: $2 adults, $1 children 6–12. Open May–Nov., 1st and 3rd Sun. each month, rides at 11, 1, and 3.*

On the south shore of Rangeley Lake, **Rangeley Lake State Park** (tel. 207/864–3858) offers superb lakeside scenery, swimming, picnic tables, a boat ramp, showers, and camping sites set well apart in a spruce and fir grove.

Western Lakes and Mountains for Free

Bridgton Historical Society Museum, housed in a former fire station built in 1902, displays artifacts of the area's history and materials on the local narrow-gauge railroad. *Gibbs Ave., tel. 207/647–5145. Admission free. Open June–Aug., Mon.–Sat. 1–4.*

Naples Historical Society Museum includes a jailhouse, a bandstand, and slides of the Cumberland and Oxford Canal and the Sebago–Long Lake steamboats. *Village Green, Rte. 302, no phone. Admission free. Open July–Aug., Tues.–Fri. 10–4, Sat. 10–1.*

What to See and Do with Children

Sandy River & Rangeley Lakes Railroad, Phillips

Songo River Queen II, a 92-foot stern-wheeler, takes passengers on hour-long cruises on Long Lake and longer voyages down the Songo River and through Songo Lock. *Rte. 302, Naples Causeway, tel. 207/693–6861. Admission: Songo River ride, $7 adults, $4 children; Long Lake cruise, $4 adults, $3* *children. July–Labor Day, 5 trips daily; June and Sept., weekends.*

Off the Beaten Track

Sabbathday Lake Shaker Museum on Route 26, 20 miles north of Portland, is part of one of the oldest Shaker communities in the United States (established in the late 18th century) and the last one in Maine. Nine members continue to farm crops and herbs, and visitors are shown the meeting house of 1794—a paradigm of Shaker design—and the ministry shop with 14 rooms of Shaker furniture, folk art, tools, farm implements, and crafts of the 18th to early 20th centuries. An extended tour (July and August only) includes the laundry, the herb department, and the spin house. A gift shop has Shaker crafts, candy, spices, books, and records. On Sunday, the Shaker day of prayer, the community is closed to visitors. *Rte. 26, New Gloucester, tel. 207/926–4597. Admission: introductory tour, $3 adults, $1.50 children 6–12; extended tour, $4.50 adults, $2.25 children. Open Memorial Day–Columbus Day., Mon.–Sat. 10–4:30.*

Shopping

Antiques Bridgton **Wales & Hamblen Antique Center** (134 Main St., tel. 207/647–8344), the region's best-known antiques store, displays the goods of 30 dealers: quilts, jewelry, country furniture, wicker, and Depression glass.

Hanover **The Lyons' Den** (Rte. 2, near Bethel, tel. 207/364–8634), a great barn of a place, carries glass, china, tools, prints, rugs, and some furniture.

Herbs **Chamomile Farm Herbs** (Stephens Rd., Rangeley, tel. 207/864–5261), a beautifully situated farm, sells dried herbs, wreaths, and farm crafts. Lunch is served and farm tours are offered.

Pottery **Bonnema Potters** (Lower Main St., Bethel, tel. 207/824–2821) features modern designs in plates, lamps, tiles, vases.

T-shirts **Groan & McGurn** (Main St., Bethel, tel. 207/824–2425) bills itself as a tourist trap; the bait is unusual T-shirts with Maine motifs: moose, raccoons, etc.

Sports and Outdoor Activities

Canoeing The Saco River (near Fryeburg) is a favorite route, with a gentle stretch from Swan's Falls to East Brownfield (19 miles) and an even gentler, scenic stretch from East Brownfield to Hiram (14 miles). Rangeley and Mooselookmeguntic lakes are good for scenic canoeing.

For canoe rentals, try **Canal Bridge Canoes** (Rte. 302, Fryeburg Village, tel. 207/935–2605), **Mooselookmeguntic House** (Haines Landing, Oquossoc, tel. 207/864–3627), **Rangeley Region Sport Shop** (Main St., Rangeley, tel. 207/864–5615), or **Saco River Canoe and Kayak** (Rte. 5, Fryeburg, tel. 207/935–2369).

Camping *See* National and State Parks and Forests, below. **Maine Campground Owners Association** (655 Main St., Lewiston 04240, tel. 207/782–5874) has a statewide listing of private campgrounds.

Hunting and Fishing Freshwater fishing for brook trout and salmon is at its best in May, June, and September, and the Rangeley area is especially popular with fly-fishermen. Nonresident freshwater anglers over the age of 12 must have a fishing license, which is available at many sporting-goods and hardware stores and at local town offices. Fishing is permitted from ice-out through September. The deep woods of the Rangeley area are popular with hunters. Game includes woodcock and partridge, deer and bear. The season for deer is usually the first three weeks of November; for game birds, usually October through November. State regulations are strictly enforced; licenses, available at town offices and many sporting-goods and hardware stores, are required of all hunters 10 years old or older. The **Department of Inland Fisheries and Wildlife** (284 State St., Augusta 04333, tel. 207/289–2043) can provide further information.

Recommended guides in the Rangeley area include: **Clayton (Cy) Eastlack** (Mountain View Cottages, Oquossoc, tel. 207/864–3416), **Grey Ghost Guide Service** (Box 24, Oquossoc, tel. 207/864–5314), and **Rangeley Region Guide Service** (Box 19HF, Rangeley, tel. 207/864–5761).

Snowmobiling The snowmobile is the principal mode of transportation in the Rangeley area during the winter months, with trails linking lakes and towns to wilderness camps. **Maine Snowmobile Association** (Box 77, Augusta 04330) has information on Maine's nearly 8,000-mile Interconnecting Trail System.

Water Sports Sebago, Long, Rangeley, and Mooselookmeguntic lakes are the most popular areas for sailing and motorboating. For rentals, try **Grant's Kennebago Camps** (Kennebago Lake, tel. 207/864–3608), **Long Lake Marina** (Rte. 302, Naples, tel. 207/693–3159), **Mountain View Cottages** (Rte. 17, Oquossoc, tel. 207/864–3416), **Naples Marina** (Naples Causeway, Naples, tel. 207/693–6254), **Rangeley Watersports** (Main St., Rangeley, tel. 207/864–3440), or **Sunny Breeze Sports** (Rte. 302, Naples, tel. 207/693–3867).

National and State Parks and Forests

Grafton Notch State Park (tel. 207/824–2912), on Route 26, 14 miles north of Bethel on the New Hampshire border, offers unsurpassed mountain scenery, picnic areas, caves to explore, swimming holes, and camping. You can take an easy nature walk to Mother Walker Falls or Moose Cave and see the spectacular Screw Auger Falls; or you can hike to the summit of Old Speck Mountain, the state's third-highest peak. If you have the stamina and the equipment, you can pick up the Appalachian Trail here, hike over Saddleback Mountain, and continue on to Katahdin. The **Maine Appalachian Club** (Box 283, Augusta 04330) publishes a map and trail guide.

Rangeley Lake State Park (tel. 207/864–3858) has 50 campsites on the south shore of the lake (*see* Exploring the Western Lakes and Mountains, above).

Sebago Lake State Park (tel. 207/693–6613, June 20–Labor Day, 207/693–6231, other times) has 300 campsites on the lake's north shore (*see* Exploring the Western Lakes and Mountains, above).

White Mountain National Forest straddles New Hampshire and Maine. Although the highest peaks are on the New Hampshire side, the Maine section includes lots of magnificent rugged terrain, camping and picnic areas, and hiking opportunities from hour-long nature loops to a 5½-hour scramble up Speckled Mountain—with open vistas at the summit. *Evans Notch Ranger District, FRD 2, Box 2270, Bethel 04217, tel. 207/824–2134. Open weekdays 8–4:30.*

Dining and Lodging

Bethel has the largest concentration of inns and bed-and-breakfasts, and its Chamber of Commerce (tel. 207/824–3585) has a central lodging reservations service.

Bethel Dining
★

Four Seasons Inn. The three small dining rooms of the region's front-running gourmet restaurant reveal tables draped with linens that brush the hardwood floors, birds and flowers in the wallpaper, and prim bouquets on the tables. The dinner menu is classic French: escargot, caviar, sautéed mushrooms, or onion soup to start; tournedos, beef Wellington, chateaubriand, veal Oscar, and bouillabaisse for entrées. *63 Upper Main St., tel. 207/824–2755. Reservations advised. Dress: casual but neat. AE, MC, V. Closed Nov.–Dec., May. Closed Mon. Dinner only. Expensive.*

The Back Stage. A funky, occasionally rowdy, totally informal place for unwinding after a day on the slopes, the Back Stage is furnished with all the charm of an airplane hangar. The fare is burgers, barbecued chicken and ribs, buffalo wings, onion soup, and nacho melt. The jukebox is loud, and dance bands perform Friday and Saturday. *Summer St., tel. 207/874–3003. No reservations in ski season. Dress: casual. MC, V. Closed Mon. Nov.–Apr. Closed Mon.–Wed. May–June, Sept.–Oct. Moderate.*

Mother's Restaurant. This gingerbread house furnished with wood stoves and bookshelves is a cozy place to enjoy the likes of veal with ginger and lime; broiled trout; and a variety of pasta offerings. In summer one can dine on the porch. *Upper Main St., tel. 207/824–2589. Reservations accepted. Dress: casual. MC, V. Closed Wed. Moderate.*

Bethel Lodging

Bethel Inn and Country Club. Bethel's grandest accommodation, once a rambling country inn on the town common, is now a full-service resort offering golf, a health club, and conference facilities. Guest rooms in the main inn, sparsely furnished with Colonial reproductions and George Washington bedspreads, are the most desirable, if not very large; the choice rooms have fireplaces and face the mountains over the golf course. Four cottages nearby on the town common also offer rooms in a plain, old-fashioned style. The 80 two-bedroom condos on the fairway, whose updated Colonial style echoes the inn decor, are clean and a bit sterile, but all units face the mountains. The health club facility has Nautilus, rowing, and cross-country skiing machines, exercycles, two saunas, a game room with billiards, a heated outdoor pool, and a Jacuzzi. The formal dining room, done in lemon yellow with pewter accents, serves elaborate dinners of roast duck, prime rib, lobster, scampi, and swordfish. *Village Common, Box 49, 04217, tel. 207/824–2175 or 800/654–0125, fax 207/824–2233. 57 rooms with bath, 80 condo units. Facilities: restaurant, tavern with weekend entertainment, all-weather tennis court, 18-hole golf course, health club, conference center. AE, CB, D, DC, MC, V. Rates are MAP or EP. Expensive–Very Expensive.*

Four Seasons Inn. This three-story, lemon yellow, domed Victorian white elephant on Main Street has ornate guest rooms decked out with velvet Victorian sofas, cut-glass and china knickknacks, canopied beds (a round bed in room 10), rag dolls, and lace and swag curtains. You can have morning coffee served in your room, and tea and petit fours await you at four in the afternoon. *63 Upper Main St., 04217, tel. 207/824–2755 or 800/ 227–7458. 15 rooms, 5 with bath. AE, MC, V. Closed Nov.– Dec., May. Moderate.*

L'Auberge. Tucked away in a meadow off the town common, the former carriage house of the Bethel Inn has been cleverly converted to an intimate bed-and-breakfast. Sunny guest rooms have brass beds, antique oak dressers, stenciling on the walls, and exposed beams. Number 8, the former hayloft, has a large four-poster, cathedral ceiling with sky mural, and dressing room. In winter you can cross-country ski from the back door. Two small dining rooms serve Continental Italian fare: linguine with meatballs; manicotti; and veal scaloppine. *Mill Hill Rd., 04217, tel. 207/824–2774. 7 rooms with bath. MC, V. Moderate.*

Sudbury Inn. The classic white-clapboard inn on Main Street offers good value, basic comfort, and a convenient location. Guest rooms sport country antiques, white bedspreads, and window shades. On weekends, second-floor rooms get the drumbeats of the bands performing in the basement pub; third-floor rooms are quieter and more spacious. The parlor's fireplace, brick-red furniture, and pressed-tin ceiling are warm and welcoming. The dining room (upholstered booths and square wood tables) has a country charm; the dinner menu runs to prime rib, sirloin au poivre, broiled haddock, and lasagne. The pub, with a large-screen TV, is a popular hangout. *Box 369, 04217, tel. 207/824–2174. 15 rooms with bath, 3 suites. Facilities: restaurant, pub. AE, D, MC, V. Inexpensive– Moderate.*

Bridgton Dining **Black Horse Tavern.** The gray, barnlike building on the main stem houses a country-style restaurant with a shiny bar, horse blankets and stirrups for decor, and an extensive menu of Mexican and Cajun specialties. A predominantly young crowd dines here on pan-blackened swordfish or sirloin; scallop pie; tortillas; chicken Creole; and ribs. Starters include nachos, buffalo wings, and chicken and smoked sausage gumbo. *8 Portland St., tel. 207/647–5300. No reservations. Dress: casual. MC, V. Moderate.*

Bridgton Lodging **Noble House.** Set amid white pines on a hill on a quiet residential street overlooking Highland Lake and the White Mountains, the stately bed-and-breakfast with the wide porch dates from the turn of the century. The parlor is dominated by a grand piano and fireplace; in the dining room beyond, hearty breakfasts (fruit, eggs, blueberry pancakes, waffles, muffins) are served family-style on china and linen. Guest rooms are small and a bit spartan in their furnishings. The honeymoon suite, a single large room, has a lake view, a whirlpool bath, and white wicker furniture. The Staples Suite on the third floor (white wicker furniture, fabrics in greens and browns) offers the most space and quiet. *Box 180, 04009, tel. 207/647–3733. 10 rooms, 7 with bath; 1 suite. Facilities: croquet, canoe, pedal boat, dock, swimming float. No credit cards. Closed mid-Oct.– mid-June. Moderate–Very Expensive.*

Center Lovell Lodging

Center Lovell Inn. The rambling white inn on Route 5 has more than a fabulous view: Spacious guest rooms in the main inn have rag rugs, maple wardrobes, floral wallpaper; rooms in the refurbished former barbershop next door are only slightly less appealing, with lower ceilings and sparser furnishings. The front rooms command the view. In the pretty little dining room—open to nonguests by reservation only—dinner entrées include veal marsala; baked filet of Maine sole stuffed with shrimp; and shrimp baked and stuffed with sea crab. *Rte. 5, 04016, tel. 207/925–1575. 11 rooms, 7 with bath; 1 suite. AE, MC, V. Closed Nov.–Apr. Rates are MAP. Inexpensive–Moderate.*

Naples Dining

Epicurean Inn. The rambling pink Victorian building on the edge of town, originally a stagecoach stop, serves classic French and New American cuisine in its small dining rooms done in muted colors, with wood floors and paisley drapes. Entrées can include roast duck, shrimp curry, tournedos with Stilton, and coho salmon. *Rte. 302, tel. 207/693–3839. Reservations advised. Dress: casual but neat. AE, DC, MC, V. No lunch. Closed Mon., Tues. Expensive.*

Naples Lodging

Augustus Bove House. Built as the Hotel Naples in 1850, the brick bed-and-breakfast at the crossroads of Routes 302 and 114 looks as though it was last renovated about a century ago. Nothing matches; the color schemes run riot on rugs, bedspreads, and wallpaper; yet you get good value—king-size beds in some rooms, lake views from the front rooms, full breakfast, and a location convenient to water activities. *R.R. 1, Box 501, 04055, tel. 207/693–6365. 12 rooms (summer), 6 rooms (winter), 5 with bath. Facilities: rental boat. AE, D, MC, V. Inexpensive–Moderate.*

Oquossoc Dining

Oquossoc House. Stuffed bears and bobcats keep you company as you dine on lobster, prime rib, filet mignon, or pork chops. The lunch menu promises chili, fish chowder, and lobster roll. *Junction Rtes. 17 and 4, tel. 207/864–3881. Reservations required on summer weekends. Dress: casual. Inexpensive–Moderate.*

Oquossoc Lodging

Oquossoc's Own Bed and Breakfast. A stay in one of the bedrooms in this house "in town" can resemble a visit with a favorite aunt. The decor is knotty pine, fluffy shag rugs, and country kitsch. Hearty dinners require a reservation. *Box 27, 04964, tel. 207/864–5584, 5 rooms with bath. MC, V. Inexpensive.*

Rangeley Dining

Red Onion. This busy two-tier restaurant looks like a Swiss ski chalet and serves lasagne, goulash, liver and onions, and pizza. An outdoor deck is used for dining in summer. *Main St., tel. 207/864–5022. No reservations. Dress: casual. No credit cards. Inexpensive.*

Rangeley Lodging

Country Club Inn. This retreat, built in the 1920s on the Mingo Springs Golf Course, enjoys a secluded hilltop location and sweeping lake and mountain views. The inn's baronial living room has a cathedral ceiling, a fieldstone fireplace at each end, and game trophies. Guest rooms downstairs in the main building and in the motel-style wing added in the 1950s are cheerfully if minimally decorated with wood paneling or bright wallpaper. The dining room—open to nonguests by reservation only—is a glassed-in porch where the linen-draped tables are set well apart and the menu features roast duck with cherry sauce and filet mignon. A charge is made for pets. *Box 680, Mingo Loop Rd., 04970, tel. 207/864–3831. 19 rooms with bath. Facilities: restaurant, outdoor pool, lounge, golf course. MC, V. Closed Apr.–mid-May, mid-Oct.–Dec. 25. Rates are MAP. Expensive.*

The Arts

Rangeley Friends of the Arts (Box 333, Rangeley, tel. 207/864–5571) sponsors musical theater, fiddlers' contests, rock and jazz, pipers, and other summer fare, mostly at Lakeside Park.

Sebago–Long Lake Region Chamber Music Festival (Bridgton Academy Chapel, North Bridgton, tel. 207/627–4939) schedules concerts from mid-July to mid-August.

The North Woods

Maine's north woods, a vast area of the north central section of the state, does not reward auto touring. Those who stay in their cars will see a dense curtain of evergreens that parts only occasionally to reveal a glimpse of lake or mountain. The way to experience this region is by canoe or raft, hiking trail, or on a fishing or hunting trip. In the north woods the three great theaters for these activities are Moosehead Lake, Baxter State Park, and the Allagash Wilderness Waterway.

Important Addresses and Numbers

Visitor Information

Baxter State Park Authority (64 Balsam Dr., Millinocket 04462, tel. 207/723–5140).

Millinocket Chamber of Commerce (Box 5, Millinocket 04462, tel. 207/723–4443).

Moosehead Lake Region Chamber of Commerce (Box 581MI, Greenville 04441, tel. 207/695–2702).

North Maine Woods (Box 421, Ashland 04732, tel. 207/435–6213), a private organization, publishes maps, canoeing guides, and lists of outfitters, camps, and campsites.

Emergencies

Police (Greenville, tel. 207/695–3835; Millinocket, tel. 207/723–9731).

Getting Around the North Woods

By Plane Charter flights from Bangor to smaller towns and remote lake and forest areas can be arranged with flying services, which will transport you and your gear and help you find a guide: **Currier's Flying Service** (Greenville Jct., tel. 207/695–2778), **Folsom's Air Service** (Greenville, tel. 207/695–2821), **Jack's Flying Service** (Greenville, tel. 207/695–3020), **Scotty's Flying Service** (Patten, tel. 207/528–2528).

By Car A car is essential to a negotiating this vast region but may not be useful to someone spending a vacation entirely at a wilderness camp. While public roads are scarce in the north country, lumber companies maintain private roads that are often open to the public (sometimes by permit only). When driving on a logging road, always give lumber company trucks the right of way. Be aware that loggers often take the middle of the road and will neither move over nor slow down for you.

Exploring the North Woods

Moosehead Lake, Maine's largest, offers more in the way of rustic camps, restaurants, guides, and outfitters than any other northern locale. Its 420 miles of shorefront, owned—like much of the north woods—almost entirely by paper manufacturers, is virtually uninhabited. Flat, straight, unpaved logging roads cut through the woods, but much of the lake area is accessible only by floatplane, boat, or canoe.

The logical base for a Moosehead Lake expedition is **Greenville,** the largest town on the lake and the spot for canoe rentals, wilderness outfitters, and several rustic hotels. Greenville's **Moosehead Marine Museum** (tel. 207/695–2716) has exhibits on the local logging industry and the steamship era on Moosehead Lake, with photos of Rockwood's renowned Mount Kineo Hotel, an immense 19th-century summer hotel that was torn down in the 1940s. The museum also runs the SS *Katahdin,* a steamer from 1914 that plies the lake daily from June to September.

Almost 20 miles north of Greenville on Route 6/15 is **Rockwood,** on the western side of Moosehead Lake, another good starting point for a wilderness trip or family vacation on the lake. Rockwood has an even more striking location than Greenville, for the dark mass of Mt. Kineo, a sheer cliff that rises 1,860 feet out of the lake, looms over the town just across the narrows.

On the eastern side of the lake, to the south, 8 miles to the northeast of Greenville, **Lily Bay State Park** (tel. 207/695–2700) has a campground with sites along the shore, two boat-launching ramps, and a swimming beach.

Lily Bay Road continues northeast to the outpost of Kokadjo on First Roach Pond, where one can have a snack or a meal at **Kokadjo's Store** (tel. 207/695–2904). It's another 20 miles to Ripogenus Dam, the center for white-water trips on the West Branch of the Penobscot and flatwater canoe trips on Chesuncook Lake. A dirt road parallels the West Branch, with occasional breathtaking views of Katahdin opening to the north.

The same road takes you to the turnoff to the southern entrance to **Baxter State Park** (tel. 207/723–5140), which can also be reached conveniently from the town of Millinocket about 24 miles to the southeast. Baxter is the jewel in the crown of northern Maine, a 200,000-acre wilderness area that surrounds **Katahdin,** Maine's highest mountain (5,267 feet at Baxter Peak). Katahdin's magnificence draws thousands of hikers every year for the daylong climb to the summit and the stunning views of woods, mountains, and lakes from the hair-raising Knife Edge Trail along its ridge. Roaring Brook Campground, which you can drive to in the park, gives direct access to the quickest way up Katahdin. Katahdin Stream and Nesowdnehunk Field campgrounds, both reached by the park's Perimeter Road, put you on the west side of Katahdin.

Because the crowds at Katahdin can be formidable on clear summer days, those who seek a greater solitude might choose to tackle instead one of the 45 other mountains in the park, all accessible from a 150-mile trail network. South Turner can be climbed in a morning (if you're fit), and it affords a great view of Katahdin across the valley. On the way you'll pass Sandy Stream Pond, where moose are to be seen at dusk. The Owl, the Brothers, and Doubletop Mountain are good day hikes. The more remote Russell Pond campsite is accessible only by a long hike through the woods; there are tent sites on the pond, lean-tos, a bunkhouse, and canoe rentals. And from here you can hike on to outlying wilderness sites on Wassataquoik Lake.

The camping season in Baxter State Park is mid-May to mid-October, and it's important that you reserve in advance by mail when you plan to camp inside the park. Camping is permitted only in authorized locations, and when campgrounds are full, you will be turned away. For driving in the park, the 50-mile Perimeter Road makes a semicircle around the western side of the park; maximum speed is 20 miles per hour.

Still more remote is the **Allagash Wilderness Waterway,** a 92-mile corridor of lakes and rivers that cuts across 170,000 acres of wilderness. The waterway begins at the northwest corner of Baxter and runs north to the town of Allagash, 10 miles from the Canadian border. **Ripogenus Dam,** 30 miles northwest of Millinocket on lumbering roads, is the most popular jumping-off point for Allagash trips. The Allagash allows some of the most challenging white-water canoeing in the Northeast, superb scenery, fishing in the warmer months, and endless snowmobiling in the winter, when as much as 20 feet of snow buries the north.

The Allagash rapids are ranked classes I and II (very easy and easy), but that doesn't mean the river is a piece of cake; river conditions vary greatly with the depth and volume of water, and even a class I rapid can hang your canoe up on a rock, capsize you, or spin you around in the wink of an eye. On the lakes, strong winds can halt your progress for days. The Allagash should not be undertaken lightly or without advance planning; the complete course requires from seven to 10 days. The Maine Department of Conservation, Bureau of Parks and Recreation (State House Station 22, Augusta 04333, tel. 207/289–3821, May–Oct.; 207/723–8518, Nov.–Apr.) can provide information on camping and canoeing in the Allagash area. The best bet for a novice is to go with a guide; a good outfitter will help you plan your route and provide your craft and transportation.

Those with their own canoe who want to go it alone can take the Telos Road north from Ripogenus Dam, putting in at Chamberlain Bridge at the southern tip of Chamberlain Lake, or at Allagash Lake, Churchill Dam, or Umsaskis Bridge.

Sports and Outdoor Activities

Camping Reservations for state park campsites can be made through the **Maine Forest Service** (tel. 207/289–3821). The state maintains primitive backcountry sites that are available without charge on a first-come, first-served basis; **Maine Forest Service, Department of Conservation** (State House Station 22, Augusta 04333, tel. 207/289–2791) has maps and information.

North Maine Woods (Box 421, Ashland 04732, tel. 207/435–6213) maintains many wilderness campsites on commercial forest land; early reservations are recommended.

Maine Publicity Bureau (97 Winthrop St., Hallowell 04347, tel. 207/289–2423) publishes a listing of private campsites and cottage rentals.

Canoeing One popular and easy route follows the Upper West Branch of the Penobscot River from Lobster Lake (just east of Moosehead Lake) to Chesuncook Lake. At the head of Chesuncook Lake you can stop at the tiny wilderness settlement of Chesuncook Village, which has a church, an inn, a few houses, and a spectacularly remote setting. From here you can paddle on Chesuncook Lake to Ripogenus Dam in a day.

The Aroostook River from Little Munsungan Lake to Fort Fairfield (100 miles) is best run in late spring. More challenging routes include the Passadumkeag River from Grand Falls to Passadumkeag (25 miles with class I–III rapids); the East Branch of the Penobscot River from Matagamon Wilderness Campground to Grindstone (38 miles with class I–III rapids); and the West Branch of the Pleasant River from Katahdin Iron Works to Brownville Junction (10 miles with class II–III rapids).

The Mount Everest of Maine canoe trips is the 110-mile route on the St. John River from Baker Lake to Allagash Village, with a swift current all the way and two stretches of class III rapids (*see* Exploring the North Woods, above, for details of the Allagash Wilderness Waterway).

Most canoe rental operations will arrange transportation, help you plan your route, and provide a guide when you need one. Transport to wilderness lakes can be arranged through the flying services listed above (*see* Getting Around the North Woods by Plane, above).

Allagash Canoe Trips (Greenville, tel. 207/695–3668) furnishes equipment and guides for use on the Allagash and Penobscot rivers.

Allagash Sporting Camp (Allagash, tel. 207/398–3555) rents canoes and camping equipment and provides guides.

Frost Pond Camps (Greenville, tel. 207/695–2821) provides equipment and guided trips on the Allagash.

North Country Outfitters (Rockwood, tel. 207/534–2242) rents equipment and sponsors guided trips on the Allagash and Penobscot rivers.

Hunting and Fishing Salmon, trout, and togue lure thousands of fisherfolk to the region from ice-out in early May to September, and the hardiest return in winter for the ice-fishing. Licenses, required of all freshwater fishermen over the age of 12, may be purchased at many sporting goods and hardware stores and outfitters. Hunters penetrate the woods, marshes, hillsides, and rivers of the north woods in November and early December in pursuit of deer, bear, pheasant, partridge, and moose (limited by lottery). The season for each animal is different, so you must be certain of the regulations—which are strictly enforced. Licenses, available at town offices and sporting-goods and hardware stores, are required of all hunters 10 years old or over. Applicants for an adult firearms hunting license must show proof of having previously held an adult license to hunt with firearms or having successfully completed an approved hunter safety course. **Maine's Department of Inland Fisheries**

and Wildlife (284 State St., Augusta 04333, tel. 207/289–2043) can provide additional information on hunting and fishing regulations.

Guides are available through most wilderness camps, sporting goods stores, and canoe outfitters. For assistance in finding a guide, contact **Maine Professional Guides Association** (Box 591, Ellsworth 04605, tel. 207/667–8807) or **North Maine Woods.**

A few well-established guides are **Gilpatrick's Guide Service** (Box 461, Skowhegan 04976, tel. 207/453–6959), **Maine Guide Fly Shop and Guide Service** (Box 1202, Main St., Greenville 04441, tel. 207/695–2266), **Professional Guide Service** (Box 346, Sheridan 04775, tel. 207/435–8044), and **Taiga Outfitters** (RFD 1, Box 147–8, Ashland 04732, tel. 207/435–6851).

Rafting   The Kennebec and West Branch of the Penobscot River offer thrilling white-water rafting (guides are strongly recommended for these trips). Because weather and river conditions are crucial factors, you should always call ahead, even when you have made a reservation.

The following outfitters lead trips down the West Branch of the Penobscot, Kennebec, and Dead rivers: **Adventure River Expeditions** (Box 101, The Forks 04985, tel. 207/663–2249), **Crab Apple Whitewater** (Crab Apple Acres Inn, The Forks 04985, tel. 207/663–2218), **Eastern River Expeditions** (Box 1173, Greenville 04441, tel. 207/695–2411 or 800/634–7238), **Maine Whitewater** (Suite 454, Bingham 04920, tel. 207/622–2260, Oct.–Apr.; 207/672–4814, May–Sept.), **Northern Outdoors** (Box 100, The Forks 04985, tel. 207/663–4466), and **Voyagers Whitewater** (Rte. 201, The Forks 04985, tel. 207/663–4423).

Dining and Lodging

Greenville and Rockwood offer the largest selection of restaurants and accommodations in the region. Casual dress is the rule at dinner.

Greenville Dining   **Greenville Inn.** Two dining rooms overlook Moosehead Lake. A third, with ornate cherry and mahogany paneling and ladderback chairs, has a subdued, gentlemanly air. The Continental menu, revised daily, reflects the owners' Austrian background: shrimp with mustard dill sauce; fresh salmon marinated in olive oil and basil; veal cutlet with mushroom cream sauce. Popovers accompany the meal. *Norris St., tel. 207/695–2206. Reservations advised. D, MC, V. Closed Apr. Dinner only. Moderate.*
Lake View Manor Restaurant. The cedar-shingle building's spacious dining room looks onto Moosehead Lake and Squaw Mountain. An enclosed lakeside porch allows dining in summer; the winter dining room, hung with paintings of local scenes, is warmed by a fire in the big stone fireplace. Filet mignon, lobster pie, and sirloin with shrimp and scallops are typical fare. *Lily Bay Rd., tel. 207/695–3810. Reservations advised. MC, V. Closed Dec.; closed Sun.–Wed. Jan.–Apr.; closed Sun.–Tues. May–June, Labor Day–Nov.; closed Sun. July–Labor Day. Dinner only. Moderate.*

Greenville Lodging   **Greenville Inn.** A rambling gray-and-white structure, built a century ago as the retreat of a wealthy lumbering family, the inn stands on a rise over Moosehead Lake, a block from town. Indoors the cherry and mahogany paneling, Oriental rugs, and

leaded glass create an aura of masculine ease. Two of the spare-
ly furnished, sunny bedrooms have fireplaces; two have lake
views; and two clapboard cottages were built in the 1960s. *Norris St., 04441, tel. 207/695–2206. 6 rooms, 4 with bath; 1 suite; 2
cottages. D, MC, V. Moderate.*

Wilson's on Moosehead Lake. Wilson's claims to be the oldest
continuously operated sporting camp on Moosehead Lake. The
log cabins, situated at the headwaters of the Kennebec River,
halfway between Greenville and Rockwood, cater to anglers,
hunters, and families in summer. Cabins have two to five bedrooms, and kitchens are fully equipped. There's a one-week
minimum stay, mid-June to Labor Day; guide service is available; leashed pets are accepted. *Greenville Jct. 04442, tel. 207/
695–2549. 15 cottages with bath. Facilities: private beach,
dock, barbecue. MC, V. Inexpensive–Moderate.*

Chalet Moosehead. Just 50 yards off Route 6/15, the efficiencies, motel room, and cottages are right on Moosehead Lake.
The attractive grounds lead to a private beach, pets are welcome, and no minimum stay is required. *Box 327, Greenville
Jct. 04442, tel. 207/695–2950. 9 rooms with bath, 1 cabin with
bath. Facilities: beach, canoes, volleyball. MC, V. Inexpensive.*

**Millinocket Dining
and Lodging**

Pamola Motor Lodge. Located off the highway in Millinocket,
this is the closest motel to Baxter State Park. The rooms have
standard motel furnishings—king and queen-size beds, TV—
and the restaurant does steaks, chops, lobster, chicken parmigiana, and spaghetti and meatballs. *973 Central St., 04462, tel.
207/723–9746. 30 rooms with bath, 3 efficiencies. Facilities:
restaurant, lounge, hot tub, outdoor pool. AE, D, MC, V. Inexpensive.*

**Rockwood Dining
and Lodging**

The Birches Resort. The family-oriented resort offers the full
north-country experience: Moosehead Lake, birch woods, log
cabins, and boats for rent. The turn-of-the-century main lodge
has four guest rooms, a living room dominated by a fieldstone
fireplace, and a dining room overlooking the lake. The dining
room is open to the public for dinner; the fare is chiefly steak
and lobster. Most guests occupy one of the 17 cottages that
sleep from two to 15 people. An additional charge is made for
pets; Full American Plan is available. *Box 81, 04448, tel. 207/
523–7305. 4 lodge rooms, 2 with bath; 17 cottages with bath.
Facilities: dining room; boats, kayaks, canoes, sailfish for
rent; private marina; outdoor hot tub and sauna; game room.
AE, D, MC, V. Dining room closed late Nov.–Dec., Apr. Moderate.*

Rockwood Lodging

Tomhegan. A 10-mile drive from Rockwood will bring you to
this rustic retreat, circa 1910, on the shores of Moosehead
Lake. Boardwalks connect eight log cabins, most with two bedrooms, all with kitchen, and the lodge has efficiencies. The
lodge will find you a hunting or fishing guide, and in winter you
can cross-country ski the miles of logging roads that connect
with the property. Cabins have a one-week minimum stay in
July and August, a two-night minimum at other times. Management planned a restaurant for 1990. *Box 308, 04478, tel.
207/534–7712. 4 efficiencies; 8 cabins with bath. Facilities:
marina, cross-country skiing. MC, V. Inexpensive–Moderate.*

Rockwood Cottages. Eight white cottages with blue trim on
Moosehead Lake, off Route 15 and convenient to the center of

Rockwood, are ideal for families; they have fully equipped kitchens, cribs are provided, and pets are welcome. Cottages sleep two to seven, and there is a one-week minimum stay in July and August. *Box 176, 04478, tel. 207/534-7725. 8 cottages. Facilities: dock, rental craft. MC, V. Inexpensive.*

Index

Personal Itinerary

Departure *Date*

Time

Transportation

Arrival *Date*   *Time*

Departure *Date*   *Time*

Transportation

Accommodations

Arrival *Date*   *Time*

Departure *Date*   *Time*

Transportation

Accommodations

Arrival *Date*   *Time*

Departure *Date*   *Time*

Transportation

Accommodations

Personal Itinerary

Arrival *Date*   *Time*

Departure *Date*   *Time*

Transportation

Accommodations

Arrival *Date*   *Time*

Departure *Date*   *Time*

Transportation

Accommodations

Arrival *Date*   *Time*

Departure *Date*   *Time*

Transportation

Accommodations

Arrival *Date*   *Time*

Departure *Date*   *Time*

Transportation

Accommodations

Personal Itinerary

Arrival   *Date*   *Time*

Departure   *Date*   *Time*

Transportation

Accommodations

Arrival   *Date*   *Time*

Departure   *Date*   *Time*

Transportation

Accommodations

Arrival   *Date*   *Time*

Departure   *Date*   *Time*

Transportation

Accommodations

Arrival   *Date*   *Time*

Departure   *Date*   *Time*

Transportation

Accommodations

Personal Itinerary

Arrival   *Date*   *Time*

Departure   *Date*   *Time*

Transportation

Accommodations

Arrival   *Date*   *Time*

Departure   *Date*   *Time*

Transportation

Accommodations

Arrival   *Date*   *Time*

Departure   *Date*   *Time*

Transportation

Accommodations

Arrival   *Date*   *Time*

Departure   *Date*   *Time*

Transportation

Accommodations

Addresses

Name

Address

Telephone

Name

Address

Telephone

Name

Address

Telephone

Name

Address

Telephone

Name

Address

Telephone

Name

Address

Telephone

Name

Address

Telephone

Name

Address

Telephone

Name

Address

Telephone

Name

Address

Telephone

Name

Address

Telephone

Name

Address

Telephone

Name

Address

Telephone

Name

Address

Telephone

Name

Address

Telephone

Name

Address

Telephone

Addresses

Name

Address

Telephone

Name

Address

Telephone

Name

Address

Telephone

Name

Address

Telephone

Name

Address

Telephone

Name

Address

Telephone

Name

Address

Telephone

Name

Address

Telephone

Name

Address

Telephone

Name

Address

Telephone

Name

Address

Telephone

Name

Address

Telephone

Name

Address

Telephone

Name

Address

Telephone

Name

Address

Telephone

Name

Address

Telephone

Name

Address

Telephone

Fodor's Travel Guides

U.S. Guides

Alaska
Arizona
Boston
California
Cape Cod
The Carolinas & the
  Georgia Coast
The Chesapeake
  Region
Chicago
Colorado
Disney World & the
  Orlando Area

Florida
Hawaii
The Jersey Shore
Las Vegas
Los Angeles
Maui
Miami & the Keys
New England
New Mexico
New Orleans
New York City
New York City
  (Pocket Guide)

New York State
Pacific North Coast
Philadelphia
The Rockies
San Diego
San Francisco
San Francisco
  (Pocket Guide)
The South
Texas
USA
The Upper Great
  Lakes Region

Virgin Islands
Virginia & Maryland
Waikiki
Washington, D.C.

Foreign Guides

Acapulco
Amsterdam
Australia
Austria
The Bahamas
The Bahamas
  (Pocket Guide)
Baja & the Pacific
  Coast Resorts
Barbados
Belgium &
  Luxembourg
Bermuda
Brazil
Budget Europe
Canada
Canada's Atlantic
  Provinces
Cancun, Cozumel,
  Yucatan Peninsula
Caribbean
Central America
China

Eastern Europe
Egypt
Europe
Europe's Great
  Cities
France
Germany
Great Britain
Greece
The Himalayan
  Countries
Holland
Hong Kong
India
Ireland
Israel
Italy
Italy's Great Cities
Jamaica
Japan
Kenya, Tanzania,
  Seychelles
Korea

Lisbon
London
London Companion
London
  (Pocket Guide)
Madrid & Barcelona
Mexico
Mexico City
Montreal &
  Quebec City
Morocco
Munich
New Zealand
Paris
Paris (Pocket Guide)
Portugal
Puerto Rico
  (Pocket Guide)
Rio de Janeiro
Rome
Saint Martin/
  Sint Maarten
Scandinavia

Scandinavian Cities
Scotland
Singapore
South America
South Pacific
Southeast Asia
Soviet Union
Spain
Sweden
Switzerland
Sydney
Thailand
Tokyo
Toronto
Turkey
Vienna
Yugoslavia

Special-Interest Guides

Bed & Breakfast
  Guide to the Mid-
  Atlantic States

Bed & Breakfast
  Guide to New
  England
Cruises & Ports
  of Call

A Shopper's Guide
  to London
Health & Fitness
  Vacations
Shopping in Europe

Skiing in North
  America
Sunday in New York
Touring Europe